Menopause and Hormone Replacement

Edited by

Hilary Critchley, Ailsa Gebbie and Valerie Beral

RCOG Press

It was not possible to refer all the material back to the authors or discussants but it is hoped that the proceedings have been reported fairly and accurately.

Hilary OD Critchley MD FRCOG FRANZCOG
Professor of Reproductive Medicine and Consultant Gynaecologist, Centre for Reproductive Biology, University of Edinburgh, The Chancellor's Building, 49 Little France Crescent, Edinburgh EH16 4SB

Ailsa Gebbie MBChB FRCOG MFFP DCH
Consultant in Community Gynaecology, Family Planning Centre, 18 Dean Terrace, Edinburgh EH4 1NL

Valerie Beral MD FRCOG FRCP
Professor of Epidemiology, Cancer Research UK Epidemiology Unit, University of Oxford, Gibson Building, Radcliffe Infirmary, Woodstock Road, Oxford OX2 6HE

Published by the **RCOG Press** at the
Royal College of Obstetricians and Gynaecologists
27 Sussex Place, Regent's Park
London NW1 4RG

www.rcog.org.uk

Registered Charity No. 213280

First published 2004

© Royal College of Obstetricians and Gynaecologists 2004

ISBN 1-904752-11-X

RCOG Editor: Andrew Welsh
Index: Liza Furnival
Design: Karl Harrington, FiSH Books, London
Printed by Henry Ling Ltd, The Dorchester Press, Dorchester DT1 1HD

RMONE REPLACEMENT

RCOG Press

Since 1973 the Royal College of Obstetricians and Gynaecologists has regularly convened Study Groups to address important growth areas within obstetrics and gynaecology. An international group of eminent scientists and clinicians from various disciplines is invited to present the results of recent research and to take part in in-depth discussions. The resulting volume, containing the papers presented and also edited transcripts of the discussions, is published within a few months of the meeting and provides a summary of the subject that is both authoritative and up-to-date.

Some previous Study Group publications available

Contents

Participants

Mary Armitage
Member of the Committee on Safety of Medicines (CSM) and Chairman of the
Expert Working Group on HRT; Clinical Vice-President, Royal College of Physicians
of London; Consultant Physician and Endocrinologist, Department of Endocrinology,
Royal Bournemouth Hospital, Castle Lane East, Bournemouth BH7 7DW, UK.

David H Barlow
Nuffield Professor of Obstetrics and Gynaecology and Head of Department,
Nuffield Department Obstetrics and Gynaecology, University of Oxford, Level 3,
The Women's Centre, John Radcliffe Hospital, Headington, Oxford OX3 9DU, UK.

Valerie Beral
Professor of Epidemiology, Cancer Research UK Epidemiology Unit, University of
Oxford, Gibson Building, Radcliffe Infirmary, Woodstock Road, Oxford OX2 6HE,
UK.

Helen M Buckler
Consultant Endocrinologist and Honorary Senior Lecturer, Department of
Endocrinology, University of Manchester, Hope Hospital, Salford, Manchester
M6 8HD, UK.

Henry G Burger
Professor and Emeritus Director, Prince Henry's Institute of Medical Research,
Monash Medical Centre, PO Box 5152, Clayton, Victoria 3168, Australia.

Linda D Cardozo
Professor of Urogynaecology, Department of Urogynaecology, 3rd Floor, Golden
Jubilee Wing, King's College Hospital, Denmark Hill, London SE5 9RS, UK.

Kristof Chwalisz
Therapeutic Area Head, Women's Health, TAP Pharmaceutical Products Inc.,
675 North Field Drive, Lake Forest, IL 60045, USA.

Hilary OD Critchley
Professor of Reproductive Medicine and Consultant Gynaecologist, Centre for
Reproductive Biology, University of Edinburgh, The Chancellor's Building,
49 Little France Crescent, Edinburgh EH16 4SB, UK.

Back row (from left to right): Bill Miller, Robin Wilson, Henry Burger, David Sturdee, Malcolm Whitehead, Kristof Chwalisz.
Middle row (from left to right): David Purdie, Ross Prentice, Gordon Lowe, David Barlow, John Studd, Joan Pitkin, Stephen Evans, Cecilia Magnusson, John Stevenson
Front row (from left to right): Declan Murphy, Linda Cardozo, Helen Buckler, Sarah Gray, Valerie Beral, Hilary Critchley, Ailsa Gebbie, Anna Glasier, Mary Armitage, Margaret Rees, Mary Ann Lumsden

Heather A Cubie
R&D Director and Consultant Clinical Scientist, Royal Infirmary of Edinburgh,
51 Little France Crescent, Edinburgh EH16 4SA, UK.

Stephen JW Evans
Professor of Pharmacoepidemiology, London School of Hygiene and Tropical
Medicine, London WC1 7HT, UK.

Ailsa Gebbie
Consultant in Community Gynaecology, Family Planning Centre, 18 Dean Terrace,
Edinburgh EH4 1NL, UK.

Sarah Gray
GP Specialist, Lower Lemon Street Surgery, 18 Lemon Street, Truro TR1 2LZ, UK.

Gordon DO Lowe
Professor of Vascular Medicine, University of Glasgow, Cardiovascular and Medical
Division, Royal Infirmary, 10 Alexandra Parade, Glasgow G31 2ER, UK.

Mary Ann Lumsden
Reader, Honorary Consultant in Obstetrics and Gynaecology, 3rd Floor, Queen
Elizabeth Building, Glasgow Royal Infirmary, 10 Alexandra Parade, Glasgow
G31 2ER, UK.

Cecilia MK Magnusson
Researcher, Department of Medical Epidemiology and Biostatistics, Karolinska
Institutet, Stockholm, 17177, Sweden.

William Miller
Professor, Edinburgh Breast Unit Research Group, Paderewski Building,
Western General Hospital, Edinburgh EH4 2XU, UK.

Declan GM Murphy
Professor of Psychiatry and Brain Maturation and Honorary Consultant Psychiatrist,
Department of Psychological Medicine, Room M216, Institute of Psychiatry,
De Crespigny Park, London SE5 8AF, UK.

Ross L Prentice
Professor of Biostatistics, University of Washington, and Member, Public Health
Sciences Division, Fred Hutchinson Cancer Research Center, 1100 Fairview Avenue
North, POB 19024, Seattle, WA 98109-1024, USA.

David W Purdie
Consultant, Edinburgh Osteoporosis Centre, 1 Wemyss Place, Edinburgh EH3 6EH,
UK.

John C Stevenson
Reader and Consultant Metabolic Physician, Royal Brompton and Harefield NHS
Trust, Sydney Street, London SW3 6NP, UK.

David W Sturdee
Consultant Obstetrician and Gynaecologist, Department of Obstetrics and
Gynaecology, Solihull Hospital, Birmingham Heartlands and Solihull Hospitals NHS
Trust, Lode Lane, Solihull B91 2JL, UK.

Malcolm Whitehead
Consultant Gynaecologist, Gynae-Endocrine Clinic, 3rd Floor, Golden Jubilee Wing,
King's College Hospital, Denmark Hill, London SE5 9RS, UK.

A Robin M Wilson
Consultant Radiologist, Breast Institute, City Hospital, Hucknall Road, Nottingham
NG5 1PB, UK.

Discussants

Joan Pitkin
Consultant Gynaecologist, Directorate of Obstetrics and Gynaecology, Northwick
Park and St. Mark's Hospital, Watford Road, Harrow, Middlesex HA5 5QF, UK.

Margaret Rees
Reader in Reproductive Medicine, Honorary Consultant in Medical Gynaecology,
Level 4, Women's Centre, John Radcliffe Hospital, Oxford OX3 9DU, UK.

John W W Studd
Consultant Obstetrician and Gynaecologist, Department of Gynaecology, Chelsea
& Westminster Hospital, 369 Fulham Road, London SW10 9NH, UK.

Additional contributors

Emily Banks
NHMRC Fellow, National Centre for Epidemiology and Population Health,
Australian National University, Canberra ACT 0200, Australia.

Diana Bull
Statistician, Cancer Research UK Epidemiology Unit, Gibson Building,
Radcliffe Infirmary, Oxford OX2 6HE, UK.

Michael Craig
Section of Brain Maturation, Department of Psychological Medicine, PO Box 50,
Institute of Psychiatry, De Crespigny Park, London SE5 8AF, UK.

Barbara Crossley
Study Coordinator, Cancer Research UK Epidemiology Unit, Gibson Building,
Radcliffe Infirmary, Oxford OX2 6HE, UK.

William Cutter
Section of Brain Maturation, Department of Psychological Medicine, PO Box 50,
Institute of Psychiatry, De Crespigny Park, London SE5 8AF, UK.

Lorraine Dennerstein
Professor and Director of Office for Gender and Health, Department of Psychiatry,
The University of Melbourne, Royal Melbourne Hospital, Melbourne, Victoria,
Australia.

Toral Gathani
Surgical Registrar, Cancer Research UK Epidemiology Unit, Gibson Building,
Radcliffe Infirmary, Oxford OX2 6HE, UK.

Anna Glasier
Director of Family Planning and Well Women Services, NHS Lothian and Honorary
Professor, University of Edinburgh and London School of Hygiene and Tropical
Medicine, 18 Dean Terrace, Edinburgh EH4 1NL, UK.

Jane Green
Clinical Epidemiologist, Cancer Research UK Epidemiology Unit, Gibson Building,
Radcliffe Infirmary, Oxford OX2 6HE, UK.

Britt-Marie Landgren
Professor, Department of Clinical Science, Division of Obstetrics and Gynaecology,
Huddinge University Hospital, SE14186, Stockholm, Sweden.

Janet Nooney
Scientific Assessor, Medicines and Healthcare Products Regulatory Agency,
Market Towers, 1 Nine Elms Lane, London SW8 5NQ, UK.

Ray Norbury
Section of Brain Maturation, Department of Psychological Medicine, PO Box 50,
Institute of Psychiatry, De Crespigny Park, London SE5 8AF, UK.

Gillian Reeves
Staff Scientist, Cancer Research UK Epidemiology Unit, Gibson Building,
Radcliffe Infirmary, Oxford OX2 6HE, UK.

David Robertson
Associate Professor and Principal Research Fellow, Prince Henry's Institute of
Medical Research, Monash Medical Centre, PO Box 5152, Clayton, Victoria,
Australia.

Dudley Robinson
Sub-specialty Trainee – Urogynaecology, Department of Urogynaecology, 3rd Floor,
Golden Jubilee Wing, King's College Hospital, Denmark Hill, London SE5 9RS,
UK.

Preface

It has been known for centuries that women in their midlife years experience menopausal symptoms as an unpleasant manifestation of declining ovarian function. Oestrogen replacement is a highly effective treatment for these symptoms, which can significantly affect quality of life and wellbeing. In the UK, the prescribing of hormone replacement therapy (HRT) to treat menopausal symptoms began gradually in the 1950s and reached a peak around 2002. At that stage it was estimated that approximately one-third of women aged 45–60 years were users. Data from large observational studies published in the 1990s suggested that HRT appeared to have an additional role in the prevention of chronic disease in older women. As a consequence, the indications for prescribing HRT increased to include prevention of cardiovascular disease, osteoporosis and Alzheimer's disease as clinicians were keen to promote use for these apparent important benefits.

However, the past two years have seen a steady decline in prescribing rates as a number of key publications have added greatly to our knowledge on the benefits and risks of HRT. In particular, the Women's Health Initiative trial that was commenced in the early 1990s was expected to confirm the protective effect of oestrogen on the vascular system. This large randomised trial's costs were enormous and the results failed to demonstrate the expected cardiovascular protection of HRT. In the UK, the Million Women Study, a very large observational study performed through breast screening centres, has confirmed the increased risk of breast cancer associated with use of HRT. Other recent studies and trials have been in broad agreement with these two major publications.

This recent changing evidence base for prescribing of HRT has attracted huge media interest that has led to confusion and great anxiety, especially among women themselves. Prescribing of HRT lies mainly in the primary care domain but with leadership and specialist help available from menopause and gynaecological services. It is difficult for healthcare professionals to grasp rapid therapeutic changes and alter prescribing habits particularly when the lay press reports emerging data in a sensationalist and often inaccurate way. The Committee on Safety of Medicines (CSM) in the UK has played a key role in providing timely and independent advice to professionals and the general population, as new information about the effects of HRT has emerged. Caution is also required when recommending alternatives to HRT in the absence of any real data indicating either their efficacy or safety.

The 47th Study Group of the RCOG met in February 2004 to debate all these issues concerning the role of HRT in menopause management. Clinicians, epidemiologists and scientists scrutinised the data and, although consensus was not achieved in all areas, greater understanding and agreement did occur. Without doubt, HRT will continue to be prescribed for women with severe menopausal symptoms but some of the other indications will now be relegated to the archives of history. It has taken many decades to reach our current level of knowledge of HRT and the situation may still change. We hope that the work of this Study Group of the RCOG will lead the way for a greater understanding of the complex balance of risks and benefits of HRT for each menopausal woman considering such therapy.

Hilary Critchley
Ailsa Gebbie
Valerie Beral

SECTION 1

THE MENOPAUSE – WHAT IS IT?

Chapter 1

Endocrinology of the menopause and menopause transition

Henry Burger, David Robertson, Britt-Marie Landgren
and Lorraine Dennerstein

Introduction and definitions

The menopausal transition has been defined by both the World Health Organization and the International Menopause Society as that period of time before the final menstrual period (FMP) when variability in the menstrual cycle is usually increased.[1,2] Neither body provided a specific definition of the meaning of increased variability. A workshop was held in 2001 (The Stages of Reproductive Aging Workshop, STRAW) to propose a staging system for reproductive ageing in women.[3] That workshop recognised two stages of the transition with some ambiguity regarding the definition of entry into the first stage. Thus in the report of the workshop it is stated that 'a woman's menstrual cycles remain regular in stage –2 (early menopausal transition) but the duration changes by seven days or more (e.g. regular cycles are now every 24 instead of 31 days). However in the text figure for the STRAW staging system (Figure 1.1), stage –2 is characterised as showing 'variable cycle length' (more than seven days different from normal). The second stage was defined by the occurrence of two or more 'skipped' cycles and at least one intermenstrual interval of 60 days or more. For the purposes of this manuscript, two different criteria for the early transition have been used.

In data from the Melbourne Women's Midlife Health Project,[4] self-report of cycle irregularity after previous regular cycles was used to define entry into the early perimenopause or early menopausal transition. In data from a longitudinal Swedish/Australian study of the transition, the first cycle of three or more in a series of 10 where the length was less than 23 or greater than 35 days was used to define the onset of the first stage of the transition.[5] In the Melbourne study the second stage of the transition used a definition of three months of amenorrhoea while the Swedish study included definitions of 60 and 90 days of amenorrhoea.

Ovarian function and the menopausal transition

Although neuroendocrine changes may contribute to the onset of the menopausal transition,[6] in this manuscript the major factor determining its onset is considered to be a fall in ovarian follicle numbers to a critical level. Richardson et al.[7] documented follicle numbers as a function of age: their study concentrated particularly on women whose menstrual cycles had become irregular or who had become postmenopausal

Final Menstrual Period
(FMP)

Stages:	**-5**	**-4**	**-3**	**-2**	**-1**	**0**	**+1**	**+2**
Terminology:	**Reproductive**			**Menopausal Transition**			**Postmenopause**	
	Early	Peak	Late	Early	Late*		Early*	Late
				Perimenopause				
Duration of Stage:	variable			variable		(a) 1 yr	(b) 4 yrs	until demise
Menstrual Cycles:	variable to regular	regular		variable cycle length (*>7 days different from normal*)	≥2 skipped cycles and an interval of amenorrhea (≥60 days)	Amen x 12 mos	none	
Endocrine:	normal FSH		↑FSH	↑FSH			↑FSH	

Stages most likely to be characterized by vasomotor symptoms   ↑= *elevated*

Figure 1.1. The stages of female reproductive ageing; reproduced with permission from Soules *et al.*[3] (*Fertility and Sterility*, © 2001 American Society for Reproductive Medicine)

(Figure 1.2). Ovarian follicle numbers fall steadily with age, the fall appearing to accelerate at around the age of 38. Mean follicle numbers in women over the age of 45 but continuing to cycle regularly are approximately 1000/ovary whereas this number falls to approximately 100/ovary in those whose menstrual cycles have become irregular. In postmenopausal ovaries few if any follicles can be found.

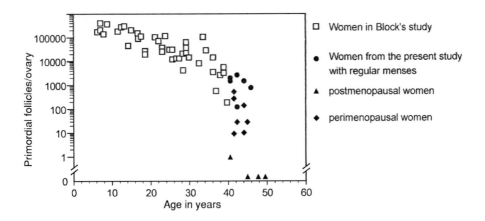

Figure 1.2. Ovarian follicle numbers as a function of age: □ women in Block's study[18] of 44 girls and women aged 7–44 years; ● women >45 years with regular menses; ◆ women >45 years with irregular menses (perimenopausal women); ▲ postmenopausal women; reproduced with permission from Richardson *et al.*[7] (*The Journal of Clinical Endocrinology & Metabolism*, © 1987 The Endocrine Society)

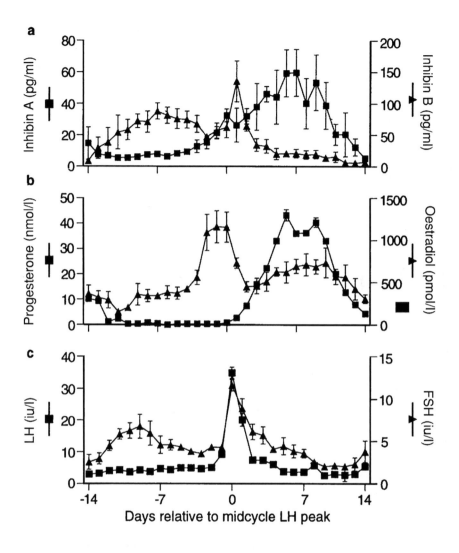

Figure 1.3. Plasma concentrations of (a) inhibin A and inhibin B, (b) oestradiol and progestogen, and (c) luteinising hormone (LH) and follicle-stimulating hormone (FSH) during the menstrual cycle; data displayed with respect to day of midcycle LH peak; reproduced with permission from Groome *et al.*[19] *(The Journal of Clinical Endocrinology & Metabolism*, © 1996 The Endocrine Society)

The marked fall in ovarian follicle numbers is associated with changes in hormone secretion. Under normal circumstances, ovarian function is driven by the gonadotrophins, follicle-stimulating hormone (FSH) and luteinising hormone (LH), which stimulate follicular development and the secretion of the ovarian steroids, and the inhibins, ovarian peptides that inhibit the secretion of FSH. During reproductive life, secretion of FSH in the follicular phase of the cycle is under dual inhibitory feedback control by oestradiol and inhibin B. The latter is a product of the pool of ovarian antral follicles. Inhibin A, on the other hand, is a product of the dominant follicle and the corpus luteum (Figure 1.3).[8]

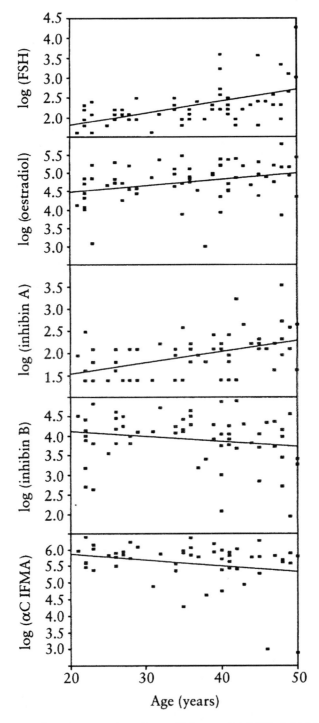

Figure 1.4. Log-transformed concentrations of serum FSH, oestradiol, inhibin A, inhibin B, and α-subunit immunoactivity (C-terminal segment of α-subunit immunofluorometric assay) as a function of age ($n = 59$–63); reproduced with permission from Burger *et al.*[9] (*Climacteric*, www.tandf.co.uk)

Endocrinology of reproductive ageing

A number of studies have examined the endocrinology of reproductive ageing, particularly with respect to follicular phase hormone concentrations. For example, Burger et al.[9] measured serum FSH, the inhibins and oestradiol in the first few days of the menstrual cycle in 66 healthy and regularly cycling female volunteers aged 20–50. FSH levels remained relatively constant until age 40 and mean FSH levels subsequently rose, although in some individual women they remained unchanged while in others considerably elevated FSH levels were observed. Oestradiol levels also increased with increasing age and inhibin B fell nonsignificantly (Figure 1.4). When the relationship between FSH and inhibin B was examined in women younger or older than 40, there was no statistically significant relationship under the age of 40 but over the age of 40 there was a significant inverse relationship between inhibin B and FSH (Figure 1.5). When log(FSH) was modelled as a function of log(inhibin B) and log(oestradiol), only the relationship with inhibin B was found to be statistically significant. The investigators concluded that inhibin B but not oestradiol was a significant independent predictor of FSH. This data amplified the original observations of Klein et al.,[10] who studied 13 normally ovulating women aged 20–25 and 20 aged 40–45, selected because they had been noted to have elevated follicular phase serum FSH levels. These investigators observed that the older women had statistically significantly higher FSH levels and particularly lower inhibin B levels than the younger controls, whereas oestradiol was somewhat higher in the older women and inhibin A did not differ between the two groups (Figure 1.6).

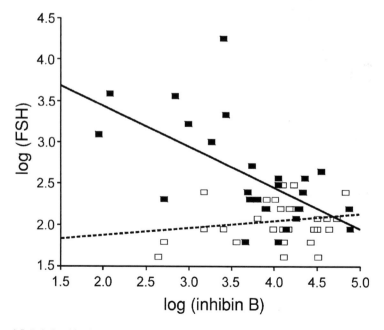

Figure 1.5. Relationships between log (FSH) and log (inhibin B) in two age groups, 20–39 years (□) and 40–50 years (■); there was no significant correlation between the two hormones in the younger age group ($r = 0.19$, not significant), dashed line, but in the older group there was a significant inverse correlation ($r = -0.61$, $P < 0.0001$), solid line; FSH = follicle-stimulating hormone; reproduced with permission from Burger et al.[9] (*Climacteric*, www.tandf.co.uk)

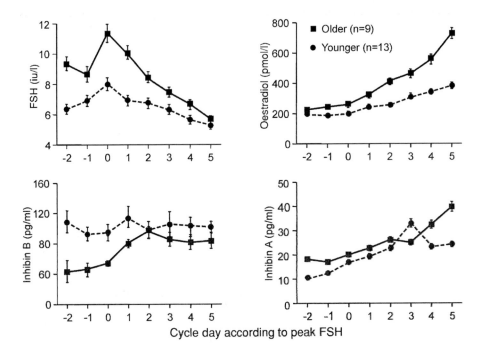

Figure 1.6. Mean ± SEM concentrations of (clockwise from top left) follicle-stimulating hormone (FSH) (*P* < 0.01), oestradiol (*P* < 0.01), inhibin A (*P* = 0.61), and inhibin B (*P* = 0.04), according to the day of maximal FSH concentration (peak FSH = day 0); SEM = standard error of the mean; reproduced with permission from Klein *et al.*[10] (*The Journal of Clinical Endocrinology & Metabolism*, © 1996 The Endocrine Society)

To summarise the endocrinology of reproductive ageing, there is a fall in ovarian follicle numbers with an increased serum FSH during the follicular phase seen in some women. In those women there is an inverse relationship of raised FSH levels with decreased inhibin B, presumably reflecting the fact that a critically low number of follicles has been reached. In grouped data, FSH rises, inhibin falls and oestradiol is well maintained, presumably owing to the increased FSH levels.

Endocrinology of the menopausal transition

The major data presented for the present manuscript comes from the Melbourne Women's Midlife Health Project.[4,11] For this project 2001 women aged 45–55 were initially recruited for a cross-sectional study using telephone numbers selected randomly from a computerised database of the Melbourne telephone directory. Of these, 438 who were still cycling were recruited for a longitudinal study involving annual interview and blood sampling. An informative analysis from this study was undertaken in year 3 where women were grouped into four categories or stages:

1. those still cycling regularly
2. those who reported a change in cycle frequency, classified as early perimenopausal
3. those who had had no menses for three months but had bled within the preceding 12 months, classified as late-perimenopausal
4. those who had had 12 months or more of amenorrhoea, classified as postmenopausal.[12]

Early perimenopausal women exhibited a profound fall in follicular phase concentrations of inhibin B while FSH was slightly raised compared with premenopausal women and there was no change in inhibin A or oestradiol. The late perimenopausal women, however, did show marked falls in oestradiol and inhibin A together with marked rises in FSH, changes that were similar to those observed in the postmenopausal women. Thus a selective fall in inhibin B concentrations appeared to be the initial endocrine event marking the onset of menstrual cycle irregularity (Figure 1.7).

Studies of individual women as they enter the menopausal transition show a high degree of within- and between-subject variation in the levels of the gonadotrophins and the sex steroids. Thus, in one example of this variation (Figure 1.8),[13] FSH levels, measured on several occasions during the initial long cycle marking the onset of the menopausal transition, were in the young reproductive age range, in the postmenopausal range, or somewhere in the intermediate ranges, whereas oestradiol levels varied inversely.

We have undertaken a longitudinal study of late reproductive ageing and the menopausal transition.[5] Twelve normal women initially aged 45–47 were studied for 36–98 months until FMP was identified. Starting with the onset of a menstrual bleed, blood sampling occurred three times weekly for four weeks, on an annual basis until the year of FMP. Daily menstrual diaries were kept with indications of spotting, bleeding, absence of bleeding or failure to record data. Cycles were classified endocrinologically as ovulatory cycles, cycles with defective luteal phase, and anovulatory cycles with evidence of continued oestradiol production (levels > 100 pmol/l). Among the latter, the possibility that ovulation occurred subsequent to the four-week sampling interval could not be excluded. Thus the designation 'anovulatory' may not always have been correct but was applicable to the sampling interval. The data were analysed in blocks of 10 cycles up to FMP and also in terms of changes during the early and late menopause transition as defined earlier. In the last 10 cycles prior to FMP, 62% were classified as anovulatory cycles and 38% were ovulatory cycles. Thirty-one to 40 cycles before FMP all cycles studied were ovulatory cycles. These cycles showed no changes in follicular phase hormonal profiles over the 4–9 year time period of observation whereas the anovulatory cycles were characterised by elevated FSH and LH and elevated ratios of FSH to inhibin A and FSH to inhibin B. These cycles were also of longer duration.

It was noteworthy that anovulatory cycles were observed only within the last 30 cycles prior to FMP, and that ovulatory cycles were frequently seen after entry into both the early and late menopausal transitions. While the transition is a period when the frequency of anovulatory cycles increases, ovulatory cycles continue to occur.

Ovulatory cycles in general showed 'normal' amounts and durations of menstrual blood loss, but in two women no menses occurred after ovulatory cycles were

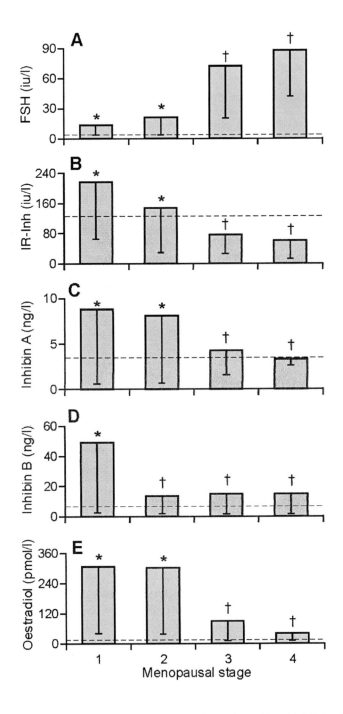

Figure 1.7. Geometric mean levels (with lower 95% confidence intervals) of (a) follicle-stimulating hormone (FSH), (b) immunoreactive inhibin (IR-INH), (c) inhibin A, (d) inhibin B, and (e) oestradiol as a function of menopausal status; menopausal stages are given in the text; values with the same superscript (* or †) are not statistically different; values with differing superscripts differ, $P < 0.05$; reproduced with permission from Burger *et al.*[12] (*Clinical Endocrinology*, © 1998 Blackwell Science Ltd)

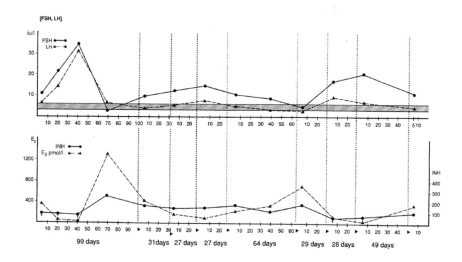

Figure 1.8. Concentrations of follicle-stimulating hormone (FSH), luteinising hormone (LH), oestradiol (E₂) and immunoreactive inhibin (INH) in a volunteer studied at the onset of the menopausal transition; the vertical dotted lines represent times of menses; the horizontal shaded bar represents the young-normal range for FSH; note the marked fluctuations in hormone levels; reproduced with permission from Hee et al.[13] (*Maturitas*, © 1993 Elsevier)

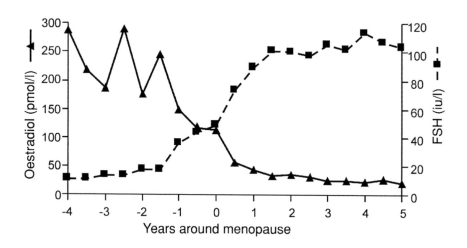

Figure 1.9. Geometric means of follicle-stimulating hormone (FSH) and oestradiol in relation to the final menstrual period (FMP); the horizontal axis represents time with respect to the FMP; reproduced with permission from Burger et al.[15] (*The Journal of Clinical Endocrinology & Metabolism*, © 1999 The Endocrine Society)

recorded. Menses associated with anovulatory cycles were generally abnormal. In two women sampling occurred starting with FMP – hence no bleeding occurred afterwards. Some cycles were associated with prolonged spotting, and some were followed by a normal menses, particularly in long cycles, raising the possibility that ovulation may have occurred after the four-week sampling interval had ceased. As had been indicated in other earlier studies, the reason for the occurrence of the final menses, i.e. failure to bleed, could not be deduced from this study where ovulatory cycles could occur without succeeding menstruation.

The above studies used reference points of cycle irregularity for data from single samples obtained in the follicular phase, or actual data from cycles with thrice-weekly serum samples. When FSH and oestradiol are measured in relation to prospectively defined final menses (without reference to menstrual history), oestradiol levels have fallen to approximately 50% of their premenopausal concentrations and FSH has risen to approximately 50% of its finally attained levels at the time of FMP (Figure 1.9).[15] It should be noted that there is no significant change in total serum testosterone concentrations across the time of the FMP and during the menopausal transition. Testosterone concentrations have been shown to fall by about 50% between the ages of 20 and 40 or 45[16] but there is no significant change around the time of the menopause (Figure 1.10).

Summary and comment on mechanisms

There is a fall in follicle numbers with age and when the numbers are low inhibin B secretion declines. FSH levels appear to remain in the reproductive age range when ovulatory cycles continue but rise in cycles that no longer show normal ovulatory characteristics. The frequency of anovulatory cycles increases in the last 30 cycles before FMP. There is a late fall in oestradiol and inhibin A as FSH rises. Testosterone levels together with dehydroepiandrosterone sulphate (DHEAS) fall substantially between the ages of 20 and approximately 45 but show little change in relation to the menopause transition.

The mechanisms that lead to menstrual cycle irregularity may include a fall in follicle numbers to critically low levels, and hence the development of temporary ovarian nonresponse to FSH stimulation. FSH concentrations rise but fail to elicit the secretion of oestradiol for some days or weeks. In some cycles the nonresponse does not persist, follicular development occurs and this in turn may lead to ovulation. Evidence for this has been presented in a large study involving daily urine collections over a number of cycles.[17] In that study the variability in the initiation of oestradiol responses was related to cycle length and FSH concentrations, with higher FSH being related to later onset of response.

The hormonal changes of the transition are thus complex, variable and unpredictable. Measurement of FSH or oestradiol is unreliable for characterisation of menopausal status.

Acknowledgements

The authors acknowledge the generous donation of kits for the measurement of inhibin A and B by Professor Nigel Groome, Oxford Brookes University, UK. Mr Nick Balasz and staff in the Department of Biochemistry at Monash Medical Centre undertook the majority of hormonal assays for our studies. Emma Dudley provided much helpful statistical assistance. Our studies were supported by grants from the Australian

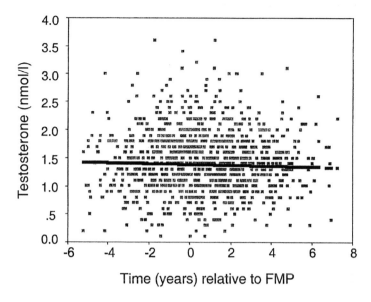

Time (years) relative to FMP

Figure 1.10. Observed testosterone levels across the menopausal transition, with linear regression fit (solid line); the horizontal axis represents time with respect to final menstrual period (FMP); reproduced with permission from Burger et al.[16] (*The Journal of Clinical Endocrinology & Metabolism,* © 2000 The Endocrine Society)

National Health and Medical Research Council and by an unrestricted grant from Organon for the endocrine investigations.

References

1. World Health Organization. *Research on the Menopause in the 90s.* Technical Report Series 866. Geneva: World Health Organization; 1996.
2. McKinlay SM, Brambilla DJ, Posner JG. The normal menopausal transition. *Maturitas* 1992;14:103–15.
3. Soules MR, Sherman S, Parrott E, Rebar R, Santoro N, Utian W, et al. Executive summary: Stages of Reproductive Aging Workshop (STRAW). *Fertil Steril* 2001;76:874–8.
4. Dennerstein L, Smith AM, Morse C, Burger HG, Green A, Hopper J, et al. Menopausal symptomatology: the experience of Australian women. *Med J Aust* 1993;159:232–6.
5. Landgren BM, Collins A, Csemiczky G, Burger HG, Baksheev L, Robertson DM. Menopause transition: annual changes in serum hormonal patterns over the menstrual cycle in women during a nine-year period prior to menopause. *J Clin Endocrinol Metab* 2004;89:2763–9.
6. Wise PM, Smith MJ, Dubal DB, Wilson ME, Rau SW, Cashion AB, et al. Neuroendocrine modulation and repercussions of female reproductive aging. In: Means AR, editor. *Recent Progress in Hormone Research.* Bethesda: The Endocrine Society; 2002. Vol. 57, p. 235–56.
7. Richardson SJ, Senikas V, Nelson JF. Follicular depletion during the menopausal transition: evidence for accelerated loss and ultimate exhaustion. *J Clin Endocrinol Metab* 1987;65:1231–7.
8. Burger HG, Dudley EC, Robertson DM, Dennerstein L. Hormonal changes in the menopause transition. In: Means AR, editor. *Recent Progress in Hormone Research.* Bethesda: The Endocrine Society; 2002. Vol. 57, p. 257–75.
9. Burger HG, Dudley E, Mamers P, Groome N, Robertson DM. Early follicular phase serum FSH as a function of age: the roles of inhibin B, inhibin A and estradiol. *Climacteric* 2000;3:17–24.

10.   Klein NA, Illingworth PJ, Groom NP, McNeilly AS, Battaglia DE, Soules MR. Decreased inhibin B secretion is associated with the monotropic rise of FSH in older, ovulatory women: a study of serum and follicular fluid levels of dimeric inhibin A and B in spontaneous menstrual cycles. *J Clin Endocrinol Metab* 1996;81:2742–5.

11.   Burger HG, Dudley EC, Hopper JL, Shelley JM, Green A, Smith A, *et al.* The endocrinology of the menopausal transition: a cross-sectional study of a population-based sample. *J Clin Endocrinol Metab* 1995;80:3537–45.

12.   Burger HG, Cahir N, Robertson DM, Groome NP, Dudley E, Green A, *et al.* Serum inhibins A and B fall differentially as FSH rises in perimenopausal women. *Clin Endocrinol (Oxf)* 1998;48:809–13.

13.   Hee J, MacNaughton J, Bangah M, Burger HG. Perimenopausal patterns of gonadotrophins, immunoreactive inhibin, estradiol and progesterone. *Maturitas* 1993;18:19–20.

14.   Burger HG, Dudley EC, Hopper JL, Groome N, Guthrie JR, Green A, *et al.* Prospectively measured levels of serum follicle-stimulating hormone, estradiol, and the dimeric inhibins during the menopausal transition in a population-based cohort of women. *J Clin Endocrinol Metab* 1999;84:4025–30.

15.   Zumoff B, Strain GW, Miller LK, Rosner W. Twenty-four hour mean plasma testosterone concentration declines with age in normal premenopausal women. *J Clin Endocrinol Metab* 1995;80:1429–30.

16.   Burger HG, Dudley EC, Cui J, Dennerstein L, Hopper JL. A prospective longitudinal study of serum testosterone dehydroepiandrosterone sulphate and sex hormone binding globulin levels through the menopause transition. *J Clin Endocrinol Metab* 2000;85:2832–8.

17.   Miro F, Parker SW, Aspinall LJ, Coley J, Ellis JE. Menstrual irregularity during the menopausal transition is caused by delayed ovarian responsiveness to FSH, The Endocrine Society 85th Annual Meeting, 19–22 June 2003, Philadelphia, USA. Abstract P2-206, p. 356.

18.   Block E. Quantitative morphological investigations of the follicular system in women; variations at different ages. *Acta Anat (Basel)* 1952;14:108–23.

19.   Groome NP, Illingworth PJ, O'Brien M, Pai R, Rodger FE, Mather JP, *et al.* Measurement of dimeric inhibin B throughout the human menstrual cycle. *J Clin Endocrinol Metab* 1996;81:1401–5.

Chapter 2

Metabolic effects of the menopause and hormone replacement therapy

John C Stevenson

Introduction

Coronary heart disease (CHD) is a major cause of death in women over 60 years, being at least six times more common than breast cancer. Approximately 50% of women develop CHD in their lifetime, with 30% dying from the disease.[1] CHD is uncommon in premenopausal women, especially non-smokers, but loss of ovarian function is associated with adverse metabolic changes and increased CHD risk. Thus the menopause is an important CHD risk factor unique to women. Ovarian hormones are thought to protect against CHD, so the adverse effects of oestrogen deficiency on the cardiovascular system could theoretically be prevented, or to some extent reversed, by hormone replacement therapy (HRT). It is important to understand the mechanisms by which HRT could be beneficial, or in any way harmful, to women in terms of cardiovascular disease (CVD).

Menopause effects on metabolic risk factors for CHD

Menopause results in an increased incidence of cardiovascular disease,[2] particularly CHD. Because of the close association between menopause and chronological age, an effect of menopause on CHD incidence has often proved difficult to demonstrate. But it has been shown that premature menopause results in the premature development of CHD.[3]

The menopause and lipids and lipoproteins

Lipids and lipoproteins are important in the development of atheromatous disease. The menopause results in adverse changes in lipids and lipoproteins, with increases in total cholesterol, triglycerides and low-density lipoprotein (LDL) cholesterol, and decreases in high-density lipoprotein (HDL) and HDL_2 cholesterol.[4] There may also be increases in other atherogenic lipoproteins such as lipoprotein (a)[5] and small dense LDL particles.[6] The latter are the most atherogenic, as they are more readily cleared through scavenger mechanisms than by the apolipoprotein B_{100} (apoB$_{100}$) receptors. Thus they are more likely to become lodged in the sub-endothelial space. Lipoprotein (a) is atherogenic largely because of its propensity for retention in the arterial wall, but it may also compete with fibrinogen and inhibit fibrinolysis. High levels of lipoprotein (a) are associated with increased risk of CHD in some populations. However, in other populations where LDL levels are low,[7] there does not appear to be an increased risk of CHD in the presence of raised lipoprotein (a) levels. It is thus possible that high lipoprotein (a) concentrations signify increase CHD risk only when LDL levels are also raised. As yet, it is not known whether changing lipoprotein (a) levels has any clinical impact on CHD risk. Triglycerides may be a particular risk factor for CHD in women. Increased endogenous triglycerides levels are associated with low HDL and HDL_2 cholesterol, insulin resistance and adverse changes in haemostatic parameters. Increased intake of exogenous triglycerides results in increased chylomicron remnants, which are themselves atherogenic.

The menopause and glucose and insulin metabolism

Insulin resistance is considered to be a pivotal metabolic disturbance in the pathogenesis of CHD.[8] Women with diabetes have a higher incidence of CHD than men with diabetes, suggesting that insulin resistance may be particularly important in women. Although there are age-related effects, menopause itself results in changes in insulin metabolism.[9] While there is no immediate change in circulating insulin concentrations, this disguises significant decreases in pancreatic insulin secretion and insulin elimination. There is also no immediate change in insulin resistance at the menopause,[9,10] but there is a progressive decrease in insulin sensitivity, producing an increase in insulin resistance, with time. Thus postmenopausal women become increasingly insulin resistant, which in turn results in a relative hyperinsulinaemia, as shown by an increase in the insulin response to a glucose challenge.[11] Insulin resistance is associated with many other factors that increase CHD risk, such as dyslipidaemia, adverse coagulation changes, central obesity and vascular smooth-muscle proliferation.

Effects on body fat and on haemostasis

Menopause results in an overall increase in body fat, but of more importance is that it causes a redistribution of fat in the male pattern.[12] This central adiposity is linked to a number of adverse metabolic changes, such as dyslipidaemia and insulin resistance. The effect of menopause on haemostatic factors has not been extensively elucidated, but there appear to be increases in fibrinogen, factor VII and plasminogen activator inhibitor-1 (PAI-1).[13]

HRT may reverse some of these changes described above, but the effects vary according to the type of oestrogen or progestogen used, and to their route of administration.[14]

HRT effects on metabolic risk factors for CHD

HRT and lipids and lipoproteins

Oestrogen lowers total cholesterol, irrespective of type of steroid or route of administration, and this effect is maintained in the long term while on treatment.[15] This lowering of cholesterol results primarily from a decrease in LDL cholesterol concentrations due to an upregulation of $apoB_{100}$ receptors. Oral oestrogen appears to be a little more effective than transdermal oestrogen in this respect. Oral HRT appears to increase the proportion of small dense LDL particles,[16] but it also increases their clearance from the circulation. Thus their shortened residence time in the circulation could reduce the likelihood of their retention in the arterial wall. Transdermal oestradiol does not decrease LDL particle size.[17] Small dense LDL particles may be more susceptible to oxidative damage that leads to foam cell production and the generation of atheroma, but oestrogen helps protect LDL against oxidative damage.[18] Oestrogen also improves the postprandial clearance of potentially atherogenic lipoprotein remnants,[19] which again will help towards the prevention of atheroma. Oestrogen also lowers the levels of lipoprotein (a), another lipoprotein risk marker for CHD.

Orally administered oestrogen increases HDL cholesterol, and particularly the HDL_2 subfraction that is thought to confer a protective effect against atherosclerosis development primarily through reverse cholesterol transport. Oestrogen acts by inhibiting hepatic lipase activity and by increasing the hepatic synthesis of apolipoprotein AI, the main protein component of HDL and HDL_2. While transdermal oestradiol appears to have a less marked effect on HDL cholesterol than oral oestrogen,[20] it does increase HDL_2. However, it also causes a reduction in HDL_3, which contains a significant amount of apolipoprotein AII, increased levels of which are associated with vascular lesions in animal models. Thus a reduction in HDL_3 could theoretically be a beneficial effect for CHD risk.

The type and route of administration of oestrogen determines its effects on triglycerides. Oestrogens primarily affect endogenous triglyceride concentrations. Conjugated equine oestrogens (CEE) cause an increase in triglycerides,[20] an effect which is pharmacological and results from the hepatic first-pass effect of this steroid. Orally administered oestradiol has a smaller effect on raising triglycerides, but transdermal oestradiol causes a reduction in triglycerides,[20] which is a physiological effect of oestradiol.

Progestogens have differing effects on lipids and lipoproteins, depending on their androgenicity and perhaps on their overall dosage.[21] The addition of progestogens to oestrogen therapy has no adverse effect in terms of lowering of LDL, since, although they increase LDL production, they also increase its clearance. Androgenic progestogens, such as norgestrel, reverse the HDL-raising effect of oestrogen[20] because they increase hepatic lipase activity. It is not known whether this reduction in HDL reflects any impairment in remnant clearance or in reverse cholesterol transport, thus the clinical significance of lowering HDL remains to be determined. In contrast, certain non-androgenic progestogens, such as dydrogesterone, have little negative impact on oestrogen-induced increases in HDL and HDL_2,[22] while others, such as medroxyprogesterone acetate (MPA), clearly attenuate the increases. Testosterone-derived progestogens, such as levonorgestrel, decrease triglyceride levels by reducing secretion of very-low-density lipoprotein (VLDL). C-21 progestogens do not prevent the increase in triglycerides induced by oral oestrogens. Thus combined oestrogen-progestogen HRT may lead to an increase in HDL but at the expense of an increase in triglycerides, or lead to a decrease in triglycerides but at the expense of a decrease, or no increase, in HDL. Which change is more important in terms of CHD benefit remains unknown but, when all these changes in lipids and lipoproteins are considered together, the various changes seen with most HRT combinations are likely to be beneficial overall. However, in certain clinical situations such as dyslipidaemia or diabetes, some HRT regimens will be potentially more beneficial than others.

HRT and glucose and insulin metabolism

Oestrogen affects glucose and insulin metabolism. Oral administration of 17β-oestradiol to postmenopausal women brings changes in glucose and insulin concentrations suggestive of an improvement in insulin resistance, whereas transdermal oestradiol is fairly neutral in its effects.[23] In contrast, alkylated oestrogens, such as ethinyl oestradiol, and CEE may raise insulin levels and impair glucose tolerance.[24]

Progestogen addition may modify the effects of oestrogen on glucose and insulin metabolism, depending on the type of progestogen used. Testosterone-derived progestogens, such as norgestrel, may increase insulin resistance.[25] Norethisterone acetate given orally may also have a negative effect,[23] but when given transdermally it has little impact.[25] Non-androgenic progestogens such as dydrogesterone have little adverse effect,[22] although MPA has unwanted effects.

HRT effects on body fat and on haemostasis

HRT has the effect of preventing or reversing the menopausal deposition of central fat.[26] It does not itself cause a significant increase in body fat, although it is a popular misconception that HRT causes weight gain.

Oestrogen affects coagulation and fibrinolysis, increasing both pro-coagulant and fibrinolytic activity. The effects of HRT on haemostasis are somewhat complex.[14,27] There is a reduction in certain pro-coagulant factors linked with atheroma development, such as fibrinogen and factor VII, but oral oestrogen also increases thrombogenesis. It is likely that the initiation of oestrogen therapy causes a transient imbalance between coagulation and fibrinolysis, thereby causing a short-term increase in thromboembolism risk, which disappears as these processes gradually readjust and come back into a balance. The non-oral administration of oestrogen may limit or even avoid this adverse effect.[17,28,29] Progestogens are probably fairly neutral in their effects on haemostasis.

HRT metabolic effects influencing vascular function

Infusions of physiological doses of oestrogen directly into the coronary arteries of women with CHD have been shown to reverse the paradoxical vasoconstrictor effect of acetylcholine seen in vessels with disturbed endothelial function.[30] This vasodilatory effect may be due to an acute oestrogen receptor-dependent effect on the nitric oxide synthase (NOS) pathway, which leads to increased levels of endothelial nitric oxide synthase (eNOS)[31] and increased production of the potent vasodilator NO. The addition of physiological doses of oestrogen to human endothelial cells stimulates NO release via endothelial cell-surface oestrogen receptors.[32] The reversal of the acetylcholine effect by oestrogen may therefore be the result of enhanced NO production from the endothelial cells in the coronary artery. NO is involved in regulation of blood pressure, platelet function, inhibition of vascular smooth-muscle proliferation and expression of adhesion molecules. HRT has been shown to lower the levels of the cell adhesion molecules E-selectin and vascular cell adhesion molecule-1 (VCAM-1) in postmenopausal women with hypercholesterolaemia[33] and in healthy postmenopausal women.[17,34] Oestrogens also reduce the release of the potent vasoconstrictor endothelin-1 by vascular endothelial cells.[35]

There is also evidence that oestrogens act independently of the endothelium, possibly by acting through ion channels. The arterial vasodilatation produced by the addition of 17β-oestradiol to isolated rings of rabbit coronary artery is still evident when the vascular endothelium has been removed.[36] Oestrogen modulates calcium channels in the smooth-muscle cell membranes of blood vessels and in cardiac myocytes: it inhibits calcium-induced contraction of coronary artery rings in a dose-dependent manner, inhibits inward calcium currents, and reduces intracellular free calcium in isolated cardiac myocytes.[37] In addition, oestrogen activates BK_{Ca} channels to cause coronary artery relaxation.[38]

Arterial function may also be affected by oestrogen via changes in the renin–angiotensin system. Women with enhanced angiotensin-1 conversion (as a result of the deletion allele of the ACE gene polymorphism) have impaired NO release from the vascular endothelium.[39] The ACE gene deletion allele has been shown to be associated with CHD, particularly in women.[40] HRT has been shown to reduce circulating ACE activity.[41,42]

Elevated levels of C-reactive protein (CRP) are associated with increased CHD risk,[43] and HRT has an effect on these levels. Oral HRT has been shown to increase CRP concentrations, whereas transdermal HRT appears to have no effect.[44]

Abnormal deposition and remodelling of vascular extracellular matrix is an important process involved in the pathogenesis and progression of atheroma, and restoration of the normal regulation of these processes may inhibit atherogenesis. A key group of enzymes involved in these processes is the matrix metalloproteinases (MMPs) and their tissue inhibitors (TIMPs). MMPs are zinc-dependent enzymes responsible for the degradation of extracellular matrix components such as collagen and proteoglycans, and they have been implicated in the development of CVD.[45] There is some evidence that they may contribute significantly to atheromatous plaque rupture,[46] and they may well be involved with plaque progression and regression. We have shown in cultures of human vascular smooth-muscle cells that oestradiol increases MMP release in a dose-dependent manner.[47] It is therefore possible that modest increases in MMPs, produced by low doses of oestrogen, may counteract increased vascular collagen deposition, while high levels of MMPs, produced by high doses of oestrogen, could promote atheromatous lesions and destabilise plaques.

The effects described above may in part explain the apparent early harm to the cardiovascular system seen in randomised clinical trials of HRT using cardiac events as clinical outcomes. These studies have used a relatively high starting dose of oestrogen for the age of the women, and they have shown an early increase in events with HRT use, but a later decrease in events.[48,49] It is thus quite conceivable that the relatively high dose of oestrogen used in these trials has initial, and transient, adverse effects on haemostasis and on vascular remodelling, resulting in the lack of benefit, or even early harm, seen in the first years of these studies. Further studies are clearly needed to establish the optimal doses, types and routes of administration of HRT for CHD.

Conclusions

Menopause results in various metabolic changes that would be expected to increase CHD risk. These include adverse changes in lipids and lipoproteins, and in glucose and insulin metabolism. There is overwhelming biological evidence for a beneficial effect of HRT on the cardiovascular system at the cellular, tissue and whole animal levels. This involves both metabolic and direct arterial effects. The failure of randomised clinical trials to show overall benefit on hard endpoints may be explained by transient adverse effects on haemostasis and vascular remodelling, resulting from the use of inappropriately high starting doses of oestrogen. There is a clear and urgent need for other randomised clinical trials with hard CHD endpoints using different HRT regimens. Until the results of such trials are available, no clear recommendations can be given for HRT use in the prevention and treatment of CHD.

Addendum

The recent publication of the oestrogen-only arm results of the Women's Health Initiative (WHI) study[50] could support the concept that doses of oestrogen that are inappropriately high for the age of the woman are more likely to have adverse CHD effects. The paper showed that, with a daily dose of 0.625 mg CEE, the hazard ratio for CHD in women aged 50–59 years was 0.56 (95% CI 0.30–1.03) whereas for women aged 70–79 years it was 1.04 (95% CI 0.75–1.44), although the study was not sufficiently powered to show significant differences in sub-group analyses. Overall, there was an absolute risk reduction per 10 000 person-years of five fewer CHD events, and the global index was slightly in favour of oestrogen-only therapy (absolute risk reduction in events of two per 10 000 person-years).

References

1. Kuhn FE, Rackley CE. Coronary artery disease in women: risk factors, evaluation, treatment and prevention. *Arch Intern Med* 1993;153:2626–36.
2. Gordon T, Kannel WB, Hjortland MC, McNamara PM. Menopause and coronary heart disease. The Framingham Study. *Ann Intern Med* 1978;89:157–61.
3. Sznajderman M, Oliver MF. Spontaneous premature menopause, ischaemic heart disease and serum lipids. *Lancet* 1963;i:962–4.
4. Stevenson JC, Crook D, Godsland IF. Influence of age and menopause on serum lipids and lipoproteins in healthy women. *Atherosclerosis* 1993;98:83–90.
5. Abbey M, Owen A, Suzakawa M, Roach P, Nestel PJ. Effects of menopause and hormone replacement therapy on plasma lipids, lipoproteins and LDL-receptor activity. *Maturitas* 1999;33:259–69.
6. Campos H, McNamara JR, Wilson PWF. Differences in low density lipoprotein subfractions and apolipoproteins in premenopausal and postmenopausal women. *J Clin Endocrinol Metab* 1988;67:30–5.
7. Crook D, Howell R, Sidhu M, Edmonds DK, Stevenson JC. Elevated serum lipoprotein(a) levels in young women with endometriosis. *Metabolism* 1997;46:735–9.
8. Godsland IF, Stevenson JC. Insulin resistance: syndrome or tendency? *Lancet* 1995;346:100–3.
9. Walton C, Godsland IF, Proudler AJ, Wynn V, Stevenson JC. The effects of the menopause on insulin sensitivity, secretion and elimination in non-obese, healthy women. *Eur J Clin Invest* 1993;23:466–73.
10. Toth MJ, Sites CK, Eltabbakh GH, Poehlman ET. Effect of menopausal status on insulin-stimulated glucose disposal: comparison of middle-aged premenopausal and early postmenopausal women. Diabetes Care 2000;23:801-6.
11. Proudler AJ, Felton CV, Stevenson JC. Ageing and the response of plasma insulin, glucose and C-peptide concentrations to intravenous glucose in postmenopausal women. *Clin Sci* 1992;83:489–94.
12. Ley CJ, Lees B, Stevenson JC. Sex- and menopause-associated changes in body-fat distribution. *Am J Clin Nutr* 1992;55:950–4.
13. Stevenson JC. Metabolic effects of the menopause and oestrogen replacement. In: Barlow DH, editor. *Baillière's Clinical Obstetrics and Gynaecology. The Menopause: Key Issues*. London: Ballière Tindall; 1996. p. 449–67.
14. Stevenson JC. Cardiovascular effects of estrogens. *J Steroid Biochem Mol Biol* 2000;74:387–93.
15. Whitcroft SI, Crook D, Marsh MS, Ellerington MC, Whitehead MI, Stevenson JC. Long-term effects of oral and transdermal hormone replacement therapies on serum lipid and lipoprotein concentrations. *Obstet Gynecol* 1994;84:222–6.
16. van der Mooren MJ, de Graaf J, Demacker PN, de Haan AF, Rolland R. Changes in the low-density lipoprotein profile during 17 beta-oestradiol-dydrogesterone therapy in postmenopausal women. *Metabolism* 1994;43:799–802.
17. Stevenson JC, Oladipo A, Manassiev N, Whitehead MI, Guilford S, Proudler AJ. Randomized trial of effect of transdermal continuous combined hormone replacement therapy on cardiovascular risk markers. *Br J Haematol* 2004;124:802–8.
18. Sack MN, Rader DJ, Cannon RO. Oestrogen and inhibition of oxidation of low density lipoproteins in postmenopausal women. *Lancet* 1994;343:269–70.

19. Westerveld HT, Kock LAW, van Rijn JM, Erkelens DW, de Bruin TWA. 17 beta-Estradiol improves postprandial lipid metabolism in postmenopausal women. *J Clin Endocrinol Metab* 1995;80:249–53.

20. Crook D, Cust MP, Gangar KF, Worthington M, Hillard TC, Stevenson JC, *et al.* Comparison of transdermal and oral estrogen/progestin hormone replacement therapy: effects on serum lipids and lipoproteins. *Am J Obstet Gynecol* 1992;166:950–5.

21. Stevenson JC. Hormone replacement therapy and lipids. *Menopause Review* 1997;2:15–20.

22. Crook D, Godsland IF, Hull J, Stevenson JC. Hormone replacement therapy with dydrogesterone and 17 beta-oestradiol: effects on serum lipoproteins and glucose tolerance during 24 month follow up. *Br J Obstet Gynaecol* 1997;104:298–304.

23. Spencer CP, Godsland IF, Cooper AJ, Ross D, Whitehead MI, Stevenson JC. Effects of oral and transdermal 17beta-estradiol with cyclical oral norethindrone acetate on insulin sensitivity, secretion, and elimination in postmenopausal women. *Metabolism* 2000;49:742–7.

24. Spellacy WN, Buhi WC, Birk SA. The effects of estrogens on carbohydrate metabolism: glucose, insulin and growth hormone studies on one hundred and seventy one women ingesting Premarin, mestranol and ethinyl estradiol for six months. *Am J Obstet Gynecol* 1972;114:378–92.

25. Godsland IF, Gangar K, Walton C, Cust MP, Whitehead MI, Wynn V, *et al.* Insulin resistance, secretion, and elimination in postmenopausal women receiving oral or transdermal hormone replacement therapy. *Metabolism* 1993;42:846–53.

26. Gambacciani M, Ciaponi M, Cappagli B, Piaggesi L, De Simone L, Orlandi R, *et al.* Body weight, body fat distribution, and hormonal replacement therapy in early postmenopausal women. *J Clin Endocrinol Metab* 1997;82:414–7.

27. Winkler UH. Menopause, hormone replacement therapy and cardiovascular disease: a review of haemostaseological findings. *Fibrinolysis* 1992;6 Suppl 3:5–10.

28. Fox J, George AJ, Newton JR, Parsons AD, Stuart GK, Stuart J, *et al.* Effect of transdermal oestradiol on the haemostatic balance of menopausal women. *Maturitas* 1993;18:55–64.

29. Scarabin PY, Oger E, Plu-Bureau G; EStrogen and THromboEmbolism Risk Study Group. Differential association of oral and transdermal oestrogen-replacement therapy with venous thromboembolism risk. *Lancet* 2003;362:428–32.

30. Collins P, Rosano GM, Sarrel PM, Ulrich L, Adamopoulos S, Beale CM, *et al.* 17 beta-Estradiol attenuates acetylcholine-induced coronary arterial constriction in women but not men with coronary heart disease. *Circulation* 1995;92:24–30.

31. Wingrove CS, Garr E, Pickar JH, Dey M, Stevenson JC. Effects of equine oestrogens on markers of vasoactive function in human coronary artery endothelial cells. *Mol Cell Endocrinol* 1999;150:33–7.

32. Stefano GB, Prevot V, Beauvillain JC, Cadet P, Fimiani C, Welters I, *et al.* Cell-surface estrogen receptors mediate calcium-dependent nitric oxide release in human endothelia. *Circulation* 2000;101:1594–7.

33. Koh KK, Cardillo C, Bui MN, Hathaway L, Csako G, Waclawiw MA, *et al.* Vascular effects of estrogen and cholesterol-lowering therapies in hypercholesterolemic postmenopausal women. *Circulation* 1999;99:354–60.

34. Koh KK, Bui MN, Mincemoyer R, Cannon RO. Effects of hormone therapy on inflammatory cell adhesion molecules in postmenopausal healthy women. *Am J Cardiol* 1997;80:1505–7.

35. Wingrove CS, Stevenson JC. 17 beta-Oestradiol inhibits stimulated endothelin release in human vascular endothelial cells. *Eur J Endocrinol* 1997;137:205–8.

36. Jiang CW, Sarrel PM, Lindsay DC, Poole-Wilson PA, Collins P. Endothelium-independent relaxation of rabbit coronary artery by 17 beta-oestradiol *in vitro*. *Br J Pharmacol* 1991;104:1033–7.

37. Jiang C, Poole-Wilson PA, Sarrel PM, Mochizuki S, Collins P, MacLeod KT. Effect of 17 beta-oestradiol on contraction, Ca^{2+} current and intracellular free Ca^{2+} in guinea-pig isolated cardiac myocytes. *Br J Pharmacol* 1992;106:739–45.

38. White RE, Darkow DJ, Falvo Lang JL. Estrogen relaxes coronary arteries by opening BK_{Ca} channels through a cGMP-dependent mechanism. *Circ Res* 1995;77:936–42.

39. Buikema H, Pinto YM, Rooks G, Grandjean JG, Schunkert H, van Gilst WH. The deletion polymorphism of the angiotensin converting enzyme gene is related to phenotypic differences in human arteries. *Eur Heart J* 1996;17:787–94.

40. Schuster H, Wienker TF, Stremmler U, Noll B, Steinmetz A, Luft FC. An angiotensin converting enzyme gene variant is associated with acute myocardial infarction in women but not in men. *Am J Cardiol* 1995;76:601–3.

41. Proudler AJ, Ahmed AIH, Crook D, Fogelman I, Rymer JM, Stevenson JC. Hormone replacement therapy and serum angiotensin-converting enzyme activity in postmenopausal women. *Lancet* 1995;346:89–90.

42. Proudler AJ, Cooper A, Whitehead MI, Stevenson JC. Effect of oestrogen-only and oestrogen-progestogen replacement therapy upon circulating angiotensin I-converting enzyme activity in postmenopausal women. *Clin Endocrinol* 2003;58:30–5.

43. Pradhan AD, Manson JE, Rossouw JE, Siscovick DS, Mouton CP, Rifai N, *et al.* Inflammatory biomarkers, hormone replacement therapy, and incident coronary heart disease: prospective analysis from the Women's Health Initiative observational study. *JAMA* 2002;288:980–7.

44. Post MS, van der Mooren MJ, Stehouwer CD, van Baal WM, Mijatovic V, Schalkwijk CG, *et al.* Effects of transdermal and oral oestrogen replacement therapy on C-reactive protein levels in postmenopausal women: a randomised, placebo-controlled trial. *Thromb Haemost* 2002;88:605–10.

45. Dollery CM, McEwan JR, Henney AM. Matrix metalloproteinases and cardiovascular disease. *Circ Res* 1995;77:863–8.

46. Galis ZS, Sukhova GK, Lark MW, Libby P. Increased expression of matrix metalloproteinases and matrix degrading activity in vulnerable regions of human atherosclerotic plaques. *J Clin Invest* 1994;94:2493–503.

47. Wingrove CS, Garr E, Godsland IF, Stevenson JC. 17beta-oestradiol enhances release of matrix metalloproteinase-2 from human vascular smooth muscle cells. *Biochim Biophys Acta* 1998;1406:169–74.

48. Hulley S, Grady D, Bush T, Furberg C, Herrington D, Riggs B, *et al.* Randomized trial of estrogen plus progestin for secondary prevention of coronary heart disease in postmenopausal women. Heart and Estrogen/progestin Replacement Study (HERS) Research Group. *JAMA* 1998;280:605–13.

49. Manson JE, Hsia J, Johnson KC, Rossouw JE, Assaf AR, Lasser NL, *et al.*; Women's Health Initiative Investigators. Estrogen plus progestin and the risk of coronary heart disease. *N Engl J Med* 2003;349:523–34.

50. Anderson GL, Limacher M, Assaf AR, Bassford T, Beresford SA, Black H, *et al.*; Women's Health Initiative Steering Committee. Effects of conjugated equine estrogen in postmenopausal women with hysterectomy: the Women's Health Initiative randomized controlled trial. *JAMA* 2004;291:1701–12.

Chapter 3

Timing of the menopause and its specific effects on health and wellbeing: epidemiology of the menopause

Cecilia Magnusson

Introduction

Despite being ubiquitous in women's lives, the menopause has received much attention from the medical establishment. It has also been the subject of great myths in the lay population. A wide range of diseases, syndromes and symptoms has, over the course of history, been attributed to the waning ovarian hormone production of the menopause. The list includes maladies ranging from hysterical flatulence, through 'declining femininity', to sheer madness.[1]

The biological effects of the menopause are not easily disentangled from those of confounding factors. Firstly, the ageing process, a universally important health determinant, coincides with the postmenopausal state. Secondly, the sociocultural expectations of the menopause transition, which is a period of 'crisis and loss', interferes with perceptions of menopausal health effects.

Attitudes towards the menopause

In 1966, the now infamous Dr Robert Wilson published his bestseller *Feminine Forever* on menopause and HRT.[2] He wrote 'Without estrogen replacement women are destined to become sexless caricatures of their former selves…the equivalent of a eunuch.' and 'With estrogen breasts and genitals will not shrivel. Such women will be much more pleasant to live with and will not become dull and unattractive.' These astonishing statements are perhaps too extreme to be paid any undue attention in a contemporary discussion of menopausal health and attitudes towards the menopause.

However, variations on the same theme are well represented in the scientific literature of today. For example, Benagiano and Primiero[3] state in a publication in 2001 that:

Growing evidence indicates that the process of ageing differs in a considerable way in the two sexes. This difference may, at least in part, be due to sex-related differences in the regulation of stress response mediators. In addition, variability in the mitochondrial genome also displays a sex-specific impact on longevity. Restricting the discussion to longevity in the female, a paramount role must be given to sex hormones in improving a woman's ageing. Indeed, it is the fall in oestradiol production that qualitatively changes the ageing perspective in the human female, since oestrogen secretion plays a major role in guaranteeing a woman's psycho-physical equilibrium during the fertile period.

This theme is contrasted by findings from a Swedish study on women's own views on the menopause.[4] The investigators followed 148 women, randomly selected from the general population of Stockholm, for four years until they were 53 years of age. Psychological interviews and implementation of rating scales, health screening and hormonal characterisation were conducted annually. Half of the study participants were then hormone replacement therapy (HRT) users, while the two residual 25% were peri- or postmenopausal, respectively, based on self-reports. Half of the women (51%) had a positive attitude to menopause, while 24% had a negative and 25% a neutral attitude. A positive attitude entailed views of the menopause such as that it constituted a developmental phase associated with an increased self-awareness and a stronger personal identity.

Timing of the menopause

Natural menopause is retrospectively defined as the last menstrual period before the absence of menses for 12 consecutive months without obvious cause (such as pregnancy), and usually occurs around the age of 50.[5]

Most studies of age at natural menopause pertain to Caucasian women, although one international study reported on the variability in reproductive factors across populations in Europe, the Americas, Asia, Australia and Africa.[6] The study comprised 18 997 women from 13 centres in 11 countries interviewed between 1979 and 1988 and surveyed with the same questionnaire. Median age at natural menopause was reported to range between 49 and 52 years.

Timing of menopause does not appear to vary substantially with ethnicity, although some studies of non-Caucasian women suggest that African women and Hispanic women of Mexican descent might have an earlier age at menopause than Caucasian women, while Japanese and Malaysian women report a median age at menopause similar to that for Caucasian women.[6-8] However, methodological obstacles, such as varying definitions of the menopause and considerable measurement error, obscure the picture.

Furthermore, age at menopause does not seem to demonstrate any clear secular trend.[9] Amundsen and Diers[10] have published interesting data from historical material indicating that median age at menopause did not differ much from 50–51 years in classical Greece and Rome. Earlier arguments that age at menopause is increasing with time have been re-evaluated in the light of new methodological insights.[9]

Determinants of timing of the menopause

Many factors have been suggested to be involved as determinants of age at menopause. Many of these, however, lack consistency in scientific reporting. This might be due to the fact that a considerable part of the variation may be attributable to genetic factors.

A Medline search only identified one classical twin study reporting on heritability of age at menopause.[11] This study comprised 275 monozygotic and 353 dizygotic female twin pairs, and the data suggested that additive genetic and unique environmental factors interact. After adjustment for confounding, the heritability for age at menopause was found to be 63%. Both early and late menopause were significantly influenced by genetic factors. Age at menopause and age at menarche were not correlated, suggesting that the genetic factors behind timing of the menopause were not mediated through the genetic effect on age at menarche.

The most consistent finding regarding other determinants for age at menopause has been that of smoking. There is a growing body of evidence that current, but not former, smokers stop menstruating 1–2 years before nonsmokers.[7] It has been hypothesized that the causal pathway between smoking and the advance of menopause is through a toxic effect of the polycyclic aromatic hydrocarbons in cigarette smoke on ovarian follicles.[7] Yet, if such an effect is not irreversible, this hypothesis is incompatible with the lack of impact of former smoking.

With varying consistency, studies have found that an earlier natural menopause is also associated with low educational attainment, unemployment, nulliparity or having fewer children, never having used oral contraceptives, low relative weight, and being on a weight reduction programme.[7] McKinlay concludes in her review from 1985, that only smoking has been dependably reported to be associated with onset of menopause.[9] All other reported potential determinants either have a very small influence on age at menopause or are inadequately adjusted for covariates, including smoking.[9]

Health effects of the menopause

The impact of the menopause, regarded as a physiological process entailing a decline in ovarian hormone secretion, on health is not easily assessed. In particular, methodological shortcomings, such as problems with definitions and measurement errors, and strong biases distort findings. It is thus difficult to interpret the findings from observational studies of health effects of the menopause. Therefore, results mostly from randomised clinical trials of the influence of HRT, which may be considered as a reversion of the physiological alterations of menopause, are presented below.

Classical menopausal symptoms

The symptoms most often associated with menopausal transition are bleeding irregularities and vasomotor and urogenital symptoms. The prevalence of vasomotor symptoms in women around menopause is reported to range from 44% in unselected samples to as high as 70%.[5,12] It is well known that such symptoms tend to wane with time. Vasomotor symptoms seem causally related to oestrogen deficiency, since their occurrence is associated with fluctuating follicle-stimulating hormone (FSH) and oestradiol levels and HRT is proven to relieve them.[13–15]

There are few studies on the prevalence of urogenital symptoms and the results are divergent.[16] It may be true that many women are reluctant to admit urinary incontinence, leading to an underestimation of the problem. Vaginal dryness seems to be related to declining hormone levels, while the association with urinary incontinence is controversial.[16] Results from the Heart and Estrogen/Progestin Replacement Study (HERS) trial reported an increased prevalence of urinary incontinence after HRT, casting doubt on such an association.[17]

Menstrual bleeding pattern has also been correlated to hormonal changes during transition to menopause.[16]

Recent Swedish data indicate that the experience of menopausal symptoms may be influenced by psychosocial factors. A qualitative study comprising 130 women aged 48 years, randomly selected from the background population, showed that optimistic and neutral expectations of the menopause were associated with low levels of symptom reporting, whereas pessimistic appraisal was significantly related to elevated symptom scores.[4] Furthermore, out of the symptoms rated, only vasomotor symptoms and joint pain, but not negative mood, decreased sexual desire, memory problems, sleep-related symptoms, vaginal dryness, urogenital problems, vitality or increased sexual desire, were associated with menopausal status in an earlier analyses of the material.[18] The other symptoms were more strongly related to psychosocial factors, lifestyle and attitude to menopause.

At least 25% of women in clinical trials report significant improvement in their vasomotor symptoms when taking placebo, further supporting the idea that menopausal symptoms are indeed dependent on factors over and above hormone levels.[19]

Quality of life

Two major randomised clinical trials have reported on the impact of HRT on quality of life: the Women's Health Initiative (WHI)[15] and HERS.[14] The findings are reviewed below.

The completed arm of WHI, the combined oestrogen-progestogen hormone trial, comprised 16 608 postmenopausal women aged 50 to 79 years who did not report any serious medical conditions and had an intact uterus at baseline.[15] The women were randomly assigned to treatment with oestrogen plus progestogen (0.625 mg of conjugated equine oestrogen plus 2.5 mg of medroxyprogesterone acetate, in 8506 women) or placebo (in 8102 women). Quality of life measures were collected at baseline and at one year in all women and at three years in a subgroup of 1511 women.

The WHI investigators have published on the impact of HRT on quality of life scores for different measures: general health, physical functioning, role limitations due to physical problems, bodily pain, energy and fatigue, social functioning, role limitations due to emotional problems, mental health, modified mini-mental state examination, depression score, sleep disturbance and satisfaction with sex.[15] After one year of follow-up, combined oestrogen-progestogen treatment had a statistically significant effect on three of these measures: physical functioning, bodily pain and sleep disturbance. These effects were, however, trivial: the mean benefits of the three measures were 0.8 points on a 100-point scale, 1.9 points on a 100-point scale and 0.4 points on a 20-point scale, respectively. The influences of HRT on measures of health-related quality of life were all slighter than the smallest possible intra-personal change.

The WHI investigators also reported on quality of life outcomes at three years of follow-up.[15] Then, HRT conferred no statistically significant benefits. The impact of HRT among subgroups was also analysed. Women in the youngest age stratum (50–54 years) reporting moderate or severe vasomotor symptoms are of specific interest, since they potentially have a more pronounced effect of HRT on wellbeing due to symptom relief. Oestrogen and progestogen improved vasomotor symptoms and resulted in a small benefit in terms of sleep disturbance but no benefit in terms of the other quality of life outcomes.

The WHI findings have been actively debated since their publication. One of the major criticisms is that women participating in the WHI are different from postmenopausal women in general. In particular, they did not perceive their menopausal symptoms, if any, as disabling, since they were willing to risk being assigned to placebo. Thus, symptom relief has been argued not to be important in their appraisal of wellbeing. Second, the instruments used may not have been sensitive enough to measure changes in the outcomes of interest. Third, the rate of adherence to the study regimen was 74% in the oestrogen-plus-progestogen group and 81% in the placebo group at one year. Noncompliance can dilute the results when data are analysed according to the intention-to-treat principle.[20]

The smaller HERS trial comprised 2763 postmenopausal women aged 50–79 years with a documented coronary artery disease.[14] The study participants were randomly assigned to treatment with 0.625 mg of conjugated equine oestrogen plus 2.5 mg of medroxyprogesterone acetate or placebo.

In contrast to the WHI findings, Hlatky et al.[14] concluded that the effect of HRT on quality of life was modified by the presence of menopausal symptoms. Their main results are summarised in Table 3.1. Women with flushes at baseline had a statistically significant improvement in mental health as well as a reduction in depressive symptoms after hormonal treatment. No effect was seen on energy/fatigue or physical functioning. Interestingly, the opposite pattern was noted in women without flushes. Symptom-free women thus experienced a statistically significant *negative* influence of hormones on physical functioning as well as energy/fatigue, while mental health and depressive symptoms were unaffected.

The HERS investigators also found that, regardless of HRT, women experiencing menopausal symptoms had significantly worse quality of life scores at study entry and during follow-up, compared with women without symptoms.[14] Furthermore, analyses of clinical and sociodemographic characteristics such as chest pain, low educational level, history of heart failure and diabetes hypertension showed a much more pronounced impact on quality of life than HRT.[14]

Chronic disease

Age at menopause has been hypothesised to be associated with a number of conditions. Few of these associations stand scientific scrutiny if the menopause is seen as a purely physiological event independent of ageing, psychosocial factors and other confounders (smoking, most importantly).

Breast cancer is a prominent exception. There is compelling evidence that ovarian hormones have a principal role in the development of breast cancer, and entering the postmenopausal state has, for decades, been known to protect from breast cancer.[21] In a report from the Million Women study,[22] the relative risk of breast cancer was, among never users of HRT, 0.75 (95% CI 0.68–0.82) for perimenopausal women and 0.63

Table 3.1. Quality of life scores according to study regimen in the HERS trial, by self-reported flushing at baseline; data from Hlatky et al.[14]

Outcome measure	Difference in mean quality of life score over follow-up					
	Flushes (n=434)			No flushes (n=2325)		
	HRT[a]	Placebo	P	HRT[a]	Placebo	P
Physical function[b]	−3.1	−2.2	0.42	−4.2	−3.3	0.04
Energy/fatigue[c]	−2.3	−2.4	0.99	−4.6	−3.1	0.03
Mental health[d]	+2.6	−0.5	0.04	−0.6	−1.1	0.4
Depressive symptoms[e]	−0.5	+0.007	0.01	−0.08	+0.06	0.08

[a] Hormone replacement therapy: 0.625 mg of conjugated equine oestrogen plus 2.5mg of medroxyprogesterone acetate; [b] Assessed using the 12-item Duke Activity Status Index; [c] Measured using a 4-item RAND-scale, graded from 0 (worst) to 100 (best); [d] Measured using the RAND mental health inventory, a 5-item scale that assesses anxiety and depression, with scores ranging from 0 (worst) to 100 (best); [e] Assessed by the 8-item scale according to Burnam et al, graded from 4 (worst) to −8.2 (best)

(95% CI 0.58–0.68) for postmenopausal women, compared with premenopausal women. These are observational data, but the inverse of menopause, i.e. HRT, has been clearly shown to increase breast cancer risk in the WHI. Lastly, the age-specific incidence curve for breast cancer is strongly indicative of a relationship between menopause and breast cancer (Figure 3.1). Breast cancer incidence increases rapidly with age up to age 50, after which there is a marked decline in the rate of increase. This pattern can be compared with the corresponding curve for fatal myocardial infarction (Figure 3.2), which has no clear trend break at menopause and where the shape of the curves is not dissimilar between women and men, although they are shifted approximately five years apart.

Oestrogen deficiency is also clearly related to a decline in bone mineral density, and thus menopause is known to confer an increased risk of osteoporotic fractures.[23] HRT has been shown in trials to be effective in the prevention of such fractures and is also protective of colorectal cancer.[24]

Mortality

Age at natural menopause has also been related to all-cause mortality in a number of observational studies. For example, women with natural menopause prior to age 40 years had a 50% higher mortality rate than those reporting menopause at age 50 years or older in a US study.[25] Women whose menopause occurred between ages 40 and 50 years did, however, not have an increased mortality compared with those whose menopause occurred at an older age. Snowdon et al.[26] reported a 95% versus 35% increase in all-cause mortality associated with natural menopause occurring before age 40 years and at 40–49 years, respectively, compared with menopause at age 50 years or older. Jacobsen et al.[27] investigated the association between age at natural menopause and all-cause mortality in a Norwegian cohort study comprising 19 731 postmenopausal women followed from 1961 through to 1997. They found some evidence of a weak association, with 1.6% (95% CI 0.6–2.7) reduced mortality per three years' increase in age at menopause.

In contrast, when longevity in women after bilateral salpingo-oophorectomy (BSOE), not given HRT, was investigated in a Swedish study, a different pattern emerged.[28] Nilsson et al. explored the association in a long-term follow-up study of a historical cohort of young women undergoing BSOE in the early 20th century at the General Hospital, Malmo, Sweden. They found no difference in life expectancy in 152 women with an early menopause caused by BSOE, as compared with national statistics of contemporary women. However, the mortality pattern was somewhat different with fewer deaths due to cancer, particularly breast cancer.

Several complex causes may underlie the observed relation between earlier age at menopause and mortality, including genetic factors, behavioural and environmental exposures, hormonal mechanisms and health-related factors. In particular, smoking is an important confounder of any assessment of the impact of age at menopause on health. Thus, the negative association noted in some studies may be due to residual confounding by smoking.

Conclusions

How can we summarise the psychological and physical health effects of the menopausal transition? Over the latter part of the 20th century, the medical view has largely been that the menopause has an important negative influence on women's

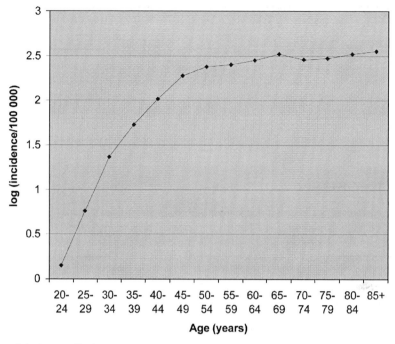

Figure 3.1. Age-specific breast cancer log incidence in Sweden 1995; data from the National Board of Health and Welfare, Sweden[29]

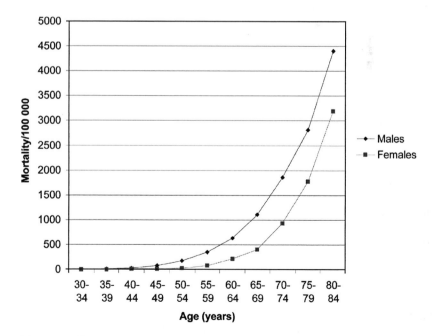

Figure 3.2. Age-specific ischaemic heart disease mortality in Sweden, 1969; data from the National Board of Health and Welfare, Sweden[29]

wellbeing and that it should be treated. Historically, physicians have treated a plethora of symptoms, all claimed to be related to reproductive function, with surgical castration (in the past, a procedure with extreme mortality) or 'substitution' with ovarian, placental or urinary extracts. These products were later discovered not to include any active hormones, in spite of their popularity and reported dramatically rejuvenating effects.[1] This is possibly the first illustration of the placebo effect of HRT.

These attitudes diverge from the findings of some studies exploring women's own views. Olofsson and Collins[18] concluded that their results 'supported the view of the menopause as a developmental phase associated with an increased self-awareness and a stronger personal identity. More than half the women held a positive view of the menopause, whereas the remaining proportion of women had either a negative or a neutral attitude.'

The classic symptoms of the menopause, vasomotor symptoms, vaginal dryness and bleeding irregularities, do indeed seem to be due to hormonal changes.[5] However, they are not present in all women, and their significance seems to vary substantially between individuals and with sociocultural factors. There is also strong evidence that menopause-induced ovarian failure causes an increased risk of osteoporotic fractures.[23]

However, the suggested negative impact of declining hormone levels on a wide array of other disorders lacks firm scientific support. The WHI trial has shown increased risks of cardiovascular disease, stroke and dementia in women with HRT, diametrically opposing widely held beliefs.[24] The trialists found a clinically unimportant, but statistically significant, positive effect of HRT on only three out of 13 measures of quality of life.[15] Prior trials have found that use of HRT has little or no overall effect on anxiety, affective symptoms or mental health but results in worsening physical function and energy levels, compared with placebo.[13,14] In conclusion, if HRT is regarded as the reverse of menopause, the hormonal changes correlated with menopause do not appear to impair quality of life in women in general. For the subgroup of women with hot flushes, mental health and depressive symptoms may be more pronounced.[14]

Therefore, the findings from the only sizeable randomised clinical trials on HRT, the reverse of menopause in terms of hormone levels, are in conflict with those from observational studies on health effects of the menopause.

Bias is a likely explanation for discrepancies between studies of randomised placebo-controlled design versus observational design. The associations between menopause and development of cancer and cardiovascular and other chronic diseases are influentially confounded by the two most important health determinants: age and smoking. Age and smoking also influence the perception of quality of life and menopausal symptoms. However, psychological and social factors also modulate women's experience of wellbeing and these may be even more important.[4] Menopause often coincides with major life events such as the death of a parent, children leaving home and an altered status on the labour market. In addition, Western societies are characterised by a reverence of youth and physical appearance. There are thus many factors apart from changing hormone levels – physical, psychological as well as sociocultural – that render midlife a demanding period for women.

In conclusion, the menopause has become medicalised and is viewed by some in the medical profession as a deficiency syndrome. This approach is problematic and such negative predictions of the menopause, when transferred to women themselves, might decrease their ability to cope with possible symptoms and hinder potential self-development.

References

1. Banks E. From dogs' testicles to mares' urine: the origins and contemporary use of hormonal therapy for the menopause. *Fem Rev* 2002;72:2–25.
2. Wilson RA. *Feminine Forever*. London: WH Allen; 1966.
3. Benagiano G, Primiero FM. Menopause, a global perspective. *Reprod Biomed Online* 2001;2:204–11.
4. Busch H, Barth-Olofsson HS, Rosenhagen S, Collins A. Menopausal transition and psychological development. *Menopause* 2003;10:179–87.
5. Hagsta TA, Janson, PO. The epidemiology of climacteric symptoms. *Acta Obstet Gynecol Scand* 1986;134(Suppl):59.
6. Morabia A, Costanza MC. World Health Organization Collaborative Study of Neoplasia and Steroid Contraceptives. International variability in ages at menarche, first livebirth, and menopause. *Am J Epidemiol* 1998;148:1195–205.
7. Gold EB, Bromberger J, Crawford S, Samuels S, Greendale GA, Sioban DH, *et al*. Factors associated with age at natural menopause in a multiethnic sample of midlife women. *Am J Epidemiol* 2001;153:865–74.
8. Thomas F, Renaud F, Benefice E, De Meeus, Guegan JF. International variability of ages at menarche and menopause: patterns and main determinants. *Hum Biol* 2001;73:271–90.
9. McKinlay SM, Bifano NL, McKinlay JB. Smoking and age at menopause in women. *Ann Intern Med* 1985;103:350–6.
10. Amundsen DW, Diers CJ. The age of menopause in classical Greece and Rome. *Hum Biol* 1970;42:79–86.
11. Sneider H, MacGregor AJ, Spectors TD. Genes control the cessation of a woman's reproductive life: a twin study of hysterectomy and age at menopause. *J Clin Endocrinol Metab* 1998;83:1875–80.
12. Hammar M, Berg G, Fahreus L, Larsson-Cohn U. Climacteric symptoms in an unselected sample of Swedish women. *Maturitas* 1984;6:345–50.
13. Greendale GA, Reboussin BA, Hogan P, Barnabei VM, Shumaker S, Johnson S, *et al*. Symptom relief and side effects of postmenopausal hormones: results from the Postmenopausal Estrogen/Progestin Interventions Trial. *Obstet Gynaecol* 1998;92:982–8.
14. Hlatky MA, Boothroyd D, Vittinghoff E, Sharp P, Whooley MA. Quality-of-life and depressive symptoms in postmenopausal women after receiving hormone therapy: results from the Heart and Estrogen/Progestin Replacement Study (HERS) trial. *JAMA* 2002;287:591–7.
15. Hays J, Ockene JK, Brunner RL, Kotchen JM, Manson JE, Patterson RE, *et al*. Effects of estrogen plus progestin on health-related quality of life. *N Engl J Med* 2003;348:1839–54.
16. Larson B, Collins A, Landgren BM. Urogenital and vasomotor symptoms in relation to menopausal status and the use of hormone replacement therapy (HRT) in healthy women during transition to menopause. *Maturitas* 1997;28:99–105.
17. Grady D, Brown JS, Vittinghoff E, Applegate W, Varner E, Snyder T. Postmenopausal hormones and incontinence: The Heart and Estrogen/Progestin Replacement Study. *Obstet Gynecol* 2001;97:116–20.
18. Olofsson AS, Collins A. Psychosocial factors, attitude to menopause and symptoms in Swedish perimenopausal women. *Climacteric* 2000;3:33–42.
19. Girdler SS, O'Briant C, Steege J, Grewen K, Light KC. A comparison of the effect of estrogen with or without progesterone on mood and physical symptoms in postmenopausal women. *J Womens Health Gend Based Med* 1999;8:637–46.
20. Cheung AM. Estrogen plus progestin did not improve health-related quality of life in postmenopausal women 50 to 79 years of age. *ACP J Club* 2003;139:60.
21. Kelsey JL, Gammon MD, John EM. Reproductive factors and breast cancer. *Epidemiol Rev* 1993;15:36–47.
22. Beral V; Million Women Study Collaborators. Breast cancer and hormone-replacement therapy in the Million Women Study. *Lancet* 2003;362:419–27.
23. Kritz-Silverstein D, Barrett-Connor E. Early menopause, number of reproductive years, and bone mineral density in postmenopausal women. *Am J Public Health* 1993;83:983–8.
24. Kocjan T, Prelevic GM. Hormone replacement therapy update: who should we be prescribing this to now? *Curr Opin Obstet Gynecol* 2003;15:459–64.
25. Cooper GS, Sandler DP. Age at natural menopause and mortality. *Ann Epidemiol* 1998;8:229–35.
26. Snowdon DA, Kane RL, Beeson WL, Burke GL, Sprafka JM, Potter J, *et al*. Is early natural menopause a biologic marker of health and aging? *Am J Public Health* 1989;79:709–14.
27. Jacobsen BK, Heuch I, Kvale G. Age at natural menopause and all-cause mortality: a 37-year follow-up of 19,731 Norwegian women. *Am J Epidemiol* 2003;57:923–9.

28.   Nilsson PM, Nilsson E, Svanberg L, Samsioe G. Longevity after early surgical menopause – the long-term effect of a permanent cessation of reproductive function and female sex hormone loss. *Eur J Obstet Gynecol Reprod Biol* 2003;110:63–5.
29.   The National Board of Health and Welfare, Sweden [http://www.sos.se/epc/epceng.htm].

Chapter 4

Effect of hormone replacement therapy on symptoms

Ailsa Gebbie and Anna Glasier

Introduction

In the UK, women approaching menopause face the decision of whether or not to take hormone replacement therapy (HRT). HRT has high levels of lay awareness and has received widespread media publicity in recent years, much of it negative criticism. From the perspective of the provider, HRT has had a rapidly changing clinical evidence base. The main indication for use of HRT in the UK has always been relief of menopausal symptoms. Women with unpleasant menopausal symptoms need support from well-informed healthcare professionals who are sympathetic to their individual experiences and provide information adapted to their situations. A woman's experience of the menopause is closely linked with her physical and social environment.[1] Women should be fully informed about HRT and in control of their personal use of it.[2] The use of HRT should be negotiated between the woman and her healthcare adviser for a particular time and stage of life and then regularly reviewed.

Vasomotor symptoms

Vasomotor symptoms comprise hot flushes and night sweats, and may also be associated with palpitations and faintness. Hot flushes are the most characteristic manifestation of the menopause and, to date, their exact pathophysiology remains unknown. A complex mechanism somehow links declining oestrogen levels to alterations in brain neurotransmitters and instability in the hypothalamic thermoregulatory centres located in anterior hypothalamic nuclei.[3] Various hypotheses have been suggested and a temporal association with pulsatile pituitary release of luteinising hormone has been demonstrated.[4]

Hot flushes are a subjective sensation of heat caused by a sudden, transient peripheral vasodilatation in skin blood vessels. At night, hot flushes are often associated with sweating. Although vasomotor symptoms can occur in association with other conditions, they are a common climacteric symptom affecting up to 80% of women.[5] Around 10–20% of women find vasomotor symptoms severe and intolerable. Almost one-third of postmenopausal women will report symptoms that last up to five years after natural menopause and hot flushes can persist for up to 15 years in 20% of women.[6] The average hot flush lasts around four minutes, but they can last for just a few seconds or as long as ten minutes.[6] Some women experience flushes several times a week whereas others notice them several times an hour.[7] Hot flushes have not been the subject of much clinical interest or research perhaps because they are not fatal and are usually self-limiting.[8]

Insomnia is another common menopausal symptom. Hot flushes are associated with a change in sleep pattern, in particular an increase in stage 4 (deep non-rapid eye movement) sleep and a latency or shortened rapid eye movement period.[9] Nocturnal vasomotor activity is highly disruptive to sleep patterns, with fatigue and lethargy as a consequence in the symptomatic menopausal woman.

Effect of HRT on vasomotor symptoms

Since vasomotor symptoms are caused by lack of endogenous oestrogen, it follows logically that HRT will alleviate the problem. The use of oestrogen in the treatment of menopausal symptoms was first described and documented by Brown-Sequard in the mid-19th century.[10]

The effect of HRT on vasomotor symptoms has been the subject of a Cochrane systematic review.[11] In HRT trials, only high-quality randomised, placebo-controlled, double-blind studies can obviate concerns regarding confounding issues and it has been known for decades that there is a marked placebo effect on menopausal symptoms.[12] Owing to the large number of studies in the literature, the Cochrane review was restricted to the effect of oral HRT versus placebo in well-conducted, randomised, placebo-controlled, double-blind trials of at least three months duration. From 99 references originally identified, 21 studies meeting the Cochrane selection criteria were included. Study participants totalled 2511. Their data show that oral HRT (both oestrogen-only and combined HRT) is a highly effective agent in the treatment of vasomotor symptoms compared with placebo, with a sustained effect in clinical trials of between three months and three years duration. There was a significant reduction in the weekly hot flush frequency for HRT compared with placebo (weighted mean difference -17.46, 95% CI -24.72 to -10.21). This was equivalent to a 77% reduction in frequency (95% CI 58.2–87.5%) for HRT relative to placebo. Symptom severity was also significantly reduced compared with placebo (OR 0.13, 95% CI 0.08–0.22). However, women randomised to placebo experienced a 50.8% (95% CI 41.7–58.5%) reduction in hot flushes between baseline and end of study.

It was beyond the scope of the Cochrane analysis to differentiate between various oral HRT products, combinations, dosages or regimens. Although the analysis was restricted to oral HRT, other randomised trials show efficacy of various routes of administration, dosages and combinations of HRT in relieving menopausal symptoms.[13,14] The Postmenopausal Estrogen/Progestin Interventions Trial (PEPI), which formed a large component of the Cochrane Collaboration data, did not show any benefit of oestrogen-progestogen combinations over oestrogen alone.[15] The synthetic steroid tibolone has combined oestrogenic, androgenic and progestogenic activity. It has shown efficacy in respect of vasomotor symptoms and randomised studies comparing tibolone with several HRT regimens show similar reduction in vasomotor symptoms.[16,17]

The natural history of hot flushes in an untreated group has not been extensively studied prospectively. Within the PEPI study, the difference in hot flush symptoms reporting between treated and untreated women diminished between years 1 and 3, compatible with the observed pattern of diminishing hot flushes over time in the placebo group.[15] Many women will note a return of hot flushes when HRT is discontinued abruptly. This is an area that is ill-understood and a survey has shown that prescribers lack confidence in managing this stage.[18]

Conclusion

Because of the causal association between hot flushes and declining oestrogen levels, HRT has traditionally been the mainstay of treatment. It is highly effective in relieving vasomotor symptoms compared with placebo and more efficacious than any other known therapy. Tibolone is also effective.

Libido and sexual dysfunction

Libido is defined as sexual energy or the desire to have sex. Loss of libido and other female sexual dysfunctions are complex and composite issues affected by many factors in addition to hormonal status. A woman's motivation for sex is mainly influenced by her emotional intimacy with her partner and tends to be largely responsive rather than spontaneous.[19] It has proven difficult to link serum levels of sex steroids with sexual functioning. The prevalence of sexual dysfunction in the population generally is high and increases with advancing age. There has been increased interest in the study of sexual function in older women over the past decade as, until recently, sexual decline and dysfunction in middle-aged women were thought simply to be natural consequences of ageing and hormonal decline. Most prospective studies have documented that perimenopausal and menopausal women remain sexually active but at a lower frequency.[20] Common sexual dysfunctions most often reported in perimenopausal and postmenopausal women are dyspareunia from inadequate vaginal lubrication and a lessening of sexual desire and responsiveness. One community study of sexual dysfunction among middle-aged women identified one-third of women as having defined sexual dysfunction. The investigators found that 17% had impaired sexual interest, 17% had vaginal dryness and 16% had infrequent orgasm. Sexual dysfunction was statistically significantly associated with increasing age, past psychiatric disease and marital disharmony. Despite the high frequency of problems, only 4% stated that they would seek help for a sexual problem.[21]

The study of sexual function is not an easy task and most data are still obtained by questionnaire rather than by any objective physiological or anatomic response measurements. Randomisation and placebo control within trials on sexual dysfunction are extremely important as there are numerous possible confounding variables and a marked placebo response.

Urogenital atrophy

Lack of oestrogen results in profound changes within the vaginal environment, causing decreased vaginal blood flow and reduced secretions and thus an increase in vaginal pH. These changes result in symptoms of inadequate lubrication with sexual arousal and a need for a longer period of sexual stimulation before vaginal lubrication for penetration is adequate. The role of oestrogen in the treatment of these symptoms is discussed in Chapter 17.

Sexual desire and responsiveness

Decreased sexual function in women following the menopause is potentially due in part to loss of both oestrogen and androgen. Although several trials have reported that HRT improves sexual desire in women following the menopause it is difficult to establish whether this is simply a domino effect from improved general wellbeing.

There is no body of scientific evidence proving that oestrogen specifically improves libido in clinical trials and, anecdotally, clinicians find highly variable responses. Postmenopausal women treated with HRT have an increase in sex hormone-binding globulin which may actually reduce the amount of free testosterone.[22]

A systematic review published in 2003 of randomised, placebo-controlled trials in female sexual dysfunction in postmenopausal women found that many therapies in clinical practice, including HRT, are not supported by adequate evidence.[23] Only one study was found where HRT significantly improved sexual desire and arousal during the week of hormone use compared with time when no treatment was administered.[24] However, the absence of a pure placebo group prevented any real conclusions on the effect of oestrogen on sexual function in postmenopausal women. Studies involving administration of progestogens alone have found deleterious effects on sexual functioning.[25]

Testosterone

Several investigators have reported improvement in sexual function in postmenopausal women treated with a combination of oestrogen and testosterone but only a minority of the studies are randomised and placebo-controlled.[26] There seems a clear rationale for testosterone replacement in women who have undergone bilateral oophorectomy and have significantly low serum testosterone levels.[27] Studies that have looked at administration of testosterone in supraphysiological doses show definite improvements in sexual parameters in postmenopausal women.[28]

However, the above-mentioned systematic review identified two trials of combined oestrogen and androgen therapy that qualified for their review.[23] In the first trial of only 20 women, the combined oestrogen-androgen combination significantly increased sexual sensation, desire, and frequency of intercourse versus oestrogen-alone but did not change the frequency of sexual fantasies, vaginal lubrication and pain during intercourse.[29] In a slightly larger randomised study of 75 women following hysterectomy and bilateral oophorectomy, there was a significant improvement in sexual function among treated women compared with the placebo group.[30] The drop-out rate in the active treatment group was high owing to androgen-related adverse effects. Sherwin and Gelfand[31] found that changes in sexual desire when testosterone was administered to oophorectomised women correlated with plasma testosterone levels but not with oestradiol levels.

A transdermal testosterone matrix patch for women with hypoactive sexual desire is being developed and will avoid some of the undesirable effects associated with both oral and implant therapy.[30]

Tibolone

Several small randomised trials on tibolone which were questionnaire-based showed improvement in sexual desire compared with both placebo and conventional HRT.[32,33] One small randomised trial of tibolone versus placebo in 38 women showed significantly improved vaginal blood flow and arousability in the tibolone group.[34]

Conclusion

Standard HRT preparations have not been demonstrated to improve libido *per se* although, in symptomatic women, HRT does improve wellbeing and might thereby improve libido indirectly. Tibolone and HRT combinations containing androgens do appear to improve sexual desire and further assessment of these agents for this indication is required.

Depression

The association between menopause and clinical depression is complex and controversial. The prevalence of depression is consistently higher in women than in men, from the age of puberty until the age of 55 years.[35] In a woman's middle years when tangible physiological changes occur, it is tempting to ascribe mood fluctuations to underlying hormonal events. While the concurrence of the two events is suggestive of causality, this in itself does not provide proof that one has caused the other. Most studies have found that hormone levels are no different in depressed menopausal women compared with non-depressed women[36] but the Harvard Study of Moods and Cycles[37] did find that a lifetime history of major depression was associated with an early decline in ovarian function based on endocrine parameters. High rates of depression have been found among women attending menopause clinics[38] but psychiatric symptoms are increased in all hospital outpatient attenders.[39] In a critical review of the data on menopause and depression, Nicol-Smith[40] stated that there was insufficient evidence to conclude that natural menopause with its accompanying changes in hormones or psychosocial factors exclusive to middle age puts women at increased risk of depression.

Studies on the effect of HRT on depression are beset by methodological problems as they need to be controlled for the secondary effects of reduction in vasomotor symptoms and type or dosage of HRT used. Despite the apparent lack of association between depression and menopause *per se*, there is some evidence of benefit of HRT in clinically significant depressive disorders, particularly when given in high dosages.[41] One study of 50 depressed women showed remission in 68% of women treated with 100 μg oestradiol patches compared with 20% of women in the placebo group.[42] It has also been postulated that HRT may work synergistically with an antidepressant such that women could be treated with lower doses of a selective serotonin reuptake inhibitor (SSRI) if they were concurrently on HRT.[43] In addition, there is some evidence that menopause appears to exacerbate pre-existing psychological disturbances. Further research is clearly required in this field but, at the present time, if a menopausal woman is diagnosed with depression the primary treatment is standard psychiatric management not oestrogen.[44]

Depressed mood, mood swings and poor memory and concentration are all symptoms associated with menopause. Whether these symptoms are distinct menopausal entities or occur predominantly as a domino effect as a consequence of vasomotor symptoms or insomnia is still not clear. Women with these mood-related symptoms at the time of the perimenopause may have a previous history of premenstrual syndrome or postnatal depression. It is also important to bear in mind that depressed mood and depressive disorders are often related less to the menopause than to the vicissitudes of life generally, such as ageing parents, teenage children, marital disharmony, poor employment opportunities. etc.[45] One meta-analysis of 14 randomised controlled trials and 12 cohort studies showed oestrogen improved depressed mood.[46] However, a systematic review published two years earlier of 111 articles on psychological symptoms in menopausal women receiving HRT concluded that no clear conclusion could be drawn with respect to HRT and its effect on psychological symptoms.[41] It has been suggested that HRT may exert a nonspecific 'mental tonic' effect in non-depressed women and one well-designed study demonstrated higher depression scores in women receiving placebo compared with hormone groups,[31] but again this is difficult to separate out from the effect of HRT on overall wellbeing in symptomatic women. In the Heart and Estrogen Replacement Study (HERS)[47] of 2763 women with pre-existing cardiovascular disease randomised to HRT or placebo, depressive symptoms significantly improved in symptomatic women compared with women without flushes at study entry (–0.5 versus +0.007, $P = 0.01$) over three years. However, there were no differences over time according to treatment assigned.

It is well established that women taking combined HRT find any beneficial effect on their mood with oestrogen therapy may be attenuated by the addition of progestogens.[48]

Conclusion

It is still not established whether HRT is effective as a treatment strategy for women with clinical unipolar depression. Further research is required in this area. HRT improves depressed mood in the perimenopause, particularly in women with a past history of premenstrual syndrome and postnatal depression. It is still unclear whether this is primarily a domino effect as a result of improved wellbeing in symptomatic women.

Quality of life

It would seem entirely logical that if women with unpleasant menopausal symptoms take HRT then their quality of life would improve significantly.[49] However, this has been a difficult area to evaluate as studies are very sensitive to the quality of life weights assigned by different health states affected by HRT and they use varying quality of life tools. Studies looking at this field generally have very small sample sizes and the rating scale method tends to exaggerate the gain in quality of life compared with other methods.

One widely quoted Swedish study[50] looked at quality of life issues in over 100 women with menopausal symptoms before and after commencing HRT. The improvements in quality of life with both the rating scale and the time trade-off methods with HRT are about double for women with severe symptoms compared with those with mild symptoms. This larger improvement was due to the lower quality of life without HRT for the women initially with severe symptoms. In the same study the willingness of women to pay out of their own money for HRT was investigated. The proportion of women that were willing to pay a certain price is the same or higher for women with severe symptoms for every price. Women with both mild and severe menopausal symptoms were willing to pay large sums of money for HRT which were well above the treatment costs associated with HRT.

Women who participated in the HERS study[47] completed quality of life questionnaires at baseline and analyses were carried out over the first three years of follow-up. Women were randomised to HRT or placebo. Women with menopausal symptoms at baseline demonstrated definite improvements in mental health compared with the placebo group, in addition to depressive symptoms, although quality of life generally declined during follow-up in the entire cohort.

It has been argued in the past that all women – even older women without menopausal symptoms – experience a 'feel good factor' when they take HRT. There is now clear evidence from the Women's Health Initiative study[51] that this is not the case. This randomised, double-blind placebo-controlled trial involving over 16 000 women provided an excellent opportunity to examine the relationship between HRT and health-related quality of life measures in largely asymptomatic women. Quality of life measures were collected at baseline and at one year in all women and at three years in a subgroup of 1511 women. Within the trial, HRT did not result in significant effects on general wellbeing or energy levels. Use of HRT was associated with a statistically significant but small benefit in terms of sleep disturbance and physical functioning after one year. At three years, there were no significant benefits in terms of any quality of life outcomes. There was definite benefit in women in the perimenopausal age group with moderate-to-severe vasomotor symptoms in terms of improved vasomotor symptoms and sleep disturbance but no benefit in terms of other quality of life outcomes.

Conclusion

HRT appears to improve quality of life in perimenopausal women with menopausal symptoms. Improvement in quality of life measures is directly related to severity of symptoms. However, recent studies have demonstrated that HRT does not significantly improve wellbeing in women who are largely asymptomatic in terms of menopausal symptoms, although there has been criticism of how well-validated the quality of life tools used were.

Summary

Hormone replacement therapy is a highly effective treatment for vasomotor symptoms and, as a direct consequence of this benefit, causes an improvement in depressed mood, libido and quality of life. It is still unclear whether HRT has a role in the management of women with unipolar depression and whether it specifically improves depressed mood independent of the effect on vasomotor symptoms. Small randomised controlled trials suggest that tibolone is effective in the management of both vasomotor symptoms and sexual dysfunction, and that HRT preparations containing androgens improve sexual desire and responsiveness.

References

1. Ballard KD, Kuh DJ, Wadworth MEJ. The role of the menopause in women's experiences of the 'change of life'. *Sociol Health Illn* 2001;23:397–424.
2. Grady D, Rubin SM, Petitti DB, Fox CS, Black D, Ettinger B, *et al.* Hormone therapy to prevent disease and prolong life in postmenopausal women. *Ann Intern Med* 1992;117:1016–37.
3. Lomax P. Pathophysiology of postmenopausal hot flushes. In: Schonbaum E, editor. *The Climacteric Hot Flush. Progress in Basic and Clinical Pharmacology*, vol. 7. Basel: Karger; 1991. p. 61–82.
4. Casper RF, Yen SSC, Wilkes MM. Menopausal flushes: a neuroendocrine link with pulsatile luteinising hormone secretion. *Science* 1979;205:823–5.
5. Porter M, Penney G, Russell D, Russell E, Templeton A. A population based survey of women's experience of the menopause. *Br J Obstet Gynaecol* 1996;103:1025–8.
6. Kronenberg F. Hot flashes: phenomenology, quality of life and search for treatment options. *Exp Gerontol* 1994;29:319–36.
7. Stearns V, Ullmer L, Lopez JF, Smith Y, Isaacs C, Hayes D. Hot flushes. *Lancet* 2002;360:1851–61.
8. Sturdee D. The hot flush: the enigma of the climacteric. *Climacteric* 2001;4:1–3.
9. Woodward S, Freedman RR. The thermoregulatory effects of menopausal hot flashes on sleep. *Sleep* 1994;17:497–501.
10. Richardson RG. *The Menopause – A Neglected Crisis*. Queensborough, Kent: Abbot Laboratories; 1973.

11.   MacLennan A, Lester S, Moore V. Oral oestrogen replacement therapy versus placebo for hot flushes. *Cochrane Database Syst Rev* 2001;(1):CD002978.

12.   Campbell S, Whitehead M. Oestrogen therapy and the menopausal syndrome. *Clin Obstet Gynecol* 1977;4:31–47.

13.   Utian WH, Burry KA, Archer DF, Gallagher JC, Boyett RL, Guy MP, *et al.* Efficacy and safety of low, standard, and high dosages of an estradiol transdermal system (Esclim) compared with placebo on vasomotor symptoms in highly symptomatic menopausal patients. The Esclim Study Group. *Am J Obstet Gynecol* 1999;181:71–9.

14.   Studd J, Pornel B, Marton I, Bringer J, Varin C, Tsouderos Y, *et al.* Efficacy and acceptability of intranasal 17 beta-oestradiol for menopausal symptoms: randomised dose-response study. Aerodiol Study Group. *Lancet* 1999;353:1574–8. Erratum in: *Lancet* 1999;354:780.

15.   Greendale GA, Reboussin BA, Hogan P, Barnabei VM, Shumaker S, Johnson S, *et al.* Symptom relief and side effects of postmenopausal hormones: results from the Postmenopausal Estrogen/Progestin Interventions Trial. *Obstet Gynecol* 1998;92:982–8.

16.   Hammar M, Christa S, Nathorst-Boos J, Rud T, Garre K. A double-blind, randomised trial comparing the effects of tibolone and continuous combined hormone replacement therapy in postmenopausal women with menopausal symptoms. *Br J Obstet Gynaecol* 1998;105:904–11.

17.   Egarter C, Huber J, Leikermoser R, Haidbauer R, Pusch H, Fischl F, *et al.* Tibolone versus conjugated estrogens and sequential progestogen in the treatment of climacteric complaints. *Maturitas* 1996;23:55–62.

18.   Cogliano M, Gebbie AE. Impact of the women's health initiative study. *Br J Gen Pract* 2004;54:301–2.

19.   Basson R. Female sexual response: the role of drugs in the management of sexual dysfunction. *Obstet Gynecol* 2001;98:350–3.

20.   Bachman GA. Sexual function in the perimenopause. *Obstet Gynecol Clin North Am* 1993;20:379–89.

21.   Osborn M, Hawton K, Gath D. Sexual dysfunction among middle aged women in the community. *BMJ* 1988;296:959–62.

22.   Davis SR. Androgen replacement in women: a commentary. *J Clin Endocrinol Metab* 1999;84:1886–91.

23.   Modelska K, Cummings S. Female sexual dysfunction in postmenopausal women: systematic review of placebo-controlled trials. *Am J Obstet Gynecol* 2003;188:286–93.

24.   Sherwin BB. The impact of different doses of estrogen and progestin on mood and sexual behaviour in postmenopausal women. *J Clin Endocrinol Metab* 1991;72:336–43.

25.   Dennerstein L, Burrows GD, Wood C. Hormones and sexuality: effects of oestrogen and progestogen. *Obstet Gynecol* 1980;56:316–22.

26.   Sherwin B. Use of combined estrogen-androgen preparations in the postmenopause: evidence from clinical studies. *Int J Fertil Womens Med* 1998;43:98–103.

27.   Nathorst-Boos J, von Schoultz H. Psychological reactions and sexual life after hysterectomy with and without oophorectomy. *Gynecol Obstet Invest* 1992;34:97–101.

28.   Burger HG, Hailes J, Nelson J, Menelaus M. Effect of combined implants of estradiol and testosterone on libido in postmenopausal women. *BMJ* 1987;294:936–7.

29.   Sarrel P, Dobay B, Wiita B. Estrogen and estrogen-androgen replacement in postmenopausal women dissatisfied with estrogen-only therapy: sexual behaviour and neuro-endocrine responses. *J Reprod Med* 1998;43:847–56.

30.   Shifren JL, Braunstein GD, Simon JA, Casson PR, Buster JE, Redmond GP, *et al.* Transdermal testosterone treatment in women with impaired sexual function after oophorectomy. *N Engl J Med* 2000;343:682–8.

31.   Sherwin B, Gelfand MM. Sex steroids and effect in the surgical menopause. A double blind, cross over study. *Psychoneuroendocrinology* 1985;10:177–87.

32.   Palacios S, Menendez C, Jurado AR, Castano R, Vargas JC. Changes in sex behaviour after menopause: effects of tibolone. *Maturitas* 1995;22:155–61.

33.   Nathorst-Boos J, Hammar M. Effect on sexual life – a comparison between Tibolone and a continuous estradiol-northethisterone acetate regimen. *Maturitas* 1997;26:15–20.

34.   Laan E, van Lunsen RHW, Everaerd W. The effects of tibolone on vaginal blood flow, sexual desire and arousability in postmenopausal women. *Climacteric* 2001;4:28–41.

35.   Pearlstein T, Rosen K, Stone AB. Mood disorders and menopause. *Endocrinol Metab Clin North Am* 1997;26:279–94.

36.   Ballinger B. Psychiatric aspects of the menopause. *Br J Psychiatry* 1990;156:773–87.

37.   Harlow BL, Wise LA, Otto MW, Soares CN, Cohen LS. Depression and its influence on reproductive endocrine and menstrual cycle markers associated with perimenopause. The Harvard Study of Moods and Cycles. *Arch Gen Psychiatry* 2003;60:29–36.

38.   Hay AG, Bancroft J, Johnstone EC. Affective symptoms in women attending a menopause clinic.

Br J Psychiatry 1994;164:513–6.

39.   Mayou R, Hawton K. Psychiatric disorder in the general hospital. *Br J Psychiatry*
1986;144:28–34.

40.   Nicol-Smith L. Causality, menopause and depression: a critical review of the literature. *BMJ*
1996;313:1229–32.

41.   Pearce J, Hawton K, Blake F. Psychological and sexual symptoms associated with the menopause
and the effects of hormone replacement therapy: a review. *Br J Psychiatry* 1995;167:163–73.

42.   Soares C, Almeida OP, Joffe H, Cohen LS. Efficacy of estradiol for the treatment of depressive
disorders in perimenopausal women. *Arch Gen Psychiatry* 2001;58:529–34.

43.   Landau C, Milan FB. Assessment and treatment of depression during the menopause: a
preliminary report. *Menopause* 1996;3:201–7.

44.   Gath D, Iles S. Depression and the menopause. *BMJ* 1990;300:1287–8.

45.   Greene JS, Cooke DJ. Life stress and symptoms at the climacterium. *Br J Psychiatry*
1980;136:486–91.

46.   Zweifel JE, O'Brien WH. A meta-analysis of the effect of HRT upon depressed mood.
Psychoneuroendocrinology 1997;22:189–212.

47.   Hlatky MA, Boothroyd D, Vittinghoff E, Sharp P, Whooley MA; Heart and Estrogen/Progestin
Replacement Study (HERS) Research Group. Quality-of-life and depressive symptoms in
postmenopausal women after receiving hormone therapy: results from the Heart and
Estrogen/Progestin Replacement Study (HERS) trial. *JAMA* 2002;287:591–7.

48.   Smith RN, Holland ES, Studd JWW. The symptomatology of progestogen intolerance. *Maturitas*
1994;2:87–91.

49.   Daly E, Gray A, Barlow D, McPherson K, Vessey M. Measuring the impact of menopausal
symptoms on quality of life. *BMJ* 1993;307:836–40.

50.   Zethraeus NJ, Johannesson M, Henriksson P, Strand RT. The impact of hormone replacement
therapy on quality of life and willingness to pay. *Br J Obstet Gynaecol* 1997;104:1191–5.

51.   Hays J, Ockene JK, Brunner RL, Kotchen JM, Manson JE, Patterson RE, *et al*. Effects of
estrogen plus progestin on health-related quality of life. *N Engl J Med* 2003;348:1839–54.

Chapter 5

The menopause – what is it?

Discussion

Discussion following Professor Burger's paper

Gebbie: Do you see a time when we will be measuring inhibin B levels to help us manage our patients clinically?

Burger: I find it very difficult to forecast that – there is still a lot of variability of data. It is very hard to extrapolate what the significance of inhibin is in terms of aspects of ovarian function including potential fertility. We know that inhibin B has been used in an attempt to provide practical predictability for assisted reproductive technology programmes and the data are quite variable. I think there is no real consensus about it. I do not see it yet but I do not exclude it categorically.

Critchley: There has been interest in younger women and particularly women who might have had radiotherapy or chemotherapy and the ability to identify an incipient onset of menopause. With regard to the other ovarian hormone, anti-müllerian hormone (AMH), I know the evidence is very early, but perhaps in combination with inhibin B and a measurement of either ovarian volume or if you are able to count antral follicles – do you see a combination as being predictive of menopause? I ask because you quite clearly show that a measurement of follicle-stimulating hormone (FSH) is not.

Burger: I think that what you said is the right direction to be thinking – that is where the evidence is going. But, as you say, it is very early. You may recall a study published in *JCEM* in November.[1] It was a detailed study involving ultrasonography and inhibin B measurements amongst others, no AMH measurements, and showed a statistically significant but again practically doubtful difference in early follicular phase less than 10 mm follicle counts, determined by ultrasonography. This was a group of older women characterised as having experienced quite some degree of 'menstrual irregularity' compared with young women. The difference in early follicular phase follicle counts was something like 4.7 versus 3.4, but with a quite a big spread of overlap between the two groups. Inhibin B was also lower in the older group but again with quite a degree of overlap between the two. I think the problem will be to find a marker upon which you could put sufficient reliability to provide reliable predictions.

Sturdee: Thank you, Professor Burger. I think that as a clinician one of the most common problems we have in our gynaecology clinics is trying to predict when the menopause is going to occur in women who have symptoms that might require treatment of one type or another. Particularly if we are having to weigh up whether surgery is appropriate. If, sometime in the future, we are able to have some measure that will tell us you will reach the menopause in six months' time or so, it would make a tremendous difference to the management of countless women in gynaecology clinics.

Burger: The Melbourne group with our Melbourne Women's Midlife Health Project has made some attempt to get at that predictability, or the ability to make those sort of predictions. Some authors have used a combination of FSH and change in menstrual cycle frequency where the interval between shortest and longest menses exceeds a certain cut-off point – I think it was 40 days. If you have a combination of those two situations then you could make broad predictions as to how soon the final menses would occur from our analysis of our prospectively recorded menstrual diary data. That is one of the few attempts I have seen to make that sort of prediction. I think we all have the clinical experience, which I think makes this area so difficult, of the woman who says that a year ago she had four months where her periods were irregular and she had lots of hot flushes and now for the last six months she has had perfectly regular cycles and no symptoms at all. So even though perhaps my presentation would have implied that there is a sequential progression from late reproductive age to early transition to late transition, I do not think in practice that is actually true for all women. I think it is true for some but others will go from early transitions back to cycle regularity then to late transitions then some more cycle regularity, etc. I do not think any of those time markers is sufficiently reliable, at least from my analysis of the data, to be able to make secure predictions about timing ultimately.

Critchley: You showed that there is no change in testosterone as women approach menopause, yet we have seen data, from Dr Gebbie, that perhaps in the group of women with loss of libido there was a benefit for tibolone and androgens. Do you have any comment there?

Burger: I think this is an extremely difficult and very topical area. As I mentioned, the data that have been published by a number of groups show that the levels of dehydroepiandrosterone sulphate (DHEAS) and testosterone fall very substantially between the ages of 20 and 45 years or thereabouts. There is on average about a 50% fall. Then from there on there is not very much more change across the menopausal transition. There is some published data that suggests that although DHEAS continues to fall, testosterone may, if anything, start to rise again in the late 50s, early 60s. In the Melbourne Women's Midlife Health Project study[2] that we have done, we have attempted to determine whether in a group of unselected women from the community there is any correlation between their change in sexual function and their change in testosterone level. We have not been able to find such a correlation. One of the criticisms that can quite validly be made of our data is that at the time when we made those analyses we used a testosterone assay, which was probably not as sensitive as ideally it should have been. There are huge problems in measuring testosterone concentrations in the normal female range and a number of papers have been published recently showing just how unreliable most testosterone assays in the female range actually are. So there are methodological difficulties about making the measurement, there are difficulties about making the association – and the major conclusions about the testosterone–libido relationship have really come from trials where testosterone has been administered. Now, if you look at most of those trials that have shown positive outcomes, the administered agent has raised testosterone, even free testosterone or bioavailable testosterone concentration, into either the absolutely top end of the normal range or usually into the lower end of the supra-normal range. So, how much is physiology, how much is pharmacology, how much is a pharmacological effect of testosterone is very difficult to sort out. There is no question that as a clinician I see quite a lot of women referred who appear to have isolated loss of libido. It is often associated with unexplained tiredness and lack of energy but without any, at least obviously, discernible other contributory factors and in women who are adequately oestrogenised. Many of those women respond to testosterone supplementation, but some do not. I have no way of telling which individual is going to respond and which is not. So I think the relationship is complex. We have been bedevilled, as Dr Gebbie very correctly pointed out, by lack of adequately validated sexual functioning assessments, and that is starting now to improve. I think it is still an area that is very muddy indeed.

Studd: There was an old story, 20 or 30 years ago from Peter van Keep about the transition phase where they reported that the climacteric symptoms were at their worst in the two or three years before periods ceased? Has your Melbourne Women's Midlife Health Project confirmed that?

Burger: No, we have looked at the relationship between prospectively determined final menses and the prevalence of symptoms. In our study the maximal prevalence would be in the first year: in that first postmenopausal year from final menstrual period for the next 12 months. But there is not much difference from the one year before that, in that there is a broad peak of symptoms that progressively increases as you come up to the final menses and then turns over and progressively goes down again. But as pointed out again earlier, 20% of women – at least – would have symptoms still five years out from the final menses.

Discussion following Dr Stevenson's paper

Prentice: I really enjoyed your remarks. In discussing possible early elevation in cardiovascular disease following initiation of HRT, you mentioned increases in thrombogenesis and adverse vascular remodelling as likely mechanisms. Then later on you mentioned that these mechanisms may be oestrogen dose-dependent. I just wondered if you could elaborate on that, especially the latter point?

Stevenson: On the vascular remodelling, the reason for suggesting that is that we know that the matrix metalloproteinases (MMPs) are key enzymes involved in vascular remodelling. We also know that the production of MMPs is influenced by oestrogens and certainly in cell culture experiments you can show very clearly dose-dependent effects of oestrogen on the production of the MMPs.

Prentice: Is MMP-9 the most pertinent marker?

Stevenson: MMP-2 and then MMP-9 seem to be the most relevant ones. So that is the basis for the hypothesis. The difficulties, of course, are that we do not get a good handle on the tissue inhibitors so just measuring MMP activity does not necessarily give you an accurate picture of what is actually happening at the tissue level. Nevertheless, it is as good as we have got as the basis behind it.

Critchley: Can I just extend that? We also know that elsewhere in the body progestogens will have quite a profound effect on MMPs, so how do we then bring in the balance of the oestrogen effect and the progestogen effect on these local mediators of remodelling? Do we know in the vascular system elsewhere in the body what effect the different progestogens have?

Stevenson: We have some indirect evidence of some of the different progestogens, but it is largely from surrogate measurements, such as flow-mediated dilatation. The problem there is that in the studies that have been done, even though some of them are randomised, they tend to be small studies. What is even more confusing is that some of them disagree with each other. There is no clear-cut pattern that has emerged so far. So we are very limited in terms of knowing the vascular effects of progestogens in so far as we cannot do any sort of direct assessments. Obviously, to do a study of clinical endpoints with different progestogens would be wonderful but who is going to fund it? Or even do it?

Evans: Thank you for your talk. Just incidentally, you did not comment on the Framingham study.[3] Although they found an increased cardiovascular risk in postmenopausal women, they also found a harmful effect of HRT in their observational data. But what I wanted to ask you was whether you have looked at C-reactive protein (CRP) and the effects of that? It is fairly consistent that all the regimens, even the ones in a sense that one does not like such as the conjugated equine oestrogens with medroxyprogesterone acetate (MPA), have been shown to have beneficial effects on lipids, but yet this has not translated into good clinical outcomes. CRP might be something that has a harmful effect, particularly an early one.

Stevenson: Just to comment on the Framingham HRT data, obviously in the first publication it was suggested that there was harm but in the subsequent publication[4] they decided to change their mind on that. So it is rather inconsistent. In terms of CRP, it is not something that we have actually looked at ourselves, although we are just in the process of analysing measurements from our Women's Hormone Intervention Secondary Prevention (WHISP) study, where we have measured CRP. We know that oral HRT does seem to increase CRP but transdermal HRT does not. There is a clear difference there. But the problem comes when you look at other so-called inflammatory markers, where although you may see an increase in CRP, you are seeing at the same time a decrease in some of the cell adhesion molecule concentrations. So it is very hard to understand whether this is just an effect on the hepatic CRP production or whether it reflects the vasculature and I do not think anybody really knows at the present time.

Lowe: Firstly, just a point of information on CRP – we have a paper at present in the *New England Journal of Medicine*.[5] It is a big meta-analysis and shows that the predictive value of CRP for arterial disease is about half of what it is alleged to be in the Boston study.[6] So, with respect to the causal relevance of CRP, it is much less a risk predictor for coronary heart disease or stroke than has been alleged. Secondly, the biological mechanism by which it may increase risk is not known. I think Dr Prentice may wish to add to this – the most recent study of Women's Health Initiative[6] showed no interaction between baseline CRP and increased risks of coronary heart disease or stroke.

Prentice: I think we only published it for stroke but what you have said is true.

Chwalisz: Dr Stevenson, you mentioned in your presentation that both MPA and conjugated oestrogens reduce insulin resistance. In the Women's Health Initiative study, Dr Prentice had a relatively high number of obese women. Do we know the effect of these compounds in obese versus non-obese women?

Stevenson: In terms of glucose and insulin metabolism?

Chwalisz: Yes, and cardiovascular risks.

Stevenson: Well , I do not know what will come out of the Women's Health Initiative on that – it is difficult to predict. I think that I said the MPA may increase insulin resistance and we certainly have evidence for that. Whether conjugated equine oestrogen would actually increase insulin resistance *per se*, I do not know because our own studies of conjugated equine oestrogen where we have directly measured insulin sensitivity, have not shown any effect *per se* of the oestrogens. The conjugated equine oestrogens have effects on insulin dynamics in other respects rather than the actual tissue resistance to insulin. So I cannot answer your question there.

Prentice: The only information I would add is that in our combined hormone trial we did look at the magnitude of coronary heart disease and stroke elevation as a function of body mass index (BMI) and did not see evidence of an interaction – we were not especially well powered to identify it, but at least there is no evidence there and that has been brought out in separate papers on those outcomes.

Armitage: You reminded us dutifully about the differential effects and that is something we struggled with at the Committee on Safety of Medicines, so often we lump it all together as generic HRT and we have got to remember the different metabolic effects of the route and the different products and combinations. There are lots of different trials of secondary prevention but they used a transdermal preparation and 17β-oestradiol. So I wondered what numbers you had in your WHISP study – you said it was a pilot study – and are you intending to recruit more because will you not need big numbers and a long length of time to show any impact?

Stevenson: Absolutely. In the PHASE study[7] we used a transdermal oestradiol, you are absolutely right. The concern I have had about the secondary prevention studies of coronary disease has been not so much the type of oestrogen but more the starting dose. Because you are getting women in their late 60s and 70s and the PHASE study uses a huge dose of 80 μg of oestradiol. Even for a 50-year old menopausal woman we usually start them on 50 μg. So, if they have used the 25 μg starting point it would have been interesting to see what effect they would have had there. The ESPRIT study[8] has published data on mortality but they did not publish data that I have seen on actual event incidence and, as you know, they saw an early decrease in mortality that was not quite statistically significant but then seemed to be coming back. It is a very difficult study, to my mind, to interpret and a bit pointless in interpreting it because I do not think that many of us who are practical clinicians are going to be using menopausal oestrogens in the general population that are not hysterectomised.

Armitage: So what is going to happen with WHISP?

Stevenson: Well, we did a pilot study at the request of the Medical Research Council, and having done the pilot study we said we would like to do the full study. However, the Medical Research Council said they did not think that the climate was right.

Discussion following Dr Magnusson's paper

Prentice: One point about a very nice presentation – I am quite sure I am remembering correctly that we neither actively excluded women that had severe vasomotor symptoms or discouraged them from the Women's Health Initiative. It just happened that rather a few chose to go through the washout period and joined the trial.

Studd: I am surprised you even mention the quality of life studies because I do not know anybody who took them seriously. But, as you say, the women are mostly without symptoms. The wrong preparation was used in the wrong population. If you did have appropriate treatments for women with flushes, sweats, vaginal dryness, insomnia and depression, given by well-informed clinicians, you would not have a result of no improvement with HRT. It would be impossible.

Critchley: Professor Studd, is this a point of clarification or can we come back to this in the discussion? I think it is discussion rather than clarification.

Lowe: Dr Magnusson, you showed us two curves to stimulate discussion, so I think we should discuss them. I guess the levelling off of the breast cancer will be discussed tomorrow, but I would like to return to the cardiovascular data and the so-called cardiovascular protection of menopause. Dr Stevenson just spoke about the data from Framingham and said that there is a limited age range – and the data a little questionable. Whereas Dr Magnusson showed us one of these lifetime risks curves – men are always five years ahead and women are five years behind – but on this curve there was not even a blip to suggest an increase in female risk of cardiovascular disease at the menopause. This stage has now been discussed by cardiovascular epidemiologists for ten years with published UK national data and data from other countries including Japan, and nowhere in the world is there an increase in postmenopausal risk. The only people who seem still to believe this now are people who make HRT and possibly a few gynaecologists. So this is one area we might have a discussion about – can we finally bury this increase in menopausal risk of coronary heart disease?

Evans: Can I just make a comment before Dr Stevenson responds to that? That is, if you are going to look at it you have got to plot, in my view, log of age against log of rate. You will then see quite clear patterns with cancers that show this change at the menopause, which you do not see in coronary heart disease.

Stevenson: I just get rather concerned about people showing straight lines or curves or whatever plotting against age and saying that there is no inflection at the time of the menopause in terms of coronary disease. I would be absolutely astonished if there was, quite honestly. We have heard beautifully from Professor Burger that the menopause is not just an overnight event. Also, of course, if you are getting the metabolic changes that might lead to an increase in coronary disease, then you are not going to be seeing an effect of those for probably 10 to 20 years anyhow. What I would expect to see on a cross-sectional basis would just be a continued increase. The difficulties, of course, are that you have age-related factors as well. As I said earlier, it is very hard to tease the two out. However, I can give you an example: if you look at cholesterol levels with age in women you see exactly the same pattern – the curve going upwards and no inflection at the age of 50 years. But if you then do a study where you look specifically to see a menopause effect, there is a clear menopause effect, at least in our studies, in some of the Danish studies and in some of the North American studies. It is not universal, because Professor Burger's study has not yet shown that, but that could be because you are still in the menopause transition rather than being clearly pre- or clearly postmenopause. So, a straight line does not exclude an effect of menopause.

Whitehead: Yes, the cardiovascular epidemiologists have always ignored the data generated from surgical menopause and, in particular, surgical oophorectomy. If you look at those data, there is a doubling in risk of arterial disease within something like five to seven years after surgery. You have abrupt loss of ovarian function and you then see a dramatic rise in incidence of arterial disease. There is the Women's Health Initiative data. I agree with Dr Stevenson. If you ever have a continuum of a decline of function of organs producing a very potent hormone and the increase in risk is very small and that continuum is at least four, perhaps six years, you may not see an abrupt rise around the time of menopause in arterial disease risk. But if you take the ovaries out suddenly, then the risk jumps out at you.

Critchley: Dr Magnusson, do you want to make any comment about Mr Whitehead's comment about surgical oophorectomy? Do you have data?

Magnusson: No, I just want to comment on the curves. I agree with people saying that you cannot draw a conclusion from just curves on data. But what is interesting in the comparison of these two curves is that in the case of breast cancer you actually see something, which is probably due to menopause. In the case of coronary heart disease you do not see anything that speaks in favour of an effect of menopause, but you do not see anything that speaks in the opposite direction either.

Stevenson: Considering the side of your slide where you put myocardial infarction, were you not surprised when you were looking at those curves for coronary disease that there was not a drop at the menopause?

Magnusson: Well, not really, if you consider that oestrogen is not very important at all. Maybe the difference that people see between those two curves in men and women might be due to something occurring in males, the higher testosterone levels that are an established factor for cardiovascular disease. Do you see what I mean? In males, if that is the explanation for the shift between the curves in men and women, some people tend to argue that the explanation is that oestrogen protects women and testosterone does not harm men, but perhaps we need to think that males have something that makes them different from women and that might harm then.

Stevenson: To my knowledge the evidence would be that if you look at testosterone levels within the physiological range, the higher your testosterone level, the less coronary heart disease you have. And the only way that testosterone harms you apart from your prostate is making you take part in violent activities at sporting events.

Pitkin: Can I go on to quality of life? I quite agree with you that observational studies here are problematic because psychosocial and cultural determinants would impact on a woman's perception of quality of life. So you need randomised controlled trials. The problem, which I would quite like your view on, is two-fold. One is the high placebo effect in some studies, and I believe the Women's Health Initiative did have that. The other is the fact that the Women's Health Initiative did not use a validated quality of life tool. It did not use the Women's Health Questionnaire – which I am sure you are aware has been a valuable tool over the last 20 years – a 20 or 30 page document published by the European regulatory body on quality of life as outcome measures in clinical trials on drug and hormone therapies and which includes of course hypertension, diabetes and HRT – where they have looked very critically at interpersonal, inter-observer error, test/re-test reliability and the whole set of very specific criteria for how and when you cannot use quality of life data and how you should incorporate it into trials. Now, unfortunately, Women's Health Initiative does not meet those criteria at all, because they did not use quality of life as outcome measures. They only used one sexual health question and most of their markers are biomedical markers looking at response, which you would use more to look at response to treatment for medical disorders rather than more nebulous things like, as Dr Gebbie has pointed out, the difficulty of teasing the warp and the weft from insomnia, libido and general non-coping at this time. Which is why you have to use validated quality of life tools. So, what I really want is your opinion because we are using the Women's Health Initiative as a gold standard but we are talking about this as whether or not that is valid, given the placebo effect and the lack of quality of life validated tools.

Magnusson: I am not an expert in this area, but I feel strongly that if the observational data are so problematic we have to at least consider the only randomised controlled data that we have.

Pitkin: I think it is most unfortunate because it was a study where we really needed randomised controlled data because you cannot use observational studies – it is unfortunate that it does not use those tools. There are lots of small studies that do not have anything like the numbers which have looked specifically using quality of life tools, particularly, the Women's Health Questionnaire which has been validated now for use in several countries, including Sweden, Denmark and Italy and, of course, it was designed for the UK. It is also validated for all sorts of different languages. These studies have much smaller numbers – that is the problem. They are randomised controlled trials and they deal mainly with symptomatic women to see if there is improvement in vasomotor symptoms. But they do all show a degree of improvement in other domains. Women's Health Questionnaire uses eight domains, 30 different items in eight domains, and a number of these smaller randomised controlled trials show distinctive improvement in sexual function, sleep patterns, and general copability, not just in vasomotor symptoms. So I think, although it is much smaller, it is very difficult to say that the improvement in quality of life is only secondary and a domino effect, secondary to vasomotor symptoms. Also, there have been one or two studies that have begun to show changes in sleep pattern, not just because of vasomotor symptoms waking people up, because they are drenched in sweats and flushes but changes in the actual frequencies of rapid eye movement, REM sleep patterns – which is probably a primary effect. So, I appreciate it is a huge study and I appreciate the other studies have maybe 300 or 400 women, so you have not got the same numbers but you are showing definite benefits in several domains and I wonder if you could comment on that.

Magnusson: I think maybe we should take the opportunity of all the expertise gathered in this room today to discuss these issues, because it is a matter of consensus and discussion.

Critchley: I think we should give Dr Prentice an opportunity to respond because obviously he has studied this with the Women's Health Initiative study.

Prentice: I am also not an expert in quality of life measures. Can I ask when the Women's Health Questionnaire that you recommended became available?

Pitkin: Myra Hunter published WHQ in the early 1990s – it is a very standard internationally recognised tool.

Prentice: The Women's Health Initiative was being designed in 1992.

Whitehead: Myra Hunter and I worked together at King's on that for ten years. It came out in the late 1980s.

Prentice: Our quality of life instruments may not have the emphasis that you would like. We had a substantial committee of behavioural scientists who spent some months combing the literature. Why your preferred tool did not appear to be available on that I am not sure. But at least in a randomised trial to the extent that you are measuring pertinent outcomes, the distinction between intervention and control should be valid.

Burger: I think there is a more general comment that is relevant to this topic. I think we should remember why the Women's Health Initiative trial was undertaken. It was undertaken in the early 1990s because the practice was growing, in the USA in particular, of recommending HRT as a means of protecting women from getting heart disease. So it was done in older, postmenopausal women to answer this question. The data from it was then analysed to look at a whole lot of other outcomes, which were not primary outcomes, and which it could be debated were not relevant outcomes for the study. Most clinicians in the world treat women who are symptomatic around the time of menopause with HRT. I think it is not appropriate for us to extrapolate data from a chronic prevention trial for coronary heart disease to the management of perimenopausal and early postmenopausal symptomatic women. It is just not appropriate to extrapolate the data from one to the other. It is important to look at the Women's Health Initiative, which has got a lot of very useful information, but I do not think the analysis of quality of life data should then be used to say HRT does not improve quality of life even in the target population, which is quite different from the volunteers, the people that were recruited for the Women's Health Initiative study.

Armitage: That was going to be my point. It does not worry me at all that the quality of life questionnaire might not have been appropriate for the study. I would not expect it to make these women better. That was Professor Studd's point. These women were in their 60s, they did not have vasomotor symptoms anyway, HRT was being given to healthy women to see if their cardiovascular outcomes were better, not to address these quality of life symptoms. So I do not think it worries us at all whether or not the quality of life questionnaire was appropriate although I expect it may not have been.

Gray: That may well be taken in the academic field. But across all the newspapers it has been 'Hormone replacement therapy does not work – paper says there is no quality of life improvement'. Women come in very concerned because they say 'Well it works for me and this is what I want'. So, my practice is to tell women that the evidence was drawn from this particular trial population and then they have gone away happy, because they have realised where the numbers come from. It would have been nice had that explanation been published as well.

Buckler: I would just like to make a point – one of my menopause nurses has just completed a community audit over three primary care trusts where she was basically looking at HRT uptake in relation to the type of general practice and access to practice nurses and women's screening. One of the things that has come out of that is that over 80% of women that are taking HRT are actually taking it for vasomotor symptoms, not other psychological or quality of life issues. So it has been shown that this is the one area where we are sure that it does work.

Discussion following Dr Gebbie's paper

Critchley: I know we are already discussing your paper, Dr Gebbie, but I guess it leads to you.

Gebbie: I think that links in with what Miss Pitkin said and there are interesting data coming out about direct effects of HRT on sleep – some interesting trials. I have put more data on that in the chapter.

Whitehead: Can I just take on Professor Burger's sentiments? I think we have to distinguish clearly between what the Women's Health Initiative did and why it was done, and the treatment of symptomatic women. If I see a patient in the clinic who has loss of genital sensation, loss of clitoral sensation and does not enjoy having intercourse, of course she is going to respond to oestrogens. I do not need a paper from North America done in an entirely inappropriate group of women as far as I am concerned in my clinical practice, to tell me HRT does not work in that group. Dr Gray's point is well taken about how we disseminate the information from these large-scale studies so as not only not to frighten the patient, but also so that we keep the primary care physicians on side. Because, certainly where I work in the NHS in south-east London, we are now having GPs and primary care trusts who will not prescribe HRT because they say it is too dangerous. So we are now left where we were in the early 1970s, with symptomatic women who cannot get treatment to relieve their symptoms. Is that really what we set out to do when we set up these large randomised controlled trials? Because, if that is the endpoint, I think we scored a spectacular own goal and that is why we must bear in mind Professor Burger's comments about keeping the treatment of early postmenopausal symptomatic women quite separate from interpretation of large-scale randomised controlled trials in older largely asymptomatic women.

Critchley: That is a helpful comment that I think we might return to when we are discussing our consensus views.

Murphy: Dr Gebbie, I thought your talk was great and very clear and I do not disagree with any of your data, but I mention it as an example of how something said by somebody in one field, taken out of context, can affect practice in other fields. For example, although HRT should not be used as a first-line treatment for depression, some people may wish to use it as an adjunctive treatment in people who have not responded to the usual clinical approaches. Depression is associated with massive morbidity and a very significant mortality. It is one of the NHS aims to reduce morbidity and mortality for depression. We are constantly striving to improve our treatments for it. I would not use oestrogens as a first-line treatment for depression. I would never recommend it – just as I would never use thyroxine as a first-line treatment for depression. There is no good evidence that thyroxine is a good treatment for depression. Nevertheless, it is a valuable and adjunctive treatment, which undoubtedly saves the lives of women with clinically significant depressive disorder. Now, that does not mean that ergo it is a great treatment for the disorder. It means that it is a treatment that we need to bear in mind which potentially has significant effects. The key word is potentially. There is nothing wrong with the words potential or probable but the difficulty comes when people on both sides of the camp have entrenched positions and that can very significantly impact upon your colleagues in other fields in their clinical work, and also in the research they are trying to do. I guess that is just the point we were trying to raise.

Evans: I think it will probably be helpful to be reminded of the regulatory position regarding medicines. I would entirely support what Mr Whitehead said that if we look at vasomotor symptoms all hormone replacement therapies are licensed for vasomotor symptoms. There is no doubt that it is effective. Any GP who says, when there is a licensed medicine for vasomotor symptoms, that it is too dangerous to use, is I think not appreciating what the licensing process is. At the same time, there has never been in the UK an HRT that is licensed for prevention of coronary heart disease. I would entirely agree with Professor Burger and others who have said that in the context of lots of people using it largely on the basis of improvements in lipids for which we had good evidence of benefit but for clinical events for which we have still no good evidence that HRT improves coronary heart disease events. It may be that other doses or routes might be effective. We still have not got clinical event evidence on that and that is why it is not licensed. I think that the regulators have been really heavily attacked at times but it seems to me they have served women well in licensing it for things that are really good and not licensing it for things for which there was no evidence. I liked what Dr Gebbie said and if only people would go through with that kind of approach, to say where is the strong evidence, where have we got conclusive benefit and so on. An individual practitioner can clearly give almost anything they like. But you cannot license something until you have conclusive evidence on it, but you can give it. It may well be for libido you give tibolone, because there is probably benefit there. But as far as I know the manufacturers have not yet applied for a licence for that. One day they will if they obtain good evidence.

Pitkin: I just would like to compliment Dr Gebbie on the presentation – I agree it was extremely clear. I think one of the problems is trying to tease out all of these different items: libido, depressed mood, quality of life. If you remember the graph of female sexual arousal as you move up to the climax before resolution – cerebral factors feed in far more, perhaps, in women than in men. I think we do not necessarily have validated tools for sexual function at the moment. But it is not just about the orgasmic platform of vaso-congestion. There is a whole tranche of cerebral effects that feed in to the arousal mechanism of the female and into more nebulous issues such as quality of life, and whether you get on with your husband and whether you have pre-existing sexual problems prior to the menopause. They all come in there and then it is very difficult to tease all the bits and pieces out. I quite agree that the majority of surveys show that women come for vasomotor symptoms predominantly but they are all much more reticent to come for the touchy-feely matters such as sexual dysfunction, not getting on very well with the partner, or indeed leakage and urogenital dryness. They are all there but they may not be what they come with. Sometimes the surveys do not always show the impact of the other domains that quality of life covers and that is the difficulty. That is why some of these areas became a bit more woolly when we are trying to be so objective about things.

References

1. Santoro N, Isaac B, Neal-Perry G, Adel T, Weingart L, Nussbaum A, *et al*. Impaired folliculogenesis and ovulation in older reproductive aged women. *J Clin Endocrinol Metab* 2003;88:5502–9.
2. Dennerstein L, Randolph J, Taffe J, Dudley E, Burger H. Hormones, mood, sexuality, and the menopausal transition. *Fertil Steril* 2002;(4 Suppl 4):S49–54.
3. Wilson PW, Garrison RJ, Castelli WP. Postmenopausal estrogen use, cigarette smoking, and cardiovascular morbidity in women over 50. The Framingham Study. *N Engl J Med* 1985;313:1038–43.
4. Stampfer MJ, Colditz GA. Estrogen replacement therapy and coronary heart disease: a quantitative assessment of the epidemiologic evidence. *Prev Med* 1991;20:47–63.
5. Danesh J, Wheeler JG, Hirschfield GM, Eda S, Eiriksdottir G, Rumley A, *et al*. C-reactive protein and other circulating markers of inflammation in the prediction of coronary heart disease. *N Engl J Med* 2004;350:1387–97.
6. Manson JE, Hsia J, Johnson KC, Rossouw JE, Assaf AR, Lasser NL, *et al.*; Women's Health Initiative Investigators. Estrogen plus progestin and the risk of coronary heart disease. *N Engl J Med* 2003;349:523–34.
7. Clarke SC, Kelleher J, Lloyd-Jones H, Slack M, Schofield PM. A study of hormone replacement therapy in postmenopausal women with ischaemic heart disease: the Papworth HRT atherosclerosis study. *BJOG* 2002;109:1056–62.
8. Cherry N, Gilmour K, Hannaford P, Heagerty A, Khan MA, Kitchener H, *et al.*; ESPRIT team. Oestrogen therapy for prevention of reinfarction in postmenopausal women: a randomised placebo controlled trial. *Lancet* 2002;360:2001–8.

SECTION 2

EFFECTS OF HRT ON THE CARDIOVASCULAR SYSTEM AND BONES

Chapter 6

Postmenopausal hormone replacement therapy in relation to cardiovascular disease and cognition

Ross Prentice

Introduction and overview of findings

Many observational studies, and meta-analyses thereof,[1,2] have reported that postmenopausal hormone replacement therapy (HRT) is associated with a 40–50% lower coronary heart disease (CHD) risk and a lower overall mortality rate. Observational studies of HRT and stroke have yielded mixed results, with most reporting neutral or modest associations.[3] Observational studies of HRT and venous thromboembolism (VTE) have been fairly consistent[3] in indicating some risk elevation, especially during the early years of use. The HRT summarised in these studies was predominantly unopposed oestrogen (E-alone), with few studies distinguishing E-alone therapy from combined oestrogen plus progestogen (E + P) therapy. When this distinction was made, there was typically no clear difference between E-alone and E+P with respect to cardiovascular disease (CVD) risk.

The potential benefits of HRT for CHD were supported generally by the Postmenopausal Estrogen/Progestin Interventions (PEPI) randomised controlled trial that compared various HRT preparations in terms of CVD risk factors[4] and other intermediate outcomes. E-alone and three E + P regimens were found to lower low-density lipoprotein cholesterol (LDL-C) substantially and to increase high-density lipoprotein cholesterol (HDL-C). The inclusion of a progestogen had variable effects on the HDL-C increase. Effects on other CVD risk factors were generally neutral or favourable.

With this background, the results[5] of the Heart and Estrogen/Progestin Replacement Study (HERS) were met with surprise and scepticism[6,7] when this secondary prevention trial among postmenopausal women with established CHD found no overall differences in CHD incidence between active and placebo groups over an average 4.1 years of follow-up with some elevation in risk during the first year of E+P use. HERS studied the most commonly used combined HRT regimen in the USA, comprising daily 0.625 mg of conjugated equine oestrogen (CEE) and 2.5 mg of medroxyprogesterone acetate (MPA) (Prempro, Wyeth-Ayerst) among women with uterus. This same regimen was simultaneously under study among predominantly healthy postmenopausal women with uterus as part of the Women's Health Initiative (WHI) randomised controlled trial.[8] The E + P trial in WHI was stopped early in July 2002 when the external Data and Safety Monitoring Board assessed that risks exceeded benefits over an average 5.2 year follow-up period. Incidence rate increases for CHD, stroke, VTE and breast cancer were only partially offset by incidence rate reductions for colorectal cancer and hip fractures, diseases that each contributed to a pre-specified global index for risk-versus-benefit trial monitoring.[8]

Several other trials of HRT preparations among women with CVD in relation to the progression of coronary artery atherosclerosis or coronary events have also been concluded. The Estrogen Replacement and Atherosclerosis (ERA) trial[9] compared daily 0.625 mg CEE, and 0.625 mg CEE plus 2.5 mg MPA, with placebo with respect to the progression of coronary artery atherosclerosis among 309 postmenopausal women with angiographically verified coronary disease, and found no difference in progression over an average 3.2 year follow-up period. Similarly, the Women's Angiographic Vitamin and Estrogen (WAVE) trial[10] randomised 423 postmenopausal women with coronary atherosclerosis to daily 0.625 mg CEE plus 2.5 mg MPA if with uterus, versus placebo, and found no benefit and a potential for harm over an average 2.8 years between angiograms. The Papworth HRT Atherosclerosis Study (PHASE)[11] randomised 255 postmenopausal women with established ischaemic heart disease to 2.5 mg transdermal 17β-oestradiol or placebo if post-hysterectomy, or to a sequential transdermal combination of the same oestrogen and 4 mg norethisterone versus placebo if with uterus. A nonsignificant elevation in the primary outcome, comprising hospitalised unstable angina, myocardial infarction or cardiac death among women assigned to active therapy, was observed over the average 30.8 month follow-up period. The oestrogen therapy for prevention of reinfarction trial (ESPRIT)[12] randomly assigned 1017 postmenopausal women who survived a myocardial infarction to daily oestradiol valerate (2 mg) or placebo, and found that the frequency of reinfarction or cardiac death did not differ between the two groups at 24 months. Also, the Women's Estrogen-Progestin Lipid-Lowering Hormone Atherosclerosis Regression Trial (WELL-HART)[13] randomised 226 postmenopausal women with coronary atherosclerosis to 1 mg oral micronised 17β-oestradiol for 12 days per month, the same oestrogen plus 5 mg MPA for 12 days per month, or placebo, and found that neither HRT regimen affected the progression of coronary atherosclerosis over a 3.3 year median follow-up period. Hence, none of these trials indicate cardioprotection for the HRT regimens studied.

In addition, two small trials examined the effects of 17β-oestradiol alone,[14] or in combination with gestodene,[15] on carotid intima-media thickness among healthy postmenopausal women. The former reported a lower progression rate over a two-year follow-up period, while the latter found no difference over a one-year period. Also, the Women's Estrogen for Stroke Trial[16] found no difference between 17β-oestradiol and placebo groups in an outcome variable of stroke or death, in a study of 664 women who had a recent stroke or transient ischaemia attack, over a 2.8 year average follow-up period, but with an indication of elevation during the first six months of use. Finally, a small secondary prevention trial of oestradiol plus norethisterone in relation to VTE stopped early based on an excess of VTE events.[17]

A number of observational studies of HRT in relation to cognitive function and dementia have also been reported. Although results have been somewhat variable, most studies among women without dementia have reported higher cognitive performance and lower dementia incidence among HRT users compared with nonusers. For example, meta-analyses[3,18] have reported reductions of about 30% in dementia incidence. In comparison, the Women's Health Initiative Memory Study (WHIMS),[19] an ancillary study to the WHI hormone trials, found an approximately two-fold elevation in probable dementia (PD) among the women studied, who were 65 or older at baseline in the WHI E+P trial. Mild cognitive impairment (MCI) was also ascertained in WHIMS, and no difference was detected between the E+P and placebo groups. In addition, studies of cognitive function among women 65 or older in the WHI

E+P trial cohort,[20] or in the WHIMS subset,[21] have found mostly neutral or slightly unfavourable effects for the CEE/MPA regimen. Finally, controlled trials in women with Alzheimer's disease[22-24] have found no beneficial effect of unopposed oestrogen on cognitive function.

A randomised placebo-controlled trial of CEE (0.625 mg daily), among 10 739 predominantly healthy women who were post-hysterectomy and in the age range 50–79 years at baseline concluded (after the RCOG meeting) as a part of the WHI.[25] This trial cohort was studied for CVD, cancer, fractures and a range of other outcomes, and the subset who were 65 years or older at baseline were eligible for the WHIMS study of cognitive performance and dementia. No overall effect of CEE on CHD was observed, but there was some elevation in stroke and VTE. Results from the corresponding component of WHIMS were recently published,[26,27] and included nonsignificant unfavourable trends in probable dementia incidence among women assigned to CEE.

The remainder of this chapter provides a more detailed summary of published findings from HERS and WHI concerning E+P and CVD, and of published findings from WHIMS and WHI concerning cognitive function and dementia in relation to E+P. A final section notes continuing activities in WHI to elucidate apparent differences between CVD results in the E+P trial and corresponding findings in a companion WHI cohort study, and to elucidate biological mechanism for early elevations in CVD risk in the years following the initiation of E+P.

Cardiovascular disease in the HERS and WHI CEE/MPA trials

The HERS study was a randomised placebo-controlled trial of daily CEE (0.625mg) plus MPA (2.5mg) among 2763 postmenopausal women with uterus who had established coronary disease. An average 11% lower LDL-C and an average 10% higher HDL-C was observed in the active versus placebo group. When the trial reached its planned termination in 1998, following a 4.1 year average follow-up period, there were 172 women with recurrent CHD in the active group compared with 176 in the placebo group.[5] The overall hazard ratio (HR) for CHD recurrence, the trial's designated primary outcome, was 0.99 (95% CI 0.80–1.22). Additionally, the estimated hazard ratio was 1.52 (95% CI 1.01–2.29), 1.00 (95% CI 0.67–1.49), 0.87 (95% CI 0.55–1.37) and 0.67 (95% CI 0.43–1.04) in the first, second, third and subsequent years from randomisation, respectively. Moreover, there were 71 CHD deaths in the active hormone group, compared with 58 in the placebo group, with a corresponding hazard ratio of 1.24 (95% CI 0.87–1.75). HERS participants continued to be followed beyond the trial termination without intervention. A report after an average 6.8 years of follow-up continued to show no overall difference in CHD recurrence rate between the active and placebo groups.[28]

HERS trial investigators also reported a nonsignificant elevation in stroke incidence (HR 1.23, 95% CI 0.89–1.70)[29] and a significant elevation in VTE incidence (HR 2.7, 95% CI 1.4–5.0)[30] over its average 4.1 years of intervention follow-up.

The WHI combined hormone trial reported primary results over its average 5.2 years of follow-up in 2002.[8] This trial involved 16 608 predominantly healthy postmenopausal women, 8506 of whom were assigned to E+P and 8102 to placebo. The slight imbalance in numbers in the two groups was because the design initially allowed women with a uterus to receive unopposed oestrogen. Following the PEPI trial results[31] indicating that long-term adherence to unopposed oestrogen was not feasible in women with a uterus, the WHI protocol was changed to randomise such women only to E+P or placebo in equal proportions. The 331 women previously randomised to E-alone were unblinded and reassigned to E+P. Eligibility for the combined hormone trial included age 50–79 at initial screening and postmenopausal, while major exclusions were related to competing risks (any medical condition likely to be associated with a predicted survival of less than three years), safety (e.g. prior breast cancer or recent other cancer), and adherence or retention concerns (e.g. alcoholism or dementia). Follow-up for clinical events occurred every six months, with annual in-clinic visits required. Information on designated symptoms and safety concerns were collected in a standardised format, and initial reports of clinical outcomes were obtained during these biannual visits. Modification of the oestrogen and progestogen dosage was allowed to manage symptoms such as vaginal bleeding and breast tenderness, and the protocol specified conditions for temporary or permanent discontinuation of medication.[8]

Definitions of CHD, stroke and VTE outcomes have been given previously.[8,32,33] Clinical outcomes were determined by local physician adjudicators and used for trial monitoring purposes. These adjudicators were centrally trained and blinded to treatment assignment and participant symptoms. CHD, stroke and VTE outcomes in the HRT trials were further adjudicated by central physician adjudicators. Confirmation rates by central adjudicators were 90% for myocardial infarction and 97% for death due to CHD, which together comprise CHD, and 95% for stroke, 98% for pulmonary embolism and 96% for deep vein thrombosis, which together comprise VTE.

Previous reports[32,33] have provided E+P versus placebo hazard ratio estimates and nominal 95% confidence intervals for CHD and stroke based on centrally adjudicated outcome data. For CHD, the hazard ratio was 1.24 (95% CI 1.00–1.54), and there were 188 CHD cases in the E+P group, compared with 147 in the control group over the average 5.6 year follow-up period until study pills were stopped (July 2002).[32] Hazard ratios for other coronary events, including revascularisation, angina, acute coronary syndrome and congestive heart failure, did not differ between E+P and placebo groups. The corresponding hazard ratio for stroke was 1.31 (95% CI 1.02–1.68), based on 151 strokes in the E+P group, compared with 107 in the placebo group, nearly 80% of which were ischaemic.[33] When analysed separately, the hazard ratio for ischaemic stroke was 1.44 (95% CI 1.09–1.90) as compared with 0.82 (95% CI 0.43–1.56) for haemorrhagic stroke. For locally adjudicated VTE,[8] the hazard ratio was 2.11 (95% CI 1.58–2.82) based on 151 cases in the E+P group and 67 in the placebo group. Corresponding estimates were 2.07 (95% CI 1.49–2.87) for deep vein thrombosis and 2.13 (95% CI 1.39–3.25) for pulmonary embolism. The WHI randomised placebo-controlled E+P trial thus provided evidence for an increased risk of CHD, stroke, and VTE over its follow-up period.

The hazard ratio in the E+P group was elevated within the first year from randomisation for CHD and VTE,[8,32] but took until the second year for stroke. Table 6.1 shows hazard ratios for each of these outcomes as a function of years since randomisation. Note that CHD risk is substantially elevated in the first two years from randomisation, whereas the stroke elevation occurs primarily between two and five years from randomisation. For either outcome, the hazard ratio estimate is close to one at more than five years from randomisation. However, a hazard ratio below one would not necessarily imply risk reduction in this time period, since higher risk E+P users have been differentially excluded from follow-up by the risk elevation at earlier times from randomisation. For VTE there is a large hazard ratio elevation in the first two years from randomisation that is subsequently reduced.

The relationship of the E+P hazard ratio to a number of baseline characteristics has also been examined.[8,32,33] The overall E+P group hazard ratio for CHD[32] did not depend

Table 6.1. E+P hazard ratios (with 95% confidence intervals) in the Women's Health Initiative (WHI) clinical trial as a function of years from randomisation

Years from randomisation	Coronary heart disease (CHD)[a]	Stroke[b]	Venous thromboembolism (VTE)[b]
<2	1.54 (1.08–2.19)	1.29 (0.82–2.04)	3.07 (1.92–4.90)
2–5	1.33 (0.95–1.86)	1.49 (1.04–2.11)	1.99 (1.33–2.99)
>5	0.70 (0.42–1.14)	1.05 (0.61–1.80)	1.09 (0.59–2.04)

[a] Cox regression analyses stratified on age, presence or absence of prior coronary event, and randomly assigned diet modification group, and adjusted for previous coronary artery bypass grafting on percutaneous transluminal coronary angioplasty;[32] [b] Cox regression analyses stratified on baseline age in five-year intervals (50–54, 55–59, 60–64, 65–69, 70–74 and 75–79)

significantly on age, years since menopause, the occurrence of hot flushes, body mass index, aspirin use or statin use, although power was limited for interaction detection. It also did not depend significantly on ethnicity, education, smoking history, the presence of prior CHD or CVD, the number of CHD risk factors, or the presence of hypertension or diabetes. The hazard ratio for CHD was also examined in relation to baseline lipids and certain inflammation and thrombosis factors. It did not depend significantly on C-reactive protein concentration, factor VIII coagulant activity or fibrinogen concentration, but a significant relationship with LDL-C was detected, with larger hazard ratios among women having a relatively high baseline value. Similarly, the overall E+P group hazard ratio for stroke[33] did not depend significantly on baseline age, years from menopause, vasomotor symptoms, use of aspirin, use of statins, or a number of demographic factors. It also did not depend significantly on baseline blood lipids, factor VIII coagulant activity or fibrinogen concentration, or on the inflammation biomarkers C-reactive protein, matrix metalloproteinase 9, E-selectin or interleukin-6. Women randomised to the E+P group experienced a small (<2 mmHg) elevation in systolic blood pressure relative to the placebo group. Including follow-up systolic blood pressure in the analysis had little effect on the E+P hazard ratio for stroke. Detailed analyses of hazard ratio interactions for VTE from the WHI E+P trial have yet to be published. As noted in the original study report,[8] there was a suggestion of a higher E+P hazard ratio for women having a VTE event prior to randomisation, compared with women without such personal history.

Cognitive function and dementia in the WHI CEE/MPA trial

The WHI HRT trials included a substantial assessment of health-related quality of life at baseline and at one year from randomisation, and in an approximate 10% subsample at three years from randomisation. E+P trial findings[20] included no significant differences between the E+P and placebo groups with respect to general health, vitality, mental health, depressive symptoms or sexual satisfaction, and significant but small (and not clinically meaningful) improvements for sleep disturbance, physical functioning and bodily pain, at one, but not three, years from randomisation. Among women 50–54 years of age with moderate-to-severe vasomotor symptoms at baseline, the E+P group experienced a small benefit compared with placebo in terms of sleep disturbance, but not for the other quality of life outcomes. Cognitive function was assessed in participants 65 years of age or older at baseline, as a part of the health-related quality of life assessment, using the modified mini-mental state examination (3MSE).[34] This examination consists of 15 parts that contain 46 separately scored items involving orientation to time, place and person, short-term memory, reading, writing, naming, verbal fluency, praxis, and graphomotor skills, leading to a score ranging from 0 (worst functioning) to 100 (best functioning). The average change from baseline (standard deviation) for the 5047 women who provided 3MSE data at baseline and at one year was 0.7 (6.0) in the E+P group compared with 0.6 (4.9) in the placebo group, with the difference nonsignificant ($P=0.40$). The change in 3MSE score from baseline to three years also was similar in the two groups ($P=0.79$).

The E+P component of the WHIMS study assessed cognitive function among a subset of non-demented WHI E + P trial women having a baseline age of 65 or older. The WHIMS study was initiated in 1996, about three years after the initiation of the E + P trial. A total of 4532 women enrolled in this component of WHIMS, 92.6% of those invited, and nearly all (4487) enrolled prior to WHI randomisation. Annual 3MSE assessments were sought from these women, and the trajectory of scores for individual women was analysed. The scores tended to improve over time in both the E + P and placebo groups, but the mean rate of increase was larger ($P=0.03$) in the placebo than in the E+P group over a 4.2 year average follow-up period, but the difference was not judged to be clinically important.[21] On the other hand, more women ($P<0.01$) in the E + P group (6.7%) compared with the placebo group (4.8%) had a clinically important, greater than two standard deviation, decline in 3MSE score during this follow-up period. The comparison of 3MSE scores between randomisation groups did not depend on baseline demographic factors (age, ethnicity, education, income), lifestyle factors (smoking, alcohol, body mass index), CVD risk factors (personal CVD history, hypertension, diabetes), aspirin or statin use, vasomotor symptoms or prior hormone use.

The occurrence of probable dementia (PD) was the primary WHIMS outcome, with mild cognitive impairment (MCI) as a secondary outcome. These outcomes were identified using the 3MSE assessments as a screening tool for cognitive impairment. Initially, a score of 72 or lower for women with eight years or fewer of education and 76 or lower among women with nine or more years of education were identified for further testing. After 16 months, these cut-off points were increased to 80 and 88, respectively, to increase sensitivity. Women having scores below the designated cut-off points were identified for comprehensive cognitive testing administered by certified technicians, and a detailed description of cognition and behavioural changes were obtained from both the participant and a reliable observer, typically a family member. These participants were also examined by a physician (geriatrician, neurologist or geriatric psychiatrist) who reviewed all pertinent data and assigned the women to one of the following three categories: no dementia, MCI or PD, based on *Diagnostic and Statistical Manual of Mental Disorders*, 4th edition.[35] If the clinician suspected PD, the woman was referred for a computed tomography scan of the brain and blood tests to rule out reversible causes of cognitive decline and dementia. A centralised adjudication committee reviewed all probable dementia cases, 50% of MCI cases and 10% of women without dementia, leading to a consensus classification. Women classified as MCI or PD continued to be screened annually with the 3MSE.

Table 6.2 shows hazard ratios for PD and MCI from the E + P component of the WHIMS study.[19] The incidence of the primary PD outcome was approximately doubled in the E +P compared with the placebo group, over the 4.1 year WHIMS follow-up, with differences beginning to emerge within a year or two following randomisation. About 50% of the PD cases were classified as Alzheimer's disease in both groups, with a small additional fraction (5–12.5%) classified as having vascular origins. Scores on

Table 6.2. E+P hazard ratios (with 95% confidence intervals) from the WHIMS study[19] for probable dementia and mild cognitive impairment

	Number of cases		Hazard ratio
	E+P	Placebo	
Probable dementia (PD)	40	21	2.05 (1.21–3.48)
Mild cognitive impairment (MCI)	56	55	1.07 (0.74–1.55)
PD or MCI	85	66	1.37 (0.99–1.89)

the 3MSE declined sharply prior to and following a PD diagnosis.[21] The incidence of mild cognitive impairment defined as poor cognitive function performance, and a report of some functional impairment (but not in a basic activity of daily living) without dementia, did not differ between the E+P and placebo groups. The hazard ratio for PD did not depend significantly on baseline age, education, smoking, history of stroke, history of diabetes, baseline 3MSE score or prior HRT. In summary, the WHIMS study among women aged 65 or older identified a small adverse effect on global cognition and, importantly, an approximate doubling of probable dementia. The effect of E+P on these outcomes among postmenopausal women younger than 65 years has not been determined. As mentioned previously, corresponding results from the WHI CEE trial were presented[26,27] subsequent to the RCOG meeting leading to this volume.

Continuing WHI activities to elucidate CEE/MPA effects on cardiovascular disease

Two WHI activities, which aim to build upon and extend the implications of the E+P trial on CVD, merit comment. One of these involves a joint analysis of trial data and data from the companion WHI Observational Study which, like the WHI HRT trials, included a personal interview to ascertain prior HRT use, as well as periodic updates of HRT use during follow-up. These analyses are attempting to identify confounding factors and other sources of bias that, when accommodated, can cause E+P hazard ratios from the two cohorts to align closely. Upon achieving such alignment, the combined strength of the two designs may lead to reliable estimates of hazard ratios for CHD, stroke and VTE for long-term E+P use, and may provide valuable assessment of the CVD effects of other E+P preparations, dosages or routes of administration.

A second continuing activity involves seeking biological explanations for the elevation in CVD risk in the early years after HRT initiation. A battery of inflammation, thrombosis and lipid markers has been obtained at baseline and at one year from randomisation for CHD, stroke and VTE cases occurring through February 2001 and matched controls. Some analyses of baseline biomarkers in relation to E+P hormone replacement have been presented but most have yet to be published, and biomarker change data have not yet been presented. Analyses to date also include genetic markers for selected candidate genes. A continuing process is identifying additional biochemical and genetic markers for the study of HRT and CVD, and a potential genome-wide scan of CHD cases and controls for a comprehensive study of genotype in relation to HRT effects on CHD is under consideration.

Acknowledgements

Supported by contract from the National Heart, Lung and Blood Institute, and by a grant from the National Cancer Institute.

References

1.   Stampfer MJ, Colditz GA. Estrogen replacement therapy and coronary heart disease: a quantitative assessment of the epidemiologic evidence. *Prev Med* 1991;20:47–63.
2.   Grady D, Rubin SM, Pettiti DB, Fox CS, Black D, Ettinger B, *et al.* Hormone therapy to prevent disease and prolong life in postmenopausal women. *Ann Intern Med* 1992;117:1016–37.
3.   Nelson HD, Humphrey LL, Nygren P, Teutsch SM, Allan JD. Postmenopausal hormone replacement therapy: scientific review. *JAMA* 2002;288:872–81.
4.   The Writing Group for the PEPI Trial. Effects of estrogen or estrogen/progestin regimens on heart disease risk factors in postmenopausal women. The Postmenopausal Estrogen/Progestin Interventions (PEPI) Trial. *JAMA* 1995;273:199–208. Erratum in: *JAMA* 1995;274:1676.
5.   Hulley S, Grady D, Bush T, Furberg C, Herrington D, Riggs B, *et al.* Randomized trial of estrogen plus progestin for secondary prevention of coronary heart disease in postmenopausal women. Heart and Estrogen/progestin Replacement Study (HERS) Research Group. *JAMA* 1998;280:605–13.
6.   Whitehead M, Stampfer M. HERS – a missed opportunity [editorial]. *Climacteric* 1998;1:170–1.
7.   Utian WH. HER and HERS findings – has the ground shifted [editorial]? *Menopause Management* 1998:5.
8.   Rossouw JE, Anderson GL, Prentice RL, LaCroix AZ, Kooperberg C, Stefanick ML, *et al.*; Writing Group for the Women's Health Initiative Investigators. Risks and benefits of estrogen plus progestin in healthy postmenopausal women. Principal results from the Women's Health Initiative randomized controlled trial. *JAMA* 2002;288:321–33.
9.   Herrington DM, Reboussin DM, Brosnihan KB, Sharp PC, Shumaker SA, Snyder TE, *et al.* Effects of estrogen replacement on the progression of coronary-artery atherosclerosis. *N Engl J Med* 2000;343:522–9.
10. Waters DD, Alderman EL, Hsia J, Howard BV, Cobb FR, Rogers WJ, *et al.* Effects of hormone replacement therapy and antioxidant vitamin supplements on coronary atherosclerosis in postmenopausal women: a randomized controlled trial. *JAMA* 2002;288:2432–40.
11. Clarke SC, Kelleher J, Lloyd-Jones H, Slack M, Schofield PM. A study of hormone replacement therapy in postmenopausal women with ischaemic heart disease: the Papworth HRT atherosclerosis study. *BJOG* 2002;109:1056–62.
12. Cherry N, Gilmour K, Hannaford P, Heagerty A, Khan MA, Kitchener H, *et al.*; ESPRIT team. Oestrogen therapy for prevention of reinfarction in postmenopausal women: a randomised placebo controlled trial. *Lancet* 2002;360:2001–8.
13. Hodis HN, Mack WJ, Azen SP, Lobo RA, Shoupe D, Mahrer PR, *et al.*; Women's Estrogen-Progestin Lipid-Lowering Hormone Atherosclerosis Regression Trial Research Group. Hormone therapy and the progression of coronary-artery atherosclerosis in postmenopausal women. *N Engl J Med* 2003;349:535–45.
14. Hodis HN, Mack WJ, Lobo RA, Shoupe D, Sevanian A, Mahrer PR, *et al.* Estrogen in the prevention of atherosclerosis. A randomized, double-blind, placebo-controlled trial. *Ann Intern Med* 2001;135:939–53.
15. Angerer P, Stork S, Kothny W, Schmitt P, von Schacky C. Effect of oral postmenopausal hormone replacement on progression of atherosclerosis. A randomized controlled trial. *Arterioscler Thromb Vasc Biol* 2001;21:262–8.
16. Viscoli CM, Brass LM, Kernan WN, Sarrel PM, Suissa S, Horwitz RI. A clinical trial of estrogen-replacement therapy after ischemic stroke. *N Engl J Med* 2001;345:1243–9.
17. Hoibraaten E, Qvigstad E, Arnesen H, Larsen S, Wickstrom E, Sandset PM. Increased risk of recurrent venous thromboembolism during hormone replacement therapy. *Thromb Haemost* 2000;84:962–7.
18. Yaffe K, Sawaya G, Lieberburg I, Grady D. Estrogen therapy in postmenopausal women: effects on cognitive function and dementia. *JAMA* 1998;279:688–95.
19. Shumaker SA, Legault C, Rapp SR, Thal L, Wallace RB, Ockene JK, *et al.* Estrogen plus progestin and the incidence of dementia and mild cognitive impairment in postmenopausal women. The Women's Health Initiative Memory Study: a randomized controlled trial. *JAMA* 2003;289:2651–62.

20. Hays J, Ockene JK, Brunner RL, Kotchen JM, Manson JE, Patterson RE, *et al.* Effects of estrogen plus progestin on health-related quality of life. *N Engl J Med* 2003;348:1839–54.
21. Rapp SR, Espeland MA, Shumaker SA, Henderson VW, Brunner RL, Manson JE, *et al.* Effect of estrogen plus progestin on global cognitive function in postmenopausal women. The Women's Health Initiative Memory Study: a randomized controlled trial. *JAMA* 2003;289:2663–72.
22. Henderson VW, Paganini-Hill A, Miller BL, Elble RJ, Reyes PF, Shoupe D, *et al.* Estrogen for Alzheimer's disease in women: randomized, double-blind, placebo-controlled trial. *Neurology* 2000;54:295–301.
23. Mulnard RA, Cotman CW, Kawas C, van Dyck CH, Sano M, Doody R, *et al.* Estrogen replacement therapy for treatment of mild to moderate Alzheimer disease: a randomized controlled trial. *JAMA* 2000;283:1007–15.
24. Wang PN, Liao SQ, Liu RS, Liu CY, Chao HT, Lu SR, *et al.* Effects of estrogen on cognition, mood, and cerebral blood flow in AD: a controlled study. *Neurology* 2000;54:2061–6.
25. Anderson GL, Limacher M, Assaf AR, Bassford T, Beresford SA, Black H, *et al.*; Women's Health Initiative Steering Committee. Effects of conjugated equine estrogen in postmenopausal women with hysterectomy: the Women's Health Initiative randomized controlled trial. *JAMA* 2004;291:1701–12.
26. Espeland MA, Rapp SR, Shumaker SA, Brunner R, Manson JE, Sherwin BB, *et al*; Women's Health Initiative Memory Study. Conjugated equine estrogens and global cognitive function in postmenopausal women: Women's Health Initiative Memory Study. *JAMA* 2004;291:2959–68.
27. Shumaker SA, Legault C, Kuller L, Rapp SR, Thal L, Lane DS, *et al.* Conjugated equine estrogens and incidence of probable dementia and mild cognitive impairment in postmenopausal women. *JAMA* 2004;291:2947–58.
28. Grady D, Herrington D, Bittner V, Blumenthal R, Davidson M, Hlatky M, *et al.*; HERS Research Group. Cardiovascular disease outcomes during 6.8 years of hormone therapy: Heart and Estrogen/progestin Replacement Study follow-up (HERS II). *JAMA* 2002;288:49–57. Erratum in: *JAMA* 2002;288:1064.
29. Simon JA, Hsia J, Cauley JA, Richards C, Harris F, Fong J, *et al.* Postmenopausal hormone therapy and risk of stroke: The Heart and Estrogen-progestin Replacement Study (HERS). *Circulation* 2001;103:638–42.
30. Grady D, Wenger NK, Herrington D, Khan S, Furberg C, Hunninghake D, *et al.* Postmenopausal hormone therapy increases risk of venous thrombolic disease: The Heart and Estrogen/Progestin Replacement Study. *Ann Intern Med* 2000;132:689–96.
31. The Writing Group for the PEPI Trial. Effects of hormone replacement therapy on endometrial histology in postmenopausal women. The Postmenopausal Estrogen/Progestin Interventions (PEPI) Trial. *JAMA* 1996;275:370–5.
32. Manson JE, Hsia J, Johnson KC, Rossouw JE, Assaf AR, Lasser NL, *et al.*; Women's Health Initiative Investigators. Estrogen plus progestin and the risk of coronary heart disease. *N Engl J Med* 2003;349:523–34.
33. Wassertheil-Smoller S, Hendrix SL, Limacher M, Heiss G, Kooperberg C, Baird A, *et al.* Effect of estrogen plus progestin on stroke in postmenopausal women. The Women's Health Initiative: a randomized trial. *JAMA* 2003;289:2673–84.
34. Teng EL, Chui HC. The Modified Mini-Mental State (3MS) examination. *J Clin Psychiatry* 1987;48:314–8.
35. American Psychiatric Association. *Diagnostic and Statistical Manual of Mental Disorders, Fourth Edition, Text Revision (DSM-IV-TR®).* Arlington: American Psychiatric Publishing Inc; 2000.

Chapter 7

Hormone replacement therapy and venous thromboembolism

Gordon Lowe

Introduction

Venous thromboembolism (VTE) comprises deep vein thrombosis of the leg (DVT) and pulmonary embolism (PE). Acute DVT presents with clinical symptoms in the leg (pain or swelling) in about 1 per 1000 persons per year in the general populations of Western countries. Its acute complication, PE, presents most commonly as clinical symptoms in the chest (e.g. breathlessness, chest pain, haemoptysis) in a further 0.5 per 1000 persons per year in such populations.[1] About 30% of patients presenting with PE die within seven days of presentation, usually rapidly if they present as massive PE (with sudden death, or with syncope or shock). In contrast, fewer than 5% of patients presenting with DVT die within seven days.[1] About 30% of VTE survivors develop recurrent VTE within ten years, and about 30% (often those with recurrent DVT) develop the post-thrombotic leg syndrome (PLS: venous stasis with chronic pain, swelling, dermatitis and often ulceration) within 20 years.[1] Prophylaxis of DVT and its complications (PE, death and PLS) is paramount.[1,2]

VTE is a multifactorial disease.[1,3] Risk factors include increasing age, obesity, varicose veins, immobility (lower limb trauma or paralysis, or hospitalisation for trauma, surgery or medical illness), malignancy, central venous catheters or trans-venous pacemakers, and intravenous drug self-use.[1,2] Risk factors among women include pregnancy[4] and use of combined oral contraceptives (COCs) or oral hormone replacement therapy (HRT).[5-7] These risk factors may promote venous thrombogenesis through one or more of Virchow's classical three pathways:

- damage to the vein wall (lower limb trauma or surgery, central venous catheters or pacemakers, or intravenous drug self-use[8])
- venous stasis (age, obesity, varicose veins, pregnancy, immobility)
- activation of blood coagulation (age, obesity, trauma, surgery, medical illness, malignancy, pregnancy, use of COCs or oral HRT).[1-7]

Rosendaal and colleagues in Leiden have, through epidemiological studies such as the Leiden Thrombophilia Study (LETS), highlighted the importance of multiple gene–environment interactions in the multifactorial disease of VTE.[3,5-7] There is growing evidence that VTE results from increasing interactions throughout life between multiple common genetic prothrombotic states (thrombophilias) and the multiple environmental challenges listed above.[3] The interaction of oestrogens (modified by progestogens) with (genetic) thrombophilias to increase risk of VTE in a supra-additive manner provides the best example to date of gene–environment interaction as a cause of cardiovascular disease.

High levels of endogenous oestrogens are believed to be a major cause of the ten-fold increased risk of VTE during pregnancy and the puerperium. They increase plasma levels of several coagulation factors, decrease the levels of several coagulation inhibitors, and hence increase activation of blood coagulation.[4] While the teleological explanation of these changes is to limit the risk of excessive peripartum haemorrhage, they also increase the risk of VTE during pregnancy and the puerperium: such risks can be reduced by selective anticoagulant prophylaxis in women at high risk (e.g. thrombophilias, previous VTE) which reduces excessive activation of blood coagulation.[2]

Oral administration of exogenous synthetic oestrogens and progestogens, as used in COCs, was reported to increase the risk of VTE shortly after their introduction in the 1960s.[5,6,9,10] This risk was associated with oestrogen doses above 50 μg but, despite reductions in dose, COC use retains a significant increase in risk not only of VTE (two- to three-fold higher) but also of arterial atherothrombotic disease including myocardial infarction, stroke and peripheral arterial disease.[5,6] The risk of VTE is about two-fold higher with third-generation COCs compared with second-generation COCs, probably owing to different effects of the relevant progestogens on oestrogen-induced activation of blood coagulation.[6]

HRT was for many years considered a 'perceived panacea' for peri- and postmenopausal women. While initially designed and introduced to Western countries in the 1960s to reduce perimenopausal symptoms such as vasomotor sweats and hot flushes, and also because of its potential to reduce osteoporotic fractures, efficacy in symptom relief has been clarified only recently by placebo-controlled trials,[11,12] as has their effect on risk of fractures.[13,14] Owing to the myth of a 'perimenopausal increase in risk' of coronary heart disease (CHD) and stroke in women,[15,16] as well as observational studies that could not adjust for several biases,[17] HRT was also promoted for prevention of CHD and stroke. However, randomised controlled trials have shown that HRT not only does not reduce the risk of CHD and stroke, but indeed increases the risk.[7] As with COCs, it is likely that these increases in risk of arterial thrombosis reflect activation of blood coagulation by exogenous oral oestrogens.[7] Such activation of coagulation is also the likely explanation of the two- to three-fold increased risk of VTE in users of HRT, which has been established beyond doubt within the past decade.[7,14,18,19]

What is the risk of VTE in users of HRT?

Six small studies on risk of VTE in users of HRT versus nonusers were reported between 1974 and 1992. They were not powered to detect a two-fold increase in risk, and had restricted validity.[20] Hence they showed lack of evidence, rather than evidence of lack of risk. However, there was a general opinion that the 'physiological' doses of 'natural' oestrogens in oral HRT preparations might be less thrombogenic than 'pharmacological' doses of synthetic oestrogens in COC preparations. In 1991, one review stated that the notion that HRT could increase the risk of VTE was based on 'medical superstition'.[21] Following publication of the six initial studies,[22–27] a randomised trial[28] and larger case–control or cohort studies[29–32] were published in 1995 and 1996, which collectively suggested that HRT use increased the risk of VTE two- to three-fold, a similar relative risk to that associated with COC use. These findings have been confirmed by further case–control or cohort studies, as well as five further randomised trials.[33-44] Four recent systematic reviews of these studies have each confirmed similar relative risks (estimated mean RR 2.1–2.4; 95% CIs 1.4–3.2).[6,14,18,19] These estimates do not change significantly according to study design, quality score or presence of baseline CHD.[19] As with COCs, the risk is highest in the first year of use,[19] with no evidence of increased risk after cessation of HRT. There appears to be no association of VTE risk with type of oral HRT (type or dose of oestrogen, or unopposed oestrogen versus combined preparations) (see Addendum). Transdermal HRT is associated with a lesser risk of VTE compared with oral preparations. A pooled analysis of the three studies of transdermal HRT[29,33,44] indicates a relative risk of 1.25 (95% CI 0.80–1.95; fixed effects model) (Stephen Evans, personal communication, 2004).

The calculated absolute extra risk of VTE associated with oral HRT use is 4 (95% CI 3–5) extra cases per 1000 users over five years in women aged 50–59 years, and 9 (95% CI 4–14) extra cases per 1000 users over five years in women aged 60–69 years (i.e. almost 1%).[45] Hence the absolute extra risk of VTE is nearly ten times higher in a woman using oral HRT in her 60s, compared with a women using COC in her 20s or 30s. This ten-fold increase in absolute risk (for a similar relative risk of 2–3) reflects the exponential increase in risk of VTE with age which occurs in women as well as in men.

Possible mechanisms by which oral HRT increases risk of VTE

The epidemiological data suggest that current oral HRT use increases the risk of VTE through reversible prothrombotic effects, particularly during the first year of use, when thrombosis may be precipitated especially in women with constitutional increased risk of VTE (thrombophilias). A summary of possible mechanisms is given here.

Reduced inhibition of blood coagulation

Excessive blood coagulation is normally prevented by three distinct inhibitory pathways, each of which inhibits different activated coagulation factors:

- antithrombin, which is a direct inhibitor of thrombin, factor Xa and factor IXa, and is activated either by endogenous heparans (which line blood vessel walls) or by therapeutic heparins
- activated protein C (APC); like antithrombin, protein C is a circulating endogenous inhibitor of blood coagulation; thrombin activates protein C, through interactions with endothelial thrombomodulin and the endothelial protein C receptor; together with its cofactor, protein S, APC inactivates factors Va and VIIIa; hence the protein C pathway acts as a negative feedback loop, controlling excessive thrombin formation
- tissue factor pathway inhibitor (TFPI), which is another circulating endogenous inhibitor of blood coagulation, and which inhibits the tissue factor–factor VIIa complex.

Congenital deficiencies of antithrombin,[46-48] protein C[46-48] and protein S[46,47] are associated with increased relative risk (about 5–6) of VTE. Hence they are found in less than 1% of the general population, but in about 5–6% of consecutive patients with proven VTE.[49] Deficiency of TFPI has also been associated with risk of VTE.[50]

Both endogenous and exogenous oestrogens reduce plasma levels of these coagulation inhibitors. Pregnancy is associated with low protein S, while COC and oral HRT use are both associated with decreases in antithrombin, protein S and TFPI.[20,50–71] The latter effect may increase tissue factor activity.[66] Conflicting results have been reported for the effects of COC or oral HRT on protein C,[51,56–59,63–65,67,68] possibly because protein C levels may increase as a compensatory response to COC- or oral HRT-induced resistance to APC (see below).

Resistance to APC was described as a new familial thrombophilia by Dahlback and colleagues in 1993.[72] While commonly associated with a mutation in coagulation factor V (the Leiden mutation[73]), which confers resistance to its inactivation by APC, there are several other causes of APC resistance in the general population,[49] including other mutations in factor V,[49] the prothrombin 20210A mutation,[74] pregnancy[49] and COC use.[49,51,75–83] A greater effect on APC resistance is a plausible mechanism for the greater risk of VTE with third-generation, compared with second-generation, COCs.[5,6,77,81–83] In 1994, Vandenbroucke and colleagues[84] reported from the Leiden Thrombophilia Study (LETS) a supra-additive increased risk of VTE in oral contraceptive users who were carriers of the factor V Leiden mutation (Table 7.1). The probable explanation is a gene–environmental interaction whereby the combination of the factor V Leiden mutation and COC use increases APC resistance, precipitating thrombosis.[3,5,6,84]

In 1996, in a *Lancet* editorial commenting on three studies[29–31] reporting an increased risk of VTE with HRT use, Vandenbroucke and Helmerhorst[85] suggested that future studies of HRT and VTE 'should focus on measuring haemostatic factors that might modulate the risk, in particular the various factors on the blood's own anticoagulation system, the protein C/S system and its most common alteration, APC-resistance and the underlying factor V Leiden mutation'. Shortly thereafter, Lowe *et al.*[78,79] reported an epidemiological study of APC resistance and the factor V Leiden mutation which showed that HRT users had a similar increase in APC resistance to COC users. They suggested that this phenotype could be a common mechanism through which several risk factors for VTE might promote thrombosis: HRT as well as COC use, obesity, high factor VIII, pregnancy, and the factor V Leiden mutation. They also suggested that further cross-sectional and prospective studies should examine the effects of HRT preparations on APC resistance and interactions with risk of VTE, and whether such relations are interactive.[78] They subsequently confirmed the effect of oral (but not transdermal) HRT on APC resistance in a larger epidemiological study.[7] Prospective studies have confirmed the effect of oral HRT on APC resistance[64,67,86,87] as well as the absence of an effect of transdermal HRT in increasing APC resistance.[88] The mechanisms remain to be defined, but may include changes in protein S and TFPI[64] or factor VIII.[89]

To determine whether HRT use increased the risk of VTE in women with thrombophilias, Lowe and colleagues[48] restudied women in the Oxfordshire case–control study of the risk of first, idiopathic VTE.[29] Risk of VTE was associated with low antithrombin, low protein C, increased APC resistance, high coagulation factor IX and high fibrin D-dimer (a marker of activated coagulation and fibrinolysis). On multivariate analysis, VTE risk was independently associated with APC resistance, low antithrombin and high factor IX. In a model from this study[48] increasing combinations of thrombophilias result in an exponential increase in VTE risk, which at any level of risk is increased about three-fold by use of oral HRT. Subsequently, the association of VTE with HRT use and APC resistance was shown to be due to a supra-additive risk for HRT use and the factor V Leiden mutation,[90] as previously shown for COC use and the factor V Leiden mutation,[84] and subsequently confirmed by a report from the Heart and Estrogen/Progestin Replacement Study (HERS)[91] (Table 7.1).

Table 7.1. Studies showing supra-additive interactions between factor V Leiden, exogenous hormone use and the risk of venous thromboembolism (VTE); after Rosendaal et al.[6] with permission (*Journal of Thrombosis and Haemostasis*, © 2003 Blackwell Publishing)

Hormone use	Factor V Leiden	Relative risk	95% confidence interval
Combined oral contraceptives:[84]			
–	–	1.0	
+	–	3.7	2.2–6.3
–	+	6.9	1.8–28.3
+	+	34.7	7.4–224
Hormone replacement therapy:[90]			
–	–	1.0	
+	–	3.2	1.7–6.0
–	+	3.9	1.3–11.2
+	+	15.5	3.1–76.7
Hormone replacement therapy:[91]			
–	–	1.0	
+	–	3.7	1.4–9.4
–	+	3.3	1.1–9.8
+	+	14.1	2.7–72.4

The likely explanation for these data is that oral HRT (like COCs) increases APC resistance, interacting with factor V Leiden, lowers antithrombin, and (as discussed below) increases plasma levels of factor IX and fibrin D-dimer. Hence oral HRT amplifies prothrombotic pathways and precipitates thrombosis particularly among women with relevant constitutional thrombophilias.[7]

Increased coagulation factors and activation

Several studies have reported that oral HRT (like COC) increases plasma levels of factor VII, especially combined preparations.[19,52–55,86] There are conflicting reports concerning fibrinogen, factor VIII, or other coagulation factors.[52–55,86] A cross-sectional study observed increased levels of factor IX in oral HRT users,[86] and in the Oxfordshire case–control study oral HRT increased the risk of VTE in women with high factor IX levels, which were associated with risk of VTE.[48]

Several studies have reported that oral HRT (like COC) increases plasma levels of coagulation activation markers (prothrombin fragment F1 + 2, thrombin–antithrombin complexes, fibrin D-dimer).[52–56,58,59,66,70,92–94] This has been attributed to reduced coagulation inhibition and increased coagulation factor levels. In the Oxfordshire case–control study, D-dimer levels were associated with risk of VTE.[48]

Effects on fibrinolysis

Like COCs,[51] oral HRT preparations increase 'fibrinolytic potential' by increasing plasma levels of plasminogen and tissue plasminogen activator (t-PA) activity, and decreasing levels of plasminogen activator inhibitor (PAI-1).[52–55,68,71,86,92–94] While such effects have been proposed to 'balance' coagulation activation,[95] the lack of association of fibrinolytic variables with risk of VTE argues against this hypothesis.[96,97]

Effects on activation of inflammation

Like COCs, oral HRT preparations increase plasma levels of C-reactive protein (CRP).[66,70,86,98–101] While the Oxfordshire case–control study observed the highest levels of CRP in women with idiopathic VTE who were also HRT users,[102] the lack of association of CRP with VTE risk in a large prospective study[103] casts doubt on the hypothesis that CRP plays a role in venous thrombogenesis.

Effects of transdermal HRT on coagulation, fibrinolysis and inflammation

In contrast to oral HRT, transdermal HRT does not appear to have significant effects on blood coagulation, fibrinolysis or inflammation.[59,86,92,94,101,104,105] This may reflect the lack of a 'first-pass' effect of high doses of oestrogens in the portal vein on hepatic plasma protein synthesis, which follows oral ingestion.[51,86] This lack of effect on blood coagulation is a plausible explanation for the lesser association of transdermal HRT use (compared with oral HRT use) with risk of VTE.

Recommendations for HRT prescription in clinical practice

National guidelines in the UK[2,45,106] currently recommend that women considering oral HRT should be advised of the small absolute increased risk of VTE. They should be aware of the symptoms and signs of VTE, and advised to seek medical help rapidly if these develop.[106] A personal and family history should be taken of VTE, and additional risk factors, such as obesity and varicose veins, should be assessed. A personal history of VTE is usually a contraindication to oral HRT, owing to the high risk of recurrence.[40] A history of VTE in a first- or second-degree family member is a relative contraindication to oral HRT, irrespective of the results of thrombophilia screening. Such women (as well as women with known thrombophilia) should be referred to a centre or specialist with expertise in thrombophilia for counselling, and consideration of thrombophilia screening.[2,106] Transdermal HRT may be preferred to oral HRT in women at increased risk of VTE, because current evidence shows a lesser association with VTE risk[44] and lesser changes in haemostasis or inflammation. If HRT is given to a woman with previous VTE, the risk of recurrent VTE should be discussed carefully, and she should be advised to report any symptoms promptly. Prophylactic anticoagulant therapy may be considered, but the risk of bleeding (which can be fatal) should be fully discussed.[106]

Routine thrombophilia screening of women commencing HRT is not currently recommended, because the balance of benefits, risks (e.g. psychological, insurance loading) and costs awaits evaluation.[2,106]

HRT use increases the risk of VTE in women undergoing elective surgery or emergency surgery for trauma.[37] The Scottish Intercollegiate Guidelines Network guideline recommends that for women currently (or recently) using oral HRT who are undergoing elective major surgery, medical practitioners should discuss stopping oral HRT (as with COC), and consider specific antithrombotic prophylaxis according to overall risk factors for VTE.[2] In practice, most HRT users will merit routine prophylaxis because they are usually aged over 40 years.[2,106] Antithrombotic prophylaxis should be given routinely in oral HRT users undergoing emergency surgery.[2] The UK Royal College of Obstetricians and Gynaecologists guideline[106] recommends that HRT does not require to be routinely stopped prior to surgery provided that appropriate thromboprophylaxis, such as low-dose unfractionated or low-molecular-weight heparin, with or without thromboembolic deterrent stockings, is used.

Acknowledgements

I thank Ruth Simpson for typing the manuscript and Professor Stephen Evans for performing the pooled analysis of transdermal HRT studies.

Addendum

Since the Study Group meeting and preparation of this manuscript, the oestrogen-only arm of the WHI trial has reported its principal findings.[107] Consistent with previous observational studies and randomised trials, there were increased hazard ratios in the active treatment group for DVT (HR 1.47; 95% CI 1.04–2.08) and PE (HR 1.34; 95% CI 0.87–2.06). A 'complier' model estimated a higher risk of PE (HR 1.99).

References

1. Heit JA, Silverstein MD, Mohr DN, Petterson TM, Lohse CM, O'Fallon WM, *et al*. The epidemiology of venous thromboembolism in the community. *Thromb Haemost* 2001;86:452–63.
2. Scottish Intercollegiate Guidelines Network. *SIGN 62: Prophylaxis of Venous Thromboembolism.* Edinburgh: Scottish Intercollegiate Guidelines Network; 2002 [www.sign.ac.uk].
3. Rosendaal FR. Venous thrombosis: a multicausal disease. *Lancet* 1999;353:1167–73.
4. Greer IA. Epidemiology, risk factors and prophylaxis of venous thromboembolism in obstetrics and gynaecology. *Baillieres Clin Obstet Gynaecol* 1997;11:403–30.
5. Rosendaal FR, Helmerhorst FM, Vandenbroucke JP. Oral contraceptives, hormone replacement therapy and thrombosis. *Thromb Haemost* 2001;86:112–23.
6. Rosendaal FR, Van Hylckama Vlieg A, Tanis BC, Helmerhorst FM. Estrogens, progestogens and thrombosis. *J Thromb Haemost* 2003;1:1371–80.
7. Lowe GDO. Hormone replacement therapy and cardiovascular disease. *J Intern Med* (in press).
8. McColl MD, Tait RC, Greer IA, Walker ID. Injecting drug use is a risk factor for deep vein thrombosis in women in Glasgow. *Br J Haematol* 2001;112:641–3.
9. Jordan WM. Pulmonary embolism. *Lancet* 1961;ii:1146–7.
10. Stadel BV. Oral contraceptives and cardiovascular disease. *N Engl J Med* 1981;305:612–18.
11. MacLennan A, Lester S, Moore V. Oral oestrogen replacement therapy versus placebo for hot flushes. *Cochrane Database Syst Rev* 2001;(1):CD002978.
12. Hlatky MA, Boothroyd D, Vittinghoff E, Sharp P, Whooley MA; Heart and Estrogen/Progestin Replacement Study (HERS) Research Group. Quality-of-life and depressive symptoms in postmenopausal women after receiving hormone therapy: results from the Heart and Estrogen/Progestin Replacement Study (HERS) trial. *JAMA* 2002;287:591–7.
13. Torgerson DJ, Bell-Seyer SE. Hormone replacement therapy and prevention of nonvertebral fractures: a meta-analysis of randomised trials. *JAMA* 2001;285:2891–7.
14. Beral V, Banks E, Reeves G. Evidence from randomised trials on the long-term effects of hormone replacement therapy. *Lancet* 2002;360:942–4.
15. Tunstall-Pedoe H. Myth and paradox of coronary risk and the menopause. *Lancet* 1998;351:1425–7.
16. Lawlor DA, Ebrahim S, Davey-Smith G. Role of endogenous oestrogen in aetiology of coronary heart disease. *BMJ* 2002;325:311–2.
17. Grodstein F, Clarkson TB, Manson JE. Understanding the divergent data on postmenopausal hormone therapy. *N Engl J Med* 2003;348:645–50.
18. Oger E, Scarabin PY. Assessment of the risk for venous thromboembolism among users of hormone replacement therapy. *Drugs Aging* 1999;14:55–61.
19. Miller J, Chan BK, Nelson HD. Postmenopausal estrogen replacement and risk for venous thromboembolism: a systematic review and meta-analysis for the US Preventive Services Task Force. *Ann Intern Med* 2002;136:680–90.
20. Hoibraaten E. *Hormone Replacement Therapy and Risk of Venous Thromboembolism.* Thesis, University of Oslo, 2001 (ISBN 82-499-008-2).
21. Young RL, Goepfert AR, Foldzieher HW. Estrogen replacement therapy is not conducive of venous thromboembolism. *Maturitas* 1991;13:189–92.
22. Boston Collaborative Drug Surveillance Program. Surgically confirmed gallbladder disease,

venous thromboembolism, and breast tumours in relation to postmenopausal estrogen therapy. *N Engl J Med* 1974;290:15–19.

23. Petitti DB, Wingerd J, Pellegrin F, Ramcharan S. Risk of vascular disease in women. Smoking, oral contraceptives, noncontraceptive estrogens, and other factors. *JAMA* 1979;242:1150–4.

24. Nachtigall LE, Nachtigall RH, Nachtigall RD, Beckman EM. Estrogen replacement therapy II: a prospective study in the relationship to carcinoma and cardiovascular and metabolic problems. *Obstet Gynecol* 1979;54:74–9.

25. Hammond CB, Jelovesh FR, Lee KL, Creasman WT, Parker RT. Effects of long-term estrogen replacement therapy. I. Metabolic effects. *Am J Obstet Gynecol* 1979;133:525–36.

26. Quinn DA, Thompson BT, Terrin ML, Thrall JH, Athanasoulis CA, McKusisk KA, *et al*. A prospective investigation of pulmonary embolism in women and men. *JAMA* 1992;268:1689–96.

27. Devor M, Barrett-Connor E, Renvall M, Feigal DJ, Ramsdell J. Estrogen replacement therapy and the risk of venous thrombosis. *Am J Med* 1992;92:275–82.

28. The Writing Group for the PEPI Trial. Effects of estrogen or estrogen/progestin regimens on heart disease risk factors in postmenopausal women. The Postmenopausal Estrogen/Progestin Interventions (PEPI) Trial. *JAMA* 1995;273:199–208.

29. Daly E, Vessey MP, Hawkins MM, Carson JL, Gough P, Marsh S. Risk of venous thromboembolism in users of hormone replacement therapy. *Lancet* 1996;348:977–80.

30. Jick H, Derby LE, Myers MW, Vasilakis C, Newton KM. Risk of hospital admission for idiopathic venous thromboembolism among users of post menopausal oestrogens. *Lancet* 1996;348:981–3.

31. Grodstein F, Stampfer MJ, Goldhaber SZ, Manson JE, Colditz GA, Speizer FE, *et al*. Prospective study of exogenous hormones and risk of pulmonary embolism in women. *Lancet* 1996;348:983–7.

32. Daly E, Vessey MP, Painter R, Hawkins MM. Case–control study of venous thromboembolism risk in users of hormone replacement therapy. *Lancet* 1996;348:1027.

33. Perez Gutthann S, Garcia-Rodriguez LA, Castellsague J, Duque Oliart A. Hormone replacement therapy and the risk of venous thromboembolism: population based case–control study. *BMJ* 1997;314:796–800.

34. Varas-Lorenzo C, Garcia-Rodriguez L, Cattaruzzi C, Troncon M, Agostinis L, Perez-Gutthann S. Hormone replacement therapy and the risk of hospitalisation for venous thromboembolism: a population-based study in southern Europe. *Am J Epidemiol* 1998;147:387–90.

35. Grady D, Furberg C. Venous thromboembolic events associated with hormone replacement therapy. *JAMA* 1997;278:477.

36. Hulley S, Grady D, Bush T, Furberg C, Herrington D, Riggs B, *et al*. Randomized trial of estrogen plus progestin for secondary prevention of coronary heart disease in postmenopausal women. Heart and Estrogen/progestin Replacement Study (HERS) Research Group. *JAMA* 1998;280:605–13.

37. Grady D, Wenger NK, Herrington D, Khan S, Furberg C, Hunninghake D, *et al*. Postmenopausal hormone therapy increases risk for venous thromboembolic disease. The Heart and Estrogen/progestin Replacement Study. *Ann Intern Med* 2000;132:689–96.

38. Hoibraaten E, Abdelnoor M, Sandset PM. Hormone replacement therapy with estradiol and risk of venous thromboembolism: a population-based case–control study. *Thromb Haemost* 1999;82:1218–21.

39. Herrington DM, Reboussin DM, Brosnihan KB, Sharp PC, Shumaker SA, Snyder TE, *et al*. Effects of estrogen replacement on the progression of coronary-artery atherosclerosis. *N Engl J Med* 2000;343:522–9.

40. Hoibraaten E, Qvigstad E, Arnesen H, Larsen S, Wickstrom E, Sandset PM. Increased risk of recurrent venous thromboembolism during hormone replacement therapy: results of the randomised, double-blind, placebo-controlled estrogen in venous thromboembolism trial (EVTET). *Thromb Haemost* 2000;84:961–7.

41. Viscoli CM, Brass LM, Kerran WN, Farrell PM, Fuissa S, Horwitz RI. A clinical trial of estrogen-replacement therapy after ischaemic stroke. *N Engl J Med* 2001;345:1243–9.

42. The ESPRIT Team. Oestrogen therapy for prevention of reinfarction in postmenopausal women: a randomised placebo-controlled trial. *Lancet* 2002;360:2001–8.

43. Rossouw JE, Anderson GL, Prentice RL, LaCroix AZ, Kooperberg C, Stefanick ML, *et al*.; Writing Group for the Women's Health Initiative Investigators. Risks and benefits of estrogen plus progestin in healthy postmenopausal women: principal results fom the Women's Health Initiative randomized controlled trial. *JAMA* 2002;288:321–33.

44. Scarabin P-Y, Oger E, Plu-Bureau G, on behalf of the Estrogen and ThromboEmbolism Risk (ESTHER) Study Group. Differential association of oral and transdermal oestrogen-replacement therapy with venous thromboembolism risk. *Lancet* 2003;362:428–32.

45. Committee on Safety of Medicines. HRT: update on the risk of breast cancer and long term safety.

Current Problems in Pharmacovigilance 2003;29:1–3 [http://www.mca.gov.uk].

46. Lane DA, Mannucci PM, Bauer KA, Bertina RM, Bochkov NP, Boulyjenkov V, et al. Inherited thrombophilia: Part 1. Thromb Haemost 1996;76:651–62.

47. Lane DA, Mannucci PM, Bauer KA, Bertina RM, Bochkov NP, Boulyjenkov V, et al. Inherited thrombophilia: Part 2. Thromb Haemost 1996;76:824–34. Erratum in: Thromb Haemost 1997;77:1047.

48. Lowe G, Woodward M, Vessey MP, Rumley A, Gough P, Daly E. Thrombotic variables and risk of idiopathic venous thromboembolism in women aged 45–64 years: relationships to hormone replacement therapy. Thromb Haemost 2000;83:530–5.

49. Nicolaes GA, Dahlback B. Congenital and acquired activated protein C resistance. Semin Vasc Med 2003;3:33–46.

50. Dahm A, van Hylckama Vlieg A, Bendz B, Rosendaal F, Bertina RM, Sandset PM. Low levels of tissue factor pathway inhibitor (TFPI) increase the risk of venous thrombosis. Blood 2003;101:4387–92.

51. Kluft C, Lansink M. Effect of oral contraceptives on haemostasis variables. Thromb Haemost 1997;78:315–26.

52. Stanwell-Smith R, Meade TW. Hormone replacement therapy for menopausal women: a review of its effects on haemostatic function, lipids, and blood pressure. Adverse Drug React Acute Poisoning Rev 1984;4:187–210.

53. Winkler UH. Menopause, hormone replacement therapy and cardiovascular disease: a review of haemostaseological findings. Fibrinolysis 1992;6 Suppl 3:5–10.

54. Meade TW. Hormone replacement therapy and haemostatic function. Thromb Haemost 1997;78:765–9.

55. Thijs A, Stehouwer CDA. Changes of hemostatic variables during hormone replacement therapy. Semin Vasc Med 2003;3:85–92.

56. Nabulsi AA, Folsom AR, White A, Patsch W, Heiss G, Wu KK, et al. Association of hormone replacement therapy with various cardiovascular risk factors in postmenopausal women. N Engl J Med 1993;328:1069–75.

57. Sporrong T, Mattsson LA, Samsioe G, Stigendal L, Hellgren M. Haemostatic changes during continuous oestradiol-progestogen treatment of postmenopausal women. Br J Obstet Gynaecol 1990;97:939–44.

58. Caine YG, Bauer KA, Barzegar S, ten Cate H, Sacks FM, Walsh BW, et al. Coagulation activation following estrogen administration to postmenopausal women. Thromb Haemost 1992;68:392–5.

59. Scarabin PY, Alhenc-Gelas M, Plu-Bureau G, Taisne P, Agher R, Aiach M. Effects of oral and transdermal estrogen/progesterone regimens on blood coagulation and fibrinolysis in postmenopausal women. A randomised controlled trial. Arterioscler Thromb Vasc Biol 1997;17:3071–8.

60. Bonduki CE, Lourenco DM, Baracat E, Haidar M, Noguti MA, da Motta EL, et al. Effect of estrogen-progestin hormonal replacement therapy on plasma antithrombin III of postmenopausal women. Acta Obstet Gynecol Scand 1998;77:330–3.

61. Hahn L, Mattsson L-A, Andersson B, Tengborn L. The effects of oestrogen replacement therapy on haemostatic variables in postmenopausal women with non-insulin-dependent diabetes mellitus. Blood Coagul Fibrinolysis 1999;10:81–6.

62. van Baal WM, Emeis JJ, van der Mooren MJ, Kessel H, Kenemans P, Stehouwer CD. Impaired procoagulant–anticoagulant balance during hormone replacement therapy? A randomised, placebo-controlled 12-week study. Thromb Haemost 2000;83:29–34.

63. Hoibraaten E, Os I, Seljeflot I, Andersen TO, Hofstad A, Sandset PM. The effects of hormone replacement therapy on hemostatic variables in women with angiographically verified coronary artery disease: results from the estrogen in women with atherosclerosis study. Thromb Res 2000;98:19–27.

64. Hoibraaten E, Mowinckel MC, de Ronde H, Bertina RM, Sandset PM. Hormone replacement therapy and acquired resistance to activated protein C: results of a randomised, double-blind, placebo-controlled trial. Br J Haematol 2001;115:415–20.

65. Hoibraaten E, Qvigstad E, Andersen TO, Mowinckel MC, Sandset PM. The effects of hormone replacement therapy (HRT) on hemostatic variables in women with previous venous thromboembolism – results from a randomised, double-blind, clinical trial. Thromb Haemost 2001;85:775–81.

66. Koh KK, Ahn JY, Kim DS, Han SH, Shin MS, Ryu WS, et al. Effect of hormone replacement therapy on tissue factor activity, C-reactive protein, and the tissue factor pathway inhibitor. Am J Cardiol 2003;91:371–3.

67. Sidelmann JJ, Jespersen J, Andersen LF, Skouby SO. Hormone replacement therapy and hypercoagulability. Results from the Prospective Danish Climacteric Study. BJOG

2003;110:541–7.

68. Gottsater A, Rendell M, Hultehn UL, Berntorp E, Mattiason I. Hormone replacement therapy in healthy postmenopausal women: a randomised, placebo-controlled study of effects on coagulation and fibrinolytic factors. *J Intern Med* 2001;249:237–46.

69. Peverill RE, Teede HJ, Smolich JJ, Malan E, Kotsopoulos D, Tipping PG, *et al*. Effects of combined oral hormone replacement therapy on tissue factor pathway inhibitor and factor VII. *Clin Sci* 2001;101:93–9.

70. Luyer MD, Khosla S, Owen WG, Miller VM. Prospective randomised study of effects of unopposed estrogen replacement therapy on markers of coagulation and inflammation in postmenopausal women. *J Clin Endocrinol Metab* 2001;86:3629–34.

71. Bladbjerg EM, Madsen JS, Kristensen SR, Abrahamsen B, Brixen K, Mosekildes L, *et al*. Effect of long-term hormone replacement therapy on tissue factor pathway inhibitor and thrombin-activatable fibrinolysis inhibitor in healthy postmenopausal women: a randomised controlled study. *J Thromb Haemost* 2003;1:1208–14.

72. Dahlback B, Carlsson M, Svenson PJ. Familial thrombophilia due to a previously unrecognised mechanism characterised by poor anticoagulant response to activated protein C. *Proc Natl Acad Sci U S A* 1993;90:1004–8.

73. Bertina RM, Koeleman BP, Koster T, Rosendaal FR, Dirven RJ, de Ronde H, *et al*. Mutation in blood coagulation factor V associated with resistance to activated protein C. *Nature* 1994;369:64–7.

74. Castaman G, Tosetto A, Simioni M, Ruggeri M, Madeo D, Rodeghiero F. Phenotypic APC resistance in carriers of the A20210 prothrombin mutation is associated with an increased risk of venous thrombosis. *Thromb Haemost* 2001;86:804–8.

75. Olivieri O, Friso S, Manzato F, Guella A, Bernardi F, Lunghi B, *et al*. Resistance to activated protein C in healthy women taking oral contraceptives. *Br J Haematol* 1995;91:465–70.

76. Henkens CM, Bom VJ, Seiren AJ, van der Meer J. Sensitivity to activated protein C; influence of oral contraceptives and sex. *Thromb Haemost* 1995;73:402–4.

77. Rosing J, Tans G, Nicolaes GA, Thomassen MC, van Oerle R, van der Ploeg PM, *et al*. Oral contraceptives and venous thrombosis: different sensitivities to activated protein C in women using second- and third-generation oral contraceptives. *Br J Haematol* 1997;97:233–8.

78. Lowe GDO, Rumley A, Woodward M, Reid E. Oral contraceptives and venous thromboembolism [letter]. *Lancet* 1997;349:1623.

79. Lowe GDO, Rumley A, Woodward M, Reid E, Rumley J. Activated protein C resistance and the FV: R506Q mutation in a random population sample: associations with cardiovascular risk factors and coagulation variables. *Thromb Haemost* 1999;81:918–24.

80. Rosing J, Middeldorp S, Curvers J, Christella M, Thomassen LG, Nicolaes GA, *et al*. Low-dose oral contraceptives and acquired resistance to activated protein C: a randomised cross-over study. *Lancet* 1999;354:2036–40.

81. Middeldorp S, Meijers JC, van den Ende AE, van Enk A, Bouma BN, Tans G, *et al*. Effects on coagulation of levonogestrel- and desogestrel-containing low-dose oral contraceptives: a cross-over study. *Thromb Haemost* 2000;84:4–8.

82. Tans G, Curvers J, Middeldorp S, Thomassen MC, Meijers JC, Prins MH, Bouma BN, *et al*. A randomised cross-over study on the effects of levonorgestrel- and desogestrel- containing oral contraceptives on the anticoagulant pathways. *Thromb Haemost* 2000;84:15–21.

83. Kemmeren JM, Algra A, Meijers JC, Bouma BN, Grobbee DE. Effects of second and third generation oral contraceptives and their respective progestogens on the coagulation system in the absence or presence of the factor V Leiden mutation. *Thromb Haemost* 2002;87:199–205.

84. Vandenbroucke JP, Koster T, Briet E, Reitsma PH, Bertina RM, Rosendaal FR. Increased risk of venous thrombosis in oral-contraceptive users who are carriers of factor V Leiden mutation. *Lancet* 1994;344:1453–7.

85. Vandenbroucke JP, Helmerhorst FM. Risk of venous thrombosis with hormone-replacement therapy. *Lancet* 1996;348:972.

86. Lowe GDO, Upton MN, Rumley A, McConnachie A, O'Reilly DSJ, Watt GCM. Different effect of oral and transdermal hormone replacement therapies on Factor IX, APC resistance, t-PA, PAI and C-reactive protein: a cross-sectional population survey. *Thromb Haemost* 2001;86:550–6.

87. Post MS, Rosing J, Van Der Mooren MJ, Zweegman S, Van Baal WM, Kenemans P, *et al*.; Ageing Women and the Institute for Cardiovascular Research-Vrije Universiteit (ICaR-VU). Increased resistance to activated protein C after short-term oral hormone replacement therapy in healthy postmenopausal women. *Br J Haematol* 2002;119:1017–23.

88. De Mitrio V, Marino R, Cicinelli E, Galantino P, Di Bari F, Giannoccaro F, *et al*. Beneficial effects of postmenopausal hormone replacement therapy with transdermal estradiol on sensitivity to activated protein C. *Blood Coagul Fibrinolysis* 2000;11:75–182.

89. Marcucci R, Abbate R, Fedi S, Gori AM, Brunelli T, Bruni V, *et al*. Acquired activated protein C

resistance in postmenopausal women is dependent on factor VIII:c levels. *Am J Clin Pathol* 1999;111:769–72.

90.   Rosendaal FR, Vessey M, Rumley A, Daly E, Woodward M, Helmerhorst FM, *et al.* Hormonal replacement therapy, prothrombotic mutations and the risk of venous thrombosis. *Br J Haematol* 2002;116:851–4.

91.   Herrington DM, Vittinghoff E, Howard TD, Major DA, Owen J, Reboussin DM, *et al.* Factor V Leiden, hormone replacement therapy, and risk of venous thromboembolic events in women with coronary disease. *Arterioscler Thromb Vasc Biol* 2002;22:1012–17.

92.   Koh KK, Mincemoyer R, Bui MN, Csako G, Pucino F, Guetta V, *et al.* Effects of hormone replacement therapy on fibrinolysis in postmenopausal women. *N Engl J Med* 1997;336:683–90.

93.   Teede HJ, McGrath BP, Smolich JJ, Malan E, Kotsopoulos D, Liang YL, *et al.* Postmenopausal hormone replacement therapy increases coagulation activity and fibrinolysis. *Arterioscler Thromb Vasc Biol* 2000;20:1404–9.

94.   Vehkavaara S, Silveira A, Hakala-Ala-Pietila T, Virkamaki A, Hovatta O, Hamsten A, *et al.* Effects of oral and transdermal estrogen replacement therapy on markers of coagulation, fibrinolysis, inflammation and serum lipids and lipoproteins in postmenopausal women. *Thromb Haemost* 2001;85:619–25.

95.   Astrup T. The haemostatic balance. *Thromb Diath Haemorrh* 1958;2:347–57.

96.   Ridker PM, Vaughan DE, Stampfer MJ, Manson JE, Shen C, Newcomer LM, *et al.* Baseline fibrinolytic state and the risk of future venous thrombosis. A prospective study of endogenous tissue-type plasminogen activator inhibitor. *Circulation* 1992;85:1822–7.

97.   Crowther MA, Roberts J, Roberts R, Johnston M, Stevens P, Skingley P, *et al.* Fibrinolytic variables in patients with recurrent venous thrombosis: a prospective cohort study. *Thromb Haemost* 2001;85:390–4.

98.   van Baal WM, Kenemans P, van der Mooren M, Kessel H, Emeis J, Stehouwer CDA. Increased C-reactive protein levels during short-term hormone replacement therapy in healthy postmenopausal women. *Thromb Haemost* 1999;81:925–8.

99.   Cushman M, Legault C, Barrett-Connor E, Stefanick ML, Kessler C, Judd HL, *et al.* Effect of postmenopausal hormones on inflammation-sensitive proteins: the Postmenopausal Estrogen/Progestin Interventions (PEPI) Study. *Circulation* 1999;100:717–22.

100.   Cushman M, Meilahn EN, Psaty BM, Kuller LH, Dobs AS, Tracy RP. *et al.* Hormone replacement therapy, inflammation, and hemostasis in elderly women. *Arterioscler Thromb Vasc Biol* 1999;19:893–9.

101.   Zegura B, Keber I, Sebestjen M, Koenig W. Double-blind, randomised study of estradiol replacement therapy on markers of inflammation, coagulation and fibrinolysis. *Atherosclerosis* 2003;168:123–9.

102.   Lowe G, Rumley A, Woodward M, Vessey M. C-reactive protein, idiopathic venous thromboembolism and hormone replacement therapy. *Thromb Haemost* 2000;84:730–1.

103.   Tsai AW, Cushman M, Rosamond WD, Heckbert SR, Tracy RP, Aleksic N, *et al.* Coagulation factors, inflammation markers, and venous thromboembolism: the Longitudinal Investigation of Thromboembolism Etiology (LITE). *Am J Med* 2002;113:636–42.

104.   Fox J, George AJ, Newton JR, Parsons AD, Stuart GR, Stuart J, *et al.* Effect of transdermal oestradiol on the haemostatic balance of menopausal women. *Maturitas* 1993;18:55–64.

105.   The Writing Group for the estradiol clotting factors study. Effects on haemostasis of hormone replacement therapy with transdermal estradiol and oral sequential medroxyprogesterone acetate: a 1-year, double-blind, placebo-controlled study. *Thromb Haemost* 1996;75:476–80.

106.   Greer IA, Walker ID. *Hormone Replacement Therapy and Venous Thromboembolism.* Royal College of Obstetricians and Gynaecologists Guideline No. 19. London: RCOG Press; 2004.

107.   Anderson GL, Limacher M, Assaf AR, Bassford T, Beresford SA, Black H, *et al.*; Women's Health Initiative Steering Committee. Effects of conjugated equine estrogen in postmenopausal women with hysterectomy: the Women's Health Initiative randomized controlled trial. *JAMA* 2004;291:1701–12.

Chapter 8

Hormone replacement therapy and osteoporosis

David W Purdie

Background

Although abnormal and excessive porosity of the aged skeleton – osteoporosis – has been recognised archaeologically for centuries, it is only within the past 60 years that the natural history of the condition has been gradually worked out, and the means developed for its detection, prevention and treatment. Initially regarded as a diagnosis in itself, osteoporosis has now been correctly assigned as a risk factor for the fragility fractures that constitute a major public health issue in contemporary Western societies. Scientific examination of the problem began with the work of Fuller Albright and his observation that the operation of bilateral oophorectomy was causally related to loss of bone tissue, particularly from the trabecular skeleton, and to subsequent osteoporosis and fracture.[1]

Albright's findings led naturally to examination of the influence of the natural menopause upon bone physiology. It has been shown that the loss of circulating oestrogen among postmenopausal women exerts a profound influence on bone behaviour from the cellular to the topographical level and that restoration of premenopausal levels of circulating oestrogen would arrest the bone loss occasioned by its withdrawal. Although there are many causes of osteoporosis, which affect both sexes, all other causes are dwarfed by the preponderance of the disease in oestrogen-deficient women. The old term of postmenopausal osteoporosis remains useful in defining both the causative event and that sector of the population upon which the greatest burden of disease falls.

Oestrogen and the skeleton

The relationship between oestrogen and osteoporosis is complex but centres on two interrelated phenomena: the effect of oestrogen deficiency upon (a) bone tissue itself, specifically the mechanisms influencing bone turnover, and upon (b) extra-skeletal mechanisms of calcium conservation in the gut and renal tubules.

The withdrawal of oestrogen at menopause inaugurates an approximate decade of accelerated bone loss, i.e. from around age 50 to 60, after which bone loss slows to become asymptotic with the age-related bone loss that had already been underway, albeit more slowly, during the premenopausal decade from around age 40. This age-related loss is broadly parallel to the rate of bone loss in age-matched men and continues lifelong in both sexes. Thus women have a double jeopardy with their two sequential phases of bone loss, whereas men have only one phase, the age-related phase, since they do not experience a natural midlife withdrawal of testosterone, a principal bone conservator. In both sexes, sex steroid actions and biomechanical strain applied to the skeleton are the principal agents for the conservation of bone mass. Major losses of bone do not occur if both these are in normal operation, apart from in exceptional circumstances such as in certain malabsorptive states or in prolonged corticosteroid exposure.

Oestrogen and bone turnover

The central effects of oestrogen deficiency on skeletal turnover are mediated through (a) an increase in the rate of recruitment of the units of turnover, the basic multicellular units (BMUs), and (b) an imbalance between bone formation and bone resorption in BMUs, in favour of the latter. A healthy adult will have around 400 000 BMUs operational at any one time, with an individual and collective balance between bone resorption, the first phase of BMU activity, and the final phase, bone formation.

The precise mechanism whereby a particular bone surface is selected to become the site of a new BMU is still unknown but it is agreed that oestrogen applies a physiological restraint, or brake, to the recruitment process.[2] In the newly activated BMU, oestrogen deficiency first operates by prolonging the life and activity of the bone-resorbing cell, the multinucleate, motile osteoclast, whose rate of apoptosis (programmed cell death) is reduced. Thus, the excavation of the cavity in the bone surface, normally some three weeks in length, proceeds to a greater depth and extent than otherwise. When the formation phase begins, the osteoblasts, charged with the approximately 16 week long refill of the preformed cavity, are also impeded by oestrogen lack and fail, both in numbers and activity, to make good the deficit. The result is that when the cycle ends there is a residual cavity due to the net loss of bone. If the BMU is sited on a trabecula in the clinically relevant sites of spine, distal radius or femoral neck, a process of weakening of the trabecular network is underway. When the cycle comes round again at the same or an adjacent site, the deficiency increases and ultimately may result in a perforation of that trabecula with consequent loss of shock absorbency.[3]

The ability of trabecular bone to fulfil its function of transmitting applied force away into the trabecular network and thus absorbing, depleting and dissipating mechanical stress is contingent on the trabeculae being adequate in terms of (a) number, (b) thickness and (c) connectedness. It is noteworthy that in ageing men, while the trabeculae do thin down, they tend to retain their connectedness to the network whereas in women the thinning is compounded by perforation and hence a disproportionate loss of resilience.

Oestrogen and bone cells

In the late 1980s our understanding of oestrogen action on the skeleton was dramatically expanded with the identification of oestrogen receptors (ERs) on all three of the principal species of bone cell, osteoclasts, osteoblasts and osteocytes,[4] with the first two containing androgen receptors as well. Of the two ER types, oestrogen receptor-α (ERα) is the principal bone receptor. It has, however, been suggested that non-genomic actions of oestrogen, i.e. those acting via cell surface reception and cytosolic second messenger(s) such as mitogen-activated protein kinase (MAPK) – and not requiring ER involvement – may be important in mediating the hormone's bone actions. The role of cytokines in modulating oestrogen action on bone cells is a major area of enquiry. Numerous intermediaries, including interleukin-1 (IL-1) and interleukin-6 (IL-6), are produced in bone marrow and are subject to oestrogen restraint. In the rat, oophorectomy normally results in accelerated bone loss but this is inhibited by selective removal of the above cytokines and also by non-availability of tumour necrosis factor-α (TNF-α), whose production by T cells is enhanced by oestrogen deficiency. Both IL-1 and TNF-α stimulate production of the central stimulator of osteoclast differentiation, RANKL, and thus are modifiable by oestrogen, which of itself does not appear directly to modulate RANKL or its receptor. Oestrogen deficiency also appears to be associated with a reduction in osteoprotegerin, which acts as a decoy receptor for RANKL.

Thus, the place of oestrogen as a physiological or natural bone conservator is supported by a substantial body of *in vitro* and *in vivo* evidence. Restoration of physiological circulating levels of oestrogen reverses these increases in cytokine production within 30 days.[5]

Oestrogen and the mechanostat

As noted above, the two main circumstances in which rapid bone loss occurs in humans are oestrogen deficiency and inactivity. Attempts to link the two have borne fruit with the observation that the cell that functions as the strain gauge or mechanoreceptor is the osteocyte. This cell is supplied with ER.[6] It has now been demonstrated that oestrogen deficiency impairs the ability of the osteocyte to sense the application of strain and even to survive.[7] Thus, it seems that both lack of strain – or disuse – and lack of oestrogen contribute to a common pathway promoting bone loss through poor osteoblast production and/or activity.

Extra-skeletal actions of oestrogen

With the decline of the postmenopausal rapid phase of bone loss, skeletal mass does not stabilise but the rate of loss declines to that seen in the fifth decade, a rate roughly parallel to that in men. The mechanism whereby the rapid-phase loss declines is not known for certain but is believed to relate to strain. Subjected to increased load factors with the depletion of the network, the surviving trabeculae react by forming bone. This thickens them, but whether or not the process also includes re-bridging of trabecular perforations is unclear.

The mechanism at the centre of slow-phase bone loss is increased parathyroid hormone (PTH) production consequent upon a relative failure of calcium conservation by bowel and kidney. PTH is released when the sensory apparatus of the parathyroids detect a decline to the set-point in plasma ionised calcium. The normal concentration of this ion in plasma, 2.25–2.55 mmol/l, is subjected to the most rigorous three-fold regulation and control – by PTH, by 1,25-dihydroxy vitamin D and by calcitonin – since cellular functions such as motility and mitosis are dependent upon the gated admission of extracellular calcium. Thus the all-important level of plasma ionised calcium is sensitive to any process that restricts the availability of the mineral – and there are two such that occur with ageing.

The efficiency of absorption of calcium from the gut, itself promoted by PTH, declines with age[8] and this route of admission of calcium to the system is thus impaired. Furthermore, the conservation of calcium by the renal tubules, again PTH-sensitive, also declines with age[9] and both processes together contribute to what has been called calcium wasting. Both gut and renal handling of calcium are sensitive to oestrogen. The hormone stimulates absorption of calcium from the gut[10] and promotes renal tubular reabsorption of calcium.[11] Overall, it has been shown in controlled trials[12] that older women receiving oestrogen therapy as HRT exhibit levels of serum PTH and bone turnover markers[13] identical to those in younger postmenopausal subjects. However in the oestrogen-deficient elderly, the operation of gut- and kidney-mediated calcium loss imposes a tendency for reduction in plasma calcium which is sensed by the parathyroids.

The result is a defence of the plasma calcium by a low-level grumbling hyperparathyroidism, not sufficient to produce, in itself, any abnormality in plasma calcium, but sufficient to initiate a progressive and sustained drain upon and make inroads into the calcium reserves held in the skeleton. The mobilisation of the reserve involves, indeed requires, bone loss.

Thus both the processes of bone loss, the initial postmenopausal rapid (IPR) phase and the later postmenopausal slow (LPS) phase, are seen to be oestrogen sensitive. The IPR phase affects mainly endosteal surfaces, hence trabecular bone, and is eventually restrained and then halted biomechanically. In contrast, the PTH-driven LPS phase affects all surfaces – both trabecular and compact bone – and, without intervention, has no natural restraint and is hence lifelong.

Oestrogen replacement

It was therefore logical that the use of oestrogen replacement therapy (ET) in postmenopausal women should be tested to ascertain if such regimens would arrest, or reverse, the full effects of oestrogen deficiency imposed by the menopause. Would ET slow the recruitment of new BMUs, rebalance bone formation and bone resorption within the BMU, return levels of bone turnover markers to normal, protect bone mineral density (BMD) and, most importantly, reduce the rate of fragility fracture? As randomised controlled trials (RCTs), provide the best means of addressing the perennial problems of the play of chance, the presence of biases and the operation of confounding variables, they are considered below.

It will be seen that a substantial body of the RCT evidence relates to the surrogate endpoint of BMD. This is for two reasons: firstly, techniques for measurement of BMD, principally dual-energy X-ray absorptiometry (DXA), have been available since 1988 and, secondly, regulatory authorities initially did not insist, as they now do, upon presentation of fracture data as a primary endpoint for efficacy in RCTs of agents seeking a licence to prevent or treat osteoporosis.

In 1998, a systematic review of ET trials up to and inclusive of 1995[13] detected some 37 RCTs and in only one[14] were fracture data presented. This trial appears below in the section on fracture data.

A further meta-analysis on the efficacy of ET in preventing and treating osteoporosis in postmenopausal women was published in 2002.[15] These authors used the Cochrane Collaboration method for identifying RCTs as modified by the Cochrane Musculoskeletal Group.[16] A total of 57 RCTs were identified in this manner, of which 47 were prevention studies and 10 were treatment studies – the latter defined as trials where the inclusion criteria required a prevalent osteoporotic fracture.

Oestrogen and bone mineral density

The meta-analysis by Wells et al.[15] pooled the data from all 55 studies reporting BMD endpoints, including both ET and oestrogen plus progestogen (EPT) regimens. The BMD changes from baseline at one and two years are detailed in Table 8.1.

Table 8.1. Changes from baseline in bone mineral density at one and two years for women on HRT (95% confidence intervals in brackets)

Skeletal site of BMD measurement	1-year BMD % change	2-year BMD % change
Lumbar vertebrae	+5.4% (4.24–6.46%)	+6.8% (5.63–7.89%)
Femoral neck	+2.5% (1.16–3.83%)	+4.1% (3.45–4.80%)
Distal radius	+3.0% (2.32–3.73%)	+4.5% (3.68–5.36%)

These values, at all sites and at both time points, were statistically significant compared with untreated controls. Funnel plots detected no evidence of publication bias. When the prevention studies were set against the treatment trials no statistical difference in BMD behaviour was found. In all studies, the spine appeared the most sensitive to oestrogen, followed by the distal radius, with the hip proving the least sensitive. This is widely believed to reflect a bone site's construction, with areas such as spine, with their higher trabecular bone component, proving the most amenable to ET.

Wells et al. also looked at the effects of ET versus EPT but found no significant differences. However, when oestrogen dose regimens were grouped into low, medium and high, a clear dose response effect was found. In the light of concerns over the safety of ET and the need to apply the lowest effective dosage, and to lower the dosage progressively as women age, it is of note that a significant gain in BMD was found at all sites with dosages equivalent to 0.3 mg conjugated equine oestrogen (CEE) daily. This dosage of CEE (not currently available in the UK) has been confirmed as efficacious by Lindsay et al.[17] in a report not included in the meta-analysis by Wells et al. Subsequent to this meta-analysis, other RCTs reporting the effect of ET regimens on BMD were reviewed by Gallagher[5] and were in general agreement with the BMD changes reported by Wells et al.

Oestrogen and fracture data

Despite the strong relationship between BMD and fracture risk, with the risk approximately doubling for each standard deviation fall in BMD, robust data on oestrogen and fracture prevention have been hard to obtain. There have been no RCTs of ET in which hip fracture was a primary outcome. In their meta-analysis of RCTs published in 2002, Wells et al.[15] identified seven studies presenting fracture data. Five studies, those of Lufkin et al.,[14] Greenspan et al.,[18] Wimalawansa,[19] Hulley et al.[20] and Alexandersen et al.,[21] presented data on vertebral fracture. The numbers in these studies are, with the exception of the Hulley et al. Heart and Estrogen/Progestin Replacement Study (HERS), relatively small and consequently the confidence intervals are wide (Table 8.2). None of these studies produced clear evidence of protection in that, although the point estimates are encouraging, in all cases the confidence intervals include unity.

Some of the above studies also looked at the effect of ET on non-vertebral fracture, as did the studies Komulainen et al.[22] and Hosking et al.[23] (Table 8.3). Again, no convincing evidence of anti-fracture efficacy can be seen. Wells et al.[15] calculated that the weighted relative risk for vertebral fractures was 0.66 (95% CI 0.41–1.07) while that for non-vertebral fractures was 0.87 (95% CI 0.71–1.08).

Table 8.2. Relative risk of vertebral fractures for women on HRT

Study	Number in study	RR (95% CI)
Lufkin et al., 1992[14]	75	0.63 (0.28–1.43)
Greenspan et al., 1998[18]	425	0.70 (0.66–7.65)
Wimalawansa, 1998[19]	72	0.40 (0.09–1.80)
Hulley et al., 1998[20]	2763	0.69 (0.34–1.38)
Alexandersen et al., 1999[21]	50	2.78 (0.12–65.9)

A further meta-analysis was reported by Torgerson and Bell-Syer[24] in which 22 trials were included and in which the objective was to quantify the effects of ET on non-vertebral fractures in women with osteoporosis. Here, a significant effect was found, with the overall RR being 0.73 (95% CI 0.56–0.94). When the women were stratified by age, those younger than 60 showed a stronger anti-fracture effect with a relative risk of 0.67 (95% CI 0.49–0.55) compared with those older than 60 whose reduction in relative risk was not significant at 0.88 (95% CI 0.77–1.08). With respect to vertebral fractures, these authors also analysed 13 trials and found a pooled relative risk of 0.67 (95% CI 0.45–0.98). The upper confidence interval limit is close to unity and this study was criticised over the ascertainment of vertebral fracture in some of the component papers.

Subsequent studies with fracture endpoints

Observational studies

The Study of Osteoporotic Fractures (SOF) group[25] reported that in their large prospective cohort study of US women older than 65 those currently on ET had a one-third reduction in non-vertebral fractures – a relative risk of 0.66 (95% CI 0.54–0.80). Subgroup analysis indicated that the best results occurred in those starting ET within five years of menopause, and showed efficacy in hip fracture prevention in the older than 75 group. In younger postmenopausal women, and again in a prospective cohort design, Randell et al.[26] showed that in current users the risk of any fracture was 0.67 (95% CI 0.55–0.81). In a systematic review in 2001 of 11 observational studies, Grady and Cummings[27] reported a significant reduction in hip fracture in ET users, with a relative risk of 0.75 (95% CI 0.68–0.84). One of the most comprehensive studies was

Table 8.3. Relative risk of non-vertebral fractures for women on HRT

Study	Number in study	RR (95% CI)
Greenspan et al., 1998[18]	425	0.70 (0.22–2.22)
Komulainen et al., 1997[22]	464	0.40 (0.16–0.99)
Wimalawansa, 1998[19]	72	1.00 (0.07–14.79)
Hulley et al., 1998[20]	2763	0.94 (0.75–1.19)
Hosking et al., 1998[23]	1609	0.98 (0.29–3.34)
Alexandersen et al., 1999[21]	50	0.31 (0.03–2.76)

reported by the Swedish Hip Fracture Study Group.[28] In this population-based case–control study, 1327 women with hip fracture aged 50–81 were compared in terms of their ET exposure with 3262 matched controls. In summary, the current users had a relative risk of 0.35 (95% CI 0.24–0.53). No difference was found in the route of oestrogen delivery and the effect was largely dissipated by five years of discontinuation.

Interventional studies

The HERS study[20] was primarily designed to examine the effect of ET on the secondary prevention of cardiovascular disease but it also looked at fracture as a secondary outcome. There was no reduction in fracture risk at the spine or at other non-vertebral sites. This lack of efficacy was attributed by the authors to the paucity of clinical osteoporosis among this group.

However, the Women's Health Initiative (WHI)[29] study came to a different conclusion. This study was also primarily designed to examine the effect of HRT on the cardiovascular system but this time in 8506 women without a history of myocardial infarction or stroke receiving CEE plus medroxyprogesterone acetate (MPA). Here, the risk of hip fracture, compared with the 8102 controls, was reported as a hazard ratio and was 0.66 (95% CI 0.45–0.98). In absolute terms, this indicates five fewer hip fractures per 10 000 women per year. For vertebral fractures, the authors reported a hazard ratio of 0.66 (96% CI 0.45–0.98), which was similar to that for the hip. For all osteoporotic fractures, excluding hip, spine, fingers and toes, the hazard ratio was 0.77 (95% CI 0.69–0.86).[29]

The oestrogen/progestogen arm of this study was halted at 5.2 years owing to the increased risk of breast cancer in the treatment group reaching a limit preset by the Data Safety Monitoring Board. The oestrogen-only arm has now also been discontinued, but no fracture data from this arm are yet published. The average age of women in the WHI study was in the mid-60s.[29] In younger postmenopausal women, however, Komulainen et al.[30] had shown in a five-year RCT, subsequent to the paper cited above,[22] that ET significantly reduced the incidence of non-vertebral fracture to a relative risk of 0.29 (95 % CI 0.10–0.90) while Mosekilde et al.,[31] reporting five-year RCT data from the Danish Osteoporosis Prevention Study and specifically looking at distal radial fracture, found a relative risk of 0.45 (95% CI 0.22–0.90).

Other oestrogenic agents

Tibolone, a non-oestrogenic steroid that is metabolised to two oestrogenic metabolites *in vivo*, has been shown to conserve BMD in randomised trials and is the subject of a large RCT – the LIFT trial – with fracture primary endpoints. This agent has been styled a selective tissue-specific oestrogen activity regulator (STEAR) by its manufacturer in order to differentiate it from other licensed agents in the field, since it is neither a conventional oestrogen nor a selective oestrogen receptor modulator (SERM).

Raloxifene, the first SERM to be licensed for the treatment of osteoporosis, has been shown in an RCT, the MORE trial,[32] to confer protection against vertebral fracture. In this study of 7705 osteoporotic women with and without prevalent fracture, randomised to two doses of raloxifene or placebo, treated women had a relative risk of 0.60 (95% CI 0.50–0.70). When separately analysed for prevalent vertebral fracture in women on 60 mg/day (the licensed regimen), the relative risk rose to 0.70 (95 % CI

0.56–0.86), emphasising yet again the necessity of intervention prior to first fracture. There is no evidence to date of significant protection by raloxifene against non-vertebral fractures.

Conclusions

The oestrogens are physiological regulators of bone turnover, catabolism and anabolism. If withdrawn, for whatever reason, bone turnover accelerates and resorption outpaces formation with consequent bone loss. If sustained, this may lead to osteoporosis and risk of fragility fracture in the postmenopausal woman. Replacement oestrogen slows turnover, rebalances bone resorption and formation, and prevents bone loss. Interventional studies in both osteoporotic and non-osteoporotic populations indicate anti-fracture efficacy at all relevant sites.

Future research should concentrate firstly on identifying the minima of oestrogen exposure consistent with anti-fracture efficacy at the hip. Secondly, oestrogenic compounds with bone specificity which will avoid adverse effects centred on the cardiovascular system and the breast should be developed.

References

1.   Albright F, Smith PH, Richardson AM. Postmenopausal osteoporosis. *JAMA* 1941;116:2465–74.
2.   Manolagas SC. Birth and death of bone cells: basic regulatory mechanisms and implications for the pathogenesis and treatment of osteoporosis. *Endocr Rev* 2000;21:115–37.
3.   Parfitt AM, Mathews CH, Villanueva AR, Kleerekoper M, Frame B, Rao DS. Relationships between surface, volume, and thickness of iliac trabecular bone in aging and in osteoporosis. Implications for the microanatomic and cellular mechanisms of bone loss. *J Clin Invest* 1983;72:1396–409.
4.   Tomkinson A, Gevers EF, Wit JM, Reeve J, Noble BS. The role of estrogen in the control of rat osteocyte apoptosis. *J Bone Miner Res* 1998;13:1243–50.
5.   Gallagher JC. The effect of estrogen on bone. In: Favus MJ, editor. *Primer on the Metabolic Bone Diseases.* Washington DC: ASBMR; 2003. Ch. 53.
6.   Damien E, Price JS, Lanyon LE. Mechanical strain stimulates osteoblast proliferation through the estrogen receptor in males as well as females. *J Bone Miner Res* 2000;15:2169–77.
7.   Eastell R, Yergey AL, Vieira NE, Cedel SL, Kumar R, Riggs BL. Interrelationship among vitamin D metabolism, true calcium absorption, parathyroid function, and age in women: evidence of an age-related intestinal resistance to 1,25-dihydroxyvitamin D action. *J Bone Miner Res* 1991;6:125–32.
8.   Nordin BE, Need AG, Morris HA, Horowitz M, Robertson WG. Evidence for a renal calcium leak in postmenopausal women. *J Clin Endocrinol Metab* 1991;72:401–7.
9.   Gallagher JC, Riggs BL, DeLuca HF. Effect of estrogen on calcium absorption and serum vitamin D metabolites in postmenopausal osteoporosis. *J Clin Endocrinol Metab* 1980;51:1359–64.
10.   McKane WR, Khosla S, Burritt MF, Kao PC, Wilson DM, Ory SJ, et al. Mechanism of renal calcium conservation with estrogen replacement therapy in women in early postmenopause – a clinical research center study. *J Clin Endocrinol Metab* 1995;80:3458–64.
11.   Khosla S, Atkinson EJ, Melton LJ 3rd, Riggs BL. Effects of age and estrogen status on serum parathyroid hormone levels and biochemical markers of bone turnover in women: a population-based study. *J Clin Endocrinol Metab* 1997;82:1522–27.
12.   McKane WR, Khosla S, Risteli J, Robins SP, Muhs JM, Riggs BL. Role of estrogen deficiency in pathogenesis of secondary hyperparathyroidism and increased bone resorption in elderly women. *Proc Assoc Am Physicians* 1997;109:174–80.
13.   O'Connell D, Robertson J, Henry D, Gillespie W. A systematic review of the skeletal effects of estrogen therapy in postmenopausal women. II. An assessment of treatment effects. *Climacteric* 1998;1:112–23.
14.   Lufkin EG, Wahner HW, O'Fallon WM, Hodgson SF, Kotowicz MA, Lane AW, et al. Treatment of postmenopausal osteoporosis with transdermal estrogen. *Ann Intern Med* 1992;117:1–9.
15.   Wells G, Tugwell P, Shea B, Guyatt G, Peterson J, Zytaruk N, Robinson V, et al.; Osteoporosis

Methodology Group and The Osteoporosis Research Advisory Group. Meta-analyses of therapies for postmenopausal osteoporosis. V. Meta-analysis of the efficacy of hormone replacement therapy in treating and preventing osteoporosis in postmenopausal women. *Endocr Rev* 2002;23:529–39.

16. Dickersin K, Scherer R, Lefebvre C. Identifying relevant studies for systematic reviews. *BMJ* 1994;309:1286–91.

17. Lindsay R, Gallagher JC, Kleerekoper M, Pickar JH. Effect of lower doses of conjugated equine estrogens with and without medroxyprogesterone acetate on bone in early postmenopausal women. *JAMA* 2002;287:2668–76.

18. Greenspan S, Bankhurst A, Bell N. Effects of alendronate and estrogen alone and in combination on bone mass and turnover in postmenopausal osteoporosis [Abstract 1107]. *J Bone Miner Res* 1998;S174.

19. Wimalawansa SJ. A four-year randomized controlled trial of hormone replacement and bisphosphonate, alone or in combination, in women with postmenopausal osteoporosis. *Am J Med* 1998;104:219–26.

20. Hulley S, Grady D, Bush T, Furberg C, Herrington D, Riggs B, *et al.* Randomized trial of estrogen plus progestin for secondary prevention of coronary heart disease in postmenopausal women. Heart and Estrogen/progestin Replacement Study (HERS) Research Group. *JAMA* 1998;280:605–13.

21. Alexandersen P, Riis BJ, Christiansen C. Monofluorophosphate combined with hormone replacement therapy induces a synergistic effect on bone mass by dissociating bone formation and resorption in postmenopausal women: a randomized study. *J Clin Endocrinol Metab* 1999;84:3013–20.

22. Komulainen M, Tuppurainen MT, Kroger H, Heikkinen AM, Puntila E, Alhava E, *et al.* Vitamin D and HRT: no benefit additional to that of HRT alone in prevention of bone loss in early postmenopausal women. A 2.5-year randomized placebo-controlled study. *Osteoporos Int* 1997;7:126–32.

23. Hosking D, Chilvers CE, Christiansen C, Ravn P, Wasnich R, Ross P, *et al.* Prevention of bone loss with alendronate in postmenopausal women under 60 years of age. Early Postmenopausal Intervention Cohort Study Group. *N Engl J Med* 1998;338:485–92.

24. Torgerson DJ, Bell-Syer SE. Hormone replacement therapy and prevention of nonvertebral fractures: a meta-analysis of randomized trials. *JAMA* 2001;285:2891–7.

25. Cauley JA, Seeley DG, Ensrud K, Ettinger B, Black D, Cummings SR. Estrogen replacement therapy and fractures in older women. Study of Osteoporotic Fractures Research Group. *Ann Intern Med* 1995;122:9–16.

26. Randell KM, Honkanen RJ, Kroger H, Saarikoski S. Does hormone-replacement therapy prevent fractures in early postmenopausal women? *J Bone Miner Res* 2002;17:528–33.

27. Grady D, Cummings SR. Postmenopausal hormone therapy for prevention of fractures: how good is the evidence? *JAMA* 2001;285:2909–10.

28. Michaelsson K, Baron J, Fahramand B. Hip fractures and estrogen in the Swedish Hip Fracture Study. *BMJ* 1998;366:1842–44.

29. Rossouw JE, Anderson GL, Prentice RL, LaCroix AZ, Kooperberg C, Stefanick ML, *et al.*; Writing Group for the Women's Health Initiative Investigators. Risks and benefits of estrogen plus progestin in healthy postmenopausal women. Principal results from the Women's Health Initiative randomized controlled trial. *JAMA* 2002;288:321–33.

30. Komulainen MH, Kroger H, Tuppurainen MT, Heikkinen AM, Alhava E, Honkanen R, *et al.* HRT and Vit D in prevention of non-vertebral fractures in postmenopausal women; a 5 year randomized trial. *Maturitas* 1998;31:45–54.

31. Mosekilde L, Beck-Nielsen H, Sorensen OH, Nielsen SP, Charles P, Vestergaard P, *et al.* Hormonal replacement therapy reduces forearm fracture incidence in recent postmenopausal women – results of the Danish Osteoporosis Prevention Study. *Maturitas* 2000;36:181–93.

32. Ettinger B, Black DM, Mitlak BH, Knickerbocker RK, Nickelsen T, Genant HK, *et al.* Reduction of vertebral fracture risk in postmenopausal women with osteoporosis treated with raloxifene: results from a 3-year randomized clinical trial. Multiple Outcomes of Raloxifene Evaluation (MORE) Investigators. *JAMA* 1999;282:637–45. Erratum in: *JAMA* 1999;282:2124.

Chapter 9

Effects of HRT on the cardiovascular system and bones

Discussion

Beral: This last session of today is about the effects of HRT on the cardiovascular systems and bones. Our first speaker is Dr Ross Prentice from Seattle in the USA. He very modestly describes himself as a biostatistician with not much knowledge in this area, and not much to contribute. But I just would like to say that Dr Prentice is probably one of the most eminent biostatisticians in the world, very widely recognised, not necessarily for his work on HRT but certainly for his work in biostatistics so if some of you want to ask questions about methodology, he is the right person to ask. I thought I would introduce him as one of the principal investigators of the Women's Health Initiative but he tells me that there are no principal investigators of the Women's Health Initiative. It is just lots of investigators who are scattered around the USA but he, and his colleagues, have run the Women's Health Initiative Co-ordinating Centre and done the analyses. I hope he will correct me if I am wrong, but the publications that come out have actually been analysed by Dr Prentice and his group although there are other authors who write up the analyses. But the data analysis is largely under his and his colleagues' direction. So he is going to talk specifically about ischaemic heart disease and stroke and then later tomorrow he is talking about dementia and other aspects. But I think you will have an opportunity if you wish to ask methodological questions.

Discussion following Dr Prentice's paper

Rees: I do not know if I have missed it but do you have data on the dropout and patient travel from HRT users and nonusers to either group and the dropout in the HRT users group in the observational study?

Prentice: In the case of the clinical trial we have published that information in the original *JAMA* paper.[1] We use a rather strict criterion, of continuing to take 80% or more of the assigned pills in the given six-month period and the dropout from intervention rates there increased from randomisation up to about 40% after five years of use. It was a bit higher, maybe 5% higher, in the intervention group versus the placebo group.

Rees: Do you have similar data for the observational study?

Prentice: It is not the same quality of data because in the clinical trial the women come in, at least annually and some every six months, and there are pill counts and pill weighing involved. In the observational study we update essentially annually the hormone use patterns.

Rees: But have you got data in the observational study in the oestrogen plus progestogen group?

Prentice: Dropout there is defined as just stopping use of it. I think our experience was more like community use in the USA where the dropout rates are quite high, much higher than in our trial.

Rees: But what was it?

Prentice: I cannot give you a number on that right now. If I have to hazard a guess, probably by the end of the average five-and-a-half years of follow-up it was the same in our cohort study as in the clinical trial and was probably at least half.

Lumsden: You said right at the beginning that you had two very similar populations. Was it that you tried to recruit women into the randomised comparison and if they did not take part, they were then recruited into observational, or were they recruited from different pools?

Prentice: Generally it was a common recruitment and if the woman proved ineligible or uninterested in the clinical trial she was given the opportunity to participate and join the cohort study. So in the case of HRT, a major reason for the women who chose the observational trial, and many women chose not to participate in the clinical trial, was that they had already made a decision on HRT. Many of these women went into the observational study. There is a minor departure from that in that the HRT clinical trial recruitment was by far the most difficult in the overall programme. Some clinics of the 40 participating centres had to do separate HRT recruitment near the end for the clinical trial to get sufficient numbers of women in, but it was a tiny fraction of the total.

(The discussion following the cognitive function aspects of Dr Prentice's paper appears in Chapter 15)

Discussion following Professor Lowe's paper

Whitehead: Are you are quite confident that non-oral HRT does not increase the risk of venous thromboembolism?

Lowe: If you look at the evidence from the three studies reported so far,[2-4] the odds ratio is close to 1.

Gray: Is there, in your opinion, any value in using low-dose aspirin as prophylaxis, or very-low-dose warfarin?

Lowe: One study, I think the Heart and Estrogen/Progestin Replacement Study (HERS), did look at that and suggested a possible protective effect of aspirin. One study suggested a 25–30% reduction in risk of venous thromboembolism in patients treated for arterial disease. So aspirin does reduce the risk of venous thromboembolism a bit.

Gray: What about low-dose warfarin?

Lowe: No study has looked at that, to my knowledge.

Discussion following Professor Purdie's paper

Burger: If you accept the Women's Health Initiative evidence[5] that combined HRT reduced fracture risk even in women of normal or somewhat diminished but not osteoporotic bone density levels, is there any evidence that any intervention reduces fracture risk in women other than those who already have osteoporosis?

Purdie: I suspect that the reduction in fracture in the Women's Health Initiative came from that subset of women in the study who were in fact osteoporotic. But we do not know that because their bone mineral densities were not measured at entry.

Prentice: In a subsample of three of the 40 clinics, bone mineral density was measured at baseline and at a couple of later points in time. We have not published any of those data yet but they might be insightful.

Evans: In regard to that, the fracture paper does publish something on it. It does give the relative risk there and it does give you the amount. You are right in the sense that most of the fractures are in those at high risk, not particularly necessarily those who were osteoporotic, but in those who were elderly.

General discussion

Cardiovascular effects

Whitehead: Dr Prentice, the revised paper on HRT and cardiovascular risk, which was published in the *New England Journal of Medicine*, says that when looking at the adjusted data there is no overall excess risk of coronary heart disease.

Prentice: The lower end of the confidence interval is right around 1, that is true, but that is a lot different than saying there is no indication of elevation.

Whitehead: This is the first opportunity that we have had to actually talk to somebody from the Women's Health Initiative who has been involved in the study about some of the things that we do not really understand and are quite important to those of us who see patients. I am very curious about the year five data, for all the clinical outcomes, because they seem to suddenly show an increased ischaemic heart disease risk. It is not just in ischaemic heart disease risk, it is in venous thromboembolism risk and it is in breast cancer risk too. It would suggest to me, if it was just one clinical endpoint that was awry, you would say well perhaps something strange has gone on but it is right across the board. This suggests to me that there is something more in the administration that has gone wrong. Why were these disparate clinical endpoints and do we suddenly have a problem in year five?

Beral: If Dr Prentice could just answer, whether it is in fact the case that in year five the results differ significantly from the other years?

Prentice: The answer is no, even though it kind of sticks out like a sore thumb. Part of the answer is also most evident in the initial publication where the outcomes are being ascertained. There may have been some differential at that point in the ascertainment when you get to year five and beyond. Many of the events have taken place very recently and the outcome process takes some time. The later publications would be the better source there. As I recall it is not so evident in them, but there is probably still some little bump at year five and I think it is probably largely not quite having complete data on the outcome at the time the trial ended. But it is somewhat anomalous and even though not significant it sticks out and we do not really have a clear explanation. It is certainly a better analysis to look at it more broadly. Normally the outcome process is pretty efficient but when you start cutting the data this finely and dealing with very recently occurring events then it takes some months for central adjudication to be completed. So, that is the most likely reason, I think, in the early report.

Evans: Can I just illustrate that the hazard ratio in the paper you are talking about is 1.45 in year five. The confidence interval is 0.81 to 2.59. One problem is with the amount of data available in year five, and the actual number of events is very low. So the confidence intervals are so wide. When you deal with lots of trials of this kind, to find odd blips here and there is not at all surprising.

Studd: But what is the hazard ratio, because there was a big dip in the number of placebos?

Evans: The annualised percentage in the placebo group is 0.28 that year, the year before was 0.32, the year before that it was 0.19, the year before that 0.35, the year before that was 0.29. These things can fluctuate up and down and I can just promise you that if you are a statistician you see this.

Prentice: We are talking about two different papers here. Mr Whitehead is taking them out of the 2002 *JAMA* publication[1] where year five had a larger hazard ratio than in the *New England Journal of Medicine* publication[6] where, as Professor Evans was just describing, the placebo group rates did not have very great variation.

Evans: The confidence interval is 0.81 to 2.59 and these are the annual percentages – they just go up and down. I think that if you are a statistician you just accept that numbers wave up and down a great deal and you are not going to pay a lot of attention to odd little blips. You can over-interpret these little bumps which go up and down incredibly.

Whitehead: It is just that in all the clinical endpoints, whether you are looking at breast cancer, venous thromboembolism or ischaemic heart disease, they all suddenly seem to have fewer events in the placebo group in year five. I just ask whether there was there any explanation because there is no overriding biological mechanism which joins those three different clinical endpoints together.

Prentice: Well I think the answer I gave is a big part of it. The data are bouncing around a little bit as Professor Evans showed, but not as dramatically as in the earlier report which you are referring to, which did look rather anomalous at year five. I think it really is a matter of the outcome data being less mature at that time than a couple of months later.

Lumsden: Dr Prentice, in your cohort study, did you follow up the women who opted not to take HRT?

Prentice: Yes.

Lumsden: Are the data as you would expect?

Prentice: Two-thirds of those women in the cohort study were not HRT users. We have the data and we have already made this initial use of them. This is actually the first analysis of the HRT data in our cohort study and I purposefully did not show any results from that until our clinical trial was complete in an effort to try not to confuse the message.

Stevenson: I would like to make two points. Firstly, you say the reason for doing the Women's Health Initiative trial was in terms of looking for any effect on coronary heart disease. If I were to design a study to do that, coronary heart disease is a disease of elderly people if you are talking about women more than men. So if you are going to design a study to do that, would not you want to actually select populations who were at increased risk of coronary heart disease? I just have concerns that if you were to look for effects on pneumonic consolidation with an antibiotic, if you gave them to normal people rather than those with pneumonia you might not see such a good outcome, and your risk–benefit might not be too good. So I think there is a big problem in trying to do studies of prevention of coronary heart disease in a general population setting.

The second point that I would make about your presentation is related to the surrogate markers you were showing. I think there is always a big concern about what they mean. Particularly with respect to the ERA trial[7] which still to my mind has not given me a good explanation as to why in the placebo group the coronary atheroma progression is greater in those who use statins or aspirin than in those who smoke or who are hypertensive – one could get the wrong messages from that.

Prentice: I will not try to defend the atherosclerosis progression trials. The designers of the HRT trials had this overriding hope to try to get useful information on benefit versus risk in some summary fashion for normal women, which drove the design to a considerable extent. You are right, if one selected on coronary heart disease risk factors, a much smaller study could have been done but it seemed important to try to learn...

Stevenson: Back then to what I said earlier – should we really be giving medicines to people that do not need them?

Prentice: I guess the point in the USA, and I think it is not very different here, is that these medicines were being used by a large number of people and we already heard that the majority of the women were using them for menopausal symptoms but a growing fraction for other reasons. Older women were being prescribed HRT or continuing longer than previously. I think that is a question for the public health need to answer benefit versus risk questions in that group of women.

Critchley: Dr Prentice, I do not think you have shown any data, but do we have any on transdermal oestrogen? We have heard suggestions that it might be an attractive way of giving women oestrogen and it avoids the problems of venous thromboembolism, Professor Purdie has shown us some protective data at a very low dose. What do we know about transdermal oestrogens?

Prentice: I am sure others are much more expert to answer that question but in our Women's Health Initiative context it is only in our cohort study that there is a little information on that topic. The number of transdermal oestradiol users was actually too small to make a sensible comparison. We did a few other comparisons beyond those that are shown, putting the entire oestradiol group together versus either conjugated equine oestrogen or oestrone sulphate preparations and did not see differences between those. But that begs the question whether the transdermal administration would have benefit. I think it is an important topic, as is the lower dose of conjugated equine oestrogen or oestradiol.

Venous thromboembolism

Gebbie: Dr Lowe, how much of this should we be informing our patients about? It would actually be quite simple to change most women onto patches. Over the years of running menopausal clinics I have seen quite a few venous thromboembolic events in women on oestrogen. What is the feeling about this clinically?

Lowe: The background to this is that we have three studies of transdermal HRT here.[8] Dr Scarabin presented his study[8] to the International Society on Thrombosis and Haemostasis, and in the discussion he put up a slide looking at all three of these studies, adjusted for risk factors. I recall that the relative risk was close to 1.

Evans: I just redid the meta-analysis essentially based on the confidence intervals presented in the RCOG document[9] so it would not be regarded as precise. The pooled estimate for a fixed effect is 1.25. The confidence interval is 0.8 to 1.95, but it does not eliminate the possibility that there is still an increased risk with transdermal preparations.

Lowe: What I might suggest is that we need to do a proper meta-analysis of these three studies in which an adjustment is made for the usual risk factors. Because it may be that the studies differed in different types of prospectus. My second point is what goes on your skin in France may be quite different from what goes on your skin in Britain.

Gray: It is likely to be mostly gel in France, whereas the British use predominantly patches. There is a potential difference in the bioavailability with the two routes. The pattern of use is different and we do not know whether gel, because it has much more of a peak and trough type of delivery as compared with patches with a more even delivery, would make any difference.

Lowe: So my answer to Dr Gebbie then is, as always, we need more data. But I think what you can say to your patients and what my chapter would certainly say is that there appears to be a lesser risk of venous thromboembolism associated with transdermal preparations in general. But as always we need more data, we need more studies, but it still looks safer.

Purdie: I have certainly prescribed transdermal oestrogens for those women with an increased risk of thrombosis. I think transdermals have suffered because they come under the umbrella of HRT and everyone has being saying all these years that HRT causes venous thromboembolism, but we do need to distinguish between them, and your paper has very clearly demonstrated that. So one of the things that I think should come out from this meeting is that there is a major difference in the effects of transdermal and oral, not only in this respect but as Dr Stevenson showed us, too, with lipids.

Barlow: The Daly paper,[2] from my memory, specifically addresses idiopathic venous thromboembolism. Some papers look at venous thromboembolism across the board, not just idiopathic. Is there anything inherently different in what is understood about whether a factor might affect the idiopathic compared with simply raising the general thrombosis risk.

Lowe: In the 22 studies, most have no detail at all as to whether they were idiopathic or associated with risk factors. None of the studies in the RCOG guideline give much detail and that is why none of the three meta-analyses will tell you about a difference in relative risk, for example, or absolute risk between the different risk factors. But there is an adverse effect, as I said, particularly for age, which is an entirely reasonable extrapolation of the data and application of the epidemiology of venous thromboembolism. It makes sense to apply the best estimate of relative risk from the studies to the absolute risk in that individual woman based on factors such as age, obesity, varicose veins, etc.

Glasier: Is the difference that people have always told us about between natural oestrogens and synthetic oestrogens such as ethinyl oestradiol in respect of venous thromboembolism risk purely related to this old idea that the pill was bad for you and HRT was not. Or is there some real difference?

Lowe: Well, the relative risk I would assess as being the same. It follows a very similar pattern. It is what I would expect in terms of looking at the effect of combined oral contraceptives (COCs) and oral HRT on the biomarkers and triangulating that against the association of the biomarkers with risk of venous thromboembolism. So I think your suggestion that COC is bad and HRT good was wrong. But to be fair, people did not have the spectrum of assays to look at differences in haemostasis in the past. We certainly had very little knowledge about thrombophilias.

Glasier: But it is an important point, not so much for HRT as for contraception, because if patch is good and oral is bad then for young women taking contraception, the patch might be better than oral pills.

Lowe: Well, what we would suggest now that patch contraceptives are coming in is to do some studies of biomarkers, ideally randomising women to oral versus patch.

Evans: Just a point of clarification is that I think in some senses at the Committee on Safety of Medicines (CSM) we got it wrong back in 1996 when the studies on HRT and venous thromboembolism came out. I was the lead assessor and I am responsible because we based our estimates of the absolute risk on studies that had looked at idiopathic cases only. All three studies, and in fact the fourth major study that came out just in 1997,[2,3,10,11] that we did have available to us then, had all looked at idiopathic cases. If you look at idiopathic cases it seems to me that the relative risk does not change. I cannot tell you whether any of the mechanisms are any different but the relative risk is remarkably consistent, and consistent with the Women's Health Initiative and HERS and consistent across age, etc. But the absolute risk is quite different. We totally underestimated the absolute risk of venous thromboembolism back in 1996. It was only when the trial data came out,[1,12,13] when we saw relatively unselected people in the studies, that we found this notably higher, possibly a factor of 10 to a factor of 100 out in the absolute risk. The same happened to some degree over second- and third-generation COCs, when we underestimated the risk. The point is that the epidemiologists, it is classic pharmaco-epidemiology from Martin Vessey, say you must study idiopathic cases to find causal factors, and that is absolutely right. But when you translate it into public health benefit, you do not exclude all the people who are excluded from the studies. Anyone who could have had the slightest hint of a risk factor other than age and obesity was excluded from the epidemiological studies and consequently the absolute estimate was quite wrong.

Gray: We are now coming into the realms of low-dose HRT. Do we have any evidence that all oral preparations carry the same risk regardless of dose because some of the data you have given suggested that that was not the case. Are we going to draw a clear distinction between oral and non-oral or do we need to look at the various different routes – gels, implants, nasal sprays, rings – or are they all going to be able to be massed into one. How detailed is our sub-analysis going to have to be?

Lowe: In the meta-analysis of the trials of HRT and venous thromboembolism most of the data was oral. You are looking across different countries with use of different preparations and there is no obvious difference between opposed and unopposed oral HRT. Beyond that you cannot go. You do not have data on the spread of preparations that you have now available on the market. All you can go by is what is published and I am sure it is not representative given that many of these studies started ten years ago with what you prescribed then. Nevertheless, these studies provide the best estimate of relative risk and I suggest you base your calculations on a relative risk of three, bearing in mind that women are quite interested in what is going to happen in that first year and not in several years down the line, and apply that to the estimated absolute risk of venous thromboembolism in that woman. Now we do need better tools for working out some magic formula that says age and years and body mass index and granny had a deep vein thrombosis, but we do not have that degree of perfection. But we can make an estimate. I think the revised CSM tables, not the original ones, actually provide us with a good starting point. So it gives you a number of excess cases per thousand users for women in their 50s, or women in their 60s. If you want, you could then double that for a woman who is obese, body mass index greater than 30, or you could add on a bit again for varicose veins, or you could then multiply that by three and you come up with some ballpark figure. I think that is the best you can do. When a woman asks which of the 150 preparations is safer, we do not have a clue. All we can go by is the limitations of the studies, which suggest a relative risk of three.

Critchley: You mentioned that we need to understand about what influences the biomarkers. We are talking about oestrogens here in a very generic way. The first thing we have to remember is that if you give oral ethinyl oestradiol in the pill or you give oral Premarin® (conjugated equine oestrogen), if it goes to the liver it is going to be metabolised to oestrone whereas if you give it transdermally you have 17β-oestradiol. So the first question we have to ask is what ligand it is, is it oestrone or oestradiol? We need to see that it is going to then have a downstream effect on your biomarker and that then determines, once you know what your ligand is, what is your optimal receptor type that it is going to bind to, to then have your effect on the biomarker. So I just make a plea that we actually need to understand so much more about the biology of what is actually going on. To complicate it even further, each individual will have a different metabolising enzyme repertoire, which will then affect the availability of that ligand. So, somebody said that we need to forget about steroid biology – I do not think we should, I think it is part of this whole picture.

Lowe: It is very complicated. What I think I tried to say is that HRT has many effects, which if you sum them up would appear to explain the thrombogenesis. Quantitating those effects and saying, well which key changes in clotting give you thrombosis, you can only speculate on. If you ask me I would say lowering of the three main inhibitor systems, probably, is the most important. Because, in particular, you see oral HRT having exactly the same percentage change as COCs, and we know that they both increase the relative risk of venous thromboembolism three-fold. The problem is that very few relevant receptors in the liver have been identified for these coagulation pathways, so we do not even know what the receptors are. Then, as you say, what about the effects of the different types of oestrone, oestradiol etc., I do not know. So I agree with your statement but I cannot really clarify except to say from epidemiological studies coupled with randomised and community studies of women taking oral hormones we think we have a general direction of where to go. But it would clearly be up to the pharmaceutical industry to do further research and say what are these receptors and what do the different formulations do in animals and then in women, etc. So I think the pathways are becoming clearer and we now see the kind of pathways that we should be focusing such research on.

Whitehead: To answer the question about the late 1970s and early 1980s, we relied largely on the data from the group at the University of South Manchester in Wythenshawe. They studied COCs and then HRT and said COCs caused more marked changes in the laboratory-derived factors that were being investigated. It was that which gave rise to the belief that HRT would cause less problem with coagulation.

When you talk about oral oestrogens, are there differences between 17β-oestradiol and conjugated equine oestrogens that we know about? Because you would predict that there would be.

Lowe: We tried to group them by types of oestrogen but there is just not enough data. For reasons you can well understand, no manufacturer is going to compare their drug against several other manufacturer's compounds because there is always a risk that it will be shown to be significantly worse. So that is the problem. You have multiple studies done with multiple study designs, each usually only of a single product, sometimes if you are lucky with a control group – sometimes if you are lucky a randomised placebo-controlled design, sometimes if you are lucky more than three months. So the quality of the data is not good. It is getting better but there is certainly not enough data to answer your question about the effects of different preparations. Unfortunately, studies such as the Postmenopausal Estrogen/Progestin Interventions (PEPI) trial[14] and the MRC[15] quite reasonably really just looked at fibrinogen and lipids because at the time we did not realise the importance of looking at other variables in the coagulation system.

Studd: Going back to COCs and oestradiol, we have all had the view in the past that ethinyl oestradiol is stronger and more potent that oestradiol. It is interesting that our patients with premature menopause coming for egg donation are all on some sort of HRT these days. We are surprised to find out that the women who have taken COCs for many years have much lower bone density than the women who have taken oestradiol for the same number of years. That applies both for cross-sectional and longitudinal studies. So somehow ethinyl oestradiol is not as effective in protecting bone. We used 100 mg oestradiol patches for treatment of severe premenstrual syndrome by stopping ovulation, stopping all cyclical symptoms. It is interesting that even on that dose it stops ovulation in most women. That does not mean it is contraceptive – you would need many more studies measuring efficacy.

Stevenson: I was surprised by the Scarabin paper[8] because, if I recall correctly, it did not show any dose effects on risk of venous thromboembolism. It showed the difference between the oral and the non-oral, and it showed the timing of the events, that it was higher in the first year and then seemed to diminish. But I think I am right to say that they did not show any dose events and that surprises me because I think that the dose is still, even for venous thromboembolism, incredibly important. We have a paper in press at the moment in the *British Journal of Haematology*[16] with a standard dose of transdermal HRT, showing that it does have effects on some of the coagulation and fibrinolytic indices. Yet, in the WHISP study we have a low-dose oral HRT, where we have no change in things such as activated protein C (APC) resistance, D-dimers etc. So again I just wonder, if you are going to change to a transdermal preparation in somebody who, for example, is going to go for surgery, you probably ultimately should give it in a low dose as well.

Lowe: Looking at the recent studies, very few have actually looked at different doses of HRT. The assays are getting better but you still need to do an adequately powered study to show dose dependencies. I fully agree with all you say and I am sure that absence of seeing a dose effect does not mean it is not there; it might be that we have not looked hard enough for it. I think it is very important that we look at different doses within the HRT range.

Barlow: In 1996, when the papers came out in the *Lancet*, the British Menopause Society held a working group that led to a monograph[17] which several of us here, including you, participated in. We were working along the lines no doubt based on the idiopathic risk in the data. We were talking, for women in their early 50s, of a risk of about one in 10 000 per year and we were saying that the tripling of that was taking us to three in 10 000. Therefore the excess was about two in 10 000 and many, many presentations over the years have used that sort of statistic – two in 10 000 per year excess risk. You were talking in your presentation about an increase in risk of about four in 1000 over five years, which is 40 in 10 000 in the five years, and that if you annualise that, approximating, it is about eight in 10 000 as the excess as opposed to two in 10 000 which we have all been quoting – a very important difference.

Lowe: This goes back to Professor Evans's point, that everybody probably has underestimated the risk. People have largely ignored venous thromboembolism but the epidemiology has really caught up in the past few years and we are all much more aware that it is more common than stroke.

Chwalisz: I would like to give an example from pharmacology that not all oestrogens are created equal with regard to hepatic oestrogenic effects. There is a very important publication showing that ethinyl oestradiol increases some oestrogenic liver parameters at very low doses,[18] such as 5 μg/day, a dose which is not sufficient for oral contraception. So the liver is extremely sensitive to some oestrogens. We addressed this question a long time ago in an attempt to develop oestrogens that would not have such marked impact on the liver. There are rat studies showing that it is possible to create oestrogen molecules that will act as oestrogens in the periphery, but will not undergo a first-pass effect in the liver.[19] This example from pharmacology shows that it is perhaps possible to design better oestrogens.

Miller: You have not mentioned much about the effects of raloxifene or tamoxifen. I am presuming that you would bring these into the same sort of concept by the fact that the liver is actually seeing these as oestrogens.

Lowe: There is no easy answer with raloxifene and tamoxifen. They do appear on the current data to treble the risk of venous thromboembolism, which is interesting. They do not, in the papers I have read, change the biomarkers, which complicates the story.

Beral: I would like to make one point about transdermals – I think in that in Scarabin's case–control study[8] it is my impression that the prevalence of use of transdermal preparations was too low in the control. So I am a little bit worried that the comparison group may be distorted and I think that one needs at least another piece of evidence before you start promulgating the idea that the transdermals are very different from other types of HRT.

Bone effects

Stevenson: Professor Purdie, if you look at the reduction in hip fracture that is shown by the Women's Health Initiative data in an officially non-osteoporotic population and compare that to the same data that you can extract from the study of osteoporotic fractures with one of the bisphosphonates, then the efficacy of HRT looks much better than the bisphosphonate. So my question is, do you think that we really have any viable alternatives for prevention of osteoporosis in women that have a risk of osteoporosis but without established disease?

Purdie: We have good data on bisphosphonates with prevention of all types of fracture, including hip particularly. But the great concern about the bisphosphonates, which must come into any of the discussions very early, is whether we are to give them long-term to women in their early postmenopause? That is the concern that many of us have had in the light of recent statements by the CSM. But younger women in their 50s who are at higher risk of osteoporosis, with densitometry showing higher degrees of osteopenia or early osteoporosis, must now start with bisphosphonates. We do not have data, to my knowledge, beyond nine to ten years of safety on bisphosphonates, whereas we can reasonably be assured that the oestrogens have been operating as bone protectors for about 200 000 years. The oestrogens are the natural conservators of bone, whereas bisphosphonates are unknown to human biochemistry. To put that in context, we have seen no major problems with bisphosphonates at the moment – morphometric and biochemical studies show normal bone up to ten years – but it was noticeable at the recent meeting of the American Society for Bone and Mineral Research (ASMBR) that several studies are continuing in the USA involving bisphosphonates. There were patients taking bisphosphonate for two years, having a gap of two to three years, reassessment, and then perhaps another pulse. So there is concern out there about the long-term safety of bisphosphonates as the number one alternative to oestrogens, and I think research has to continue on both fronts. We need better oestrogens, we need better bisphosphonates, we need longer data to assure ourselves that they are safe long-term. If not in the bone field, the great angst about bisphosphonates is that they tend to turn off or tone down the normal housekeeping of bone, the normal turnover of bone, the removal of old bone, which is essential for the vitality of bone. The long-term fear is that we might ironically wind up, although there is no evidence yet, with a more fragile skeleton.

Lumsden: I wonder if you could expand on this dose effect on bone. We were led to believe for a very long time that there was a lower limit in dosage of oestrogen that is bone-protective or bone-sparing. Now this is changing but yet I think that one can draw the conclusion from the literature that the effect on bone does tend to be dose-dependent because if you look at women who have implants they tend to have very dense bones, and why we can suddenly come down to 12.5 µg?

Purdie: We do not know yet, but you are quite right – the major meta-analysis[20] showed a clear dose–response effect. Therefore the reduction to 12.5 µg transdermally showing bone gain at the hip was really quite remarkable. The authors have commented, of course, that if 12.5 µg transdermally is protective, what happens when you go down to 6.3 µg. Where is the lower limit and when does bone pass below the operative horizon of the oestrogen? We simply do not know.

Lumsden: What is the circulating oestradiol level at: 12.5 µg or lower?

Purdie: That was not reported in the abstracts. As I mentioned earlier, the ability of oestrogens to protect the older skeleton is inversely related to the ambient oestradiol. Women with more circulating oestradiol do not respond as well to oestrogens as women with lower levels. We know that as skeletons age through the 60s and 70s, even the 80s, the ambient oestradiol, although it is low, is still operational. In one very elegant study,[21] residual oestradiol in women in their eighth decade was switched off using aromatase inhibitors and the investigators found a very substantial rise in the bone markers. That, by the way, has very important implications for the treatment of breast cancer with aromatase inhibitors. The paper in the *Lancet* just 18 months ago, the ATAC study,[22] showed an excess of fracture in women treated with aromatase inhibitors. So the answer to the question is that we do not know how low we could go but we have to find out, and soon. I look forward to data on mammographic density, especially from these low-dose and ultra-low-dose studies in the USA, to see if there is any change in mammographic density with this ultra-low dose. Because, as we all know, breast density has been a major problem with conventional oestrogens and appears to be relevant to the breast cancer problem.

Studd: There is a stampede at the moment for the lowest possible dose from every manufacturer, trying every single route. It is reassuring but surprising that oestrogen works in such small doses without endometrial stimulation. We all know that the benefits in the bone are dose-dependent. I can understand the reflex of going for the lowest possible dose with a dangerous adverse effect. What I really would like to know, and it is a very sincere question to everybody, is there any really good evidence that the adverse effects of HRT are dose-dependent within reason? Professor Beral did not show it for breast cancer in the million women study and Scarabin did not find an increased risk of venous thromboembolism with transdermal oestradiol. I am talking about the preparations in general use. Is there any real evidence that the risks are dose-dependent?

Beral: The data that Dr Prentice showed are the first I have ever seen suggesting a dose–response relationship for cardiovascular disease. Does anyone else wish to comment?

Stevenson: Well, I think it is an important question. Professor Purdie, I wanted to comment about your use of aromatase inhibitors. I think you do have an interesting setting here because postmenopausal breast cancer patients are now being treated long-term to some degree with aromatase inhibitors and clearly aromatase inhibitors take circulating oestrogen levels through the floor. If you are trying to measure them, it is hard work in postmenopausal women – they really are so low. I guess the surprise that I have from the ATAC study that you just mentioned is not that there is an increase in fractures and so forth, but that there is not a greater increase. It just seems to be that all these women by and large are going to have almost immeasurable levels of oestrogen, and in a way you might expect that they would all really have a pretty high risk of developing bone fractures. I wonder why that is not the case and it would seem to me that there must be local factors that are not non-oestrogenic which actually prevent bone loss or prevent fractures in those women.

Purdie: I think one of the reasons is that there will, of course, be a spectrum of ambient bone mineral density in the women beginning to receive their aromatase inhibitors. And perhaps the fractures that appeared in the ATAC study were from those patients who concomitantly had low bone density at entry. I think we need more prospective data on patients receiving aromatase inhibitors and to see what the true incidence of fractures is going to be. We need to examine these women carefully, instrumentally before starting their aromatase inhibitor and decide with our colleagues in breast surgery and oncology as to whether we should use them or perhaps use tamoxifen, which of course confers a degree of protection as it is a selective oestrogen receptor modulator (SERM).

Stevenson: I totally agree with you, but I just want to clarify one of your conclusions, where you said we should concentrate on identifying a minimum of oestrogen exposure consistent with anti-fracture efficacy. I am not sure how easy that is going to be if in fact you are taking the extreme of postmenopausal women treated with aromatase inhibitors who virtually have no oestrogen: in these women it may actually be very little oestrogen that will protect them. As you said in a throwaway remark, in one of the studies it may actually be that the lower the oestrogen the greater the efficacy.

Purdie: One other aspect of the whole oestrogen story worth mentioning is that there is an agent under examination at the moment that appears to confer bone protection or rather to act on the skeleton as a conventional oestrogen, but non-genomically. It appears to act through either one or more surface receptors and then a second messenger. That is another area of development which we should, I think, consider and discuss for the future because if this agent does not have an action on the reproductive tract again it is on the line of development we are looking for.

Barlow: Steve Cummings[23] and his co-workers looked at the endogenous oestrogen levels in women with the very lowest oestrogen levels and the next nearly variable levels. They were seeing differences in bone density. I think it was bone density rather than fracture, but we were seeing differences even at the lowest, to the even lower levels, which would fit the same idea.

Lumsden: We know that there are non-genomic progesterone receptors and I am sure that once we have done the studies, there will be non-genomic oestrogen receptors as well. So I think we always have to keep in mind that although it has not been described, these agents might have effects.

Armitage: In our rush to find safer preparations, we should not prejudge the outcome of clinical studies that we do not have, in terms of the relative risks of different doses or in terms of the efficacy. From the amount of time it has taken to get the information that we have now got, I do not know how easily those questions will be answered.

Professor Purdie, what are your thoughts about anorexic girls, because we have heard recently in the news, in the last week or two, about how much more prevalent this is and how aware we need to be about their bones. We know that their bones are very considerably worse than just from the loss of gonadal steroids and I am also interested in John's comment that COCs seems to protect less than HRT. I have always used HRT in anorexic girls.

Purdie: Anorexic girls are a unique group and a very difficult group to handle. I have used both HRT and COC to deliver oestrogens to these young women and I have been almost invariably depressed by the results obtained. One or two studies from the USA have suggested that androgens might be better, dehydroepiandrosterone (DHEA) has been the subject of one or two trials now and has allegedly shown bone mineral density gains in these women. You also have to be extremely careful not to suggest that whatever you are using might improve appetite, which will lead to almost immediate rejection of the drug by the patient.

References

1.   Rossouw JE, Anderson GL, Prentice RL, LaCroix AZ, Kooperberg C, Stefanick ML, *et al.*; Writing Group for the Women's Health Initiative Investigators. Risks and benefits of estrogen plus progestin in healthy postmenopausal women: principal results fom the Women's Health Initiative randomized controlled trial. *JAMA* 2002;288:321–33

2.   Daly E, Vessey MP, Hawkins MM, Carson JL, Gough P, Marsh S. Risk of venous thromboembolism in users of hormone replacement therapy. *Lancet* 1996;348:977–80.

3.   Perez Gutthann S, Garcia Rodriguez LA, Castellsague J, Duque Oliart A. Hormone replacement therapy and risk of venous thromboembolism: population based case-control study. *BMJ* 1997;314:796–800.

4.   Varas-Lorenzo C, Garcia-Rodriguez LA, Cattaruzzi C, Troncon MG, Agostinis L, Perez-Gutthann S. Hormone replacement therapy and the risk of hospitalization for venous thromboembolism: a population-based study in southern Europe. *Am J Epidemiol* 1998;147:387–90.

5.   Cauley JA, Robbins J, Chen Z, Cummings SR, Jackson RD, LaCroix AZ, *et al.*; Women's Health Initiative Investigators. Effects of estrogen plus progestin on risk of fracture and bone mineral density: the Women's Health Initiative randomized trial. *JAMA* 2003;290:1729–38.

6.   Manson JE, Hsia J, Johnson KC, Rossouw JE, Assaf AR, Lasser NL, *et al.*; Women's Health Initiative Investigators. Estrogen plus progestin and the risk of coronary heart disease. *N Engl J Med* 2003;349:523–34.

7.   Herrington DM, Reboussin DM, Brosnihan KB, Sharp PC, Shumaker SA, Snyder TE, *et al.* Effects of estrogen replacement on the progression of coronary-artery atherosclerosis. *N Engl J Med* 2000;343:522–9.

8.   Scarabin P-Y, Oger E, Plu-Bureau G, on behalf of the Estrogen and ThromboEmbolism Risk (ESTHER) Study Group. Differential association of oral and transdermal oestrogen-replacement therapy with venous thromboembolism risk. *Lancet* 2003;362:428–32.

9.   Greer IA, Walker ID. *Hormone Replacement Therapy and Venous Thromboembolism*. Royal College of Obstetricians and Gynaecologists Guideline No. 19. London: RCOG Press; 2004.

10.   Grodstein F, Stampfer MJ, Goldhaber SZ, Manson JE, Colditz GA, Speizer FE, *et al.* Prospective study of exogenous hormones and risk of pulmonary embolism in women. *Lancet* 1996;348:983–7.

11.   Jick H, Derby LE, Myers MW, Vasilakis C, Newton KM. Risk of hospital admission for idiopathic venous thromboembolism among users of postmenopausal oestrogens. *Lancet* 1996;348:981–3.

12.   Grady D, Wenger NK, Herrington D, Khan S, Furberg C, Hunninghake D, *et al.* Postmenopausal hormone therapy increases risk for venous thromboembolic disease. The Heart and Estrogen/progestin Replacement Study. *Ann Intern Med* 2000;132:689-9-6.

13.   Hulley S, Grady D, Bush T, Furberg C, Herrington D, Riggs B, *et al.* Randomized trial of estrogen plus progestin for secondary prevention of coronary heart disease in postmenopausal women. Heart and Estrogen/progestin Replacement Study (HERS) Research Group. *JAMA* 1998;280:605–13.

14.   Cushman M, Legault C, Barrett-Connor E, Stefanick ML, Kessler C, Judd HL, *et al.* Effect of postmenopausal hormones on inflammation-sensitive proteins: the Postmenopausal Estrogen/Progestin Interventions (PEPI) Study. *Circulation* 1999;100:717–22.

15.   Medical Research Council's General Practice Research Framework. Randomised comparison of oestrogen versus oestrogen plus progestogen hormone replacement therapy in women with hysterectomy. *BMJ* 1996;312:473–8.

16.   Stevenson JC, Oladipo A, Manassiev N, Whitehead MI, Guilford S, Proudler AJ. Randomized trial of effect of transdermal continuous combined hormone replacement therapy on cardiovascular risk markers. *Br J Haematol* 2004;124:802–8.

17.   *Hormone Replacement Therapy and Venous Thromboembolism*. Round Table Series. London: Royal Society of Medicine; 1997.

18.   Mandel FP, Geola FL, Lu JK, Eggena P, Sambhi MP, Hershman JM, *et al.* Biologic effects of various doses of ethinyl estradiol in postmenopausal women. *Obstet Gynecol* 1982;59:673–9.

19.   Elger W, Barth A, Hedden A, Reddersen G, Ritter P, Schneider B, *et al.* Estrogen sulfamates: a new approach to oral estrogen therapy. *Reprod Fertil Dev* 2001;13:297–305.

20.   Wells G, Tugwell P, Shea B, Guyatt G, Peterson J, Zytaruk N, *et al.*; Osteoporosis Methodology Group and The Osteoporosis Research Advisory Group. Meta-analyses of therapies for postmenopausal osteoporosis. V. Meta-analysis of the efficacy of hormone replacement therapy in treating and preventing osteoporosis in postmenopausal women. *Endocr Rev* 2002;23:529–39.

21.   Heshmati HM, Khosla S, Robins SP, O'Fallon WM, Melton LJ 3rd, Riggs BL. Role of low levels of endogenous estrogen in regulation of bone resorption in late postmenopausal women. *J Bone Miner Res* 2002;17:172–8.

22.   Baum M, Budzar AU, Cuzick J, Forbes J, Houghton JH, Klijn JG, *et al.*; ATAC Trialists' Group. Anastrozole alone or in combination with tamoxifen versus tamoxifen alone for adjuvant treatment of postmenopausal women with early breast cancer: first results of the ATAC randomised trial. *Lancet* 2002;359:2131–9. Erratum in: *Lancet* 2002;360:1520.

23.   Stone K, Bauer DC, Black DM, Sklarin P, Ensrud KE, Cummings SR. Hormonal predictors of bone loss in elderly women: a prospective study. The Study of Osteoporotic Fractures Research Group. *J Bone Miner Res* 1998;13:1167–74.

SECTION 3

EFFECTS OF HRT ON CANCER, THE BREAST AND THE BRAIN

Chapter 10

The endometrium, problematic bleeding and endometrial cancer

David Sturdee

Introduction

During the fertile premenopausal years, the endometrium is uniquely endowed with a complex monthly cycle of proliferation, differentiation, breakdown and regeneration. This high cellular turnover, conditioned by ovarian hormones and growth factors, has many opportunities of losing its regulatory controls, such as during the menopausal transition when cycles are frequently irregular and anovulatory. Despite this, significant endometrial disease is uncommon in premenopausal women. After the menopause and in the absence of exogenous hormone stimulation, the endometrium will generally become thin and atrophic, while still retaining the ability to respond to oestrogen and progestogen. Sequential regimens of oestrogen and progestogen hormone replacement therapy (HRT) are intended to mimic the cyclic stimulation of the endometrium and will usually produce a similar response with proliferative and secretory changes.

The ideal HRT will not only provide relief from menopausal symptoms, prevention of osteoporosis and possibly reduction in cardiovascular disease, but will also protect the endometrium from hyperplasia or carcinoma. In postmenopausal women who have not been taking oestrogen therapy, the incidence of endometrial cancer is relatively low at about one per 1000 women per year.[1] One of the recognised risk factors for endometrial cancer is a delayed or late menopause and because HRT effectively prolongs the menopausal age it can be an additional risk factor. So, despite our increasing knowledge of the effect of hormones on the endometrium, endometrial cancer remains a significant risk for postmenopausal women taking HRT.

Unopposed oestrogen

Unopposed oestrogen therapy causes endometrial proliferation initially but a gradually increasing incidence of hyperplasia with prolonged unopposed stimulation. The PEPI trial[2] studied 596 postmenopausal women who were randomised to placebo, unopposed oestrogen, continuous or sequential HRT over 36 months and found that those receiving oestrogen alone – 0.625 mg conjugated equine oestrogen (CEE) – were significantly more likely to develop simple (27.7%), complex (22.7%), or atypical (11.7%) hyperplasia than the placebo group (simple 0.8%, complex 0.8%, atypical 0.7%; $P > 0.001$). More recently, a Cochrane review of all the appropriate studies found that after six months of unopposed oestrogen the odds ratio was 5.4 (95% CI 1.4–20.9) and after 36 months 16.0 (9.3–27.5).[3]

One might expect that lower-dose unopposed oestrogen therapy would be associated with less risk of hyperplasia, and Notelowitz et al.[4] reported a 1.7% rate of hyperplasia in women receiving 0.3 mg unopposed esterified oestrogen for two years, which was similar to that in the control women. However, a further case–control study has found a five-fold higher risk of developing endometrial cancer in women taking 0.3 mg unopposed CEE daily compared with untreated women.[5]

There is no evidence that use of the weaker oestrogen – oestriol – either vaginally or orally will have any less effect on the risk of endometrial hyperplasia.[6]

For over 25 years it has also been recognised that unopposed oestrogen is associated with a significantly increased risk of endometrial cancer, with relative risks ranging from 1.4 to 12.0,[7,8] and that this increases with the duration of unopposed therapy up to a relative risk of 15.0 (Table 10.1).[9] A cohort study in California of 5160 women reported a relative risk of 10 in women who had taken unopposed oestrogen,[10] equivalent to an absolute risk of endometrial cancer of 1 per 100 women per year. In a meta-analysis by Grady et al.,[11] the overall relative risk of endometrial cancer in oestrogen users as compared with nonusers was 2.3 and again with increases associated with duration of use. Furthermore, it is not widely recognised that the risk of endometrial cancer remains increased for many years after stopping unopposed oestrogen therapy.[12] Even after 15 years or more without therapy, there is still a significantly increased relative risk of 5.8 (95% CI 2.0–17).[10] To counteract this risk, progestogen has been added to oestrogen therapy in a sequential regimen for usually 10–14 days in each cycle, with the intention of imitating the normal premenopausal ovarian cycle. This form of HRT should also produce a regular bleed, which for older women in particular is unsatisfactory. Continuous combined regimens have thus been developed that contain oestrogen and progestogen every day ('continuous combined oestrogen-progestogen replacement therapy', CCEPT), and by avoiding a cycle, there is no period-type bleed.

Oestrogen causes endometrial proliferation by increasing the number of oestrogen/progesterone receptors, and also by increasing the mitotic rate in the glandular cells of the endometrium. The administration of progestogen during oestrogen therapy causes a downregulation of the receptors, and induction of 17β-oestradiol dehydrogenase, which converts oestradiol to the less-active oestrone, thereby reducing the oestrogenic stimulus.[13] The histological evidence of a progestogenic effect is a change from a proliferative to a secretory endometrium from which hyperplasia is less likely to develop.

Table 10.1. Endometrial cancer risk with unopposed oestrogens: some case–control studies

Study	Year	Relative risk	
		Ever use	Long-term
Smith et al.[66]	1975	4.5	–
Ziel and Finkle[67]	1975	7.6	13.9
Gray et al.[68]	1977	3.1	11.6
Horwitz and Feinstein[8]	1978	12.0	5.2
Antunes et al.[9]	1979	6.0	15.0
Weiss et al.[1]	1979	7.5	8.2
Shapiro et al.[60]	1980	3.9	6.0
Weiderpass et al.[6]	1999	–	6.2

Endometrial response to sequential oestrogen-progestogen HRT

The addition of progestogen in sequential regimens of HRT reduces the incidence of hyperplasia. In 1985 Varma[14] reported on 398 patients and found that the addition of progestogen for seven days in each cycle did not prevent hyperplasia. Paterson et al.[15] found that after seven days of progestogen in each month the incidence of hyperplasia was reduced to 3–4%, after ten days of progestogen it was 2%, and the maximum protective effect was achieved with 12–13 days of progestogen.[16,17] As a result, there has been some complacency about the protective effect of sequential HRT regimens. However, these early studies were of relatively short duration with biopsies usually being taken after 6–9 months of therapy. More recent studies with longer duration of HRT have raised concern about the protection of the endometrium. In the largest published study of this type,[18] 1192 women who were taking standard sequential regimens of HRT for a mean of 3.29 years (median 2.56 years; 5th to 95th centile: 0.77–8.49 years) had endometrial aspiration biopsies taken by Pipelle® during the progestogen phase of a cycle (Table 10.2). As expected, a large proportion (47.4%) had a secretory endometrium, but complex hyperplasia was found in 5.5% and atypical hyperplasia in 0.7%. There were no significant differences in the prevalence of hyperplasia between regimens containing 10 or 12 days of progestogen in each cycle.[18]

A prospective cohort follow-up study of 23 244 women for a mean of 5.7 years did not, however, show an increase in the risk of endometrial carcinoma associated with sequential oestrogen and progestogen regimens.[19] But a more recent case–control study of women aged 45–74 years found that, among women who were taking sequential HRT regimens with at least ten days of progestogen in each cycle, the relative risk of endometrial cancer was not increased with up to five years' use, but with more than five years' use there was a relative risk of endometrial cancer of 2.5 (95% CI 1.1–5.5).[20]

Malignant potential of endometrial hyperplasia

There is a continuing debate about the implications of endometrial hyperplasia, and the potential for progression to carcinoma. Much of this is due to the many different terminologies that have been used to describe hyperplasia[21] and the poor reproducibility of endometrial diagnoses among pathologists.[22,23] For this reason,

Table 10.2. Endometrial histology during sequential oestrogen-progestogen replacement therapy for a mean of 3.29 years; reproduced with permission from Sturdee et al.[18]

Endometrial histology	Women (n)	Proportion (%)
Unassessable	214	18.0
Inactive/atrophic	90	7.6
Proliferative	180	15.1
Secretory	565	47.4
Menstrual	32	2.7
Pseudodecidual	11	0.9
Complex hyperplasia	65	5.5
Atypical hyperplasia	8	0.7
Carcinoma	0	0.0
Other	27	2.3
Total	1192	–

regulatory authorities require at least two pathologists blinded to treatment in any study of a new HRT regimen.[24,25] In the clinical situation, the finding of endometrial hyperplasia will usually prompt the clinician to take some action such as treatment with progestogen or surgery. There are, therefore, few data on the natural history of untreated hyperplasia. In a prospective study of 51 women with endometrial hyperplasia followed for six months, Terakawa et al.[26] found that in 69% (35/51) of the women the endometrium became normal during the observation period but the findings persisted in 17% (6/35) of those with simple hyperplasia, in 25% (1/4) of those with complex hyperplasia, in 14% (1/7) of those with simple atypical hyperplasia, and in 80% (4/5) of those with complex atypical hyperplasia. In three of the women with simple hyperplasia there was progression to complex atypical hyperplasia at the end of six months. However, although evidence on the long-term outcome is limited, the general consensus is that endometrial hyperplasia without atypia has a low potential for malignant progression, but the presence of cytological atypia increases the risk considerably.[22,23,27]

In addition, there is a low background prevalence of endometrial hyperplasia and carcinoma in postmenopausal women. In a study of 801 asymptomatic peri- and postmenopausal women, Archer et al.[28] found a 5.2% prevalence of hyperplasia, with atypia in 0.6%. There was one case of endometrial adenocarcinoma. A further study of endometrial biopsy specimens from 2964 women before taking HRT found that from 68.7% of the women they were atrophic, 23.5% were proliferative, 0.5% were secretory, 0.6% had hyperplasia, 0.07% had adenocarcinoma, and in 6.6% of the women the biopsies were insufficient for classification.[29] It is from data such as these that clinical management guidelines for HRT suggest that it is not obligatory to perform an endometrial biopsy in every woman prior to starting HRT.

Bleeding during sequential oestrogen-progestogen HRT

Sequential regimens of oestrogen and progestogen are intended to produce a regular and predictable bleed, similar to menstruation, and this is so for at least 77% of postmenopausal women.[30] While most women will accept this as a small price to pay for the benefits of HRT, bleeding remains one of the most common causes for patient dissatisfaction and poor long-term adherence to therapy, particularly if it is irregular, as may happen in about 8% of women on such therapy.[30] Clinicians would also wish that the timing of the bleed during sequential therapy might provide some guide to the state of the endometrium. This had been suggested by Padwick et al.[31] in 1986, who considered that bleeding on or after day 11 from the start of the progestogen phase was indicative of adequate progestogenic effect and endometrial protection. However, that study was based on only 96 women, none of whom presented with endometrial hyperplasia; moreover, it was assumed that hyperplasia develops from a proliferative endometrium and that secretory transformation indicates adequate progestogenic protection of the endometrium. A large UK multicentre study investigated the timing of the bleed in 413 postmenopausal women who had been taking standard sequential regimens of HRT with 10 or 12 days of progestogen per cycle for a mean of 2.7 years.[32] For most women, bleeding started around day 13 after starting progestogen and there was no correlation between endometrial histology and the time of onset of bleeding. In particular, 37 of 65 cases with complex hyperplasia and four of eight with atypia had regular bleeds after day 11. It is therefore quite clear that regular bleeding during sequential HRT is not a helpful guide to the state of the endometrium or the presence of hyperplasia (Figure 10.1). Irregular, breakthrough or too-heavy bleeding is

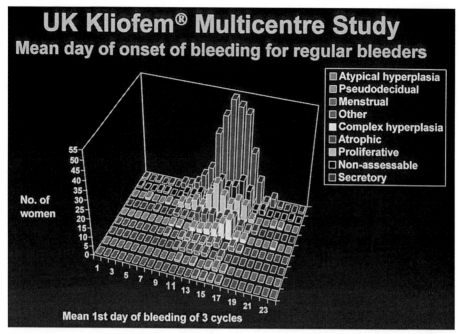

Figure 10.1. Endometrial histology in postmenopausal women taking sequential oestrogen-progestogen and the mean first day of bleeding over three cycles from the start of the progestogen phase; the data are in reverse order from the list in the box with secretory data in the upper file and atypical hyperplasia at the bottom; reproduced with permission from Sturdee[69]

unacceptable for both patient and prescriber if continued beyond the first few months. The amount of bleeding is dose-dependent and often a change of regimen with increased progestogen or a lower dose of oestrogen will resolve the problem.

Long cycle therapy

As monthly sequential therapy results in a cyclical bleed, which is inconvenient in some women and may reduce compliance, attempts have been made to limit the frequency of bleeding by longer sequential cycles ranging from three to six months. However, David *et al.*[33] demonstrated that simple hyperplasia of the endometrium develops after three cycles of unopposed oestrogen (Table 10.3). Ettinger *et al.*[34] have also reported on 214 women using CEE and medroxyprogesterone acetate (MPA) to see whether the progestogen could be given quarterly instead of monthly without increasing the risk of endometrial hyperplasia. Hyperplasia was found in 1.5% of 199 women completing follow-up, which was similar to the 0.9% prevalence found as a baseline risk. The quarterly MPA resulted in longer bleeds (7.7 ± 2.9 versus 5.4 ± 2.0 days) and more reports of heavy bleeds (31.1% versus 8.0%) and unscheduled bleeding (15.5% versus 16.8%). Nevertheless, the women reported a 4:1 preference for the quarterly regimen compared with a monthly sequential regimen.

Table 10.3. Endometrial histology before and after one, two and three cycles of unopposed 17β-oestradiol 2 mg/day for 21 days, and after the fourth cycle consisting of 17β-oestradiol 2 mg/day for 21 days with additional norethisterone acetate (NETA) 1 mg/day for the last 10 days; data from David et al.[33]

	Atrophic	No tissue	Proliferative	Secretory	Simple hyperplasia
Before HRT	44	52	4	0	0
After month 1	71	11	18	0	0
After month 2	13	3	84	0	0
After month 3	4	1	80	0	15
After month 4 + NETA for 10 days	3	16	3	78	0

A randomised prospective controlled trial with a quarterly sequential HRT regimen reported that simple hyperplasia without cytological atypia developed at the end of the oestrogen phase, which was independent of the oestrogen dose, but was converted to an inactive or atrophic endometrium by the addition of gestodene for 12 days.[35] The authors claimed that this combination offered good cycle control but no statistical analysis of the results was offered, and only 30 women were studied.

Thus, three months is generally considered to be the maximum interval for adding the progestogen. However, the Scandinavian Long Cycle Study Group[36] reported a four-year study of 240 early postmenopausal women. They found that the incidence of endometrial pathology (simple, complex or atypical hyperplasia or carcinoma) was significantly higher in the 12-week cycle group ($P = 0.0003$) with an annual incidence of 5.6%, compared with 1% in the monthly cycle group. They further confirmed that long cycle therapy resulted in more irregular bleeding but reported no improved compliance. Another study from Finland found that long cycle HRT was associated with a higher relative risk of endometrial pathology than monthly cycle HRT, with a standardised incidence ratio for the quarterly cycle of 2.0 (95% CI 1.6–2.6), compared with a standardised incidence ratio for the monthly cycle of 1.3 (95% CI 1.1–1.6),[37] giving further support to the previous studies.

All these data indicate that progestogens will reduce the risk of endometrial hyperplasia and carcinoma, but the duration of progestogen in each cycle is important and should be for at least ten days. Furthermore, there may still be a risk with long-term use of monthly sequential HRT and more so with long cycle regimens.

Continuous combined therapy

The biochemical and morphological changes in the endometrium induced by progestogen are maintained as long as progestogen is administered.[38] If this is continuous, the proliferative effect of oestrogen will be prevented, and the endometrium should become atrophic. This was the rationale for the introduction of CCEPT, since without any cycle or a progestogen phase, and with no tissue to be shed, there should not be any bleeding,[39] whereas the benefits should be the same as for sequential therapy.[40]

Bleeding

Although the main aim of CCEPT is to avoid cyclical bleeding, all studies of CCEPT have found a high incidence of bleeds, particularly in the first three months, varying from 50% to 80%.[30,39] This occurs more often in women who are within one year of the menopause, rather than in postmenopausal women, probably as a result of some residual ovarian activity. There is no consensus on when such bleeding should be considered abnormal, but persistent bleeding beyond nine months of CCEPT or starting after a long break without any loss should be investigated for other causes by techniques such as ultrasound, endometrial biopsy and hysteroscopy. An endometrial polyp or submucous fibroid may be found but the majority of women bleed without any obvious underlying pathology.[41] Progestogens are known to cause changes in endometrial vascular morphology and to increase the activity of potent growth factors, such as vascular endothelial growth factor (VEGF). VEGF induces angiogenesis and contributes to vascular permeability and vasodilatation. Disturbances in other cytokines and alterations in endometrial apoptosis may also contribute to changes in vascular fragility and breakthrough bleeding.[42] The mechanism of abnormal bleeding with HRT and especially CCEPT is poorly understood at present, and ironically bleeding is sometimes more common in women taking CCEPT than unopposed oestrogen.

Endometrium

Several studies have confirmed that an atrophic endometrium is achieved with CCEPT in 90–100% of women, even after only three months of treatment, with daily doses of progestogen as low as 0.25 mg norethisterone acetate or 2.5 mg MPA. After one year of treatment with CEE 0.625 mg and MPA 2.5 or 5.0 mg daily, Woodruff and Pickar[43] found endometrial hyperplasia without atypia in less than 1% of women, which is lower than the background rate in postmenopausal women. The Cochrane review[3] reported that endometrial hyperplasia may be less likely with CCEPT than a sequential regimen, in particular with long duration of therapy (OR 0.3; 95% CI 0.1–0.97). Endometrial cancer has also only rarely been reported in women taking CCEPT, and most of these cases had other risk factors.[44-46]

Hill et al.[47] assessed the risk of endometrial cancer in 969 women taking CCEPT. They found a relative risk of 0.6 (95% CI 0.3–1.3), concluding that there was no increased risk for endometrial cancer over the baseline and that there may even be a decreased risk. Archer et al.[48] reported a randomised trial of 625 women using a transdermal CCEPT regimen of oestradiol and norethisterone acetate, which also prevented endometrial hyperplasia. Both of these studies, however, were of relatively short duration (72 and 12 months, respectively), so the long-term effects are not known.

In the PEPI trial,[2] conducted over three years, there were no recorded cases of complex hyperplasia in women on CCEPT, compared with 1.7% of 118 women treated with sequential HRT and 0.8% of women taking a placebo. Another study of CCEPT using oestrone sulphate and MPA over a two-year period also reported no cases of endometrial hyperplasia.[49]

In the UK, a multicentre study[18] of 751 women who had previously been taking sequential HRT and 445 untreated postmenopausal women (total 1196) completed 9 months of CCEPT with oestradiol 2 mg and norethisterone acetate 1 mg daily. There were no cases of endometrial hyperplasia, and the endometrium was atrophic in more than two-thirds of women.[18] Furthermore, all the women with complex hyperplasia during the previous sequential HRT and who completed the study (*n*=42) reverted to normal endometrial patterns (Figure 10.2). Continuation of this study for five years confirmed the protective effect of this CCEPT regimen in 387 women, with over 70% having an atrophic endometrium and the remainder having other normal histology and no hyperplasia or carcinoma.[50] These data indicate the protective effect of the continuous progestogen of CCEPT regimens in not only preventing hyperplasia, but also the correction of pre-existing hyperplasia.

There is further evidence for the protective effect of CCEPT regimens from a population-based case–control study from Sweden.[6] With less than five years' use of CCEPT, the observed risk of developing endometrial carcinoma was 0.8 (95% CI 0.5–1.3) and with more than five years' use it was 0.2 (95% CI 0.1–0.8). This was in marked contrast to the risk with sequential oestrogen-progestogen where the risk after more than five years' use was 2.9 (95% CI 1.8–4.6), (Table 10.4).

The Women's Health Initiative (WHI) report,[51] following the premature termination of the continuous combined arm of this randomised controlled trial, found that after a mean of 5.3 years of CEE 0.625 mg with MPA 2.5 mg daily in 8506 women there were five cases of endometrial cancer (six cases in the placebo group) and there was no change in the risk of endometrial cancer. The hazard ratio was 0.63 (95% CI 0.47–1.47).

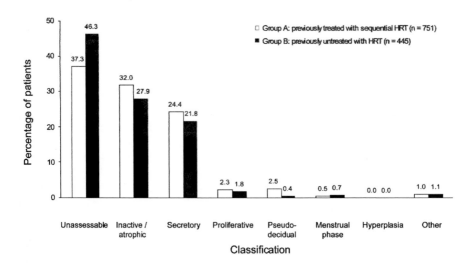

Figure 10.2. Histological results of endometrial biopsies after treatment with CCEPT (oestradiol 2 mg and norethisterone acetate 1 mg daily) for nine months; reproduced with permission from Sturdee *et al.*[18]

Table 10.4. Risk of endometrial cancer with sequential oestrogen-progestogen (E+P) and continuous combined therapy; data from Weiderpass *et al.*[6]

Duration	Odds ratio (95% CI)	
	Sequential E+P	Continuous combined
<5 years	1.5 (1.0–2.2)	0.8 (0.5–1.3)
>5 years	2.9 (1.8–4.6)	0.2 (0.1–0.8)
Per year	1.1 (1.06–1.15)	0.86 (0.77–0.97)

Breast cancer

The Million Women Study (MWS),[52] which reported on the risk of breast cancer in women attending the UK national breast screening service, indicated that the risk was significantly greater with the use of CCEPT compared with oestrogen alone. This finding prompted the following statement in the discussion: 'However, if the additional breast and endometrial cancers associated with each type of HRT are added together, there seems to be little advantage to using oestrogen-progestogen in preference to oestrogen-only HRT for women who still have a uterus.' Rather surprisingly, this suggestion has not received much comment, but if taken up would fly in the face of standard teaching and accepted practice in UK and Europe, especially over the last 35 years. An important difference between the apparent effects of oestrogen on the risks of breast and endometrial cancers is that on cessation of therapy the increased risk of breast cancer disappears after five years, whereas for endometrial cancer the risk remains increased for many years.[12] Clinical practice should not be dictated by the results from one, albeit very large, observational study. The implications and validity of such statements need critical analysis and careful consideration of all available data before influencing prescribing practice.

Tibolone

Tibolone is a synthetic hormone that has similar effects to CCEPT.[53] In the endometrium it is converted to a Δ-4 metabolite, which has no oestrogenic activity, so the endometrium is not stimulated. As with CCEPT, the endometrium is mainly kept in an atrophic state and bleeding is uncommon but there are few long-term data.[54]

Raloxifene

Raloxifene is a selective oestrogen receptor modulator (SERM) that is licensed for the treatment and prevention of osteoporosis. It has anti-oestrogenic effects on both breast and endometrial tissue, and oestrogenic benefits on bone and lipid metabolism. A randomised, double-blind trial of 7705 women over four years compared raloxifene with placebo.[55] This confirmed no endometrial stimulation and suggested that there may be a reduction in the risk of endometrial cancer in those taking raloxifene ($P = 0.23$).

A randomised controlled trial of 136 women compared the effects of raloxifene and CCEPT on the endometrium.[56] Endometrial biopsies from the women taking raloxifene revealed a normal atrophic endometrium in 94.4% and benign stimulatory endometrium in 5.6%, whereas in the women taking CCEPT there was an atrophic endometrium in 78.7%, benign stimulated endometrium in 19.1% and benign abnormal endometrium in 2.1% of biopsy specimens. Overall, there was no endometrial proliferation found with raloxifene.

Intrauterine progestogen

Postmenopausal women who have had a hysterectomy can have unopposed oestrogen replacement therapy as there is no evidence of any benefit from additional progestogen other than to protect the endometrium. It is logical therefore to deliver the progestogen directly into the endometrial cavity, which will give a high local concentration in the endometrium but with lower circulating levels than following systemic administration. An intrauterine system that delivers levonorgestrel (LNG) 20 μg/day has been available for contraception and the treatment of menorrhagia for several years (Mirena®), but many studies have also demonstrated the merits of using this route of progestogen delivery for CCEPT. Since 1991, 16 studies of intrauterine LNG in combination with different types and routes of oestrogen in 809 women have all reported no cases of endometrial hyperplasia.[57] A smaller experimental intrauterine system that delivers 10 μg/day compared with 20 μg/day with the Mirena® and is more suitable for the postmenopausal woman has also been shown to be acceptable[58] and to protect the endometrium (Figure 10.3).[59]

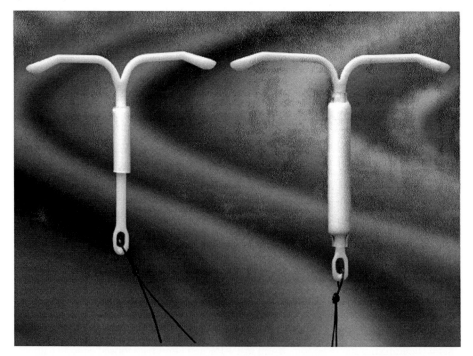

Figure 10.3. The levonorgestrel-releasing Mirena® intrauterine system (right) and the smaller experimental menopausal levonorgestrel system (MLS) (left); photograph courtesy of Prof. F Riphagen of Leiras, Turku, Finland

HRT in women who have had endometrial cancer

Some observational studies have suggested that endometrial cancers associated with HRT are less aggressive and have a better prognosis,[6,60] but there are no data to indicate a difference in histological findings. Conversely, in a population case–control study, Shapiro et al.[61] found that the tumours were more aggressive and more likely to have invaded the myometrium.

As with breast cancer, a history of endometrial cancer is usually considered to be a relative contraindication for HRT. However, there have been several retrospective studies of women who had mainly had stage I endometrial cancer and no increase in subsequent disease was found in those receiving oestrogen compared with the controls.[62-64] But these studies are likely to have an element of selection bias. In a more recent retrospective case–control study by Suriano et al.,[65] 139 women from a cohort of 249 endometrial cancer patients received oestrogen therapy after their primary cancer treatment. After 70 months there was only a 2.7% recurrence rate and a longer disease-free interval in the matched HRT group compared with a 14.7% recurrence rate in the matched control group. So, although the evidence is rather light, oestrogen does not appear to increase the rate of recurrence in women that have a history of endometrial cancer.

Conclusions

- Unopposed oestrogen therapy is associated with a significantly increased risk of developing endometrial hyperplasia and, with continued use, of carcinoma. This risk remains for many years after cessation of therapy.
- The addition of progestogen will reduce the risk of endometrial disease, but regimens should include at least ten days in each monthly cycle. After five years there is probably less protection of the endometrium. Postmenopausal women who have been taking sequential oestrogen/progestogen therapy for more than five years are at increased risk of endometrial carcinoma, and should be advised to change to a CCEPT regimen.
- During sequential oestrogen-progestogen therapy, the timing of the bleed does not give any guide to the state of the endometrium or the possible presence of hyperplasia.
- Long cycle regimens with a progestogen at less than monthly intervals may not provide adequate endometrial protection.
- For women taking long-term HRT a continuous combined oestrogen and progestogen regimen (CCEPT) should be recommended for endometrial safety.
- Selective oestrogen receptor modulator (SERM) therapy such as raloxifene may provide a suitable alternative to long-term HRT, though long-term safety data are needed.
- Intrauterine delivery of progestogen causes fewer progestogenic effects outside the uterine cavity than systemic therapy, while providing long-term protection of the endometrium.

References

1.   Weiss NS, Szekely DR, English DR, Schweid AI. Endometrial cancer in relation to patterns of menopausal estrogen use. *JAMA* 1979;242:261–4.
2.   The Writing Group for the PEPI Trial. Effects of hormone replacement therapy on endometrial

histology in postmenopausal women. The Postmenopausal Estrogen/Progestin Interventions (PEPI) Trial. *JAMA* 1996 7;275:370–5.

3.   Lethaby A, Farquhar C, Sarkis A, Roberts H, Jepson R, Barlow D. Hormone replacement therapy in postmenopausal women: endometrial hyperplasia and irregular bleeding. *Cochrane Database Syst Rev* 2000;(2):CD000402.

4.   Notelowitz M, Varner RE, Rebar RW. Minimal endometrial proliferation over a two-year period in taking 0.3mg of unopposed esterified estrogens. *Menopause* 1997;4:80–8.

5.   Cushing KL, Weiss NS, Voigt LF, McKnight B, Beresford SA. Risk of endometrial cancer in relation to use of low-dose unopposed estrogens. *Obstet Gynecol* 1998;91:35–9.

6.   Weiderpass E, Adami HO, Baron JA, Magnusson C, Bergstrom R, Lindgren A, et al. Risk of endometrial cancer following estrogen replacement with and without progestins. *J Natl Cancer Inst* 1999;91:1131–7.

7.   Henderson BE, Casagrande JT, Pike MC, Mack T, Rosario I, Duke A. The epidemiology of endometrial cancer in young women. *Br J Cancer* 1983;47:749–56.

8.   Horwitz RJ, Feinstein AR. Alternative analytic methods for case–control studies of estrogens and endometrial cancer. *N Engl J Med* 1978;299:1089–94.

9.   Antunes CMF, Stolley PD, Rosenstein MB. Endometrial cancer and estrogen use. Report of a large case control study. *N Engl J Med* 1979;300:9–13.

10.   Paganini-Hill, Ross RK, Henderson BE. Endometrial cancer and patterns of use of oestrogen replacement therapy: a cohort study. *Br J Cancer* 1989;59:445–7.

11.   Grady D, Gebretsadik T, Kerlikowske K, Ernster V, Petitti D. Hormone replacement therapy and endometrial cancer risk: a meta-analysis. *Obstet Gynecol* 1995;85:304–13.

12.   Green PK, Weiss NS, McKnight B, Voigt LF, Beresford SA. Risk of endometrial cancer following cessation of menopausal hormone use (Washington, United States). *Cancer Causes Control* 1996;7:575–80.

13.   Casper RF. Regulation of estrogen/progestogen receptors in the endometrium. *Int J Fertil Menopausal Stud* 1996;41:16–21.

14.   Varma TR. Effect of long-term therapy with estrogen and progesterone on the endometrium of post-menopausal women. *Acta Obstet Gynecol Scand* 1985;64:40–6.

15.   Paterson MEL, Wade-Evans T, Sturdee DW, Thom MH, Studd JWW. Endometrial disease after treatment with oestrogens and progestogens in the climacteric. *BMJ* 1980;280:822–4.

16.   Whitehead MI, McQueen J, Beard RJ, Minardi J, Campbell S. The effects of cyclical oestrogen therapy and sequential oestrogen therapy on the endometrium of post-menopausal women. *Acta Obstet Gynecol Scand* 1977;65:91–101.

17.   Sturdee DW, Wade-Evans T. Paterson MEL, Thom MH, Studd JWW. Relations between bleeding pattern, endometrial histology and oestrogen treatment in postmenopausal women. *BMJ* 1978;I:1575–7.

18.   Sturdee DW, Ulrich LG, Barlow DH, Wells M, Campbell MJ, Vessey MP, et al. The endometrial response to sequential and continuous combined oestrogen-progestogen replacement therapy. *BJOG* 2000;107:1392–400.

19.   Persson I, Adami HO, Bergkvist L, Lindgren A, Pettersson B, Hoover R, et al. Risk of endometrial cancer after treatment with oestrogens alone or in conjunction with progestogens: results of a prospective study. *BMJ* 1989;298:147–51.

20.   Beresford JAA, Weiss NS, Voigt LF, McKnight B. Risk of endometrial cancer in relation to use of oestrogen combined with cyclic progestogen therapy in post-menopausal women. *Lancet* 1997;349:458–61.

21.   Bergeron C, Nogales FF, Masseroli M, Abeler V, Duvillard P, Muller-Holzner E, et al. A multicentric European study testing the reproducibility of the WHO classification of endometrial hyperplasia with a proposal of a simplified working classification for biopsy and curettage specimens. *Am J Surg Pathol* 1999;23:1102–8.

22.   Bergeron C. Problems of endometrial histology interpretation. *Climacteric* 2000;3:288–93.

23.   Wells M. The endometrium and hormone replacement therapy: risk of oestrogen and endometrial cancer. In: O'Brien PMS, MacLean AB, editors. *Hormones and Cancer*. London: RCOG Press; 1999. p. 153–63.

24.   Committee for Proprietary Medicinal Products. *Points to Consider on Hormone Replacement Therapy*. London: CPMP; 13 November 1997.

25.   Food and Drug Administration HRT Working Group. *Guidance for Clinical Evaluation of Combination Estrogen-Progestin-Containing Drug Products Used for Hormone Replacement Therapy of Postmenopausal Women*. Washington, DC: FDA; 1995.

26.   Terakawa N, Kigawa J, Taketani Y, Yoskikawa H, Yajima A, Noda K, et al. The behaviour of endometrial hyperplasia: a prospective study. *J Obstet Gynaecol Res* 1997;28:223–30.

27.   Kurman RJ. The behaviour of endometrial hyperplasia. A long term study of 'untreated' hyperplasia in 170 patients. *Cancer* 1985;56:403–12.

28.   Archer DF, McIntyre-Seltman K, Wilborn WW Jr, Dowling EA, Cone F, Creasy GW, *et al.* Endometrial morphology in asymptomatic postmenopausal women. *Am J Obstet Gynecol* 1991;165:317–22.
29.   Korhonen MO, Symons JP, Hyde BM, Rowan JP, Wilborn WH. Histologic classification and pathologic findings for endometrial biopsy specimens obtained from 2964 perimenopausal and postmenopausal women undergoing screening for continuous hormones as replacement therapy (CHART 2 Study). *Am J Obstet Gynecol* 1997;176:377–80.
30.   Archer DF, Pickar JH, Bottiglioni F. Bleeding patterns in postmenopausal women taking continuous combined or sequential regimens of conjugated estrogens with medroxyprogesterone acetate. *Obstet Gynecol* 1994;83:686–92.
31.   Padwick ML, Pryse-Davies J, Whitehead MI. A simple method for determining the optimal dosage of progestin in postmenopausal women receiving estrogens. *N Engl J Med* 1986;315:930–4.
32.   Sturdee DW, Barlow DH, Ulrich LG, Wells M, Campbell MJ, Vessey MP, *et al.* Is the timing of withdrawal bleeding a guide to endometrial safety during sequential oestrogen-progestogen replacement therapy? *Lancet* 1994;344:979–82.
33.   David A, Czernobilsky B, Weisglass L. Long cyclic hormonal cycle therapy in postmenopausal women. In: Berg G, Hammar M, editors. *The Modern Management of the Menopause. Proceedings of the VII International Congress on the Menopause.* London: Parthenon Publishing; 1994. p. 463–70.
34.   Ettinger B, Selby J, Citron JT, Vangessel A. Cyclic HRT using quarterly progestin. *Obstet Gynecol* 1994;83:693–700.
35.   Boerrigter PJ, van de Weijer PHM, Baak JPA, Fox H, Haspels AA, Kenemans P, *et al.* Endometrial response in estrogen replacement therapy quarterly combined with a progestogen. *Maturitas* 1996;24:63–71.
36.   Bjarnason K, Cerin A, Lindgren R, Weber T. The Scandinavian Long Cycle Study Group. Adverse endometrial effects during long cycle hormone replacement therapy. *Maturitas* 1999;32:161–70.
37.   Pukkala E, Tulenheimo-Silfvast A, Leminem A. Incidence of cancer among women using long versus monthly cycle HRT, Finland 1994–1997. *Cancer Causes Control* 2001;12:111–15.
38.   Whitehead MI, Townsend PT, Pryse-Davies J, Ryder TA, King RJ. Effects of estrogens and progestins on the biochemistry and morphology of the postmenopausal endometrium. *N Engl J Med* 1981;305:1599–605.
39.   Mattsson L-A, Cullberg G, Samsioe G. Evaluation of a continuous combined oestrogen/progestogen regimen for climacteric complaints. *Maturitas* 1982;4:95–102.
40.   Hillard, TC. Period-free HRT. In: Sturdee DW, Olah K, Keane D, editors. *The Yearbook of Obstetrics and Gynaecology.* London: RCOG Press; 2001. p. 98–118.
41.   Nagele F, O'Connor H, Baskett TF, Davies A, Mohammed H, Magos AL. Hysteroscopy in women with abnormal uterine bleeding on hormone replacement therapy: a comparison with postmenopausal bleeding. *Fertil Steril* 1996;65:1145–50.
42.   Hickey M, Higham JM, Fraser IS. Hormone replacement therapy and irregular bleeding. *Climacteric* 2001;4:95–102.
43.   Woodruff JD, Pickar JH. Incidence of endometrial hyperplasia in postmenopausal women taking conjugated estrogens (Premarin) with medroxyprogesterone acetate or conjugated estrogens alone. The Menopause Study Group. *Am J Obstet Gynecol* 1994;170:1213–23.
44.   Leather AT, Savvas M, Studd JWW. Endometrial histology and bleeding patterns after 8 years of continuous combined oestrogen and progestogen therapy in post-menopausal women. *Obstet Gynecol* 1991;78:1008–10.
45.   McGonigle KF. Development of endometrial cancer in women on oestrogen and progestin hormone replacement therapy. *Gynecol Oncol* 1994;55:126–32.
46.   Comerci JT, Fields AL, Runowicz CD, Goldberg GL. Continuous low dose combined hormone replacement therapy and the risk of endometrial cancer. *Gynecol Oncol* 1997;64:425–30.
47.   Hill DA, Weiss NS, Beresford SA, Voigt LF, Daling JR, Stanford JL, *et al.* Continuous combined hormone replacement therapy and risk of endometrial cancer. *Am J Obstet Gynecol* 2000;183:1456–61.
48.   Archer DF, Furst K, Tipping D, Dain MP, Vandepol C. A randomized comparison of continuous combined transdermal delivery of estradiol-norethindrone acetate and estradiol alone for menopause. CombiPatch Study Group. *Obstet Gynecol* 1999;94:498–503.
49.   Nand SL, Webster MA, Baber R, O'Connor V. Bleeding pattern and endometrial changes during continuous combined hormone replacement therapy. The Ogen/Provera Study Group. *Obstet Gynecol* 1998;91:678–84.
50.   Wells M, Ulrich LG, Sturdee DW, Barlow DH, Ulrich LG, O'Brien K, *et al.* Effect on endometrium of long term treatment with continuous combined oestrogen-progestogen replacement therapy: follow up study. *BMJ* 2002;325:239–42.

51. Rossouw JE, Anderson GL, Prentice RL, LaCroix AZ, Kooperberg C, Stefanick ML, *et al.*; Writing Group for the Women's Health Initiative Investigators. Risks and benefits of estrogen plus progestin in healthy postmenopausal women: principal results fom the Women's Health Initiative randomized controlled trial. *JAMA* 2002;288:321–33.

52. Beral V; Million Women Study Collaborators. Breast cancer and hormone-replacement therapy in the Million Women Study. *Lancet* 2003;362:419–27. Erratum in: *Lancet* 2003;362:1160.

53. Moore RA. Livial: a review of clinical studies. *Br J Obstet Gynaecol* 1999;106:1–21.

54. Bruce D, Robinson J, Rymer J. Long-term effects of tibolone on the endometrium.as assessed by bleeding episodes, transvaginal scan and endometrial biopsy. *Climacteric* 2004;7:261–6.

55. Delmas PD, Bjarnason NH, Mitlak J, Ravoux AC, Shah AS, Huster WJ, *et al.* Effects of raloxifene on bone mineral density, serum cholesterol concentrations, and uterine endometrium in postmenopausal women. *N Engl J Med* 1997;337:1641–7.

56. Fugere P, Scheele WH, Shah A, Strack TR, Glant MD, Jolly E. Uterine effects of raloxifene in comparison with continuous-combined HRT in post-menopausal women. *Am J Obstet Gynecol* 2000;182:568–74.

57. Riphagen FE. Intrauterine application of progestins in hormone replacement therapy. *Climacteric* 2000;3:199–211.

58. Sturdee DW, Rantala ML, Colau JC, Zahradnik H-P, Riphagen FE. The acceptability of a small intrauterine progestogen-releasing system for continuous combined hormone therapy in early postmenopausal women. *Climacteric* (in press).

59. Raudaskoski T, Tapanainen J, Tomas E, Luotola H, Pekonen F, Ronni-Sivula H, *et al.* Intrauterine 10 microg and 20 microg levonorgestrel systems in postmenopausal women receiving oral oestrogen replacement therapy: clinical, endometrial and metabolic response. *BJOG* 2002;109:136–44.

60. Nyholm HC, Nielson AL, Norup P. Endometrial cancer in postmenopausal women with and without previous estrogen replacement treatment: comparison of clinical and histological characteristics. *Gynecol Oncol* 1993;49:229–35.

61. Shapiro S, Kaufman DW, Slone D, Rosenberg L, Miettinen OS, Stolley PD, *et al.* Recent and past use of conjugated estrogens in relation to adenocarcinoma of the endometrium. *N Engl J Med* 1980;303:485–9.

62. Creasman WT, Henderson D, Hinshaw W, Clarke-Pearson DL. Estrogen replacement therapy in the patient treated for endometrial cancer. *Obstet Gynecol* 1986;67:326–30.

63. Lee RB, Burke TW, Park RC. Estrogen replacement therapy following treatment for stage I endometrial carcinoma. *Gynecol Oncol* 1990;36:189–91.

64. Chapman JA, DiSaia PJ, Osann K, Roth PD, Gillotte DL, Berman ML. Estrogen replacement in surgical stage I and II endometrial cancer survivors. *Am J Obstet Gynecol* 1996;175:1195–200.

65. Suriano KA, McHale M, McLaren CE, Li KT, Re A, DiSaia PJ. Estrogen replacement therapy in endometrial cancer patients: a matched control study. *Obstet Gynecol* 2001;97:555–60.

66. Smith DC, Prentice R, Thompson D, Herman W. Association of exogenous estrogens and endometrial carcinoma. *N Engl J Med* 1975;293:1164–7.

67. Ziel H, Finkle W. Increased risk of endometrial carcinoma among users of conjugated estrogens. *N Engl J Med* 1975;293:1167–70.

68. Gray LA Sr, Christopherson WM, Hoover RN. Estrogens and endometrial carcinoma. *Obstet Gynecol* 1977;49:385–9.

69. Sturdee DW. HRT, the endometrium and bleeding. In: Barlow,DH, Sturdee DW, Miles A, editors. *The Effective Management of the Menopause. UK Key Advances in Clinical Practice*. London: Aesculapius Medical Press; 2002. p. 49–59.

Chapter 11

Steroid hormones and the breast

William Miller

Summary

There is considerable evidence that steroid hormones influence not only developmental processes in normal breast but also the natural history of breast cancer. Although these data come from a variety of disciplines (including physiology, epidemiology, molecular biology, pathology and endocrinology) and implicate oestrogens and progestogens, the specific hormone involvements in particular processes still remain to be clearly defined. This is especially so when considering the development of breast cancer in postmenopausal women and the influence of hormone replacement therapy (HRT). The variation in sensitivity, morphology and activity of individual breasts is large and the endocrinology of the postmenopausal breast is unusual in that levels and profiles of steroid hormones do not simply reflect those in the blood. This, together with the difficulty in accessing normal breast tissue, means there is an immediate urgency to develop appropriate experimental models of normal breast and identify surrogate markers by which to monitor tissue activity and hormonal influences.

Introduction

Steroid hormones are involved in breast development and are heavily implicated in the natural history of breast cancer.[1] This chapter will review the evidence for this. It will become obvious, however, that the influence of specific hormones on particular processes still remains to be clarified. This is especially true for processes occurring within the breast at the menopause (and the effect of HRT on these). Although central roles have been assigned to oestrogen and progestogens, data are far from consistent. In order to come to realistic conclusions, it is necessary to compensate for confounding factors and to restrict analyses to observations that are relevant.

The limitation of experimental model systems must be recognised. The mammary glands of many experimental animals may differ from the breast in terms of structure, developmental stages and sensitivity to mutagens and hormonal environment. Similarly, cell lines and xenografts may be artificial with regard to the environment in which they have been selected and maintained; sensitivity may be more dependent upon acquired characteristics and selection pressures associated with culture and xenografting than the inherent properties of epithelial cells growing *in situ* within the breast. Many studies have also employed inappropriate concentrations and delivery systems of hormones. The present review will therefore focus upon physiological measurements and epidemiological, histological, molecular and endocrinological assessments made in biopsied breast material obtained from women with and without cancer. While it is acknowledged that the latter material is often difficult to acquire and might be associated with biases, the observations are more likely to have relevance to normal and malignant processes within the breast.

Hormones and the development of the normal breast

Until puberty, the breast is relatively rudimentary and quiescent. At this time, under the stimulus of ovarian hormones, discs of stroma connective tissue develop and, within these, ducts enlarge, lengthen and branch. Simultaneously, lobular buds appear. Mature lobular alveolar units (terminal duct lobular units, or TDLUs) are the functional elements of the adult breast (Figure 11.1) and thousands may exist in each breast – even then, this epithelial component only represents a small proportion of total breast volume and the breast is largely composed of supporting fibrous tissue and fat. Although major development occurs at puberty and ovarian hormones must be implicated, the roles of individual hormones are not defined and a synergy between a multiplicity of factors probably exists. This is most graphically illustrated in women with gonadal dysgenesis and gonadotrophin deficiency in whom there is complete failure of breast development; oestrogen replacement therapy induces breast development but only in cases with an intact hypothalamic–pituitary axis.[2] The sequence of events occurring at puberty also suggests a cooperation between oestrogen

(a)   (b)

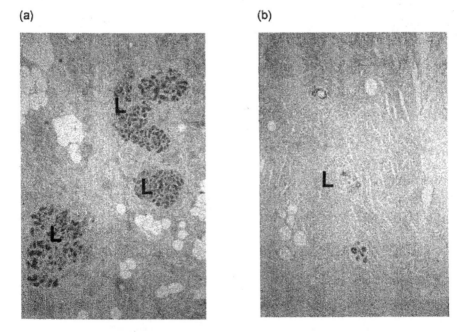

Figure 11.1. (a) A group of normal resting lobules (L) in the breast of a premenopausal woman; (b) a postmenopausal involuted lobule (L) in fibrous tissue and fat

and progesterone. Thus TDLUs do not appear until the onset of ovulatory cycles in which progesterone is secreted from a functioning corpus luteum,[3] and complete functional development of the breast does not occur until pregnancy when full secretory status and lobular differentiation occur with milk production. These changes coincide with the trophic stimulus of hormones derived from the fetal placental unit, which secretes not only steroid but also polypeptide hormones. Again, while general endocrine involvement is evident, knowledge of definitive roles for specific hormones in particular processes is often lacking.

Major changes also occur in the breast at the menopause (Figure 11.1). They are involutionary in nature and will be discussed in more detail below. Although less dramatic in degree, changes also occur in the breast during the menstrual cycle of premenopausal women and peripheral synthesis of hormones may have focal effects in the postmenopausal period (see below). The cyclic variation in proliferation and apoptosis that can be observed during the menstrual cycle is informative.[4-6] Thus, proliferative activity of luminal epithelial cells is higher in the luteal phase of the cycle (the peak of apoptosis follows that of proliferation by about three days).[4,5] This coincides with high circulating levels of oestrogen and progesterone. However, the large variation in proliferation scores between individual breasts irrespective of stage of the menstrual cycle should be noted (Figure 11.2). This suggests that there are other factors that are equally influential in determining the level of proliferation within the breast. These agents have yet to be defined although associations with growth factor and second messenger systems have been uncovered.[7]

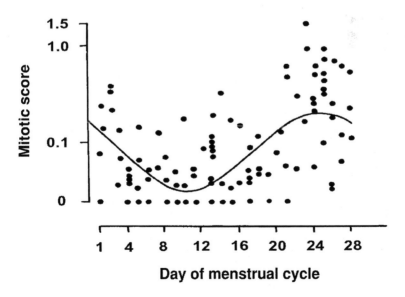

Figure 11.2. The mitotic score in TDLUs plotted against the day of the menstrual cycle of premenopausal women; data derived from Anderson *et al.*[4]

Hormones and risk of breast cancer

The aetiology of breast cancer has a strong hormonal component.[1] The disease is 100-fold more frequent in females than males and in women does not occur before puberty. Increased risk is associated with early menarche and late menopause; conversely, early menopause and pregnancy are protective. Furthermore the influence of other factors such as obesity and international distribution of breast cancer is more marked after the menopause. The effect of menopause itself on risk is particularly impressive and informative. Thus, surgical menopause is associated with a 40% reduction in risk and oophorectomy before the age of 35 years decreases risk to one-third of that in women with a natural menopause.[8] These observations suggest, firstly, that ovarian activity has a role in the majority of breast cancers occurring in women undergoing a natural menopause and, secondly, that since the breasts of women at 35 years have already been under the influence of over one-half of menstrual cycles during their lifetime, it is not simply exposure to ovarian hormones that causes cancer.

The above studies also do not pinpoint the hormones that modulate increased risk but it is natural to suspect oestrogens and progestogens as the major ovarian hormones. Further evidence for this comes from epidemiological investigations in which either oestrogen or progestogens alone or in combination have been given to women. Such studies include:

- administration during pregnancy[9]
- oral contraceptive steroids in premenopausal women[10,11]
- hormone replacement therapy (HRT) at and after the menopause.[12-17]

The consensus is now that in each of these situations risk is increased although individual reports may be negative and the effects may be relatively small. Data on HRT are presented in detail elsewhere in this volume. However, the results from meta-analyses[12,16] and individual large studies[13,15,17] indicate that current use of HRT is associated with significantly increased risk of breast cancer and the effects are substantially greater for oestrogen-progestogen combinations than for oestrogen alone and other types of HRT.

Hormones and carcinogenesis

Carcinogenesis is classically thought to be a two-stage process involving

1. initiation, in which mutational events occur
2. promotion, during which pools of susceptible cells are enlarged and/or the growth of transformed cells is selectively encouraged to realise overt invasive tumours.

Steroid hormones could potentially act both in the initiation and promotion of breast cancer (Figure 11.3). For example, it is generally accepted that agents that increase the rate of cell proliferation not only raise the likelihood of genetic mistakes,[18] but may also propagate them by replication of transformed cells, i.e. promote tumours. For this reason, evidence of proliferative potential within the breast has been sought. While the case for oestrogen's enhancing the rate of cell proliferation in glandular tissue within the breast is relatively convincing[19-21] (the main debate surrounds whether oestrogen directly stimulates oestrogen receptor-positive cells or indirectly affects receptor-negative cells via a paracrine mechanism[22]), that for progestogens is still controversial.

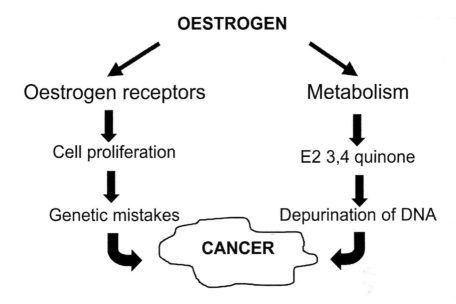

Figure 11.3. Mechanisms whereby oestrogen may act as a promoter (mediated through hormone receptors and cell proliferation) or as an initiator (mediated through metabolism and depurination of DNA) of breast cancer

The controversy is not helped by a wide range of *in vitro* and *in vivo* studies that have used a spectrum of experimental systems and differing concentrations and types of progestogen. With regard to the latter, not all 'progestogens' have the same structure and this may lead to functional differences. Synthetic progestogens may be divided into two major classes: 17α-acetoxyprogestogens and nor-testosterone derivatives. Whereas agents such as medroxyprogesterone acetate may possess glucocorticoid as well as progestational activity, nor-testosterone compounds may have androgenic, antiandrogenic and oestrogenic effects depending on the test system.[23,24]

The case for steroid hormones having direct genotoxic effect has received less attention. However, catechol metabolites of oestrogen are known to form adducts with DNA as well as generating free radicals.[25] As a result depurination and point mutation of DNA can occur, processes that can lead to cancer.

Finally, the breast is an organ that is subject to major involution and periods of quiescence, processes that can determine the pool size of cells susceptible to carcinogenesis.[26] It is thus essential to define the role of steroid hormones both as anti-involutionary agents and as cell-cycle mediators.

Normal breast, the menopause and HRT

Breast involution occurs at the menopause. This involves a decrease in glandular epithelium with a concomitant increase in the proportion of fat and connective tissue.[27,28] However, involution is not uniform and one part of the breast may lose all its lobules whereas another may retain focal lobular patterns. Persistent lobules in postmenopausal breasts appear more frequently in mastectomy specimens (for breast cancer) than in breasts examined at routine autopsy.[29] It has therefore been suggested that the presence of lobular alveolar units in postmenopausal breasts may be associated with increased risk of breast cancer.

If involution is associated with cessation of ovarian function at the menopause, it may be expected that HRT might delay these changes. While early studies were inconclusive and based on administration of oestrogens,[30] larger and more definitive studies comparing different types of HRT have now been published.[31,32] The most informative was a histological comparison of excisional biopsies performed because of mammographic abnormalities in postmenopausal women receiving either oestrogen alone, oestrogen plus progestogen or no HRT.[32] Breast epithelial density as assessed by digital tracing was significantly greater in the oestrogen and combined hormone groups compared with no HRT. Density of the combined HRT group was significantly higher than oestrogen alone and the lobular morphology of breasts exposed to combined HRT was similar to that observed during the luteal phase in premenopausal women. Additionally, proliferation scores in TDLUs in the breasts of women receiving HRT were significantly higher than in those of women not taking HRT (Figure 11.4). The increase was significantly greater in the oestrogen plus progestogen group than the oestrogen alone, such that proliferation rates in the combined group were similar to those in breasts from the luteal phase of premenopausal women. These effects of HRT reflect those seen in macaque monkeys given oestrogen and progestogen[33] and parallel the increased risk of breast cancer in women given HRT as reported in recent studies.[13-15,17] However, not all studies on surgical material from postmenopausal women given HRT have reported positive results. For example, Hargreaves et al.[31] examined a large number of subjects and found no evidence for increased cell proliferation in epithelial elements from breasts of postmenopausal women taking HRT (either oestrogen with or without progestogens) over cases not exposed to HRT. All

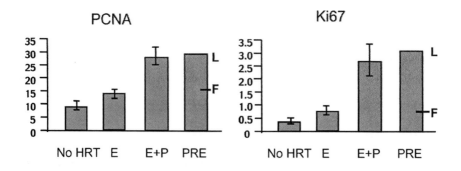

Figure 11.4. Proliferation scores in the TDLUs of premenopausal (PRE) women (F = follicular phase, L = luteal phase) and postmenopausal women either on no HRT or HRT with oestrogen only (E) or combined oestrogen and progestogen (E+P); values are means ± SD; data derived from Hofseth et al.[32]

samples had significantly lower scores than those in breasts from premenopausal women. Possible reasons for differences between the studies include:

- length of time on HRT – the Hargreaves cohort took HRT for a maximum of 5.5 years, whereas the women in the positive US investigation took HRT for as long as 20 years (there also being evidence for increased proliferation with longer time on oestrogen plus progestogen HRT[32])
- type of progestogen used – all women in the US study received MPA whereas 90% of the women in the Hargreaves study used nor-testosterone derivatives (although the recent Million Women Study on HRT found increased risk for breast cancer irrespective of the progestogen type in the combined group).[17]

The endocrinology of the postmenopausal breast

Because of the hormonal aetiology of breast cancer, considerable efforts have been expended in attempting to demonstrate that circulating hormones are associated with risk of the disease. These have generated conflicting data and it is only with the advent of meta-analyses[34] and large prospective studies[34-38] that it has been possible to present convincing evidence that high levels of oestrogens (and androgens) relate to increased risk of breast cancer. However, while these data may be used to identify groups of differing risk, they do not pinpoint with certainty individuals who will subsequently develop cancer. This is because:

- the hormone levels of cases and controls invariably fall within 'normal' reference ranges
- the majority of those who have high levels do not go on to develop cancer, and cases still occur within groups with low values.

It is clear that other factors influence susceptibility. Among these is the observation that hormone levels and profiles within the postmenopausal breast are distinctive and not necessarily reflective of those in the circulation. This is true for both malignant and non-malignant components of the breast and for several classes of steroid hormones.[39-41]

The evidence that oestrogens accumulate in breast cancers, normal epithelial elements and mammary adipose tissue in concentrations markedly in excess of those in the circulation is particularly impressive.[40] It is clear that these tissues have the ability both to concentrate oestrogens against a gradient[42,43] and to synthesise the hormones locally.[44-46] *In vivo* infusion studies have shown that the potential for uptake varies greatly between individuals, as does the relative contribution of uptake and synthesis to endogenous tissue levels (Figure 11.5).[47-49] It is important to take these local tissue factors into account when considering the effects of exogenously administered hormones such as in HRT.

Prevention of breast cancer by hormone deprivation

Surgical ablation of the ovaries, particularly early in reproductive life, markedly reduces the subsequent incidence of breast cancer. Furthermore, endocrine therapies that have in common the ability to reduce oestrogen signalling have a major role in treatment of women with established breast cancer.[50] Because of this, there are good

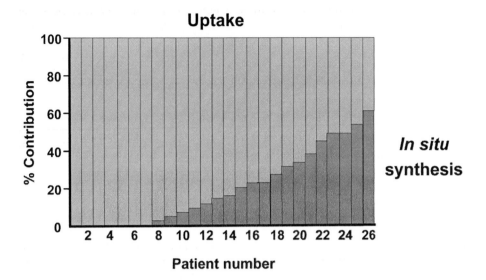

Figure 11.5. The relative contribution of uptake from the circulation and *in situ* synthesis to endogenous oestrogens in non-malignant breast tissue in postmenopausal women; data derived from Larionov *et al.*[43]

reasons to use such endocrine treatment as a preventive measure against breast cancer. Selective oestrogen receptor modulators (SERMs) such as tamoxifen and raloxifene are already showing promise in this setting.[51–53] For example, a meta-analysis published in 2003 has shown that tamoxifen in high-risk women significantly reduced incidence of breast cancer, with the hazard ratio for those taking the drug being 0.62.[54] Prevention trials are now being planned for aromatase inhibitors,[55] as there are clinical and theoretical reasons to believe that this class of drugs may be particularly effective in this setting. Thus, results from the ATAC trial[56] in which large numbers of women with early breast cancer were given either tamoxifen or the aromatase inhibitor anastrozole show substantially fewer contra-lateral breast cancers in the anastrozole arm compared with the tamoxifen group (20 versus 35 at 47 months' follow-up). This may either be because aromatase inhibitors are inherently more potent than tamoxifen or that the drugs have different mechanisms of action. Thus, tamoxifen does not reduce endogenous oestrogens whereas aromatase inhibitors do. If oestrogens are genotoxic, only aromatase inhibitors would reduce the incidence of tumours induced through this mechanism.

Conclusions

There is compelling evidence that steroid hormones play a central role in the development of normal breast and the natural history of many breast cancers. Since the female breast only develops at puberty and major involution occurs at the menopause, ovarian hormones are involved. Among these hormones, oestrogen and progesterone seem to be particularly important. However, the exact mechanisms by which individual processes are influenced still remain to be determined. Additionally, it is clear that steroid hormones interact with other factors controlling proliferation and involution of functional units within the breast (TDLUs). These factors also require to be identified and characterised if pathological abnormalities are to be avoided. This is especially true of events occurring at the menopause. While in most postmenopausal women TDLUs disappear, in others residual units exist. The reason for their preservation and the factors influencing proliferative activity within the unit are largely unknown. It is a reasonable hypothesis that local uptake/synthesis of hormones or administered hormones such as in HRT are responsible. While evidence for this may be deduced from well-designed studies, there are many discordant reports in the literature. In part, this is because of the wide variety of experimental systems used and the choice of clinical material examined. The need for more realistic models of the postmenopausal breast and precise surrogate markers of its activity is obvious.

Oestrogens and progestogens may also influence risk of breast cancer. The case for oestrogen is more convincing than that for progestogen, in that measures that particularly target oestrogen (SERMs and aromatase inhibitors) reduce the incidence of breast cancer. The exact role of progestogen is still controversial, although recent meta-analyses and large randomised studies indicate that HRT with combined oestrogen and progestogen has significantly greater effects on risk than HRT with oestrogen alone.

Finally, the endocrinology of the postmenopausal breast is distinctive, such that local levels of hormones within the breast do not simply reflect those in the circulation. Hence, measurements within the breast are likely to be more informative. Researchers should therefore be encouraged to focus their effort at the level of the breast with the recognition that susceptibility to breast cancer will be more dependent upon local influences than factors in the circulation.

Acknowledgement

The wisdom and perception of Professor TJ Anderson during detailed discussion are greatly appreciated; without these the manuscript could not have been written.

References

1. Miller WR. *Estrogen and Breast Cancer*. Austin, TX: RG Landes & Co; 1996.
2. Laron Z, Kauli R, Pertzelan A. Clinical evidence on the role of oestrogens in the development of the breasts. *Proc Roy Soc Edin* 1989;95B:13–22.
3. Bonser GM, Dosser JA, Jull TW. *Human and Experimental Breast Cancer*. Springfield, Illinois: Charles C Thomas; 1961.
4. Anderson TJ, Ferguson DJP, Raab GM. Cell turnover in the "resting" human breast: influence of parity, oral contraceptive pill, age and laterality. *Br J Cancer* 1982;46:376–82.
5. Going JJ, Anderson TJ, Battersby S, MacIntyre CCA. Proliferative and secretory activity in human breast tissue during natural and artificial menstrual cycles. *Am J Pathol* 1988;130:193–204.
6. Potten CS, Watson RJ, Williams GT, Tickle S, Roberts SA, Harris M, *et al*. The effect of age and menstrual cycle upon proliferative activity of the normal human breast. *Br J Cancer* 1988;58:163–70.
7. Battersby S, Anderson TJ, Miller WR. Patterns of cyclic AMP binding in normal human breast. *Breast Cancer Res Treat* 1994;30:153–8.
8. Trichopoulos D, MacMahon B, Cole P. Menopause and breast cancer risk. *J Natl Cancer Inst* 1972;48:605–13.
9. Greenberg ER, Barnes AB, Resseguie L, Barrett JA, Burnside S, Lanza LL, *et al*. Breast cancer in mothers given diethylstilbestrol in pregnancy. *N Engl J Med* 1984;311:1393–8.
10. Collaborative Group on Hormonal Factors in Breast Cancer. Breast cancer and hormonal contraceptives: collaborative reanalysis of individual data on 53 297 women with breast cancer

and 100 239 women without breast cancer from 54 epidemiological studies. *Lancet* 1996;347:1713–27.

11.   Althuis MD, Brogan DR, Coates RJ, Daling JR, Gammon MD, Malone KE, *et al.* Hormonal content and potency of oral contraceptives and breast cancer risk among young women. *Br J Cancer* 2003;88:50–7.

12.   Beral V, Bull D, Doll R, *et al.* Breast cancer and hormone replacement therapy: collaborative reanalysis of data from 51 epidemiological studies of 52,705 women with breast cancer and 108,411 women without breast cancer. Collaborative Group on Hormonal Factors in Breast Cancer. *Lancet* 1997;350:1047–59. Erratum in: *Lancet* 1997;350:1484.

13.   Magnusson C, Persson I, Adami HO. More about: effect of hormone replacement therapy on breast cancer risk: estrogen versus estrogen plus progestin. *J Natl Cancer Inst* 2000;92:1183–4.

14.   Ross RK, Paganini-Hill A, Wan PC, Pike MC. Effect of hormone replacement therapy on breast cancer risk: estrogen versus estrogen plus progestin. *J Natl Cancer Inst* 2000;92:328–32.

15.   Schairer C, Lubin J, Troisi R, Sturgeon S, Brinton L, Hoover R. Menopausal estrogen and estrogen-progestin replacement therapy and breast cancer risk. *JAMA* 2000;283:485–91.

16.   Beral V, Banks E, Reeves G. Evidence from randomised trials on the long-term effects of hormone replacement therapy. *Lancet* 2002;360:942–4.

17.   Beral V; Million Women Study Collaborators. Breast cancer and hormone-replacement therapy in the Million Women Study. *Lancet* 2003;362:419–27. Erratum in: *Lancet* 2003;362:1160.

18.   Preston-Martin S, Pike MC, Ross RK, Henderson BE. Epidemiologic evidence for the increased cell proliferation model of carcinogenesis. *Environ Health Perspect* 1993;101 Suppl 5:137–8.

19.   McManus MJ, Welsch CW. The effect of estrogen, progesterone, thyroxine, and human placental lactogen on DNA synthesis of human breast ductal epithelium maintained in athymic nude mice. *Cancer* 1984;54:1920–7.

20.   Laidlaw IJ, Clarke RB, Howell A, Owen AW, Potten CS, Anderson E. The proliferation of normal human breast tissue implanted into athymic nude mice is stimulated by estrogen but not progesterone. *Endocrinology* 1995;136:164–71.

21.   Clarke RB, Howell A, Anderson E. Estrogen sensitivity of normal human breast tissue *in vivo* and implanted into athymic nude mice: analysis of the relationship between estrogen-induced proliferation and progesterone receptor expression. *Breast Cancer Res Treat* 1997;45:121–33.

22.   Clarke RB, Howell A, Potten CS, Anderson E. Dissociation between steroid receptor expression and cell proliferation in the human breast. *Cancer Res* 1997;57:4987–91.

23.   Bullock LP, Bardin CW, Sherman MR. Androgenic, antiandrogenic, and synandrogenic actions of progestins: role of steric and allosteric interactions with androgen receptors. *Endocrinology* 1978;103:1768–82.

24.   Jordan VC, Jeng MH, Catherino WH, Parker CJ. The estrogenic activity of synthetic progestins used in oral contraceptives. *Cancer* 1993;71(4 Suppl):1501–5.

25.   Liehr JG. Breast carcinogenesis and its prevention by inhibition of estrogen genotoxicity. In: Miller WR, Ingle JN, editors. *Endocrine Therapy in Breast Cancer.* New York: Marcel Dekker; 2002. p. 287–301.

26.   Henson DE, Tarone RE. On the possible role of involution in the natural history of breast cancer. *Cancer* 1993;71(6 Suppl):2154–6.

27.   Prechtel K. Mastopathie und Altersabhangige Brustdrusen-veranderungen. *Fortschr Med* 1971;89:1312–15.

28.   Vorherr H. *The Breast: Morphology, Physiology and Lactation.* New York: Academic Press; 1974.

29.   Wellings SR, Jensen HM, Marcum RG. An atlas of subgross pathology of the human breast with special reference to possible precancerous lesions. *J Natl Cancer Inst* 1975;55:231–73.

30.   Miller WR, Anderson TJ. Oestrogens, progestogens and the breast. In: Studd JWW, Whitehead MI, editors. *The Menopause.* London: Blackwell Scientific Publications; 1988. p. 234–46.

31.   Hargreaves DF, Knox F, Swindell R, Potten CS, Bundred NJ. Epithelial proliferation and hormone receptor status in the normal post-menopausal breast and the effects of hormone replacement therapy. *Br J Cancer* 1998;78:945–9.

32.   Hofseth LJ, Raafat AM, Osuch JR, Pathak DR, Slomski CA, Haslam SZ. Hormone replacement therapy with estrogen or estrogen plus medroxyprogesterone acetate is associated with increased epithelial proliferation in the normal postmenopausal breast. *J Clin Endocrinol Metab* 1999;84:4559–65.

33.   Cline JM, Soderqvist G, von Schoultz E, Skoog L, von Schoultz B. Effects of hormone replacement therapy on the mammary gland of surgically postmenopausal cynomolgus macaques. *Am J Obstet Gynecol* 1996;174(1 Pt 1):93–100.

34.   Thomas HV, Reeves GK, Key TJ. Endogenous estrogen and postmenopausal breast cancer: a quantitative review. *Cancer Causes Control* 1997;8:922–8.

35.   Toniolo PG, Levitz M, Zeleniuch-Jacquotte A, Banerjee S, Koenig KL, Shore RE, *et al.* A prospective study of endogenous estrogens and breast cancer in postmenopausal women. *J Natl*

Cancer Inst 1995;87:190–7.

36. Dorgan JF, Longcope C, Stephenson HE Jr, Falk RT, Miller R, Franz C, *et al.* Serum sex hormone levels are related to breast cancer risk in postmenopausal women. *Environ Health Perspect* 1997;105 Suppl 3:583–5.

37. Thomas HV, Key TJ, Allen DS, Moore JW, Dowsett M, Fentiman IS, *et al.* A prospective study of endogenous serum hormone concentrations and breast cancer risk in premenopausal women on the island of Guernsey. *Br J Cancer* 1997;75:1075–9.

38. Hankinson SE, Willett WC, Manson JE, Colditz GA, Hunter DJ, Spiegelman D, *et al.* Plasma sex steroid hormone levels and risk of breast cancer in postmenopausal women. *J Natl Cancer Inst* 1998;90:1292–9.

39. Miller WR. Levels and patterns of estrogen within the breast, its fluids and tissues. In: Miller WR, editor. *Estrogen and Breast Cancer*, Austin, TX: RG Landes & Co; 1996. p. 95–110.

40. van Landeghem AA, Poortman J, Nabuurs M, Thijssen JH. Endogenous concentration and subcellular distribution of estrogens in normal and malignant human breast tissue. *Cancer Res* 1985;45:2900–6.

41. Vermeulen A. Human mammary cancer as a site of sex steroid metabolism. *Cancer Surv* 1986;5:585–95.

42. Miller WR. Uptake and synthesis of steroid hormones by the breast. *Endocrine Related Cancer* 1997;4:307–11.

43. Larionov AA, Berstein LM, Miller WR. Local uptake and synthesis of oestrone in normal and malignant postmenopausal breast tissues. *J Steroid Biochem Mol Biol* 2002;81:57–64.

44. Perel E, Killinger DW. The interconversion and aromatization of androgens by human adipose tissue. *J Steroid Biochem* 1979;10:623–7.

45. Miller WR. Steroid metabolism in breast cancer. In: Stoll BA, editor. *Breast Cancer: Treatment and Progress*. Oxford: Blackwell Scientific Publications; 1986. p. 156–72.

46. Miller WR, Mullen P, Sourdaine P, Watson C, Dixon JM, Telford J. Regulation of aromatase activity within the breast. *J Steroid Biochem Mol Biol* 1997;61:193–202.

47. Reed MJ, Aherne GW, Ghilchik MW, Patel S, Chakraborty J. Concentrations of oestrone and 4-hydroxyandrostenedione in malignant and normal breast tissues. *Int J Cancer* 1991;49:562–5.

48. Miller WR. Importance of intratumour aromatase and its susceptibility to inhibitors. In: Dowsett M, editor. *Aromatase Inhibition – Then, Now and Tomorrow*. London: Parthenon Publishing Group; 1994. p. 43–53.

49. James VHT, Reed MJ, Adams EF, Ghilchick M, Lai LC, Coldham NG, *et al. Proc Roy Soc Edin* 1989;95B:185–93.

50. Miller WR. Estrogens and endocrine therapy for breast cancer. In: *Estrogen and Breast Cancer*. Austin, TX: RG Landes & Co; 1996. p. 125–50.

51. Fisher B, Costantino JP, Wickerham DL, Redmond CK, Kavanah M, Cronin WM, *et al.* Tamoxifen for prevention of breast cancer: report of the National Surgical Adjuvant Breast and Bowel Project P-1 Study. *J Natl Cancer Inst* 1998;90:1371–88.

52. Cummings SR, Eckert S, Krueger KA, Grady D. The effect of raloxifene on risk of breast cancer in postmenopausal women. *JAMA* 1999;281:2124–89.

53. Lo SS, Vogel VG. Endocrine prevention of breast cancer using selective oestrogen receptor modulators (SORMs). *Best Pract Res Clin Endocrinol Metab* 2004;18:97–111.

54. Cuzick J, Powles T, Veronesi U, Forbes J, Edwards R, Ashley S, *et al.* Overview of the main outcomes in breast-cancer prevention trials. *Lancet* 2003;361:296–300.

55. Goss PE, Strasser-Weippl K. Aromatase inhibitors for chemoprevention. *Best Pract Res Clin Endocrinol Metab* 2004;18:113–30.

56. Baum M, Budzar AU, Cuzick J, Forbes J, Houghton JH, Klijn JG, *et al.*; ATAC Trialists' Group. Anastrozole alone or in combination with tamoxifen versus tamoxifen alone for adjuvant treatment of postmenopausal women with early breast cancer: first results of the ATAC randomised trial. *Lancet* 2002;359:2131–9. Erratum in: *Lancet* 2002;360:1520.

Chapter 12

Hormone replacement therapy and mammographic screening for breast cancer

Robin Wilson

Background – breast cancer and breast cancer screening

Breast cancer remains the most common malignancy in women with over one million cases diagnosed each year worldwide and it is the most common cause of female cancer death. Breast cancer is particularly common in the developed Western world where its incidence continues to increase. In the UK, one in nine women can expect to develop breast cancer at some time in their lives. In England in 2001 there were 33 829 new cases of breast cancer diagnosed in women (30% of all cancers in women) and 11 554 deaths (17% of all female cancer deaths).[1] Despite the increasing incidence, the death rate from breast cancer in England has fallen by approximately 20% across all ages and this is attributed to improved treatment, especially the use of anti-oestrogens such as tamoxifen, and earlier diagnosis, including screening.[2]

The vast majority of breast cancer is sporadic and its specific cause or causes are unknown. However, approximately 5% of breast cancer occurs in women with an inherited genetic mutation, usually one of the breast cancer susceptibility genes *BRCA1* or *BRCA2*. Breast cancer occurring in these women tends to occur at a younger age and to have more aggressive behaviour. Other than gene mutations, the most significant risk factors for breast cancer are being female and increasing age. Breast cancer is very rare under the age of 35 and less than 1% of breast cancer occurs in males. A number of other factors are known to increase the risk of breast cancer in women, including early menarche, late menopause, nulliparity, obesity, excessive alcohol consumption, prolonged use of the oral contraceptive pill and, as confirmed recently, use of hormone replacement therapy (HRT).[3]

As yet there are no proven effective methods of preventing breast cancer or of treating disease that is advanced at presentation. However, treatment of early-stage disease significantly improves the chances of cure and disease control. Therefore, current medical interventions to influence the outcome of breast cancer focus on early detection through screening of asymptomatic women and encouraging early presentation to rapid-access breast diagnosis clinics for women with breast symptoms.

Interest in screening for breast cancer began in the 1970s and 1980s when randomised controlled trials in the USA and Europe provided evidence that population screening by X-ray mammography could reduce breast cancer deaths through early detection by up to 35%. As a result, breast screening by mammography is now routinely available in most developed countries. Organised population mammographic breast screening is provided in most northern European countries. Although the efficacy of breast screening was questioned in 2001, the World Health Organization International Agency for Research on Cancer (IARC) has since re-evaluated the available evidence on breast screening and concluded that screening by mammography only can be expected to reduce mortality by 35% in women aged 50 to 70 years.[4-6] The IACR also emphasised that screening is less effective in younger women and that clinical palpation of the breast and breast self-examination do not influence breast cancer mortality.[6] Recent publications updating the Swedish trials have also reconfirmed the efficacy of mammographic screening.[7-9]

The UK National Health Service Breast Screening Programme (NHSBSP) was introduced in 1988 and now offers mammographic screening to all women of 50 years and over with invitation of women aged 50–70 years. Screening is by two-view X-ray mammography provided every three years. In 2001, 1.75 million women were invited for screening as part of the NHSBSP and 1.3 million women attended (76% of those invited) at a cost of £30 per woman screened.[1] Current performance statistics are very encouraging and it is predicted that, as a result of early detection, mammographic screening in the UK will reduce breast cancer mortality by 25% (approximately 1250 cases per year) by the year 2010.[1,2]

The relationship of mammographic breast density with breast cancer and the effectiveness of screening

Increased breast density on mammography has been shown to be a significant independent risk factor for breast cancer on a par with other moderate risk factors such as atypical epithelial hyperplasia, lobular carcinoma *in situ*, previous biopsy showing benign breast disease and family history of breast cancer.[10-22] The methodology, data and findings of these studies are well summarised in the review by Harvey and Bovbjerg.[23] The reported odds ratios of increased breast density for breast cancer in these studies are of the order of 1.8–6.0, with most studies showing an odds ratio of 4.0 or more.

Apart from the link with risk of breast cancer, breast density is of particular interest to those involved in interpreting X-ray mammograms. Breasts that are dense on mammography are difficult to interpret with an inverse relationship between increasing density and decreasing sensitivity and specificity for breast cancer.[24-27] The sensitivity of screening mammography for breast cancer increases with age. This is partly due to the changing pathological and mammographic features of breast cancer with age (breast cancer in younger women tends to be oestrogen receptor-negative, of high grade and less likely to produce easily detectable features on mammography) but is largely due to the relative decrease in mammographic background density with age. The breast tends to involute with time as the stromal and epithelial elements of the breast decrease relative to the fatty component and this process is mirrored by reducing breast density on mammography. In women aged 25–29 years, only around 11% have a fatty radiolucent mammographic background pattern while approximately one-third of women aged 75–79 years will have an entirely fatty mammographic pattern. Half of women aged 40–49 years have more then 50% breast density while only a third of women aged 75–79 years have this degree of breast density.[28] Kopans[29] has also reported similar findings and others have observed that breast density does not change dramatically with time and that there is considerable variability in breast density within all age groups.[30]

There is a wide range of breast density that is considered normal on mammography. Although breast density tends to reduce with age, there is no dramatic change in breast density associated with the menopause. In women over 50 years, the sensitivity of mammography in the fatty breast showing very little background density approaches 98% while the sensitivity in the dense breast falls to as low as 48%.[31]

Hormones and the effectiveness of mammographic breast screening

Anything that increases breast density can be expected to reduce the sensitivity of mammography for breast cancer. Two commonly occurring external factors are associated with increased breast density on mammography – high alcohol consumption and use of HRT. For alcohol, the effect is said in one study to be independent of the type of alcohol in premenopausal women but is particularly associated with white rather than red wine in postmenopausal women.[32] HRT increases mammographic breast background density in a proportion of users. It slows breast involution and is reported to be associated with an increase in mammographic density in 17–73% of users.[23,33]

The increased density effect of HRT is unpredictable and varies according to the type of therapy and how it is administered. Persson et al.[34] reported that 28% of women taking combined continuous treatment had increased mammographic density while this effect fell to 10% in those receiving cyclical therapy, 5% in those taking oestradiol only and 3% of controls. The Postmenopausal Estrogen/Progestin Interventions (PEPI) trial and other studies have also reported similar findings of mammographic density increase being most common with combined continuous therapy compared with cyclical use.[35–38] That combined oestrogen and progestogen preparations are associated most commonly with increases in mammographic density and that this increase in density is probably due to cellular proliferation in the terminal duct lobular units (TDLUs) mirrors well the reports from large studies that these preparations are also associated with the highest increase in breast cancer risk.[3,39–42] The breast appears to be highly and rapidly sensitive to the administration and withdrawal of HRT. The PEPI trial also found that density changes occurred to the greatest degree in the first year of treatment and decrease in density was observed after only two weeks of stopping treatment.[35] Further evidence that changes in mammographic density occur rapidly has been reported by Colacurci et al.[43] who found that mammographic density was not significantly different from the pretreatment density after only three weeks of stopping treatment while density increased in those who stayed on treatment. Harvey et al.[44] reported in a small study that short-term cessation of HRT (mean 15 days) led to a decrease or resolution of close to three-quarters of observed mammographic changes. On the same theme, selective oestrogen receptor modulators (SERMs) such as tamoxifen and raloxifene have been shown to reduce breast density significantly.[45–47]

The density shown on mammography is thought to reflect the amount of both stromal and epithelial tissue in the TDLUs rather than the larger ducts.[48] The various papers correlating histopathology and cytology with mammographic patterns are well summarised in the review by Harvey and Bovbjerg.[23] A study of benign breast biopsy histology found that, compared with no hormone treatment, oestrogen alone users showed a small increase in epithelial proliferation while use of combined hormone treatment was associated with significantly higher cellular proliferative indices and these changes were confined to the TDLUs, where most significant breast pathology arises.[49] This fits well with the observations that combined continuous HRT is associated with the highest risk of developing breast cancer, with the highest incidence of increasing breast density on mammography and with stimulating the appearance and growth of benign breast pathology seen on mammography, such as simple cysts and fibroadenomas. Breast cancer occurring in breasts that show increased density on mammography regardless of HRT status has also been associated with less favourable histology. Roubidoux et al.[50] have reported that breast cancers occurring in women who have significant mammographic breast density tend to be larger, of higher histological grade and oestrogen receptor-negative, although only increase in size was found to be independent of age at diagnosis. Sala et al.[51] have also reported an association between high histological grade and increased mammographic density.

Information on the effect of tibolone on breast density is sparse. Erel et al.[52] reported that tibolone has little effect on mammographic density, and another comparative study[53] has shown it is associated with increased density in only 2–6% of women compared with 46–50% of women receiving combined oestrogen and progestogen. Topical administration of oestrogen also appears not to have any significant effect on mammography with increase in density reported in no more than 2% of women.[54] Where HRT does not affect breast density it appears that it does not influence the sensitivity of screening mammography.[22,55]

The mammographic changes produced by HRT include developing focal densities in one or both breasts, enlarging masses and the appearances of new masses, but a generalised increase in density is the most common effect.[23,56,57] New masses and enlarging pre-existing masses are almost always benign, representing, most commonly, simple cysts or fibroadenomas. While the mammographic features of these abnormalities usually show that they are likely to be benign, because they are new or increasing in size, recall for further tests is required. There is clear evidence that when HRT results in any of these changes in the breast on mammography both the sensitivity and the specificity of screening mammography is reduced. The cancer detection rate falls while the number of women recalled unnecessarily for further tests or biopsy increases.

Increased breast density is associated with reduced mammographic sensitivity for the changes of breast cancer simply because the features of breast cancer are more difficult to see in the mammographically dense breast. Increased mammographic breast density is also associated with reduced specificity and with a higher proportion of false positive findings that lead to further investigations. Sensitivity is reported to be reduced by between 7% and 21%.[25,58–61] However, one large study has not shown that HRT affects mammographic sensitivity.[54] A possible explanation for this result is that 41% of the women were using topical hormone preparations with 27% using combined oestrogen and progestogen and only 12% using continuous combined HRT.[55] Further evidence of the reduced sensitivity of mammography associated with use of HRT is that users are significantly more likely to present with an interval breast cancer. Litherland et al.[59] have reported that HRT users have an overall relative risk of presenting with an interval cancer over nonusers of 1.79, with the effect most obvious in the first year after screening (RR 2.27).

The reduction in specificity associated with HRT use varies in published studies between 12% and 50%, with false positive screening outcomes occurring mainly in women screened for the second or subsequent time and particularly in those who had started HRT since their previous screening mammogram.[58,60,62,63] Analysis of the Million Women Study[64] has shown that in the region of 20% of unnecessary recalls in the NHSBSP are the direct result of HRT use. The relative risk of false positive recall was 1.64 in current users and 1.21 in past users with an effect remaining significant for five years after stopping treatment. This excess in false positive screening results is likely to be associated with significant unnecessary, and potentially avoidable, short-term anxiety in around 14 000 women per year in the NHSBSP.[65]

It is estimated that around 30% of women participating in the NHSBSP are current users of HRT and in a significant proportion of these women their use of HRT is likely to be having a significant negative effect on both the sensitivity and specificity of their screening outcomes by increasing breast density and making the mammograms more difficult to interpret. Further evidence that HRT is associated with masking of the mammographic signs of breast cancer is provided by the observations that hormone users, and particularly those using continuous combined therapy, have lower cancer detection rates at screening and are much more likely to present with an interval cancer within one year of a normal screening result (RR 2.0) (see Chapter 13).

Conclusions and recommendations

Increased breast density is a recognised independent risk factor for breast cancer and it also reduces the sensitivity and specificity of mammography by masking the visible features of breast cancer. Breast density decreases with age but a significant proportion of women even into old age will always show significant density on mammography regardless of their hormone treatment status.

HRT reduces the efficacy of screening mammography in a proportion of postmenopausal women by increasing the density of their screening mammograms and thereby increases the chances of both false negative and false positive results. As well as this masking effect, HRT independently increases users' overall risk of developing breast cancer. Increased mammographic density is particularly associated with continuous combined therapy and to a lesser extent with cyclical combined therapy. The effect of oestrogen alone on breast density appears to be significantly less while topical hormones and tibolone appear not to affect mammographic breast density significantly. Women taking or considering HRT should be made aware of the potential effects of hormone treatment on their breast cancer risk and any potential reduction in effectiveness of mammographic screening by possible increase in mammographic density. Where possible, HRT that is associated with a low incidence of inducing increased mammographic density should be considered.

The breast appears to be highly sensitive to changes in exogenous hormones. There is some evidence that stopping HRT, even for a short time, can reverse the density changes shown on mammography. Further studies are required to confirm that stopping HRT for two to three weeks will result in reduced breast density. If this is shown to be the case then consideration should be given to advising women known to have increased breast density as a result of HRT to stop therapy before attending for mammography. Similarly, SERMs could be investigated as potential short-term treatment to reduce breast density prior to mammography.

Alternatively, the possibility of using other imaging techniques less affected by breast density such as ultrasound and magnetic resonance imaging could be investigated in selected women who have a significant increase in breast density associated with HRT, although the resources required are likely to make this option prohibitive.[31,65-68]

References

1.   NHS Cancer Screening Programmes [www.cancerscreening.nhs.uk/breastscreen/index.html].
2.   Blanks RG, Moss SM, McGahan CE, Quinn MJ, Babb PJ. Effect of NHS breast screening programme on mortality from breast cancer in England and Wales, 1990-8: comparison of observed with predicted mortality. *BMJ* 2000;321:665-9.

3. Beral V; Million Women Study Collaborators. Breast cancer and hormone-replacement therapy in the Million Women Study. *Lancet* 2003;362:419–27. Erratum in: *Lancet* 2003;362:1160.
4. Olsen O, Gotzsche PC. Cochrane review on screening for breast cancer with mammography. *Lancet* 2001;358:1340–2.
5. Olsen O, Gotzsche PC. *Systematic review of screening for breast cancer with mammography.* 2001 [http://image.thelancet.com/lancet/extra/fullreport.pdf].
6. World Health Organization. *7th Handbook on Cancer Prevention.* Lyons: IARC; 2002.
7. Nystrom L, Andersson I, Bjurstam N, Frisell J, Nordenskjold, Rutqvist LE. Long-term effects of mammographic screening: update overview of the Swedish randomised trials. *Lancet* 2002;359:909–19.
8. Tabar L, Vitak B, Chen HH, Yen MF, Duffy SW, Smith RA. Beyond randomised controlled trials: organised mammographic screening substantially reduces breast carcinoma mortality. *Cancer* 2001;91:1724–31.
9. Duffy SW, Tabar L, Chen HH, Holmqvist M, Yen MF, Abdsalah S, *et al.* The impact of organised mammographic screening on breast carcinoma mortality in seven Swedish counties. *Cancer* 2002;95:458–69.
10. Boyd NF, O'Sullivan B, Campbell JE, Fishell E, Simor I, Cooke G, *et al.* Mammographic signs as risk factors for breast cancer. *Br J Cancer* 1982;45:185–93.
11. Brisson J, Merletti F, Sadowsky NL, Twaddle JA, Morrison AS, Cole P. Mammographic features of the breast and breast cancer risk. *Am J Epidemiol* 1982;115:428–37.
12. Brisson J, Morrison AS, Kopans DB, Sadowsky NL, Kalisher L, Twaddle JA, *et al.* Height and weight, mammographic features of breast tissue, and breast cancer risk. *Am J Epidemiol* 1984;119:371–81.
13. Wolfe JN, Saftlas AF, Salane M, Mammographic parenchymal patterns and quantitative evaluation of mammographic densities: a case–control study. *AJR Am J Roentgenol* 1987;148:1087–92.
14. Brisson J, Verreault R, Morrison AS, Tennine S, Meyer F. Diet, mammographic features and breast cancer risk. *Am J Epidemiol* 1989;130:14–24.
15. Saftlas AF, Hoover RN, Brinton LA, Szklo M, Olson DR, Salane M, *et al.* Mammographic densities and risk of breast cancer. *Cancer* 1991;67:2833–8.
16. Boyd NF, Byng JW, Jong RA, Fishell EK, Little LE, Miller AB, *et al.* Quantitative classification of mammographic densities and breast cancer risk: results from the Canadian National Breast Screening Study. *J Natl Cancer Inst* 1995;87:670–5.
17. Kato I, Beinart C, Bleich A, Su S, Kim M, Toniolo PG. A nested case–control study of mammographic patterns, breast volume, and breast cancer. *Cancer Causes Control* 1995;6:431–8.
18. Byrne C, Schairer C, Wolfe J, Parekh N, Salane M, Brinton LA, *et al.* Mammographic features and breast cancer risk: effect of time, age, and menopause status. *J Natl Cancer Inst* 1995;87:1622–9.
19. van Gils CH, Hendriks JH, Holland R, Karssemeijer N, Otten JD, Straatman H, *et al.* Changes in mammographic breast density and comcomitant changes in breast cancer risk. *Eur J Cancer Prev* 1999;8:509–15.
20. Lam PB, Vacek PM, Geller BM, Muss HB. The association of increased weight, body mass index, and tissue density with risk of breast cancer in Vermont. *Cancer* 2000;89:369–75.
21. Maskarinec G, Meng L. A case–control study of mammographic densities in Hawaii. *Breast Cancer Res Treat* 2000;63:153–61.
22. Carney PA, Miglioretti DL, Yankaskas BC, Kerlikowske K, Rosenberg R, Rutter CM, *et al.* Individual and combined effects of age, breast density and hormone replacement therapy on the accuracy of screening mammography. *Ann Intern Med* 2003;138:168–75.
23. Harvey JA, Bovbjerg VE. Quantitative assessment of mammographic breast density: relationship with breast cancer risk. *Radiology* 2004;230:29–41.
24. Mandelson MT, Oestreicher N, Porter PL, White D, Finder CA, Taplin SH, *et al.* Breast density as predictor of mammographic detection: comparison of interval- and screen-detected cancers. *J Natl Cancer Inst* 2000;92:1081–7.
25. Rosenberg RD, Hunt WC, Williamson MR, Gilliland FD, Wiest PW, Kelsey CA, *et al.* Effects of age, breast density, ethnicity, and estrogen replacement therapy on screening mammographic sensitivity and cancer stage at diagnosis: review of 183,134 screening mammograms in Albuquerque, New Mexico. *Radiology* 1998;209:511–18.
26. Kerlikowske K, Grady D, Rubin SM, Sandrock C, Ernster VL. Efficacy of screening mammography: a meta-analysis. *JAMA* 1995;273:149–54.
27. Coveney EC, Geraghty JG, O'Laoide R, Hourihane JB, O'Higgins NJ. Reasons underlying negative mammography in patients with palpable breast cancer. *Clin Radiol* 1994;49:123–5.
28. Stomper PC, D'Souza DJ, DiNitto PA, Arredondo MA. Analysis of parenchymal density on mammograms in 1353 women 25–79 years old. *AJR Am J Roentgenol* 1996;167:1261–5.

29.   Kopans DB. Conventional wisdom: observation, experience, anecdote, and science in breast imaging. *AJR Am J Roentgenol* 1994;162:299–303.

30.   Powell KA, Obuchowski NA, Davros WJ, Chilcote WA. Quantitative analysis of breast parenchymal density: correlation with women's age. *Acad Radiol* 1999;6:742–7.

31.   Kolb TM, Lichy J, Newhouse JH. Comparison of the performance of screening mammography, physical examination, and breast US and evaluation of factors that influence them: an analysis of 27,825 patient evaluations. *Radiology* 2002;225:165–75.

32.   Vachon CM, Kushi LH, Cerhan JR, Kuni CC, Sellers TA. Association of diet and mammographic breast density in the Minnesota breast cancer family cohort. *Cancer Epidemiol Biomarkers Prev* 2000;9:151–60.

33.   Rutter CM, Mandelson MT, Laya MB, Taplin S. Changes in breast density associated with initiation, discontinuation and continuing use of hormone replacement therapy. *JAMA* 2001;285:171–6.

34.   Persson I, Thurfjell E, Holmberg L. Effect of estrogen and estrogen-progestin replacement regimes on mammographic breast parenchymal density. *J Clin Oncol* 1997;15:3201–7.

35.   Greendale GA, Reboussin BA, Sie A, Singh HR, Olson LK, Gatewood O, et al. Effects of estrogen and estrogen-progestin on mammographic parenchymal density. Postmenopausal Estrogen/Progestin Interventions (PEPI) Investigators. *Ann Intern Med* 1999;130:261–9.

36.   Marugg RC, van der Mooren MJ, Hendriks JH, Rolland R, Ruijs SH. Mammographic changes in postmenopausal women on hormone replacement therapy. *Eur Radiol* 1997;7:749–55.

37.   Sendag F, Cosan Terek M, Ozsener S, Oztekin K, Bilgin O, Bilgen I, et al. Mammographic density chnges during different postmenopausal hormone replacement therapies. *Fertil Steril* 2001;76:445–50.

38.   Lundstrom E, Wilczek B, von Palffy Z, Soderqvist G, von Schoultz B. Mammographic breast density during hormone replacement therapy: differences according to treatment. *Am J Obstet Gynecol* 1999;188:348–52.

39.   Persson I, Weiderpass E, Bergkvist L, Bergstrom R, Schairer C. Risk of breast and endometrial cancer after estrogen and estrogen-progestin replacement. *Cancer Causes Control* 1999;10:253–60.

40.   Schaire C, Lubin J, Triosi R, Sturgeon S, Brinton L, Hoover R. Menopausal estrogen and estrogen-progestin replacement therapy and breast cancer risk. *JAMA* 2000;283:485–91.

41.   Ross RK, Paganini-Hill A, Wan PC, Pike MC. Effect of hormone replacement therapy on breast cancer risk: estrogen versus estrogen plus progestin. *J Natl Cancer Inst* 2000;92:328–32.

42.   Rossouw JE, Anderson GL, Prentice RL, LaCroix AZ, Kooperberg C, Stefanick ML, et al.; Writing Group for the Women's Health Initiative Investigators. Risks and benefits of estrogen plus progestin in healthy postmenopausal women: principal results fom the Women's Health Initiative randomized controlled trial. *JAMA* 2002;288:321–33.

43.   Colacurci N, Fornaro F, De Franciscis P, Mele D, Palermo M, del Vecchio W. Effects of short-term suspension of hormone replacement therapy on mammographic density. *Fertil Steril* 2001;76:451–5.

44.   Harvey JA, Pinkerton JV, Herman CR. Short-term cessation of hormone replacement therapy and improvement of mammographic specificity. *J Natl Cancer Inst* 1997;89:1623–5.

45.   Fisher B, Costantino JP, Wickerham DL, Redmond CK, Kavanah M, Cronin WM, et al. Tamoxifen for prevention of breast cancer: report of the National Surgical Adjuvant Breast and Bowel Project P-1 Study. *J Natl Cancer Inst* 1998;90:1371–88.

46.   Cummings SR, Eckert S, Krueger KA, Grady D, Powles TJ, Cauley JA, et al. The effect of raloxifene on risk of breast cancer in postmenopausal women: results from the MORE randomized trial. Multiple Outcomes of Raloxifene Evaluation. *JAMA* 1999;281:2189–97.

47.   Freedman M, San Martin J, O'Gorman J, Eckert S, Lippman ME, Lo SC, et al. Digitized mammography: a clinical trial of postmenopausal women randomly assigned to receive raloxifene, estrogen, or placebo. *J Natl Cancer Inst* 2001;93:51–6.

48.   Page DL, Winfield AC. The dense mammogram. *AJR Am J Roentgenol* 1986;147:487–9.

49.   Hofseth LJ, Raafat AM, Osuch JR, Pathak DR, Slomski CA, Haslam SZ. Hormone replacement therapy with estrogen or estrogen plus medroxyprogesterone acetate is associated with increased epithelial proliferation in the normal postmenopausal breast. *J Clin Endocrinol Metab* 1999;84:4559–65.

50.   Roubidoux MA, Bailey JE, Wray LA, Helvie MA. Invasive cancers detected after breast cancer screening yielded a negative result: relationship of mammographic density to tumour prognostic factors. *Radiology* 2004;230:42–8.

51.   Sala E, Warren R, McCann J, Duffy S, Luben R, Day N. Mammographic parenchymal patterns and breast cancer natural history – a case–control study. *Acta Oncol* 2001;40:461–5.

52.   Erel CT, Elter K, Akman C, Ersavasti G, Altug A, Seyisoglu H, et al. Mammographic changes in women receiving tibolone therapy. *Fertil Steril* 1998;69:870–5.

53. Lundstrom E, Christow A, Kersemaekers W, Svane G, Azavedo E, Soderqvist G, *et al*. Effects of tibolone and continuous combined hormone replacement therapy on mammographic breast density. *Am J Obstet Gynecol* 2002;186:717–22.

54. Thurfjell EL, Holmberg LH, Persson I. Screening mammography: sensitivity and specificity in relation to hormone replacement therapy. *Radiology* 1997;203:339–41.

55. Evans A. Hormone replacement therapy and mammographic screening. *Clin Radiol* 2002;57:563–4.

56. Doyle GJ, McLean L. Unilateral increase in mammographic density with hormone replacement therapy. *Clin Radiol* 1994;49:50–1.

57. Cyrlak D, Wong CH. Mammographic changes in post menopausal women undergoing hormone replacement therapy. *AJR Am J Roentgenol* 1993;161:1177–83.

58. Seradour B, Esteve J, Heid P, Jacquemier J. Hormone replacement therapy and screening mammography : analysis of the results in the Bouche du Rhone programme. *J Med Screen* 1999;6:99–102.

59. Litherland JC, Stallard S, Hole D, Cordiner C. The effect of hormone replacement therapy on the sensitivity of screening mammograms. *Clin Radiol* 1999;54:285–8.

60. Kavanagh AM, Mitchell H, Giles GG. Hormone replacement therapy and accuracy of mammographic screening. *Lancet* 2000;355:270–4.

61. Banks E, Reeves G, Beral V, Bull D, Crossley B, Simmonds M, *et al*. Impact of use of hormone replacement therapy on false positive recall in the NHS breast screening programme: results from the Million Women Study. *BMJ* 2004;328:1291–2.

62. Litherland JC , Evans AJ, Wilson ARM. The effect of hormone replacement therapy on recall rate in the National Health Service Breast Screening Programme. *Clin Radiol* 1997;52:276–9.

63. Harvey JA. Use and cost of breast imaging for postmenopausal women undergoing hormone replacement therapy. *AJR Am J Roentgenol* 1999;172:1615–19.

64. Banks E, Reeves G, Beral V, Bull D, Crossley B, Simmonds M, *et al*. Impact of use of hormone replacement therapy on false positive recall in the NHS breast screening programme: results from the Million Women Study. *BMJ* 2004;328:1291–2.

65. Warner E, Plewes DB, Shumak RS, Catzavelos GC, Di Prospero LS, Yaffe MJ, *et al*. Comparison of breast magnetic resonance imaging, mammography, and ultrasound for surveillance of women at high risk for hereditary breast cancer. *J Clin Oncol* 2001;19:3524–31.

66. Stoutjesdijk MJ, Boetes C, Jager GJ, Beex L, Bult P, Hendriks JH, *et al*. Magnetic resonance imaging and mammography in women with a hereditary risk of breast cancer. *J Natl Cancer Inst* 2001;93:1095–102.

67. Kuhl CK, Schmutzler RK, Leutner CC, Kempe A, Wardelmann E, Hocke A, *et al*. Breast MR imaging screening in 192 women proved or suspected to be carriers of a breast cancer susceptibility gene: preliminary results. *Radiology* 2000;215:267–79.

68. Brekelmans CT, Seynaeve C, Bartels CC, Tilanus-Linthorst MM, Meijers-Heijboer EJ, Crepin CM, *et al.*; Rotterdam Committee for Medical and Genetic Counseling. Effectiveness of breast cancer surveillance in BRCA1/2 gene mutation carriers and women with high familial risk. *J Clin Oncol* 2001;19:924–30.

Chapter 13

The effect of hormone replacement therapy on breast and other cancers

Valerie Beral, Emily Banks, Gillian Reeves, Jane Green, Toral Gathani, Diana Bull and Barbara Crossley

Introduction

Hormone replacement therapy (HRT) is mainly used by perimenopausal and postmenopausal women to relieve menopausal symptoms. Since the menopause occurs at an average age of about 50 years in Western countries,[1] use of HRT is most common in women in their 50s.[2-5] By the late 1990s, somewhere between 20% and 40% of women aged 50–64 years in northern Europe, the USA and Australia were using HRT, although the prevalence of use varied considerably from country to country.[2-5] Following the premature termination, in July 2002, of the Women's Health Initiative trial of the long-term effects of combined oestrogen-progestogen HRT,[6] use of HRT has declined.[5]

In considering the effects of HRT on cancer, it should be borne in mind that, among women in their 50s, the incidence of cancer of the breast is about ten times higher than the incidence of cancer at any other particular site.[7] For every 1000 UK women aged 50 years, an estimated 14 will be diagnosed with breast cancer in the next five years, whereas the corresponding figures are between one and two per 1000 for cancers of the colorectum, endometrium, ovary, cervix and lung (Figure 13.1). Breast cancer is also the most common cause of death between the ages of about 30 and 65 years[8] and, for women in their early 50s, death rates attributable to breast cancer are three to four times higher than death rates attributable to colorectal, ovarian or lung cancer (Figure 13.1). Hence, emphasis in this review will be on breast cancer, not only because of the known hormonal influences on it, but also because relatively small increases in the relative risk of breast cancer could affect substantial numbers of women.

The published evidence on the effect of different patterns of use of HRT on the incidence of and mortality from cancer is summarised here and new results are presented on the risk of breast cancer associated with different patterns of use of HRT in the Million Women Study.[4,9]

Breast cancer

Both randomised trials and observational studies have shown an increased risk of breast cancer associated with the use of combined oestrogen-progestogen HRT.[6,9-12] Observational data suggest a greater increase in the relative risk of breast cancer

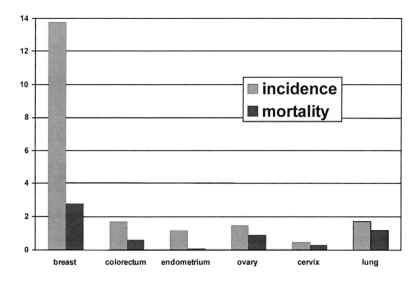

Figure 13.1. Cancer incidence and mortality from age 50 to 55 years per 1000 women in the UK, in the year 2000[7,8]

associated with the use of combined than with oestrogen-only HRT.[9,12] (Results from randomised trials support this finding – see Addendum.)

HRT and the effectiveness of mammography

Nowadays routine mammographic screening is advised in most Western countries for women between the ages of 50 and 70 years, and often at younger ages as well. These are the ages when use of HRT is most common and, since its use reduces both the sensitivity and specificity of mammography,[13] there are important consequences, both for interpreting research findings and for public health.

Women who are using HRT at the time when their mammogram is performed are more likely than never users to be recalled for further investigations that subsequently prove not to be cancer.[11,13,14] This reduction in the specificity of mammography is greatest in current users of HRT, but is also found in past users, persisting for up to five years after use of HRT has ceased.[14]

Use of HRT reduces the sensitivity of mammography, making it more likely that cancers that are already present at the time of mammography are missed and diagnosed in the 'interval' between screens.[13] For women included in the 2003 report concerning HRT and breast cancer in the Million Women Study,[9] Table 13.1 shows the relative risk of breast cancer in current and past users of HRT, subdivided according to time since recruitment into the study. All study participants had a mammogram carried out by the NHS Breast Screening Programme one week after recruitment into the study, on average. Hence, in this study, the time since recruitment is effectively the time since mammography. Incident breast cancers included in the 2003 report were all invasive breast cancers diagnosed after recruitment into the Million Women Study and notified by the Office of National Statistics (ONS).[9] These notifications are currently being

Table 13.1. Breast cancer incidence, by time since recruitment into the Million Women Study,[9] in current and past users of HRT at recruitment

Average time since recruitment (category of time since recruitment) (years)	Current users of HRT at recruitment			Past users of HRT at recruitment		
	Average duration of use of HRT at recruitment[a] (years)	Observed (expected[b]) number of breast cancers	Relative risk (95% CI) of breast cancer compared with never users of HRT	Average duration of use of HRT at recruitment[a] (years)	Observed (expected[b]) number of breast cancers	Relative risk (95% CI) of breast cancer compared with never users of HRT
0.1 (screen-detected)	6.7	1374 (1010)	1.37 (1.27–1.48)	3.3	525 (566)	0.93 (0.84–1.03)
0.7 (<1)	6.1	275 (103)	2.66 (2.15–3.30)	4.2	72 (52)	1.38 (1.03 -1.85)
1.5 (1 to <2)	6.9	550 (255)	2.16 (1.87–2.48)	4.2	161 (131)	1.23 (1.02–1.49)
2.5 (2 to <3)	6.4	559 (337)	1.66 (1.45–1.89)	4.0	158 (182)	0.87 (0.72–1.05)
3.4 (≥3)	6.1	444 (261)	1.70 (1.47–1.97)	3.3	128 (142)	0.90 (0.73–1.07)

[a] among women with breast cancer; [b] based on incidence rates in never users of HRT in the Million Women Study, and adjusted for age, time since menopause, parity and age at first birth, body mass index, region and deprivation index

Table 13.2. Breast cancer incidence, by time since recruitment into the Million Women Study,[9] in current users of oestrogen-only and oestrogen-progestogen HRT at recruitment

Average number of years since recruitment (category of time since recruitment) (years)	Current users of oestrogen-only HRT at recruitment			Past users of oestrogen-progestogen HRT at recruitment		
	Average duration of use of HRT at recruitment[a] (years)	Observed (expected[b]) number of breast cancers in current users of HRT	Relative risk (95% CI) of breast cancer in current v. never users of HRT	Average duration of use of HRT at recruitment[a] (years)	Observed (expected[b]) number of breast cancers in current users of HRT	Relative risk (95% CI) of breast cancer in current v. never users of HRT
0.1 (screen-detected)	7.6	446 (405)	1.10 (0.99–1.23)	6.3	810 (497)	1.63 (1.49–1.78)
0.7 (<1)	7.1	69 (40)	1.72 (1.28–2.32)	6.1	176 (53)	3.31 (2.62–4.19)
1.5 (1 to <2)	7.8	163 (103)	1.59 (1.31–1.94)	6.5	343 (128)	2.68 (2.29–3.13)
2.5 (2 to <3)	7.2	164 (138)	1.19 (0.99–1.43)	6.1	346 (167)	2.07 (1.79–2.40)
3.4 (≥3)	7.4	149 (105)	1.42 (1.17–1.73)	5.7	259 (130)	1.99 (1.68–2.35)

[a] among women with breast cancer; [b] based on incidence rates in never users of HRT in the Million Women Study, and adjusted for age, time since menopause, parity and age at first birth, body mass index, region and deprivation index

cross-checked against information recorded by the collaborating NHS breast screening centres on the breast cancers detected at screening in study participants. According to the ONS, 4027 of the incident invasive breast cancers included in the 2003 report[9] were diagnosed in the first 12 months after recruitment into the study. So far 2724 of these cancers have been confirmed in the records of the collaborating screening centres as having been screen-detected, and 97% of these screen-detected cancers were diagnosed within four months of recruitment. Checks have not yet been completed for the remaining 1303 cancers, but 752 of them were diagnosed four months or less after recruitment, and, for the purpose of these analyses, they are taken to be screen-detected. Some of the breast cancers diagnosed in the third and fourth year after recruitment may well have been detected at the next round of routine screening, since women are invited for routine mammography by the NHS Breast Screening Programme about once every three years. We do not have information on which of the breast cancers notified by the ONS and diagnosed in the third and fourth year after recruitment were screen-detected. However, the large majority of the invasive breast cancers diagnosed in the period from four months to two years after recruitment into the study were interval cancers, and presented symptomatically.

For current users of HRT at the time of recruitment, compared with never users, the relative risk of breast cancer is lowest for the screen-detected breast cancers, diagnosed immediately after recruitment, and highest for the interval cancers diagnosed in the first year after recruitment (Table 13.1). These results are plotted in Figure 13.2 according to the mean time since recruitment in each category, and the overall result for all current users of HRT at recruitment is shown as a dotted line. Some women would have changed their use of HRT after recruitment, but the large and highly significant differences ($P < 0.00001$) between the results for screen-detected cancers

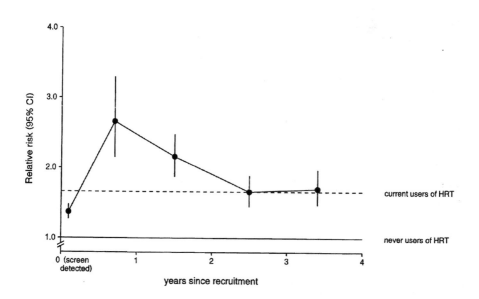

Figure 13.2. Relative risk of breast cancer in current users of HRT at recruitment into the Million Women Study[9]

and the interval cancers diagnosed less than two years after recruitment cannot be accounted for by changes in use of HRT over such a short period. Nor does it seem likely that increased surveillance of current users of HRT would account for the pattern of risk seen in Figure 13.2, since there is no reason to believe that surveillance would be the most intense immediately after mammography, and decline with time since mammography. By contrast, the pattern of risk seen in Figure 13.2 is consistent with the well-established reduced sensitivity of mammography associated with the use of HRT, with the consequent increased probability that cancers are missed at mammography and diagnosed as interval cancers instead.[13] This reduced sensitivity of mammography is likely to be due to HRT-induced increases in the mammographic density of breast tissue that mask the detection of cancers.[13]

For past users of HRT at recruitment, there is also some variation in the relative risk of breast cancer according to time since recruitment, with the largest relative risk being seen for interval cancers diagnosed soon after recruitment (Table 13.1). Even though past users of HRT do not have an overall increased risk of breast cancer, the pattern of occurrence of breast cancer in past users of HRT suggests that some cancers may have been missed at screening and diagnosed as interval cancers instead (Figure 13.3). In this population, past use of HRT has been shown to be associated with a reduced specificity of mammography and this effect lasts for up to five years.[14] The HRT-induced increase in mammographic breast density may, thus, take years to wear off completely. Any persistent increase in breast density in past users of HRT could also lower mammographic sensitivity, and the results in Figure 13.3 suggest that this might be occurring.

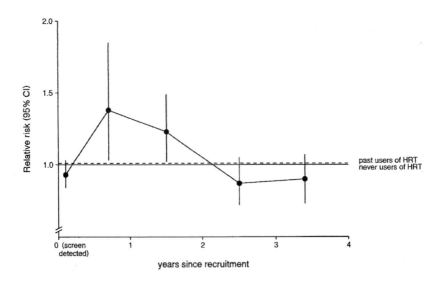

Figure 13.3. Relative risk of breast cancer in past users of HRT at recruitment into the Million Women Study[9]

Table 13.3. Breast cancer incidence, by time since recruitment into the Million Women Study,[9] for current users of HRT for <1 year and for 1–4 years at recruitment

Average number of years since recruitment (category of time since recruitment) (years)	Current users of HRT with a reported duration of use of <1 year at recruitment		Current users of HRT with a reported duration of use of 1–4 years at recruitment		
	Observed (expected[b]) number of breast cancers in current users of HRT	Relative risk (95% CI) of breast cancer in current versus never users of HRT	Average duration of use of HRT at recruitment[a] (years)	Observed (expected[b]) number of breast cancers in current users of HRT	Relative risk (95% CI) of breast cancer in current versus never users of HRT
0.1 (screen-detected)	45 (54.2)	0.83 (0.61–1.12)	2.9	381 (305)	1.25 (1.11–1.41)
0.7 (<1)	21 (5.6)	3.77 (2.33–6.12)	2.6	85 (32)	2.62 (1.97–3.50)
1.5 (1 to <2)	26 (13.5)	1.93 (1.28–2.89)	2.7	149 (78)	1.92 (1.57–2.35)
2.5 (2 to <3)	21 (17.1)	1.23 (0.79–1.91)	2.8	162 (101)	1.60 (1.32–1.94)
3.4 (≥3)	28 (13.8)	2.03 (1.37–3.01)	2.8	139 (79)	1.75 (1.42–2.16)

[a] among women with breast cancer; [b] based on incidence rates in never users of HRT in the Million Women Study, and adjusted for age, time since menopause, parity and age at first birth, body mass index, region and deprivation index

Table 13.4. Breast cancer incidence, by time since recruitment into the Million Women Study,[9] for current users of HRT for 5–9 years and for ≥10 years at recruitment

Average number of years since recruitment (category of time since recruitment) (years)	Current users of HRT with a reported duration of use of 5–9 years at recruitment			Current users of HRT with a reported duration of use of ≥10 years at recruitment		
	Average duration of use of HRT at recruitment[a] (years)	Observed (expected[b]) number of breast cancers in current users of HRT	Relative risk (95% CI) of breast cancer in current versus never users of HRT	Average duration of use of HRT at recruitment[a] (years)	Observed (expected[b]) number of breast cancers in current users of HRT	Relative risk (95% CI) of breast cancer in current versus never users of HRT
0.1 (screen-detected)	6.8	604 (403)	1.50 (1.35–1.66)	12.3	307 (216)	1.42 (1.25–1.61)
0.7 (<1)	6.6	110 (40)	2.73 (2.10–3.57)	12.6	54 (22)	2.49 (1.78–3.49)
1.5 (1 to <2)	6.8	222 (104)	2.14 (1.78–2.56)	12.8	140 (54)	2.59 (2.10–3.18)
2.5 (2 to <3)	6.7	242 (140)	1.73 (1.47–2.05)	12.0	120 (71)	1.68 (1.36–2.07)
3.4 (≥3)	6.7	190 (103)	1.84 (1.52–2.21)	13.0	77 (56)	1.37 (1.06–1.77)

[a] among women with breast cancer; [b] based on incidence rates in never users of HRT in the Million Women Study, and adjusted for age, time since menopause, parity and age at first birth, body mass index, region and deprivation index

Effect of different patterns of use

Recency of use

The totality of the available evidence from observational studies suggests that the risk of breast cancer is increased in current users of HRT, and that these effects wear off rapidly after use ceases, such that the effect has largely, if not wholly, disappeared five years after cessation.[1,9] The reduction in mammographic specificity[14] and sensitivity is greatest among current users of HRT, but is also evident in past users (Figures 13.2 and 13.3).

Type of HRT

Observational data consistently show larger relative risks associated with the use of combined oestrogen-progestogen than for oestrogen-only HRT.[9,12] Results from randomised trials are available largely for combined oestrogen-progestogen HRT.[6,10,11] (See Addendum.) Both oestrogen-only and oestrogen-progestogen HRT reduce mammographic specificity[14] and sensitivity (in that the relative risks of breast cancer associated with use of each type of HRT are lowest for screen-detected cancers, and greatest in the year after mammography – see Table 13.2 and Figure 13.4).[9]

Duration of use

Observational data show that the relative risk of breast cancer increases with increasing duration of use of HRT.[1,9,12] Table 13.3 shows results from the Million Women Study on the relative risk of breast cancer, according to time since recruitment, for women who reported at recruitment that they were current users of HRT and that their total duration of use of HRT was for less than one year and for 1–4 years, respectively. In both groups the relative risk of breast cancer is lowest for the screen-detected cancers and highest for the interval cancers diagnosed in the first year after recruitment (Table 13.3 and

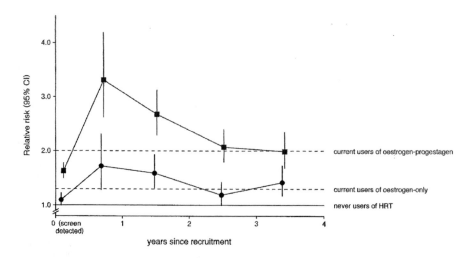

Figure 13.4. Relative risk of breast cancer in current users of oestrogen-only and oestrogen-progestogen HRT at recruitment into the Million Women Study[9]

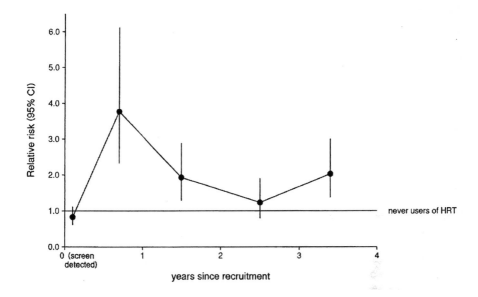

Figure 13.5. Relative risk of breast cancer in women reporting less than one year's current use of HRT at recruitment into the Million Women Study[9]

Figure 13.5), reflecting the lowered sensitivity of mammography associated with the use of HRT.[12,15] The average duration of use of HRT at recruitment was 2.8 years for women in the '1–4 years' duration category, and their relative risk of breast cancer was significantly increased at each time interval shown in Table 13.3. For the women who reported using HRT for less than one year at recruitment, the cumulative incidence of breast cancer was significantly increased compared with never users of HRT about 18 months after recruitment (Figure 13.6). Thus, results from the Million Women Study show statistically significant increases in the incidence of breast cancer with two or more years of use of HRT. However, this does not mean that use of HRT for shorter durations has no effect on breast cancer incidence. Studies would need to be even bigger than the Million Women Study to assess reliably the risk of breast cancer associated with even shorter durations of use of HRT. Randomised trials are substantially smaller than observational studies and do not have sufficient statistical power to provide reliable evidence about how long it takes for the use of HRT to increase the risk of breast cancer, nor were they designed to answer such a question. Table 13.4 shows results similar to those in Table 13.3, for women whose reported duration of use at recruitment was 5–9 years and 10 or more years, respectively. A similar pattern to that illustrated in Figure 13.2 can be seen.

Tumour characteristics, mortality and breast cancer recurrence

Breast cancers diagnosed in users of oestrogen-progestogen HRT in the Women's Health Initiative trial were, on average, significantly larger and more likely to have spread beyond the breast than the cancers diagnosed in nonusers of HRT (Table 13.5).[11]

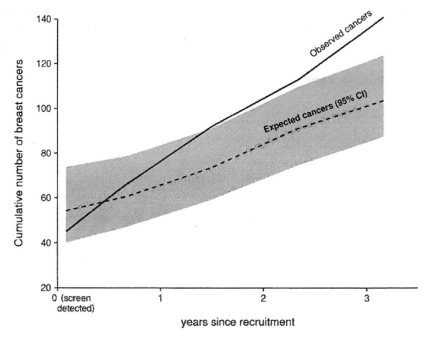

Figure 13.6. Observed and expected number of breast cancers in women reporting less than one years' use of HRT at recruitment into the Million Women Study[9]

There have been some reports that HRT increases the risk of lobular breast cancers to a greater extent than ductal cancers, but the evidence for this is inconsistent.[11,12] Women who were using HRT when they were recruited into the Million Women Study had a higher mortality from breast cancer than nonusers of HRT,[9] but the result was of borderline statistical significance, and longer follow-up is under way.

Table 13.5. Characteristics of the invasive breast cancers diagnosed in participants in the Women's Health Initiative trial[11]

	Oestrogen-progestogen	Placebo
Number of women with breast cancer/total number randomised	199/8506	150/8102
Average tumour size[a]	1.7 mm	1.5 mm
Regional/metastatic spread[a]	24%	16%
Poorly differentiated/anaplastic	31%	32%
Oestrogen receptor-positive	13%	11%
Progesterone receptor-positive	25%	20%

[a] significant difference ($P < 0.05$) between oestrogen-progestogen and placebo

The HABITS (Hormonal Replacement Therapy After Breast Cancer – Is It Safe?) trial of women with breast cancer randomised to receive HRT or not was stopped in December 2003 because of an increased incidence of adverse events in the HRT group.[16] In the 345 women followed until September 2003, the numbers of new breast cancer events in the HRT and non-HRT groups were, respectively, 11 and 2 for local recurrences, 10 and 5 for distant metastases, and 5 and 1 for contra-lateral breast cancer. The relative risk of new breast cancer events in those randomised to HRT compared with no HRT was 3.5 (95% CI 1.5–8.1).

Colorectal cancer

Both randomised trials and observational data suggest that use of HRT reduces the incidence of colorectal cancer.[2,6,10] Results from all randomised trials combined suggest about a 30% (95% CI 10–50%) reduction in the incidence of colorectal cancer associated with the use of combined HRT.[10] Observational data suggest about a 20% reduction in risk, but there is relatively little information on the effects of different types of HRT, or on the effects of duration and recency of use.[2]

Endometrial cancer

The fact that oestrogen-only HRT increases proliferation of the endometrium and the incidence of endometrial cancer has been known for almost 30 years.[17] Indeed, the main reason that progestogens are given together with oestrogens in women with a uterus is to reduce the risk of oestrogen-associated endometrial cancer. The relative risk of endometrial cancer increases with increasing duration of use of oestrogen-only HRT: the results from a meta-analysis of published studies, conducted mostly in the 1970s and 1980s, suggest a relative risk of around six for 5–9 years' use of HRT (Table 13.6).[17]

The addition of progestogen reduces the increased incidence of endometrial cancer associated with use of oestrogens-only HRT, and the more days each month that progestogens are used, the lower the relative risk is.[18,19] Overall, the results from published studies suggest a slightly increased risk of endometrial cancer, with a relative risk of about 1.3, associated with the addition of progestogens 'sequentially', that is,

Table 13.6. Summary of published results on the incidence of endometrial cancer in relation to use of HRT

	Relative risk (95% CI)
Oestrogen-only HRT[17]	
Duration <1 year	1.4 (1.0–1.8)
Duration 1–4 years	2.8 (2.3–3.5)
Duration 5–9 years	5.9 (4.7–7.5)
Duration ≥10 years	9.5 (7.4–12.3)
Sequential oestrogen-progestogen HRT[2]	
Ever versus never	1.3 (1.1–1.5)
Continuous oestrogen-progestogen HRT[20]	
Women's Health Initiative trial	0.8 (0.5–1.4)

for only part of each month.[2] Continuous use of progestogens together with oestrogens appears to result in an incidence of endometrial cancer similar to, or possibly slightly lower than, the incidence in never users of HRT.[19,20] In the Women's Health Initiative trial there was no significant difference in the incidence of endometrial cancer in women taking continuous combined oestrogen-progestogen HRT and those taking placebo (Table 13.6).[20] There is little published information on the effects on endometrial cancer of long-duration use of combined HRT, or on the persistence of effects after use ceases, although there is some evidence to suggest that the effects of oestrogen-only HRT on the endometrium may persist for some years after use of HRT stops.[18,19]

Other cancers

Observational studies suggest a possible slight increase in the risk of ovarian cancer, which may increase with increasing duration of use of HRT. Relative risks of about 1.5 have been found associated with ever use compared with never use of oestrogen-only HRT and relative risks of about 1.2 associated with oestrogen-progestogen HRT.[2,21–23] The Women's Health Initiative trial reported a relative risk of 1.58 (95% CI 0.77–3.24), based on 20 ovarian cancers in the HRT group and 12 in the placebo group.[20] Thus the available data suggest that use of HRT might perhaps increase the risk of ovarian cancer, but more information is required before this association can be clarified.

The Women's Health Initiative trial reported a statistically significantly increased incidence of abnormal Papanicolaou cervical smear results in women receiving HRT.[20] In the trial a relative risk of 1.44 (95% CI 0.47–4.42) was found, based on a total of 13 incident cervical cancers. The trial investigators concluded that further investigation of these results was warranted.

The effect of HRT on other cancers, which are generally rarer than those already mentioned, has been little studied.

Comparison of results from randomised trials and observational studies

Randomised controlled clinical trials have the advantage that the allocation of treatment (HRT versus placebo in the trials considered here) is at random, thus minimising any consequences of biased prescribing. Differential prescribing of HRT on the basis of past health, with the tendency not to prescribe HRT to women with medical problems, is well documented.[4] In the Million Women Study, for example, those with a history of breast cancer or of conditions that predispose to ischaemic heart disease tended to be less likely to be currently using HRT than women with no such history (Table 13.7). As might be expected, women with such conditions are at a substantially increased risk of death from cancer and ischaemic heart disease (Table 13.7). Differential prescribing according to medical history can seriously distort comparisons in observational studies between HRT users and nonusers in terms of their mortality from cancer and the incidence of other conditions, such as ischaemic heart disease. Since the prescribing of HRT is influenced by complex clinical judgements, no amount of statistical manipulation of results from observational studies can adjust adequately for this. The discrepancies between results from randomised trials and observational studies on the effect of HRT on survival with breast cancer and on incidence and mortality from ischaemic heart disease are largely due to this type of

%**Table 13.7.** Relationship between a history of cancer and cardiovascular disease at recruitment into the Million Women Study,[9] the prevalence of use of HRT at recruitment, and subsequent mortality in never users of HRT

Medical history at recruitment	Prevalence of use of HRT at recruitment (%)	Age-adjusted relative risk of death[a]
Breast cancer	4	84.0[b]
Other cancer	35	6.3[c]
Conditions predisposing to ischaemic heart disease:		
Diabetes	26	15.4[d]
Heart disease	31	13.7[d]
Stroke	26	13.5[d]
Hypertension	34	4.4[d]
Thromboembolism	27	3.9[d]
None of the above	34	1.0

[a] relative risk of death up to 31 December 2002 associated with a history of the condition listed versus a history of none of the conditions listed, in never users of HRT at recruitment; [b] relative risk of death from breast cancer up to 31 December 2002; [c] relative risk of death from cancer other than breast cancer up to 31 December 2002; [d] relative risk of death from ischaemic heart disease up to 31 December 2002

bias: women with clinical conditions predictive of a high risk of subsequent morbidity and mortality tend not to be prescribed HRT.

Cancer incidence is poorly predicted, if at all, by known medical conditions. There is thus less scope for the type of prescribing bias that is evident when studying cancer survival or the incidence of ischaemic heart disease. Results on cancer incidence show similar findings from randomised trials and observational studies (as described above), further indicating that prescribing biases are not of major concern with respect to cancer incidence. Some lifestyle factors do predict cancer risk, but, except for smoking and lung cancer, such factors tend to be associated with relative risks of two or less. Also, there is less variation in prescribing of HRT according to lifestyle factors than according to past health.[4] Statistical adjustments for lifestyle factors can be performed; although, for the aforementioned reasons, adjustments for factors other than menopausal status have little effect on the overall results – for incident breast cancer, at least.[1,7]

Overall, results from randomised trials must carry more weight than observational studies and, where any discrepancies exist, the trial results should take precedence. However, randomised trials have some inherent shortcomings that are relevant when considering the effects of HRT on cancer. 'Intention to treat' analyses, which are central to the proper reporting of trial results, do not permit examination of the effects of different patterns of use of HRT, such as even simple comparisons of the effect of current and past use of HRT. Furthermore, if compliance is low, as it was in the Women's Heath Initiative trial several years after recruitment, intention to treat analyses necessarily dilute the magnitude of any real effect. Trials of HRT versus placebo were set up, and sample size calculated, mainly with ischaemic heart disease as the chief outcome to be examined. Hence, the trials have little statistical power to look at specific cancers, and indeed breast cancer is the only cancer that is common enough to be studied.[6,11] Each randomised trial has tended to study one type of HRT only versus placebo, and by far the most common preparation studied is conjugated equine oestrogen (CEE) and medroxyprogesterone acetate (MPA), as this was the most widely used combined HRT preparation when the trials were set up. So questions inevitably arise about whether results from trials of one specific HRT product can be generalised to other types of HRT. Studying the effects of different types of HRT and different patterns of use requires observational data, and there is less scope for bias in such comparisons than there is when comparing users and nonusers of HRT.

Questions arise about whether trial results can be generalised to other populations, and the examination of the trial results in different subgroups, for example, by age and body mass index, and the replication of results in observational data help address that question. So far, the findings from the trials do not vary significantly between women of different ages, medical histories and behaviours, thus suggesting that the results are applicable to the general population.

Absolute risk of cancer

As described above, most of our knowledge on the effects of HRT on cancer relates to breast cancer. In Table 13.8 we have attempted to calculate the excess incidence of cancer of the breast, colorectum, endometrium and ovary for 1000 women using oestrogen-only and combined HRT from age 50 to 55 years. The estimates are made over five years only, as considerable uncertainty exists about the effect of past use of HRT for cancers other than breast cancer. Estimates are given in brackets where they are very uncertain, such as for colorectal cancer with oestrogen-only therapy or for ovarian cancer with either type of therapy.

The results of these calculations show that, when considering all cancers together, the effect of HRT on breast cancer predominates. They also show that the fewest additional HRT-associated cancers are found in women who have had a hysterectomy and use oestrogen-only therapy (estimated excess incidence of cancer of about 1 in 600 HRT users over five years). For women with a uterus, the excess incidence of cancer is greater for users of oestrogen-progestogen HRT than of oestrogen-only HRT (estimated excess incidences of about 1 in 200, and 1 in 400, respectively).

Table 13.8. Incidence of certain cancers from age 50 to 55 years in 1000 women, and estimated excess incidence associated with use of HRT for 5 years, beginning at age 50 years; figures given in parentheses are uncertain (see footnotes and text)

Cancer site	5-year incidence in 1000 never users of HRT	Excess incidence in 1000 women using:	
		oestrogen-only HRT	oestrogen-progestogen HRT
Breast	9.0[a]	+1.5[a]	+6.0[a]
Colorectum	1.7[7]	0[b]	−0.6[b]
Ovary	1.5[7]	(+0.8)[c]	(+0.3)[c]
Endometrium (in women with a uterus)	1.6[7]	+0.9[d]	(−0.3)[d]

[a] from the Million Women Study;[9] [b] from the Women's Health Initiative trial for oestrogen-progestogen HRT[6] and of oestrogen-only HRT,[25] assuming that the effects of oestrogen-only HRT are similar; [c] assuming a relative risk of 1.5 in current users of oestrogen-only HRT and 1.2 in current users of oestrogen-progestogen HRT;[2,22,23] [d] assuming that the relative risk increases by a factor of 1.2 per year of use for oestrogen-only HRT[18] and assuming a relative risk of 0.8 for users of continuous combined HRT[20]

Conclusions

Since breast cancer is far more common than other cancers at ages when women typically use HRT, the overall effect of HRT on cancer in the short term is dominated by its effect on breast cancer. To evaluate the long-term effect of HRT on all cancer, more needs to be known about the effects of different types of HRT and about the persistence of its effects in past users. Randomised trials and observational studies yield similar findings for cancer incidence, but observational studies of breast cancer survival appear to be biased, presumably by the selective prescribing of HRT to women with good-prognosis disease.[24]

Addendum

After the RCOG meeting had ended, the oestrogen-only arm of the Women's Health Initiative trial was stopped early because of an excess of stroke in the treated group.[25] At that time there was no significant difference between the oestrogen-only and placebo group for the incidence of breast cancer (RR = 0.77, 95% CI 0.59–1.01) or of colorectal cancer (RR = 1.08, 95% CI 0.75–1.55). The results for breast cancer in the Women's Health Initiative trials of oestrogen-only and oestrogen-progestogen combinations were significantly different, in line with the findings from observational studies (discussed in the main manuscript). Women in the oestrogen-only arm of the Women's Health Initiative were considerably more obese than women in the Million Women Study (45% and 18%, respectively, had a body mass index of greater than 30 kg/m^2).[26] The relative risk of breast cancer associated with use of oestrogen-only HRT has been shown to be reduced the more obese women are, and the fact that obesity was so common in the trial participants probably accounts, at least in part, for the apparently low relative risk of breast cancer found in the trial.[26]

References

1. Collaborative Group on Hormonal Factors in Breast Cancer. Breast cancer and hormone replacement therapy: collaborative reanalysis of data from 51 epidemiological studies of 52,705 women with breast cancer and 108,411 women without breast cancer. *Lancet* 1997;350:1047–59. Erratum in: *Lancet* 1997;350:1484.

2. Beral V, Banks E, Reeves G, Appleby, A. Use of hormone replacement therapy and the subsequent risk of cancer. *J Epidemiol Biostat* 1999;4:191–215.

3. Banks E, Barnes I, Baker K, Key TJ. Use of hormonal therapy for the menopause in nine European countries. In: Riboli E, Lambert E, editors. *Nutrition and Lifestyle: Opportunities for Cancer Prevention*. Lyon: IARC; 2002. p. 301–3.

4. Million Women Study Collaborators. Patterns of use of hormone replacement therapy in one million women in Britain, 1996–2000. *BJOG* 2002;109:1319–30.

5. Hersh AL, Stefanick ML, Randall SS. National use of postmenopausal hormone therapy – annual trends and response to recent evidence. *JAMA* 2004;291:47–53.

6. Rossouw JE, Anderson GL, Prentice RL, LaCroix AZ, Kooperberg C, Stefanick ML, *et al.*; Writing Group for the Women's Health Initiative Investigators. Risks and benefits of estrogen plus progestin in healthy postmenopausal women: principal results fom the Women's Health Initiative randomized controlled trial. *JAMA* 2002;288:321–33.

7. Office of National Statistics. Cancer Statistics, Registrations. *Registrations of Cancers Diagnosed in 2000, England*. Series MB1 no. 31. London: Her Majesty's Stationery Office; 2003.

8. Office of National Statistics. Mortality Statistics, Cause. *Review of the Registrar General on Deaths by Cause, Sex and Age, in England and Wales, 2000*. Series DH2 no. 27. London: Her Majesty's Stationery Office; 2001.

9. Beral V; Million Women Study Collaborators. Breast cancer and hormone-replacement therapy in

the Million Women Study. *Lancet* 2003;362:419–27. Erratum in: *Lancet* 2003;362:1160.

10.   Beral V, Banks E, Reeves G. Evidence from randomised trials on the long-term effects of hormone replacement therapy. *Lancet* 2002;360:942–4.

11.   Chlebowski RT, Hendrix SL, Langer RD, Stefanick ML, Gass M, Lane D, *et al.*; WHI Investigators. Influence of estrogen plus progestin on breast cancer and mammography in healthy postmenopausal women: the Women's Health Initiative Randomized Trial. *JAMA* 2003;289:3243–53.

12.   Li CI, Malone KE, Porter PL, Weiss NS, Tang MT, Cushing-Haugen KL, *et al.* Relationship between long durations and different regimens of hormone therapy and risk of breast cancer. *JAMA* 2003;289:3254–63.

13.   Banks E. Hormone replacement therapy and the sensitivity and specificity of breast cancer screening: a review. *J Med Screen* 2001;8:29–35.

14.   Banks E, Reeves G, Beral V, Bull D, Crossley B, Simmonds M, *et al.* Impact of use of hormone replacement therapy on false positive recall in the NHS breast screening programme: results from the Million Women Study. *BMJ* 2004;328:1291–2.

15.   Million Women Study Collaborators. Breast cancer and hormone replacement therapy: the Million Women Study. *Lancet* 2003;362:1330–1.

16.   Holmberg L, Anderson H; HABITS steering and data monitoring committees. HABITS (hormonal replacement therapy after breast cancer – is it safe?), a randomised comparison: trial stopped. *Lancet* 2004;363:453–5.

17.   Grady D, Gebretsadik T, Kerlikowski K, Ernster V, Petitti D. Hormone replacement therapy and endometrial cancer risk: a meta-analysis. *Obstet Gynecol* 1995;85:304–13.

18.   Pike MC, Peters RK, Cozen W, Probst-Hensch NM, Felix JC, Wan PC, *et al.* Estrogen-progestin replacement therapy and endometrial cancer. *J Natl Cancer Inst* 1997;89:1110–6.

19.   Weiderpass E, Adami HO, Baron JA, Magnusson C, Bergstrom R, Lindgren A, *et al.* Risk of endometrial cancer following estrogen replacement with and without progestins. *J Natl Cancer Inst* 1999;91:1131–7.

20.   Anderson GL, Judd HL, Kaunitz AM, Barad DH, Beresford SA, Pettinger M, *et al.*; Women's Health Initiative Investigators. Effects of estrogen plus progestin on gynecologic cancers and associated diagnostic procedures: the Women's Health Initiative randomized trial. *JAMA* 2003;290:1739–48.

21.   Bosetti C, Negri E, Franceschi S, Trichopoulos D, Beral V, La Vecchia C. Relationship between postmenopausal hormone replacement therapy and ovarian cancer. *JAMA* 2001;285:3089.

22.   Lacey JV, Mink PJ, Lubin JH, Sherman ME, Troisi R, Hartge P, *et al.* Menopausal hormone replacement therapy and risk of ovarian cancer. *JAMA* 2002;288:334–41.

23.   Riman T, Dickman PW, Nilsson S, Correia N, Nordlinder H, Magnusson CM, *et al.* Hormone replacement therapy and the risk of invasive epithelial ovarian cancer in Swedish women. *J Natl Cancer Inst* 2002;94:497–504.

24.   Chlebowski RT, Col N. Menopausal hormone therapy after breast cancer. *Lancet* 2004;363:440–1.

25.   Anderson GL, Limacher M, Assaf AR, Bassford T, Beresford SA, Black H, *et al.*; Women's Health Initiative Steering Committee. Effects of conjugated equine estrogen in postmenopausal women with hysterectomy: the Women's Health Initiative randomized controlled trial. *JAMA* 2004;291:1701–12.

26.   Beral V, Banks E, Reeves G; Million Women Study Collaborators. Effects of estrogen-only treatment in postmenopausal women [letter]. *JAMA* 2004 11;292:684.

Chapter 14

Oestrogen: brain ageing, cognition and neuropsychiatric disorder

Ray Norbury, Michael Craig, William Cutter,
Malcolm Whitehead and Declan Murphy

Introduction

Numerous studies have demonstrated unequivocally that oestrogen has effects on brain regions beyond those involved in gonadal regulation and reproduction.[1] Both isoforms of oestrogen receptor (ERα and ERβ) are expressed throughout the brain,[2] including areas implicated in learning, memory and higher cognitive function (e.g. hippocampus and cerebral cortex). Oestrogen can therefore significantly impact on the development, maturation and function of brain regions involved in cognition and neuropsychiatric disorder.

Over the past century, the average life expectancy of women has increased significantly yet the average age at which women reach menopause has remained essentially constant at approximately 52 years.[3] This means that women can now expect to spend around half of their adult life in postmenopausal years. The possibility that hormone replacement therapy (HRT) may protect against age-related cognitive decline and reduce the risk of age-related dementia has therefore become a major public health issue. Here we review the studies that have contributed to our understanding of the effects of oestrogen on brain ageing, cognition and neuropsychiatric disorder.

Oestrogen as a neuroprotectant

Oestrogens significantly affect the microstructure of brain regions that are crucial to higher cognitive function. In the adult female rat, hippocampal CA1 pyramidal cell dendritic spine and synapse density varies as a function of oestrus cycle. During pro-oestrus, when ovarian steroids peak, spine density is greatest. Conversely, in di-oestrus, when ovarian steroid levels are minimal, spine density reduces. In addition, ovariectomy reduces dendritic spine density in CA1, an effect that can be ameliorated or reversed by exogenous oestrogen.[4]

It has been proposed that the trophic and plastic effects of oestrogen may be due, in part, to activation of neurotrophic factors.[5] Nerve growth factor, brain-derived neurotrophic factor, neurotrophin 3, insulin-like growth factor 1, and their cognate receptors directly support neuronal viability. Oestrogen induces transcription of neurotrophic factors, and the widespread co-localisation of oestrogen receptors, neurotrophic factors and their receptors suggests that these two signalling molecules may interact to modulate cell survival.[6]

Oestrogen may also act as an antioxidant.[7] During the course of normal metabolism reactive oxygen species (ROS) are produced. These ROS have the capacity to oxidise and damage a variety of cellular constituents, including lipids, DNA and proteins. The brain has a high rate of oxygen consumption and is therefore particularly vulnerable to damage by oxidative stress. Oestrogens are inhibitors of lipid peroxidation and can, when present with intrinsic defence mechanisms against oxidative stress (e.g. glutathione peroxidase), provide protection against ROS at physiologically relevant concentrations.[8]

Gender differences in brain structure arise as a normal part of brain maturation. Females, for example, have greater myelination during adolescence than males in areas such as the superior medulla lamina.[9] It is possible that later myelination in males may render them more vulnerable to neuropsychiatric disorders such as schizophrenia. Studies have also reported that males (age range 7–17 years) show a significantly greater reduction in cerebral grey matter volume compared with females over a similar age range.[10] It has been suggested that this may be due to an accelerated rate of neuronal pruning, which may also contribute to the earlier onset and increased severity of schizophrenia in males.

We have used magnetic resonance imaging (MRI) to examine the effects of long-term oestrogen replacement therapy (ERT), started at or around the menopause, on age-related differences in regional cerebral morphology (unpublished data). Women who had never taken ERT had a greater age-related reduction in grey matter concentration in prefrontal and temporal cortex and cerebellum, suggesting that oestrogen may protect the brain from ageing in regions that are implicated in higher cognitive function and affected by Alzheimer's disease (AD). More recently, Eberling et al.[11] evaluated the effects of ERT and the selective oestrogen receptor modulator (SERM) tamoxifen in postmenopausal women using MRI and ^{18}F-fluorodeoxyglucose positron emission tomography (^{18}F-FDG PET), which is a measure of glucose metabolism. Both the tamoxifen-treated group and ERT nonusers showed lower metabolism in frontal and temporal cortex with respect to the ERT-treated group. In addition, the tamoxifen-treated group had smaller right hippocampal volumes than the ERT-treated group. The ERT nonusers had hippocampal volumes that were intermediate to the other two groups. The results from these studies provide physiological and anatomical evidence for a neuroprotective effect of oestrogen in the ageing female brain.

Functional imaging techniques have also been employed to assess the effects of oestrogen on networks subserving various aspects of cognitive function.[12] A randomised placebo-controlled cross-over study using functional magnetic resonance imaging (fMRI) found oestrogen-induced alterations in brain activation patterns during encoding and retrieval of both verbal and nonverbal stimuli.[13] Maki and Resnick[14] used PET to examine longitudinal changes in regional cerebral blood flow (rCBF) over a two-year period in women on and off HRT (both with and without adjuvant progestogen therapy). HRT use was associated with increased rCBF in the right hippocampus, parahippocampal gyrus and left middle temporal gyrus – regions implicated in learning and memory. We have shown that long-term (>5 years) users of ERT had significantly reduced age-related differences in neuronal membrane breakdown (as measured by ^{1}H magnetic resonance spectroscopy) in hippocampus and parietal lobe, and this was inversely related to performance on a visual memory task.[15] Thus, ERT may modulate age-related differences in rCBF and neuronal membrane breakdown, and this may partially explain ERT's neuroprotective effect.

Oestrogen effects on neurotransmitter systems

The cholinergic system

In rats, long-term loss of ovarian function has a negative impact on basal forebrain cholinergic function. Conversely, oestrogen replacement enhances cholinergic function as evidenced by increases in choline acetyltransferase (ChAT) activity, choline uptake and potassium-evoked acetylcholine release.[3] Muscarinic receptor density varies as a function of oestrus cycle, being highest during pro-oestrus and lowest during di-oestrous.[16] In addition, ovariectomy upregulates m_4 type muscarinic receptors in rat frontal cortex, hypothalamus and hippocampus, whereas oestrogen treatment restores binding to that seen in vehicle-treated controls.[17] Oestrogen replacement also reduces the cognitive impairment produced by the muscarinic receptor antagonist scopolamine.[18] The effect of oestrogen on markers of cholinergic function (e.g. ChAT) and hippocampal muscarinic receptors may have functional significance, especially in relation to postmenopausal memory problems and neurodegenerative disorders such as AD.

Studies in humans also suggest a beneficial effect of oestrogen on cholinergic function. We have reported significantly higher cholinergic responsivity in women taking long-term ERT compared with women who were ERT-naive (as measured by growth hormone [GH] response to oral pyridostigmine).[19] Moreover, in the long-term ERT users there was a significant positive correlation between GH response and duration of oestrogen exposure. Smith et al.[20] used single-photon emission tomography (SPET) and the radiotracer ^{123}I-iodobenzovesamicol (a marker for presynaptic cholinergic terminals) to examine the effect of long-term HRT on brain cholinergic synaptic density. They found no significant differences in regional binding indices between HRT users and nonusers. However, length of HRT treatment correlated positively with iodobenzovesamicol binding in frontal, temporal and parietal cortices. This study was an important first step and suggests that, although no main effect of HRT was found, HRT may influence the survival or plasticity of cholinergic cells. Taken together, these findings suggest that in older postmenopausal women oestrogen may be involved in the normal maintenance and physiological regulation of cholinergic projections, and that ERT can enhance the functional status of these cholinergic projections.

The serotonergic system

The 5-hydroxytryptamine$_{2A}$ ($5HT_{2A}$) receptor is important in many neuropsychiatric disorders, including depression, schizophrenia and AD.[21] The density of $5HT_{2A}$ receptors in the frontal and cingulate cortex significantly increases in rat brain during pro-oestrus.[22] In ovariectomised rats, there is an increase in central $5HT_2$ receptors and a concomitant decrease in $5HT_1$ receptors following two weeks of oestrogen-only treatment.[23] Progestogen alone had identical directional effects on receptor number, but the effect was less pronounced. However, combined treatment blocked the oestrogen-induced increase in $5HT_2$ receptors. The suggestion that oestrogen modulates expression of 5HT receptors in humans is supported by two PET studies. Moses et al.[24] reported increased $5HT_{2A}$ receptor density in a number of brain regions in women who took 8–14 weeks of ERT followed by the addition of progestogen for 2–6 weeks. Kugaya et al.[25] found significant increases in $5HT_{2A}$ binding in prefrontal regions following approximately 10 weeks of unopposed oestrogen. They also found that verbal fluency and trail making test performance, but not mood, were significantly improved by oestrogen without correlation with receptor changes. We have also shown that ERT significantly modulates the age-related reduction in serotonergic responsivity.[21] Thus, there is increasing evidence that ovarian hormones interact with the 5HT system at multiple levels and this may help provide a theoretical role for oestrogen in the regulation of mood and hormone-linked affective states.

The dopaminergic system

Previous studies have reported gender differences in maturation of the dopaminergic system that may also be influenced by oestrogen. These studies suggest that dopaminergic neurons start to develop earlier in females and then exhibit a steeper pattern of decline in midlife.[26] Older human and animal studies indicate that oestrogen modulates many aspects of dopaminergic function. It remains unclear, however, whether oestrogens enhance or suppress the dopaminergic system. Preliminary data from this group suggest that ERT may prevent the decline in dopaminergic responsivity (as measured by GH response to apomorphine challenge) in postmenopausal women (unpublished data). This may have implications for the treatment of disorders such as Parkinson's disease.

The noradrenergic system

The noradrenergic system has been implicated both in depression and cognitive processes. Both α- and β-adrenergic receptors may be upregulated by oestradiol in ovariectomised female rats.[27] There is debate regarding the effect of oestrogens on the synthesis and breakdown of noradrenaline. Oestrogen has, for example, been reported both to increase and to decrease tyrosine hydroxylase activity (an enzyme involved in noradrenaline synthesis) in the hypothalamus and striatum.[28]

Oestrogen and cognitive function

The most robust effect of oestrogen on cognitive function is in verbal memory. Prospective randomised studies of HRT versus placebo following total abdominal hysterectomy (TAH) and bilateral salpingo-oophorectomy (BSO) report a significant positive effect of oestrogens on verbal memory.[29] Performance in some cognitive tasks also varies as a function of menstrual cycle in healthy premenopausal women. During the luteal phase (characterised by high levels of oestrogen and progesterone), verbal articulation is improved whereas spatial ability is decreased,[30] a pattern that is reversed during the follicular phase (which is characterised by relatively low oestrogen and progesterone). A similar pattern of cognitive performance is also observed if subjects are tested during the pre-ovulatory oestradiol surge (to control for the potential effects of progesterone on cognitive performance), suggesting that oestrogen rather then progesterone is responsible for the observed cognitive effects.

Oestrogen and Alzheimer's disease

LeBlanc *et al.*[31] reviewed the medical literature on the use of HRT for prevention of cognitive decline and reduction of dementia in healthy postmenopausal women, and performed a meta-analysis of observational studies. Women in the studies ranged in age from 45 to 80 years. Naturally and surgically menopausal women were included, and both combination therapy and unopposed oestrogen were used. Two cohort studies,[32,33] provided the strongest evidence for a reduced risk of AD in ERT/HRT users compared with nonusers, with relative risks of 0.5 (95% CI 0.25–0.9) and 0.46 (95% CI 0.21–1.00), respectively. The results of these two cohort studies, together with those of ten case–control studies, were combined by meta-analysis. Results indicated a 34% decreased risk of AD for women using ERT/HRT (summary RR 0.66; 95% CI 0.53–0.82). There is also evidence that duration of treatment is positively correlated with reduction in risk. Zandi et al.[34] showed that the risk of developing AD was reduced by 42%, 68% and 83% among women who had used HRT for <3 years, 3–10 years and >10 years, respectively.

The Women's Health Initiative Memory Study (WHIMS)[35,36] is a double-blind randomised placebo-controlled clinical trial that has enrolled a subgroup of women from the Women's Health Initiative (WHI) study[37] to examine the effect of HRT on the incidence of mild cognitive impairment and dementia. In total, 4532 women aged 65 years or over and free of probable dementia were randomised to take combined therapy, unopposed oestrogen or placebo. The oestrogen-progestogen arm of the WHI was discontinued early (after 5.6 years instead of the intended 8.5 years) as women in the intervention group were at increased risk for heart disease, stroke, pulmonary embolism and breast cancer compared with the women receiving placebo. The WHI oestrogen-only trial, which enrolled women with a prior hysterectomy, continues and is due to report in 2005. Thus, to date, results from the combined therapy trial only are available. Cognitive assessment was performed annually by completing the modified mini-mental state examination (MMSE), and participants were followed for a mean duration of 5.2 years. Based on 3MSE results, women exhibiting evidence of cognitive impairment received more extensive neuropsychological testing and neurological evaluation to confirm diagnosis and classify dementia type.

Rapp et al.[35] reported no significant between-group differences in rate of cognitive decline. However, Schumaker et al.[36] reported that women receiving combination HRT were twice as likely to develop probable dementia over a five-year period compared with controls ($n=40$ in the HRT group and $n=21$ in the placebo group; 95% CI 1.21–3.48). However, there were no significant between-group differences in the most common classification of dementia, AD ($n=20$ [50%] in the HRT group and $n=12$ [57.1%] in the placebo group; $P=0.79$). The remaining 20 cases of dementia in the HRT group included diagnoses such as normal-pressure hydrocephalus and alcohol-related dementia, and we are not aware of any reasons why HRT should be implicated in the aetiology of these disorders. However, it is possible that HRT increased risk for stroke/vascular events, and this may have led to an increase in all-cause dementia, but no increase in rate of gradual cognitive decline or AD. Thus, results from the above studies suggest that HRT initiated in women 65 years or older has no effect on rate of cognitive decline or incidence of AD, but may increase risk for all-cause dementia through vascular events.

How, then, do we reconcile the apparent discrepancy between these data and the results from observational studies that indicate a protective affect of oestrogen against AD? The answer to this question may reside in the animal literature. Animal studies indicate that continuous oestrogen replacement or cyclic administration of oestrogen plus progestogen may prevent age-related cognitive decline and enhance cognitive performance, provided that treatment is initiated within a limited period following loss of ovarian function.[37] Beyond this window of opportunity, neurones and/or neurochemical systems may remain refractory to the effects of oestrogen. Studies currently in progress are unlikely to address this problem: the oestrogen-only arm of the WHIMS, like the combined therapy group, focuses exclusively on women over the age of 65 years. A further potential confound of the WHIMS studies is a lack of apolipoprotein E (ApoE) genotyping. The ApoE ε4 allele is associated with earlier age at onset and increased risk of AD[38] and evidence suggests that oestrogen may modulate ApoE expression.[39] Oestrogen-accentuated expression of ApoE would mean that the potential benefits of HRT would be less effective in women bearing an ε4 allele. Thus, despite good evidence suggesting that postmenopausal HRT has positive effects on age-related dementia and cognition, conclusive evidence will not be forthcoming until questions concerning timing and regimen of replacement and genotyping of individuals are properly addressed.

Oestrogen and schizophrenia

There are gender differences in pre-morbid functioning, age of onset, symptomatology and outcome of schizophrenia. For example, men have a single peak of disease onset in the early 20s, whereas women have a later age of onset and a second peak in incidence between the ages of 45 and 55 years. In addition, women are more likely to have a family history of schizophrenia, atypical or affective features and show a seasonal pattern of hospital admission. Because oestrogen has putative anti-dopaminergic/antipsychotic actions, it has been suggested that in women oestrogens may be responsible for the delay in onset of the first peak, and the second peak may be due to the decline in oestrogen levels at menopause. However, when women with schizophrenia are given adjunctive treatment with exogenous oestrogen there is a slight increase in speed of recovery but no improvement overall compared with antipsychotic medication alone.[40] Despite the lack of clear evidence for the efficacy of oestrogen as an antipsychotic, it remains plausible that ERT might protect against late-onset schizophrenia in postmenopausal women by inhibiting the development of predisposing age-related changes in brain structure and neurochemistry (e.g. in the hippocampus).

Oestrogen and depression

Epidemiological evidence suggests that vulnerable subgroups of women are more prone to suffer depression at times of reproductive change (e.g. in the postpartum period there is a peak of incidence[41]). This observation has led to studies examining the effect of ERT on depression. The small number of studies and methodological difficulties present in many have meant that at present we cannot be sure of the role of oestrogen in depression: it may be useful as a prophylaxis against postpartum depression (PPD)[42] and as a treatment for PPD,[43] and it may also have an adjunctive role in treatment-resistant depression in women.[44] Reports that oestrogen may be useful as an antidepressant in the perimenopause[45,46] are difficult to substantiate as oestrogen may only be treating menopausal symptoms with the incidental effect of reducing secondary depressive symptoms. ERT is, however, effective in reducing mild depressive symptoms after the menopause.[47] Thus, the extent to which changes in endogenous oestrogen are important in the genesis of depression remains unclear. Moreover, oestrogen cannot on current evidence be recommended as an antidepressant, except perhaps in circumstances of nonresponse to standard therapy in women.

Conclusions

The potential beneficial effects of oestrogen on cognitive ageing and age-related dementia are an important public health issue. Considerable evidence supports the role of oestrogen as a neuroprotectant, and current understanding suggests that oestrogen, initiated at or around the time of the menopause, may protect against age-related cognitive decline and reduce the risk for developing AD. However, once AD is established oestrogen is ineffective. The role of oestrogen in depression and schizophrenia remains unclear. At present, oestrogen cannot be recommended as a first-line treatment for either of these disorders, but may have a role as an adjunct therapy.

References

1.   McEwen B. Estrogen actions throughout the brain. *Recent Prog Horm Res* 2002;57:357–84.
2.   Shughrue PJ, Lane MV, Merchenthaler I. Comparative distribution of estrogen receptor-alpha and -beta mRNA in the rat central nervous system. *J Comp Neurol* 1997;388:507–25.
3.   Gibbs RB, Gabor R. Estrogen and cognition: applying preclinical findings to clinical perspectives. *J Neurosci Res* 2003;74:637–43.
4.   Woolley CS, McEwen BS. Estradiol regulates hippocampal dendritic spine density via an N-methyl-D-aspartate receptor-dependent mechanism. *J Neurosci* 1994;14:7680–7.
5.   Brinton RD. Cellular and molecular mechanisms of estrogen regulation of memory function and neuroprotection against Alzheimer's disease: recent insights and remaining challenges. *Learn Mem* 2001;8:121–33.
6.   Toran-Allerand CD, Miranda RC, Bentham WD, Sohrabji F, Brown TJ, Hochberg RB, *et al*. Estrogen receptors colocalize with low-affinity nerve growth factor receptors in cholinergic neurons of the basal forebrain. *Proc Natl Acad Sci U S A* 1992;89:4668–72.
7.   Behl C. Estrogen can protect neurons: modes of action. *J Steroid Biochem Mol Biol* 2002;83:195–7.
8.   Green PS, Gordon K, Simpkins JW. Phenolic A ring requirement for the neuroprotective effects of steroids. *J Steroid Biochem Mol Biol* 1997;63:229–35.
9.   Benes FM, Turtle M, Khan Y, Farol P. Myelination of a key relay zone in the hippocampal formation occurs in the human brain during childhood, adolescence, and adulthood. *Arch Gen Psychiatry* 1994;51:477–84.
10.   De Bellis MD, Keshavan MS, Beers SR, Hall J, Frustaci K, Masalehdan A, *et al*. Sex differences in brain maturation during childhood and adolescence. *Cereb Cortex* 2001;11:552–7.
11.   Eberling JL, Wu C, Tong-Turnbeaugh R, Jagust WJ. Estrogen- and tamoxifen-associated effects on brain structure and function. *Neuroimage* 2004;21:364–71.
12.   Maki PM, Resnick SM. Effects of estrogen on patterns of brain activity at rest and during cognitive activity: a review of neuroimaging studies. *Neuroimage* 2001;14:789–801.
13.   Shaywitz SE, Shaywitz BA, Pugh KR, Fulbright RK, Skudlarski P, Mencl WE, *et al*. Effect of estrogen on brain activation patterns in postmenopausal women during working memory tasks. *JAMA* 1999;281:1197–202.
14.   Maki PM, Resnick SM. Longitudinal effects of estrogen replacement therapy on PET cerebral blood flow and cognition. *Neurobiol Aging* 2000;21:373–83.
15.   Robertson DM, van Amelsvoort T, Daly E, Simmons A, Whitehead M, Morris RG, *et al*. Effects of estrogen replacement therapy on human brain aging: an *in vivo* ^{1}H MRS study. *Neurology* 2001;57:2114–17.
16.   van Huizen F, Tonnaer JA. Muscarinic receptor regulation and 2nd messenger responses in rat neocortex cultures. *J Recept Res* 1993;13:437–51.
17.   El-Bakri NK, Adem A, Suliman IA, Mulugeta E, Karlsson E, Lindgren JU, *et al*. Estrogen and progesterone treatment: effects on muscarinic M(4) receptor subtype in the rat brain. *Brain Res* 2002;948:131–7.
18.   Gibbs RB. Estrogen replacement enhances acquisition of a spatial memory task and reduces deficits associated with hippocampal muscarinic receptor inhibition. *Horm Behav* 1999;36:222–33.
19.   van Amelsvoort T, Murphy DG, Robertson D, Daly E, Whitehead M, Abel K. Effects of long-term estrogen replacement therapy on growth hormone response to pyridostigmine in healthy

postmenopausal women. *Psychoneuroendocrinology* 2003;28:101–12.

20.   Smith YR, Minoshima S, Kuhl DE, Zubieta JK. Effects of long-term hormone therapy on cholinergic synaptic concentrations in healthy postmenopausal women. *J Clin Endocrinol Metab* 2001;86:679–84.

21.   van Amelsvoort TA, Abel KM, Robertson DM, Daly E, Critchley H, Whitehead M, *et al.* Prolactin response to d-fenfluramine in postmenopausal women on and off ERT: comparison with young women. *Psychoneuroendocrinology* 2001;26:493–502.

22.   Sumner BE, Fink G. The density of 5-hydroxytryptamine2A receptors in forebrain is increased at pro-oestrus in intact female rats. *Neurosci Lett* 1997;234:7–10.

23.   Biegon A, Reches A, Snyder L, McEwen BS. Serotonergic and noradrenergic receptors in the rat brain: modulation by chronic exposure to ovarian hormones. *Life Sci* 1983;32:2015–21.

24.   Moses EL, Drevets WC, Smith G, Mathis CA, Kalro BN, Butters MA, *et al.* Effects of estradiol and progesterone administration on human serotonin 2A receptor binding: a PET study. *Biol Psychiatry* 2000;48:854–60.

25.   Kugaya A, Epperson CN, Zoghbi S, van Dyck CH, Hou Y, Fujita M, *et al.* Increase in prefrontal cortex serotonin 2A receptors following estrogen treatment in postmenopausal women. *Am J Psychiatry* 2003;160:1522–4.

26.   Herlenius E, Lagercrantz H. Neurotransmitters and neuromodulators during early human development. *Early Hum Dev* 2001;65:21–37.

27.   Hernandez-Diaz FJ, Sanchez JJ, Abreu P, Lopez-Coviella I, Tabares L, Prieto L, *et al.* Estrogen modulates alpha(1)/beta-adrenoceptor-induced signaling and melatonin production in female rat pinealocytes. *Neuroendocrinology* 2001;73:111–22.

28.   Beattie CW, Rodgers CH, Soyka LF. Influence of ovariectomy and ovarian steroids on hypothalamic tyrosine hydroxylase activity in the rat. *Endocrinology* 1972;91:276–9.

29.   Phillips SM, Sherwin BB. Effects of estrogen on memory function in surgically menopausal women. *Psychoneuroendocrinology* 1992;17:485–95.

30.   Hampson E. Variations in sex-related cognitive abilities across the menstrual cycle. *Brain Cogn* 1990;14:26–43.

31.   LeBlanc ES, Janowsky J, Chan BK, Nelson HD. Hormone replacement therapy and cognition: systematic review and meta-analysis. *JAMA* 2001;285:1489–99.

32.   Tang MX, Jacobs D, Stern Y, Marder K, Schofield P, Gurland B, *et al.* Effect of oestrogen during menopause on risk and age at onset of Alzheimer's disease. *Lancet* 1996;348:429–32.

33.   Kawas C, Resnick S, Morrison A, Brookmeyer R, Corrada M, Zonderman A, *et al.* A prospective study of estrogen replacement therapy and the risk of developing Alzheimer's disease: the Baltimore Longitudinal Study of Aging. *Neurology* 1997;48:1517–21. Erratum in: *Neurology* 1998;51:654.

34.   Zandi PP, Carlson MC, Plassman BL, Welsh-Bohmer KA, Mayer LS, Steffens DC, *et al*; Cache County Memory Study Investigators. Hormone replacement therapy and incidence of Alzheimer disease in older women: the Cache County Study. *JAMA* 2002;288:2123–9.

35.   Rapp SR, Espeland MA, Shumaker SA, Henderson VW, Brunner RL, Manson JE, *et al*; WHIMS Investigators. Effect of estrogen plus progestin on global cognitive function in postmenopausal women: the Women's Health Initiative Memory Study: a randomized controlled trial. *JAMA* 2003;289:2663–72.

36.   Shumaker SA, Legault C, Rapp SR, Thal L, Wallace RB, Ockene JK, *et al*; WHIMS Investigators. Estrogen plus progestin and the incidence of dementia and mild cognitive impairment in postmenopausal women: the Women's Health Initiative Memory Study: a randomized controlled trial. *JAMA* 2003;289:2651–62.

37.   The Women's Health Initiative Study Group. Design of the Women's Health Initiative clinical trial and observational study. *Control Clin Trials* 1998;19:61–109.

38.   Corder EH, Saunders AM, Strittmatter WJ, Schmechel DE, Gaskell PC, Small GW, *et al.* Gene dose of apolipoprotein E type 4 allele and the risk of Alzheimer's disease in late onset families. *Science* 1993;261:921–3.

39.   Lambert JC, Coyle N, Lendon C. The allelic modulation of apolipoprotein E expression by oestrogen: potential relevance for Alzheimer's disease. *J Med Genet* 2004;41:104–12.

40.   Kulkarni J, Riedel A, de Castella AR, Fitzgerald PB, Rolfe TJ, Taffe J, *et al.* Estrogen – a potential treatment for schizophrenia. *Schizophr Res* 2001;48:137–44.

41.   Kumar R, Robson KM. A prospective study of emotional disorders in childbearing women. *Br J Psychiatry* 1984;144:35–47.

42.   Sichel DA, Cohen LS, Robertson LM, Ruttenberg A, Rosenbaum JF. Prophylactic estrogen in recurrent postpartum affective disorder. *Biol Psychiatry* 1995;38:814–18.

43.   Gregoire AJ, Kumar R, Everitt B, Henderson AF, Studd JW. Transdermal oestrogen for treatment of severe postnatal depression. *Lancet* 1996;347:930–3.

44.   Klaiber EL, Broverman DM, Vogel W, Kobayashi Y. Estrogen therapy for severe persistent

depressions in women. *Arch Gen Psychiatry* 1979;36:550–4.
45.   Schmidt PJ, Nieman L, Danaceau MA, Tobin MB, Roca CA, Murphy JH, *et al*. Estrogen replacement in perimenopause-related depression: a preliminary report. *Am J Obstet Gynecol* 2000;183:414–20.
46.   Soares CN, Almeida OP, Joffe H, Cohen LS. Efficacy of estradiol for the treatment of depressive disorders in perimenopausal women: a double-blind, randomized, placebo-controlled trial. *Arch Gen Psychiatry* 2001;58:529–34.
47.   Epperson CN, Wisner KL, Yamamoto B. Gonadal steroids in the treatment of mood disorders. *Psychosom Med* 1999;61:676–97.

Chapter 15

Effects of HRT on cancer, the breast and the brain

Discussion

Discussion following Mr Sturdee's paper

Burger: Is there really any convincing evidence that one progestogen has a better haemostatic profile than another? It has often been said that norethisterone is superior to medroxyprogesterone acetate (MPA), for example. Do you have any comments about that?

Sturdee: It has often been said but I do not have any data that shows that. I often wonder what is behind these statements. But I do not know of any data that prove it. I do not know from the point of view of the effect on the endometrium whether different progestogens have different effects on the various growth factors and other things that influence bleeding. I do not know whether Miss Rees might know more about that than me.

Rees: A couple of years ago we published[1] the effects of different progestogens in different doses using the mouse model and found that different progestogens did have different effects. When levonorgestrel was increased in dose, the angiogenic response was reduced and that was the only gestogen that was seen to do that on a consistent basis. We looked at levonorgestrel, norethisterone, MPA, and there was another gestogen – nomegestrol. We looked at four doses, which were achievable with systemic therapy.

Barlow: In relation to the question you were just asking about both the relative effects of the progestogens, part of that statement about norethisterone versus, say, MPA might relate to milligram for milligram dose since the MPA dose is much higher than the equivalent norethisterone dose, for example for endometrial protection the 5–10 mg MPA dose equates to a 0.5–1 mg dose of norethisterone.

Critchley: I think a very important factor is that levonorgestrel is the most androgenic progestogen of them all. We have data to show that there is a profound local effect of levonorgestrel on the androgen receptor and of course it is androgens that have the most potent effect on making the endometrium atrophic.

Burger: Yet when women are treated with combinations of oestrogen and testosterone it does not appear that testosterone itself has much endometrial protective effect, at least that is the hearsay-type evidence. Again I do not know of good hard scientific data about that, but I think if you treat a woman with a uterus then you have to give her a progestogen as well.

Critchley: I think what we have to remember is that we have a cell in the uterus and it is the intracellular ratio between the oestradiol and the androgen and obviously if you are bringing in progestogen then that acts on the enzymes that convert one to being more or less potent. So not only does it affect the ratio of the steroid that the cell produces, it also affects what happens to the receptor. What levonorgestrel does, for example, is switch off the enzyme that makes the oestrogen less potent but the androgen more potent. Depending on which progestogen the cell is seeing, it shifts that balance in different directions. So I think there is an explanation for why the androgenic progestogens, for example, then act on the growth factor angiogenic endpoints that Miss Rees is describing.

Whitehead: In terms of comparing progestogens, it is very important always to remember that MPA produced by 'Smith Pharmaceuticals' may have a completely different pharmacokinetic profile to MPA produced by 'Jones Pharmaceuticals'. The bioavailability of MPA from the three different major manufacturers is quite different. That is a point that is often not, I think in terms of scientific research, fully appreciated and taken into account.

Discussion following Professor Miller's paper

Lumsden: In the two studies you quoted, did they use similar doses of oestradiol and progestogen?

Miller: There were major differences in progestogens and if you read the Hofseth paper,[2] she does actually discuss this to some extent. I think 100% of the women in that study were taking MPA, whereas 92% in the Hargreaves study[3] were taking norgestrel or another nor-progestogen. So there is a major difference there and that might very well account for the differences. Although one would have to say, and I do not want to steal Professor Beral's thunder at all, that she will no doubt be at pains to point out that in the Million Women Study it really did not seem to matter what progestogen women were taking but there are differences. There are certainly differences in the nature of the oestrogens, yes, which could account for the differences.

Evans: A minor statistical point on the Hargreaves study, because you have a 111 observations and any outliers will give you a very distorted graphical picture there. The fact that there are a lot more and therefore you get more outliers and having very different sample sizes will end up giving you a wrong visual impression of your comparison there. The other thing is that I suspect it should be shown on the log scale and, if you were to do that, I would not be surprised if there were still some significant differences if you analysed it. I do not know, obviously.

Miller: Well, I am not a statistician and I take your point. I mean it is one of the points I hope I made as I was going through, there was a big difference. It was not a matched, a good matching, numerically, it was clearly biased in terms of the control group. In the paper they made the point clearly that the differences are nonsignificant.

Studd: The proliferative effects in breasts with progestogen is very impressive and it makes me wonder whether anybody has reviewed the histology in the breast cancer cases of these reports. I ask because Ingmar Persson, from Stockholm I think, reviewed the endometrial cancers, 15 years ago. It showed that 40% were downgraded to hyperplasia or *in situ* cancers. I just thought the same thing might occur with the breast, where you have this problem with *in situ* or intra-ductal carcinoma compared with cancer. Has anybody really reviewed the pathology?

Miller: In women on HRT? I think it has been done – certainly it has been looked at with regard to the contraceptive pill. I could probably go back into the literature and get the data for you. You might have the data, Dr Magnusson.

Magnusson: Before the Women's Health Initiative, many observational studies showed that breast cancer also appeared more benign after HRT than after non-treatment. But in the Chlebowski paper[4] of the Women's Health Initiative, again we were surprised to see that they seemed more malignant after HRT – they had more positive lymph nodes, more distant metastases, and so on.

Studd: But that is a solitary paper that is giving that message, is it not?

Magnusson: In the Nurse's Health Study[5] and in the Million Women Study there seems to be an increased mortality, not only incidence, of breast cancer after HRT.

Pitkin: I am not a breast surgeon but my understanding is that you need about 10 000 breast cancers to see a 5% difference in oestrogen-positive receptors and lymph node status. I wondered if the Women's Health Initiative, I think they had about 3500 cancers, was underpowered to make that observation, although the paper indicates that there is an increased risk of oestrogen receptor-positive tumours with more node-positive status. I think you need a larger number of breast cancers to actually make a definitive decision on that.

Magnusson: The comparisons were statistically significant.

Discussion following Dr Wilson's paper

Prentice: You mentioned that in the Persson *et al.*[6] summary there was no significant difference between oestradiol only and controls in the percentage that had increased mammographic density. Was there any dose information on oestradiol or any other oestrogens?

Wilson: That is the big problem with all these studies, that there is no information at all. We are lucky we know that they were on different hormone replacement therapies, I mean that is only one trial, the other trials do show a more significant effect of oestrogen alone compared with, say, tibolone or no HRT at all. That is one of the few that actually broke it down into different types.

Lowe: What happened if you looked at individuals serially in the postmenopausal situation? Women who were not taking any hormone preparations. Can you show for certain that there are any sequential changes?

Wilson: Yes, anecdotally we know that the mammographic density decreases in the women that we have screened for 15 years. A couple of studies in the USA have actually looked at that specifically, but interestingly, one of them that was published recently showed that the decline in breast density appears to have slowed in the 1990s compared to the 1980s.[7-9] There was less decline in breast density overall in that study in mammograms in the 1990s than in the 1980s. There was no real explanation for that.

Lowe: So if you actually say that 17–73% of women who were taking HRT clearly have a change in density, is that actually underestimating, when you say it is a change? Presumably that means that whatever you take away from 100% has no change, but actually therefore underestimating the effect, because you would have normally expected there to be a decrease!

Wilson: It probably is underestimating the effect because if the breast is already dense we are not going, by the way that we assess it, to see that it has become denser. That may actually have a significant effect in those particular women.

Rees: There was a paper by Greendale *et al.*[10] which was the PEPI study, that showed only an increase in combined HRT but not oestrogen alone. They have very well defined HRT regimens! So how did the increase in breast density compare with the data that you presented?

Wilson: In my chapter I have got the PEPI study included actually, but I think the problem is that is there is a range, as I have given, of 17–73%. It is because of the inconsistencies in the way the studies were done and also the inconsistencies in the way that people assessed what represented a dense breast or not. Some people were any change, in other people it had to be a 50% change, for instance. So I am not sure I can answer that question correctly.

Rees: Can you also comment why the paper in *JAMA*,[11] which compared the mammography screening services in the USA and in the UK, concluded that you had to have double the number of mammograms in the USA to detect one cancer than you would have in the UK?

Wilson: Was it that you did not have to have double the number of mammograms but they recalled twice as many women to detect the same number of cancers? That created a lot of anxiety by the Society of Breast Imaging because they took that as a direct criticism of how radiologists in the USA behave. But it has to be said that that is true in all aspects of medicine. The medicolegal setup is different, they are going to recall a lot more subtle changes for tests in the USA than we do here. We are much more specific. Our post-predictive value of recall is much higher in this country than it is in the USA but I do not think that says anything about the mammograms. It is just the level at which the radiologist fires a recall. I do not think we can read anything into that in terms of density and HRT.

Lumsden: When we were talking about this enormous rise due to radiation risk, how can you separate that out from the fact that women who are having annual screening, presumably, are at high risk?

Wilson: The risk is a purely theoretical calculation done by a physicist working in the Northern Yorkshire region. Nobody even knows whether there is a linear relationship with radiation or whether it is a threshold, exponential process. I think they tend to take the linear relationship and that it is additive, in other words that you will be having a mammogram one year additive to the next mammogram you have done. This is purely relating to the frequency in the young age trials where women had eight successive mammograms between the ages of 40 and 48. We do not routinely screen like that – it was only for women in that trial and it was still felt that a 100 to 1 benefit outweighed the risk of radiation in that population.

Studd: With this data you have shown us, should we change our views on the frequency of mammographic screening from the formal three years in patients who are having HRT?

Wilson: I think the answer to that is no, because if HRT is having an effect on the mammogram, doing the mammogram more often does not make it easier to interpret. If it has gone dense and we cannot see the cancer, we will just not see it more frequently.

Discussion following Professor Beral's paper

Burger: One of my real concerns about the announcement of the Women's Health Initiative was that the statement was made that in that study after an average 5.2 years of use there was a 26% increase in the relative risk of breast cancer. When one read the actual paper, one found that approximately 26% of the participants had previously used HRT for some varying interval. And when the statistics were given for those who had not previously used HRT, there was no statistically significant increase for an average of 5.2 or at least after 5.2 years of use. One might have said that a more reasonable way to present the data would be to say that women who had not previously used HRT, when using HRT for an average duration of 5.2 years, did not have any increase in breast cancer risk. Now, firstly, I wanted to ask Professor Beral or Dr Prentice to make a comment on that and, secondly, how do you resolve the difference that women who never previously had HRT and then had five years had no increased risk after five years? How does the randomised controlled trial data fit with the results of a study like the Million Women Study?

Prentice: On your first point, the plan for trial reporting, from the outset, focused on overall trial data. That is why we emphasised the overall estimated 26% increase. But, as you say, when we broke it into subsets such as duration of prior use or whether or not there was prior use, the data became fine but they became rather sparse. Nevertheless, as you said, there was no evidence of increase in the group that did not have prior use. The trend with whether or not, and duration of prior use was significant or borderline significant. So I think that is a provocative point and it is probably a point that leads into some of Professor Beral's initial comments that trials are small. They seem large when you are doing them, but they are not able to address all the questions and we have to rely on interplay with observational data to look carefully at some of these finer points. I think the Million Women Study would add to our ability to make a statement on that point.

Your question about how the trial results and observational studies like the marvellous 1.3 Million Women Study fit together is a good one and I think that has not been really carefully done yet. I hope we will do something like I showed yesterday for cardiovascular disease, comparing our trial and our cohort study, where we have a lot of common data collection and so on. But we will try to look at that type of question more carefully there.

Evans: Can I just ask a point of clarification, Professor Beral? You said that the rapid effect for HRT came in quite quickly. Am I right in thinking that there are two aspects to the rapid effect? The first one is that HRT can have a rapid effect in hiding cancers. That is the point – that somebody who has a cancer that was beginning to appear prior to their using HRT, that if they were a nonuser their cancer would be detected at screening? But HRT might well then hide that cancer at screening and it is not then detected till later.

Beral: For people who use HRT for less than a year, there is no significant increase in breast cancer in the first year after recruitment. But they had fewer cancers picked up on screening than women who were not using HRT. I think some of the Women's Health Initiative data, too, showed the rapid effect on recall. I think Dr Wilson would say too that the effects on breast density occur quite rapidly, do they not?

Wilson: Yes, they do. The other interesting thing is that if you compare that to interval cancers after screening the presentation of cancers with the whole population, you do not see that pattern. You have less in year one, more in year two, and then about the same in year three. The interval cancer presentation goes up with time. So it is a masking effect and it fits with other observations of interval cancers that there is a 2.2 relative risk in the first year if you are on HRT, whereas the interval cancers tend to present much later, purely because they probably were not visible and they have just grown, whereas in the HRT users they are hidden.

Evans: Can I come back to your point, it relates to Dr Prentice's data? In the women who were never users in the Women's Health Initiative, the actual data was 114 versus 102, hazard ratio 1.06, 95% confidence interval 0.81–1.38. Now what you are saying is that there is no increase in them. What I think is that it is a classic error that people make in saying that when there is no significant difference it means that there is no increased risk. Now that confidence interval goes up to 1.38 and that includes the overall point estimate. It is clear there is no real strong heterogeneity of risk by the prior use. So to say that this shows there is not a risk, now if that risk of being one with the confidence interval 0.99–1.1, you know or 0.99–1.01 rather, then I might go with what you are saying, that the Women's Health Initiative should have gone out with a message saying that there is no real risk in there. But what they could not say was that there is no real risk in them and so I would say that your criticism of them is misplaced because you have to take into account the uncertainty. Once Dr Prentice said in his brilliant and succinct way that he had said the data are fine. It means it is a fine cut and as soon as I start fine cutting things, then the confidence intervals widen and my uncertainty becomes much greater. So I have to be very careful with that kind of interpretation.

Whitehead: I am intrigued by HRT masking cancers. If you go to the Women's Health Initiative paper, which reports the number of patients and the percentages for recall because the mammogram was unsatisfactory, it seems to run out at about 4% per annum. That is in the Women's Health Initiative, which is continuous combined oestrogen-progestogen replacement. Now would a misreading in 4% of the population come up with that sort of increase in relative risk, if continuous combined is really masking the cancer? That is one question. The second question is were the baseline mammograms of the patients who were found to have cancers, say within 18 months of being enrolled into the study, reviewed to see if there was a cancer there that had been missed?

Beral: First of all, I would say that the recall rates in the UK and in the USA are completely different. As someone said, it is a medicolegal issue and there are all sorts of reasons why the recall rate is much higher in the USA. Furthermore, in general, mammographies are done annually in the USA whereas they are only done every three years in the UK. So, actually, that aspect of the two studies is quite different in terms of the frequency of mammography. It is thus quite problematic to compare and I would not even begin to guess what would predict what. The answer regarding re-reading is no, it has not been done yet but it is in active discussion. These are not trivial questions or exercises to do.

Wilson: I do not know the details of this study – this 4% we are talking about, is that unsatisfactory mammograms?

Whitehead: That is the recall rate from the Women's Health Initiative.

Wilson: They recalled only 4%?

Whitehead: Per year, because the mammograms were unsatisfactory.

Wilson: Does unsatisfactory mean that they wanted to repeat them because they were technically unsatisfactory or because they thought there was an abnormality?

Whitehead: Sorry, it was 4% in the placebo group, but 8% in the hormone user group, so it is a 4% excess in the hormone user group.

Wilson: That is quite a low recall rate for the USA.

Whitehead: Suspicious abnormality was about 1% and highly suggestive of malignancy 0.1%. That is the data as it is reflected in the paper.

Wilson: The other paper[11] that we were talking about compared screening in three different centres in the USA with the UK. The average recall rate there was about 12–13%, compared to the UK where it is about 4–5%. You are talking about the review of the mammograms to see if anything was missed. People may be surprised to hear that the published evidence from the screening programme in the UK in the last ten years is that if you review the mammograms, 50% of the cancers are visible in retrospect. Whether you would look at the films again blind and recall it is a different thing. But if you know where it is, and you go back and look at it, there is something there in up to 50%. That is in the non-HRT group, and I think the pure effect that you are getting here is not that the HRT in the first year is causing a dramatic increase in the incidence of breast cancer but what it is doing is stopping us from seeing what was already pre-existent.

Prentice: I think I am just stating the obvious, but if an intervention preparation such as HRT affects the outcome and the ability to measure the outcome, even a randomised controlled trial does not give unbiased comparisons there. So that relates to Professor Burger's original question. It is likely in our trial, as we studied hazard ratios in relation to prior use, that there is underestimation among never users and some underestimation in the previous use categories as well. So it really adds to Professor Evans's comments about the difficulty of making a clear statement about the never user group, as to whether or not there is evidence for an increased risk there.

Lowe: Professor Beral, could you put up your last slide please, the conclusion? I know you are probably going to answer that you do not have the data but taking you up about needing to know more about different types of HRT, is there any way in which you can even speculate about dose and transdermal? Because, going on the discussion yesterday, and changing prescriptions reflect this, if there is a move to low-dose oral, or to transdermal for cardiovascular reasons, one question will be whether that will have any effect on the increased risk of breast cancer.

Beral: We published,[12] which I have not shown, that transdermal had the same effect on breast cancer, so we have already published that there was not a clear difference with transdermal. We were going to be able to look at a variety of outcomes. We have got mortality and we have got all sorts of cancer incidence, and we will do it in due course. I certainly have learned never to speculate.

Wilson: From a radiologist's point of view we would be quite keen on transdermal because it would get rid of the masking effect, according to the published literature.

Pitkin: Just for clarification in the Million Women Study, going back to the actual questionnaire that was sent out with the appointments to the patients, you asked whether they were ever on HRT or not. You asked how long they had been on HRT. You asked what preparation they were on and how long they had been on that. Now, if you have a woman who has been on HRT for three years and the most common change in primary care was from a monthly bleed to a no bleed, your data will tell you that she has been on, say, Livial® (tibolone), say for six months, but your questionnaire does not tell you what she was on the other two and half years, does it? That is actually quite relevant in terms of exposure to breast tissue, and if we think that not all oestrogens and progestogens are the same. Then we are looking at the response of breast tissue to different types of HRT, and you are covering all the types, we actually only have the data on what they had been on for now, and that may not have been what they were on longest. I wonder if there is a whole tranche of information there that we do not have, because it might be relevant. We do not know what different oestrogens and different progestogens do to breast tissue.

Beral: I cannot remember if it is in the paper or not, but we did look at people who used HRT for a long time and generally the last HRT preparation they used is the one they had used for the longest time. I cannot remember the figures now but most long-duration users have actually been using the same brand most of the time. Our main interest was oestrogen only and combined oestrogen and progestogen preparations. People do not switch between those categories – they might switch particular preparations within the groups but not between them.

The only real potential problem was with tibolone, because we did know that tibolone is in a class of its own. Half of the women who were on tibolone at the time of recruitment had actually used it exclusively and so we did special analyses, they are in the paper, for tibolone, for the women who only used tibolone. We got identical relative risks for tibolone. That was the important one to clarify, because that was where there could be carry-over effects. We are going to look at type used in follow-up data. Women do tend to change HRT brands in the beginning and then they tend to settle. This is what the data suggest.

Pitkin: Dr Prentice, there was some degree of unblinding in the Women's Health Initiative because of bleeding patterns. How much do you think that impacted on mammographic screening and the detection of cancers?

Prentice: There was noteworthy unblinding by the end of the 5.2 or ultimately 5.6 year period. I think it was approximately a quarter or thereabouts. Women had to be unblinded and the primary reason was for persistent bleeding we found. I think going back to Mr Sturdee's comments, close to 10% of women were having persistent bleeding over three or four years so those women continued with annual mammograms as part of the programme. Whether the unblinding could have affected their initiation of investigation of what leads to a breast cancer diagnosis is pure speculation. I think it is unlikely to be a major effect and that it would be a feature of any observational study and be a more serious issue there. But it could have been a feature, but the unblinding as you said was primarily for safety reasons and there was not really another option.

Discussion following Professor Murphy's paper and the cognitive function aspects of Dr Prentice's paper

Murphy: One potential difficulty is that, as Dr Prentice said, the modified mini-mental state examination is an extremely blunt instrument. For example, were I to be psychotic and unable to function and think clearly, I would score 40 on this test. That is, I would be scoring at the top, so you have got to ask whether it is a sensitive instrument and whether it is a sensitive instrument for measuring what you want to be measuring. In terms of presence or absence of dementia, undoubtedly it is. In terms of the presence or absence of mild or statistically significant changes in particular areas of cognition that you are interested in, the answer is no. The potential take-home message from this is that oestrogens do not do anything to you which is beneficial or potentially harmful as measured by the mini-mental state examination in terms of cognition when you are older. The observational studies that were published earlier suggested a significant beneficial effect in verbal memory particularly. That indeed is what is coming out on sensitive tests for verbal memory. Use of oestrogens was associated with less decline in parameters of verbal abilities and verbal memory. However, there is also evidence that it may be having negative impact on some other areas of cognition. So it is not a simple take-home message, it is quite complex and it really does depend upon the measure that you are using.

Gray: Is there any evidence of a window of opportunity and might these women who are starting oestrogen at the age of 65 years be too late for it to give benefit?

Prentice: I think that is all quite possible, so I believe the authors of these two papers[13,14] brought that point out rather strongly, it is just that one should not be quick to extrapolate.

Studd: Our cross-sectional data show that women who had long-term oestrogen therapy had better cognition than those without therapy but it has not been shown in prospective studies. So that almost is what we are implying – if you start early, at the correct sort of age for early menopausal therapy, then there might be an advantage. Professor Murphy, would you support that?

Murphy: With a caveat, yes. If you start saying treatment was not started early enough, you look like a drowning man clinging onto any straw of opportunity that is around. The question is, is it neurobiologically plausible? The most neurobiologically plausible answer is that early treatment at or around the menopause for relevant symptoms may have a significant beneficial effect. There is relatively good data, if you believe observational studies, from observational studies and from small-scale randomised controlled trials. Would I expect a woman of 64 or 65 years, who is not symptomatic in any way, shape or form, to respond cognitively to hormones? I would have much more difficulty accepting that. The very long answer to your short question is, yes, I would be moderately confident that at or around menopause there are significant beneficial effects, but I would not be confident, and perhaps the opposite, that later use would be associated with benefit.

Purdie: Is there a potential for healthy user bias, in terms of neurobiology? You know how we were misled into falsely believing observational data on cardiovascular disease. But is there a healthy lifestyle, which helps to prevent against dementia?

Murphy: Yes of course, there is a healthy user bias, in any observational study. Whatever you do you really cannot get away from that, and you have to accept that. Can you prevent dementia, Alzheimer's disease by your lifestyle? No. Can you prevent other types of dementia? Yes, you can, if you watch your diet, your alcohol intake, your cholesterol, and all those good things that we know about but do not necessarily do.

Beral: Can I just make a non-HRT comment about the healthy user effect? There were a number of studies looking at dementia in relation to use of statins, observational studies, which had relative risks of the order of 0.2, saying if you used statins the relative risk of dementia is 0.2. There was a call for use of statins routinely to prevent dementia. But when the randomised trials were done, and included younger people, the relative risk was 1.0 and there was no protection against dementia by using statins in the randomised trials. The interpretation may be that basically if someone has early disease, even if it is not recognised or not detectable on testing, then they are not the sort of people who can take routine preventive treatment. That may be one of the early signs of dementia, that people do not take early preventive treatments. I think one has to think in this context with HRT – that it is possible that when people are very early stage disease, their compliance with daily use of HRT does fall off and that this is an early indicator of subsequent dementia. One has to look at the randomised trials with respect to dementia because there are even more extreme examples in other fields where the observational data and the trials do not agree.

Lumsden: Are there are any data about premature menopause and cognition?

Murphy: There is pretty good data showing that premature menopause is associated with cognitive differences. But the premature menopause and dementia story is poor.

Critchley: In any of your mechanistic studies, either looking at the cholinergic or the serotonergic, did you see any difference in the use or the effect of oestrogen versus oestrogen plus progestogen?

Murphy: The answer to that is no, because we deliberately did not look at people with oestrogen plus progestogen. It was just oestrogen alone.

Magnusson: Coming back to the neurobiological possibility, if we agree that the observational data is problematic, what was the supporting non-observational data? In humans, you had some more observational evidence as well, did you not?

Murphy: The early small-scale randomised controlled trials in humans, not for dementia now but for normal cognition, suggested that use of oestrogens at around menopause, be it surgical or natural, significantly improved cognitive function. But those treatment interventions were relatively short-lived, for approximately three to six months. There has never been an interventional study as far as I am aware that has gone longer than a very few months in people who are perimenopausal.

Magnusson: So the evidence is very poor because the studies were small?

Murphy: It is up to you decide whether you think it is good or poor. But there is no negative study there, all the interventional studies at around menopause are positive. And they are all on the same cognitive domain, which is verbal memory.

Stevenson: Do you have a biological explanation as to why we should get an increase in dementia with HRT?

Murphy: Yes and no, but it is compete speculation. I think, firstly, let us accept the study and assume there are no faults in the study. What potential explanations could there be? One could be that you have an increase in the risk of stroke, for example, and that might be affecting cognition. That is one potential explanation and that would be entirely reasonable.

Prentice: Out of those 61 women classified as probably demented, only two or three of those had a stroke diagnosis but there could, of course, have been undetected strokes.

Murphy: So that is one potential explanation. There was a nonsignificant increase in Alzheimer's disease which contributed to the overall picture, and there is absolutely no good neurobiological explanation for that. It is slightly difficult to understand that finding because were I to accept that the treatment was going to give an increase in the prevalence of a neurodegenerative disorder, I would expect that the prodromal symptoms would also be increased. So I really do not know how to evaluate that. The other potential confound in here is that it is difficult to put the study in context because there is no information on apolipoprotein E4 (ApoE$_4$)status. The ApoE$_4$ state is the primary genetic risk factor for developing Alzheimer's disease. So although hopefully in a study of this size that should have been dealt with by randomisation, we do not know that that is the case. It is a potential bias in terms of entry into the study but also in terms of treatment response to oestrogens. There is a preliminary study from another group suggesting that your response to oestrogen also depends on your ApoE$_4$ status.

Evans: The editorial that accompanied the dementia paper noted the higher rate of vascular dementia in the treated group as 5 to 1, very small numbers, and that some of the dementia could well be caused by silent brain infarcts and so that certainly was the biological explanation offered by the editorial at the time.

Murphy: That is true but there are also other things going on in there, which are happening just as frequently, or nearly as frequently, when you add them on as a factor for dementia, such as alcoholism, normal pressure hydrocephalus and frontal lobe dementia. It is absolutely implausible that oestrogen is causing you to become an alcoholic or to give you a normal pressure hydrocephalus.

Prentice: The numbers are very small.

Glasier: Professor Murphy, is it not the fact that if you see an increase in the incidence of dementia without an increase in the incidence of mild cognitive impairment, that actually speaks in favour of the dementias more likely to be being caused by an acute event, which would strengthen your argument that perhaps it is a vascular event which is unrecognised?

Lowe: We have some unpublished epidemiological studies of an association between coagulation activation with both Alzheimer's disease and vascular dementia. A recent observational study submitted for publication amongst 1000 patients with atrial fibrillation with serial cognitive function testing showed that anticoagulation with warfarin reduces the extent of decline in cognitive function and possibly the incidence of dementia. So yet again I am afraid it is raising clotting activation as one possible mechanism. Professor Murphy, you mentioned the importance of $ApoE_4$ – is it possible for the Women's Health Initiative study to do any retrospective testing of genotype and, secondly, do oestrogens have any effects on plasma levels of $ApoE_4$?

Prentice: It would be possible since WHI has the necessary stored specimens from participating women.

Murphy: And the answer to your second question is not that I am aware of, no one has looked – as far as I know.

Beral: Just on the same point, how common is $ApoE_4$? I thought it was really rare. Do you not have to be homozygous, and what is the prevalence?

Murphy: About 12%.

Studd: What is the current story about increased vascular flow with oestrogens that is attenuated by progestogen?

Whitehead: There is some early work that it is attenuated. About 40% change back towards the pretreatment status.

Studd: But might the addition of progestogen not be important to these HRT studies?

Gray: We all have had women who have come saying they feel as if they were going mad, who come back three months later saying thank you very much I am feeling very much better. The women for whom this 'going mad' is really one of the presenting symptoms seem to be the ones that are most difficult to get off HRT. I was just wondering whether or not there has been any work done on those women to look at the cognitive effect of stopping rather than the cognitive effect of starting?

Murphy: Not that I am aware of. The only studies that I am aware of are the crossover trials which show that once you stopped oestrogens you had a worsening of your mood.

Murphy: Can I just say that although oestrogens may affect mood and may affect cognitive function they should not be used as treatment for mood disorder or for cognitive dysfunction. There will be no evidence that will support you for doing that.

Studd: For women with menopausal problems, premenstrual syndrome problems etc., their lives are transformed by appropriate HRT. It may be a dose response; it may be we are using a higher dose than the studies have been referring to. In depression resistant to antidepressants, women got better in randomised controlled trials. In the same way with premenstrual depression, women get better with high-dose transdermal oestrogens and they get worse with progestogen.

Murphy: There is mixed evidence that HRT is useful for mood. It is not a treatment indication for mood and I could not and would not recommend it as a primary treatment for mood although you may wish to consider it in a woman who has not responded to selective serotonin reuptake inhibitor (SSRI) antidepressant treatment or a woman who is not clinically depressed and feels that there is some mood disturbance which does not meet the criteria for a clinically significant depression, you might wish to consider it.

Studd: There is a body of opinion that treatment with oestrogens is a very appropriate, even first-line, treatment for, what I would call, hormone-responsive depression.

Murphy: I do not know what hormone-responsive depression is but were I to be an expert witness in the courts to defend you for treating a woman with a mood disorder with HRT as opposed to antidepressant, it would not be an easy job!

Pitkin: I think it is going back to Dr Gebbie's lecture of yesterday of how difficult it is to tease out the various factors, as we said, for example, libido. It is the same issue with mood and I think there is a difference between clinically significant affective disorders that you treat with antidepressants and the mild reactive depression that we are probably seeing in our clinics. I see a lot of professional women who come and say 'I cannot think quickly, I cannot think clearly, I am a line manager for many people, I know that my appraisals of staff are not fair, I know that I have a knee-jerk reaction, that I am disciplining and shouting at people, not being objective in my assessment of my people under me.' So I have women coming to me quite clearly with perceptions of difficulty coping, and knowing that they are not controlling their temper and they are not being objective when they are appraising staff. This is a very nebulous area that some of these women complain of which may produce a sort of mild reactive depression. I am sure that it responds to HRT.

Stevenson: Just to come back to Professor Murphy's point of saying that you should not initiate HRT for mood?

Murphy: For clinically significant depression.

Stevenson: You have got a woman who is 'going mad', you give her HRT and three months later she says 'I feel wonderful'. Then, as we have all seen now in clinical practice, so many women are being inappropriately taken off HRT and she gets much worse again off the treatment. Would you regard that as an indication for resumption of HRT? Could you defend that one in law?

Murphy: I think you would have to be guided by the needs of the individual, your clinical practice and whether you are really talking about mood or whether you are talking about sleep disturbance or recrudescence of menopausal symptoms. I think what you are saying is a recrudescence of menopausal symptoms. Then you would need to think carefully about whether your resumption of the treatment is indicated. If it was menopausal symptoms, then your treatment would be indicated.

Stevenson: But you rarely get these things in isolation, you normally see a mixture of symptoms.

Armitage: I do not really want to put a Committee on Safety of Medicines (CSM) hat on, because clinically all of us use medicines off licence. We do it all the time for the benefit of our patients. What we have to be able to do is to be prepared to defend it if it is challenged. I would not have a problem with recommending that HRT should be used predominantly for people with symptoms, most of them will be vasomotor, but we all have patients such as has been described where women are not coping, not concentrating – a good deal of that may have to do with poor sleep pattern and other things, but they exist and they get better. Now, what the CSM is recommending is that on a regular basis, we say annually, you should review the need for continuing it. I think it is a great pity if people are stopped abruptly because we know that causes a lot of rebound symptoms. If in fact it is titrated gradually and as you titrate it down the patient has recurrence of their symptoms, then you could justify, and you can, as long as you have documented that, that this recurrence of symptoms and therefore together you make an informed choice. So I do not see that it is a conflict, but what you have to do is regularly review whether there is an indication to continue.

Lowe: Can I just go back to ApoE? I strongly encourage further research on genotypes and plasma levels with respect to a possible interaction with HRT. I confirm what Professor Murphy said about the genotype having a prevalence of at least 10% in the population. Furthermore, it is known that the genotype interacts with adverse outcomes following head injuries and with stroke, from colleagues in Glasgow at the Southern General Hospital. So, if the question has been raised of possible protection or possible increased dementia in some subgroups of women, I would have thought that ApoE would be a natural candidate to look at and I strongly encourage colleagues to do that. I can send the appropriate papers to support it.

Critchley: Professor Beral, in the Women's Health Initiative study the average age of the women was about 63 years. So, two questions – firstly, how do we appropriately extrapolate that back to a message for woman in their early 50s and, secondly, obviously over that time frame from menopause to, say, 63 there are other lifestyle factors that might have a role in predisposing to breast cancer and how sure are we that it is just HRT alone?

Beral: Most of what I presented and also most of the analysis in Women's Health Initiative are relative risks. One knows that absolute risks vary with lots of factors, and age is one thing, the risks in breast cancer increase with age, and also with obesity. So to get a measure that you can compare across groups we use relative risks. In the Women's Health Initiative, and also in the Million Women Study but not so much, we have looked at different subgroups. Because the question is do the relative risks hold up? Are they consistent across different subgroups which might have different background rates? The Women's Health Initiative have published, and actually so have we, the relative risk of breast cancer that one finds in a major group and one then looks across different age groups, in the USA across different racial groups, across people with a whole range of different characteristics that might affect the outcome. So far I think it is fair to say, and I think it is partly because the Women's Health Initiative trial is small, that they have not found any significant variation in their overall results across subgroups in general. The only thing we have ever found for breast cancer is the body mass index interaction, that in general the effects are stronger in thinner people, women who are less obese. That really means, it is a crude way of testing how generalisable the result is across different subgroups that may have different baseline risks. So one looks at relative risks because they are more reliable when comparing across different groups which have got different baseline rates. If there is no variation, and generally there is not, then it is reasonable to say that one can generalise to the sort of groups that one has looked at.

What is important clinically is absolute risk – relative risks are more scientific. The Women's Health Initiative always presented both relative risks and absolute risks (in brackets, as annualised rate). Then one says, let us take these relative risks and apply them to what we think are typical rates for various subgroups. For example, the relative risks are the same for women who have had children or not, but the women who have not had children had a higher absolute risk. So it is only when one gets to the absolute risks that one has to worry about these things given that there is no evidence of variation in the effect across subgroups. The only clear evidence we have of variation across subgroups is that the breast cancer effects are stronger and the relative risks are larger in thinner women.

Prentice: In terms of the Women's Health Initiative, the only interaction with relative risk is the one that Professor Burger alluded to earlier and that is possible interaction with duration of prior use. The situation in our trial of 16 000 women, and 300 are breast cancer cases, is that we do not have great power for looking at that type of interaction. We are better off in the Million Women Study for that purpose, but still the absence of ability to detect an interaction is some distance from being able to say that we have the answer in the related subgroups.

Beral: Basically, with age the effects seem to be very similar for HRT. I think the most interesting effect is that there is no variation by age for the fracture risks which Professor Evans mentioned yesterday. There are obviously quite a lot of events so one has got more power and the relative risks were rather similar for women in their 50s, 60s and 70s – some women in their 70s at recruitment went to be in their 80s when a fracture occurred. The relative protection offered against fractures with HRT was the same for women in their 70s as in their 50s.

Armitage: Professor Miller, in your talk you mainly concentrated on oestrogen and I wonder whether there is any data at a cellular level, for example, which might throw light on the apparently bad effects of progestogens that have been identified recently?

Miller: My impression is that the actual biology of what is going on is really very fragmented. I presented you today with two studies[2,3] on the effects of HRT on the breast. If you actually wanted to look within the female breast as opposed to cell lines and so forth, there really is not very much more in the literature. It is not that I selected out one out of 70 to present to you and one out of 50 in the other direction. I mean, that is about the sum total of the data that is there. In terms of the number of samples that has been looked at, in one it was 50 against 90, in another one it was 30 against 30. When you think that Professor Beral is presenting data on the Million Women Study and when we come down to actually look at what is happening in terms of events biochemically or anatomically, the numbers are very small. I think also you have to be very careful. I did omit one study which maybe I should mention to you because you asked specifically about progestogens and it may throw some sort of light on to what might be happening and whether in fact what you are looking at is an artificial situation. There is one study which I did not talk about because I thought it was somewhat artificial. It was a French–Belgian study[15] where they got postmenopausal women to rub gels on their breast. They rubbed a placebo, oestrogen, progestogen or a combination of oestrogen plus progestogen on the breast. They did that for 14 days and then you took breast tissue at surgery to look at. It really was quite amazing but there were only around ten women in each group. If you looked at the effect of oestradiol, then the proliferation rates in the breast was 100-fold higher than the proliferation rate in the placebo group. If you looked at the effect of progestogen, the increase was around 18-fold. If you looked at the oestrogen plus progestogen, it was 15-fold, which is not the sort of data that would go along with what Professor Beral is saying, where you get an effect of oestrogen and progestogen which is greater. If you then start to look at the biochemistry or the molecular biology of what is happening as a result of administering progestogen in that sort of situation, you are going to, I would imagine, get totally different results from, for example, the study that I presented earlier. This is the problem that I have and it would be interesting to hear what is said this afternoon when it comes to looking at specific ages with anti-oestrogens and in antiprogestogens. But what you pick up when you actually look for biological effects in the literature is so very dependent upon the test system.

Whitehead: Could I comment on the HABITS study? There were two prospective randomised controlled trials of use of HRT in early breast cancer survivors in Sweden. HABITS was published last week,[16] their data showing this excess risk, but the Stockholm study, and I have seen the results from that, shows no excess risk. So we have two randomised controlled trials which are diametrically opposed in terms of their results. It is a great shame, I think, that the Stockholm study was not published in the same edition of the *Lancet*, but perhaps the manuscript was not so far advanced. I was wondering why there might be such differences, and it struck me that in the HABITS trial use of tamoxifen is only about 20% and so you have a group of women, whom if they behave like UK women, 65–70% are going to have to have a receptor-positive breast cancer, they are being given HRT without any tamoxifen cover. I just wondered whether that might have influenced the outcome? It is conjecture because the trouble is we do not actually know from the manuscript from HABITS whether the cancers occurred in women who were or were not taking tamoxifen...

Beral: In the HABITS study they do mention this other Stockholm study but it is very hard to know, if they have not published their results, how long the follow-up, and how many women and so forth. So I think until we have seen this other study published, it is very hard to comment on it. But they do actually give data in the HABITS study on what proportion of women were on tamoxifen and what proportion had oestrogen receptor-positive tumours.

Gebbie: Professor Miller, I do not know how familiar you are with tibolone, but one of the manufacturers' big selling points is that it does not increase intracellular oestrogen levels in breast tissue. I just wondered if you wanted to comment on that, and if you feel that it is relevant.

Miller: I do not really have an opinion, but I think it is important. It is very clear if in fact you were looking at the treatments of breast cancer or you are looking at the preventive issues, that you certainly should not lump together the selective oestrogen receptor modulators (SERMs) with the aromatase inhibitors. Because there are major differences, not only in terms of potency, but in terms of, as just alluded to, the mechanism of action with tamoxifen, particularly if you are looking at premenopausal women you are looking at a background of perhaps increased levels of circulating oestrogen and levels within the breast. One thing we know about aromatase inhibitors, or specific aromatase inhibitors, is that they would dramatically reduce circulating oestrogens and oestrogen levels within the breast, so there is a clear differential there. If you in fact are looking at an agent, which is a partial agonist, whether or not it has biological effects depends upon not only its potency but on the relative level of endogenous oestrogen and that really matters a lot. But I have not really thought enough about tibolone.

Critchley: Dr Wilson, if, as we heard earlier from your presentation and Professor Beral's presentation, there is a concern that HRT might be hiding a cancer and that is why we are seeing this increased risk, what would be the impact of this? Because I think there will be a lot of women who, irrespective of the data that are published, because of vasomotor symptoms or because they are younger women, will still want HRT but will be very concerned about the risk of breast cancer. What will be the impact if those women wanted to have a mammography screen before they started HRT and that became part of practice?

Wilson: I think that it appears that HRT increases your risk of breast cancer but it also appears that it masks them, and they are two separate things. The masking is the only thing that you can deal with, by changing the type of HRT women are taking. The current advice from the Royal College of Radiologists is that women should not have a screening mammogram before they start on HRT. If you are looking at women in their late 40s or early 50s, your pick-up rate would be in the region of two per 1000 mammograms. So part of it is because we could not cope with those kinds of referrals and part of it is that the pick-up rate will be very low in finding a cancer that you may have missed had you done the mammogram after women had started HRT. Where I am coming from is that it appears that the effect on mammography of the masking effect appears to be mainly associated with continuous combined therapy and less so with cyclical and even less with oestrogen alone. As far as we know, but there are only two published studies, there is no effect at all with tibolone or with topical agents. So, from a radiologist's point of view, we would be saying try not to use continuous combined therapy if you do not want the potential cancer to be masked.

Critchley: If we are getting this message then, there may be a risk from HRT but it seems to be at its lowest level with oestrogen alone and progestogens seem to be bad news. But we know from Mr Sturdee's first presentation that if you want to protect the endometrium because there still is a risk with oestrogen alone then progestogen needs to be given continuously. Is there an argument that if women are going to take oestrogen at a low dose, perhaps transdermally, that the optimum way of giving progestogen to negate these other effects should be by an intrauterine delivery route?

Studd: Perhaps it is to give a shorter duration of progestogen. There are many of us in this room, Mr Whitehead, Mr Sturdee and myself, who were involved in the early studies of the progestogen work, that 14 days was a correct dose and had a protective effect. But for years now, I have used seven days, because women hate progestogen, by and large. A large number have progestogen intolerance and I have had a routine of just giving seven days per month in women with depression who are progestogen-intolerant. On checking the endometrium, there is no excess bleeding problem or pathology and I think that could be a compromise.

Gebbie: Could I just say that for a lot of these women, everyone keeps on saying that a Mirena® is the answer. But with these you do get a well-documented levonorgestrel serum level and the manufacturers, Schering, have no mammographic data at all on what it might do to breast density as a surrogate marker for breast cancer.

Purdie: Can I just recall the paper I quoted yesterday, only in abstract form so far, that Cummings and colleagues have managed to take oestrogen down below the event horizon, as they put it, of the endometrium. There is a 12 μg/day transdermal delivery system and they looked very carefully with ultrasound at endometrial thickness and found no changes in two years of such exposure. A lot of the problems we face we have talked about over these two days are progestogen-related and it is now, I think, a matter of some urgency to establish whether or not we might safely use ultra-low-dose oestrogen without progestogen. It flies in the whole face of what we have been taught, the great outbreak of endometrial cancer in the 1970s with conventional higher-dose oestrogen is accepted without doubt, but I think we have to make a shift and be responsible for prospective studies to see if this observation is correct or not.

Studd: That is why a compromise may be a shorter duration with a small dose.

Cardozo: Surely the answer to Professor Critchley's question must be, yes, of course that is the next thing to explore. If you are looking at the risk of oestrogen being lowest when given non-orally and probably transdermally but certainly non-orally. If you are looking at giving progestogen that affects mainly the endometrium and not other target end-organs, then the next clinical trial must be with intrauterine progestogens and non-oral oestrogens as a combination.

Barlow: Many of us do that with particular patients already. Another possibility raised by all this is, if oestrogen alone, for instance, makes mammographic density more readable then we should be exploring things such as whether two months of stopping the progestogen part of your continuous combined therapy is possible, during which time most women would not bleed very much. Professor Miller, you showed in one of your very early slides the idea that pregnancy gives further differentiation of the breast tissue. We know that never having been pregnant versus having been pregnant is one of the risk factors. Is there much known about fully-differentiated breast tissue versus non-fully-differentiated breast tissue and whether hormones have different effects subsequently on it?

Miller: I think that there are. I think Roger King might be able tell you a bit more about it with regard to breast and so forth. He did some studies[17] where he actually looked at material obtained from parous women versus nulliparous women, and there clearly were different sensitivities. I think that Tom Anderson[18] in Edinburgh, who did a lot of the early work looking at the effects of the menstrual cycle and parity on the breast, was amazed at the effect that there were lobules which after pregnancy in the parous breast appear to be totally quiescent. These lobules had long-term quiescence and they therefore in many respects were not going to be susceptible, if you believe that proliferation is the reason that you actually get cancer. There would be lobules which would not in fact be susceptible and therefore perhaps part of the benefit of pregnancy was because of these lobules. We really just do not know anything about these sorts of mechanistic things – it is quite a blank canvas and is very difficult.

Beral: What do we do about the progestogenic effect on the breast? The problem is basically that if you reduce progestogens you help the breast cancer, but you do not help the endometrium. One should not start recommending things where there is no evidence and we really do need to keep to where the evidence is and maybe set up new research to look at questions but try not to jump ahead. I think the other thing is to make sure that both the breast and the endometrium are considered together because the effects of hormones there are very different on each.

Studd: Many of us have used the Mirena® intrauterine system since June 1995 when it was first licensed and we have our strong views about its value.

Beral: I am just saying that we have to be clear about what is still a research question and where the evidence is. I was going to ask Dr Magnusson, in the Weiderpass study[19] of endometrial cancer where you were one of the authors, there is a very-low-dose oestrogen used in Sweden, do you want to mention it?

Magnusson: That was oestriol used orally. Is it used here at all?

Rees: It is available in tablet form and it is used infrequently.

Cardozo: It does not work – it has one-twelfth of the bioavailability of vaginal oestriol.

Magnusson: Nevertheless, in Sweden it was frequently used for urogenital symptoms. It was shown to increase the risk of endometrial cancer.

Gray: One thing that I would like to raise again from the clinical aspect is that when you are looking at the risk–benefit equation of whether or not to use progestogens in a perimenopausal woman, you get chaotic bleeding. Do you investigate it and you have to factor in the cost and the anxiety created by unscheduled bleeding? Is it or is it not something to worry about?

Sturdee: I am sure we must still continue to advocate giving progestogen to women with a uterus. I think that giving it intrauterine is the logical way to give it because, as we know, it is only needed for the endometrium and nowhere else. There is no doubt that the current Mirena dose is far too high for our needs in a postmenopausal woman – the half-dose Mirena which is currently being researched is also too high. But the levels in the circulation are considerably less than they are with the original Mirena. So therefore one presumes it is less likely to have an effect on the breast. I think that future research should look at lowering the dose even further, down to 5 µg levonorgestrel or even less then that. I think we need to be looking at lower-dose progestogen while we are talking about lower-dose oestrogen. Professor Purdie mentioned the 12 µg patch – I would be amazed if that was effective in controlling symptoms.

Purdie: The primary endpoint of the study was bone protection. I was surprised to find protection at the femoral neck with the lower dose. But we simply do not know about symptoms.

Stevenson: Tibolone does not affect breast density adversely and does not seem to have any adverse effects in terms of breast metabolism that we are aware of. How can the observation in the Million Women Study be explained that tibolone increases breast cancer incidence? The second point is why should there be a difference? Is it purely an age effect that a women could be exposed to 17β-oestradiol endogenously for 20–40 years and yet a couple of years of exogenous use makes a huge impact on breast cancer risk?

Beral: The answer to the endogenous versus exogenous question is that in postmenopausal women endogenous hormone levels actually make quite a difference to breast cancer risk. Dividing women into three groups depending on their endogenous oestrogen levels gave relative risks of two or three, which is quite high. Regarding tibolone, I think one has to be cautious about intermediate markers. We have seen with cardiovascular disease that intermediate markers are sometimes misleading. For health policy, for example, one really has to look at real clinical disease outcomes.

Stevenson: But we have to be able to explain the observation biologically.

Beral: It took 20 years to explain smoking and lung cancer. Twenty years before it could be shown in an animal that smoking causes cancer.

Studd: Do you think there was any treatment bias in these women who possibly had benign breast disease and as people thought tibolone was protective those type of patients were given tibolone preferentially.

Beral: Well, we did look at every possible risk factor and there was nothing that came out to be different in users of tibolone and other types of HRT. It did not look like tibolone was being prescribed very selectively, although it might in some context, but there was no difference in terms of family history, body mass index, or anything else.

Burger: There is some evidence from a not very good French study[20] that suggests that progesterone may not have the same effect on the breast as the synthetic progestogen. It seems to me that this is one of the areas where we need more studies to be done as to whether progesterone is different from synthetic progestogen as far as the breast is concerned. The question that I wanted to ask again is to follow up on what seems to me to be a very significant difference between the Million Women Study and the Women's Health Initiative. If you look at the breast cancer event rate in the placebo versus the treated arm of the Women's Health Initiative, although differences start to emerge at about year four or five, for years one, two and three there are really no differences in event rates between the two arms. The two curves are really superimposable. Why is it that in the Million Women Study even very short apparent duration of use leads to a very substantial increase in apparent relative risk?

Beral: Statistical power is the issue. We had 3000 breast cancers in the oestrogen plus progestogen, and there were 200 in the Women's Health Initiative.

Prentice: Just a reminder that the lack of difference in the Women's Health Initiative in the first three years may be related to the masking of breast density somewhat. But that does not explain the difference between the Women's Health Initiative and Million Women Study. It is important to get some insight into the mechanism for the early elevation that was seen in the Million Women Study.

Beral: There is one big difference that does relate to the masking in the Women Health's Initiative. I presume women had annual mammography whereas in the Million Women Study in the UK it was every three years. Early on, there were fewer screen-detected cancers picked up in short-term users than in nonusers. It could be that with repeated mammographies you just keep on missing the cancers.

Lumsden: I feel very concerned about this idea of low-dose oestradiol when we have no data. It would seem intuitive that whereas hyperplasia with the higher dose will develop within one year, with a low dose it will take three years. There are very good data to suggest that oestradiol effects do persist after stopping treatment. So I think we need to be very cautious there. There are also a number of cases in the literature of endometrial cancer, even in the presence of the levonorgestrel intrauterine system. So this is not the panacea answer to all the problems.

Studd: Professor Beral, there are a couple of points in your study which to many of us do not make biological sense. It is the increase of breast cancer in the first year that we find surprising, and what does that have to do with oestrogen? Secondly, your survival from diagnosis of 2.4 years when, if you are talking about metastatic breast disease on diagnosis, then the survival is three years. Why is it so bad and were they receptor-positive?

Beral: We really have gone over that a lot and basically these are the results. If you look over time, women who used HRT for less than a year when they started experience an excess of breast cancer within one-and-a-half years. We have enormous statistical power. I think that is the thing I want to emphasise. But I cannot say that the excess did not occur earlier because if we had even more statistical power we, maybe, would have found it earlier. The HABITS trial[16] is rather in the same direction – very early, adverse events on breast cancer. So I think that it is suggestive that there are very early changes and we know there are early changes as well on mammography.

To answer your question about the deaths, that is as far as we followed women up. The longest duration of follow-up when we reported was four years. Follow-up is continuing and we are going to look at mortality again, in which case we will have deaths occurring later. So the only deaths we had to look at were the deaths that occurred soon after diagnosis.

Studd: But do we know whether the quick deaths were receptor-negative?

Beral: No. Several people have asked and, unfortunately we do not have receptor status. We are trying desperately to get it. Our experience is that surprisingly few women were tested for receptor status before about the year 2000.

Stevenson: Another area where there seems to be discrepancies between the Women's Health Initiative and the Million Women Study perhaps is with unopposed oestradiol. I know it has not been published yet but we know from Jacques Rousseau that there is not an increased risk of breast cancer in this group. Surely this is important to consider.

Prentice: We know that there is not evidence of an increase which is a little different from knowing that there is not an increase.

Stevenson: But it would have been stopped if there was evidence?

Prentice: I am certainly not suggesting that there is evidence. The statement that has been provided to the participating women at this point in the trial is that when the combined hormone trial was ending there was not evidence of an increase in breast cancer risk. That is the only information on the topic that has been released. Again, that has to be taken in the context of these detection issues, and it will be a complicated analysis to sort out when the data are able to be released.

Evans: Can I just show a couple of graphs to answer Dr Stevenson's question? The point is that the trial is much smaller than the Million Women Study. We know that oestrogen only has a reduced risk compared with oestrogen plus progestogen, so we would not expect to find that there was evidence from the oestrogen only in the Women's Health Initiative trial yet to stop that trial. Even if the relative risk were exactly what the Million Women Study showed, you just would not expect it to match as it is a much smaller study of the events and the relative risk we expect to be less. Can I just show here (Figure 15.1), this is the HABITS and Stockholm trials, and to say that these are diametrically opposed to each other. Again, that is the sort of thing that you see in trials. You get trials that have different results and that is why I would love to see many more trials in HRT. To say that these are diametrically opposed is not simply saying that they are totally incompatible with one another. What I would expect is that the HABITS trial has exaggerated the effect. It has stopped early. You will find that early stopping exaggerates effects. It is very likely that the Stockholm trial may have underestimated the effect. So if we were to look at the joint effect then some relative risk that was a bit less than two is actually compatible with both of them.

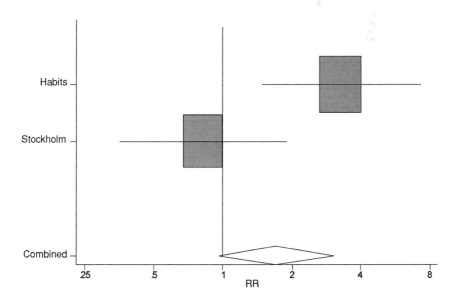

Figure 15.1. Results from breast cancer trials

Stevenson: You said that you thought that the HABITS trial, because it was stopped early, may have overestimated the effect. But the Stockholm trial was stopped early as well. They were both stopped early.

Evans: It was stopped early but only as a result of the other one.

Stevenson: Well, as a result of recruitment problems.

Evans: Yes, but that is a different issue – it is like saying that the WISDOM trial stopped early because of Women's Health Initiative in some sense. It is not stopped on data. Stockholm did not stop on data. HABITS stopped on the data.

Pitkin: I take Professor Evans's point that if you stop a study early you may exaggerate the effect. The tragedy in stopping the HABITS study, of course, is the knock-on effect, with Stockholm and the Royal Marsden and all other studies that you now cannot recruit for, so you then cannot gain any further information. I am still quite confused and concerned about the apparent differences between the Stockholm and the HABITS study. I am not sure that everyone in the HABITS group were restaged at entry to the study. I do not know what their clinical staging was and if it was reviewed within a very recent time frame of recruitment or if there was a heterogeneity of oestrogen-positive receptors across both groups. I think that the HRT preference was left to local decision making and on the analysis that appeared not to make a difference but the numbers are so small, can you say that? So there are all sorts of issues, which now are likely to be left unresolved.

The other thing that I wanted to say is on tibolone – although these trials are generally very small, there are a couple of studies[21,22] now on fine-needle aspiration of human breast tissue that show increased cellular apoptosis and decreased cellular proliferation, so clearly there have been some studies at cellular levels on tibolone and proliferation.

My third point is on ovarian cancer. We know the numbers are very much smaller but because there is no screening programme and because it presents late, it is a bigger killer. It matters to us clinicians because we are constantly asking women whether they want oophorectomy or not at the time of the hysterectomy, with little information to say whether they would have gotten ovarian cancer if we had not taken the ovaries out. One study[23] did seem to show very little difference between controls and continuous combined therapy. So we have got Mr Sturdee's study saying continuous combined therapy is best for endometrium, we are left with the feeling it is probably the least good for breast and, on the current available observational study data, it seems to be the best for ovarian cancer, better than oestrogen alone or sequential progestogens.

References

1. Hague S, MacKenzie IZ, Bicknell R, Rees MC. In-vivo angiogenesis and progestogens. *Hum Reprod* 2002;17:786–93.
2. Hofseth LJ, Raafat AM, Osuch JR, Pathak DR, Slomski CA, Haslam SZ. Hormone replacement therapy with estrogen or estrogen plus medroxyprogesterone acetate is associated with increased epithelial proliferation in the normal postmenopausal breast. *J Clin Endocrinol Metab* 1999;84:4559–65.
3. Hargreaves DF, Knox F, Swindell R, Potten CS, Bundred NJ. Epithelial proliferation and hormone receptor status in the normal post-menopausal breast and the effects of hormone replacement therapy. *Br J Cancer* 1998;78:945–9.
4. Chlebowski RT, Hendrix SL, Langer RD, Stefanick ML, Gass M, Lane D, *et al.*; WHI

Investigators. Influence of estrogen plus progestin on breast cancer and mammography in healthy postmenopausal women: the Women's Health Initiative Randomized Trial. *JAMA* 2003;289:3243–53.

5.   Colditz GA, Hankinson SE, Hunter DJ, Willett WC, Manson JE, Stampfer MJ, *et al*. The use of estrogens and progestins and the risk of breast cancer in postmenopausal women. *N Engl J Med* 1995;332:1589–93.

6.   Persson I, Thurfjell E, Holmberg L. Effect of estrogen and estrogen-progestin replacement regimes on mammographic breast parenchymal density. *J Clin Oncol* 1997;15:3201–7.

7.   Stomper PC, D'Souza DJ, DiNitto PA, Arredondo MA. Analysis of parenchymal density on mammograms in 1353 women 25–79 years old. *AJR Am J Roentgenol* 1996;167:1261–5.

8.   Kopans DB. Conventional wisdom: observation, experience, anecdote, and science in breast imaging. *AJR Am J Roentgenol* 1994;162:299–303.

9.   Powell KA, Obuchowski NA, Davros WJ, Chilcote WA. Quantitative analysis of breast parenchymal density: correlation with women's age. *Acad Radiol* 1999;6:742–7.

10.   Greendale GA, Reboussin BA, Sie A, Singh HR, Olson LK, Gatewood O, *et al*. Effects of estrogen and estrogen-progestin on mammographic parenchymal density. Postmenopausal Estrogen/Progestin Interventions (PEPI) Investigators. *Ann Intern Med* 1999;130:261–9.

11.   Smith-Bindman R, Chu PW, Miglioretti DL, Sickles EA, Blanks R, Ballard-Barbash R, *et al*. Comparison of screening mammography in the United States and the United Kingdom. *JAMA*. 2003;290:2129–37. Erratum in: *JAMA* 2004;291:824.

12.   Million Women Study Collaborators. Breast cancer and hormone replacement therapy: the Million Women Study. *Lancet* 2003;362:1330–1.

13.   Shumaker SA, Legault C, Rapp SR, Thal L, Wallace RB, Ockene JK, *et al*. Estrogen plus progestin and the incidence of dementia and mild cognitive impairment in postmenopausal women. The Women's Health Initiative Memory Study: a randomized controlled trial. *JAMA* 2003;289:2651–62.

14.   Rapp SR, Espeland MA, Shumaker SA, Henderson VW, Brunner RL, Manson JE, *et al*. Effect of estrogen plus progestin on global cognitive function in postmenopausal women. The Women's Health Initiative Memory Study: a randomized controlled trial. *JAMA* 2003;289:2663–72.

15.   Foidart JM, Colin C, Denoo X, Desreux J, Beliard A, Fournier S, de Lignieres B. Estradiol and progesterone regulate the proliferation of human breast epithelial cells. *Fertil Steril* 1998;69:963–9.

16.   Holmberg L, Anderson H; HABITS steering and data monitoring committees. HABITS (hormonal replacement therapy after breast cancer–is it safe?), a randomised comparison: trial stopped. *Lancet* 2004;363:453–5.

17.   Anderson TJ, Battersby S, King RJ, McPherson K, Going JJ. Oral contraceptive use influences resting breast proliferation. *Hum Pathol* 1989;20:1139–44.

18.   Anderson TJ, Ferguson DJ, Raab GM. Cell turnover in the "resting" human breast: influence of parity, contraceptive pill, age and laterality. *Br J Cancer* 1982;46:376–82.

19.   Weiderpass E, Adami HO, Baron JA, Magnusson C, Bergstrom R, Lindgren A, *et al*. Risk of endometrial cancer following estrogen replacement with and without progestins. *J Natl Cancer Inst* 1999;91:1131–7.

20.   de Lignieres B, de Vathaire F, Fournier S, Urbinelli R, Allaert F, Le MG, *et al*. Combined hormone replacement therapy and risk of breast cancer in a French cohort study of 3175 women. *Climacteric* 2002;5:332–40.

21.   Conner P, Christow A, Kersemaekers W, Soderqvist G, Skoog L, Carlstrom K, *et al*. A comparative study of breast cell proliferation during hormone replacement therapy: effects of tibolon and continuous combined estrogen-progestogen treatment. *Climacteric* 2004;7:50–8.

22.   Valdivia I, Campodonico I, Tapia A, Capetillo M, Espinoza A, Lavin P. Effects of tibolone and continuous combined hormone therapy on mammographic breast density and breast histochemical markers in postmenopausal women. *Fertil Steril* 2004;81:617–23.

23.   Riman T, Dickman PW, Nilsson S, Correia N, Nordlinder H, Magnusson CM, *et al*. Hormone replacement therapy and the risk of invasive epithelial ovarian cancer in Swedish women. *J Natl Cancer Inst* 2002;94:497–504.

SECTION 4

HORMONE REPLACEMENT AND WHO NEEDS IT

Chapter 16

Hormone replacement therapy: regimen and routes of administration

Mary Ann Lumsden

Introduction

Hormone replacement therapy (HRT) has two principal constituents, an oestrogen and a progestogen, and these may be present alone or in combination. Oestrogen is included because it is the most effective means of relieving symptoms associated with the menopause and a progestogen is required for non-hysterectomised women to prevent unopposed stimulation of the endometrium. It is often assumed that all oestrogens and all progestogens are similar and exert a 'class effect'. However, this is not necessarily the case and the actions can be influenced by both the type of steroid and the route of administration. The question of class effect is of vital importance since the results of the large epidemiological studies carried out in recent years are assumed to apply to all HRT regimens regardless of their constituents or the mode of delivery of the oestrogen.

Oestrogens

Oestrogens may be classified as natural or synthetic. The oestrogen most commonly prescribed worldwide is conjugated equine oestrogen (CEE), which is considered to be a natural oestrogen. This is derived from pregnant mare's urine and consists of conjugates, mainly sulphates and glucuronides, of oestrogenic compounds. These conjugates are not metabolised to oestradiol and therefore differ from the synthetic oestrogens such as oestradiol valerate or micronised oestradiol that give rise to 17β-oestradiol. This means that they differ in potency and this could influence both effectiveness and the adverse effect profile.

Routes of administration

Oestrogen can be given by a number of different routes: these can be divided into the oral and non-oral routes. The advantages and disadvantages of the most commonly used routes of administration are discussed below and shown in Table 16.1.

Oral

Oral oestrogen is subject to first-pass metabolism, with the oestrogen being absorbed through the gut and passing straight to the liver where it is metabolised. This means that the dose given is high compared with the level in the systemic circulation.

Table 16.1. Advantages and disadvantages of various routes of administration

Route of administration	Advantages	Disadvantages
Oral therapy	Ease of use Cheap Beneficial lipid effect Can be co-administered with progestogen	High dose required Variable absorption Affects liver metabolism Some elevate triglycerides
Transdermal therapy	Low dose of pure hormone Avoids liver metabolism Variable doses available	Expensive Variable absorption Less effect on lipids
Subcutaneous implant	Pure oestradiol Cheap Infrequent insertion High blood levels Avoids liver metabolism Good compliance Can co-administer testosterone Enhanced bone effects	Surgical procedure Tachyphylaxis Difficult to remove Possible prolonged release
Vaginal pessaries	Local action Can be used if systemic administration contra-indicated Cream cheap	Can be messy Rings and tablets expensive

All the non-oral routes avoid hepatic first-pass metabolism and this profoundly alters their effect on liver synthesis and metabolism. The liver is the site of many metabolic and synthetic processes. After an oral dose, the amount of oestrogen arriving at the liver is high – much higher than that achieved by the non-oral routes. This has a significant impact on carbohydrate and lipid metabolism and also influences production of proteins such as the coagulation factors.

Transdermal patches and gels

In patches, the oestradiol is incorporated into the adhesive and absorption occurs when the patch is attached firmly to the skin. First-pass metabolism is avoided, which will normally be advantageous unless the effect on lipid metabolism is felt to be desirable. Patches are applied to the skin once or twice weekly.

Oestradiol gel can be applied directly to the skin in a metered dose. This route is appealing for many women as it is easy, the gel disappears rapidly leaving no mark, and it is possible to adjust the dose with ease. It is a popular method of administering oestradiol in mainland Europe.

Subcutaneous implants

Subcutaneous implants have the convenience of being administered approximately every six months and give a high dose of oestradiol into the circulation, which can be maintained for long periods of time. They have the advantage of convenience but the disadvantage that they cannot be easily removed. Tachyphylaxis can occasionally develop when symptoms recur, as the level of hormone drops even though the amount in the circulation is still high.[1]

Local oestrogen

Oestrogen can be administered directly to the vagina in the form of creams, pessaries or rings. It is useful for women with urogenital atrophy, which is frequently associated with superficial dyspareunia. Systemic absorption does occur and appropriate vaginal rings can be used for systemic administration of oestradiol.

Nasal sprays

A nasal spray has been developed that achieves a very high level of oestradiol in the circulation within 20–30 minutes and then falls rapidly, i.e. giving essentially an oestradiol 'pulse'. Studies have demonstrated that this route is effective in relieving symptoms and can be useful for women intolerant to other routes of administration.

Class effects of oestrogen

Vasomotor symptoms

Oestrogen is the most effective means of treating hot flushes and leads to relief in over 80% of women regardless of the mode of administration.[2–4]

Bone

The relationship between osteoporosis and sex steroids is well established and can result in loss of up to 15% of the skeleton in the years following the menopause. Epidemiological evidence suggests that women who experience less exposure to endogenous oestrogen have a higher risk of osteoporosis, for example women who undergo a premature menopause. Some of the earliest evidence of a protective effect of oestrogen on bone was in the form of case–control studies and these, together with other randomised controlled trials (RCTs), have now been confirmed following the publication of results from the Women's Health Initiative (WHI).[5] Oestrogen appears to be effective regardless of the route of administration,[6–12] although there are data to suggest that there is a dose-dependent effect and women receiving subcutaneous oestradiol implants tend to have above-average bone density.

Studies have shown that lower doses of oestrogen are effective in improving bone density in women older than 65 years who are also more likely to experience adverse effects with standard doses of HRT.[13]

Cohort studies have shown that current and recent users of HRT have the lowest risk of osteoporotic fractures. There is also evidence that bone loss increases after HRT is stopped. Over the past few years, recommendations regarding prolonged use of HRT have changed dramatically and the advice is now to use HRT only in women with symptoms. For most women, this will be for less than five years. The Committee on Safety of Medicines has recommended that HRT should not necessarily be the first line for bone protection in asymptomatic women and alternatives should be carefully considered.[14]

Breast

Breast cancer is now the most commonly diagnosed malignancy in the UK and by age 74 years one in nine women will have developed breast cancer. Unsurprisingly, breast cancer is a major concern for women in the developed world. Observational data have shown that HRT confers a small, but significantly increased, risk of developing breast cancer with long-term use and this increase was the principal reason why the Women's Health Initiative study was terminated prematurely.[15] The effect of oestrogen on breast cancer risk is assumed to be a class effect although this might be contributed to by the fact that less information is available from women receiving oestrogen via a non-oral route. Most data relate to CEE and the assumption is made that it applies to all types of oestrogens

Progestogens

The progestogens commonly used include those based on the C19 steroid testosterone (such as norethisterone, levonorgestrel and norethindrone) or the C21 steroid progesterone. There are only two C21 progestogens in widespread use and these are medroxyprogesterone acetate (MPA), widely used in the USA, and dydrogesterone. The C19 steroids are a clinically important group since they are the basis for the success of hormonal contraception. They are subdivided into oestranes (C18) and gonanes (C17). Recently a derivative of spironolactone, drospirenone,[16] has been developed for use. Progestogens differ considerably in their metabolic and vascular effects. They also differ in their androgenicity but, interestingly, this is not necessarily related to whether they are C21 or C19 – one of the newer anti-androgenic progestogens (dienogest) is a C19 steroid.[17] Some of the compounds are prodrugs, metabolised to active compounds by the liver, and examples include promegestone (converted to trimegestone) and norgestimate (converted to norgestrel).

Progestogens have one common action, the change produced in oestrogen-primed endometrium, but there are large differences in their other clinical effects. In practice, clinically used progestogens have been selected because of their activity after oral administration and ability to inhibit ovulation. The pregnancy-maintaining role of progestogens (an important role for progesterone) is usually overlooked.

The biological actions of natural progesterone and synthetic progestogens are listed in Table 16.2.

Routes of administration

As with oestrogen, this may be oral, parenteral (vaginal, intramuscular, transdermal) or intrauterine.

Oral

Progestogens are normally given orally since absorption is usually rapid and gives a maximum serum concentration within 2–5 hours. They have a longer half-life than progesterone and result in stable plasma levels. Many are metabolised by the liver. Oral progesterone, even in micronised form, is variably absorbed and bioavailability is uncertain. Not all undergo first-pass metabolism, for example MPA does not bind to sex hormone-binding globulin (SHBG) and has nearly 100% bioavailability. This is also true for megestrol acetate and levonorgestrel, but not norethisterone, 40% of which is bound to SHBG.

Progestogens tend to exert fewer metabolic effects than oestrogens. However, norethisterone is metabolised to ethinyl oestradiol in the liver, which may explain the oestrogenic actions of this progestogen.

Table 16.2. Biological actions of natural progesterone and synthetic progestogens; adapted with permission from Schindler *et al.*[16] (Maturitas, © 2003 Elsevier)

Progestogen	Progestogenic	Anti-gonadotrophic	Anti-oestrogenic	Oestrogenic	Androgenic	Anti-androgenic	Glucocorticoid	Anti-mineralocorticoid
Progesterone	+	+	+	−	−	+/−	+	+
Dydrogesterone	+	−	+	−	−	+/−	−	+/−
Megestrol acetate	+	+	+	−	+/−	+	+	−
MPA	+	+	+	−	+/−	−	+	−
Norethisterone	+	+	+	+	+	−	−	−
Levonorgestrel	+	+	+	−	+	−	−	−

Transdermal

It has been said that a patch the size of a football pitch would be required to administer sufficient progesterone to provide luteal phase levels. This contrasts with oestradiol where new patch technology has permitted significant doses to be achieved after application of a small adhesive disc. Norethisterone can be administered in the form of a patch and preparations of norethisterone acetate (NETA) in combination with oestradiol are available.

Progesterone cream

Although much publicity has been given to progesterone creams, the available data from placebo-controlled trials suggest that the circulating levels of progesterone achieved, although low,[18] are sufficient to induce secretory change in the endometrium. However, the efficacy of the cream is no greater than that of a placebo.[19]

Sufficient doses of progesterone can be administered using pessaries/suppositories but, as administration may be required twice daily, acceptance of this route of administration by women in the UK is not high.

Intrauterine progestogen

Levonorgestrel can now be administered directly to the endometrium following the development of intrauterine systems. Systemic absorption of the progestogen is low thus decreasing both metabolic effects and adverse effects of the progestogen. The system lasts for five years and is likely to become an important component of HRT in the future.[20,21]

Depot preparations

These are more commonly used for contraception since large doses must be administered.

Effects of progestogens

Steroids with progestogenic activity exhibit enormous variation in their chemical structures. All bind to the progesterone receptor (PR) although binding to the different isoforms may vary. All produce characteristic changes in the oestrogen-primed endometrium but the dose required for transformation varies with route of administration and timing. The effects of the commonly used progestogens are summarised in Table 16.2.

Biological activity at the cellular level is mediated by the intracellular steroid receptors. Progestogens also bind to androgen and oestrogen receptors (AR and ER) with differing affinities, as shown in Table 16.3.

Reference to Tables 16.2 and 16.3 gives a sound pharmacological basis for the assertion that progestogens differ from each other. The receptor binding provides a plausible explanation for the effects and adverse effects of progestogens. The fact that these receptors are so widespread explains why the progestogens have such variable actions in women.

Table 16.3. Relative binding affinities of progesterone and synthetic progestogens to steroid receptors and serum binding proteins; adapted with permission from Schindler *et al.*[16] (Maturitas, © 2003 Elsevier)

Progestogen	PR	AR	ER	GR	MR	SHBG	CBG
Progesterone	50	0	0	10	100	0	36
Dydrogesterone	75	0	–	–	–	–	–
Megestrol acetate	65	5	0	30	0	0	0
MPA	115	5	0	29	160	0	0
Norethisterone	75	15	0	0	0	16	0
Levonorgestrel	150	45	0	1	75	50	0

Reference steroids: PR = progesterone receptor (promegestone = 100%); AR = androgen receptor (metribolone = 100%); ER = oestrogen receptor (17β-oestradiol = 100%); GR = glucocorticoid receptor (dexamethasone = 100%); MR = mineralocorticoid receptor (aldosterone = 100%); SHBG = sex hormone-binding globulin (dihydrotestosterone = 100%); CBG = corticosteroid-binding globulin (cortisol = 100%)

Bone-sparing effects

Some progestogens have bone-sparing effects. This is well documented for norethisterone and megestrol acetate but not for MPA. This is important if the progestogen is being given to peri- or postmenopausal women. In addition, it is well known from the literature concerning the oral contraceptive pill that there is a difference in the incidence of deep vein thrombosis (DVT). Whether this is true if the progestogen is administered alone is unclear. However, it appears that progestogens may enhance the effect of oestrogen on bone density.[22]

Effects on breast tissue

Progestogens also differ in their effect on breast tissue. This may be dose-related in that progestogens are administered at very high dosage to women with advanced oestrogen-dependent cancer, whereas there are data to suggest that some progestogens may stimulate proliferation of breast tissue.[23] In addition, they increase mammographic density and this can lead to difficulties in identifying abnormalities (see Chapter 12).

The effects of progestogens on the breast appear to differ markedly from those on the endometrium. Recent data from the Million Women Study[24] suggest that combined HRT has a greater impact on breast cancer risk than oestrogen administered alone and that this risk also differs between sequential and continuous combined regimens. Progestogens administered alone increase the risk of breast cancer although it is likely that their effects on tissues will differ according to the oestrogen status of the woman.

Cardiovascular risk factors

The effects of progestogens on cardiovascular risk factors are discussed later in this chapter.

Tibolone

This steroid has the properties of an oestrogen, androgen and progestogen. It was one of the first 'no period' regimens developed and is most suited to the fully postmenopausal woman.

It is effective in relieving hot flushing and also can be used to maintain bone density. Although it does not increase mammographic density, it is associated with an increase in the incidence of breast cancer.[24] Because of its androgenic properties it might also be useful in women with decreased libido.

Tibolone is the only preparation in the UK licensed for use as 'add back' therapy to prevent adverse effects induced by gonadotrophin-releasing hormone (GnRH) agonist administration.

HRT regimens

Millions of women worldwide take combined hormones in the form of either the combined oral contraceptive (COC) pill or HRT. Combined HRT is the regimen usually preferred by women who have a uterus, with the exception of those who have an intrauterine system such as the levonorgestrel intrauterine system, which secretes enough hormone to provide endometrial protection although systemic absorption is low and other effects of progestogens, for example on bone, are limited.

Combined regimens

When the hormones are administered together, it is possible to give a lower dose of progestogen than if it were to be given alone to relieve menopausal symptoms. The doses of the different progestogens that are required to provide endometrial protection have been clearly defined.[25,26] Perimenopausal women will take the progestogens for approximately two weeks each month while using the oestrogen continuously. This will give a regular withdrawal bleed. Older women might find a continuous combined regimen more appropriate, where a lower dose of progestogen can be administered daily. Some 'long cycle' preparations even administer oestrogen alone for ten weeks followed by combination with a progestogen for the two subsequent weeks. Whether these different regimens differ in their effects on metabolic factors or proliferation of breast tissue has not been determined conclusively.

Effects of HRT regimen on the breast

The Million Women Study suggests that the increase in breast cancer risk is less in women receiving oestrogen alone than in those receiving combination therapy.[24] This supports data from the WHI study since there was no increase in the incidence of breast cancer in those receiving CEE without a progestogen.[27] The conclusion from these trials is that progestogens actually stimulate the breast and may have a carcinogenic effect. Since the presence of oestradiol is required for synthesis of progesterone receptors, it is likely that progestogens will induce different changes when given in combination than when administered alone. However, it is not as yet clear how the various progestogens differ in this respect.

Effects of HRT regimen on venous thromboembolism and stroke

It is well known that administration of sex steroids in the form of either COC or HRT increases the risk of venous thromboembolism (VTE) and stroke.[28-30] It was initially believed that the risk with HRT was less than with COC but this is no longer thought to be the case.

The risk of a recurrent VTE is greater in women receiving oral HRT,[31] which also exacerbates the risk in women with thrombophilia.[32] However, epidemiological data suggest that there is no increase in risk with transdermal oestradiol.[33]

From studies with the COC pill, it is clear that the third-generation progestogens increase the risk of VTE more than second-generation agents. However, these progestogens are not found in standard HRT regimens and it is not clear whether the progestogen modifies the effect of oestradiol or whether the increased risk is altered by progestogen type.

The mechanism of thrombotic risk and stroke induced by HRT is unclear and involves an interaction of many different factors.[34,35]

The effect of HRT preparations on the different components of the coagulation/fibrinolysis cascade is complex[36-39] and the clinical relevance, in relation to both arterial and venous coagulation, of the documented changes uncertain. This is further complicated by the impact of varying the method of administration.[40]

Endometrial protection

The effect of progestogens on the endometrium is the only true class effect of these steroids. Unopposed oestrogen stimulates endometrial proliferation with an increase in the incidence of endometrial hyperplasia and cancer. Progesterone and the progestogens have an antiproliferative effect when given in appropriate doses.[41] Studies with progesterone cream suggest that a level of circulating progesterone much lower than that found in the luteal phase of the cycle is all that is required.[42] Protection can be achieved by intermittent or continuous administration of a progestogen and even as few as 14 days every three months may be sufficient.

The cardiovascular system

Observational studies carried out mainly in the USA in the 1960s suggested that oestrogen had a cardioprotective effect.[43,44] This sparked tremendous interest in the mechanism of action and numerous studies were performed to investigate the effect of components of HRT on the vasculature and on cardiovascular risk factors. Since publication of the Heart and Estrogen/Progestin Replacement Study (HERS) in 1998, the emphasis has shifted towards investigating why there is an apparent increase in the incidence of vascular events after initiation of HRT.[45]

Vascular effects of HRT

Oestrogen has many biological effects that are compatible with a beneficial effect on cardiovascular disease (CVD) risk even though this is not borne out in practice.[46,47] HRT has no effect on blood pressure even though some studies have demonstrated improved vascular reactivity and endothelial function with oestrogen. Oestradiol induces vasodilatation by stimulation of nitric oxide synthesis in healthy postmenopausal women and also those with diseased vessels. Studies with cynomolgus monkeys have also suggested that atheroma formation was decreased by oestrogen[48] but this has not been confirmed in the human. Transdermal oestradiol has less effect on the endothelium[49] than oral and little information is available on the effects of the addition of a progestogen.

Both oestrogen and progesterone receptors are present in the arterial wall and there is evidence that the arterial effects of both steroids are receptor mediated. It is also possible that progestogens downregulate the oestradiol receptors. Depending on their chemical structure, progestogens have different metabolic and vascular effects that may enhance or abolish those induced by oestrogen therapy. Progestogen therapy can stabilise arteries in a state of vasomotor instability, but may also induce vasoconstriction of oestrogenised vessels.[50]

HRT and lipids

Oral oestradiol improves the lipid profile, with lowered total cholesterol, higher high-density lipoprotein cholesterol (HDL-C) and lower low-density lipoprotein cholesterol (LDL-C).[51] This effect is likely to result from first-pass metabolism through the liver. CEE leads to a similar profile although its administration is associated with a significantly greater increase in triglyceride levels than that following oral oestradiol administration. Since first-pass metabolism is avoided by transdermal oestradiol, the effect on the lipid profile is less than that following oral administration.[52-57]

The effect of co-administration of progestogen depends on its androgenicity.[26] The C21 progestogens tend to be 'lipid friendly' with little modification of the changes induced by the oestrogen. The C19 progestogens tend to decrease HDL-C, resulting in an atherogenic profile. The lipid profile thus varies between the different HRT regimens.[58]

HRT and carbohydrate metabolism

In healthy postmenopausal women, CEE may either impair or leave unchanged glucose tolerance, while oral or transdermal oestradiol causes little change. CEE may also increase the insulin response to a glucose load but, in contrast, oral and transdermal oestradiol may either decrease the response or have a neutral effect.[59-61]

The increased insulin resistance observed in the luteal phase of the menstrual cycle suggests an effect of progesterone on insulin sensitivity and addition of progestogen may modify the action of oestrogen to some extent. MPA has been shown to increase insulin resistance in some studies, norethisterone has a neutral effect, and dydrogesterone may even have a beneficial action.[62,63] Little is known about the effect of progestogens when administered alone.

There have now been a number of RCTs of HRT in women with type 2 diabetes.[64-66] These have demonstrated either a fall in HbA$_{1c}$ or a neutral effect, and no adverse effect on insulin sensitivity.[67] Development of diabetes might be less common in those on HRT although the incidence of cardiovascular events is greater in diabetic women taking HRT than those not. HRT has been little used in postmenopausal women with diabetes and in the future it is likely to be prescribed even less often.

HRT and inflammation

Interest in the effect of HRT on inflammatory factors has increased since the publication of the HERS study in 1998.[45] This demonstrated that there was no difference in the number of deaths from CVD in the women who took HRT compared with those on placebo. In addition, it appeared that there was a relative increase in the likelihood of death in the first year after starting HRT with an apparent diminution over time. The early increase was also noted in the WHI study and is similar to that found in the incidence of VTE. The results of these studies were surprising since, as described above, oestradiol has many biological actions that might suggest a cardioprotective effect and observational studies had also suggested a significant decrease in the incidence in CVD in those on HRT.

Inflammation and cardiovascular disease

Vascular inflammation is central in the course of atherosclerosis. High-sensitivity C-reactive protein (hsCRP) is a sensitive but nonspecific marker of inflammation. Cellular adhesion molecules such as intercellular adhesion molecule-1 (ICAM-1), vascular cell adhesion molecule-1 (VCAM-1) and endothelial-leucocyte adhesion molecule-1 (E-selectin) are preferentially expressed by endothelium in the early stages of atherosclerosis. Inflammatory cytokines such as interleukin-6 (IL-6) and tumour necrosis factor-α (TNF-α) are considered to be pro-atherogenic whereas others such as IL-10 may have anti-atherogenic effects.[68]

The pro-atherogenic adhesion molecules also interact with both the complement and coagulation systems.[69] For example, CRP is found adjacent to complement in the centre of an atheromatous plaque.

Inflammation and HRT

One possible explanation for the increase in vascular events following initiation of HRT is that HRT has acute effects that result in activation of the coagulation cascade and/or plaque instability. These changes might explain the increase in both arterial and venous events. Inflammatory factors such as CRP, IL-6 and monocytic tissue factor (mTF) might be involved as a trigger for both systems. CRP is a known risk factor for CVD in both men and women, with increases within the normal physiological range being associated with an increased risk of heart disease.[70] It is known to be involved in the atherogenic process since it is found in macrophage-rich regions at the centre of unstable plaque and stimulates the release of cytokines that might increase the chance of plaque rupture. There are also data to suggest that its synthesis is altered by sex steroid administration.[71–76]

Effect of HRT on inflammatory mediators

The data would suggest that the mode of administration impacts on the effect of oestrogen on CRP levels. Most studies agree that oral oestradiol increases the level of CRP significantly.[77–79] However, transdermal HRT appears to have no effect.[33] This suggests that first-pass metabolism is important and this seems logical in that CRP is produced from hepatocytes. Addition of progestogens may attenuate the effect of oestrogen as demonstrated by administration of transdermal oestradiol and oral norethisterone to postmenopausal women with type 2 diabetes, where a significant decrease in CRP was demonstrated following six months of use.[80] The type of progestogen may have some impact[81,82] even when administered via an intrauterine system. Thus, in summary, oral oestradiol increases CRP levels, transdermal oestradiol has a neutral effect, and progestogens may modify the effect of the oestrogen or have little impact. The effect of different types of HRT on CRP is shown in Table 16.4.

Overall, oral oestradiol administration leads to an increase in CRP although little change in other inflammatory mediators. However, transdermal oestradiol has little effect. The addition of a progestogen appears to modify the effect of oestradiol by either neutralising the effect of oral oestradiol or causing a decrease if added to a transdermal preparation. This results in a specific effect on CRP, a known risk factor for cardiovascular disease, although whether the steroids influence only the hepatic production is unknown.

The inflammatory mediator IL-6 activates CRP and, like CRP, is increased as a result of inflammatory stimuli. However, the effect of oral oestrogen is less consistent

Table 16.4. The effect of HRT on C-reactive protein (CRP)

Study	Type of HRT	Effect on CRP
Brooks-Asplund et al.[83] (2002)	E	Increased
	E + P (in vitro)	No change
Cushman[76] (2002)	E	Increased
	E + P (various)	No change
Goudev et al.[71] (2002)	E + P (low dose) + NETA	No change
Kluft et al.[78] (2002)	E	Increased
Post et al.[91] (2002)	E (transdermal)	No change
	E (oral)	Increased
Silvestri et al.[84] (2003)	E + P (CEE + MPA)	Increased
Sattar et al.[80] (2000)	E (transdermal) + NETA	Decreased
Skouby et al.[82] (2002)	E + P (various)	Increased
	Oestradiol valerate + cyproterone acetate	No change
Stork et al.[79] (2002)	E + P (gestodene)	No change
van Baal et al.[75] (1999)	E + P (dydrogesterone)	No change
Yilmazer et al.[74] (2003)	E (transdermal) + P (MPA)	No change
	E (oral) + NETA	Increased

CEE = conjugated equine oestrogen; E = oestrogen; MPA = medroxyprogesterone acetate; NETA = norethisterone acetate; P = progestogen

than with CRP.[83] This suggests that HRT is not simply stimulating a generalised inflammatory response.[84] There are also fewer consistent effects on other factors such as the adhesion molecules that appear to be influenced by the route of administration of the oestradiol.[85,86] The effects of HRT on inflammatory mediators other than CRP are summarised in Table 16.5.

Tissue factor is an inflammatory mediator that is known to interact with the coagulation cascade via effects on factor VII. It is thus quite plausible to postulate that CRP and IL-6 might also activate the coagulation cascade and lead to a prothrombotic state. Data concerning the impact of HRT on coagulation/fibrinolysis are complex and have been subject to extensive review.[69,87] The effects are inconsistent depending on the type of preparation and the route of administration.

Factor VII is a risk factor for CVD and the effects of oestradiol are more consistent than with a number of the other factors.[88–90] Both oral and transdermal oestradiol lead to a significant decrease, suggesting that this pathway is unlikely to contribute to the prothrombotic effect of the HRT. The route of administration of oestradiol has significant impact on its effects as would be expected from the absence of first-pass metabolism with the transdermal route. This would suggest that for those women with increased risk of either arterial or venous thrombosis a transdermal delivery route might be safer than an oral preparation.

Conclusion

Exogenous sex steroids have profound actions on most body systems. These may be beneficial, such as those on bone, but may also result in deleterious adverse effects such as the increased risk of breast cancer or a thrombotic event. The lack of a protective effect against cardiovascular disease is surprising in view of the biological actions of oestrogen and the reasons for this are not clear. The differences between the routes of administration of steroids and the types themselves might form part of the explanation.

Table 16.5. The effect of HRT on inflammatory mediators, excluding C-reactive protein (CRP)

Study	Type of HRT	Mediator	Effect
Brooks-Asplund et al.[83] (2002)	E	TNF-α	Increased
		IL-6	No change
	E + P	TNF-α	Increased
		IL-6	Increased
Cushman et al.[69] (1999)	E	Alpha 1-acid glycoprotein	Decreased
	E + P	Alpha 1-acid glycoprotein	Decreased
Goudev et al.[71] (2002)	E (oral) + NETA	sICAM-1	Decreased
		sVCAM-1	Decreased
		P-selectin	Decreased
Kluft et al.[78] (2002)	E (oral)	IL-6	No change
		Serum amyloid	No change
Silvestri et al.[84] (2003)	CEE + MPA	IL-6	Decreased
		VCAM-1	Decreased
		E-selectin	Decreased
Stork et al.[79] (2002)	E + gestodene	ICAM-1	Decreased
		VCAM-1	Decreased
		E-selectin	Decreased
van Baal et al.[75] (1999)	E + dydrogesterone	E-selectin	Decreased

CEE = conjugated equine oestrogen; E = oestrogen; ICAM-1 = intercellular adhesion molecule-1; IL-6 = interleukin-6; MPA = medroxyprogesterone acetate; NETA = norethisterone acetate; sICAM-1 = soluble intercellular adhesion molecule-1; sVCAM-1 = soluble vascular cell adhesion molecule-1; VCAM-1 = vascular cell adhesion molecule-1

References

1. Templeman C, Quinn D, Hansen R, Moreton T, Baber R. An audit of oestrogen implant hormone replacement therapy. *Aust N Z J Obstet Gynaecol* 1998;38:455–60.
2. MacLennan A, Lester S, Moore V. Oral oestrogen replacement therapy versus placebo for hot flushes. *Cochrane Database Syst Rev* 2001;(1):CD002978.
3. Greendale GA, Reboussin BA, Hogan P, Barnabei VM, Shumaker S, Johnson S, et al. Symptom relief and side effects of postmenopausal hormones: results from the Postmenopausal Estrogen/Progestin Interventions Trial. *Obstet Gynecol* 1998;92:982–8.
4. Rymer J, Morris EP. Extracts from "Clinical evidence": Menopausal symptoms. *BMJ* 2000;321:1516–19.
5. Cauley JA, Robbins J, Chen Z, Cummings SR, Jackson RD, LaCroix AZ, et al.; Women's Health Initiative Investigators. Effects of estrogen plus progestin on risk of fracture and bone mineral density: the Women's Health Initiative randomized trial. *JAMA* 2003;290:1729–38.
6. Adami S, Suppi R, Bertoldo F, Rossini M, Residori M, Maresca V, et al. Transdermal estradiol in the treatment of postmenopausal bone loss. *Bone Miner* 1989;7:79–86.
7. Hutchinson TA, Polansky SM, Feinstein AR. Post-menopausal oestrogens protect against fractures of hip and distal radius. A case–control study. *Lancet* 1979;2:705–9.
8. Kiel DP, Felson DT, Anderson JJ, Wilson PW, Moskowitz MA. Hip fracture and the use of estrogens in postmenopausal women. The Framingham Study. *N Engl J Med* 1987;317:1169–74.
9. Lindsay R, Hart DM, Forrest C, Baird C. Prevention of spinal osteoporosis in oophorectomised women. *Lancet* 1980;2:1151–4.
10. Stevenson JC, Cust MP, Gangar KF, Hillard TC, Lees B, Whitehead MI. Effects of transdermal versus oral hormone replacement therapy on bone density in spine and proximal femur in postmenopausal women. *Lancet* 1990;336:265–9.
11. Paganini-Hill A, Ross RK, Gerkins VR, Henderson BE, Arthur M, Mack TM. Menopausal estrogen therapy and hip fractures. *Ann Intern Med* 1981;95:28–31.
12. Lufkin EG, Wahner HW, O'Fallon WM, Hodgson SF, Kotowicz MA, Lane AW, et al. Treatment of postmenopausal osteoporosis with transdermal estrogen. *Ann Intern Med* 1992;117:1–9.

13.   Horowitz M, Wishart JM, Need AG, Morris HA, Nordin BE. Effects of norethisterone on bone related biochemical variables and forearm bone mineral in post-menopausal osteoporosis. *Clin Endocrinol (Oxf)* 1993;39:649–55.

14.   Duff G, Committee on Safety of Medicines. Use of hormone replacement therapy in the prevention of osteoporosis: important new information. 3 December 2003 [http://medicines.mhra.gov.uk].

15.   Rossouw JE, Anderson GL, Prentice RL, LaCroix AZ, Kooperberg C, Stefanick ML, *et al.*; Writing Group for the Women's Health Initiative Investigators. Risks and benefits of estrogen plus progestin in healthy postmenopausal women: principal results fom the Women's Health Initiative randomized controlled trial. *JAMA* 2002;288:321–33.

16.   Schindler A.E. Campagnoli C, Druckmann R, Huber J, Pasqualini JR, Schweppe KW, *et al.* Classification and pharmacology of progestins. *Maturitas* 2003;46SI:S7–16.

17.   Raudrant D, Rabe T. Progestogens with antiandrogenic properties. *Drugs* 2003;63:463–92.

18.   Cooper A, Spencer C, Whitehead MI, Ross D, Barnard GJ, Collins WP. Systemic absorption of progesterone from Progest cream in postmenopausal women. *Lancet* 1998;351:1255–6.

19.   Wren BG, Champion SM, Willetts K, Manga RZ, Eden JA. Transdermal progesterone and its effect on vasomotor symptoms, blood lipid levels, bone metabolic markers, moods, and quality of life for postmenopausal women. *Menopause* 2003;10:13–18.

20.   Nilsson CG, Lahteenmaki PL, Luukkainen T, Robertson DN. Sustained intrauterine release of levonorgestrel over five years. *Fertil Steril* 1986;45:805–7.

21.   Boon J, Scholten PC, Oldenhave A, Heintz AP. Continuous intrauterine compared with cyclic oral progestin administration in perimenopausal HRT. *Maturitas* 2003;46:69–77.

22.   Delmas PD, Confavreux E, Garnero P, Fardellone P, de Vernejoul MC, Cormier C, *et al.* A combination of low doses of 17 beta-estradiol and norethisterone acetate prevents bone loss and normalizes bone turnover in postmenopausal women. *Osteoporos Int* 2000;11:177–87.

23.   Franke HR, Vermes I. Differential effects of progestogens on breast cancer cell lines. *Maturitas* 2003;46 Suppl 1:S55–8.

24.   Beral V; Million Women Study Collaborators. Breast cancer and hormone-replacement therapy in the Million Women Study. *Lancet* 2003;362:419–27. Erratum in: *Lancet* 2003;362:1160.

25.   Whitehead MI, Townsend PT, Pryse-Davies J, Ryder T, Lane G, Siddle N, *et al.* Actions of progestins on the morphology and biochemistry of the endometrium of postmenopausal women receiving low-dose estrogen therapy. *Am J Obstet Gynecol* 1982;142:791–5.

26.   Whitehead MI, Hillard TC, Crook D. The role and use of progestogens. *Obstet Gynecol* 1990;75:59S–76S; discussion 81S–83S.

27.   Anderson GL, Limacher M, Assaf AR, Bassford T, Beresford SA, Black H, *et al.*; Women's Health Initiative Steering Committee. Effects of conjugated equine estrogen in postmenopausal women with hysterectomy: the Women's Health Initiative randomized controlled trial. *JAMA* 2004;291:1701–12.

28.   Castellsague J, Perez Gutthann S, Garcia Rodriguez LA. Recent epidemiological studies of the association between hormone replacement therapy and venous thromboembolism. A review. *Drug Saf* 1998;18:117–23.

29.   Jick H, Jick SS, Gurewich V, Myers MW, Vasilakis C. Risk of idiopathic cardiovascular death and nonfatal venous thromboembolism in women using oral contraceptives with differing progestagen components. *Lancet* 1995;346:1589–93.

30.   Poulter NR, Chang CL, Farley TM, Marmot MG, Meirik O. Effect on stroke of different progestagens in low oestrogen dose oral contraceptives. WHO Collaborative Study of Cardiovascular Disease and Steroid Hormone Contraception. *Lancet* 1999;354:301–2.

31.   Hoibraaten E, Qvigstad E, Arnesen H, Larsen S, Wickstrom E, Sandset PM. Increased risk of recurrent venous thromboembolism during hormone replacement therapy – results of the randomized, double-blind, placebo-controlled estrogen in venous thromboembolism trial (EVTET). *Thromb Haemost* 2000;84:961–7.

32.   Lowe G, Woodward M, Vessey M, Rumley A, Gough P, Daly E. Thrombotic variables and risk of idiopathic venous thromboembolism in women aged 45–64 years. Relationships to hormone replacement therapy. *Thromb Haemost* 2000;83:530–5.

33.   Lowe GD, Upton MN, Rumley A, McConnachie A, O'Reilly DS, Watt GC. Different effects of oral and transdermal hormone replacement therapies on factor IX, APC resistance, t-PA, PAI and C-reactive protein – a cross-sectional population survey. *Thromb Haemost* 2001;86:550–6.

34.   Cano A, van Baal WM. The mechanisms of thrombotic risk induced by hormone replacement therapy. *Maturitas* 2001;40:17–38.

35.   Pines A, Bornstein NM, Shapira I. Menopause and ischaemic stroke: basic, clinical and epidemiological considerations. The role of hormone replacement. *Hum Reprod Update* 2002;8:161–8.

36.   Demirol A, Baykal C, Kirazli S, Ayhan A. Effects of hormone replacement on hemostasis in spontaneous menopause. *Menopause* 2001;8:135–40.

37. Douketis JD, Gordon M, Johnston M, Julian JA, Adachi JR, Ginsberg JS. The effects of hormone replacement therapy on thrombin generation, fibrinolysis inhibition, and resistance to activated protein C: prospective cohort study and review of literature. *Thromb Res* 2000;99:25–34.
38. Winkler UH, Altkemper R, Kwee B, Helmond FA, Coelingh Bennink HJ. Effects of tibolone and continuous combined hormone replacement therapy on parameters in the clotting cascade: a multicenter, double-blind, randomized study. *Fertil Steril* 2000;74:10–19.
39. Teede HJ, McGrath BP, Smolich JJ, Malan E, Kotsopoulos D, Liang YL, *et al*. Postmenopausal hormone replacement therapy increases coagulation activity and fibrinolysis. *Arterioscler Thromb Vasc Biol* 2000;20:1404–9.
40. Kroon UB, Tengborn L, Rita H, Backstrom AC. The effects of transdermal oestradiol and oral progestogens on haemostasis variables. *Br J Obstet Gynaecol* 1997;104 Suppl 16:32–7.
41. Lane G, Siddle NC, Ryder TA, Pryse-Davies J, King RJ, Whitehead MI. Dose dependent effects of oral progesterone on the oestrogenised postmenopausal endometrium. *BMJ* 1983;287:1241–5.
42. Ross D, Cooper AJ, Pryse-Davies J, Bergeron C, Collins WP, Whitehead MI. Randomized, double-blind, dose-ranging study of the endometrial effects of a vaginal progesterone gel in estrogen-treated postmenopausal women. *Am J Obstet Gynecol* 1997;177:937–41.
43. Grodstein F, Stampfer M. The epidemiology of coronary heart disease and estrogen replacement in postmenopausal women. *Prog Cardiovasc Dis* 1995;38:199–210.
44. Grodstein F, Manson JE, Stampfer MJ. Postmenopausal hormone use and secondary prevention of coronary events in the nurses' health study. a prospective, observational study. *Ann Intern Med* 2001;135:1–8.
45. Hulley S, Grady D, Bush T, Furberg C, Herrington D, Riggs B, *et al*. Randomized trial of estrogen plus progestin for secondary prevention of coronary heart disease in postmenopausal women. Heart and Estrogen/progestin Replacement Study (HERS) Research Group. *JAMA* 1998;280:605–13.
46. Wagner JD, Kaplan JR, Burkman RT. Reproductive hormones and cardiovascular disease mechanism of action and clinical implications. *Obstet Gynecol Clin North Am* 2002;29:475–93.
47. Mikkola TS, Clarkson TB. Estrogen replacement therapy, atherosclerosis, and vascular function. *Cardiovasc Res* 2002;53:605–19.
48. Clarkson TB, Anthony MS, Mikkola TS, St Clair RW. Comparison of tibolone and conjugated equine estrogens effects on carotid artery atherosclerosis of postmenopausal monkeys. *Stroke* 2002;33:2700–3.
49. Duncan AC, Petrie JR, Brosnan MJ, Devlin AM, Bass RA, Charnock-Jones DS, *et al*. Is estradiol cardioprotection a nitric oxide-mediated effect? *Hum Reprod* 2002;17:1918–24.
50. Rosano GM, Leonardo F, Sarrel PM, Beale CM, De Luca F, Collins P. Cyclical variation in paroxysmal supraventricular tachycardia in women. *Lancet* 1996;347:786–8.
51. Stevenson JC. Metabolic effects of the menopause and oestrogen replacement. *Baillieres Clin Obstet Gynaecol* 1996;10:449–67.
52. Stevenson JC, Crook D, Godsland IF, Lees B, Whitehead MI. Oral versus transdermal hormone replacement therapy. *Int J Fertil Menopausal Stud* 1993;38 Suppl 1:30–5.
53. Spencer C, Crook D, Ross D, Cooper A, Whitehead M, Stevenson J. A randomised comparison of the effects of oral versus transdermal 17beta-oestradiol, each combined with sequential oral norethisterone acetate, on serum lipoprotein levels. *Br J Obstet Gynaecol* 1999;106:948–53. Erratum in: *Br J Obstet Gynaecol* 1999;106:1107.
54. Erenus M, Karakoc B, Gurler A. Comparison of effects of continuous combined transdermal with oral estrogen and oral progestogen replacement therapies on serum lipoproteins and compliance. *Climacteric* 2001;4:228–34.
55. Karjalainen A, Heikkinen J, Savolainen MJ, Backstrom AC, Salinto M, Kesaniemi YA. Metabolic changes induced by peroral oestrogen and transdermal oestradiol gel therapy. *Br J Obstet Gynaecol* 1997;104 Suppl 16:38–43.
56. Whitcroft SI, Crook D, Marsh MS, Ellerington MC, Whitehead MI, Stevenson JC. Long-term effects of oral and transdermal hormone replacement therapies on serum lipid and lipoprotein concentrations. *Obstet Gynecol* 1994;84:222–6.
57. Chen FP, Lee N, Soong YK, Huang KE. Comparison of transdermal and oral estrogen-progestin replacement therapy: effects on cardiovascular risk factors. *Menopause* 2001;8:347–52.
58. Hanggi W, Lippuner K, Riesen W, Jaeger P, Birkhauser MH. Long-term influence of different postmenopausal hormone replacement regimens on serum lipids and lipoprotein (a): a randomised study. *Br J Obstet Gynaecol* 1997;104:708–17.
59. Fineberg SE. Glycaemic control and hormone replacement therapy: implications of the Postmenopausal Estrogen/Progestogen Intervention (PEPI) study. *Drugs Aging* 2000;17:453–61.
60. Spencer CP, Godsland IF, Cooper AJ, Ross D, Whitehead MI, Stevenson JC. Effects of oral and transdermal 17beta-estradiol with cyclical oral norethindrone acetate on insulin sensitivity, secretion, and elimination in postmenopausal women. *Metabolism* 2000;49:742–7.

61.   Saglam K, Polat Z, Yilmaz MI, Gulec M, Akinci SB. Effects of postmenopausal hormone replacement therapy on insulin resistance. *Endocrine* 2002;18:211–14.
62.   Duncan AC, Lyall H, Roberts RN, Petrie JR, Perera MJ, Monaghan S, *et al*. The effect of estradiol and a combined estradiol/progestagen preparation on insulin sensitivity in healthy postmenopausal women. *J Clin Endocrinol Metab* 1999;84:2402–7.
63.   Crook D, Godsland IF, Hull J, Stevenson JC. Hormone replacement therapy with dydrogesterone and 17 beta-oestradiol: effects on serum lipoproteins and glucose tolerance during 24 month follow up. *Br J Obstet Gynaecol* 1997;104:298–304.
64.   Andersson B. Hormone replacement therapy in postmenopausal women with diabetes mellitus: a risk-benefit assessment. *Drugs Aging* 2000;17:399–410.
65.   Perera M, Sattar N, Petrie JR, Hillier C, Small M, Connell JM, *et al*. The effects of transdermal estradiol in combination with oral norethisterone on lipoproteins, coagulation, and endothelial markers in postmenopausal women with type 2 diabetes: a randomized, placebo-controlled study. *J Clin Endocrinol Metab* 2001;86:1140–3.
66.   Stojanovic ND, Kwong P, Byrne DJ, Arnold A, Jagroop IA, Nair D, *et al*. The effects of transdermal estradiol alone or with cyclical dydrogesterone on markers of cardiovascular disease risk in postmenopausal women with type 2 diabetes: a pilot study. *Angiology* 2003;54:391–9.
67.   Palin SL, Kumar S, Sturdee DW, Barnett AH. HRT in women with diabetes – review of the effects on glucose and lipid metabolism. *Diabetes Res Clin Pract* 2001;54:67–77.
68.   Young JL, Libby P, Schonbeck U. Cytokines in the pathogenesis of atherosclerosis. *Thromb Haemost* 2002;88:554–67.
69.   Cushman M, Meilahn EN, Psaty BM, Kuller LH, Dobs AS, Tracy RP. Hormone replacement therapy, inflammation, and hemostasis in elderly women. *Arterioscler Thromb Vasc Biol* 1999;19:893–9.
70.   Albert MA, Glynn RJ, Ridker PM. Plasma concentration of C-reactive protein and the calculated Framingham Coronary Heart Disease Risk Score. *Circulation* 2003;108:161–5.
71.   Goudev A, Georgiev DB, Koycheva N, Manasiev N, Kyurkchiev S. Effects of low dose hormone replacement therapy on markers of inflammation in postmenopausal women. *Maturitas* 2002;43:49–53.
72.   Primatesta P, Falaschetti E, Poulter NR. Influence of hormone replacement therapy on C-reactive protein: population-based data. *J Cardiovasc Risk* 2003;10:57–60.
73.   Pradhan AD, Manson JE, Rossouw JE, Siscovick DS, Mouton CP, Rifai N, *et al*. Inflammatory biomarkers, hormone replacement therapy, and incident coronary heart disease: prospective analysis from the Women's Health Initiative observational study. *JAMA* 2002;288:980–7.
74.   Yilmazer M, Fenkci V, Fenkci S, Sonmezer M, Aktepe O, Altindis M, *et al*. Hormone replacement therapy, C-reactive protein, and fibrinogen in healthy postmenopausal women. *Maturitas* 2003;46:245–53.
75.   van Baal WM, Kenemans P, Emeis JJ, Schalkwijk CG, Mijatovic V, van der Mooren MJ, *et al*. Long-term effects of combined hormone replacement therapy on markers of endothelial function and inflammatory activity in healthy postmenopausal women. *Fertil Steril* 1999;71:663–70.
76.   Cushman M. Effects of hormone replacement therapy and estrogen receptor modulators on markers of inflammation and coagulation. *Am J Cardiol* 2002;90:7F–10F.
77.   Ridker PM, Hennekens CH, Rifai N, Buring JE, Manson JE. Hormone replacement therapy and increased plasma concentration of C-reactive protein. *Circulation* 1999;100:713–6.
78.   Kluft C, Leuven JA, Helmerhorst FM, Krans HM. Pro-inflammatory effects of oestrogens during use of oral contraceptives and hormone replacement treatment. *Vascul Pharmacol* 2002;39:149–54.
79.   Stork S, von Schacky C, Angerer P. The effect of 17beta-estradiol on endothelial and inflammatory markers in postmenopausal women: a randomized, controlled trial. *Atherosclerosis* 2002;165:301–7.
80.   Sattar N, Perera M, Small M, Lumsden MA. Hormone replacement therapy and sensitive C-reactive protein concentrations in women with type-2 diabetes. *Lancet* 1999;354:487–8.
81.   Skouby SO. The rationale for a wider range of progestogens. *Climacteric* 2000;3 Suppl 2:14–20.
82.   Skouby SO, Gram J, Andersen LF, Sidelmann J, Petersen KR, Jespersen J. Hormone replacement therapy: estrogen and progestin effects on plasma C-reactive protein concentrations. *Am J Obstet Gynecol* 2002;186:969–77.
83.   Brooks-Asplund EM, Tupper CE, Daun JM, Kenney WL, Cannon JG. Hormonal modulation of interleukin-6, tumor necrosis factor and associated receptor secretion in postmenopausal women. *Cytokine* 2002;19:193–200.
84.   Silvestri A, Gebara O, Vitale C, Wajngarten M, Leonardo F, Ramires JA, *et al*. Increased levels of C-reactive protein after oral hormone replacement therapy may not be related to an increased inflammatory response. *Circulation* 2003;107:3165–9.
85.   Berg G, Ekerfelt C, Hammar M, Lindgren R, Matthiesen L, Ernerudh J. Cytokine changes in

postmenopausal women treated with estrogens: a placebo-controlled study. *Am J Reprod Immunol* 2002;48:63–9.

86.   Oger E, Alhenc-Gelas M, Plu-Bureau G, Mennen L, Cambillau M, Guize L, *et al*. Association of circulating cellular adhesion molecules with menopausal status and hormone replacement therapy. Time-dependent change in transdermal, but not oral estrogen users. *Thromb Res* 2001;101:35–43.

87.   Rosendaal FR, Helmerhorst FM, Vandenbroucke JP. Oral contraceptives, hormone replacement therapy and thrombosis. *Thromb Haemost* 2001;86:112–23.

88.   Peverill RE, Teede HJ, Smolich JJ, Malan E, Kotsopoulos D, Tipping PG, *et al*. Effects of combined oral hormone replacement therapy on tissue factor pathway inhibitor and factor VII. *Clin Sci (Lond)* 2001;101:93–9.

89.   Gottsater A, Rendell M, Hulthen UL, Berntorp E, Mattiasson I. Hormone replacement therapy in healthy postmenopausal women: a randomized, placebo-controlled study of effects on coagulation and fibrinolytic factors. *J Intern Med* 2001;249:237–46.

90.   Bladbjerg EM, Skouby SO, Andersen LF, Jespersen J. Effects of different progestin regimens in hormone replacement therapy on blood coagulation factor VII and tissue factor pathway inhibitor. *Hum Reprod* 2002;17:3235–41.

91.   Post MS, van der Mooren MJ, Stehouwer CD, van Baal WM, Mijatovic V, Schalkwijk CG, *et al*. Effects of transdermal and oral oestrogen replacement therapy on C-reactive protein levels in postmenopausal women: a randomised, placebo-controlled trial. *Thromb Haemost* 2002;88:605–10.

Chapter 17

Urogenital symptoms and hormone replacement therapy

Dudley Robinson and Linda Cardozo

Introduction

Symptoms of urogenital atrophy are a manifestation of oestrogen withdrawal following the menopause and they may appear for the first time more than 10 years after the last menstrual period.[1] The female genital and lower urinary tract share a common embryological origin from the urogenital sinus and both are sensitive to the effects of female sex steroid hormones. Oestrogen is known to have an important role in the function of the lower urinary tract throughout adult life and oestrogen and progesterone receptors have been demonstrated in the vagina, urethra, bladder and pelvic floor musculature.[2-5] Oestrogen deficiency occurring following the menopause is known to cause atrophic changes within the urogenital tract[6] and is associated with urinary symptoms such as frequency, urgency, nocturia, incontinence and recurrent infection. These may co-exist with symptoms of vaginal atrophy such as dyspareunia, itching, burning and dryness.

The role of oestrogen replacement in the treatment of these symptoms of urogenital atrophy has still not been clearly defined despite several randomised trials and widespread clinical use. This paper presents an overview of the pathogenesis and management of urogenital symptoms and the role of oestrogen replacement therapy.

Epidemiology

Increasing life expectancy has led to an increasingly elderly population and it is now common for women to spend a third of their lives in the oestrogen-deficient postmenopausal state.[7] The average age of the menopause is 50 years although there is some cultural and geographical variation.[8] Worldwide in 1990 there were approximately 467 million women aged 50 years or over and this is expected to increase to 1200 million by 2030.[9] Furthermore, postmenopausal women comprise 15% of the population in industrialised countries with a predicted growth rate of 1.5% by 2020. Overall, in the developed world 8% of the total postmenopausal population have been estimated to have urogenital symptoms.[10]

Urogenital atrophy

The prevalence of symptomatic urogenital atrophy is difficult to estimate since many women accept the changes as being an inevitable consequence of the ageing process and thus do not seek help. It has been estimated that 10-40% of all postmenopausal women are symptomatic[11] although only 25% of those are thought to seek medical help. Vaginal symptoms associated with urogenital atrophy are reported by two out of three women by the age of 75 years.[12]

A study published in 2000 assessed the prevalence of urogenital symptoms in 2157 Dutch women aged 50–75 years.[13] Overall, 27% of the women complained of vaginal dryness, soreness and dyspareunia while the prevalence of urinary symptoms such as leakage and recurrent infections was 36%. When considering severity, almost 50% reported moderate to severe discomfort, although only a third had received medical intervention. Interestingly women who had previously had a hysterectomy reported moderate to severe complaints more often than those who had not.

The prevalence of urogenital atrophy and urogenital prolapse has also been examined in a population of 285 women attending a menopause clinic.[14] Overall, 51% of the women were found to have anterior vaginal wall prolapse, 27% posterior vaginal prolapse and 20% apical prolapse. In addition, 34% of the women were noted to have urogenital atrophy, with 40% complaining of dyspareunia. While urogenital atrophy and symptoms of dyspareunia were related to menopausal age, the prevalence of prolapse showed no association.

Urogenital atrophy is an inevitable consequence of the menopause but women may not always be symptomatic. A study published in 2001 looked at 69 women attending a gynaecology clinic who were asked to fill out a symptom questionnaire prior to examination and undergoing vaginal cytology.[15] Urogenital symptoms were found to be relatively uncommon and were poorly correlated with age and physical examination findings although not with vaginal cytological maturation index. Women who were taking oestrogen replacement therapy had higher symptom scores and physical examination scores. In conclusion, it would appear that urogenital atrophy is a universal consequence of the menopause although women may often be minimally symptomatic.

Urinary incontinence

The prevalence of urinary incontinence is known to increase with age, affecting 15–35% of community-dwelling women over the age of 60 years,[16] with other studies reporting a prevalence of 49% in women over 65 years.[17] Rates of 50% have been reported in elderly nursing home residents.[18] A cross-sectional population prevalence survey of 146 women aged 15–97 years found that 46% experienced symptoms of pelvic floor dysfunction defined as stress or urge incontinence, flatus or faecal incontinence, symptomatic prolapse or previous pelvic floor surgery.[19]

Little work has been done to examine the incidence of urinary incontinence although a study in New Zealand of women over the age of 65 years found 10% of the originally continent developed urinary incontinence during the three-year study period.[20]

Economic considerations

The economic cost of urogenital atrophy is difficult to estimate owing to under-reporting and also because some of the cost is borne by the women themselves without involving the health services. The cost of incontinence is slightly easier to estimate although it is still affected by under-reporting. It comprises the 'direct' costs of treatment, supplies and provision of medical staff while the 'indirect' costs relate to loss of earnings and productivity. A study performed in 1994 in Scotland estimated that the cost of pad supplies alone in the UK may be in the region of £57.3 million per year while the cost of incontinence has been estimated at $16 billion a year in the USA. More recent data from the UK has shown the annual expenditure on incontinence to be £163 million, with appliances and containment accounting for £59 million and £69 million, respectively, and the cost of drugs and surgery being £23 million and £12 million, respectively.[21]

Oestrogen receptors and hormonal factors

The effects of the steroid hormone 17β-oestradiol are mediated by ligand-activated transcription factors known as oestrogen receptors, which are glycoproteins sharing common features with androgen and progesterone receptors. The classic oestrogen receptor (ERα) was first discovered by Elwood Jensen in 1958 and cloned from uterine tissue in 1986,[22] although it was not until 1996 that the second oestrogen receptor (ERβ) was identified.[23]

Oestrogen receptors have been demonstrated throughout the lower urinary tract and are expressed in the squamous epithelium of the proximal and distal urethra, vagina and trigone of the bladder[24] but not in the dome of the bladder, reflecting its different embryological origin. Pubococcygeous muscle and the musculature of the pelvic floor have also been shown to be oestrogen-sensitive[25,26] but oestrogen receptors have not yet been identified in the levator ani muscles.[27]

The distribution of oestrogen receptors throughout the urogenital tract has been studied and both α and β receptors have been found in the vaginal walls and uterosacral ligaments of premenopausal women, although the latter was absent in the vaginal walls of postmenopausal women.[28] In addition, α receptors are localised in the urethral sphincter and when sensitised by oestrogens are thought to help maintain muscular tone.[29] Interestingly, oestrogen receptors have also been identified in mast cells in women with interstitial cystitis[30] and in the male lower urinary tract.

Progesterone and androgen receptors

In addition to oestrogen receptors, both androgen and progesterone receptors are expressed in the lower urinary tract, although their role is less clear. Progesterone receptors are expressed inconsistently, having been reported in the bladder, trigone and vagina. Their presence may be dependent on oestrogen status. In addition, while androgen receptors are present in both the bladder and urethra, their role has not yet been defined.[31]

A study published in 2000 examined the incidence of both oestrogen and progesterone expression throughout the lower urinary tract in 90 women undergoing gynaecological surgery: 33 women were premenopausal, 26 women were postmenopausal without hormone replacement therapy (HRT) and 31 women were postmenopausal and taking HRT.[32] Biopsies were taken from the bladder dome, trigone, proximal urethra, distal urethra, vagina and vesicovaginal fascia adjacent to the bladder neck. Oestrogen receptors were found to be consistently expressed in the squamous epithelia although they were absent in the urothelial tissues of the lower urinary tract of all women, irrespective of oestrogen status. Progesterone receptor expression, however, showed more variability, being mostly subepithelial, and was significantly lower in postmenopausal women not taking oestrogen replacement therapy.

Lower urinary tract function

In order to maintain continence the urethral pressure must remain higher than the intravesical pressure at all times except during micturition.[33] Oestrogens play an important role in the continence mechanism with bladder and urethral function becoming less efficient with age.[34] Elderly women have been found to have a reduced flow rate, increased urinary residuals, higher filling pressures, reduced bladder capacity and lower maximum voiding pressures.[35] Oestrogens may affect continence by increasing urethral resistance, raising the sensory threshold of the bladder or by increasing α adrenoreceptor sensitivity in the urethral smooth muscle.[36,37] In addition, exogenous oestrogens have been shown to increase the number of intermediate and superficial cells in the vagina of postmenopausal women[38] and these changes have also been demonstrated in the bladder and urethra.[12]

A prospective observational study published in 2001 assessed cell proliferation rates throughout the tissues of the lower urinary tract;[39] 59 women were studied, of whom 23 were premenopausal, 20 were postmenopausal and not taking HRT, and 16 were postmenopausal and taking HRT. Biopsies were taken from the bladder dome, trigone, proximal urethra, distal urethra, vagina and vesicovaginal fascia adjacent to the bladder neck. The squamous epithelium of oestrogen-replete women was shown to exhibit greater levels of cellular proliferation than in those women who were oestrogen-deficient.

Bladder function

Oestrogen receptors, although absent in the transitional epithelium of the bladder, are present in the areas of the trigone but have undergone squamous metaplasia.[24] Oestrogen is known to have a direct effect on detrusor function through modifications in muscarinic receptors[40,41] and by inhibition of movement of extracellular calcium ions into muscle cells.[42] Consequently, oestradiol has been shown to reduce the amplitude and frequency of spontaneous rhythmic detrusor contractions[43] and there is also evidence that it may increase the sensory threshold of the bladder in some women.[44]

Neurological control

Sex hormones are known to influence the central neurological control of micturition although their exact role in the micturition pathway has yet to be elucidated. Oestrogen receptors have been demonstrated in the cerebral cortex, limbic system, hippocampus and cerebellum,[45,46] while androgen receptors have been demonstrated in the pontine micturition centre and the pre-optic area of the hypothalamus.[47]

Urethra

Oestrogen receptors have been demonstrated in the squamous epithelium of both the proximal and distal urethra[24] and oestrogen has been shown to improve the maturation index of urethral squamous epithelium.[48] It has been suggested that oestrogen increases urethral closure pressure and improves pressure transmission to the proximal urethra, both of which promote continence.[49–52] Oestrogens have been shown to cause vasodilatation in the systemic and cerebral circulation and these changes are also seen in the urethra.[53-55] The vascular pulsations seen on urethral pressure profilometry secondary to blood flow in the urethral submucosa and urethral sphincter have been shown to increase in size following oestrogen administration,[56] while the effect is lost following oestrogen withdrawal at the menopause.

Collagen

Oestrogens are known to have an effect on collagen synthesis and they have been shown to have a direct effect on collagen metabolism in the lower genital tract.[57] Changes found in women with urogenital atrophy may represent an alteration in systemic collagenase activity,[58] and genuine stress incontinence and urogenital prolapse has been associated with a reduction in both vaginal and periurethral collagen.[59-61] There is a reduction in skin collagen content following the menopause[62] and rectus muscle fascia has been shown to become less elastic with increasing age, resulting in a lower energy requirement to cause irreversible damage.[63] Changes in collagen content have also been identified, with the hydroxyproline content in connective tissue from women with stress incontinence being 40% lower than in continent controls.[64]

Urogenital atrophy

Withdrawal of endogenous oestrogen at the menopause results in well-documented climacteric symptoms such as hot flushes and night sweats in addition to the less commonly reported symptoms of urogenital atrophy. Symptoms do not usually develop until several years after the menopause when levels of endogenous oestrogens fall below the level required to promote endometrial growth.[65] This temporal relationship would suggest oestrogen withdrawal as the cause.

Vaginal dryness is commonly the first reported symptom and is caused by a reduction in mucus production within the vaginal glands. Atrophy within the vaginal epithelium leads to thinning and an increased susceptibility to infection and mechanical trauma. Glycogen depletion within the vaginal mucosa following the menopause leads to a decrease in lactic acid formation by Döderlein's lactobacillus and a consequent rise in vaginal pH from around 4 to between 6 and 7. This allows bacterial overgrowth and colonisation with Gram-negative bacilli, compounding the effects of vaginal atrophy and leading to symptoms of vaginitis such as pruritus, dyspareunia and discharge.

Lower urinary tract symptoms

Epidemiological studies have implicated oestrogen deficiency in the aetiology of lower urinary tract symptoms, with 70% of women with urinary incontinence relating its onset to their final menstrual period.[6] Lower urinary tract symptoms have been shown to be common in postmenopausal women attending a menopause clinic, with 20% complaining of severe urgency and almost 50% complaining of stress incontinence.[66] Urge incontinence, in particular, is more prevalent following the menopause and the prevalence would appear to rise with increasing years of oestrogen deficiency.[67] There is, however, conflicting evidence regarding the role of oestrogen withdrawal at the time of the menopause. Some studies have shown a peak incidence in perimenopausal women[68,69] while other evidence suggests that many women develop incontinence at least 10 years prior to the cessation of menstruation, with significantly more premenopausal women than postmenopausal women being affected.[65,70]

Cyclical variations in the levels of both oestrogen and progesterone during the menstrual cycle have also been shown to lead to changes in urodynamic variables and lower urinary tract symptoms, with 37% of women noticing deterioration in symptoms prior to menstruation.[71] Measurement of the urethral pressure profile in nulliparous premenopausal women shows there is an increase in functional urethral length midcycle and early in the luteal phase, corresponding to an increase in plasma oestradiol.[72] Furthermore, progestogens have been associated with an increase in irritative bladder symptoms,[73,74] and with urinary incontinence in those women taking combined HRT.[75] The incidence of detrusor instability in the luteal phase of the menstrual cycle may be associated with raised plasma progesterone following ovulation and progesterone has been shown to antagonise the inhibitory effect of oestradiol on rat detrusor contractions.[76] This may help to explain the increased prevalence of detrusor overactivity found in pregnancy.[77]

Urinary tract infection is also a common cause of urinary symptoms in women of all ages. This is a particular problem in the elderly with a reported incidence of 20% in the community and over 50% in institutionalised women.[78,79] Pathophysiological changes such as impairment of bladder emptying, poor perineal hygiene and both faecal and urinary incontinence may partly account for the high prevalence observed. In addition, as previously described, changes in the vaginal flora due to oestrogen depletion may cause colonisation with Gram-negative bacilli which, in addition to causing local irritative symptoms, also act as uropathogens. These microbiological changes may be reversed with oestrogen replacement following the menopause, which offers a rationale for treatment and prophylaxis.

Oestrogens in the management of incontinence

Oestrogen preparations have been used for many years in the treatment of urinary incontinence[80,81] although their precise role remains controversial. Many of the studies performed have been uncontrolled observational series examining the use of a wide range of different preparations, dosages and routes of administration. The inconsistent use of progestogens to provide endometrial protection is a further confounding factor making interpretation of the results difficult.

In order to clarify the situation a meta-analysis from the Hormones and Urogenital Therapy (HUT) Committee has been reported.[82] Of 166 articles identified that were published in English between 1969 and 1992, only six were controlled trials and 17 were uncontrolled series. Meta-analysis found an overall significant effect of oestrogen therapy on subjective improvement in all women and for those with urodynamic stress incontinence alone. Subjective improvement rates with oestrogen therapy in randomised controlled trials ranged from 64% to 75% although placebo groups also reported an improvement of 10–56%. In uncontrolled series, subjective improvement rates were 8–89% with women with urodynamic stress incontinence showing improvement of 34–73%. However, in terms of objective fluid loss there was no significant effect. Maximum urethral closure pressure was found to increase significantly with oestrogen therapy although this outcome was influenced by a single study showing a large effect.[83]

A further meta-analysis performed in Italy has analysed the results of randomised controlled clinical trials on the efficacy of oestrogen treatment in postmenopausal women with urinary incontinence.[84] A search of the literature (1965–96) revealed 72 articles of which only four were considered to meet the meta-analysis criteria. There was a statistically significant difference in subjective outcome between oestrogen and placebo but no such difference in objective or urodynamic outcome. The authors conclude that this difference could be relevant although the studies may have lacked objective sensitivity to detect this.

The role of oestrogen replacement therapy in the prevention of ischaemic heart disease has been assessed in a four-year randomised trial, the Heart and Estrogen/progestin Replacement Study (HERS),[85] involving 2763 postmenopausal women younger than 80 years with intact uteri and ischaemic heart disease. In the study, 55% of women reported at least one episode of urinary incontinence each week, and were randomly assigned to oral conjugated oestrogen plus medroxyprogesterone acetate or placebo daily. Incontinence improved in 26% of women assigned to placebo compared with 21% receiving HRT, while 27% of the placebo group complained of worsening symptoms compared with 39% in the HRT group ($P = 0.001$). The incidence of incontinent episodes per week increased an average of 0.7 in the HRT group and decreased by 0.1 in the placebo group ($P < 0.001$). Overall, combined HRT was associated with worsening stress and urge urinary incontinence although there was no significant difference in daytime frequency, nocturia or number of urinary tract infections.

The effects of oral oestrogens and progestogens on the lower urinary tract were assessed in 32 female nursing home residents with an average age of 88 years in a study published in 2001.[86] The women were randomised to oral oestrogen and progestogen or placebo for six months. At follow-up there was no difference between severity of incontinence, prevalence of bacteriuria or the results of vaginal cultures, although there was an improvement in atrophic vaginitis in the placebo group.

Oestrogens in the management of stress incontinence

In addition to the studies included in the HUT meta-analysis, several authors have also investigated the role of oestrogen therapy in the management of urodynamic stress incontinence only. Oral oestrogens have been reported to increase the maximum urethral pressures and lead to symptomatic improvement in 65–70% of women,[49,87] although other work has not confirmed this.[88,89] Two placebo-controlled studies have examined the use of oral oestrogens in the treatment of urodynamic stress incontinence in postmenopausal women. Neither conjugated equine oestrogens and medroxyprogesterone,[90] nor unopposed oestradiol valerate[91] showed a significant difference in either subjective or objective outcomes. Furthermore, a review of eight controlled and 14 uncontrolled prospective trials concluded that oestrogen therapy was not an efficacious treatment for stress incontinence but may be useful for symptoms of urgency and frequency.[92]

A meta-analysis published in 2003 has helped to determine the role of oestrogen replacement in women with stress incontinence.[93] Of the papers reviewed, 14 were non-randomised studies, six were randomised trials (of which four were placebo-controlled) and two were meta-analyses. Interestingly, there was only a symptomatic or clinical improvement noted in the non-randomised studies while there was no such effect noted in the randomised trials. The authors conclude that currently the evidence would not support the use of oestrogen replacement alone in the management of stress incontinence.

From the available evidence, oestrogen does not appear to be an effective treatment for stress incontinence although it may have a synergistic role in combination therapy.

Two placebo-controlled studies have examined the use of oral and vaginal oestrogens with the α adrenergic agonist phenylpropanolamine used separately and in combination. Both studies found that combination therapy was superior to either drug given alone although, while there was subjective improvement in all groups,[94] there was only objective improvement in the combination therapy group.[95] This may offer an alternative conservative treatment for women who have mild urodynamic stress incontinence.

Oestrogens in the management of urge incontinence

Oestrogens have been used in the treatment of urinary urgency and urge incontinence for many years although there have been few controlled trials to confirm their efficacy. A double-blind placebo-controlled crossover study using oral oestriol in 34 postmenopausal women produced subjective improvement in eight women with mixed incontinence and in 12 women with urge incontinence.[96] However, a double-blind multicentre study of the use of oestriol (3 mg/day) in postmenopausal women complaining of urgency has failed to confirm these findings,[97] showing both subjective and objective improvement but not significantly better than placebo. Oestriol is a naturally occurring weak oestrogen that has little effect on the endometrium and does not prevent osteoporosis, although it has been used in the treatment of urogenital atrophy. Consequently, it is possible that the dosage or route of administration in this study was not appropriate for the treatment of urinary symptoms and higher systemic levels may be required.

Sustained-release 17β-oestradiol vaginal tablets (Vagifem, Novo Nordisk) have also been examined in postmenopausal women with urgency and urge incontinence or a urodynamic diagnosis of sensory urgency or detrusor overactivity. These vaginal tablets have been shown to be well absorbed from the vagina and to induce maturation of the vaginal epithelium within 14 days.[98] However, following a six-month course of treatment the only significant difference between active and placebo groups was an improvement in the symptom of urgency in those women with a urodynamic diagnosis of sensory urgency.[99] A further double-blind randomised placebo-controlled trial of 17β-oestradiol vaginal tablets has shown lower urinary tract symptoms of frequency, urgency, urge and stress incontinence to be significantly improved although there was no objective urodynamic assessment performed.[100] In both of these studies the subjective improvement in symptoms may simply represent local oestrogenic effects reversing urogenital atrophy rather than a direct effect on bladder function.

In order to try to clarify the role of oestrogen therapy in the management of women with urge incontinence, a meta-analysis of the use of oestrogen in women with symptoms of 'overactive bladder' was performed by the HUT Committee.[101] In a review of 10 randomised placebo-controlled trials, oestrogen was found to be superior to placebo when considering symptoms of urge incontinence, frequency and nocturia, although vaginal oestrogen administration was found to be superior for symptoms of urgency. In those taking oestrogens, there was also a significant increase in first sensation and bladder capacity as compared with placebo

Oestrogens in the management of recurrent urinary tract infection

Oestrogen therapy has been shown to increase vaginal pH and reverse the microbiological changes that occur in the vagina following the menopause.[102] Initial small uncontrolled studies using oral or vaginal oestrogens in the treatment of recurrent urinary tract infection appeared to give promising results,[103,104] which have unfortunately not been supported by larger randomised trials. Several studies have been performed examining the use of oral and vaginal oestrogens but these have had mixed results.

Kjaergaard and colleagues[105] compared vaginal oestriol tablets with placebo in 21 postmenopausal women over a five-month period and found no significant difference between the two groups. However, a subsequent randomised double-blind placebo-controlled study assessing the use of oestriol vaginal cream in 93 postmenopausal women during an eight-month period did reveal a significant effect.[106]

Kirkengen et al.[107] randomised 40 postmenopausal women to receive either placebo or oral oestriol and found that although both groups initially had a significantly decreased incidence of recurrent infections, after 12 weeks oestriol was shown to be significantly more effective. These findings, however, were not confirmed subsequently in a trial of 72 postmenopausal women with recurrent urinary tract infections randomised to oral oestriol or placebo. Following a six-month treatment period and a further six-month follow-up, oestriol was found to be no more effective than placebo.[108]

A randomised open parallel-group study assessing the use of an oestradiol-releasing silicone vaginal ring (Estring, Pharmacia and Upjohn, Sweden) in postmenopausal women with recurrent infections showed that the cumulative likelihood of remaining infection-free was 45% in the active group and 20% in the placebo group.[109] Estring was also shown to decrease the number of recurrences per year and to prolong the interval between infection episodes.

Oestrogens in the management of urogenital atrophy

Symptoms of urogenital atrophy do not occur until the levels of endogenous oestrogen are lower than those required to promote endometrial proliferation.[65] It is thus possible to use a low dosage of oestrogen replacement therapy in order to alleviate urogenital symptoms while avoiding the risk of endometrial proliferation and removing the necessity of providing endometrial protection with progestogens.[110] The daily dose of oestradiol used in systemic oestrogen replacement is usually 25–100 μg although studies investigating the use of oestrogens in the management of urogenital symptoms have shown that 8–10 μg of vaginal oestradiol is effective.[111] Thus only 10–30% of the dose used to treat vasomotor symptoms may be effective in the management of urogenital symptoms. Since 10–25% of women receiving systemic HRT still experience the symptoms of urogenital atrophy,[112] low-dose local preparations may have an additional beneficial effect.

In a review by the HUT Committee of oestrogen therapy in the management of urogenital atrophy, ten randomised trials and 54 uncontrolled series were examined from 1969 to 1995 assessing 24 different treatment regimens.[113] Meta-analysis of ten placebo-controlled trials confirmed the significant effect of oestrogens in the management of urogenital atrophy.

The route of administration was assessed and oral, vaginal and parenteral (transcutaneous patches and subcutaneous implants) routes were compared. Overall the vaginal route of administration was found to correlate with better symptom relief and greater improvement in cytological findings.

With regard to the type of oestrogen preparation, oestradiol was found to be most effective in reducing symptoms, although conjugated oestrogens produced the most cytological change and the greatest increase in serum levels of oestradiol and oestrone.

Finally, the effect of different dosages was examined. Low-dose vaginal oestradiol was found to be the most efficacious according to symptom relief although oral oestriol was also effective. Oral oestriol had no effect on the serum levels of oestradiol or oestrone while vaginal oestriol had minimal effect. Vaginal oestradiol was found to have a small effect on serum oestrogen although not as great as systemic preparations. In conclusion, it would appear that oestrogen is efficacious in the treatment of urogenital atrophy and low-dose vaginal preparations are as effective as systemic therapy.

The use of a continuous low-dose oestradiol-releasing silicone vaginal ring (Estring) releasing oestradiol 5–10 µg/24 hours has been investigated in postmenopausal women with symptomatic urogenital atrophy.[109] There was a significant effect on symptoms of vaginal dryness, pruritus vulvae, dyspareunia and urinary urgency with improvement being reported in over 90% of women in an uncontrolled study. The patient acceptability was high and while the maturation of vaginal epithelium was significantly improved there was no effect on endometrial proliferation.

These findings were supported by a one-year multicentre study of Estring in postmenopausal women with urogenital atrophy which found subjective and objective improvement in 90% of the women up to one year. However there was a 20% withdrawal rate, with 7% of women reporting vaginal irritation, 2% having vaginal ulceration, and 3% complaining of vaginal bleeding, although there were no cases of endometrial proliferation.[114]

Long-term safety has been confirmed by a ten-year review of the use of the oestradiol ring delivery system, which has found its safety, efficacy and acceptability to be comparable to other forms of vaginal administration.[115] A comparative study of safety and efficacy of Estring with conjugated equine oestrogen vaginal cream in 194 postmenopausal women complaining of urogenital atrophy found no significant difference in vaginal dryness, dyspareunia and resolution of atrophic signs between the two treatment groups. Furthermore, there was a similar improvement in the vaginal mucosal maturation index and a reduction in pH in both groups, with the vaginal ring being found to be preferable to the cream.[116]

Selective oestrogen receptor modulators (SERMS)

A recent development in hormonal therapy has been the development of selective oestrogen receptor modulators (SERMs). These drugs have oestrogen-like actions in maintaining bone density and in lowering serum cholesterol but have anti-oestrogenic effects on the breast[117] and do not cause endometrial stimulation.[118] In theory, partial oestrogen antagonists may lead to a downregulation of oestrogen receptors in the urogenital tract and consequently cause an increase in lower urinary tract symptoms and symptomatic urogenital atrophy. Early work would suggest that some SERMs in development (levormeloxifene and idoxifene) may increase the risk of urogenital prolapse,[119] although there were some methodological problems noted in the studies concerned. However, in an analysis of three randomised double-blind placebo-controlled trials investigating raloxifene in 6926 postmenopausal women, there appeared to be a protective effect, with fewer treated women having surgery for urogenital prolapse: 1.5% versus 0.75% ($P < 0.005$).[120] The long-term effects of SERMs on the urogenital tract remain to be determined and there is little data regarding effects on urinary incontinence and urogenital atrophy.

Conclusions

Oestrogens are known to have an important physiological effect on the female lower genital tract throughout adult life, leading to symptomatic, histological and functional changes. Urogenital atrophy is the manifestation of oestrogen withdrawal following the menopause. The use of oestrogen replacement therapy has been examined in the management of lower urinary tract symptoms as well as in the treatment of urogenital atrophy, although only recently has it been subjected to randomised placebo-controlled trials and meta-analysis.

Oestrogen therapy alone has been shown to have little effect in the management of urodynamic stress incontinence but when used in combination with an α-adrenergic agonist may lead to an improvement in urinary leakage. When considering the irritative symptoms of urinary urgency, frequency and urge incontinence, oestrogen therapy may be of benefit but this may simply represent reversal of urogenital atrophy rather than a direct effect on the lower urinary tract. The role of oestrogen replacement therapy in the management of women with recurrent lower urinary tract infection remains to be determined although there is now some evidence that vaginal administration may be efficacious. Finally, low-dose vaginal oestrogens have been shown to be have a role in the treatment of urogenital atrophy in postmenopausal women and would appear to be as effective as systemic preparations.

References

1.   Iosif CS. Effects of protracted administration of oestriol on the lower genitourinary tract in postmenopausal women. *Acta Obstet Gynecol Scand* 1992;251:115–20.
2.   Cardozo LD. Role of oestrogens in the treatment of female urinary incontinence. *J Am Geriatr Soc* 1990;38:326–8.
3.   Iosif S, Batra S, Ek A, Astedt B. Estrogen receptors in the human female lower uninary tract. *Am J Obstet Gynecol* 1981;141:817–20.
4.   Batra SC, Fossil CS. Female urethra, a target for oestrogen action. *J Urol* 1983;129:418–20.
5.   Batra SC, Iosif LS. Progesterone receptors in the female urinary tract. *J Urol* 1987;138:130–4.
6.   Iosif C, Bekassy Z. Prevalence of genitourinary symptoms in the late menopause. *Acta Obstet Gynecol Scand* 1984;63:257–60.
7.   US National Institutes of Health. Population Figures. US Treasury Department/NIH; 1991.
8.   World Health Organization. *Research on the menopause in the 1990's. Report of a WHO Scientific Group*. WHO Technical Report Series 866. Geneva: World Health Organization; 1994.
9.   Hill K. The demography of the menopause. *Maturitas* 1996;23:113–27.
10.   Barlow DH, Samsioe G, van Geelen JM. A study of European womens' experience of the problems of urogenital ageing and its management. *Maturitas* 1997;27:239–47.
11.   Greendale GA, Judd JL. The menopause: health implications and clinical management. *J Am Geriatr Soc* 1993;41:426–36.
12.   Samsioe G, Jansson I, Mellstrom D, Svanborg A. Occurrence, nature and treatment of urinary incontinence in a 70-year-old female population. *Maturitas* 1985;7:335–42.
13.   Van Geelen JM, Van de Weijer PH, Arnolds HT. Urogenital symptoms and resulting discomfort in non-institutionalised Dutch women aged 50–75 years. *Int Urogynecol J Pelvic Floor Dysfunct* 2000;11:9–14.
14.   Versi E, Harvey MA, Cardozo L, Brincat M, Studd JW. Urogenital prolapse and atrophy at menopause: a prevalence study. *Int Urogynecol J Pelvic Floor Dysfunct* 2001;12:107–10.
15.   Davila GW, Karapanagiotou I, Woodhouse S, Singh A, Huber K, Zimberg S, *et al*. Are women with urogenital atrophy symptomatic? *Obstet Gynecol* 2001;97 (4 Suppl 1):S48.
16.   Diokno AC, Brook BM, Brown MB. Prevalence of urinary incontinence and other urological symptoms in the non-institutionalised elderly. *J Urol* 1986;136:1022.
17.   Yarnell J, Voyle G, Richards C, Stephenson T. The prevalence and severity of urinary incontinence in women. *J Epidemiol Community Health* 1981;35:71–4.
18.   Ouslander JG. Urinary incontinence in nursing homes. *J Am Geriatr Soc* 1990;38:289–91.
19.   MacLennan AH, Taylor AW, Wilson AW, Wilson D. The prevalence of pelvic floor disorders and

their relationship to gender, age, parity, and mode of delivery. *BJOG* 2000;107:1460–70.

20. Kok AL, Voorhorst FJ, Burger CW, Van Houten P, Kenemans P, Jannsens J. Urinary and faecal incontinence in community residing elderly women. *Age Ageing* 1992;21:211.

21. Department of Health; 2001.

22. Green S, Walter P, Kumar V, Krust A, Bornert JM, Argos P, *et al.* Human oestrogen receptor cDNA: sequence, expression and homology to v-erbA. *Nature* 1986;320:134–9.

23. Kuiper G, Enmark E, Pelto-Huikko M, Nilsson S, Gustafsson J-A. Cloning of a novel oestrogen receptor expressed in rat prostate and ovary. *Proc Natl Acad Sci U S A* 1996;93:5925–30.

24. Blakeman PJ, Hilton P, Bulmer JN. Mapping oestrogen and progesterone receptors throughout the female lower urinary tract. *Neurourol Urodyn* 1996;15:324–5.

25. Ingelman-Sundberg A, Rosen J, Gustafsson SA. Cytosol oestrogen receptors in urogenital tissues in stress incontinent women, *Acta Obstet Gynecol Scand* 1981;60:585–6.

26. Smith P. Oestrogens and the urogenital tract. *Acta Obstet Gynecol Scand* 1993;72:1–26.

27. Bernstein IT. The pelvic floor muscles: muscle thickness in healthy and urinary-incontinent women measured by perineal ultasonography with reference to the effect of pelvic floor training. Oestrogen receptor studies. *Neurourol Urodyn* 1997;16:237–75.

28. Chen GD, Oliver RH, Leung BS, Lin LY, Yeh J. Estrogen receptor alpha and beta expression in the vaginal walls and uterosacral ligaments of premenopausal and postmenopausal women. *Fertil Steril* 1999;71:1099–102.

29. Schreiter F, Fuchs P, Stockamp K. Estrogenic sensitivity of alpha-receptors in the urethra musculature. *Urol Int* 1976;31:13–19.

30. Pang X, Cotreau-Bibbo MM, Sant GR, Theoharides TC. Bladder mast cell expression of high affinity oestrogen receptors in patients with interstitial cystitis. *Br J Urol* 1995;75:154–61.

31. Blakeman PJ, Hilton P, Bulmer JN. Androgen receptors in the female lower urinary tract. *Int Urogynecol J Pelvic Floor Dysfunct* 1997;8:S54.

32. Blakeman PJ, Hilton P, Bulmer JN. Oestrogen and progesterone receptor expression in the female lower urinary tract, with reference to oestrogen status. *BJU Int* 2000;86:32–8.

33. Abrams P, Cardozo L, Fall M, Griffiths D, Rosier P, Ulmsten U, *et al*; Standardisation Sub-committee of the International Continence Society. The standardisation of terminology of lower urinary tract function: report from the Standardisation Sub-committee of the International Continence Society. *Neurourol Urodyn.* 2002;21:167–8.

34. Rud T, Andersson KE, Asmussen M, Hunting A, Ulmsten U. Factors maintaining the intraurethral pressure in women. *Invest Urol* 1980;17:343–7.

35. Malone-Lee J. Urodynamic measurement and urinary incontinence in the elderly. In:Brocklehurst JC, editor. *Managing and Measuring Incontinence*. Proceedings of the Geriatric Workshop on Incontinence, July 1988.

36. Versi E, Cardozo LD. Oestrogens and lower urinary tract function. In: Studd JWW, Whitehead MI, editors. *The Menopause*. Oxford: Blackwell Scientific Publications; 1988. p. 76–84.

37. Kinn AC, Lindskog M. Oestrogens and phenylpropanolamine in combination for stress incontinence. *Urology* 1988;32:273–80.

38. Smith PJB. The effect of oestrogens on bladder function in the female. In: Campbell S, editor. *The Management of the Menopause and Postmenopausal Years*. Carnforth: MTP; 1976. p. 291–8.

39. Blakeman PJ, Hilton P, Bulmer JN. Cellular proliferation in the female lower urinary tract with reference to oestrogen status. *BJOG* 2001;8:813–6.

40. Shapiro E. Effect of estrogens on the weight and muscarinic receptor density of the rabbit bladder and urethra. *J Urol* 1986;135:1084–7.

41. Batra S, Anderson KE. Oestrogen induced changes in muscarinic receptor density and contractile responses in the female rat urinary bladder. *Acta Physiol Scand* 1989;137:135–41.

42. Elliott RA, Castleden CM, Miodrag A, Kirwan P. The direct effects of diethylstilboestrol and nifedipine on the contractile responses of isolated human and rat detrusor muscles. *Eur J Clin Pharmacol* 1992;43:149–55.

43. Shenfield OZ, Blackmore PF, Morgan CW, Schlossberg SM, Jordan GH, Ratz PH. Rapid effects of oestriol and progesterone on tone and spontaneous rhythmic contractions of the rabbit bladder. *Neurourol Urodyn* 1998;17:408–9.

44. Fantl JA, Wyman JF, Anderson RL, Matt DW, Bump RC. Postmenopausal urinary incontinence: comparison between non-estrogen-supplemented and estrogen-supplemented women. *Obstet Gynecol* 1988;71 (6 Pt 1):823–8.

45. Maggi A, Perez J. Role of female gonadal hormones in the CNS. *Life Sci* 1985;37:893–906.

46. Smith SS, Berg G, Hammar M, editors. *The Modern Management of the Menopause. Hormones, Mood and Neurobiology – a Summary*. Carnforth: Parthenon Publishing; 1993. p. 204.

47. Blok EFM, Holstege G. Androgen receptor immunoreactive neurones in the hypothalamic preoptic area project to the pontine micturition centre in the male cat. *Neurourol Urodyn* 1998;17:404–5.

48.   Bergman A, Karram MM, Bhatia NN. Changes in urethral cytology following estrogen administration. *Gynecol Obstet Invest* 1990;29:211–13.

49.   Rud T. The effects of estrogens and gestagens on the urethral pressure profile in urinary continent and stress incontinent women. *Acta Obstet Gynecol Scand* 1980;59:265–70.

50.   Hilton P, Stanton SL. The use of intravaginal oestrogen cream in genuine stress incontinence. *Br J Obstet Gynaecol* 1983;90:940–4.

51.   Bhatia NN, Bergman A, Karram MM. Effects of estrogen on urethral function in women with urinary incontinence. *Am J Obstet Gynecol* 1989;160:176–81.

52.   Karram MM, Yeko TR, Sauer MV, Bhatia NN. Urodynamic changes following hormonal replacement therapy in women with premature ovarian failure. *Obstet Gynecol* 1989;74:208–11.

53   Gangar KF, Vyas S, Whitehead M, Crook D, Meire H, Campbell S. Pulsatility index in internal carotid artery in relation to transdermal oestradiol and time since menopause. *Lancet* 1991;338:839–42.

54   Jackson S, Vyas S. A double blind, placebo controlled study of postmenopausal oestrogen replacement therapy and carotid artery pulsatility index. *Br J Obstet Gynaecol* 1998;105:408–12.

55   Penotti M, Farina M, Sironi L, *et al.* Long term effects of postmenopausal hormone replacement therapy on pulsatility index of the internal carotid and middle cerebral arteries. *Menopause, The journal of the North American Menopause Society* 1997;4:101–4.

56   Versi E, Cardozo LD. Urethral instability: diagnosis based on variations in the maximum urethral pressure in normal climacteric women. *Neurourol Urodyn* 1986;5:535–41.

57   Falconer C, Ekman-Ordeberg G, Ulmsten U, Westergren-Thorsson G, Barchan K, Malmstrom A. Changes in paraurethral connective tissue at menopause are counteracted by estrogen. *Maturitas* 1996;24:197–204.

58   Kushner L, Chen Y, Desautel M, Moak S, Greenwald R, Badlani G. Collagenase activity is elevated in conditioned media from fibroblasts of women with pelvic floor weakening. *Int Urogynecol J Pelvic Floor Dysfunct* 1999;10:34(S1).

59.   Jackson S, Avery N, Shepherd A, Abrams P, Bailey A, *et al.* The effect of oestradiol on vaginal collagen in postmenopausal women with stress urinary incontinence. *Neurourol Urodyn* 1996;15:327–8.

60.   James M, Avery N, Jackson S, Bailey A, Abrams P. The pathophysiological changes of vaginal skin tissue in women with stress urinary incontinence: a controlled trial. *Int Urogynecol J Pelvic Floor Dysfunct* 1999;10:35(S1).

61.   James M, Avery N, Jackson S, Bailey A, Abrams P. The biochemical profile of vaginal tissue in women with genitourinary prolapse: a controlled trial. *Neurourol Urodyn* 1999;18:284–5.

62.   Brincat M, Moniz CF, Studd JWW. Long term effects of the menopause and sex hormones on skin thickness. *Br J Obstet* Gynaecol 1985;92:256–9.

63.   Landon CR, Smith ARB, Crofts CE, Trowbridge EA. Biochemical properties of connective tissue in women with stress incontinence of urine. *Neurourol Urodyn* 1989;8:369–70.

64.   Ulmsten U, Ekman G, Giertz G, Malmstrom A. Different biochemical composition of connective tissue in continent and stress incontinent women. *Acta Obstet Gynecol Scand* 1987;66:455.

65.   Samsioe G. Urogenital ageing – a hidden problem. *Am J Obstet Gynecol* 1998;178:S245–9.

66.   Cardozo L. The lower urinary tract in peri- and postmenopausal women. In: Cardozo LD, Tapp A, Versi E, Samsioe G, Bonne Erickson P, editors. *The Urogenital Deficiency Syndrome.* Bagsverd, Denmark: Novo Industri AS; 1987. p. 10–17.

67.   Kondo A, Kato K, Saito M, *et al.* Prevalence of hand washing incontinence in females in comparison with stress and urge incontinence. *Neurourol Urodyn* 1990;9:330–1.

68.   Thomas TM, Plymat KR, Blannin J, Meade TW. Prevalence of urinary incontinence. *BMJ* 1980;281:1243–5.

69.   Jolleys JV. Reported prevalence of urinary incontinence in a general practice. *BMJ* 1988;296:1300–2.

70.   Burgio KL, Matthews KA, Engel B. Prevalence, incidence and correlates of urinary incontinence in healthy, middle aged women. *J Urol* 1991;146:1255–9.

71.   Hextall A, Bidmead J, Cardozo L, Hooper R. Hormonal influences on the human female lower urinary tract: a prospective evaluation of the effects of the menstrual cycle on symptomatology and the results of urodynamic investigation. *Neurourol Urodyn* 1999;18:282–3.

72.   Van Geelen JM, Doesburg WH, Thomas CMG. Urodynamic studies in the normal menstrual cycle: the relationship between hormonal changes during the menstrual cycle and the urethral pressure profile. *Am J Obstet Gynecol* 1981;141:384–92.

73.   Burton G, Cardozo LD, Abdalla H, Kirkland A, Studd JWW. The hormonal effects on the lower urinary tract in 282 women with premature ovarian failure. *Neurourol Urodyn* 1992;10:318–19.

74.   Cutner A, Burton G, Cardozo LD, Wise BG, Abbot D, Studd JWW. Does progesterone cause an irritable bladder? *Int Urogynecol J Pelvic Floor Dysfunct* 1993;4:259–61.

75.   Benness C, Gangar K, Cardozo LD, Cutner A. Do progestogens exacerbate urinary incontinence

in women on HRT? *Neurourol Urodyn* 1991;10:316–18.

76.   Elliot RA, Castleden CM. Effect of progestagens and oestrogens on the contractile response of rat detrusor muscle to electrical field stimulation. *Clin Sci* 1994;87:342.

77.   Cutner A. *The Urinary Tract in Pregnancy*. MD Thesis. London: University of London; 1993.

78.   Sandford JP. Urinary tract symptoms and infection. *Ann Rev Med* 1975;26:485–505.

79.   Boscia JA, Kaye D. Asymptomatic bacteria in the elderly. *Infect Dis Clin North Am* 1987;1:893–903.

80.   Salmon UL, Walter RI, Gast SH. The use of oestrogen in the treatment of dysuria and incontinence in postmenopausal women. *Am J Obstet Gynecol* 1941;14:23–31.

81.   Youngblood VH, Tomlin EM, Davis JB. Senile urethritis in women. *J Urol* 1957;78:150–2.

82.   Fantl JA, Cardozo LD, McClish DK; the Hormones and Urogenital Therapy Committee. Estrogen therapy in the management of incontinence in postmenopausal women: a meta-analysis. First report of the Hormones and Urogenital Therapy Committee. *Obstet Gynecol* 1994;83:12–18.

83.   Henalla SM, Hutchins CJ, Robinson P, Macivar J. Non-operative methods in the treatment of female genuine stress incontinence of urine. *Br J Obstet Gynaecol* 1989;9:222–5.

84.   Zullo MA, Oliva C, Falconi G, Paparella P, Mancuso S. [Efficacy of oestrogen therapy in urinary incontinence. A meta-analytic study]. [Italian] *Minerva Ginecol* 1998;50:199–205.

85.   Grady D, Brown JS, Vittinghoff E, Applegate W, Varner E, Synder T. Postmenopausal hormones and incontinence: the Heart and Estrogen/progestin Replacement Study. *Obstet Gynecol* 2001;97:116–20.

86.   Ouslander JG, Greendale GA, Uman G, Lee C, Paul W, Schnelle J. Effects of oral estrogen and progestin on the lower urinary tract among female nursing home residents. *J Am Geriatr Soc* 2001;49:803–7.

87.   Caine M, Raz S. The role of female hormones in stress incontinence. In: Proceedings of the 16th Congress of the International Society of Urology, Amsterdam, The Netherlands.

88.   Wilson PD, Faragher B, Butler B, Bullock D, Robinson EL, Brown ADG. Treatment with oral piperazine oestrone sulphate for genuine stress incontinence in postmenopausal women. *Br J Obstet Gynaecol* 1987;94:568–74.

89.   Walter S, Wolf H, Barlebo H, Jansen H. Urinary incontinence in postmenopausal women treated with oestrogens: a double-blind clinical trial. *Urol Int* 1978;33:135–43.

90.   Fantl JA, Bump RC, Robinson D, McClish DK, Wyman JF. Efficacy of estrogen supplementation in the treatment of urinary incontinence. The Continence Program for Women Research Group. *Obstet Gynecol* 1996;88:745–9.

91.   Jackson S, Shepherd A, Brookes S, Abrams P. The effect of oestrogen supplementation on post-menopausal urinary stress incontinence: a double-blind, placebo controlled trial. *Br J Obstet Gynaecol* 1999;106:711–18.

92.   Sultana CJ, Walters MD. Estrogen and urinary incontinence in women. *Maturitas* 1994;20:129–38

93.   Al-Badr A, Ross S, Soroka D, Drutz HP. What is the available evidence for hormone replacement therapy in women with stress urinary incontinence? *J Obstet Gynaecol Can* 2003;25:567–74.

94.   Beisland HO, Fossberg E, Moer A, Sander S. Urethral sphincteric insufficiency in postmenopausal females: treatment with phenylpropanolamine and estriol separately and in combination. A urodynamic and clinical evaluation. *Urol Int* 1984;39:211–16.

95.   Hilton P, Tweddel AL, Mayne C. Oral and intravaginal oestrogens alone and in combination with alpha adrenergic stimulation in genuine stress incontinence. *Int Urogynecol J Pelvic Floor Dysfunct* 1990;12:80–6.

96.   Samsioe G, Jansson I, Mellstrom D, Svanberg A. Urinary incontinence in 75 year old women. Effects of oestriol. *Acta Obstet Gynecol Scand* 1985;93:57.

97.   Cardozo L, Rekers H, Tapp A, Barnick C, Shepherd A, Schussler B, *et al.* Oestriol in the treatment of postmenopausal urgency: a multicentre study. *Maturitas* 1993;18:47–53.

98.   Nilsson K, Heimer G. Low-dose oestradiol in the treatment of urogenital oestrogen deficiency – a pharmacokinetic and pharmacodynamic study. *Maturitas* 1992;15:121–7.

99.   Benness C, Wise BG, Cutner A, Cardozo LD. Does low dose vaginal oestradiol improve frequency and urgency in postmenopausal women *Int Urogynecol J Pelvic Floor Dysfunct* 1992;3:281.

100.   Eriksen PS, Rasmussen H. Low-dose 17 beta-estradiol vaginal tablets in the treatment of atrophic vaginitis: a double-blind placebo controlled study. *Eur J Obstet Gynecol Reprod Biol* 1992;44:137–44.

101.   Cardozo L, Versi E, McClish D, Lose G; Hormones and Urogenital Therapy Committee. 4th Report of the Hut Committee. *Acta Obstet Gynecol Scand* (in press).

102.   Brandberg A, Mellstrom D, Samsioe G. Low dose oral estriol treatment in elderly women with urogenital infections. *Acta Obstet Gynecol Scand Suppl* 1987;140:33–8.

103.   Parsons CL, Schmidt JD. Control of recurrent urinary tract infections in postmenopausal women. *J Urol* 1982;128:1224–6.

104.   Privette M, Cade R, Peterson J, Mars D. Prevention of recurrent urinary tract infections in postmenopausal women. *Nephron* 1988;50:24–7.
105.   Kjaergaard B, Walter S, Knudsen A, Johansen B, Barlebo H. [Treatment with low-dose vaginal estradiol in post-menopausal women. A double-blind controlled trial]. [Danish]. *Ugeskr Laeger* 1990;152:658–9.
106.   Raz R, Stamm WE. A controlled trial of intravaginal estriol in postmenopausal women with recurrent urinary tract infections. *N Engl J Med* 1993;329:753–6.
107.   Kirkengen AL, Anderson P, Gjersoe E, *et al.* Oestriol in the prophylactic treatment of recurrent urinary tract infections in postmenopausal women. *Scand J Prim Health Care* 1992;10:142.
108.   Cardozo LD, Benness C, Abbott D. Low dose oestrogen prophylaxis for recurrent urinary tract infections in elderly women. *Br J Obstet Gynaecol* 1998;105:403–7.
109.   Eriksen B. A randomized, open, parallel-group study on the preventive effect of an estradiol-releasing vaginal ring (Estring) on recurrent urinary tract infections in postmenopausal women. *Am J Obstet Gynecol* 1999;180:1072–9.
110.   Mettler L, Olsen PG. Long term treatment of atrophic vaginitis with low dose oestradiol vaginal tablets. *Maturitas* 1991;14:23–31.
111.   Smith P, Heimer G, Lindskog, Ulmsten U. Oestradiol releasing vaginal ring for treatment of postmenopausal urogenital atrophy. *Maturitas* 1993;16:145–54.
112.   Smith RJN, Studd JWW. Recent advances in hormone replacement therapy. *Br J Hosp Med* 1993;49:799–809.
113.   Cardozo L, Bachmann G, McClish D, Fonda D, Birgerson L. Meta-analysis of estrogen therapy in the management of urogenital atrophy in postmenopausal women: second report of the Hormones and Urogenital Therapy Committee. *Obstet Gynecol* 1998;92:722–7.
114.   Henriksson L, Stjernquist M, Boquist L, Cedergren I, Selinus I. A one-year multicenter study of efficacy and safety of a continuous, low-dose, estradiol-releasing vaginal ring (Estring) in postmenopausal women with symptoms and signs of urogenital aging. *Am J Obstet Gynecol* 1996;174:85–92.
115.   Bachmann G. Estradiol-releasing vaginal ring delivery system for urogenital atrophy. Experience over the past decade. *J Reprod Med* 1998;43:991–8.
116.   Ayton RA, Darling GM, Murkies AL, Farrell EA, Weisberg E, Selinus I, *et al.* A comparative study of safety and efficacy of continuous low dose oestradiol released from a vaginal ring compared with conjugated equine oestrogen vaginal cream in the treatment of postmenopausal urogenital atrophy. *Br J Obstet Gynaecol* 1996;103:351–8.
117.   Park WC, Jordan VC. Selective estrogen receptor modulators (SERMS) and their roles in cancer prevention. *Trends Mol Med* 2002;8:82–8.
118.   Silfen SL, Ciaccia AV, Bryant HU. Selective estrogen receptor modulators: tissue selectivity and differential uterine effects. *Climacteric* 1999;2:268–83.
119.   Hendrix SL, McNeeley SG. Effect of selective estrogen receptor modulators on reproductive tissues other than endometrium. *Ann N Y Acad Sci* 2001;949:243–50.
120.   Goldstein SR, Neven P, Zhou L, Taylor YL, Ciacca AV, Plouffe L. Raloxifene effect on frequency of surgery for pelvic floor relaxation. *Obstet Gynecol* 2001;98:91–6.

Chapter 18

Hormone replacement and who needs it

Discussion

Discussion following Dr Lumsden's paper and Professor Cardozo's paper

Pitkin: I think none of us will treat urodynamically proven stress incontinence with oestrogens but, bearing in mind Mark Brincat's[1-3] work on connective tissue collagen elasticity which we have not mentioned yet, are you aware of any evidence to show that oestrogens in conjunction with pelvic floor exercises have a synergistic effect on improving urodynamically proven stress incontinence? I think there were a couple of papers showing that bladder neck surgery with preoperative oestrogen might be better than bladder neck surgery on atrophic tissue.

Cardozo: To answer the second question first – there is a study that looked at colposuspension and the variables of women entering that trial showed that there was a higher cure rate with colposuspension in women who had been oestrogenised compared with women who had not, which was very interesting because there was no association with age, obesity and various other factors. So that was one study, but of course that was not a primary endpoint of the study. There have been no large studies which have looked at pelvic floor exercises with and without oestrogens in postmenopausal women, which is very unfortunate because I am absolutely certain that in women with urodynamic stress incontinence oestrogens as an adjunct are effective but it is very difficult to prove and to undertake large controlled studies. With regard to Mark Brincat's work, I do not think anyone has really looked at that. I have not seen any further literature on it.

Beral: Can I just ask a point of fact – you said you did not want to discuss the Cochrane reviews, but I think they are quite important. So if you could just explain to us why your review came to different conclusions than the Cochrane review.

Cardozo: The Cochrane review is based on the literature that is available and one of the early trials that looked at the effect of oestriol showed a very low P value for oestriol being more effective than placebo in women with incontinence, unclassified incontinence, because it was before the time of urodynamic studies. All women with incontinence were treated either with placebo or with oral oestriol. When you actually analysed the data, there were only 12 subjects in the study in the oestrogen arm. So the fact that it was significant on the 0.5 P value really did not mean that it was clinically significant or clinically relevant. It was included as one of the studies in that particular

Cochrane database, which skews the data quite considerably. The conclusions which the Cochrane authors drew were that there was possibly an effect of systemic oestrogen on incontinence. But if you divide down incontinence into stress incontinence and incontinence associated with irritative symptoms, then the effect is lost.

Beral: So how does your conclusion differ from the Cochrane one?

Cardozo: In that if you separate stress incontinence from all types of incontinence, there is no effect of oestrogens on stress incontinence. Whereas the Cochrane collaboration looked at all types of incontinence, because they could not subdivide it into stress incontinence and urge incontinence. So what I was trying to draw your attention to was the fact that you cannot treat incontinence as one disorder.

Beral: For the other outcomes, was the Cochrane review conclusion the same?

Cardozo: It was the same.

Beral: So the difference was only for incontinence by separating out stress, thank you very much.

Prentice: Professor Cardozo, a point of information: there is a completed paper from the combined hormone trial in the Women's Health Initiative on urinary incontinence, which makes the separation between stress and urge. It was completed about three months ago but I am not exactly sure where it is in the publication queue.

Cardozo: So it is not published yet? I am not aware of those data and I thought I trawled fairly carefully.

Prentice: This is just for the group's interest.

Cardozo: And what did it show?

Prentice: I cannot tell you – but Susan Hendrix is the lead author and gynaecologist, if you wish to contact her.

Critchley: I was interested in the comments you made about selective oestrogen receptor modulators (SERMs) and the relationship to urogenital prolapse. Could you say a little bit more about that? And was it all SERMs or a particular one?

Cardozo: No, it was not all SERMs. It was a Novo Nordisk one and there is a Pfizer one: there are two.

Chwalisz: There were, in fact, two: levormeloxifene and idoxifene. Both of them were more oestrogenic than raloxifene but it still induced this adverse event, which in fact was noted during phase III trials. In addition, there were some sub-endometrial changes in the form of cysts observed in the studies. I do not know which was the most important effect to make the company terminate the studies – the prolapse or the endometrial stimulation.

Gebbie: Just to clarify then – what effect does raloxifene have on urogenital atrophy and prolapse?

Cardozo: There is no evidence that raloxifene increases urogenital prolapse and there are no data on raloxifene in relation to urogenital symptoms.

Gebbie: So we do not know if raloxifene helps atrophic vaginitis or not then.

Burger: Are we aware of any difference between various progestogens in terms of their irritative or counterbalancing effect?

Cardozo: Unfortunately, there have not been any specific studies targeted at progestogens because the perceived wisdom is that progestogens make urinary and lower genital symptoms worse and therefore there has been no indication to study them and the only way they have been studied is a by-product of combined HRT.

Gray: Has there been any guidance for the long-term use of topical oestrogens in much older women?

Cardozo: The only guidance that there has been is that if you are giving only oestriol not more than three times a week or oestradiol (Vagifem®) not more than twice a week, surveillance is not needed unless there is symptomatic evidence of bleeding or some other change and that a progestogen is not needed in the studies that have been carried out to date. But I do not know of any very long-term data, apart from ten years in the Scandinavian series. There have been up to ten-year data reported.

Glasier: In the interests of time, the questions have started to stray from questions of fact to a general discussion, so I think it would be sensible to finish the discussion about urogenital problems and then go back to Dr Lumsden. So is there anything else anyone wants to raise in relation to Professor Cardozo's talk?

Purdie: Just a small point, speaking as an editor of a Cochrane group – I think it would be really important, if you have not already done so, since all these reviews are updated or they go off the web eventually, that you feed your concerns to them about that review, so that when they then redo it they really keep a focus on that aspect.

Cardozo: It has been done. But also, this year there is going to be a World Health Organization international consultation on incontinence, which is the third review of its type. That will be the first review since the Cochrane review on oestrogens for incontinence was reported, which means that that body, which is quite substantial, will feed back to the Cochrane database. I think that is quite important. It is not that they have done anything wrong with the data, it is just the conclusions they have drawn do not make a distinction, which is unfortunate.

Beral: Can I just check? At lunchtime when we left off the discussion, we were discussing oral oestriol. Although I know you are talking about topical therapy now, Scandinavia seems to be leading in this field. I wonder if we could ask Dr Magnusson to talk about the work that she has been involved in in looking at endometrial cancer risk because there is an increased risk of endometrial cancer associated with oestriol.

Magnusson: With oral oestriol, I think I told you, there is about a two-fold increase in endometrial cancer risk after long time.

Beral: How long?

Magnusson: I should get the data before I answer that, but we could not see anything with topical therapy. However, our results were criticised because we did not have the power to really tease out the effect of oestriol so people were still suspecting that there could be something with the topical group as well.

Beral: But can I ask – that was oestriol on its own? Because many of the Scandinavian preparations combine oestradiol and oestriol together in their oral preparations and I have not seen any increase in endometrial cancer with the vaginal oestriol preparation.

Magnusson: The oral preparations contained oestriol only.

Beral: And at a dose of?

Magnusson: 1 or 2 mg.

Whitehead: Can I make a comment about oestriol? Oestriol is not a weak oestrogen – it is called a weak oestrogen but once oestriol binds to the receptor it initiates exactly the same cellular response as does oestradiol or oestrone. Oestriol was believed to interfere with oestradiol stimulation of responsive cells and that is why oestriol was added to oestradiol, the aim being to try to damp down oestradiol stimulation. I think it is important to remember that oestriol is the only oestrogen with which we come into contact, which is water-based – it is water-soluble. Most of it is excreted within minutes of absorption through the kidney, it is not protein-bound to any great extent. If you go back to the late 1970s work from Uppsala in Sweden, it was shown very nicely that if you give oestriol three times a day orally, you can get exactly the same endometrial proliferation that you can with oestradiol once a day. It is all down to dose and frequency of administration, but do not think oestriol is a weak oestrogen – if you give 1 mg/day orally, it may be weak. But if you give enough, you will get normal endometrial response.

Cardozo: You do not get the same endometrial response when it is given topically though. It has been measured over many years in Scandinavian countries. they have led on using topical oestrogens and in all of their reported studies of vaginal oestriol and low-dose vaginal oestradiol, there has not been endometrial stimulation.

Chwalisz: There are studies with oestriol esters, it is a form of depot formulation of oestriols and it maintains relatively high oestriol levels. After application of an ester, oestriol is extremely potent – as potent as oestradiol! It is just a pharmacokinetic characteristic of oestriol after all administrations. I would fully agree with your comment.

Glasier: If there are no other points on urogynaecology, is there anything we should discuss in relation to Dr Lumsden's paper on regimens and routes of administration?

Beral: Can I just ask for clarification because I am certainly not in my field? For the C-reactive protein (CRP), I was not clear whether you were implying that it was a marker of changes in clotting factors.

Lumsden: Well I think that the original hypothesis was that oral oestrogen stimulated an inflammatory response, which causes the rise in CRP. This interacts with the coagulation cascade so you have two things happening, and Professor Lowe will correct if I am wrong. One would be an increase in plaque instability and the second would be an activation of coagulation, both of which would increase the likelihood of venous and arterial thrombotic episodes. But I think that was the original hypothesis and why we set out to do what we did along with many other people. But I think that as the data have developed it becomes less clear. I think assessing plaque instability is incredibly difficult and that is probably one of the limiting factors of the studies that have been done. But my original thoughts were that inflammation came first and coagulation afterwards but I suspect Professor Lowe might disagree on that.

Lowe: It is important to differentiate between venous and arterial thrombosis. Venous, as I hoped to convince you yesterday, seems to be all about clotting. There are very few studies on CRP and venous thromboembolism but there is one large American prospective study[4] that shows that baseline CRP has no association with the incidence of clinical venous thromboembolism. That is where the data stands. There is an association between CRP and arterial disease and it is a risk predictor, as I said yesterday. A paper[5] in press suggests that it is about half as strong as a previous literature suggested and funnel plots suggest it was selective publication of positive results. Having said that, it is still a predictive factor for arterial disease but, again as I said yesterday, the hypothesis that CRP tells you about plaque instability is still a hypothesis. There is little direct data and there is little evidence that HRT, I think from the latest trials, modifies coronary artery disease in terms of progression of atherosclerosis although that may not be the same as plaque rupture. Until we have a selective inhibitor of CRP, we cannot really test its biological possibility. Having said that, I think it is worth measuring, as in the studies you have done, because it is a good indicator of the first-pass effect on the liver. So even though it is just a marker of what it is doing to the liver, that might still be a useful thing to study in terms of to what effect is the liver synthesising potential inflammatory mediators in general.

Beral: It is not at all clear to me which comes first and that seems to be really important. Could it not be the thrombotic events causing inflammation, i.e. the other way around? It does not seem logical to me the way it is but it is not my specialist area.

Lowe: We have been interested in which comes first: is it inflammation or clotting? There are relationships – if you compare, say, fibrinogen or fibrin D-dimer for prediction of coronary heart disease events with CRP, CRP loses out. One interpretation of which is that clotting comes first and clotting then may be inflammatory. But that is very controversial.

Stevenson: Just following on from yesterday, where the starting dose of oestrogen may be absolutely crucial in terms of whether you are going to get vascular benefit or harm, were you able to look at any dose effect on your measurements, CRP for example?

Lumsden: Unfortunately not, because, as the women were truly postmenopausal and were largely asymptomatic, we started with the 1 mg dose. We will have data on circulating oestradiol levels in all the women but I have not got all the data at the moment and so we cannot look at any correlations. There are correlations with certain coagulation factors and circulating oestradiol levels which we found from other studies using different types of HRT administration. But I think it is difficult to be sure – I had thought that what I would say in reviewing the data was that 2 mg raised your CRP a lot, 1 mg a bit and transdermal not all. But the literature does not support that.

Prentice: You mentioned CRP and interleukin-6 (IL-6), did you also look at E-selectin and matrix metalloproteinases (MMPs)?

Lumsden: We have not looked at that, no. I think from the literature the effect seems to be rather variable. I think a lot of the problem with the studies I have read is that they are not placebo-controlled. Some use a reference group and whether that explains some of the lack of differences I do not know.

Prentice: We do have nested case–control studies of heart disease, stroke and venous disease that are actually completed but have not yet been published. I had a question that is maybe naive but, since these inflammatory factors or coagulation factors are markers for an early rise in vascular disease, has anyone looked at inflammatory factors in relation to cancers?

Lowe: There is a collaboration study on fibrinogen – 200 000 people in prospective studies, and the paper has just been written. It will answer that question with interesting results, that is that fibrinogen is a predictor of heart attacks and strokes, and also of total mortality, the major part of which is cancer mortality. So it makes you wonder whether clotting factors and inflammatory factors are necessarily just related to cardiovascular disease, or do they tell us something more general about the body's responses to various stresses, some of which could be, for example, pre-malignant conditions. So, as always, the data will raise more questions than answers.

Pitkin: Well, I think we have come on to the essence of these three days, which, as a clinician, is balancing the risks and benefits. I think what I am hearing listening to my colleagues here is that when you are looking at data and statistics, they are in an infinite number of shades of grey. We are told the data is fine but clinicians also have shades of grey. We have to balance what we are getting in terms of figures with what we are going to do with patients sitting in front us, given that every woman is different, with different goals and aspirations and different risk factors of her own, and her family's risk factors to go with it.

References

1.   Raine-Fenning NJ, Brincat MP, Muscat-Baron Y. Skin aging and menopause: implications for treatment. *Am J Clin Dermatol* 2003;4:371–8.
2.   Baron YM, Brincat MP, Galea R. Increased reduction in bone density and skin thickness in postmenopausal women taking long-term corticosteroid therapy: a suggested role for estrogen add-back therapy. *Climacteric* 1999;2:189–96.
3.   Brincat M, Moniz CJ, Studd JW, Darby A, Magos A, Emburey G, *et al*. Long-term effects of the menopause and sex hormones on skin thickness. *Br J Obstet Gynaecol* 1985;92:256–9.
4.   Tsai AW, Cushman M, Rosamond WD, Heckbert SR, Tracy RP, Aleksic N, *et al*. Coagulation factors, inflammation markers, and venous thromboembolism: the longitudinal investigation of thromboembolism etiology (LITE). *Am J Med* 2002;113:636–42.
5.   Danesh J, Wheeler JG, Hirschfield GM, Eda S, Eiriksdottir G, Rumley A, *et al*. C-reactive protein and other circulating markers of inflammation in the prediction of coronary heart disease. *N Engl J Med* 2004;350:1387–97.

SECTION 5

THE BALANCE BETWEEN RISKS AND BENEFITS OF HORMONE REPLACEMENT

Chapter 19

Short-duration use of hormone replacement therapy

David Barlow

Introduction

Hormone replacement therapy (HRT) has been the standard approach to the management of symptoms associated with oestrogen withdrawal in the perimenopause and postmenopause for decades. An additional role for HRT in the modulation of postmenopausal health resulted from the encouraging data that emerged from observational studies of the health of postmenopausal women who used HRT. These studies supported a role for HRT initially in the management and prevention of osteoporosis, then in the prevention of coronary heart disease, and most recently in reduction in the risks of colorectal cancer and Alzheimer's disease.

Since HRT use is associated with potential risk as well as potential benefit, there has been great interest in working out how the risk–benefit balance applies in various clinical scenarios. The major randomised controlled trials (RCTs) have provided large-scale clinical endpoint trial data for the first time. The findings of these trials have triggered a major and currently continuing reappraisal of the place of HRT in clinical management because not all of the findings were as expected.

The use of HRT has been under greatly increased scientific, public and media attention as a result of the publication of the two American RCTs, the Heart and Estrogen/Progestin Replacement Study (HERS)[1] and the Women's Health Initiative (WHI).[2] The observational UK Million Women Study (MWS)[3] has further focused negative publicity on HRT in relation to breast cancer risk. The American studies examined the effects of continuous combined HRT used by 'healthy' (WHI) or 'cardiac compromised' (HERS) postmenopausal women. In WHI, the women were treated for an average of 5.2 years and in HERS the women were treated for an average of 4.1 years, prolonged to 6.8 years in an extension study (HERS II).[4] These studies have made a substantial contribution to the reappraisal of the use of HRT for long-term general health benefit. This use of HRT implies relatively extended durations of treatment and as a result is generally distinct from its use for symptom relief in the menopausal transition and the early postmenopause. Obviously, for some women HRT use for perimenopausal symptom relief may be extended subsequently to become long-term therapy. The main issues that must be addressed in considering short-duration use are:

- defining short-duration use
- reasons why women would use HRT for short duration – usually for symptom relief

- adverse effects women might experience with HRT
- risks of short-duration use.

Short-duration use of HRT will generally be for the relief of menopausal symptoms, of which the most common are vasomotor symptoms such as hot flushes. Symptom relief will usually continue for the duration of treatment but symptoms may return when treatment is stopped. It is known that many women use HRT for quite a short time, often less than one year, but for symptom relief it is very reasonable to consider that a woman would use it for at least two years before she would consider stopping to see if the symptoms return. If that approach is taken, then it is important that should symptoms return on stopping HRT, women should be given the opportunity to restart HRT and take it for a further reasonable period before trying to stop again, so that overall use of HRT might extend to three to four years. A practical working definition of short-duration use for the purpose of this chapter is to consider use up to five years HRT. Within this definition, the majority of women will be those in the perimenopause and early postmenopausal years and they will generally be under 60 years of age. These women correspond to the youngest subset of the WHI study and the expected duration of use will be well within the period of time covered in that study. It is reasonable to expect that women in this age group (below 55 or below 60 years) will generally have a low absolute risk of significant disease but that breast cancer will be a real concern for many of them.

Thus a woman might well have initiated HRT for symptom relief and, having achieved this, may be continuing with HRT in order to maintain her 'symptom-relieved' status. If the woman is symptomatic off HRT and continues to use HRT beyond five years for symptom relief then that symptom relief should be added to the benefit side of the risk–benefit equation and may have a critical effect on the balance of benefit and risk.

In general, use of HRT for less than five years for symptom relief is straightforward in terms of weighing up benefit and risk since relief of distressing symptoms can be added to the benefits and some risks will be minimised. This compares with the long-term HRT picture, where the benefit side of the equation often does not involve symptom relief and the risks may be more prominent. The impact of risk may be lower in short-duration HRT use by these early postmenopausal women because the overall HRT cumulative exposure will be lower but also because these younger women will probably have a lower absolute risk of adverse clinical events on which any increased risk must make an impact.

Since the women using short-duration HRT will generally be below 55 or 60 years of age, it is possible to extrapolate from the trials about the impact of risk associated with HRT in the context of the often lower absolute risk of events in this age group compared with older women. The duration of treatment involved in the WHI study is in keeping with short-duration treatment and so it provides useful clinical endpoint data on the major risk issues to be considered. The 50–59 year subgroup of the WHI trial participants coincides with this age group of interest, whereas the whole WHI age spectrum was from 50 to 79 years, but it is important not to over-interpret subgroup results since the study was powered to address its endpoints in the whole study population. The analyses of WHI have provided information on the ten-year subgroups showing actual numbers of events and the annualised percentage rate for most of the clinical events of interest.

Symptoms of the menopause

Vasomotor symptoms

The menopausal transition brings symptoms for many women and the occurrence of these has been the subject of many studies. The findings vary with the methodology of the studies but generally there is an increase in the prevalence of vasomotor symptoms through the menopausal transition and beyond with this decreasing after the first few years of the postmenopause. The analysis of patterns of symptoms by age and sex in middle age by Bungay et al.[5] showed peaks of prevalence of flushing and sweating closely associated with the mean age of menopause, coinciding with it or occurring a little after it. In a prospective longitudinal study of the menopausal transition, Dennerstein et al.[6] reported that general somatic symptoms peaked in the perimenopause but vasomotor symptoms increased through the transition. Again in Melbourne, Guthrie et al.[7] reported that 29% of women with 3–12 months of amenorrhoea and 37% of postmenopausal women experienced hot flushes several times a day. In total, 13% of premenopausal women, 37% of perimenopausal women and 62% of postmenopausal women reported having had at least one hot flush in the previous two weeks.

Psychological symptoms

A range of psychological symptoms are also seen to have increased prevalence around the time of the menopause and again these gradually improve with increasing time beyond the menopause. Bungay et al.[5] reported that a group of minor psychological symptoms, including lack of confidence, poor concentration and poor memory, also peaked around the menopause but these peaks of prevalence were less prominent and were associated with an age just preceding the mean age of menopause. Hunter et al.[8] studied 474 women aged between 45 and 55 years in detail and observed which symptoms increased in prevalence over the menopausal transition (Table 19.1).

Table 19.1. The average percentage of pre-, peri- and postmenopausal non-hysterectomised women aged 45–55 years ($n = 474$) not using HRT experiencing problems in each symptom group; reproduced with permission from Hunter et al.,[8] (Maturitas, © 1988 Elsevier)

Symptom group	Premenopausal A (%)	Perimenopausal B (%)	Postmenopausal C (%)	Significance
Vasomotor	18	47	58	$P < 0.001$; A < B < C
Somatic	31	38	37	NS
Depressed mood	17	25	25	$P < 0.001$; A < B,C
Anxiety/fears	33	36	37	NS
Sleep problems	35	44	49	$P < 0.005$; A < B < C
Sexual problems	23	28	35	$P < 0.04$; A < B < C
Cognitive difficulties	46	48	51	NS

NS = not significant

Urogenital symptoms

In contrast to the symptoms that relate to the menopausal transition and the early postmenopausal years, urogenital symptoms of oestrogen deficiency tend to start with the menopause but can continue for many years thereafter since they result from the continuing low oestrogen state and may affect women in all the decades of postmenopausal life. This symptom cluster is often referred to as urogenital ageing (UGA) and includes symptoms such as urinary frequency, symptoms suggestive of recurrent urinary tract infection, urgency, vaginal irritation and dryness and superficial dyspareunia.

A population survey of 2000 women across the UK aged 55–85 years found that 49% reported menopausal urogenital symptoms at some time but no more than 11% were currently affected by individual symptoms; however, where they occurred these were often of long duration.[9] Approximately 12% of those women who reported dyspareunia and/or vaginal dryness claimed a severe problem but many did not seek professional advice, often because of embarrassment.[9] Similar results were observed in a population survey of women across Europe, with 30% of the women reporting significant UGA symptoms, of whom 60% made efforts to alleviate their problems.[10]

In general, if these symptoms are to be relieved in the long term they would require long-term treatment, but they are highly amenable to local therapy, which should not carry the same risks as systemic HRT (see Chapter 17). It is important that health professionals be aware of the many potential urogenital symptoms that might occur and make it easy for women to discuss these because for many this is an embarrassing topic and there is a strong likelihood that the problem will recur when any short-term treatment is stopped.[9]

HRT and relief of menopausal symptoms

The most common use of HRT is for the relief of vasomotor symptoms and there is extensive trial literature demonstrating the efficacy of HRT in this area, both in placebo-controlled crossover studies and in placebo-controlled randomised trials. Examples are the classic 1975 placebo-controlled crossover trial of Coope et al.[11] (Figure 19.1) and the 1998 randomised placebo-controlled trial of Notelovitz et al.[12] (Figure 19.2). Indeed, every new HRT preparation is tested for efficacy against hot flushes as part of the licensing process.

The evidence concerning the efficacy of HRT in improving psychological symptoms is much less clear-cut. There are studies suggesting benefit and others questioning this. All clinicians treating women with HRT for psychological symptoms will have observed some women who achieve substantial improvement in their psychological picture when given HRT and these benefits will often be sustained for considerable periods of time. It is never possible to fully exclude a placebo effect in such anecdotal experience, although placebo effects are often not sustained. When HRT is given in randomised placebo-controlled trials, the concomitant relief of vasomotor symptoms and related insomnia leaves open the argument that any improvement in psychological symptoms is a secondary effect. An example of a randomised placebo-controlled study indicating psychological benefit from HRT is that of Sherwin and Gelfand,[13] in which women having a surgical menopause were given sex steroids, and which was controlled with women given placebo and women who had hysterectomy with ovarian conservation (Figure 19.3).

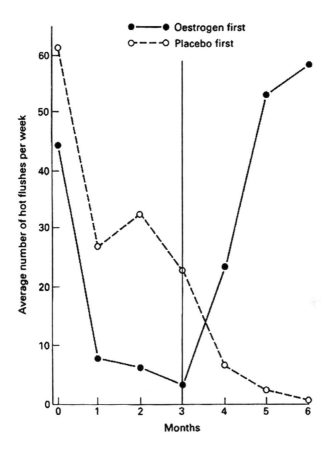

Figure 19.1. Hot flush count during a six-month crossover trial with Premarin® 1.25 mg/day; reproduced with permission from Coope *et al.*[11] (BMJ, © BMJ Publishing Group)

Evidence from surveys suggests that women are most likely to use HRT if they have had a hysterectomy, presumably as a result of factors such as the greater distress reported by women after hysterectomy, especially if there has been a surgical menopause, and the simplicity of HRT after hysterectomy since vaginal bleeding is not an issue. A study of 424 women in the community in Glasgow found a gradient of reported menopausal symptom distress, with 42% of postmenopausal women, 57% of hysterectomised women and 76% of oophorectomised women reporting having experienced a need for treatment for menopausal symptoms.[14] Thirty-seven percent of the women reported ever-use of HRT and 28% reported current use. Overall in this sample of women in the mid-1980s, HRT was predominantly used by the hysterectomised and oophorectomised women (15/33) compared with 29/188 of the postmenopausal women. This was even more notable for the use of HRT beyond 3 years where this applied to 9/33 of the oophorectomised women but only three of the 188 postmenopausal women.[14] This low prevalence of use is consistent with the reported past use by older women surveyed in the mid-1990s (Table 19.2).[9] In that study, only 13% of the ex-users of oral HRT reported having used it for more than three years and 53% reported use for less than six months.

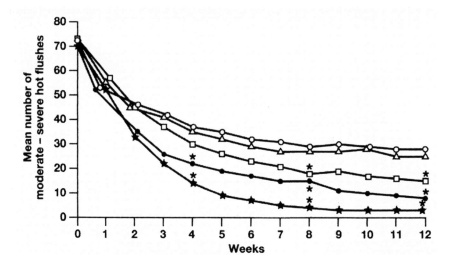

Figure 19.2. Hot flush weekly weighted score in a placebo-controlled randomised trial of oral 17β-oestradiol in 333 symptomatic women who were at least six months beyond their last menstrual period (mean age 51 years, range 40–63 years); placebo (*open circles*), 0.25 mg (*open triangles*), 0.5 mg (*open squares*), 1 mg (*solid circles*), 2 mg (*asterisks*) 17β-oestradiol; stars indicate statistically significant difference versus placebo; reproduced with permission from Notelovitz et al.[29]

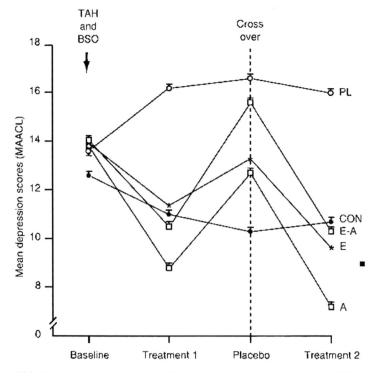

Figure 19.3. Mean depression scores (± SEM) in women having hysterectomy (TAH) with bilateral oophorectomy (BSO) followed by treatment with oestrogen (E), androgen (A) or both (E-A); control groups were women having TAH and BSO given placebo (PL) and women having hysterectomy with ovarian conservation (CON); reproduced with permission from Sherwin and Gelfand[13] (Psychoneuroendocrinology, © 1985 Elsevier)

In general, it should be emphasised that HRT users are a subset of the population usually motivated by the desire to obtain relief from menopausal symptoms and that much of the use, especially in women with an intact uterus, is relatively short-term.

Other potential benefits

Reduced colorectal cancer risk

The whole WHI population experienced less colorectal cancer but there are no age-specific figures. The overall hazard ratio was favourable but not significant at 0.63 (adjusted 95% CI 0.32–1.24), indicating annualised rates of 10 per 10000 cases in the HRT group and 16 per 10000 in the placebo group. This represents a reduction of 6 cases per 10000 women per year across a 50–79 year age band. There is insufficient trial-based information to indicate that a reduction in colorectal cancer will be experienced by those under 60 years of age during five years of treatment with HRT.

Reduced fracture risk

The WHI trial confirmed the strong evidence from secondary endpoint trials that HRT has an impact on osteoporosis and that fracture reductions are demonstrable in a large RCT.[15] There is a consensus that treatment of osteoporosis using antiresorptive agents such as HRT is not associated with significant effects many years after the cessation of the treatment. The time course of the loss of a treatment effect is thought to be over a number of years. Women using HRT in their 50s should therefore not expect to see continuing benefit when they are in their 70s and approaching the age when hip fracture becomes a significant issue. It can be postulated that the skeletal effect of HRT will not be a major factor in the decision making on short-term use of HRT but the WHI data do indicate that even during treatment of five years' duration below 60 years there is a clinical benefit, as illustrated in Table 19.3. This shows that there is no relevant hip fracture effect in women below 60 years but that there is a reduction in the annualised rates of all fractures, particularly for the women under 55 years where the rates were 105 per 10000 for HRT and 153 per 10000 for placebo, a difference of 48 fractures per 10000 women per year. The equivalent difference for the 55–59 age group was 11 fractures per 10000 women per year. Even without consideration of nonclinical vertebral fractures, which were not assessed in the WHI study, the evidence concerning the fracture reduction benefit is sufficient to be considered an additional benefit to the treatment of symptoms in women using short-duration HRT.

Table 19.2. Awareness and usage of HRT; reproduced with permission from Barlow *et al.*[9]

	Total	55–64 years	65–74 years	>74 years	>84 years
Total	2045	675	690	661	113
Never heard of HRT	9%	4%	6%	17%	24%
Never used HRT	79%	72%	84%	80%	75%
Ever used HRT	12%	23%	9%	2%	1%
Current HRT use	6%	13%	2%	1%	0

Table 19.3. Fractures reported in the WHI study for a mean of 5.2 years of HRT; presented as numbers of events and as annualised percentage rates (in brackets), as well as hazard ratios with 95% confidence intervals; reproduced with permission from Cauley *et al.*[15] (JAMA, © 2003 American Medical Association)

Age group	E + P group	Placebo group	Hazard ratio with 95% CI
All fractures			
Whole study 50–79 years	733 (1.52)	896 (1.99)	0.76 (0.69–0.83)
50–54 years	67 (1.05)	90 (1.53)	0.68 (0.49–0.93)
55–59 years	124 (1.18)	126 (1.29)	0.91 (0.71–1.16)
Hip fracture			
Whole study 50–79 years	52 (0.11)	73 (0.16)	0.67 (0.47–0.96)
50–59 years	1 (0.01)	5 (0.03)	0.17 (0.07–1.43)

E + P = oestrogen plus progestogen

Adverse effects of HRT

The best established adverse effect of using HRT is the risk of inducing vaginal bleeding. If the HRT is in a cyclical formulation, as is used in perimenopausal and early menopausal women, then bleeding will be expected on a monthly basis. The acceptability of this to women is variable and generally it is expected that women would prefer not to bleed. For women who are in the established postmenopause, continuous combined preparations tend to be favoured and these can offer bleeding profiles that will not be associated with bleeding for most women. Archer *at al.*[16] have demonstrated that the addition of continuous low-dose oral progestogen (norethisterone acetate) to oral 17β-oestradiol can result in patterns of bleeding or spotting that provide a majority of women with immediate freedom from bleeding, and that most of the minority who do experience these symptoms become bleed-free (Figure 19.4). This is in contrast to the pattern with women who are given only oestradiol, where the initial experience is absence of bleeding but with an increasing percentage bleeding as time passes.

Other adverse effects of HRT use tend to be relatively uncommon. Breast discomfort is a feature of the first month or two of treatment but usually resolves quite quickly after this. Abdominal cramps can be reported in women on cyclical preparations in relation to the episodes of bleeding and some women may retain fluid and be concerned about weight gain. Overall adverse effects tend to be less of an issue than concern about risks.

Risks with short-duration HRT

Health professionals and patients are familiar with having to weigh up the potential benefits of proposed treatments against adverse effects and risks. This is especially the case in surgical specialties where the formal process of informed written consent is well established. With the use of drug therapies, the process is one of informed consent but generally without written consent, although patients would expect to be informed of adverse effects and risks. Where the need for treatment is strong the coexistence of some degree of risk is accepted, and this is the situation when a woman is seeking relief from distressing menopausal symptoms. Different standards might be considered to

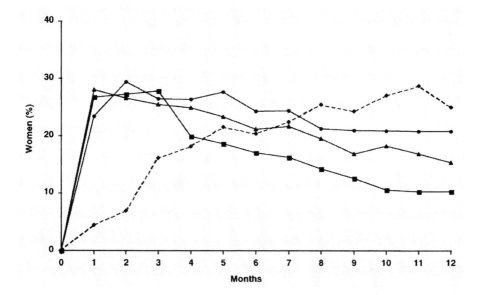

Figure 19.4. Frequency of bleeding (with or without spotting) in women randomised to receive daily 1 mg oral 17β-oestradiol alone (*dashed line*), or in combination with either oral norethisterone acetate (NETA) 0.1 mg (*ovals*), 0.25 mg (*triangles*) or 0.5 mg (*squares*); the 1 176 women, aged 44 to 82 years, were at least one year postmenopausal; reproduced with permission from Archer *et al.*[16]

apply where the patient is not ill but is using a drug intervention in order to reduce the risk of a future health problem. In this case, the issue of risk associated with the intervention gains in prominence since the chance of an adverse occurrence might be on the same scale as the hoped-for benefit.

The principal risks to be considered in association with HRT use in the early postmenopause are well defined: thromboembolism risk, breast cancer risk and, now, risk of coronary heart disease or stroke.

Thromboembolism risk

The general public have a long experience of associating the use of exogenous sex hormones with thromboembolism risk. This issue has been prominent in relation to the oral contraceptive pill for many years and has been a major factor in the limitation of pill use in the later reproductive years, especially in cigarette smokers. Since 1996 there has been observational evidence indicated a doubling or tripling of the risk of idiopathic venous thromboembolism, particularly in the early phase of treatment in the first year.[17–19] Those observations have been confirmed in the WHI RCT[2] where the hazard ratio for the whole study population across the age range 50 to 79 years was 2.11 (adjusted 95% CI 1.26–3.55). With annualised rates of 34 per 10 000 for the HRT group and 16 per 10 000 for the placebo group, the difference was 18 per 10 000 women. This was substantially higher for both arms than was estimated from observational studies but several of those had been restricted to idiopathic thromboembolism and excluded women with predisposing risk factors. There is currently no breakdown of the thromboembolism events by age group in the WHI reports so we do not know whether the higher rates relate to the effect of thromboembolism in the older women in the study or whether the difference represents the inclusion of all thrombotic events.

Women below 60 years using short-duration HRT will be running a risk of thromboembolism since it is a feature of the early phase of treatment, but it is not clear how much of the relatively high rate reported for the WHI women applies to the younger decade in the study. It is now well established that women who have a personal or family history of venous thromboembolism require particular assessment (see Chapter 7). All HRT users should be told about this possible risk so that they can report a potential problem.

Endometrial cancer risk

The association between oestrogen therapy and risk of endometrial cancer was probably the first major problem to appear in the HRT field. The adverse evidence of risk in unopposed oestrogen users resulted in a reappraisal of treatment strategies that led to the oestrogen plus progestogen regimens introduced in the 1980s. Those new regimens were referred to as cyclical or sequential and involved monthly bleeds for most users as the price paid for endometrial safety. 'Continuous combined' regimens have since been developed because they offer freedom from vaginal bleeding to most women, thus rendering the HRT more acceptable. The cyclical regimens have remained predominant for HRT use in perimenopausal women but continuous combined regimens now predominate in postmenopausal use. There is no evidence to suggest that appropriately used cyclical or continuous combined short-duration HRT regimens are associated with endometrial pathology but there are observational data indicating that use of cyclical HRT in excess of five years is associated with increased risk of endometrial cancer.[20,21] The observational evidence suggests that continuous combined HRT is not associated with increased risk and may offer reduced risk of endometrial cancer below that of untreated women.[21] The women in the arm of WHI that has been reported were using continuous combined HRT and no increased risk was found, with 58 endometrial cancers occurring in the study over the 5.6 years of mean exposure.[22] Just over 10% of the women in both groups had previous exposure to unopposed oestrogen. The hazard ratio for endometrial cancer across the whole age spectrum, 33% of whom were under 60 years, was 0.81 (95% CI 0.48–1.36) based on 27 endometrial cancers in the HRT group and 31 in the placebo group. The annualised rates were six per 10 000 women in the HRT group and seven per 10 000 in the placebo group.[22] On this evidence, women using short-duration HRT are likely to be free of any increased endometrial cancer risk whether using cyclical or continuous combined regimens.

Breast cancer risk

Breast cancer can be a devastating disease associated with early death, and women's perceptions and concerns about using HRT are often shaped by the media coverage given to this particular topic. The debate about whether symptomatic women should use HRT often focuses on the severity of symptoms weighed against the spectre of breast cancer risk. The general view, based on the epidemiology as collated in the Collaborative Group on Hormonal Factors in Breast Cancer re-analysis in 1997,[23] was that less than five years use of HRT was associated with only a very small increment in risk of 2–3% per year of use. The Beral *et al.*[23] reanalysis was a landmark in bringing together a very large body of data on this question. The paper calculated that five years' use of predominantly oestrogen-only HRT from age 50 would be associated with an increase in prevalence of breast cancer from 45 to 47 women per 1000 by age 70 years. This estimate of two extra cancers per thousand women is not a trivial matter but is probably much smaller than the extent of risk perceived by many women. The more recent observational Million Women Study[3] has suggested that the risk is higher for short-term use of even two years. The evidence from WHI has been presented in some detail by Chlebowski et al.,[24] indicating concordance between WHI and the Collaborative reanalysis[23] of the observational literature.

Table 19.4 presents the most relevant data from WHI on the question of short-duration HRT.[24] This indicates the annualised percentage rates and hazard ratios for breast cancer comparing the HRT group with the placebo group on an intention to treat basis. The below-60 age group is identified, as is the group of women across the whole study who had no previous HRT use. This is the group most relevant to the consideration of short-duration use. However, we do not have information specifically for the 50–59 year age group who had no previous HRT use. Similarly, we have the year-by-year statistics only for the whole age spectrum of the study. If such subgroup data were available, their value would be undermined by the limited power of the subgroup analysis. Therefore, the messages for short-duration use in women under 60 years should be interpreted cautiously since the lack of statistical significance cannot be taken as proof of no difference. The first three years of treatment were not associated with a numeric increase in risk and the absolute rates were lowest in the youngest decade of the study with annualised rates for invasive breast cancer of 31 per 10 000 in the HRT group and 26 per 10 000 in the placebo group. Thus the suggested increase in risk would be of the order of five women in 10 000 per year. This would appear to be the appropriate level of risk to communicate to women in this decade considering using HRT for symptom relief.

Cardiovascular disease and stroke

The epidemiological literature on coronary artery disease had suggested that risk would be reduced in HRT users[25] and the observational studies on stroke suggested that the effect would be either neutral or a slight benefit.[26] The WHI study did not confirm these suggestions and raises the possibility of increased risk. With short-duration use, cardiovascular benefit was not a significant issue and it is the questions of whether

Table 19.4. Invasive breast cancer in the WHI study; presented as numbers of cases and as annualised percentage rates (in brackets), as well as hazard ratios with 95% confidence intervals; reproduced with permission from Chlebowski et al.[24]

Age group	E+P group	Placebo group	Hazard ratio with 95% CI
50–59 years	52 (0.31)	40 (0.26	1.20 (0.80–1.82)
Whole study 50–79 years	199 (0.41)	150 (0.33)	1.24 (1.01–1.54)
Whole study and no previous hormones			
50–79 years	141 (0.40)	121 (0.36)	1.09 (0.86–1.39)
50–79 years, year 1	7 (0.11)	14 (0.23)	0.48 (0.19–1.20)
50–79 years, year 2	15 (0.24)	22 (0.37)	0.65 (0.34–1.25)
50–79 years, year 3	19 (0.31)	19 (0.33)	0.96 (0.51–1.82)
50–79 years, year 4	35 (0.58)	23 (0.40)	1.45 (0.85–2.45)
50–79 years, year 5	28 (0.54)	17 (0.34)	1.61 (0.88–2.94)

E + P = oestrogen plus progestogen

coronary heart disease or stroke risks are increased that remain relevant. Since both coronary artery disease and stroke have low absolute risk in the age group being considered here, the relative risk indicated by WHI will result in a small effect on women because of the low absolute risk. In women aged 50–59 years, the annualised coronary heart disease event rate for the HRT group was 22 per 10 000 and 17 per 10 000 for the placebo group so that the numeric difference was five events per 10 000 women per year and the hazard ratio was reported as 1.27 (95% CI 0.7–2.2).[27] For stroke the annualised rates for the 50–59 year age group were 14 per 10 000 and 10 per 10 000 in the HRT and placebo groups, respectively, with the numeric difference 4 per 10 000 per year.[28] Again, there was a nonsignificant hazard ratio of 1.46 (95% CI 0.77–2.79) but again this was a subgroup analysis.

We thus have the statistics that 10 000 women in the age range we are considering who use HRT face approximate annual risks of five coronary events, four stroke events and five invasive breast cancers more than if they do not use HRT. The thromboembolism statistic suggested from the observational studies is in the region of an extra two events per 10 000 per year but the WHI study (for the age spectrum 50–79 years) reported the possibility of an extra 18 per 10 000 thromboembolism events per year. As before, with ovarian cancer we do not have figures for the decade of age of interest, but for the whole population the hazard ratio was nonsignificant at 1.58 (95% CI 0.77–3.24) and the annualised rates were four per 10 000 for the HRT group and three per 10 000 for the placebo group.[22]

Balanced alongside these figures when a woman is trying to decide what to do in order to relieve distressing symptoms of the menopause is the likelihood that vasomotor symptoms can be estimated to be relieved at an annualised rate of at least 9 500 per 10 000 women. With somatic and psychological symptoms, the results are less predictable but a conservative estimate would be that several thousand women per 10 000 would achieve benefit. For vaginal symptoms, good responses can be expected but if these are the only problem then local therapy might be preferable since it bypasses the risks we are considering.

Table 19.5 therefore provides a speculation on the benefit–risk equation to be considered by women suffering distressing menopausal vasomotor symptoms. These are conservative estimates, including the assumption that 30% of untreated women will have relief from vasomotor symptoms either by using placebo or doing nothing.

Table 19.5. Estimates of annualised rates relevant to decision making by women seeking relief of distressing menopausal vasomotor symptoms; assumptions have been made cautiously with respect to expected benefit from HRT and the risks marked by *, with numbers in parentheses, are based on WHI data for the whole WHI age spectrum (50–79 years), which is likely to overestimate the absolute risk faced by women below 60 years; the possible beneficial effect on endometrial cancer risk has not been considered in this modelling of decision making in short-duration HRT use

Condition	Rate (per 10 000 women per year)		
	HRT users	Placebo users	Difference (HRT – placebo)
Vasomotor symptoms	500	7000	−6500
All fractures	105	153	−48
Colon cancer*	(10)	(16)	−6
Breast cancer	31	26	+5
Ovarian cancer*	(4)	(3)	+1
Coronary disease	22	17	+5
Stroke	14	10	+4
Thromboembolism*	(34)	(16)	+18

Conclusions

The long-term use of HRT is currently controversial as a result of the data that have emerged in the past few years. Short-duration use of HRT, mainly for symptom relief in peri- and early postmenopausal women, is much less controversial because greater weight can be given to the benefit side of the equation and some aspects of the risk side of the equation are less prominent, as indicated in Table 19.5. Women affected by distressing symptoms have the potential for a substantial improvement in symptomatology and a reduction in the risk of 'all fractures' during their short-duration treatment, against which they must weigh a number of risks that are all at a low level. Individual decision making will determine the woman's action. It is to be hoped that women seeking symptom relief by means of HRT are given the appropriate advice on benefit and risk and the opportunity to use HRT in this way if they wish. There are currently anecdotal reports that women are being discouraged from using HRT for symptom relief because of the recent adverse publicity attached to HRT, which is unjustified and is not evidence-based.

References

1.   Hulley S, Grady D, Bush T, Furberg C, Herrington D, Riggs B, *et al.* Randomized trial of estrogen plus progestin for secondary prevention of coronary heart disease in postmenopausal women. Heart and Estrogen/progestin Replacement Study (HERS) Research Group. *JAMA* 1998;280:605–13.
2.   Rossouw JE, Anderson GL, Prentice RL, LaCroix AZ, Kooperberg C, Stefanick ML, *et al.*; Writing Group for the Women's Health Initiative Investigators. Risks and benefits of estrogen plus progestin in healthy postmenopausal women: principal results fom the Women's Health Initiative randomized controlled trial. *JAMA* 2002;288:321–3.
3.   Beral V; Million Women Study Collaborators. Breast cancer and hormone-replacement therapy in the Million Women Study. *Lancet* 2003;362:419–27. Erratum in: *Lancet* 2003;362:1160.
4.   Grady D, Herrington D, Bittner V, Blumenthal R, Davidson M, Hlatky M, *et al.*; HERS Research Group. Cardiovascular disease outcomes during 6.8 years of hormone therapy: Heart and Estrogen/progestin Replacement Study follow-up (HERS II). *JAMA* 2002;288:49–57. Erratum in: *JAMA* 2002;288:1064.
5.   Bungay GT, Vessey MP, McPherson CK. Study of symptoms in middle life with special reference to the menopause. *BMJ* 1980;281:181–3.
6.   Dennerstein L, Smith AM, Morse C, Burger H, Green A, Hopper J, *et al.* Menopausal symptoms in Australian women. *Med J Aust* 993;159:232–6.
7.   Guthrie JR, Dennerstein L, Hopper JL, Burger HG. Hot flushes, menstrual status, and hormone levels in a population-based sample of midlife women. *Obstet Gynecol* 1996;88:437–42.
8.   Hunter M, Battersby R, Whitehead MI. Relationships between psychological symptoms, somatic complaints and menopausal status. *Maturitas* 1988;8:217–28.
9.   Barlow DH, Cardozo LD, Francis RM, Griffin M, Hart DM, Stephens E, *et al.* Urogenital ageing and its effect on sexual health in older British women. *Br J Obstet Gynaecol* 1997;104:87–91.
10. Barlow DH, Samsioe G, van Geelen JM. A study of European womens' experience of the problems of urogenital ageing and its management. *Maturitas* 1997;27:239–47.
11. Coope J, Thomson JM, Poller L. Effects of "natural oestrogen" replacement therapy on menopausal symptoms and blood clotting. *BMJ* 1975;4:139–43.
12. Notelovitz M, Arce J-C, Nanavati N, Huang WC. One milligram 17beta-estradiol is the optimal dose for treatment of moderate to severe vasomotor symptoms: a dose-response study. *Menopause* 1998;5:251.
13. Sherwin BB, Gelfand MM. Sex steroids and affect in the surgical menopause: a double-blind, cross-over study. *Psychoneuroendocrinology* 1985;10:325–35.
14. Barlow DH, Grosset KA, Hart H, Hart DM. A study of the experience of Glasgow women in the climacteric years. *Br J Obstet Gynaecol* 1989;96:1192–7.
15. Cauley JA, Robbins J, Chen Z, Cummings SR, Jackson RD, LaCroix AZ, *et al.*; Women's Health Initiative Investigators. Effects of estrogen plus progestin on risk of fracture and bone mineral density: the Women's Health Initiative randomized trial. *JAMA* 2003;290:1729–38.
16. Archer DF, Dorin MH, Heine W, Nanavati N, Arce JC for the Endometrium Study Group. Uterine

bleeding in postmenopausal women on continuous therapy with estradiol and norethindrone acetate. *Obstet Gynecol* 1999;94:323–9.

17. Daly E, Vessey MP, Hawkins MM, Carson JL, Gough P, Marsh S. Risk of venous thromboembolism in users of hormone replacement therapy. *Lancet* 1996;348:977–80.

18. Jick H, Derby LE, Myers MW, Vasilakis C, Newton KM. Risk of hospital admission for idiopathic venous thromboembolism among users of postmenopausal oestrogens. *Lancet* 1996;348:981–3.

19. Grodstein F, Stampfer MJ, Goldhaber SZ, Manson JE, Colditz GA, Speizer FE, *et al.* Prospective study of exogenous hormones and risk of pulmonary embolism in women. *Lancet* 1996;348:983–7.

20. Beresford SAA, Weiss NS, Voigt LF, McKnight B. Risk of endometrial cancer in relation to use of oestrogen combined with cyclic progestagen therapy in postmenopausal women. *Lancet* 1997;349:458–61.

21. Weiderpass E, Adami HO, Baron JA, Magnusson C, Bergstrom R, Lindgren A, *et al.* Risk of endometrial cancer following estrogen replacement with and without progestins. *J Natl Cancer Inst* 1999;91:1131–7.

22. Anderson GL, Judd HL, Kaunitz AM, Barad DH, Beresford SA, Pettinger M, *et al.*; Women's Health Initiative Investigators. Effects of estrogen plus progestin on gynecologic cancers and associated diagnostic procedures: the Women's Health Initiative randomized trial. *JAMA* 2003;290:1739–48.

23. Collaborative Group on Hormonal Factors in Breast Cancer. Breast cancer and hormone replacement therapy: collaborative reanalysis of data from 51 epidemiological studies of 52,705 women with breast cancer and 108,411 women without breast cancer. *Lancet* 1997;350:1047–59. Erratum in: *Lancet* 1997;350:1484.

24. Chlebowski RT, Hendrix SL, Langer RD, Stefanick ML, Gass M, Lane D, *et al.*; WHI Investigators. Influence of estrogen plus progestin on breast cancer and mammography in healthy postmenopausal women: the Women's Health Initiative Randomized Trial. *JAMA* 2003;289:3243–53.

25. Grady D, Rubin SM, Petitti DB, Fox CS, Black D, Ettinger B, *et al.* Hormone therapy to prevent disease and prolong life in postmenopausal women. *Ann Intern Med* 1992;117:1016–37.

26. Finucane FF, Madans JH, Bush TL, Wolf PH, Kleinman JC. Decreased risk of stroke among postmenopausal hormone users: result from a national cohort. *Arch Int Med* 1993;153:73–9.

27. Manson JE, Hsia J, Johnson KC, Rossouw JE, Assaf AR, Lasser NL, *et al.*; Women's Health Initiative Investigators. Estrogen plus progestin and the risk of coronary heart disease. *N Engl J Med* 2003;349:523–34.

28. Wassertheil-Smoller S, Hendrix SL, Limacher M, Heiss G, Kooperberg C, Baird A, *et al.*; WHI Investigators. Effect of estrogen plus progestin on stroke in postmenopausal women: the Women's Health Initiative: a randomized trial. *JAMA* 2003;289:2673–84.

29. Notelovitz M, Lenihan JP, McDermott M, Kerber IJ, Nanavati N, Arce J. Initial 17beta-estradiol dose for treating vasomotor symptoms. *Obstet Gynecol* 2000;95:726–31.

Chapter 20

Disease incidence associated with long-term use of hormone replacement therapy

Emily Banks, Gillian Reeves and Stephen Evans

Introduction

Until very recently it has been difficult to provide a meaningful answer to the longstanding question of how use of hormone replacement therapy (HRT) affects a woman's overall risk of disease, because reliable data on the relationship between use of HRT and important outcomes, particularly cardiovascular disease (CVD), have been limited. The early publication of results from the oestrogen-progestogen arm of the Women's Health Initiative (WHI) randomised trial[1] and the publication of results regarding HRT and breast cancer from the Million Women Study,[2] together with the availability of data from other studies,[3,4] means that it is now possible to arrive at broad estimates of the overall effect of combined oestrogen-progestogen HRT on the risk of major potentially life-threatening disease. However, uncertainty remains about the effects of oestrogen-only HRT on the risk of CVD and a number of other conditions, and about the effect of duration of use and the persistence of effects after use of HRT has ceased, for most types of HRT.

'Long-term' use of HRT is assumed to refer to use of HRT for more than one or two years. This paper examines the evidence to date regarding the effects of around five years' use of HRT on health, focusing on major potentially life-threatening conditions, including breast, colorectal and endometrial cancers, coronary heart disease (CHD), stroke, pulmonary embolism (PE) and hip fracture. These conditions have been primary and secondary outcomes of the major randomised trials of HRT.

To appreciate the impact of use of HRT on disease incidence, it is important to keep in perspective the absolute frequency of these conditions among women in their 50s and 60s. Among women aged 50–59 years, breast cancer is by far the most common major potentially life-threatening condition, with around 12 per 1000 women who are not using HRT expected to develop the disease over a five-year period (Table 20.1). Among the same 1000 women over a five-year period, around 5 would be expected to experience incident CHD (defined as either myocardial infarction or coronary artery disease death) and the incidence of stroke, colorectal cancer, PE and hip fracture is each estimated at around 1–3 per 1000 (Table 20.1). Among women aged 60–69 years not using HRT and followed for five years, the incidence of breast cancer and CHD is similar (at around 15 and 16.5 per 1000, respectively), the incidence of stroke is around 10–11 per 1000, the incidences of colorectal cancer and hip fracture are each about 7–8 per 1000, and 4 per 1000 would be expected to have a PE (Table 20.2). These figures demonstrate that breast cancer remains important throughout the 50–70 year age period

Table 20.1. Estimated incidence of various conditions according to use of HRT among 1000 healthy postmenopausal women in Western countries aged 50–59 years over a five-year period; based on data from the Women's Health Initiative[1,3,17]

Condition	Never user of HRT	User of oestrogen + progestogen HRT for 5 years
Breast cancer	12.0	15.2
Colorectal cancer	3.2	2.0
Coronary heart disease	5.0	6.1
Stroke	3.2	4.4
Pulmonary embolism	1.6	3.2
Hip fracture	1.5	1.0
Total	**26.5**	**31.9**

and CVD becomes increasingly important when women are in their 60s. Hip fracture is also much more common among women in their 60s compared with their 50s. However, its incidence is still half of that of breast cancer among women in their 60s (Table 20.2).

Methods

This paper reviews the current published evidence on the effects of long-term use of HRT, with emphasis on results from randomised trials and large-scale meta-analyses. First, the published data are examined in terms of the relative risks for the association between use of HRT and the risk of major clinical disease, separately according to HRT type and duration of use where possible. Analysis is done on a relative risk scale since this tends to be consistent across different risk groups. The available evidence regarding the absolute risk of disease in relation to use of HRT is then reviewed, since it is absolute risks that are relevant to the risk–benefit balance.

Table 20.2. Estimated incidence of various conditions according to use of HRT among 1000 healthy postmenopausal women in Western countries aged 60–69 years over a five-year period; based on data from the Women's Health Initiative[1,3,17]

Condition	Never user of HRT	User of oestrogen + progestogen HRT for 5 years
Breast cancer	15.0	19.0
Colorectal cancer	8.0	5.0
Coronary heart disease	16.5	20.0
Stroke	10.5	14.5
Pulmonary embolism	4.0	8.0
Hip fracture	7.5	5.0
Total	**61.5**	**71.5**

Evidence regarding HRT and major clinical conditions

Breast cancer

There is consistent evidence from randomised trials and observational studies that use of HRT increases the risk of breast cancer.[2,3,5,6] The overall evidence suggests that the risk is increased while women are taking HRT and that the effects wear off soon after use of HRT ceases, returning to levels of risk found in never users of HRT within a few years after ceasing use. Among current users of HRT the relative risk of breast cancer increases with increasing duration of use. The available evidence indicates that all types of HRT, including tibolone, increase the risk of breast cancer but that use of combined oestrogen-progestogen HRT increases breast cancer incidence to a greater extent than other types of HRT.[2] Compared with never users of HRT, the relative risks of breast cancer among women who have used oestrogen-only and combined oestrogen-progestogen HRT for one to four years were found to be 1.25 (95% CI 1.10–1.41) and 1.74 (95% CI 1.60–1.89), respectively, in the Million Women Study.[2]

Colorectal cancer

Data from randomised trials and observational studies indicate that women using HRT have a reduced risk of colorectal cancer.[1,3,7] Overall, randomised trials find a relative risk of 0.64 (95% CI 0.45–0.92) for those randomised to combined conjugated equine oestrogen (CEE) and medroxyprogesterone acetate (MPA) versus placebo.[3] The effect of other specific types of HRT, including oestrogen-only HRT and tibolone, on colorectal cancer is unknown, nor is it known how long the effects of combined HRT persist, or if effects vary according to the duration of use of HRT.

Endometrial cancer

It is now accepted that use of oestrogen-only HRT increases the risk of endometrial cancer in women with an intact uterus.[7–9] The relative risk of endometrial cancer increases with increasing duration of use of oestrogen-only HRT. The limited available evidence suggests that these effects wear off comparatively slowly after use stops, but it is unclear how long they last.[8,9] The addition of progestogen to oestrogen reduces the raised risk of endometrial cancer, and the more days per month progestogen is used, the greater the protection appears to be. Current use of continuous combined oestrogen-progestogen HRT brings endometrial cancer incidence rates down to levels similar to, or possibly slightly lower than, those in never users. The Women's Health Initiative trial reported a relative risk of endometrial cancer of 0.81 (95% CI 0.48–1.36) with continuous combined CEE and MPA after 5.6 years of follow-up.[10] The effect of tibolone on endometrial cancer is uncertain. It is also unknown how long the effects of combined HRT persist.

Coronary heart disease

Overall, randomised trials indicate no significant association between use of HRT and the risk of CHD (non-fatal myocardial infarction and cardiac death combined), with a summary relative risk of 1.11 (95% CI 0.98–1.26) in women randomised to HRT compared with those randomised to placebo (Figure 20.1). While most of the available evidence relates to use of combined oestrogen-progestogen HRT containing CEE and MPA, the limited data on other preparations indicate no significant difference between

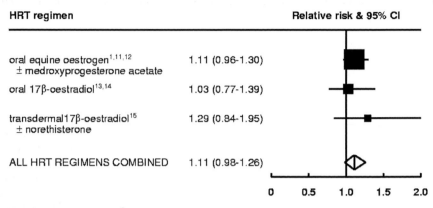

HRT regimen — **Relative risk & 95% CI**

HRT regimen	Relative risk & 95% CI
oral equine oestrogen[1,11,12] ± medroxyprogesterone acetate	1.11 (0.96-1.30)
oral 17β-oestradiol[13,14]	1.03 (0.77-1.39)
transdermal 17β-oestradiol[15] ± norethisterone	1.29 (0.84-1.95)
ALL HRT REGIMENS COMBINED	1.11 (0.98-1.26)

Test for heterogeneity: $\chi^2_2 = 0.74$, p=0.7

Figure 20.1. Incidence of coronary heart disease in major randomised trials of HRT, according to the HRT regimen used.

the effect on CHD of this formulation and other types of HRT, including transdermal preparations (Figure 20.1).[11–15]

Although the combined randomised trial data for HRT and CHD do not demonstrate any significant effect on risk, concerns have been raised by the results of the two largest randomised trials published to date that the relative risk of CHD varies according to time since therapy has commenced.[16,17] Table 20.3 presents a summary of the results for CHD in the Heart and Estrogen/Progestin Replacement Study (HERS) and the WHI randomised trials, showing the relative risk of CHD in women randomised to oestrogen-progestogen HRT compared with placebo, separately for the first and subsequent years of follow-up. The overall relative risk of incident CHD during the first year of follow-up is 1.63 (95% CI 1.18–2.24) and differs significantly from the overall relative risk of 0.99 (95% CI 0.89–1.14) for CHD occurring in the

Table 20.3. Relative risk of coronary heart disease (non-fatal myocardial infarction and coronary artery disease death combined) among women randomised to oestrogen-progestogen HRT compared with placebo, in the Heart and Estrogen/Progestin Replacement Study and Women's Health Initiative randomised trials, during the first and subsequent years of follow-up

Study	Relative risk (95% CI) of coronary heart disease in women randomised to oestrogen-progestogen HRT compared to placebo	
	During first year of follow-up	During subsequent years of follow-up
Heart and Estrogen/Progestin Replacement Study[11]	1.52 (1.01–2.29)	0.92 (0.77–1.09)
Women's Health Initiative[17]	1.81 (1.09–3.01)	1.14 (0.89–1.45)[a]
Summary	**1.63 (1.18–2.24)**	**0.99 (0.89–1.14)**

Test for heterogeneity: summary first versus subsequent years of follow-up: $\chi^2_1 = 7.9$, $P = 0.005$; [a] obtained by summarising the hazard ratios[17] for years 2 to ≥6

subsequent years of follow-up (Table 20.3). This suggests that the risk of adverse CHD events with use of oestrogen-progestogen HRT may be high in the first year after commencement of use. What is clear is that there is no randomised trial evidence that shows any protective effect of HRT on CHD.

Stroke

Randomised trials are consistent in finding an increased risk of stroke among women randomised to take HRT, compared with those randomised to placebo, with a summary relative risk of 1.27 (95% CI 1.06–1.51).[3] There is also observational evidence that HRT increases the risk of stroke.[18] It is not clear whether the relationship between HRT and stroke varies according to the subtype of stroke. None of the individual trials to date has found a significant difference between the effect of HRT on ischaemic or haemorrhagic stroke,[13,19,20] and a summary of data from trials with appropriate information does not demonstrate significant heterogeneity between the relative risk of ischaemic stroke and the relative risk of haemorrhagic stroke in women randomised to oestrogen-progestogen HRT compared with placebo (χ_1^2(heterogeneity) = 0.7, $P = 0.4$; Table 20.4). However, there were only 63 cases of haemorrhagic stroke in the combined trial data, so the power to investigate the difference in these relationships is limited. It is also uncertain to what extent effects on stroke persist after use of HRT ceases, nor is it known whether effects vary with the specific type of HRT or the duration of use.

Pulmonary embolism

Women randomised to take HRT have around twice the risk of having a PE, compared with women randomised to placebo.[3] These data are consistent with findings from observational studies demonstrating an elevated risk of venous thromboembolism (VTE) in women using HRT, compared with never users.[21,22] Data from randomised trials show the greatest elevation in the risk of VTE in the first year after starting use, and in the WHI there was a significant trend of declining (but still elevated) relative risks of VTE over the five years of follow-up.[1,16]

Table 20.4. Relative risk of different subtypes of stroke in women randomised to oestrogen-progestogen HRT compared with those randomised to placebo in three randomised trials

	Relative risk (95% CI) of stroke in women randomised to oestrogen-progestogen HRT compared with placebo	
	Ischaemic stroke	Haemorrhagic stroke
Heart and Estrogen/Progestin Replacement Study[20]	1.18 (0.83–1.67)	1.65 (0.47–5.72)
Women's Estrogen for Stroke Trial[13]	1.11 (0.74–1.67)[a]	1.34 (0.41–4.32)[a]
Women's Health Initiative[19]	1.44 (1.09–1.90)	0.82 (0.43–1.56)
Summary	**1.27 (1.06–1.55)**	**1.01 (0.61–1.70)**

Test for heterogeneity: ischaemic versus haemorrhagic stroke: $\chi_1^2 = 0.7$, $P = 0.4$; [a] obtained by summarising the hazard ratios for fatal and non-fatal stroke subtypes

Fractured neck of femur

Randomised trials and observational studies find that the risk of hip fracture is reduced by around 30–40% in women currently taking HRT, compared with never users (Table 20.1).[3,23] The effect of HRT on fracture appears to wear off once use ceases, with no significant protective effect of HRT on fracture apparent in past users.[24-26] Although evidence is limited, there does not appear to be any large difference between the protective effect of oestrogen-only or oestrogen-progestogen HRT on fracture.[24-26]

Relative risk according to women's personal characteristics

The cause-specific relative risks associated with use of HRT have not been found to vary significantly for women with varying background risks of disease or personal characteristics, including age, ethnic background, history of serious illness, smoking patterns, family history and use of various medications.[1-3,5] However, there is evidence from observational studies that the relative risk of breast cancer associated with use of HRT is greater in leaner compared with fatter women.[2,5]

Use of HRT and the absolute incidence of disease

At this stage, a robust assessment of the effect of use of HRT on the risk of major disease is possible for use of oestrogen-progestogen HRT only, since randomised data regarding the effect of oestrogen-only HRT and other types of HRT are limited. The absolute incidences of breast cancer, colorectal cancer, CHD, stroke, PE and hip fracture among users of oestrogen-progestogen HRT and nonusers of HRT are presented, based on data from the WHI randomised trial. Women participating in this trial were in their mid-60s, on average, during the trial, and overall incidence rates from the trial in users and nonusers of HRT are assumed to apply to women aged 60–69 years. Since the cause-specific relative risks for women randomised to oestrogen-progestogen HRT compared with placebo found in the trial did not vary significantly by age, the ratio of incidence rates at age 50–59 years compared with age 60–69 years is assumed to be the ratio of age-specific rates typical of women in developed countries: 0.8 for breast cancer,[5] 0.3 for CHD and stroke,[27] 0.4 for PE,[27] 0.4 for colorectal cancer,[28] and 0.2 for hip fracture.[29] All analyses are by 'intention to treat' and, because the average period of randomisation is around five years, they are assumed to reflect use of oestrogen-progestogen HRT of around five years' duration. The incidences of the different conditions in the tables are added together, giving equal weight to each condition.

Use of oestrogen-progestogen HRT among women 50–59 years old

Among 1000 postmenopausal women aged 50–59 years who have never used HRT, an estimated 26.5 women would develop one of the six conditions of interest over a five-year period (Table 20.1). If these women used oestrogen-progestogen HRT for five years, the number diagnosed with these conditions would increase to an estimated 31.9 per 1000 women, resulting from an excess of breast cancer, CHD, stroke and PE of around 7.1 per 1000 women and a deficit of colorectal cancer and hip fracture of around 1.7 per 1000.

Use of oestrogen-progestogen HRT among women 60–69 years old

Among 1000 postmenopausal women aged 60–69 years who have never used HRT, an estimated 61.5 women would develop one of the six conditions of interest over a five-year period (Table 20.2). If these women used oestrogen-progestogen HRT for five years, the number diagnosed with these conditions would increase to 71.5 per 1000 women, resulting from an extra 15.5 cases of breast cancer, CHD, stroke and PE and 5.5 fewer cases of colorectal cancer and hip fracture.

Discussion

Main findings

At the ages examined here, long-term use of oestrogen-progestogen HRT is associated with greater harm than benefit, in terms of major clinical conditions. The net absolute excess of harmful events associated with use of oestrogen-progestogen HRT is higher in women aged 60–69 years than in women aged 50–59 years. Breast cancer is the most common serious condition in women aged 50–69 years and its incidence is strongly related to use of HRT; it therefore makes the largest contribution to the overall risk–benefit analysis.

Our summary estimates and overall risk versus benefit assessment give equal weight to each of the conditions examined here. Women considering use of HRT may place different emphasis on different conditions, as part of an informed decision on whether or not to use it. The figures presented here relate to relatively common, potentially life-threatening conditions and do not consider the effect of HRT on other conditions, such as deep vein thrombosis, vertebral fracture, incontinence, gall bladder disease and endometrial hyperplasia. There is very good evidence that HRT improves vasomotor symptoms in perimenopausal women, and for some these symptoms continue postmenopausally. While it is possible to estimate the likely effect of HRT on these conditions, it is difficult to compare them directly and meaningfully to one another and to weight them alongside potentially life-threatening conditions. They are therefore not included in the risk–benefit analyses. Although dementia is associated with high subsequent mortality, it is also not included in the risk–benefit equation, as reliable data are too limited at present. The only randomised data available on the relationship between HRT and the risk of dementia are from the WHI, which found a significantly increased risk of incident dementia in women randomised to take oestrogen-progestogen HRT, compared with placebo. However, this is based on a total of only 61 incident cases of probable dementia.[30] Data from randomised trials do not suggest any meaningful beneficial effect of HRT on quality of life in women without menopausal symptoms.[31,32]

Use of oestrogen-only HRT

The findings presented here relate predominantly to oestrogen-progestogen HRT, because of the limitations of the data currently available on oestrogen-only HRT. However, it is possible to speculate on the possible overall effects of oestrogen-only HRT, based on the current evidence. The available data indicate that use of oestrogen-only HRT results in a lesser increase in the risk of breast cancer than use of oestrogen-progestogen HRT[2] and that, among women with a uterus, use of oestrogen-only HRT results in a greater increase in the risk of endometrial cancer than use of oestrogen-progestogen HRT. The limited data on coronary disease do not suggest large differences in risk according to use of different types of HRT, however, it is not possible to quantify reliably the effects of oestrogen-only HRT on risk (Figure 20.1).

Based on data from the Million Women Study, among 1000 postmenopausal women starting use of HRT at age 50 years, five years' use of oestrogen-only HRT is estimated to increase the absolute incidence of breast cancer by around 1.5 per 1000 users, while five years' use of oestrogen-progestogen HRT is estimated to increase the number of breast cancers by around 6 per 1000 users.[2] Among women with a uterus, five years' use of oestrogen-only HRT, starting at age 50 years, would be expected to increase the incidence of endometrial cancer by around 2.3 per 1000 women (assuming a background incidence of 1.5 per 1000 women aged 50–54 years over a five-year period and relative risks of 1.4 and 2.8 for <1 and 1–4 years' use of oestrogen-only HRT compared with never users, respectively[33]). Use of combined oestrogen-progestogen HRT, particularly where progestogen is taken throughout the cycle, does not appear to result in substantial changes in endometrial cancer incidence.[10] This means that for women with a uterus in their early 50s, five years' use of oestrogen-only HRT appears to result in a somewhat lower total number of extra breast and endometrial cancers than five years' use of combined oestrogen-progestogen HRT (3.8 for oestrogen-only versus 6 for oestrogen-progestogen HRT). Although the magnitude of the effect of oestrogen-only HRT on other conditions is uncertain, its harmful effects on these would have to be considerably larger than the effects of oestrogen-progestogen in order to offset the extra breast cancers resulting from use of oestrogen-progestogen HRT.

Another implication of these findings is that, although there is likely to be an excess of harmful events in women who have had a hysterectomy and are using oestrogen-only HRT, the overall excess of harmful events is likely to be smaller than that seen in women with a uterus using either oestrogen-only or oestrogen-progestogen HRT. Results from the oestrogen-only arm of the WHI randomised trial are expected to be available in 2005 and will provide much-needed randomised evidence on the effects of oestrogen-only HRT.

Methodological considerations

The relative and absolute risks used in this paper are by 'intention to treat' within the randomised trials, as this provides an unbiased estimate of the relationship between use of HRT and disease. However, since a substantial proportion of women (25–42%) ceased taking the study medications over the course of the two larger trials,[1,16] these are likely to be underestimates of the true effect of current use of HRT. There is a possibility of slight bias towards higher adverse effects because of the fact that the WHI oestrogen-progestogen HRT arm stopped early but this is likely to be much less than bias induced by noncompliance. It has been suggested that those taking HRT are more likely to go to their doctor with breast problems and so are more likely to be diagnosed with cancer. The WHI trial found that mammography rates on treatment and placebo were similar so this was not an explanation of their results. In the Million Women Study all women were participating in a breast screening programme and any difference in rates of GP attendance could not explain the increase in the number of screen-detected cancers. It is possible that more HRT users attended screening but this does not bias the within-study comparison of users and nonusers.

A key element of making the available evidence regarding HRT and disease risk applicable and meaningful to the broader population is the translation of relative risks into absolute risks. This translation is possible because the relative risks of disease associated with the use of HRT in the relevant randomised trials do not vary significantly according to women's background characteristics, and can therefore be reasonably generalised to the broader population. The translation of relative risks into absolute risks also depends on the availability of reliable age-specific disease incidence rates from a suitable population, which presents more challenging issues.

Difficulties arise in obtaining reliable age-specific incidence rates of relevant diseases among women eligible to use HRT. For cancer outcomes, reliable incidence rates are available through cancer registries. For other conditions, such as stroke and hip fracture, it is less clear which rates are most appropriate. Some hospital-based statistics are available for these conditions.[34,35] However, these rates may count women more than once and include women who are frail and ill, and who would not typically use HRT. It is for these reasons that the quantitative review on which much of this paper is based uses incidence rates from the WHI to estimate age-specific absolute incidences of disease in users and nonusers of HRT. If rates from hospital statistics were used to estimate absolute incidences for conditions such as stroke and hip fracture, then the absolute excess and reduction in the respective incidences of these conditions associated with use of HRT would be larger than those presented here.

Generalisability and validity

Some critics of the WHI have argued that the women, aged 50–79 years, included in the study were particularly unhealthy, in that 36% were hypertensive or were using antihypertensive medications, 1.8% had had a myocardial infarction, 2.8% had angina, 0.8% had had a stroke and 69% were overweight (i.e. they had a body mass index of 25 or greater). This, together with the fact that the mean age of participants at recruitment was around 63 years, has been used as grounds to question the validity of the trial in examining the effect of HRT in the primary prevention of disease and the generalisability of the results, especially to women outside the USA.[36,37] Aside from the fact that the overall effects of combined HRT found in the WHI did not vary significantly by age, past medical history or use of other medications the women in the study do not appear to differ dramatically from women in the general population on a number of measures. For example, among women aged 50–64 years from the general population in the UK who joined the Million Women Study, although the prevalence of obesity (i.e. body mass index 30 or greater) was considerably lower than in the WHI population, 3.8% reported previous heart disease, 1.0% reported having had a stroke in the past and 15% reported current treatment for hypertension.[38] Considered broadly, the current evidence suggests that, for most conditions, the findings from the WHI and other trials are likely to be generalisable and probably provide the most appropriate background incidence rates at present.

The overall results shown here relate to hypothetical groups of 1000 healthy postmenopausal women aged 50–59 and 60–69 years, and represent the estimated average effect of HRT on the absolute risk of various conditions. However, the absolute risk of a particular condition will vary according to a woman's background risk of disease: the higher her background risk of a particular condition, the greater will be the absolute effect of use of HRT, in terms of both risks and benefits. Thus, women with a family history of breast cancer are likely to experience a greater absolute excess incidence of breast cancer if they use HRT, compared with women who do not have relatives with breast cancer, and women with osteoporosis are likely to have a greater absolute reduction in hip fracture incidence compared with women without osteoporosis. It should be noted that even among women at an increased risk of having a fracture, the WHI found no net benefit of use of HRT.[23] Age is by far the strongest risk factor for hip fracture and the rates for this increase dramatically above age 70 years, so that the benefit of HRT use in older women may be higher. However, stroke rates also increase a great deal with age, so that the risk–benefit balance is still unlikely to be favourable at higher ages. The problem is that the most common pattern of HRT use, starting at ages around 50 years and stopping soon thereafter, is unlikely to confer later benefit on fracture rates.[24-26]

For most conditions, including breast cancer, endometrial cancer, colorectal cancer, PE and fracture, the results regarding the effect of HRT from randomised trials and observational studies are in accordance with one another. For CHD, findings have appeared to be less consistent. Observational studies have reported finding a decreased risk of CHD in women using HRT compared with nonusers.[39,40] In apparent contrast, randomised trials do not show a significant beneficial effect of HRT on CHD.[3] A possible explanation for these findings is that women who use HRT have a lower pre-existing risk of CHD than nonusers. This is evidenced by the fact that women who use HRT are less likely than nonusers to have a history of conditions predisposing to incident CHD, including previous heart disease, diabetes mellitus, stroke, VTE and hypertension, as well as having a generally more favourable cardiovascular risk profile.[41-44] Findings from the Million Women Study also suggest that among women with conditions such as diabetes mellitus and clotting disorders, those with more severe disease are less likely to use HRT than those with milder disease, indicating that straightforward adjustment for the presence or absence of disease is unlikely to account completely for the bias resulting from preferential prescribing of HRT to healthier women.[41] Because the predisposing conditions for myocardial infarction are well known, biased prescribing of HRT to women without early signs of or risk factors for CVD is a specific problem for observational studies examining the relationship between HRT and CHD and stroke. These issues do not apply in the same way to observational studies of HRT and other conditions, such as cancer or fracture, where disease onset is less predictable and prescribing is less likely to be biased by known risk factors. For other CVD, particularly for VTE, observational and randomised evidence have been consistent in terms of relative effects, although observational studies have tended to underestimate rates of VTE in HRT users, owing to concentration on idiopathic cases.

Concerns have also been raised that the lack of protection against CHD seen in the randomised trials might be a consequence of the specific type of HRT used in the HERS and the WHI, i.e. CEE and MPA.[45] However, based on the current available evidence, the lack of protection against CHD is statistically consistent across the trials published to date, regardless of the specific HRT used (Figure 20.1). Finally, it has also been argued that HRT needs to be initiated around the time of the menopause and prior to the development of atherosclerosis in order to prevent future CHD.[36,37] This hypothesis is not supported by the finding in the randomised trials that the effects of HRT on CHD do not vary significantly by age, nor do they differ significantly between women with and without a past history of CVD.[3,11,17]

The reason for the apparent variation in the risk of CHD and VTE according to year of follow-up found in the randomised trials is not known. However, it is possible that there are sub-groups of women at high risk of clotting who cease using HRT once they have a CVD event. The remaining pool of users would then be at a lower risk of a cardiovascular event with use of HRT, so the apparent decline could be due to this 'survivor' effect. Declining adherence to treatment is also likely to result in attenuation of risks with increasing time since randomisation.

The findings regarding the protective effect of oestrogen-progestogen HRT on colorectal cancer are puzzling. Colorectal cancer does not show a notable change in rate around the menopause nor are there marked male–female differences in rate or large differences in risk associated with reproductive patterns. Yet, the reduction in the relative risk of colorectal cancer among users of oestrogen-progestogen HRT is comparable to, or greater than, the elevation in relative risk seen for breast cancer, which is strongly related to hormonal and reproductive risk factors. The nature of the relationship between colorectal cancer and HRT, together with possible aetiological mechanisms, therefore requires further clarification.

Use of HRT by women with a premature menopause

Because randomised trials and observational studies have tended to focus on women aged 50 years and over, data regarding the effects of use of HRT on younger women are lacking. Information to guide prescription of HRT to women with a premature menopause is therefore extremely limited. Estimation of the absolute effects of HRT in this particular group is also made more difficult by the fact that it is hard to predict how premature menopause would affect the background rates of many of the relevant conditions. If the relative risks of disease associated with use of HRT in postmenopausal women aged 50 years and over are assumed to apply to postmenopausal women under 50 years, then two general points can be made. First, because background rates of disease are lower in younger compared with older women, the overall absolute excess of breast cancer, stroke and PE and reduction in colorectal cancer and hip fracture among women using HRT in their 40s is likely to be smaller than that seen among women using HRT in their 50s and 60s. Secondly, because breast cancer is less steeply age-related than colorectal cancer and hip fracture, breast cancer is of greater relative importance at young ages. Hence the overall effect of use of HRT by women in their 40s will be dominated by its effects on breast cancer.

Mortality

Evidence regarding the effect of HRT on overall mortality and on mortality from various conditions is inevitably limited and the existing randomised trials are too small to be able to provide much-needed reliable evidence on cause-specific mortality and HRT. However, the evidence that is available suggests that use of HRT increases mortality from breast cancer[2] and that use of oestrogen-only HRT increases mortality from endometrial cancer.[7] A 2002 review of randomised trials found a summary relative risk of death of 1.03 (95% CI 0.90–1.18) in women randomised to HRT compared with those randomised to placebo, indicating that HRT used for about five years does not appear to have an immediate, substantial and nonspecific effect on mortality.[3]

Outstanding questions

This paper is based on the current available evidence regarding HRT and disease risk. There are a number of outstanding questions relating to the effects of HRT. In particular, evidence on the effects of different types of HRT on the risk of many diseases is lacking, as is information on the effects of duration of use and persistence of effects after use has ceased. While randomised controlled trials provide unbiased data regarding the effects of HRT, the number of trial participants developing major incident disease is relatively small, and deaths are even fewer. For example, a summary of the available randomised evidence yields a total of around 360 women with incident breast cancer, 140 with incident colorectal cancer and 160 with a fractured neck of femur.[3] This means that for rare but important conditions, such as endometrial and ovarian cancer, and cause-specific mortality, existing trials will be unable to provide reliable information on the effects of HRT. These limitations aside, the current evidence indicates that long-term use of oestrogen-progestogen HRT results in greater harm than benefit, in terms of the conditions considered here.

Acknowledgements

We thank Valerie Beral for her comments on the manuscript and Adrian Goodill for creating Figure 20.1.

Addendum

The results from the oestrogen-only arm of the Women's Health Initiative were published in April 2004, after the early cessation of this trial.[46] This increases dramatically the amount of randomised information available regarding the effects of oestrogen alone on major diseases and this addendum aims to take note of these new results, which were published too recently to be incorporated into the main body of this chapter.

The oestrogen-only arm of the WHI trial randomised 10 739 women who had had a hysterectomy to receive either 0.625 mg CEE daily or placebo. The trial found a significantly elevated risk of stroke and a significantly reduced risk of hip fracture in women randomised to oestrogen-only HRT compared with placebo, with relative risks of 1.39 (95% CI 1.10–1.77) and 0.61 (95% CI 0.41–0.91), respectively. The incidences of CHD (0.91, 95% CI 0.75–1.12), breast cancer (0.77, 95% CI 0.59–1.01), PE (1.34, 95% CI 0.87–2.06) and colorectal cancer (1.08, 95% CI 0.75–1.55) did not differ significantly between the groups.

Broad consideration of the published evidence to date, incorporating these results, indicates that there is no significant beneficial effect of either oestrogen-only or combined oestrogen-progestogen HRT on the risk of CHD and that use of either type of HRT results in an elevated risk of stroke and PE and a reduction in the risk of hip fracture. Randomised controlled trials and observational studies find a substantial increase in the risk of breast cancer among users of combined oestrogen-progestogen HRT. Breast cancer risk is increased to a lesser extent among users of oestrogen-only HRT, although results from trials and observational studies remain consistent with a small increase in risk compared with women who have never used HRT.[47] The data raise the possibility that use of oestrogen-progestogen HRT may reduce the risk of colorectal cancer to a greater extent that use of oestrogen-only HRT, although the evidence is too limited for any meaningful conclusions to be reached at this stage.

Overall, the data indicate that long-term use of HRT is unlikely to result in a net benefit, in terms of the conditions considered here. Use of oestrogen-progestogen HRT appears to be associated with a greater excess of adverse events than use of oestrogen-only HRT.

References

1.   Rossouw JE, Anderson GL, Prentice RL, LaCroix AZ, Kooperberg C, Stefanick ML, *et al.*; Writing Group for the Women's Health Initiative Investigators. Risks and benefits of estrogen plus progestin in healthy postmenopausal women: principal results fom the Women's Health Initiative randomized controlled trial. *JAMA* 2002;288:321–33.

2.   Beral V; Million Women Study Collaborators. Breast cancer and hormone-replacement therapy in the Million Women Study. *Lancet* 2003;362:419–27. Erratum in: *Lancet* 2003;362:1160.

3.   Beral V, Banks E, Reeves G. Evidence from randomised trials on the long-term effects of hormone replacement therapy. *Lancet* 2002;360:942–4.

4. Beral V, Banks E, Reeves G. Long term effects of hormone replacement therapy. *Lancet* 2003;361:254–5.

5. Collaborative Group on Hormonal Factors in Breast Cancer. Breast cancer and hormone replacement therapy: collaborative reanalysis of data from 51 epidemiological studies of 52,705 women with breast cancer and 108,411 women without breast cancer. *Lancet* 1997;350:1047–59. Erratum in: *Lancet* 1997;350:1484.

6. Chlebowski RT, Hendrix SL, Langer RD, Stefanick ML, Gass M, Lane D, et al.; WHI Investigators. Influence of estrogen plus progestin on breast cancer and mammography in healthy postmenopausal women. *JAMA* 2003;289:3243–53.

7. Beral V, Banks E, Reeves G, Appleby P. Use of HRT and the subsequent risk of cancer. *J Epidemiol Biostat* 1999;4:191–215.

8. Pike MC, Peters RK, Cozen W, Probst-Hensch NM, Felix JC, Wan PC, et al. Estrogen-progestin replacement therapy and endometrial cancer. *J Natl Cancer Inst* 1997;89:1110–6.

9. Weiderpass E, Adami HO, Baron JA, Magnusson C, Bergstrom R, Lindgren A, et al. Risk of endometrial cancer following estrogen replacement with and without progestins. *J Natl Cancer Inst* 1999;91:1131–7.

10. Anderson GL, Judd HL, Kaunitz AM, Barad DH, Beresford SA, Pettinger M, et al.; Women's Health Initiative Investigators. Effects of estrogen plus progestin on gynecologic cancers and associated diagnostic procedures: the Women's Health Initiative randomized trial. JAMA 2003;290:1739–48.

11. Grady D, Herrington D, Bittner V, Blumenthal R, Davidson M, Hlatky M, et al.; HERS Research Group. Cardiovascular disease outcomes during 6.8 years of hormone therapy. *JAMA* 2002;288:49–57. Erratum in: *JAMA* 2002;288:1064.

12. Waters DD, Alderman EL, Hsia J, Howard BV, Cobb FR, Rogers WJ, et al. Effects of hormone replacement therapy and antioxidant vitamin supplements on coronary atherosclerosis in postmenopausal women: a randomized controlled trial. *JAMA* 2002;288:2432–40.

13. Viscoli CM, Brass LM, Kernan WN, Sarrel PM, Suissa S, Horwitz RI. A clinical trial of estrogen-replacement therapy after ischemic stroke. *N Engl J Med* 2001;345:1243–9.

14. The ESPRIT team. Oestrogen therapy for the prevention of reinfarction in postmenopausal women: a randomised placebo controlled trial. *Lancet* 2002;360:2001–8.

15. Clarke SC, Kelleher J, Lloyd-Jones H, Slack M, Schofiel PM. A study of hormone replacement therapy in postmenopausal women with ischaemic heart disease: the Papworth HRT atherosclerosis study. *BJOG* 2002;109:1056–62.

16. Hulley S, Grady D, Bush T, Furberg C, Herrington D, Riggs B, et al. Randomized trial of estrogen plus progestin for secondary prevention of coronary heart disease in postmenopausal women. Heart and Estrogen/progestin Replacement Study (HERS) Research Group. *JAMA* 1998;280:605–13.

17. Manson JE, Hsia J, Johnson KC, Rossouw JE, Assaf AR, Lasser NL, et al.; Women's Health Initiative Investigators. Estrogen plus progestin and the risk of coronary heart disease. *N Engl J Med* 2003;349:523–34.

18. Grodstein F, Manson JE, Colditz GA, Willett WC, Speizer FE, Stampfer MJ. A prospective, observational study of postmenopausal hormone therapy and primary prevention of cardiovascular disease. *Ann Intern Med* 2000;133:933–41.

19. Wassertheil-Smoller S, Hendrix SL, Limacher M, Heiss G, Kooperberg C, Baird A, et al.; WHI Investigators. Effect of estrogen plus progestin on stroke in postmenopausal women: the Women's Health Initiative: a randomized trial. *JAMA* 2003;289:2673–84.

20. Simon JA, Hsia J, Cauley JA, Richards C, Harris F, Fong J, et al. Postmenopausal hormone therapy and risk of stroke: The Heart and Estrogen-progestin Replacement Study (HERS). *Circulation* 2001;103:638–42.

21. Daly E, Vessey MP, Hawkins MM, Carson JL, Gough P, Marsh S. Risk of venous thromboembolism in users of hormone replacement therapy. *Lancet* 1996;348:977–80.

22. Daly E, Vessey MP, Painter R, Hawkins MM. Case–control study of venous thromboembolism risk in users of hormone replacement therapy. *Lancet* 1996;348:1027.

23. Cauley JA, Robbins J, Chen Z, Cummings SR, Jackson RD, LaCroix AZ, et al.; Women's Health Initiative Investigators. Effects of estrogen plus progestin on risk of fracture and bone mineral density: the Women's Health Initiative randomized trial. *JAMA* 2003;290:1729–38.

24. Michaelsson K, Baron JA, Farahmand BY, Johnell O, Magnusson C, Persson PG, et al. Hormone replacement therapy and risk of hip fracture: population based case-control study. The Swedish Hip Fracture Study Group. *BMJ* 1998;316:1858–63.

25. Weiss NS, Ure CL, Ballard JH, Williams AR, Daling JR. Decreased risk of fractures of the hip and lower forearm with postmenopausal use of estrogen. *N Engl J Med* 1980;303:1195–8.

26. Cauley JA, Seeley DG, Ensrud K, Ettinger B, Black D, Cummings SR. Estrogen replacement therapy and fractures in older women. *Ann Intern Med* 1995;122:9–16.

27.   Peto R, Lopez A, Borham J. *Mortality from Smoking in Developed Countries 1950–2000*. Oxford: Oxford University Press; 1994.
28.   Parkin DM, Whelan SL, Ferlay J, Raymond L, Young J. *Cancer Incidence in Five Continents*. Scientific Publication No. 143. Lyon: IARC; 1997.
29.   McCormick A, Fleming D, Charlton S. *Morbidity Statistics from General Practice. Fourth National Study, 1991–92*. Office of Populations Census and Surveys, Series MB5, No. 3. London: HM Stationery Office; 1995.
30.   Shumaker SA, Legault C, Rapp SR, Thal L, Wallace RB, Ockene JK, *et al.*; WHIMS Investigators. Estrogen plus progestin and the incidence of dementia and mild cognitive impairment in postmenopausal women: the Women's Health Initiative Memory Study: a randomized controlled trial. *JAMA* 2003;289:2651–62.
31.   Hays J, Ockene JK, Brunner RL, Kotchen JM, Manson JE, Patterson RE, *et al.*; Women's Health Initiative Investigators. Effects of estrogen plus progestin on health-related quality of life. *N Engl J Med* 2003;348:1839–54.
32.   Hlatky MA, Boothroyd D, Vittinghoff E, Sharp P, Whooley MA; Heart and Estrogen/Progestin Replacement Study (HERS) Research Group. Quality-of-life and depressive symptoms in postmenopausal women after receiving hormone therapy: results from the Heart and Estrogen/Progestin Replacement Study (HERS) trial. *JAMA* 2002;287:591–7.
33.   Grady D, Gebretsadik T, Kerlikowske K, Ernster V, Petitti D. Hormone replacement therapy and endometrial cancer risk: a meta-analysis. *Obstet Gynecol* 1995;85:304–12.
34.   Bacon WE, Maggi S, Looker A, Harris T, Nair CR, Giaconi J, *et al*. International comparison of hip fracture rates in 1988–89. *Osteoporos Int* 1996;6:69–75.
35.   Malmgren R, Bamford J, Warlow C, Sandercock P, Slattery J. Projecting the number of patients with first ever strokes and patients newly handicapped by stroke in England and Wales. *BMJ* 1989;298:656–60.
36.   Radford N, Church T. Risks of postmenopausal hormone replacement. *JAMA* 2002;288:2819.
37.   Speizer F. Risks of postmenopausal hormone replacement. *JAMA* 2002;288:2819–20.
38.   The Million Women Study Collaborative Group. The Million Women Study: design and characteristics of the study population. *Breast Cancer Res* 1999;1:73–80.
39.   Grodstein F, Stampfer M. The epidemiology of coronary heart disease and estrogen replacement in postmenopausal women. *Prog Cardiovasc Dis* 1995;38:199–210.
40.   Grodstein F, Stampfer MJ, Manson JE, Colditz GA, Willett WC, Rosner B, *et al*. Postmenopausal estrogen and progestin use and the risk of cardiovascular disease. *N Engl J Med* 1996;335:453–61. Erratum in: *N Engl J Med* 1996;335:1406.
41.   Million Women Study Collaborators. Patterns of use of hormone replacement therapy in one million women in Britain, 1996–2000. *BJOG* 2002;109:1319–30.
42.   Barrett-Connor E, Brown WV, Turner J, Austin M, Criqui MH. Heart disease risk factors and hormone use in postmenopausal women. *JAMA* 1979;241:2167–9.
43.   Matthews KA, Kuller LH, Wing RR, Meilahn EN, Plantinga P. Prior to use of estrogen replacement therapy, are users healthier than nonusers? *Am J Epidemiol* 1996;143:971–8.
44.   Rodstrom K, Bengtsson C, Lissner L, Bjorkelund C. Pre-existing risk factor profiles in users and non-users of hormone replacement therapy: prospective cohort study in Gothenberg, Sweden. *BMJ* 1999;319:890–3.
45.   Chan NN, Tong PC, Chow CC, Chan JC. Long-term effects of hormone replacement therapy. *Lancet* 2003;361:254.
46.   Anderson GL, Limacher M, Assaf AR, Bassford T, Beresford SA, Black H, *et al.*; Women's Health Initiative Steering Committee. Effects of conjugated equine estrogen in postmenopausal women with hysterectomy: the Women's Health Initiative randomized controlled trial. *JAMA* 2004;291:1701–12.
47.   Beral V, Banks E, Reeves G; Million Women Study Collaborators. Effects of estrogen-only treatment in postmenopausal women [letter]. *JAMA* 2004 11;292:684.

Chapter 21

The balance between risks and benefits of hormone replacement

Discussion

Discussion following Professor Barlow's paper

Burger: I saw that in the adverse events outcome you calculated, I think, it was an additional six per 10 000 women per year for cardiovascular events.

Barlow: Taken from the Manson paper.[1]

Burger: The Manson paper said that there was actually no relative risk increase for women who were less than nine years postmenopausal. They divided women by whether they were nine years or less postmenopausal, then I think it was 10–19, and then 20+ years. In the less than nine years the hazard ratio was about 0.85 or 0.89, which would seem to be the more relevant figure to use in actually saying that there probably would not be an increased cardiovascular event rate in this group of women being treated for symptoms.

Barlow: I very much agree with what you just said. What I quite deliberately did was to try always to use as bad a scenario as I could find. I was trying to take reasonably as adverse a difference as it has been quoted, just as I tried to be as helpful to the placebo response as possible – in that I could be seen as someone who was in favour of the treatment of symptomatic women. I wanted to try not to whitewash the other side of these figures, so I did not try to, in any way, downgrade what that might look like being on the other side of the equation. You know I could have taken the other line of years since menopause, but I felt it was actually easier to get to the figures across the range of issues by taking a ten year age band which is so nicely given to us.

Beral: It was quite an interesting idea, your last figure, but one of the problems is that the measures are not actually in the same units. The top one is a prevalence figure, whereas the other figures below are all incidence figures. So it is actually not directly comparing like with like because the incidence figures are per year of use and all those incidence figures will double in a year but the prevalence figures will stay the same. It is an interesting idea but they are actually not the same units and I think you need to think about that a bit. The other thing that I would say is about the fractures. I think it is not necessarily fair to put a fractured finger in the same context as a colon cancer. So some of those fractures, although quite important, are just not in the same league as the other events. This is the point about duration of use: the longer you use it, the more those numbers accumulate.

Barlow: I wondered when I made the slides whether I should leave that part out. I just put it in to show the numbers, if you like. I think the real question is maybe what do you do if this is the experience for the whole group and we are talking about two years of treatment or four years of treatment, maybe one takes the annualised figures and multiplies them by four for a table like this.

Gray: Can one assess in any way the impact of the recalls for mammography because you cannot measure anxiety although that is always the question about screening programmes? But certainly some of the women presumably were subjected to triple assessment with biopsies. But nonetheless it does represent significant workload and significant anxiety. Is there any way of getting a handle on that?

Barlow: I am sure there would be. If you are on cyclical HRT then there is the question of what, if any, monitoring you are going to do with the uterine situation versus using continuous combined. So you have got interventional things to think about depending on which route you choose.

Lowe: I think this kind of table is what everybody wants. I hope tomorrow morning we will discuss how this can be put in the form of easy communication to patients, GPs, or whatever. But if I were a woman, I would think that, well, these are average kind of things but I am an individual woman. I wonder, based on discussions yesterday and today, whether you could produce a kind of ready-reckoner for a woman – maybe this is done already or somebody is developing it – in which you could factor in several easy things such as age, smoking and obesity which have an interaction both for cancer and cardiovascular disease. Then try to come back with a kind of individualised form of this, which might be more applicable to the individual woman.

Barlow: The answer is yes, but it is having the tools to do so. It is knowing what to factor into that ready-reckoner to make it work. But to an extent it would be possible.

Pitkin: Well, it has been tried to some extent with bones and fracture prevention, to try to predict people who might be more at risk of fracture, and some studies have shown some success and others have found that these indexes have not worked. So perhaps it would be a bit more difficult than it sounds on face value. I get slightly concerned when we start doing that because it is the same as integrated care pathways and protocols and guidelines. They are only guidelines and protocols and they are becoming more and more carved into tablets of stone with less and less individuality for individual cases and freedom for the clinician. That becomes quite medically and legally relevant, but it could be looked at.

Gray: From the GP point of view, I perceive that a lot of the problem that we have is that the women do not appreciate that those studies were on an average age of 63, which I think a lot of their GPs do not appreciate either. We need to make this age-specific, literally the ten-year cohorts or, even better still, five-year cohorts. If that could be produced for the individual's risk without integrating the risks that would still be helpful.

Lumsden: I think that one of the problems with the ready-reckoner is that my understanding is that for most women the fear of breast cancer actually outweighs absolutely everything else. Telling them that they might have a very small chance of having a venous thromboembolism or something else is not as significant as the chance of breast cancer. What we need to get across to them, I think, is the likelihood of that above everything else. The picture that came out of the *Lancet* 1997 paper[2] of the different increases of breast cancer with different duration of use is one of the most useful things that I have ever had in my clinic. If we could have something like that maybe for what is really important for the women in question.

Studd: I think Dr Lumsden is both right and wrong in this respect. It depends on how well the women feel. When you balance the quality of life, it is not just vasomotor symptoms, it is insomnia, it is being wide awake, it is energy, it is libido, marital harmony, anxiety, even depression. It is very difficult in fact to persuade women to come off therapy if you are doing your job and if you have targeted the right symptoms with the right treatments. I will give an example: I have 100 consecutive patients who are using implants for ten years, and I ask them whether they want to come off therapy or not. They are all well, they are mostly on oestradiol and testosterone, mostly on the lowest dose, E25, T25. Out of 100 only three want to come off and can be persuaded to stop. In the questionnaire there is a line – 'are you aware that there is almost certainly an increased risk of breast cancer?' Yes, they are aware of that but, nevertheless, they are feeling well and they do not want to come off, and you stress breast cancer. These women say 'I realise that there is a small extra risk, but I feel well, I do not want to go back to being mad, or depressed with loss of energy.' When you ask them what symptoms they get when the implants wear off after six months, it is not flushes and sweats, it is loss of energy, confidence, concentration and libido, and depression. These people are not interested in short-term therapy once they are well. If they are not better, there is no problem. But the problem is with women who feel better.

Pitkin: I think that is true and that is the grey area with short-term therapy and long-term therapy. Short-term people want to continue then merge on into the long-term problem. There is a fine transition. A lot of women do not want to come off, exactly as you say, and if we factor in a plan such as Professor Lowe has just mentioned, it has to include these other symptoms, albeit more nebulous and less complained of, not just vasomotor symptoms all the time.

Barlow: If you are to bring other symptoms in there, say, psychological symptoms, I do not know what the placebo response would be. It would certainly be something. But the difference would be that you would know within a few weeks or a couple of months whether you are actually getting any effect on the symptom. If you are not, the woman is just not going to stay on the stuff anyway, if she is, and she is getting the benefit, then it is the same thing.

Barlow: I think one thing I want to say about the MHRA statement on HRT and osteoporosis in December 2003 is that they were quite clearly saying that they were talking about long-term treatment in asymptomatic women. They were not talking about anything like this. The message is getting lost in the system and with the media. The GPs, for whatever reason, do not want to be doing this sort of treatment and it is these women who are getting caught up in all this.

Magnusson: Can I just ask, since I have no clinical experience whatsoever, what happens if women use short-term HRT? Does that mean that they just postpone their menopausal symptoms, or is it a totally different story when you come off it after three years?

Pitkin: It is very individual. Some women will come off it and will be very happy and some will come off it and not be happy, even if you phase it down gradually.

Magnusson: That seems important, if you are going through the same experience at the age of 50 or the age of 53.

Pitkin: Subjectively, and this is subjectively, by 55 I would say probably about 40% will come off happily without any symptoms and 60% will have some symptomatology. You would either have to restart or you certainly have to climb down very slowly. We would all say something slightly different as a ballpark figure from clinical practice, if you asked each of us.

Rees: Professor Barlow and I did a study with Janet Brockie[3] many years ago that showed that by the age of 60 less than 10% of women were actually still flushing. So, if you stop HRT too early you are quite likely to have flushes because you were due to flush anyway but it is much less the later you stop. But there is this small cohort of women who come to specialist menopause clinics – they are not seen in primary care – who will continue to flush to the end of their days and simply require oestrogen.

Burger: One other point, your calculations are clearly based on 0.625 mg of conjugated equine oestrogen and 2.5 mg of Provera® (medroxyprogesterone acetate, MPA). From such data as is available the suggestion would be that the rates of many of the problems would be less and the rate of cure of symptoms would not be too different if you used doses that are two-thirds of that or even a bit less.

Barlow: Maybe, but I do not know a substantial trial that proves that. But the point of doing it this way was: this is per 10 000 women per year. If you go to many GPs, if you go to women, they will maybe think the numbers are ten-or twenty-fold larger than those they see in the media. It was to try to get a feel for the scale of numbers that I did it this way. I think they are much smaller numerators than the public and many GPs think. But I am not trying to negate the fact that breast cancer is a huge concern.

Discussion following Professor Evans's paper

Stevenson: With regard to the implication you made about the coronary heart disease findings in the observational studies, you said that lifestyle affects coronary heart disease risk, which is absolutely right, and therefore there will be the healthy user bias with the HRT users.

Evans: It is more subtle than a healthy user. Healthy user is a technical term in epidemiology and it is not just a healthy user effect.

Stevenson: Lifestyle clearly affects fractures but yet you do not see the disparity between the observational studies and the randomised trials for osteoporosis. Another point that I would make is that for coronary heart disease, which is the most peculiar of all the things you have looked at, I still think that we can explain in rational biological terms the early harm, later benefit concept. So far, we have only looked at one HRT regimen in a couple of sets of women.

Evans: Now I would entirely agree with you in terms of the regimens and they could have different effects. I disagree with you over osteoporosis and the coronary heart disease – I think there are special factors for coronary heart disease. For example, the fact that somebody with diabetes will have much less chance of ending up in trials. People with a family history, you would think that perhaps particularly in the USA, during the time that the Women's Health Initiative was started, that those at high risk of coronary heart disease might be given HRT because of beliefs it might be protective. It turned out that this was not nearly as true as you might expect.

Stevenson: Did you know that diabetes is a risk factor for osteoporosis as well?

Evans: Yes, diabetes is a risk factor for osteoporosis, but nothing like a strong risk factor like it is for coronary heart disease. Am I wrong on that?

Stevenson: No, I agree, it is not a strong risk factor.

Evans: I think they are not quite the same thing. Exercise is probably the biggest lifestyle factor, I would have thought, for osteoporosis. Again, Dr Prentice showed that exercise in the observational studies for the Women's Health Initiative users was at a higher level than that of the nonusers.

Burger: We know that there is a huge amount of experimental data for the beneficial effects of oestrogens on the vascular system. We also know that diseased arteries lack oestrogen receptors and do not respond in the same favourable haemodynamic way to the administration of oestrogen as do healthy arteries. We know that there are data from cynomolgus monkey models of vascular disease in which atherosclerosis is induced experimentally where it is clear that if oestrogen is introduced into gonadectomised animals at the same time as the atherogenic stimulus, there is 70% reduction in atheroma formation. If you wait until the animal has been atherosclerotic for three or four years, then there is no benefit at all. So the potential explanation of the difference between the observational and the interventional study is that the observational studies studied women who had received hormones from the time of menopause when they still presumably had healthy arteries, whereas in the Women's Health Initiative it is very likely that a high number of the subjects would have diseased arteries by the time they entered the study. I think it is something we have not discussed before.

Evans: I think that is a reasonable theory and something that is possible. However, the really odd thing is that when we take statins, statins work both in primary prevention and in secondary prevention and in people at a great variety of risk levels, a variety of ages, people who have established disease, and so you have an entirely different effect in terms of statins. So I do not think you can regard HRT as being in the same class, and so some of your argument is partly special pleading. I think this is simply one of those uncertainties.

Purdie: You posed the question: does five years of oestrogen produce prevention of hip fracture at the age of 80? Well, I think the best data to answer that comes from the Swedish hip fracture prevention group,[4] and the answer is five years of oestrogen gives you hip fracture protection for five years, at the very most.

Evans: I think that is the point and that is the conclusion of the Royal College of Physicians of Edinburgh[5] and the case–control studies[6,7] seem to show that. The only thing I would say is that the power that they would have for detecting a difference like that might be quite small. Because you might think that you have kept your bone density a little bit higher, but the problem is that in practice even if it does give you a tiny residual effect it will be overwhelmed by the effect of age by the time you are 80.

Pitkin: When you were talking about ovarian cancer, you said that more women who were on HRT had a hysterectomy, and that hysterectomy is protective. I think it is fairly clear that in both of the studies that have looked at hysterectomy as being protective for ovarian cancer, it is short-lived protection. The general theory is that it may have been that the ovaries were visualised at the time of surgery and if they appeared peculiar then they were removed. If they were not peculiar then they were not. But it is not a long-term protective effect and although two studies have shown an effect on hysterectomy, it is not maintained.

Evans: I think the point, though, is that if you have failed to stratify by hysterectomy status, you can end up with a misleading result. That is certainly what Professor Beral's systematic review said.

Pitkin: If women are hysterectomised, they will have oestrogen alone and most observational studies show that that has a bigger ovarian cancer effect than continuous combined which is the same as placebo.

Beral: I think basically for ovarian cancer we do not really know and, as I said earlier, unfortunately the trials are not really going to help us enormously. We will have to get observational data and be very careful about it.

Burger: I can see biologically why HRT may cause breast cancer but I cannot see how it can cause ovarian cancer, particularly when we have really overwhelming data that the pill in younger women is protective against ovarian cancer.

Beral: I think at the moment we just do not know.

Evans: I think it has caused headlines in terms of the media and so on, but I do not think it comes into the risk–benefit equation in any important way. What is of concern, of course, is that if it does have an adverse effect then the case fatality rate for ovarian cancer is so much higher than the case fatality rate for breast cancer, so that would be concerning, if it did have an effect. In some sense, I would agree with you that it is surprising we do not find it to be protective.

Pitkin: I think if we are looking at balancing long-term risks and benefits and what we do for the short term and for the long term, it is very important here to say that all the studies have been looking at 50- and 60-year olds, and we really cannot extrapolate all this data down to people with premature ovarian failure. which GPs are already doing.

Gebbie: I think Mr Whitehead is going to cover that specifically in his presentation.

Pitkin: I would like to ask Professor Miller about those small studies on tibolone,[8,9] on reduction in cell proliferation on fine-needle aspiration, with biopsies in humans.

Miller: I do not have experience of tibolone. Can I comment on the question of fine-needle aspirates because that was part of the study and it may have some relevance on how valid the results on tibolone are? I tried in my talk to give the impression that if you are really interested in events that occur within the breast, then to make some study of the breast itself is in fact quite valid. The difficulty, of course, is getting hold of material from breasts that are not coming to surgery for some sort of problem. I suppose the idea that you could stick a needle in the breast and come up with material is a reasonable approach. I think in the absence of anything else I would encourage that but I do have major concerns. You really need to define what the question is you want to look at and it seems to me that there is a heterogeneity in the postmenopausal breast. If in fact you take a very small sample then the worry is that it is not representative of what you are looking at. So you really need to know to some degree what you are sticking the needle into. I think the sample size has relevance, as well, as to what you can do. We saw in those studies where although they had a biopsy of material, they could only get relevant information out of two-thirds of the samples that they looked at. That is because of the events, that they were trying to measure were just not of sufficient frequency so that you could actually get reliable results. If in fact you go down to fine-needle aspirates, the quality of those aspirates are quite variable in postmenopausal women. Many of them are acellular. Certainly many of them will not have sufficient material such that you could actually measure proliferation. If you go down to apoptosis, and I spent a lot of time looking down the microscope in sections trying to assess apoptosis, in the postmenopausal woman we are talking about events which are of hazard value 0.1%, so the number of cells that you have to count in order to get really meaningful results are quite high. I have a lot of question marks about results that are published on apoptotic events in fine-needle aspirates from postmenopausal breasts.

Gebbie: I think we should move on from tibolone, I think there simply is not the data or the expertise in this room to go into it in any more depth.

Cardozo: I think it is quite important that we firm up on what our view is going to be, or whether we are going to be divided, on advising women who have a strong family history of osteoporosis regarding the timing and duration of prophylactic oestrogen, if they choose to take them. Having listened to what has been said, there is considerable divided opinion on this, and I think that we need to be absolutely certain that we put forward an evidence-based statement that is not biased. I think this needs to come from the people who are knowledgeable in that area.

Gebbie: How should we take this forward?

Critchley: Well, I think if somebody around the table has some evidence that will help us formulate a view then we should hear it now.

Beral: I was just going to say that the evidence of family history of osteoporosis as a risk factor for osteoporosis is not very strong. I think if we had evidence that it was a major risk factor, we could move on from there. As I have said in other meetings, the main risk factor for having a family history of osteoporosis is having a mother who lived a long time – a long-lived mother is the main risk factor for family history of osteoporosis. So we just have to be careful about what we are doing.

Armitage: In the Royal College of Physicians guidelines for osteoporosis, it said that maternal hip fracture is an independent risk factor. I think the trouble is that family history of osteoporosis is much too vague and everyone has got a grandmother that has lost a bit of height and whatever. But I think a maternal hip fracture, almost by definition, implies the older age group.

Whitehead: I was somewhat taken aback by some of the comments yesterday that bisphosphonates form an effective alternative to HRT for hip fracture, because I do not think the data is there. I am sure many of you have seen the type of presentation before where we have basically got various treatments, starting with calcitonin in on the left here, raloxifene, risedronate and then Fosamax® (alendronate), and basically this is the percentage increase in spinal bone mineral density, but with all of these there is about a 50% reduction in vertebral fracture risk. Anything seems to work as far as the spine is concerned. If we get the data on hip, these are not head-to-head comparisons, but we have here the raloxifene trial where raloxifene does not appear to reduce hip fracture risk. We have got two alendronate studies, FIT 1 and FIT 2: now this was significant by one patient, this patient is worth its weight in gold to Merck Sharp & Dohme, the P value was at 0.047. FIT 2 showed no significant effect of alendronate on hip fracture risk. The only data with risedronate on hip fracture risk does not show a significant reduction in hip fracture risk. There is only one risedronate database which shows a significant reduction in risk of hip fracture with the active agent. Now, if you go to the paper, the group here in whom there was a significant reduction in hip fracture risk is very strange. They have all had a couple of fractures already, they have a t score on average of about −4.4. That is not the type of patient I see in my clinic, who is concerned about prophylaxis against hip fracture because her mother died of a fat embolism at the age of 58, immediately following her hip fracture. So I do not think that the data for bisphosphonates show a really effective prevention of hip fracture. Are there any data at the moment in younger groups of women perhaps with better bones? I think in that group the only data we have got really showing that an agent is effective is the Women's Health Initiative data for HRT. That is my point.

Evans: Can I just make a point here? We should not go on statistical significance only. What counts in some senses is the uncertainty in those trials. Most of those studies are underpowered to be able to detect hip fracture.

Prentice: Just for my recall, FIT 2 were persons that had somewhat reduced t scores but were not osteoporotic?

Whitehead: Correct, yes.

Prentice: Were there sizeable numbers of clinical events?

Whitehead: I mean if you put FIT 1 and FIT 2 together then you just get statistical significance. That is because of the effect in the FIT 1 trial.

Discussion following Mr Whitehead's paper

Gebbie: Can I just ask one question very quickly. There is one subgroup of women with premature menopause that we have run into a problem with and these are women who have had treatment for cancer, mainly lymphomas. They had a lot of mantle radiation, which is associated with a very high risk of subsequent breast cancer. All the oncologists are telling them to stop HRT. I wondered if anybody else in the room has had experience with this.

Miller: There is a circular that has come around from the Department of Health to all these women who had mediastinal radiation saying that they have an increased risk in the range of 1 in 3 to 1 in 7 of breast cancer. It suggests all sorts of strategies of management including bilateral mastectomies and annual mammography. I think it is appalling and very worrying.

Gebbie: Are the statistics wrong?

Miller: Well, it has come from the Department of Health.

Beral: I think the absolute risks they are quoting are really far too high and I have been involved in discussions with people who have got data in this country that really contradict what the experts have said. But, regardless of that, I think there are really two issues about this premature menopause business. There are women with a premature menopause because they are being treated for cancer, and I really think they have to be considered separately from people who have spontaneous premature menopause where they do not have some declared past history of cancer. I think people who have a history of cancer, the common ones as you said are probably breast cancer and lymphomas, where people have had radiation treatment, both of those groups are at an increased risk of breast cancer. Maybe it is not as high as the advice that is going around, but certainly radiation treatment at young age does increase the risk of breast cancer and I think it is true to say that neither the Women's Health Initiative trial nor the Million Women Study have women who are younger than 50 years. In our international collaborative study, the Collaborative Group on Hormonal Factors In Breast Cancer,[10] there were women who were younger than 50 and had early menopause. There was no suggestion that the relative risks varied by age of diagnosis, so the same relative risks would apply at younger age as at older ages. There is no reason to believe that it is different and so it goes back to the absolute risk. If the baseline risk of breast cancer is very high with women, say, who have been treated with radiation or because they have had a one breast cancer, I think one can assume the background rates are high and that the effects of HRT will multiply up in the same way. So I think one has to be cautious about a blanket statement that people who have had an early menopause, particularly for treatment for cancer, can be treated with HRT without a problem. On the other hand, women who have had an oophorectomy or premature menopause are at low risk of breast cancer. So, given that they are already at low risk, it is another matter whether one wants to increase their low risk by giving them HRT.

Whitehead: The trouble is they are symptomatic.

Beral: That is right, but then one has to treat it as a symptomatic issue. But the idea should not be promulgated that it does not matter, that you can just give HRT and that the HRT will not affect breast cancer risk until you are 50. It is back to what the baseline rates would be and whether you are multiplying onto a small background rate or onto a higher background rate.

Whitehead: When I am talking to patients, I would use your 1997 figures, which state that normal ovarian function in women during their late 40s increases risk of breast cancer by 2.8% per annum. That is what you published then.

Critchley: Mr Whitehead, we were particularly asked by the RCOG Consumers'

Forum to include some discussion about add-back HRT. I think what we have to remember as well is that gonadotrophin-releasing hormone (GnRH) analogues are not just used for women with endometriosis. They are being used now as a medical option for fibroids and I think therefore we need to have some view about add-back in younger women with either endometriosis or with fibroids who are often on these analogues for not months, but years. This was something we were particularly requested to address in our programme.

The second question pertains to this problem of premature menopause and young girls and we are talking about, again, a very heterogeneous group. We are talking about girls who may be born with no ovaries, women with Turner's syndrome. We are talking about the survivors of childhood cancer, we will have one in 700 of the population – those will be boys and girls but, you know, significant numbers of young women. We are talking about children, adolescents, that may need to have 10, 20 or 30 years of HRT. Now can you deprive a 15-year old or a 20-year old of oestrogen because if you were a normal 20-year old you would see physiological levels of oestradiol every month if you were ovulating. That has got to have some role in the bone mass that you retain as an adolescent which will have a role in your later fracture risk. So, to be a bit provocative, we would not deprive a diabetic of insulin, we would not deprive somebody who was hypothyroid, so I think we do have to separate out the very young woman who, if you like, needs replacement of steroid that their body would have normally produced. I agree with Mr Whitehead that the teenager in the disco does not want to have a pack of HRT fall out but is combined oral contraception (COC) suitable? What is the ideal form of HRT in these young girls who actually need replacement or therapy because they are deprived of hormone? It is a whole different argument as to whether they need a physiological replacement regimen – we just do not know. We give them that but we do not have the long-term data. It is a huge area but I feel we cannot leave the topic of premature menopause without addressing it because, you are right, these young girls are on HRT and are coming to us and saying 'Well, can we stay on this?'

Gray: Whilst the younger woman may get protection from breast cancer by having lost her ovarian function, and thereby the relative risk multiplying effect will work for her, surely the comparison is actually her peers who would normally be producing the oestrogen naturally, so for her physiological replacement with physiological doses is not a risk increase, it is simply levelling the playing field.

Beral: I think it has to be explained like that. Women need to know their risks if they were not on treatment. I think it is complicated and I am not trying to suggest what the management should be. I am just saying that the underlying risks of breast cancer that you are changing and low to start with and that it is important for you and your patients to recognise that. That has to be acknowledged and in this instance you have to use individual management. All I am saying is that one cannot assume there is no effect by adding HRT, and if the underlying risk is low you are still increasing that risk by giving HRT.

Rees: Two philosophical points: is menstruation harmful to health and, if we do not give oestrogen to young girls who have had a premature menopause, we are then saying that menstruation is harmful to health. The second thing is that we would not have these anxieties about the COC pill given to a 20-year old who needs contraception.

Gebbie: A very valid point, thank you.

Cardozo: I am very worried about the subsets of girls with anorexia and who may be oestrogen-deprived for many years. They are now being advised by their GP that it is not safe to take oestrogens in the doses in which we think it should be prescribed, rather than the COC pill. It is unacceptable to most of them to take the combined pill because they are below the age when they should be having sexual intercourse, so they have parental and teacher pressure put on them not to take the pill. I think this is something that we need to address in our recommendations.

Whitehead: They have a problem that, if you re-oestrogenise, in terms of their bone status the effect of the oestrogen is often minimal and I suspect because they simply are not getting enough vitamins and minerals.

Cardozo: My involvement is, in a way, peripheral as they are referred to us because of their very high incidence of urinary tract symptoms. You may or may not know that girls with anorexia nervosa also have very high prevalence of irritative urinary symptoms: frequency, urgency and nocturia, which rule their lives and can impair their quality of life considerably. This can be partly addressed by giving them oestrogen supplementation. But of course that is perceived as being as disadvantageous because of their body image and they do not want to put on weight or they do not want to get bigger breasts and so on. There needs to be some long-term strategy because they are often oestrogen-deprived for many years at a time in their lives when their bone build-up would be greatest and their oestrogen-sensitive tissues are being deprived. If they are being given advice not to take the treatment they need, I think this is obviously terribly harmful for their future lives.

Studd: We published some data years ago on giving transdermal oestrogens or oestradiol for these girls with anorexia with three or five years of amenorrhoea and terrible bones. The effect on the bones was superb – very good indeed. What is interesting is that although they are terrified of putting on weight, they did not mind having their periods. They quite like having periods. Their whole idea of this dieting was not to become amenorrhoeic and that was a worthwhile correction for them.

Armitage: Just to come back to the premature menopause again – because I think this is so important. When the recent advice came out before Christmas from the Committee on Safety of Medicines,[11] we put out a statement saying, trying to reassure, that if you were less than the average age of menopause, i.e. less than 50, then the advice did not apply to you, then you go up to 50. We did that actually without the studies, which I think is probably unusual for us, without the confirmatory studies. Certainly the clinicians amongst us felt very much what is being expressed is that you are just bringing back to the physiological – I mean you would not oophorectomise girls to reduce their risk of breast cancer so why would you not restore them back to where nature would have intended it. I have become very anxious when Professor Beral has talked about perhaps that is not right. So, Professor Beral, when you are saying you are multiplying it up, is it fair to say that actually in the young girls their absolute risk of breast cancer is so low, that even if you do multiply it up it does not matter?

Beral: I think that this is a clinical situation and involves, as you say, specific consideration of individual cases. But the idea that HRT has different effects when you are young and whether it is reasonable to say to people 'Well, you know you would be at very low of breast cancer, but if you do this you will be the same as everybody else.' Breast cancer is the most common cause of death for women from age 30 years to about 60 – it is so widespread that it is the condition that people fear. If you say to someone 'Well, if you have premature menopause when you are 40, just spontaneously, you actually will have a very low risk of breast cancer for the rest of your life!" some people might say that they are quite happy about that and not wish to take HRT to bring their risk up to the same level as other women. I just think you should be giving women that option.

Armitage: Would you say that to a women with Turner's syndrome or a 20- or 30-year old?

Beral: No, not to a women with Turner's syndrome but some people with an early menopause would say 'Oh, OK, that is fine.'

Armitage: Mr Whitehead's definition was less than 40 years.

Whitehead: That is the accepted definition.

Armitage: I think most of us would be totally comfortable if you are less than 40 you really would feel happy to say, well we are putting it back to baseline. I suppose where it becomes a grey area is in the 43-, 44-year olds, who have quite a lot of symptoms, and are still having regular or quite erratic periods.

Gebbie: It all comes down to individual choice and informed consent.

Whitehead: Can I just come back to your paper in 1997? What you published then was that each year of normal ovarian function increased risk of breast cancer by 2.8%. If it was oestrogen only, that the oestrogen only was increasing the risk by 2.3%. I would have suspected that if we had oestrogen plus progestogen it most probably would be back to 2.8%.

Beral: The risk of breast cancer is much higher with oestrogen plus progestogen. It is not replacing with oestrogen plus progestogen. Breast cancer incidence with combined HRT is higher in comparison with each year of menopause. It is quite complicated but it is not the right argument to use to say that use of HRT is just the same as if you had a later menopause. It is not correct.

References

1. Manson JE, Hsia J, Johnson KC, Rossouw JE, Assaf AR, Lasser NL, *et al*.; Women's Health Initiative Investigators. Estrogen plus progestin and the risk of coronary heart disease. *N Engl J Med* 2003;349:523–34.
2. Collaborative Group on Hormonal Factors in Breast Cancer. Breast cancer and hormone replacement therapy: collaborative reanalysis of data from 51 epidemiological studies of 52,705 women with breast cancer and 108,411 women without breast cancer. *Lancet* 1997;350:1047–59. Erratum in: *Lancet* 1997;350:1484.
3. Brockie JA, Barlow DH, Rees MC. Menopausal flush symptomatology and sustained reflex vasoconstriction. *Hum Reprod* 1991;6:472–4.
4. Michaelsson K, Baron JA, Johnell O, Persson I, Ljunghall S. Variation in the efficacy of hormone replacement therapy in the prevention of hip fracture. Swedish Hip Fracture Study Group. *Osteoporos Int* 1998;8:540–6.

5. Consensus Conference on Hormone Replacement Therapy. *J Royal Coll Phys Edin* 2004;34 Suppl 13.

6. Michaelsson K, Baron JA, Farahmand BY, Johnell O, Magnusson C, Persson PG, *et al*. Hormone replacement therapy and risk of hip fracture: population based case-control study. The Swedish Hip Fracture Study Group. *BMJ* 1998;316:1858–63.

7. Yates J, Barrett-Connor E, Barlas S, Chen YT, Miller PD, Siris ES. Rapid loss of hip fracture protection after estrogen cessation: evidence from the National Osteoporosis Risk Assessment. *Obstet Gynecol* 2004;103:440–6.

8. Conner P, Christow A, Kersemaekers W, Soderqvist G, Skoog L, Carlstrom K, *et al*. A comparative study of breast cell proliferation during hormone replacement therapy: effects of tibolon and continuous combined estrogen-progestogen treatment. *Climacteric* 2004;7:50–8.

9. Valdivia I, Campodonico I, Tapia A, Capetillo M, Espinoza A, Lavin P. Effects of tibolone and continuous combined hormone therapy on mammographic breast density and breast histochemical markers in postmenopausal women. *Fertil Steril* 2004;81:617–23.

10. Collaborative Group on Hormonal Factors in Breast Cancer. Breast cancer and hormonal contraceptives: collaborative reanalysis of individual data on 53 297 women with breast cancer and 100 239 women without breast cancer from 54 epidemiological studies. *Lancet* 1996;347:1713–27.

11. Duff G, Committee on Safety of Medicines. Use of hormone replacement therapy in the prevention of osteoporosis: important new information. 3 December 2003 [http://medicines.mhra.gov.uk].

SECTION 6

ALTERNATIVE STRATEGIES FOR TREATMENT OF MENOPAUSAL SYMPTOMS

Chapter 22

Selective steroid receptor modulators: new therapeutic options for the treatment of peri- and postmenopausal disorders

Kristof Chwalisz

Introduction

The ovarian hormones oestrogen, progesterone and, to some extent, testosterone maintain female reproductive functions and regulate the activity of various target tissues via oestrogen (ER), progesterone (PR) and androgen (AR) receptors that are widely distributed throughout the body. Steroid hormone receptors are present in the reproductive tract and in various cells of the cardiovascular, neural, musculoskeletal, gastrointestinal and immune systems. These hormones are beneficial, and often obligatory for women during their reproductive age, providing a biological advantage for premenopausal women. In fact, protective effects of oestrogen on the cardiovascular and central nervous systems have been found in various animal models, and epidemiological studies showed an increased risk for coronary heart disease (CHD) after menopause; risks for other disorders, such as stroke and dementia also seem to increase with age.

The classic preventive approach to postmenopausal hormone replacement therapy (HRT) was based on the assumption that this biological advantage can be maintained after menopause by simply substituting the ovarian hormone oestrogen, possibly for a woman's entire life. Is this assumption correct? The results of the Women's Health Initiative (WHI) study, a study anticipated to provide definitive answers about health benefits and risks of postmenopausal HRT, challenged this assumption and many other dogmas in this area. The WHI study dramatically changed the view of the role of oestrogen, and HRT overall, in the management and prevention of postmenopausal osteoporosis and CHD. The WHI trials confused millions of women and physicians throughout the world, and abruptly created a new landscape in postmenopausal therapy. Many postmenopausal women lost confidence in HRT and simply stopped treatments, even in the presence of vasomotor symptoms.

However, patients continue to require care, and there is a clear medical need for new preventive and therapeutic approaches throughout the stages of reproductive ageing. Some women suffer from various symptoms relating to hormonal imbalance several years before the menopause. Perimenopausal transition is still a largely unstudied period of a woman's life that is often characterised by changes in menstrual pattern, fluctuations in reproductive hormones, and clinical symptoms, including abnormal uterine bleeding, vasomotor and urogenital symptoms, and decrease in libido.[1] There is also an urgent medical need for new, non-hormonal treatments for vasomotor symptoms that culminate around the menopause.

Although oestrogen therapy is currently the most effective treatment of menopausal symptoms and is still recommended for short-term use, many women now refuse using any hormonal treatments, primarily because of the fear of breast cancer. Osteoporosis represents the major health-economic problem of postmenopausal women. A 50-year old woman in the USA has a 40% lifetime risk of an osteoporotic fracture. We are currently facing a demographic revolution as the growth in the number of people of age 65 years and older is greater than that of the general population; those of age 85 years and older are the fastest growing segment.[2] Geripause is a newly defined postmenopausal phase that includes women over the age of 65 years.[2] Geripause is characterised by continuous loss of lean body mass (sarcopenia),[3] which may lead to frailty.[4,5] An effective treatment of frailty is not currently available.

The past ten years have witnessed the introduction of several new treatments for osteoporosis. The bisphosphonates alendronate and risedronate and the selective oestrogen receptor modulator (SERM) raloxifene are the most widely used antiresorptive agents. These agents slow bone turnover and, therefore, increase bone mineral density. This effect reflects, however, not an increase in bone mass, but an increase in mineral content. Although bisphosphonates represent an effective and safe alternative to oestrogens as an antiresorptive strategy, there is a need for effective, orally active anabolic drugs that increase bone strength by stimulating bone formation. Anabolic therapy, to induce bone formation, is still underdeveloped. For example, the currently available anabolic agent teriparatide, a recombinant peptide fragment of parathyroid hormone that restores bone in patients with severe osteoporosis, must be administered by means of daily subcutaneous injections.[6,7]

Recent advances in the molecular biology of steroid receptors show, however, that steroidal hormones elicit very complex tissue- and cell-specific responses in the body that are modulated by nontranscription signalling pathways. This complexity was underestimated in the past. The different stages of a woman's life are characterised by specific changes in reproductive hormones that are accompanied by metabolic changes.[1,8–10] We are now starting to understand how steroid hormones exhibit tissue-specific responses during the different periods of a woman's life. This brief review describes recent advances in ER, PR and AR pharmacology, outlines our current understanding of tissue-selective action of selective steroid hormone receptor modulators, addresses problems and deficiencies of current postmenopausal therapies, and outlines potential future developments in this area.

Selective receptor modulators (SRMs)

Most of the effects of the steroid hormones oestradiol, progesterone and active androgens (testosterone and 5α dihydrotestosterone [DHT]) are mediated by their cognate receptors ER, PR and AR that belong to the superfamily of nuclear steroid receptors.[11] The nuclear receptor superfamily comprises a large and diverse group of eukaryotic transcription factors that control many biological functions, including embryonic development, reproduction, tissue growth and differentiation, and hormone-mediated homeostasis. The natural ligands of some members of this family are still unknown. The steroid hormone receptors are, however, relatively well characterised, and a number of synthetic ligands, which exhibit high-affinity binding to nuclear steroid receptors, have been synthesised during the past 20 years. These compounds were key to understanding the functions of steroid receptors *in vivo*. ER, PR and AR ligands, with both agonist and antagonist activities, are now available and clinically used.

Historically, tamoxifen played a key role in the conceptualisation and discovery of selective receptor modulators (SRMs) and should be considered as the prototypical selective oestrogen receptor modulator (SERM). Careful evaluation of tamoxifen effects *in vivo* revealed that this compound exhibits oestrogen-like (agonist) effects in bone and the endometrium while exerting antagonist effects in the breast and central nervous system (CNS).[12-14] This discovery led to reclassification of tamoxifen as a SERM. Today, SRMs are defined as a class of nuclear receptor ligands that exert selective agonist or antagonist effects on target tissue of a particular steroid hormone.[15] They should be distinguished from 'pure' steroid receptor agonists and antagonists. This functional definition is based on the presence of tissue-selective effects of steroid hormone receptor modulators. SRMs mimic the effects of a natural receptor ligand in some tissues while opposing its effects in other tissues. These compounds often act as partial agonists or antagonists, depending on cells or tissue and the presence or absence of the respective natural ligand. Partial agonists or antagonists, irrespective of the dose, exhibit pharmacological effects that are weaker than those of the 'pure' agonists and antagonists.

More recently, selective progesterone receptor modulators (SPRMs) and selective androgen receptor modulators (SARMs) have been synthesised and pharmacologically characterised. Clinically relevant tissue-selective effects must be present before a compound can be classified as an SRM.[15]

Tissue selectivity of SRMs

For many years, the molecular basis of tissue selectivity was unknown. However, the discovery of nuclear coregulators (i.e. coactivators and corepressors) provided an explanation of this phenomenon. Coregulators are nuclear proteins that form multiple complexes with nuclear receptors and modulate their transcriptional activity.[15] Coactivators enhance transcriptional activity of nuclear receptors, whereas corepressors elicit inhibitory effects on the receptors. It has been postulated that the relative balance of coactivator and corepressor expression, within the given target cell, determines the relative agonist versus antagonist activity of SRMs.[15]

'Pure' steroid receptor antagonists seem to change the conformation of the steroid receptor such that it conversely favours interaction with corepressors or inhibits interactions with coactivators; in contrast, agonists or partial agonists promote the expected interaction of the nuclear receptor with coactivators. For example, agonist-mediated induction of transcriptional activation is associated with the recruitment of coactivators, such as steroid receptor coactivator-1 (SRC-1), receptor coactivator-2 (SRC-2), receptor coactivator-3 (SRC-3), cAMP response element binding (CREB) binding protein (CBP) and other coactivators, whereas an antagonist-liganded steroid receptor is able to recruit corepressors, for example nuclear receptor corepressor (NCoR), and/or inhibits association with coactivators.[16-18] (Figure 22.1) It is known that the availability of both coactivators and corepressors is dependent on tissue and hormonal milieu. Thus, cell type- and promoter-specific differences in coregulator recruitment determine the tissue selectivity of SRMs. To date, more than 50 coactivators have been cloned and characterised and the list is still growing.[15] Figure 22.1 presents a simplified model of action of SRMs and the role of coregulators.

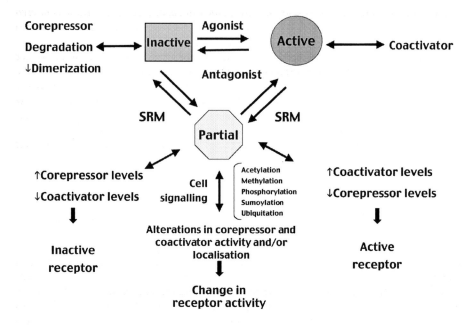

Figure 22.1. Simplified model of the interaction between steroid hormone receptors and coregulators explaining the relative agonist/antagonist activity of SRMs; in the presence of agonist, nuclear receptors, in the active conformation, interact well with coactivators and are transcriptionally active; in the presence of antagonists, receptors adopt an inactive conformation and preferentially interact with corepressors, resulting in loss of transcriptional activity; in the presence of SRMs, nuclear receptors adopt a conformational intermediate between the active and inactive state and, therefore, have the potential to interact with either coactivators or corepressors, and exert partial activity; the activity of SRM-occupied receptors depends on the relative expression of coactivators and corepressors in a given cell environment and the effects of cell signalling on coregulator subcellular localisation and/or activity; reproduced with permission from Smith and O'Malley[15] (Endoctine Reviews, © 2004 The Endocrine Society)

Nontranscription cellular signalling

Although coregulator function is the key to understanding tissue specificity of SRMs,[15] other factors, including the tissue-specific distribution of steroid receptor isoforms and cellular signalling, e.g. via phosphorylation, have been recognised as important genomic and non-genomic mechanisms that determine the cell- and tissue-specific responses to nuclear receptor ligands (Figure 22.1).[19,20] Cellular signalling pathways, e.g. those activated by growth factors, cytokines, or newly discovered membrane G-protein-coupled steroid receptors,[21,22] can influence the activity and subcellular localisation of coregulators, as well as nuclear receptors. These factors modulate the interaction between nuclear receptors and coregulators, and change their effects on gene expression via various enzymatic activities, including phosphorylation, acetylation, methylamines, sumoylation and ubiquitation (Figure 22.1).[15,20]

Overall, recent molecular studies show that the effects of steroidal hormones *in vivo* are regulated by extremely complex mechanisms that are highly regulated in a cell- and tissue-specific manner. The original models of steroid hormone action, whereby an agonist simply bound and converted its cognate receptor to its active form, no longer describe the action of nuclear receptor ligands. A growing understanding of the mechanisms responsible for tissue and cell selectivity of SRMs could lead to the development of new non-hormonal strategies for postmenopausal therapy. New SERMs, SPRMs and SARMs, discussed below, represent the most exiting new opportunities for peri- and postmenopausal therapy. These compounds have the potential to elicit the beneficial effects of 'pure' agonists while avoiding their undesirable action.

Selective oestrogen receptor modulators (SERMs)

ER pharmacology

Oestrogen effects are mediated by at least two genetically different receptors, ERα and ERβ, that share some similarities in their binding domain but seem to elicit very different effects.[23,24] 17β-oestradiol (E_2) is the natural ligand for ERα and most likely for ERβ. Upon binding of an agonist, the receptors undergo conformational changes leading to formation of either homodimers (ERβ/ERβ or ERα/ERα) or heterodimers (ERα/ERβ) in a cell-specific manner.

The role of both ER isoforms has been defined by both studies with genetically engineered mice either lacking or overexpressing ERα or ERβ, and pharmacological studies with receptor isoform-specific agonists and antagonists.[25–28] Whereas ERα clearly mediates most oestrogenic effects in the reproductive tract, bone, CNS and the cardiovascular system, the role of ERβ is still poorly defined. Studies in mice with selective ablation of ERβ and experiments with ERβ-specific ligands suggest that this receptor plays an important role in inflammation. ERβ-specific agonists have shown efficacy in animal models with bowel disease and rheumatoid arthritis,[29] indicating that oestrogen plays a more important role than previously thought. Activated ER isoforms can interact with target genes directly by binding to specific, high-affinity oestrogen response elements within specific gene promoters, or indirectly through protein–protein interaction with various transcription factors, such as activator protein 1 (AP1) and specificity protein 1 (Sp1).[30] ER can also inhibit transcriptional activity by inhibiting the activity (transrepression) of certain transcription factors, such as nuclear factor kappa B (NF-κB), explaining, at least in part, the anti-inflammatory effects of E_2 observed in some models of inflammation.[29,30]

17β-oestradiol, the natural ER ligand, exerts a variety of effects on the reproductive tract, and skeletal, cardiovascular and central nervous systems. These effects have been extensively studied in animal models and humans. Whereas the effects of oestrogens on the reproductive tract and bone are similar in animals and humans, there is a clear discrepancy between animal and human studies concerning their beneficial effects on the cardiovascular system and CNS. The WHI failed to demonstrate any beneficial effects of oestrogen substitution on the cardiovascular and central nervous systems, which are clearly seen in animal models. The exact reason for this discrepancy is unclear and might relate to various factors, including compound-specific effects, pharmacokinetics, study design and others.

Whereas most animal studies used the natural ER ligand E_2, the majority of large clinical studies, including WHI, employed the most frequently prescribed continuous combined oestrogen plus progestogen products in the USA, which contain oral conjugated equine oestrogen (CEE), with and without the progestogen medroxyprogesterone acetate (MPA). CEE, a mixture of various steroids extracted from pregnant mare urine, contains at least ten oestrogens, and a number of other compounds with less defined activity.[31] The pharmacologically active oestrogens are sulphated ovarian oestrogens, oestrone (E_1) and E_2, and several equine oestrogens not secreted by the human ovary. Even though CEE has been used for a long time, the pharmacological properties are poorly defined, mostly because of pharmacokinetic differences of individual components, their ability to interact with different ER isoforms, and unknown tissue-specific responses.

The pharmacokinetic aspects of oestrogen pharmacology are particularly important in this respect. Orally administered CEE (as well as other oral oestrogens) undergoes an excessive passage through the hepatic portal circulation, resulting in unusually high concentrations of parent compounds and their active metabolites in the liver cells that contain ER. Orally administered oestrogens, acting via ER, modulate the synthesis of various physiologically important liver proteins and enzymes involved in lipid metabolism, including angiotensinogen,[32,33] C-reactive protein (CRP),[34] IGF-1,[34] activated protein C, lipoproteins,[35] steroid hormone binding proteins (SHBG and CBG),[32] etc. Both raloxifene and tamoxifen, which act in the liver as ER agonists, induce similar effects after oral administration.[36] Whereas most human studies, including WHI, employed orally administered oestrogen, most animal studies used the subcutaneous or intramuscular route of oestrogen administration, such as osmotic minipumps, pellets or subcutaneous injections in an oily vehicle. These treatments, which somewhat mimic ovarian E_2 production, produce systemic hormone concentration without the initial passage through the hepatic circulation. It should be stressed that circulating ovarian oestrogens, as well as transdermally administered oestrogens, have been shown to have none or minimal effects on liver parameters at physiological concentrations.[32–35]

SERM drugs available

Although tamoxifen is the prototypic, first-generation SERM,[13] it has been used in medicine as an ER antagonist for the treatment of breast cancer. Raloxifene, the second-generation SERM, has to be considered as the first-in-class SERM that has been specifically developed for postmenopausal therapy based on its partial agonist and antagonist properties. The divergent effects of the SERMs tamoxifen and raloxifene on the endometrium are perfect examples of how coregulators influence the tissue-selective effects of SRMs. In the breast, both tamoxifen and raloxifene act as ER antagonists. In the uterus, however, tamoxifen acts as an ER agonist, whereas raloxifene is an ER antagonist. In the breast, both compounds promote the recruitment of corepressors to ER target promoters.[37] However, in the endometrium, tamoxifen, but not raloxifene, is able to recruit the coactivator SRC-1.[37]

Although tamoxifen exerts a protective effect on the breast, and has agonist (antiresorptive) activity in the human skeleton, it cannot be used for the prevention of osteoporosis because of its oestrogenic effects on the endometrium and increased risk of endometrial hyperplasia and cancer. Raloxifene does not have any oestrogen agonist activity on the endometrium but shows antiresorptive effects in bone and protective effects on the breast.[38] However, raloxifene is a potent ER antagonist in the CNS, which explains its potential to induce hot flushes.[39] In addition, the antiresorptive effects of raloxifene on bone are relatively weak. Therefore, there is a need for SERMs with increased potency on bone and no antagonistic effects on the CNS.

The introduction of raloxifene into postmenopausal therapy may soon be followed by third-generation SERMs. Indeed, a number of third-generation SERMs, such as lasofoxifene,[40] arzoxifene[41] and bazodoxifene,[42] are currently under development for treatment and prevention of osteoporosis and prevention of breast cancer.[43] Although these SERMs do not seem to induce hot flushes, they are unable to prevent them. A fourth-generation SERM, with selective agonist activity in the CNS sufficient to prevent hot flushes in postmenopausal women, has not yet been discovered. Interestingly, lasofoxifene is currently being developed in combination with a classical oestrogen for the treatment of menopausal symptoms.[44] This example shows that tissue-selective effects of SERMs can still be improved in the future. Table 22.1 presents the major pharmacodynamic effects of first-, second- and third-generation SERMs in humans.

Selective progesterone receptor modulators (SPRMs)

PR pharmacology

The human PR exists in two forms: hPR-A and hPR-B (Figure 22.2(a)). In contrast to ER isoforms, which are products of two genes, both PR isoforms are derived from the same gene by the use of two different promoters.[45] The hPR is formed by a DNA

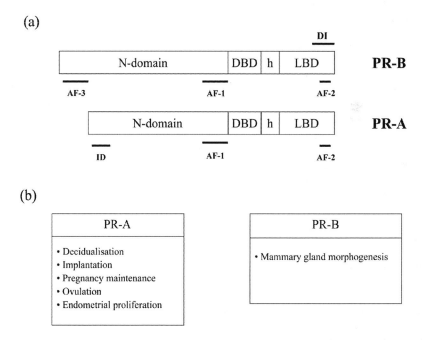

Figure 22.2. (a) Structure of human PR-A and PR-B isoforms showing domain organisation; N-domain, DBD (DNA binding domain), LBD (ligand binding domain), AF-1, AF-2, AF-3 (transcription activation domain), ID (inhibitor domain), DI (dimerization domain); (b) major functions of PR isoforms *in vivo* based on studies in mice with selective PR-A or PR-B ablation

Table 22.1. Pharmacodynamic effects of SERMs; adapted from Anthony et al.[43,73]

Site of action		Ligands			
	Oestrogens (E_2, E_1)	First generation (tamoxifen)	Second generation (raloxifene)	Third generation (lasofoxifene, arzoxifene, bazodoxifene, etc.)	Fourth generation ideal SERM (hypothetical)
Bone	Agonist	Agonist	Agonist	Agonist	Agonist
Breast	Agonist	Antagonist	Antagonist	Antagonist	Antagonist
Endometrium	Agonist	Partial agonist	Antagonist	Antagonist	Antagonist
CNS (hot flushes)	Agonist	Antagonist	Antagonist	No effect	Agonist
Coagulation (DVT, PE)	Agonist	Agonist	Agonist	?	Antagonist
Vagina	Agonist	Antagonist	Antagonist	Antagonist (partial agonist)?	Agonist

DVT = deep vein thrombosis; PE = pulmonary embolism

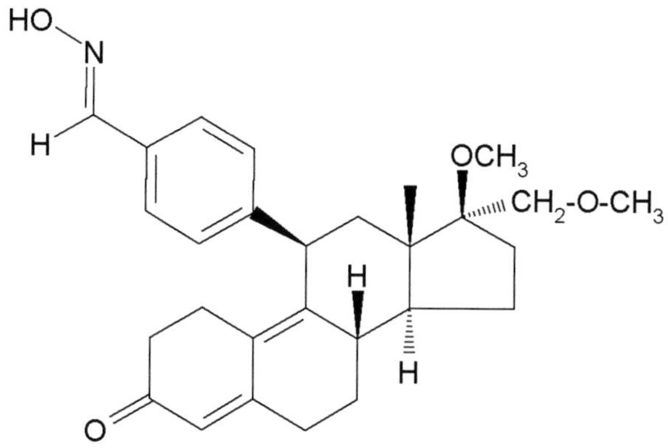

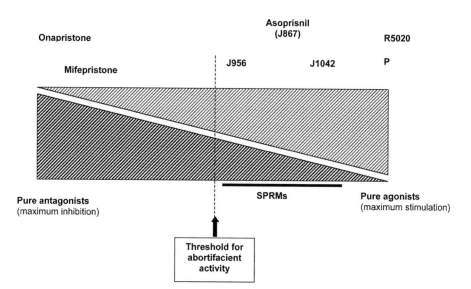

Figure 22.3. Chemical structure of asoprisnil (J867); benzaldehyde,4-[(11β,17β)-17-methoxy-17-(methoxymethyl)-3-oxoestra-4,9-dien-11-yl]-,1-oxime

Figure 22.4. Spectrum of antagonist and agonist activities of various PR ligands based on animal *in vivo* models; onapristone is an example of a 'pure' PR antagonist; mifepristone is a PR antagonist with marginal agonist activity in some *in vitro* models – it acts as a PR antagonist *in vivo*; the SPRMs asoprisnil (J867), J912 and J1042 are partial PR agonists/antagonists in various animal models – they exhibit marginal or absent labour-inducing (abortifacient) activity; progesterone (P) and promegestone (R5020) are 'pure' PR agonists; modified with permission from Chwalisz *et al.*[60] (Annals of the New York Academy of Sciences, © 2002 New York Academy of Sciences)

binding domain (DBD), carboxyl terminal ligand domain (LBD), N-terminal domain, and three transcriptional domains (AF-1, AF-2 and AF-3), which provide a surface for interaction with coactivator complexes. The B isoform differs from hPR-A by an N-terminal extension, an AF-3 domain, responsible for coactivator recruitment resulting in two transcription factors with both overlapping and distinct gene-regulatory activity *in vitro*.[15] Within *in vitro* systems (cell-free preparations and cell lines), hPR-B is a much stronger activator of gene transcription; however, hPR-A has transrepression activity and in cells containing multiple nuclear receptors can inhibit or modulate transactivation effects of both hPR-B and ER.[46] The functions of PR isoforms *in vivo* have been recently characterised based on studies in mice with selective ablation of PR-A and PR-B[27,28] (Figure 22.2(b)). Surprisingly, selective ablation of PR-A produced a phenotype characterised by infertility, severe endometrial hyperplasia, anovulation and ovarian abnormalities in the presence of normal mammary gland response to progesterone. In contrast, mice with selective ablation of PR-B were fertile and did not show altered responses to progesterone in the uterus, but exhibited severely disrupted pregnancy-induced mammary gland morphogenesis. Overall, both *in vitro* and *in vivo* studies indicate that PR-A and PR-B can profoundly affect the biological responses to progesterone and synthetic PR ligands.[27,28,47] Since the hPR-A/hPR-B ratio can vary in different physiological and pathological situations, the ultimate response to a ligand may be determined by cell concentration of the specific isoform.[48,49]

PR-mediated effects and breast proliferation

The WHI study, and other clinical studies employing continuous oestrogen plus progestogen regimens, observed a slight, but significant, increase in breast cancer risk. These findings are consistent with animal studies described above and clinical experience with progestogens. Mammary gland development is predominantly postnatal and is controlled by a complex interplay between the reproductive hormones E_2, progesterone and prolactin, and local growth factors.[50] There is growing evidence that progesterone is an important mitogen in the epithelial breast cells, which is in contrast to its inhibitory effects on the endometrial epithelial cells.[51] PR antagonists suppress mammary gland proliferation and inhibit growth of PR-positive mammary gland tumours in experimental settings, whereas progestogens have an opposite effect in these models.[52] There is also clinical evidence indicating proliferative effects of progesterone and progestogens in the breast. The mitotic activity in normal breast tissue peaks during the luteal phase, and synthetic progestogens clearly increase mammographic breast density,[53–55] an effect which is accompanied by an increase in the expression of proliferation markers.[56] Overall, both clinical and preclinical studies suggest that progesterone acts as a primary mitogen in the postmenopausal breast where E_2 levels are much lower, whereas oestrogen is the key proliferative factor in the premenopausal breast.[50]

SPRM drug available

Asoprisnil (J867) has recently been characterised as a prototype of a novel class of 11β-benzaldoxime-substituted SPRMs and the first-in-class SPRM to reach an advanced stage of clinical development for the treatment of uterine fibroids (Figure 22.3).[57,58]

Figure 22.4 shows examples of PR ligands with varying degrees of PR antagonist or agonist activities *in vivo,* including the 'pure' antagonist onapristone, 'almost pure' PR antagonist mifepristone and the 'pure' PR agonists progesterone and promegestone

(R5020). The SPRMs asoprisnil, its metabolite J912 and J1042 exhibit partial (mixed) PR agonist and antagonist activities in animals and humans, and differ, therefore, from PR antagonists and agonists. J1042 is the most agonistic SPRM. The SPRMs also show a high degree of endometrial selectivity and marginal labour-inducing effects in pregnancy models.[57]

The partial PR agonist effects are clearly seen in the rabbit endometrium and guinea pig vagina (Figure 22.5).[59] Unlike classical progesterone antagonists such as mifepristone and onapristone, asoprisnil showed only marginal labour-inducing activity during midpregnancy and was completely ineffective in inducing preterm parturition in the guinea pig.[57] In non-human primates, asoprisnil at high doses completely eliminated menstrual cyclicity, induced endometrial atrophy, and showed antiproliferative effects in the mammary gland in the presence of follicular phase oestradiol concentrations.[57,60]

Asoprisnil is the first drug that effectively controls endometrial bleeding at the endometrial level by targeting the function of spiral arteries. Early clinical studies in normal volunteers consistently demonstrated that asoprisnil suppresses menstruation in the absence of breakthrough bleeding, irrespective of the effects on ovulation.[61] Clinical results from a double-blind placebo-controlled study in subjects with uterine fibroids reported that asoprisnil was effective in decreasing the leiomyoma volume, suppressing endometrial proliferation and substantially reducing uterine bleeding.[62,63] Unlike continuous administration of progestogens or oestrogen plus progestogen combinations, treatment with asoprisnil is not associated with breakthrough bleeding and spotting. Overall, these studies indicate that asoprisnil holds promise as a new treatment for abnormal uterine bleeding and symptomatic leiomyomata, which are very common during perimenopause.

Selective androgen receptor modulators (SARMs)

AR pharmacology

ARs are widely expressed in various tissues; natural androgens play an important role in promoting and maintaining bone strength, increasing muscle mass, decreasing fat tissue and enhancing libido in both males and females.[64] The role of androgens is relatively unexplored, but more recently the state of androgen deficiency has been defined as a specific clinical condition in women, generally characterised by sexual dysfunction.[65,66] Androgens exhibit both antiresorptive and anabolic effects on bone, which is in contrast to oestrogens that exhibit mostly antiresorptive effects in bone.[67] In advanced age, the loss of anabolic effects of androgens on muscle plays an important role in the development of frailty in both females and males.[4] Importantly, there is abundant clinical and experimental evidence that androgens normally inhibit mammary epithelial proliferation and breast growth.[55,68]

SARM drugs available

Androgens have been known for a long time to exhibit positive effects on vasomotor symptoms, muscle and bone in postmenopausal women. Their use, however, has been limited due to negative effects on lipids and androgenic adverse effects, such as acne, hirsutism and voice change. SARMs are not yet available for clinical studies. However, there is interest in developing orally active SARMs, and experimental compounds exhibiting tissue-selective effects *in vivo* have already been reported in the

(a)

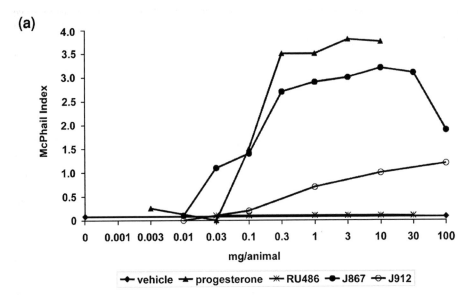

(b)

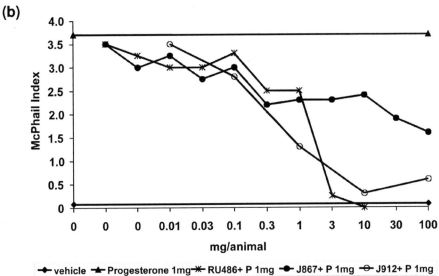

Figure 22.5. The effects of asoprisnil (J867), its metabolite J912, and the reference compounds progesterone and mifepristone on the rabbit endometrium. (a) Agonist activity. Animals received vehicle only, progesterone, mifepristone, asoprisnil or J912: progesterone showed maximal agonist effect, mifepristone had no agonist activity, asoprisnil exhibited a pronounced agonist effect, while J912 was modestly agonistic; (b) Antagonist activity. Animals were primed with oestrogen for 5 days, then treated for 7 days with vehicle, progesterone 1 mg/day ('P 1 mg'), mifepristone + P 1 mg, asoprisnil + P 1 mg, or J912 + P 1 mg, at the dosages shown: asoprisnil was a partial antagonist, showing only weak effects at up to 100 mg/day, purified J912 was a partial antagonist up to 1 mg/day, nearly abolishing progesterone effects at 10 mg/day (well above therapeutic plasma concentrations), mifepristone, in contrast, showed strong antagonist effects, completely blocking progesterone induction at 3 mg/day; modified with permission from Elger et al.[72] (Steroids, © 2000 Elsevier)

literature.[69,70] Non-virilising SARMs, with anabolic effects on bone and muscle, have the potential of becoming a treatment of choice for osteoporosis and frailty during late menopause and geripause. In addition, SARMs have the potential to improve sexual function in women,[66] unlike the currently available agents with anabolic effects on bone, such as parathyroid hormone analogues (PTHa),[6,7] or strontium ranelate.[71]

Conclusions

The synthesis of new SRMs with tissue-specific effects and recent discoveries in the field of steroid receptor action, together with advances in understanding the biology of menopausal transition and ageing, offer the promise of new therapeutic strategies for the prevention and treatment of perimenopausal symptoms and postmenopausal disorders. Cloning and characterisation of coregulator molecules provide a key to understanding the pharmacology of tissue-specific responses of hormones and SRMs.[15] These discoveries offer hope to millions of women seeking non-hormonal therapies of postmenopausal disorders.

New third-generation SERMs with improved efficacy should soon become available for the prevention of osteoporosis and breast cancer. With the understanding of the mechanisms determining tissue specificity, it is likely that an 'ideal' SERM will be discovered for the treatment of vasomotor symptoms. New SPRMs have the potential to treat abnormal uterine bleeding in perimenopausal women, and SARMs represent a potential new option for the prevention and treatment of osteoporosis and frailty.

New therapeutic strategies to treat menopausal symptoms and postmenopausal disorders are urgently needed. Development of new drugs for postmenopausal therapy is not going to be an easy task. Clinical outcomes, rather then surrogate parameters, will be needed to prove the efficacy of new therapies. In addition, long-term safety data will be required to meet the enormous expectations of women, physicians and regulatory agencies.

The WHI challenged the concept of HRT. However, as our knowledge of cell-specific effects of SRMs is increasing, improved therapies are likely to emerge. These changing developments should be viewed as an opportunity to restore the confidence of patients and practising physicians in the pharmaceutical industry and academic research regarding the appropriate dissemination of research data. An effort to elevate the level of responsibility by the pharmaceutical community is warranted so that anticipated results do not conflict with final data. This commitment is important to guarantee the scientific balance that will protect the science and value of future therapies.

References

1.   Soules MR, Sherman S, Parrott E, Rebar R, Santoro N, Utian W, *et al*. Stages of Reproductive Aging Workshop (STRAW). *J Womens Health Gend Based Med* 2001;10:843–8.
2.   Eskin BA. *The Menopause: Comprehensive Management*. New York: Parthenon Publishing Group; 2000. p. 299.
3.   Roubenoff R, Castaneda C. Sarcopenia – understanding the dynamics of aging muscle. *JAMA* 2001;286:1230–1.
4.   Roubenoff R. Sarcopenia and its implications for the elderly. *Eur J Clin Nutr* 2000;54 Suppl 3:S40–7.
5.   Fried LP, Tangen CM, Walston J, Newman AB, Hirsch C, Gottdiener J, *et al*.; Cardiovascular Health Study Collaborative Research Group. Frailty in older adults: evidence for a phenotype. *J Gerontol A Biol Sci Med Sci* 2001;56:M146–56.
6.   Neer RM, Arnaud CD, Zanchetta JR, Prince R, Gaich GA, Reginster JY, *et al*. Effect of

parathyroid hormone (1-34) on fractures and bone mineral density in postmenopausal women with osteoporosis. *N Engl J Med* 2001;344:1434–41.

7.   Orwoll ES, Scheele WH, Paul S, Adami S, Syversen U, Diez-Perez A, *et al*. The effect of teriparatide [human parathyroid hormone (1-34)] therapy on bone density in men with osteoporosis. *J Bone Miner Res* 2003;18:9–17.

8.   Zapantis G, Santoro N. The menopausal transition: characteristics and management. *Best Pract Res Clin Endocrinol Metab* 2003;17:33–52.

9.   Santoro N. The menopause transition: an update. *Hum Reprod Update* 2002;8:155–60.

10.   Santoro N, Crawford SL, Allsworth JE, Gold EB, Greendale GA, Korenman S, *et al*. Assessing menstrual cycles with urinary hormone assays. *Am J Physiol Endocrinol Metab* 2003;284:E521–30.

11.   Tsai MJ, O'Malley BW. Molecular mechanisms of action of steroid/thyroid receptor superfamily members. *Annu Rev Biochem* 1994;63:451–86.

12.   Love RR, Mazess RB, Barden HS, Epstein S, Newcomb PA, Jordan VC, *et al*. Effects of tamoxifen on bone mineral density in postmenopausal women with breast cancer. *N Engl J Med* 1992;326:852–6.

13.   Jordan VC, Robinson SP. Species-specific pharmacology of antiestrogens: role of metabolism. *Fed Proc* 1987;46:1870–4.

14.   Jordan VC. Antiestrogens and selective estrogen receptor modulators as multifunctional medicines. 1. Receptor interactions. *J Med Chem* 2003;46:883–908.

15.   Smith CL, O'Malley BW. Coregulator function: a key to understanding tissue specificity of selective receptor modulators. *Endocr Rev* 2004;25:45–71.

16.   Jackson TA, Richer JK, Bain DL, Takimoto GS, Tung L, Horwitz KB. The partial agonist activity of antagonist-occupied steroid receptors is controlled by a novel hinge domain-binding coactivator L7/SPA and the corepressors N-CoR or SMRT. *Mol Endocrinol* 1997;11:693–705.

17.   Wagner BL, Norris JD, Knotts TA, Weigel NL, McDonnell DP. The nuclear corepressors NCoR and SMRT are key regulators of both ligand- and 8-bromo-cyclic AMP-dependent transcriptional activity of the human progesterone receptor. *Mol Cell Biol* 1998;18:1369–78.

18.   McDonnell DP. The molecular determinants of estrogen receptor pharmacology. *Maturitas* 2004;48 Suppl 1:7–12.

19.   Wong CW, McNally C, Nickbarg E, Komm BS, Cheskis BJ. Estrogen receptor-interacting protein that modulates its nongenomic activity-crosstalk with Src/Erk phosphorylation cascade. *Proc Natl Acad Sci U S A* 2002;99:14783–8.

20.   Leonhardt SA, Boonyaratanakornkit V, Edwards DP. Progesterone receptor transcription and non-transcription signaling mechanisms. *Steroids* 2003;68:761–70.

21.   Zhu Y, Rice CD, Pang Y, Pace M, Thomas P. Cloning, expression, and characterization of a membrane progestin receptor and evidence it is an intermediary in meiotic maturation of fish oocytes. *Proc Natl Acad Sci U S A* 2003;100:2231–6.

22.   Thomas P, Zhu Y, Pace M. Progestin membrane receptors involved in the meiotic maturation of teleost oocytes: a review with some new findings. *Steroids* 2002;67:511–17.

23.   Lindberg MK, Weihua Z, Andersson N, Moverare S, Gao H, Vidal O, *et al*. Estrogen receptor specificity for the effects of estrogen in ovariectomized mice. *J Endocrinol* 2002;174:167–78.

24.   Nilsson M, Dahlman-Wright K, Gustafsson JA. Nuclear receptors in disease: the oestrogen receptors. *Essays Biochem* 2004;40:157–67.

25.   Couse JF, Korach KS. Estrogen receptor null mice: what have we learned and where will they lead us? *Endocr Rev* 1999;20:358–417.

26.   Schomberg DW, Couse JF, Mukherjee A, Lubahn DB, Sar M, Mayo KE, *et al*. Targeted disruption of the estrogen receptor-alpha gene in female mice: characterization of ovarian responses and phenotype in the adult. *Endocrinology* 1999;140:2733–44.

27.   Conneely OM, Mulac-Jericevic B, Lydon JP. Progesterone-dependent regulation of female reproductive activity by two distinct progesterone receptor isoforms. *Steroids* 2003;68:771–8.

28.   Mulac-Jericevic B, Conneely OM. Reproductive tissue selective actions of progesterone receptors. *Reproduction* 2004;128:139–46.

29.   Harris HA, Albert LM, Leathurby Y, Malamas MS, Mewshaw RE, Miller CP, *et al*. Evaluation of an estrogen receptor-beta agonist in animal models of human disease. *Endocrinology* 2003;144:4241–9.

30.   Hall JM, Couse JF, Korach KS. The multifaceted mechanisms of estradiol and estrogen receptor signaling. *J Biol Chem* 2001;276:36869–72.

31.   Bhavnani BR. Estrogens and menopause: pharmacology of conjugated equine estrogens and their potential role in the prevention of neurodegenerative diseases such as Alzheimer's. *J Steroid Biochem Mol Biol* 2003;85:473–82.

32.   Chetkowski RJ, Meldrum DR, Steingold KA, Randle D, Lu JK, Eggena P, *et al*. Biologic effects of transdermal estradiol. *N Engl J Med* 1986;314:1615–20.

33.   Elger W, Barth A, Hedden A, Reddersen G, Ritter P, Schneider B, *et al*. Estrogen sulfamates: a

new approach to oral estrogen therapy. *Reprod Fertil Dev* 2001;13:297–305.

34. Vongpatanasin W, Tuncel M, Wang Z, Arbique D, Mehrad B, Jialal I. Differential effects of oral versus transdermal estrogen replacement therapy on C-reactive protein in postmenopausal women. *J Am Coll Cardiol* 2003;41:1358–63.

35. Oger E, Alhenc-Gelas M, Lacut K, Blouch MT, Roudaut N, Kerlan V, *et al.* Differential effects of oral and transdermal estrogen/progesterone regimens on sensitivity to activated protein C among postmenopausal women: a randomized trial. *Arterioscler Thromb Vasc Biol* 2003;23:1671–6.

36. Reindollar R, Koltun W, Parsons A, Rosen A, Siddhanti S, Plouffe L Jr. Effects of oral raloxifene on serum estradiol levels and other markers of estrogenicity. *Fertil Steril* 2002;78:469–72.

37. Shang Y, Brown M. Molecular determinants for the tissue specificity of SERMs. *Science* 2002;295:2465–8.

38. Barrett-Connor E. Raloxifene: risks and benefits. *Ann N Y Acad Sci* 2001;949:295–303.

39. Davies GC, Huster WJ, Lu Y, Plouffe L Jr, Lakshmanan M. Adverse events reported by postmenopausal women in controlled trials with raloxifene. *Obstet Gynecol* 1999;93:558–65.

40. Ke HZ, Foley GL, Simmons HA, Shen V, Thompson DD. Long-term treatment of lasofoxifene preserves bone mass and bone strength and does not adversely affect the uterus in ovariectomized rats. *Endocrinology* 2004;145:1996–2005.

41. Suh N, Glasebrook AL, Palkowitz AD, Bryant HU, Burris LL, Starling JJ, *et al.* Arzoxifene, a new selective estrogen receptor modulator for chemoprevention of experimental breast cancer. *Cancer Res* 2001;61:8412–15.

42. Biskobing DM. Novel therapies for osteoporosis. *Expert Opin Investig Drugs* 2003;12:611–21.

43. Anthony M, Dunn BK, Sherman S. Selective Estrogen Receptor Modulators (SERMs). *Ann N Y Acad Sci* 2001;949:383.

44. Lyttle CR, Komm BS, Cheskis BJ. Estrogens: from classical endocrine action to tissue selective action. *Ernst Schering Res Found Workshop* 2004:1–21.

45. Richer JK, Jacobsen BM, Manning NG, Abel MG, Wolf DM, Horwitz KB. Differential gene regulation by the two progesterone receptor isoforms in human breast cancer cells. *J Biol Chem* 2002;277:5209–18.

46. Giangrande PH, McDonnell DP. The A and B isoforms of the human progesterone receptor: two functionally different transcription factors encoded by a single gene. *Recent Prog Horm Res* 1999;54:291–313;discussion 313–14.

47. Ismail PM, Amato P, Soyal SM, DeMayo FJ, Conneely OM, O'Malley BW, *et al.* Progesterone involvement in breast development and tumorigenesis – as revealed by progesterone receptor "knockout" and "knockin" mouse models. *Steroids* 2003;68:779–87.

48. Mote PA, Bartow S, Tran N, Clarke CL. Loss of co-ordinate expression of progesterone receptors A and B is an early event in breast carcinogenesis. *Breast Cancer Res Treat* 2002;72:163–72.

49. Sartorius CA, Shen T, Horwitz KB. Progesterone receptors A and B differentially affect the growth of estrogen-dependent human breast tumor xenografts. *Breast Cancer Res Treat* 2003;79:287–99.

50. Clarke RB. Steroid receptors and proliferation in the human breast. *Steroids* 2003;68:789–94.

51. Pike MC, Spicer DV. Hormonal contraception and chemoprevention of female cancers. *Endocr Relat Cancer* 2000;7:73–83.

52. Schneider MR, Michna H, Habenicht UF, Nishino Y, Grill HJ, Pollow K. The tumour-inhibiting potential of the progesterone antagonist Onapristone in the human mammary carcinoma T61 in nude mice. *J Cancer Res Clin Oncol* 1992;118:187–9.

53. Lundstrom E, Wilczek B, von Palffy Z, Soderqvist G, von Schoultz B. Mammographic breast density during hormone replacement therapy: effects of continuous combination, unopposed transdermal and low-potency estrogen regimens. *Climacteric* 2001;4:42–8.

54. Lundstrom E, Wilczek B, von Palffy Z, Soderqvist G, von Schoultz B. Mammographic breast density during hormone replacement therapy: differences according to treatment. *Am J Obstet Gynecol* 1999;181:348–52.

55. Conner P, Svane G, Azavedo E, Soderqvist G, Carlstrom K, Graser T, *et al.* Mammographic breast density, hormones, and growth factors during continuous combined hormone therapy. *Fertil Steril* 2004;81:1617–23.

56. Hofseth LJ, Raafat AM, Osuch JR, Pathak DR, Slomski CA, Haslam SZ. Hormone replacement therapy with estrogen or estrogen plus medroxyprogesterone acetate is associated with increased epithelial proliferation in the normal postmenopausal breast. *J Clin Endocrinol Metab* 1999;84:4559–65.

57. DeManno D, Elger W, Garg R, Lee R, Schneider B, Hess-Stumpp H, *et al.* Asoprisnil (J867): a selective progesterone receptor modulator for gynecological therapy. *Steroids* 2003;68:1019–32.

58. Chwalisz K, DeManno D, Garg R, Larsen L, Mattia-Goldberg C, Stickler T. Therapeutic potential for the selective progesterone receptor modulator asoprisnil in the treatment of leiomyomata. *Semin Reprod Med* 2004;22:113–19.

59.   Elger W, Bartley J, Schneider B, Kaufmann G, Schubert G, Chwalisz K. Endocrine pharmacological characterization of progesterone antagonists and progesterone receptor modulators with respect to PR-agonistic and antagonistic activity. *Steroids* 2000;65:713–23.

60.   Chwalisz K, Garg R, Brenner RM, Schubert G, Elger W. Selective progesterone receptor modulators (SPRMs): a novel therapeutic concept in endometriosis. *Ann N Y Acad Sci* 2002;955:373–88;discussion 389–93, 396–406.

61.   Chwalisz K, Elger W, McCrary K, Beckman P, Larsen L. Reversible suppression of menstruation in normal women irrespective of the effect on ovulation with the novel selective progesterone receptor modulator (SPRM) J867. *J Soc Gynecol Invest* 2002;9 Suppl 1:abstract 49.

62.   Chwalisz K, Lamar Parker R, Williamson S, Larsen L, McCrary K, Elger W. Treatment of uterine leiomyomas with the novel selective progesterone receptor modulator (SPRM). *J Soc Gynecol Invest* 2003;10 (2 Suppl):abstract 636.

63.   Chwalisz K, Larsen L, McCrary K, Edmonds A. Effects of the novel selective progesterone receptor modulator (SPRM) Asoprisnil on bleeding patterns in subjects with leiomyomata. *J Soc Gynecol Invest* 2004;11 (2 Suppl):abstract 728.

64.   Mooradian AD, Morley JE, Korenman SG. Biological actions of androgens. *Endocr Rev* 1987;8:1–28.

65.   Bachmann G, Bancroft J, Braunstein G, Burger H, Davis S, Dennerstein L, *et al*. Female androgen insufficiency: the Princeton consensus statement on definition, classification, and assessment. *Fertil Steril* 2002;77:660–5.

66.   Cameron DR, Braunstein GD. Androgen replacement therapy in women. *Fertil Steril* 2004;82:273–89.

67.   Notelovitz M. Androgen effects on bone and muscle. *Fertil Steril* 2002;77 Suppl 4:S34–41.

68.   Dimitrakakis C, Zhou J, Bondy CA. Androgens and mammary growth and neoplasia. *Fertil Steril* 2002;77 Suppl 4:S26–33.

69.   Negro-Vilar A. Selective androgen receptor modulators (SARMs): a novel approach to androgen therapy for the new millennium. *J Clin Endocrinol Metab* 1999;84:3459–62.

70.   Yin D, Gao W, Kearbey JD, Xu H, Chung K, He Y, *et al*. Pharmacodynamics of selective androgen receptor modulators. *J Pharmacol Exp Ther* 2003;304:1334–40.

71.   Meunier PJ, Roux C, Seeman E, Ortolani S, Badurski JE, Spector TD, *et al*. The effects of strontium ranelate on the risk of vertebral fracture in women with postmenopausal osteoporosis. *Obstet Gynecol Surv* 2004;59:526–7.

72.   Elger W, Bartley J, Schneider B, Kaufmann G, Schubert G, Chwalisz K. Endocrine pharmacological characterization of progesterone antagonists and progesterone receptor modulators with respect to PR-agonistic and antagonistic activity. *Steroids* 2000;65:713–23.

73.   Anthony M, Williams JK, Dunn BK. What would be the properties of an ideal SERM? *Ann N Y Acad Sci* 2001;949:261–78.

Chapter 23

Alternative treatments for vasomotor symptoms

Helen Buckler

Introduction

Vasomotor flushing is one of the most distressing symptoms of the menopausal syndrome. About 80% of all women experience this symptom and around 40% of women will seek medical help for it.[1] Up to 50% of women continue to have symptoms for more than five years.[2,3]

A hot flush is characterised by a sudden sensation of heat or burning that occurs in the upper body and can be accompanied by perspiration. Palpitations, sensations of weakness, vertigo and dizziness can also accompany or even precede the hot flush. The sensation lasts around four minutes on average but can range from 30 seconds to five minutes.[4] Hot flushes can interfere with sleep, leading to sleep deprivation and chronic fatigue with subsequent mood changes. Irritability, poor concentration and memory problems can occur as a consequence. The cause of vasomotor symptoms is unknown but appears to be related to a dysfunction of the thermoregulatory centres in the hypothalamus caused by oestrogen withdrawal. It is still unclear how decreasing and fluctuating levels of oestrogen result in hot flushes.

There is no doubt that oestrogen therapy is highly effective at relieving hot flushes. However, this option may not be acceptable to all women for reasons that may vary from contraindications such as the risks of breast or endometrial cancer to subjective concerns such as fear of undesired vaginal bleeding or adverse effects. With the recent publications from the Women's Health Initiative[5] and Million Women Study,[6] women are becoming increasingly concerned about the use of oestrogen therapy. As a result, critical evaluation of alternative therapies is essential for the clinician to help advise women regarding non-oestrogen therapy and to provide information regarding their safety and efficacy.

A number of both steroid and nonsteroidal agents have been used to treat vasomotor symptoms. Common problems encountered when reviewing the data and assessing the efficacy of these include a very marked placebo effect and inter-study variability. Trials that are not placebo-controlled are therefore not useful. Alternative agents most commonly employed include progestogens or progesterone, phyto-oestrogens, clonidine, selective serotonin re-uptake inhibitors (SSRIs) and other antidepressants, gabapentin and veralipride, and black cohosh and other herbal remedies.

Progestogens and progesterone

A progestogen is combined with oestrogen in hormone replacement therapy (HRT) for women with an intact uterus to protect against the development of endometrial hyperplasia and carcinoma. Progestogens alone, particularly medroxyprogesterone acetate and megestrol acetate have, however, also been used to treat hot flushes in women following breast cancer and could be used in women with endometrial carcinoma where oestrogen is contraindicated.

Two double-blind studies have demonstrated that medroxyprogesterone acetate in a dose of 20 mg/day can significantly decrease hot flushes by 74–90%.[7,8] Depot medroxyprogesterone acetate (DMPA) at doses of 50 mg, 100 mg or 150 mg 3-monthly can also relieve hot flushes although the 150 mg dose was most effective.[9] DMPA in a dose of 150 mg has also been found to be as effective as 0.625 mg of conjugated oestrogens in relieving hot flushes.[10] Megestrol acetate (20 mg twice daily) can also prevent hot flushes in menopausal women.[11] Hot flushes were reduced by 85% by megestrol acetate but only by 21% in the placebo group. In the treatment group, 74% had a decrease by 50% or more in the frequency of their hot flushes. Medroxyprogesterone acetate and megestrol acetate are very similar drugs and the available data suggest that they have equivalent effects on hot flushes, although no direct comparison has been undertaken. The specific mechanism for the reduction of hot flushes by progestogens is not well understood. Medroxyprogesterone acetate does not appear to cause any oestrogenic effect on vaginal cells, suggesting that it does not act by being converted into oestrogen-like compounds.[7] Progestogens can have adverse effects such as irregular uterine bleeding, depression, headache, weight gain and vaginal atrophy. This can limit the usefulness of these agents in some women. There is also concern about the possible association of these agents with an increased cardiovascular risk,[12] and also now the possibility of their association with increased risk of breast cancer.[5,6]

Synthetic progestogens are normally used in clinical practice rather than oral administration of progesterone as they are more resistant to hepatic metabolism. There is up to a ten-fold variation in the bioavailability of various progestogens following oral administration.[13] The doses of progestogens required are therefore in need of further evaluation. Progestogens can be administered transdermally but are only currently available in combination with 17β-oestradiol as sequential or cyclical HRT. Oral administration of progesterone results in rapid metabolism and inactivation by the liver, and therefore high doses may need to be given, which may induce marked sedative effects.[14] Intramuscular administration of progesterone is painful and intravaginal administration is inconvenient, and there is currently no evidence for its role in relieving hot flushes.

Non-prescription progesterone cream is widely available and is being used by many women in the hope that it will relieve their menopausal symptoms and prevent bone loss. However the progesterone levels after administration of transdermal progesterone cream appear to be very low. Cooper and co-workers[15] performed a randomised double-blind placebo-controlled crossover study to evaluate the absorption, metabolism and urinary excretion of progesterone administered transdermally in postmenopausal women. The study used two to four times the manufacturer's recommended dose of progesterone cream (Progest, Oregon, USA, 3.5 mg/g) and achieved median circulating progesterone levels of 2.9 nmol/l (range 0.7–15 nmol/l). Mean serum concentrations of progesterone of 1.6–3.3 ng/l have been reported after the administration of 60 mg of progesterone cream transdermally daily.[16] The levels in these studies are unlikely to help vasomotor symptoms although this still needs clarification. Topical progesterone cream (20 mg daily) has been shown in a placebo-controlled trial to cause a reduction in vasomotor symptoms.[17] Eighty-three percent of the women receiving progesterone cream showed improvement or resolution of vasomotor symptoms compared with 19% of the women receiving placebo. There was no change in bone mineral density. It may well be that if a sufficient amount of transdermal progesterone can be administered then it will alleviate vasomotor symptoms but long-term benefit and safety need to be established.

Phyto-oestrogens

A phyto-oestrogen is a plant-derived compound that is structurally and functionally related to oestrogens and their active metabolites. They can have agonistic, partial agonistic or antagonistic interactions with oestrogen receptors and could be considered natural selective oestrogen receptor modulators (SERMs). There are several classes of phyto-oestrogens or isoflavonoids. They are found in legumes, wholegrain products, fruit, vegetables, cow's milk and meat. The most commonly ingested source of isoflavonoids is soy protein, which contains the isoflavonoids daidzein and genistein. Another source often used is red clover. The pharmacodynamics and pharmacokinetics of phyto-oestrogens are poorly understood.

There are several mechanisms via which phyto-oestrogens may have an action on specific target tissues. Some of the actions are mediated through the oestrogen receptors ERα and ERβ. Most phyto-oestrogens bind preferentially to ERβ[18] whereas 17β-oestradiol binds with equal affinity to ERα and ERβ. The cellular action of phyto-oestrogens may well vary therefore depending on the relative levels of ERα and ERβ, the presence of co-activators and co-repressors, and the nature of the response element with which the receptors interact on the oestrogen-regulated genes. They can also have an effect on sex hormone binding globulin[19] and can have an antioxidant[20] and antiandrogen effect.[21] Different phyto-oestrogens probably have varying effects as their biological action is complex.

The interest in phyto-oestrogens in the menopause originates from epidemiological data that show that less than 25% of Japanese and oriental women going through the menopause complain of hot flushes[22] compared with 80% of American women.[23] It has been suggested that this difference is due to the Asian diet, which is rich in phyto-oestrogens. The traditional Japanese diet contains 200 mg per day of phyto-oestrogens.[24]

Results from studies evaluating phyto-oestrogen-rich diets have suggested that the oestrogenic and therapeutic responses in menopausal women vary. Some of the variation between trials derives from differences in sample size, type of phyto-oestrogen used, duration of evaluation as well as a tendency of hot flushes to resolve with time.

Several randomised controlled trials have tested the hypothesis that supplementing the diet with soy relieves menopausal symptoms. Results are far from conclusive but some studies do suggest a positive, although often moderate, effect. A small reduction in hot flushes was reported in postmenopausal women treated with soy protein (60 g) in comparison with casein although 25% of subjects dropped out and adverse effects were common.[25] Soy extract tablets (50 mg), soy isoflavone extracts (50 mg) and isoflavone supplements showed improvement in hot flushes compared with placebo.[26–28] These studies found about 45% reduction in hot flushes compared with a reduction with placebo of around 30%. This modest decrease compares with a 90% or greater reduction in hot flushes with oestrogen treatment. Whether much higher doses of phyto-oestrogens would have a greater beneficial effect on the reduction of hot flushes is unknown. However two studies of longer duration (six months) have shown no effect of an isoflavone-rich diet (80.4 mg) or soy-derived isoflavones (72 mg) on hot flushes.[29,30] Five other randomised controlled trials showed no benefit of soy on menopausal symptoms.[31–35] Over-the-counter preparations of isoflavones extracted from red clover were no better at relieving menopausal symptoms and hot flushes than placebo.[36,37] A large study of 252 postmenopausal women evaluated red clover-derived isoflavones in two different products (82 mg/day and 57 mg/day isoflavones) but although after 12 weeks there was a significant reduction in hot flushes there was no difference between the treatment and placebo groups.[38]

Conclusive recommendations are lacking regarding the use of dietary phyto-oestrogens to treat common menopausal symptoms. However there are some data indicating a cardioprotective effect of soy protein[39,40] and epidemiological studies support a high phyto-oestrogen-containing diet as protective against breast cancer.[41] It is not known whether some phyto-oestrogens have adverse effects and, in particular, little is known about the long-term safety of dietary soy.

Although they are popular, phyto-oestrogens have not been demonstrated to be effective in treating menopausal symptoms. There are some results, however, that are sufficiently encouraging to suggest that this area warrants further research with longer-term studies.

Black cohosh

Black cohosh, or *Actaea racemosa* (formerly referred to as *Cimicifuga racemosa*), is a herb native to eastern North America. It has traditionally been used among native Americans for the treatment of a variety of female disorders.

The roots are thought to contain compounds with oestrogenic properties. However, black cohosh also contains other compounds that act independently of the oestrogen receptor and have a central action mediated by dopaminergic receptors. There are many preparations of black cohosh on the market and each may be extracted by a different method. Black cohosh has been recommended for sleep disturbances, mood disorders and hot flushes. However, some of the evidence to support these recommendations is from open-label trials that do not take the placebo effect into account. A randomised controlled trial of black cohosh showed no conclusive evidence of benefit.[42] However, a study published in 2002 compared a black cohosh preparation (CR BNO 1055) with conjugated oestrogens and placebo[43] and the authors concluded that CR BNO 1015 was equally effective as conjugated oestrogens (0.625 mg) at relieving menopausal symptoms. Symptoms of vaginal atrophy were significantly improved by CR BNO 1015. However, the improvement in some menopausal symptoms was not significantly greater for CR BNO 1015 than placebo. CR BNO 1055 did not affect the uterus but appeared to have beneficial effects on bone turnover. It may therefore have some SERM effects.

Other herbal preparations

Various other herbal preparations have been tried to treat the symptoms of the menopause. These include dong quai, evening primrose oil, agnus castus, wild yam, St John's wort, vitamin E and ginseng. None of these preparations in randomised controlled trials or observational studies have been shown to be effective for the relief of hot flushes.

Clonidine

It was noted that women taking α-adrenergic agonists for hypertension appeared to suffer fewer hot flushes. The α-adrenergic agonist clonidine had also been noted to reduce flushing in individuals with phaeochromacytomas and possibly improve mental functioning.[44,45] The mechanism of action is thought to involve altering hypothalamic neurotransmitters, resulting in stabilisation of the thermoregulatory centre. Clonidine is the most common α-adrenergic agonist used for hot flushes and has been shown to provide better symptomatic relief of hot flushes than placebo.[46-50] Doses of 50–400 μg/day have been used. The response to clonidine appears to be dose-dependent and the mean rate of hot flush occurrence has been decreased by up to 46% with a dose of 400 μg. However, at this dose, adverse effects such as insomnia, syncope, sedation and dry mouth are common.[49] Clonidine has been compared with oestrogen and although clonidine significantly reduced hot flushes, oestrogen was more effective.[51] Transdermal clonidine has also been shown to be useful.[52] The alternative α-adrenergic agonist lofexidine can also reduce hot flushes but this is also associated with significant adverse effects.[53] Methyldopa can be helpful but again its use is limited by adverse effects.[54,55]

Antidepressants

As with clonidine, clinicians noticed that women prescribed SSRIs for depression had fewer hot flushes. It has been postulated that serotonin is involved in the pathogenesis of hot flushes,[56] and if this is the case then SSRIs would be expected to be helpful in their treatment. Animal studies suggest that serotonin plays an important role in thermoregulation and that the temperature increase associated with hot flushes may be linked to an overloading of serotonin receptor sites in the hypothalamus.

The SSRI fluoxetine has been evaluated for the treatment of hot flushes in breast cancer survivors and in women at high risk of breast cancer. Fluoxetine 20 mg/day reduced hot flushes by 50% whereas placebo only decreased them by 36%.[57] The alternative SSRI paroxetine (20 mg/day) also reduced the hot flush score by 75% in breast cancer survivors and there were significant improvements in depression, sleep, anxiety and quality of life score.[58] Paroxetine controlled release was used in a double-blind placebo-controlled study of postmenopausal women without breast cancer.[59] One hundred and sixty five women were included and randomised to 12.5 or 25 mg/day of paroxetine or placebo. The reduction in hot flush frequency was 62% with the lower dose and 65% with the higher dose, which was significantly better than placebo.

Venlafaxine is an antidepressant that inhibits both noradrenaline and serotonin uptake. It has been reported in an open-label trial of breast cancer patients to decrease hot flush frequency by 50%.[60] In a placebo-controlled trial it was also effective and the decrease in hot flushes was greatest with higher doses (up to 150 mg/day).[61]

These drugs are generally well tolerated and may provide an alternative to oestrogen treatment in the management of hot flushes. The specific dosages of these agents required for treating hot flushes are not known and may well be lower than those recommended for depression. Although these agents are generally well tolerated there are fewer adverse effects with lower dosages. The duration of benefit of antidepressant treatment for hot flushes also remains unknown.

Gabapentin and veralipride

There have been some studies examining the use of gabapentin for the relief of hot flushes. Gabapentin is a γ-amino butyric acid analogue that is used as an anticonvulsant and for the relief of neuropathic pain. The mechanisms by which it could help hot flushes are not known and appear independent of γ-amino butyric acid receptors. Two pilot studies have suggested a reduction in hot flushes after initiation of gabapentin treatment.[62,63] A randomised controlled trial showed a significant reduction in severe hot flushes with gabapentin (900 mg/day) compared with placebo.[64] The dose used as an anticonvulsant is normally 3000–3600 mg/day. However, even with a lower dose adverse effects of somnolence, fatigue, tremor, nausea, oedema and ataxia are common.

The antidopaminergic agent veralipride has been shown to be as effective as conjugated oestrogens for the treatment of hot flushes.[65] However adverse effects including galactorrhoea and weight gain are likely to limit its use.[66]

Behavioural therapies

Behavioural therapies and relaxation techniques have been tried for the reduction of hot flushes. It is difficult to obtain an appropriate control group as it is impossible to blind for this type of intervention. Paced respiration as rhythmic deep breathing has been found to decrease the frequency of hot flushes.[67,68] As a control group, non-therapeutic α-wave electroencephalographic bio-feedback was used, which was ineffective. It therefore appears that slow deep breathing exercises can modulate the frequency of hot flushes, although only modestly. The authors suggest that this effect is by modulating elevated central sympathetic activation that may be involved in the initiation of hot flushes.

Relaxation therapy has not been found to decrease the frequency of hot flushes but may decrease the intensity.[69] Psychological treatment combined with HRT can be helpful in relieving some menopausal symptoms but is no better than HRT alone in relieving vasomotor symptoms.[70] Exercise has been recommended for the treatment of hot flushes and may show some benefit.[71,72] Lifestyle issues such as smoking and high body mass index may increase a woman's risk for hot flushes.[73] As these factors are potentially modifiable, it may be important to further elucidate lifestyle factors that are associated with a risk of hot flushes. Preventive measures can then be targeted for women at greatest risk.

Summary

For many years women have sought alternative therapies for menopausal symptoms. The highly publicised findings from the Women's Health Initiative and the Million Women Study have further increased this demand. Clinicians are being placed under increasing pressure to find safe alternative medications to HRT.

It is important to offer help and therapy to alleviate vasomotor and menopausal symptoms where quality of life is affected. No therapy for vasomotor symptoms has stood the test of time as well as oestrogen therapy. The use of HRT is entirely justifiable to reduce symptoms around the time of the perimenopause, although it is not appropriate for all women because of co-existing problems, adverse effects or personal preference.

Herbal products are increasingly popular but women can be confused as to which supplements to use. They also have concerns regarding their long-term safety and interactions with other medications they are taking. In addition, there is lack of consensus among experts regarding the appropriate dosages, length of treatment and possible drug interactions.

The phyto-oestrogens or isoflavones are probably safe and may potentially have a cardioprotective effect and an anti-oestrogen effect on the breast. The results of studies using phyto-oestrogens for vasomotor symptoms are at present far from uniform but some suggest a beneficial although modest effect. Phyto-oestrogens can be considered as naturally occurring selective oestrogen receptor modulators, and development of SERMs with an oestrogen agonist effect on vasomotor symptoms plus favourable oestrogen antagonist effects would be ideal.

Just because a product is natural does not mean that it is safe. Herbal products may have little effect but may actually cause harm. A herb or plant may not be the same natural compound when it is formulated into a capsule or tablet. Herbal preparations may vary widely in their content and dosages and therefore may not provide a consistent and reliable effect.

Although unlicensed for this indication, some antidepressants, including venlafaxine, fluoxetine and paroxetine, appear to reduce the frequency of hot flushes. These agents are generally well tolerated. HRT, through its action in alleviating hot flushes and sleep disturbances, may also improve mood and wellbeing in postmenopausal women as a domino effect. In this respect, antidepressants may also help menopausal women who have low mood and reduced wellbeing.

Lifestyle modifications such as maintaining normal body mass and stopping smoking should be considered in perimenopausal women. Information and advice regarding behavioural therapies, relaxation and exercise can also be given at this time.

References

1. Dennerstein L. Wellbeing, symptoms and the menopausal transition. *Maturitas* 1996;23:47–57.
2. Thompson B, Hart SA, Durnod. Menopausal age and symptomatology in general practice. *J Biosoc Sci* 1973;5:71–82.
3. Stearns V, Ullmer L, Lopez JF, Smith Y, Isaacs C, Hayes D. Hot flushes. *Lancet* 2002;360:1851–61.
4. Meldrum DR, Shamonki IM, Frumar AM, Tataryn IV, Chang RJ, Judd HL. Elevations in skin temperature of the finger as an objective index of postmenopausal hot flashes: standardization of the technique. *Am J Obstet Gynecol* 1979;135:713–7.
5. Rossouw JE, Anderson GL, Prentice RL, LaCroix AZ, Kooperberg C, Stefanick ML, *et al.*; Writing Group for the Women's Health Initiative Investigators. Risks and benefits of estrogen plus progestin in healthy postmenopausal women: principal results From the Women's Health Initiative randomized controlled trial. *JAMA* 2002;288:321–33.
6. Beral V; Million Women Study Collaborators. Breast cancer and hormone-replacement therapy in the Million Women Study. *Lancet* 2003;362:419–27. Erratum in: *Lancet* 2003;362:1160.
7. Schiff I, Tulchinisky D, Cramer D, Ryan KJ. Oral medroxyprogesterone in the treatment of postmenopausal symptoms. *JAMA* 1980;244:1443–5.
8. Albrecht BH, Schiff I, Tulchinisky D, Ryan KJ. Objective evidence of placebo on oral medroxyprogesterone acetate therapy to diminish menopausal vasomotor symptoms. *Am J Obstet Gynecol* 1981;139:631–5.
9. Morrison J, Martin D, Blair R, Anderson G. The use of medroxyprogesterone acetate for the relief of climacteric symptoms. *Am J Obstet Gynecol* 1980;138:99–104.
10. Lobo RA, McCormick W, Singer F, Roy S. Depo-medroxyprogesterone acetate compared with conjugated estrogens for the treatment of postmenopausal women. *Obstet Gynecol* 1984;63:1–5.
11. Loprinzi CL, Michalak JC, Quella SK, O'Fallon JR, Hatfield AK, Nelimark RA, *et al.* Megestrol acetate for the prevention of hot flashes. *N Engl J Med* 1994;331:347–52.
12. Vasilaki SC, Jick H, del Mar Melero-Montes M. Risk of idiopathic venous thrombo embolism in users of progestogens alone. *Lancet* 1999;354:1610–11.
13. Paqualini JR. Progestins present and future. *J Steroid Biochem Mol Biol* 1996;59:357–63.
14. Arafat ES, Hargrove JT, Maxson WS, Desiderio DM, Wentz AC, Anderson RN. Sedative and hypnotic effects of oral administration of micronised progesterone may be mediated through its metabolites. *Am J Obstet Gynecol* 1988;159:1203–9.
15. Cooper A, Spencer C, Whitehead MI, Ross D, Barnard GJ, Collins WP. Systemic absorption of progesterone from Progest cream in postmenopausal women. *Lancet* 1998;351:1255–6.
16. Burry KA, Patton PE, Hermsmeyer K. Percutaneous absorption of progesterone in postmenopausal women treated with transdermal estrogen. *Am J Obstet Gynecol* 1999;180 (6 Pt 1):1504–11.

17.   Leonetti H, Longo S, Anasti J. Trandermal progesterone cream for vasomotor symptoms and postmenopausal bone loss. *Obstet Gynecol* 1999;94:225–8.
18.   Kuiper GG, Lemmen JG, Carlsson B, Corton JC, Safe SH, van der Saag PT, *et al*. Interaction of estrogenic chemicals and phytoestrogens with estrogen receptor beta. *Endocrinology* 1998;139:4252–63.
19.   Carusi D. Phytoestrogens as hormone replacement therapy: an evidence-based approach. *Prim Care Update Ob Gyns* 2000;7:253–9.
20.   Rohrdanz E, Ohler S, Tran-Thi QH, Kahl R. The phytoestrogen daidzein affects the antioxidant enzyme system of rat hepatoma H4IIE cells. *J Nutr* 2002;132:370–5.
21.   Saito M, Mitsui T, Mizuno T. Genistein represses the induction of prostatic bugs by testosterone. *J Soc Biol* 2000;194:95–7.
22.   Locke M. *Encounters With Ageing: Mythologies of Menopause in Japan and North America*. Berkeley and Los Angeles: University of California Press; 1993.
23.   Notelovitz M. Estrogen replacement therapy indications and agents selection. *Am J Obstet Gynecol* 1989;161:8–17.
24.   Cassidy A, Bingham S, Setchell KD. Biological effects of a diet of soy protein rich in isoflavones on the menstrual cycle of premenopausal women. *Am J Clin Nutr* 1994;60:333–40.
25.   Albertazzi P, Pansini F, Bonaccorsi G, Zanotti L, Forini E, De Aloysio D. The effect of dietary soy supplementation on hot flushes. *Obstet Gynecol* 1998;91:6–11. Erratum in: *Obstet Gynecol* 2001;98:702.
26.   Scambia G, Mango D, Signorile PG, Anselmi Angeli RA, Palena C, Gallo D, *et al*. Clinical effects of a standardized soy extract in postmenopausal women: a pilot study. *Menopause* 2000;7:105–11.
27.   Upmalis DH, Lobo R, Bradley L, Warren M, Cone F, Lamia C. Vasomotor symptom relief by soy isoflavone extract tablets in postmenopausal women – a multi-centre double-blind randomized placebo controlled trial. *Menopause* 2000;7:236–42.
28.   Han KK, Soares JM, Haider MA, de Lima GR, Baracat EC. Benefits of soy isoflavone therapeutic regimen on menopausal symptoms. *Obstet Gynecol* 2002;99:389–94.
29.   St German A, Peterson CT, Robinson JG, Lee Alekel D. Isoflavone rich or isoflavone poor soy protein does not reduce menopausal symptoms during 24 weeks of treatment. *Menopause* 2001;8:17–21.
30.   Penotti M, Fabio E, Modena AB, Rinaldi M, Omodeiu Vigamo P. The effect of soy derived isoflavones on hot flushes, endometrial thickness, the pulsatility index of the uterine and cerebral arteries. *Fertil Steril* 2003;79:1112–17.
31.   Murkies AL, Lombard C, Strauss BJ, Wilcox G, Burger HG, Morton MS. Dietary flour supplementation decreases post-menopausal hot flushes: effect of soy and wheat. *Maturitas* 1995;21:189–95.
32.   Wilcox G, Burger HG, Morton MS, Brzezinski A, Aldercreutz H, Shaoul R, *et al*. Short term effects of phyto-oestrogen rich diet on postmenopausal women. *Menopause* 1997;4:89–94.
33.   Dalais FS, Rice GE, Wahlqvist ML, Grehan M, Murkies AL, Medley G, *et al*. Effects of dietary phyto-oestrogens in postmenopausal women. *Climacteric* 1998;1:124–9.
34.   Knight DC, Howells JB, Eden JA, Howes LH. Effects on menopausal symptoms and acceptability of isoflavone containing soy powder dietary supplementation. *Climacteric* 2001;4:13–18.
35.   Van Patten CL, Olivotto IA, Chambers GK, Gelmon KA, Hislop TG, Templeton E, *et al*. Effect of soy phytoestrogens on hot flashes in postmenopausal women with breast cancer: a randomized, controlled clinical trial. *J Clin Oncol* 2002;20:1449–55.
36.   Knight D, Howells JB, Eden JA. The effect of Promensil an isoflavone extract on menopausal symptoms. *Climacteric* 1999;2:79–84.
37.   Baber RJ, Templeman C, Moreton T, Kelly GE, West L. Randomized placebo controlled trial of an isoflavone supplement and menopausal symptoms in women. *Climacteric* 1999;2:85–92.
38.   Tice JA, Ettinger B, Ensrud K, Wallace R, Blackwell T, Cummings SR. Phytoestrogen supplements for the treatment of hot flashes: the Isoflavone Clover Extract (ICE) Study: a randomized controlled trial. *JAMA* 2003;290:207–14.
39.   Anderson JW, Johnstone BM, Cook-Newall ME. Better analysis of the effects of soy protein intake on serum lipids. *N Engl J Med* 1995;333:276–82.
40.   Clarkson TB, Anthony MS, Morgan TM. Inhibition of postmenopausal atherosclerosis progression: a comparison of the effects of conjugated equine estrogens and soy phytoestrogens. *J Clin Endocrinol Metab* 2001;86:41–7.
41.   Aldercreutz H. Epidemiology of phytoestrogens. *Baillieres Clin Endocrinol Metab* 1998;12:605–23.
42.   Jacobson JS, Troxel AB, Evans J, Klaus L, Vahdat L, Kinne D, *et al*. Randomized trial of black cohosh for the treatment of hot flashes among women with a history of breast cancer. *J Clin Oncol* 2001;19:2739–45.

43. Wuttke W, Seidlova-Wuttke D, Gorkow C. The Cimicifuga preparation BNO 1055 vs. conjugated estrogens in a double-blind placebo-controlled study: effects on menopause symptoms and bone markers. *Maturitas* 2003;44 Suppl 1:S67–77.
44. Ginsburg J, O'Reilly B. Effect of oral Clonidine on the vascular effects of stressful mental arithmetic in menopausal women. *J Cardiovasc Pharmacol* 1987;10:S138–41.
45. Metz SA, Halter JB, Porte D Jr, Robertson RP. Suppression of plasma catecholamines and flushing by clonidine in man. *J Clin Endocrinol Metab* 1978;46:83–90.
46. Eddington RF, Shagnon JP, Steinberg WN. Clonidine (Dixarit) for menopausal flushing. *Can Med Assoc J* 1980;123:23–36.
47. Bolli P, Simpson FO. Clonidine in menopausal flushing: a double-blind trial. *N Z Med J* 1975;82:196–7.
48. Clayden JR, Bell JW, Pollard P. Menopausal flushing – a double-blind trial of non-hormonal medication. *BMJ* 1974;1:409–12.
49. Laufer LR, Erlik Y, Meldrum DR, Judd HL. Effect of clonidine on hot flashes in postmenopausal women. *Obstet Gynecol* 1982;60:583–6.
50. Salni T, Punnonen R. Clonidine in the treatment of menopausal symptoms. *Int J Gynaecol Obstet* 1979;16:422–6.
51. Barr W. Problems related to menopausal women. *S Afr Med J* 1975;49:437–9.
52. Nagamani N, Kelver ME, Smith ER. Treatment of menopausal hot flushes with transdermal administration of Clonidine. *Am J Obstet Gynecol* 1987;156:561–5.
53. Jones KP, Ravnikar V, Schiff I. A preliminary evaluation of the effect of lofexidine on vasomotor flushes in post-menopausal women.*Maturitas* 1985;7:135–9.
54. Nesheim BI, Saetre T. Reduction of menopausal hot flushes by methyldopa. A double blind crossover trial. *Eur J Clin Pharmacol* 1981;20:413–16.
55. Hammond MG, Hatley L, Talbert LM. A double-blind study to evaluate the effect of methyldopa on menopausal vasomotor symptoms. *J Clin Endocrinol Metab* 1984;58:1158–60.
56. Berendsen HH. The role of serotonin in hot flushes. *Maturitas* 2000;36:155–64.
57. Loprinzi CL, Sloan JA, Perez EA, Quella SK, Stella PJ, Mailliard JA, *et al*. Phase III evaluation of fluoxetine for treatment of hot flashes. *J Clin Oncol* 2002;20:1578–83.
58. Stearns V, Isaacs C, Rowland J, Crawford J, Ellis MJ, Kramer R, *et al*. A pilot trial assessing the efficacy of paroxetine hydrochloride (Paxil) in controlling hot flashes in breast cancer survivors. *Ann Oncol* 2000;11:17–22.
59. Stearns V, Beebe KL, Iyengar M, Dube E. Paroxetine controlled release in the treatment of menopausal hot flashes: a randomized controlled trial. *JAMA* 2003;289:2827–34.
60. Loprinzi CL, Pisansky TM, Fonseca R, Sloan JA, Zahasky KM, Quella SK, *et al*. Pilot evaluation of venlafaxine hydrochloride for the therapy of hot flashes in cancer survivors. *J Clin Oncol* 1998;16:2377–81.
61. Barton D, La VB, Loprinzi C, Novotny P, Wilwerding MB, Sloan J. Venlafaxine for the control of hot flashes: results of a longitudinal continuation study. *Oncol Nurs Forum* 2002;29:33–40.
62. Loprinzi L, Barton DL, Sloan JA, Zahasky KM, Smith de AR, Pruthi S, *et al*. Pilot evaluation of gabapentin for treating hot flashes. *Mayo Clin Proc* 2002;77:1159–63.
63. Guttuso TJ Jr. Gabapentin's effects on hot flashes and hypothermia. *Neurology* 2000;54:2161–3.
64. Guttuso T Jr, Kurlan R, McDermott MP, Kieburtz K. Gabapentin's effects on hot flashes in postmenopausal women: a randomized controlled trial. *Obstet Gynecol* 2003;101:337–45.
65. Wesel S, Bourguignon RP, Bossumer WB. Veralipride versus conjugated oestrogens – a double-blind study in the management of menopausal hot flushes. *Curr Med Res Opin* 1984;8:696–700.
66. Verbeke K, Dhont M, Vandekerckhove D. Clinical and hormonal effects of long-term veralipride treatment in post-menopausal women. *Maturitas* 1988;10:225–30.
67. Freedman RR, Woodward S. Behavioral treatment of menopausal hot flushes – evaluation by ambulatory monitoring. *Am J Obstet Gynecol* 1992;167:202–7.
68. Freedman RR, Woodward S, Brown B. Biochemical and thermoregulatory effects of behavioural treatment for menopausal hot flushes. *Menopause* 1995;2:211–18.
69. Irvin JH, Domar AD, Clark C, Zuttermeister PC, Friedman R. The effects of relaxation response training on menopausal symptoms. *J Psychosom Obstet Gynaecol* 1996;17:202–7.
70. Anart MT, Kuadros JL, Herrera J. Hormonal and psychological treatment – therapeutic alternative for menopausal women. *Maturitas* 1998;29:203–13.
71. Prince RL, Smith M, Dick IM, Price RI, Webb PG, Henderson NK, *et al*. Prevention of postmenopausal osteoporosis. A comparative study of exercise, calcium supplementation, and hormone-replacement therapy. *N Engl J Med* 1991;325:1189–95.
72. Ivarsson T, Spetz AC, Hammar M. Physical exercise and vasomotor symptoms in postmenopausal women. *Maturitas* 1998;29:139–46.
73. Whiteman MK, Staropoli CA, Langenberg PW, McCarter RJ, Kjerulff KH, Flaws JA. Smoking, body mass, and hot flashes in midlife women. *Obstet Gynecol* 2003;101:264–72.

Chapter 24

Alternative strategies for treatment of menopausal symptoms

Discussion

Discussion following Dr Chwalisz's paper

Beral: Can I just raise a question about progestogens and antiprogestogens and breast cancer because of our earlier discussion? There are a lot of data which do suggest that, certainly for postmenopausal women, giving progestogens together with oestrogen is much worse than oestrogen alone. In reading around, and speaking to a number of people here, there is a literature that asks the question 'why do we not use antiprogestogens for breast cancer prevention?' There has been so much work on anti-oestrogens but not that much, as I understand it, on antiprogestogens. I was going to ask you about RU486 – mifepristone – and also about the new compound that you mentioned. Are they opposing or similar, and does anyone have any data on breast cancer risk, on long-term safety and such like, about mifepristone?

Chwalisz: I have to explain here that mifepristone exhibited quite good efficacy in animal models of breast cancer[1] but did not show positive clinical effects. There is one phase II Canadian study with mifepristone[2] in a favourable group of women with PR-positive recurrent breast cancer who had received no prior therapy. This study showed little efficacy of mifepristone. However, the 'pure' PR antagonist onapristone, used as a first-line therapy, did show efficacy in subjects with breast cancer in a small clinical study.[3] Unfortunately, the development of this compound has been terminated because of its adverse liver effects. Overall these studies are too small to make any conclusions about efficacy of PR antagonists in breast cancer. It would be important, however, to develop compounds acting selectively on PR-A or PR-B isoforms for preventive strategies. Theoretically, it should be possible to develop an HRT regimen with an oestrogen and a selective progesterone receptor modulator (SPRM), which has no stimulatory effects on breast, but there is still a long way from the laboratory to the clinic. Progestogen is clearly a mitogen in the breast and both animal and human data support this view.

Glasier: There are very few clinical studies and the one or two that there have been are in the treatment of breast cancer.[4] There are lots of studies of cell lines and if you have a progesterone receptor and you feed the cell line mifepristone then you inhibit or reduce growth. But there is an enthusiasm, certainly in Edinburgh, for developing a contraceptive with low-dose antigestogens or SPRMs and I think that the line between the two is very fine. So there is an exciting potential for doing that.

Beral: You have done studies, but I think on very small numbers of women?

Glasier: We have never been able to look at the breast – we have only looked at uterus and ovulation. It is very difficult to get breast tissue from normal women who are volunteering for studies.

Chwalisz: We are doing mammograms in our phase III programme with asoprisnil. However, these studies are being performed in premenopausal women who already have increased breast density, so it is uncertain whether we will be able to demonstrate any effect. We do not yet have this data, and perhaps we will need more studies to determine SPRM effects on breast. I agree with you that it is an exciting opportunity, but we need to do more work to determine whether this type of molecule decreases breast density and proliferation.

Miller: Can I ask you a specific question? Your results in the monkeys are very interesting, particularly with regard to breast. But these monkeys, are they premenopausal monkeys?

Chwalisz: Yes, these are premenopausal monkeys which were treated in this particular study for nine months with relatively high doses of asoprisnil.[5]

Miller: So, what you are antagonising there is in fact natural progesterone.

Chwalisz: Yes, some of these monkeys were cycling although some of them become amenorrhoeic at the beginning of the study. What we know from these studies is that the oestrogen levels were relatively high. Similarly, we have not found any inhibitory effects of asoprisnil on oestrogen levels in humans, so this particular compound may modulate the responses of oestrogen, luteal phase progesterone, and may directly affect the tissue.

Miller: You must know from the preclinical basic biology in development of the drug whether if in fact you load the progesterone receptors with synthetic progestogens, such as those used in HRT and so on, you antagonise to the same degree or not? Is it an effect irrespective of what is sitting on the progesterone receptor?

Chwalisz: Yes, we previously used bioassays to evaluate the effects of various progestogens on breast proliferation, You can see a dramatic increase in density of epithelial tissue with almost every progestogen, so what we observe here is a class effect. There might be an inhibitory effect of androgens on breast proliferation, which is still unexplored in my opinion. The antigestogens, mifepristone and onapristone, clearly suppress breast proliferation. They even suppress the effects of oestrogen on breast proliferation in animal models. So, progesterone receptor, antagonised with mifepristone or onapristone, has an inhibitory activity on oestrogen responses in the breast even in the absence of progesterone. This is what the preclinical studies show.

Stevenson: With regard to your comment on the selective androgen receptor modulators (SARMs), a couple of points. First of all, in your list of bone-anabolic agents you need to include fluoride, strontium, and oestrogen. So we do have some anabolic agents to bone, although they do have drawbacks. I would encourage you to actually look for the vascular effects of the SARMs, as well as the other effects you are looking at, because they could be very important.

Chwalisz: Yes, thank you for this comment. In asoprisnil studies we are currently looking for evidence supporting the vascular hypothesis of amenorrhoea. It would be important to address the effects of SPRMs and SARMs on different vascular beds. I agree with you that this is an important issue.

Whitehead: If a drug is developed, any drug to reduce the risk of breast cancer, and the drug is successful, and the drug is taken for five years or ten years or even fifteen years, what happens when patients eventually stop the drug? Is this the ideal drug for the pharmaceutical industry because the drug is started and then subjects never stop it because of the worry that there is going to be a rebound of excess risk?

Chwalisz: Raloxifene is probably prescribed because of this potential effect on reducing breast cancer, which is still not fully explored.

Studd: But is it licensed for that?

Chwalisz: It is not licensed for that but prescribed nevertheless.

Miller: I think tamoxifen is definitely but raloxifene is not.

Gebbie: But the patient expectation is of reduced risk of breast cancer?

Chwalisz: The patient perspective is that there is a very strong interest in having a compound which will prevent breast cancer, particularly in the USA.

Whitehead: But if you stop raloxifene, do you get a rebound excess risk in breast cancer?

Chwalisz: We do not know and I am not aware of any data. In fact, the company is doing a lot of studies in this area to demonstrate this preventive effect, but I am not aware of the data. Most of them are still unpublished.

Purdie: Can I just comment on that, as an investigator in the Multiple Outcomes of Raloxifene Evaluation (MORE) study?[6] We have repeatedly asked Eli Lilly to maintain sufficient statistical power to see if patients discontinuing raloxifene exhibit any form of rebound in breast cancer and have yet to have a satisfactory answer from them on that.

Miller: There are data to address that question. It is not, admittedly, a straight-on risk. There is a huge experience with use of tamoxifen in the adjuvant treatment of breast cancer. It is very clear that they have looked at large trials where in fact the length of the duration has actually been looked at. The data suggest that if you treat for five years with tamoxifen, then the recurrence rates are less than if you treat for two years. So there is a progressive benefit up to five years. The great worry is that once you actually treat beyond five years, although the numbers in the studies are smaller, because normally people stop at five years, the suggestion is that actually the rate starts to increase. The suggestion is that there is a rebound effect. We really do not know what the molecular changes are, but there seem to be reductive changes occurring within the tumour, where the tumour now instead of seeing tamoxifen as an anti-oestrogen is starting to see it as an oestrogen and therefore it is contraindicated to actually continue beyond five years. That may not be the same across the board though.

Whitehead: You are talking about breast cancer recurrence, but I am talking about new breast cancers.

Miller: That is slightly different but there is a point which perhaps needs to be teased out too. If we are talking about breast cancer prevention then what we are actually talking about is the carcinogenic process. If we are talking about the carcinogenic process then these sorts of observations in proliferating so-called 'normal' breasts are really important. But if what you are actually talking about is the appearance of breast cancer, particularly over a short term, then the natural history of breast cancer suggests that you are not necessarily looking at an inhibition of the carcinogenic process. What you are probably looking at is the retardation or abolition of occult tumours which are actually appearing. If that is the case, then the recurrence data becomes relevant.

Whitehead: Because you would expect them to start growing again when you withdraw the suppressor.

Discussion following Dr Buckler's paper

Barlow: I thought it was a very nicely comprehensive presentation you gave on alternative treatments that can be adopted for women with flushes. With regard to progestogen, one thing I would like to add is that the progestogen norethisterone was not mentioned and it is quite widely used in doses from 5 mg down to 1 mg on a continuous basis and it is quite effective in reducing hot flushes, their intensity or taking them away altogether, and it also gives protection to the skeleton at the same time. There are a number of trials[7,8] showing that. Also, with low-dose oestrogen therapy and continuous combined therapy there is some trial evidence from randomised controlled trials[9] that adding a low dose of norethisterone to the oestrogen may give extra benefit in the secondary endpoints measures such as bone density. So I just wanted to add that norethisterone sits alongside medroxyprogesterone acetate (MPA) and megestrol.

Buckler: I would agree with that and I think clinically actually we probably use norethisterone more. But, in fact, from the primary outcome of vasomotor symptoms in just straightforward menopausal women rather than women receiving GnRH-analogues, etc., there is actually no randomised controlled data on norethisterone on its own.

Lumsden: Dr Buckler, high-dose progestogens have been used in the treatment of advanced breast cancer for a long time. I wonder if you could comment on the sort of dosages that are often used in HRT when progestogens are used to try to treat symptoms because it seems to be very variable. Also, I would have thought it was quite possible that the effect of the progestogen would be altered by co-administration with oestrogen, as you have with combined HRT, because of the effects of oestrogen on progesterone receptor synthesis.

Buckler: Addressing the first question, I would have though that the doses that have been used in breast cancer when progestogens have been given in an attempt to treat are actually much higher than you need for hot flushes. I suspect that it may be possible for us to use lower doses than actually have been investigated. Certainly using norethisterone, I think you can often get some relief of hot flushes with doses lower relative to the doses that have been used of MPA and megestrol acetate. I agree, I think from the point of view of effects on the breast, I am sure if you are giving progestogen and oestrogen together it is a very different scenario. I think that it is a slight concern, as you know, that we just do not have any safety data.

Prentice: I had a question for Dr Buckler about dose: you mentioned that 20 mg of MPA was effective for hot flushes, what about the standard 2.5 mg dose *per se*?

Buckler: It is not known – we do not know. I suspect that 2.5 mg of MPA would not reduce hot flushes but that is just an opinion. But certainly 5 mg of norethisterone can reduce hot flushes, although that has not been well studied, it is just anecdotal from clinical practice.

Prentice: Just a point of clarification about black cohosh: you mentioned a couple of small randomised trials[10,11] that, you said, showed no benefit but you also said it was compared to oestrogen. Is there is no absolute benefit?

Buckler: No, oestrogen was a lot more effective.

Cardozo: I would like to take issue with something that Dr Buckler said. Most overweight women would like to be thin and most women who smoke would like not to smoke. If you go to your GP with a problem like hot flushes and you are told to go away and lose weight and stop smoking, all that is is counter-productive. It stops you having a social life and there is no evidence whatsoever that it helps your hot flushes. This happens all the time with incontinent women, they go to the doctor and they are told to lose weight and stop smoking, they miss out on their social activities, they cannot take exercise because they wet themselves and they become depressed and need to be treated for a co-morbidity. So I think before we advise women to do things which affect their lifestyle, we have to think whether there is any evidence whatsoever that it is going to improve their prime symptom.

Buckler: I agree totally and I did not mean to give the impression that if a woman comes with hot flushes the first thing you do is to tell them to stop smoking and lose weight, and take up jogging. I think it was really just, perhaps, that it gives us an opportunity to offer some general healthcare advice. Also perhaps the other thing is that if there are factors that we know make hot flushes worse then it may be that we should try and make women aware of that early on. But I agree totally that suggesting somebody loses weight to sort their problems out is unrealistic.

Cardozo: It must not come as a recommendation from this group that we give women counterproductive advice for which there is no evidence whatsoever.

Chwalisz: I would like to make a comment on norethisterone. It is a unique progestogen because it is probably the only progestogen that is oestrogenic. Ethinyl oestradiol is one of the active metabolites of norethisterone and is the reason why this compound is more effective in reducing hot flushes than other progestogens.

Beral: One comment about breast cancer and progestogens: in the Million Women Study, out of the million we have 618 women who took progestogens only and there were 9 breast cancers amongst them. It is in the paper, and the relative risk was 2.02 and it was actually significantly increased. But 618 out of a million – it is not very commonly prescribed alone. Another question about the antidepressants for you and maybe for others too. As you have shown, several trials have demonstrated that a range of antidepressants seem to work and we were talking earlier that a lot of women feel depressed and anxious. HRT is often prescribed for this reason, combined with menopausal symptoms. What is your view about the idea that if depression is a major problem then women should use some of these antidepressants only as an initial therapy. Because there have been quite long follow-up studies of antidepressants and certainly in the long term they not only treat the depression, the current one, but they actually prevent recurrences of depression very effectively. I do not think – obviously it is not being taken by as many women as HRT but there do not seem to be serious effects even with long-term use. So I just wonder what people think of antidepressants as a first-line therapy?

Buckler: I think it is very reasonable. I think the difficulty perhaps is if you have a woman who goes to see the GP or even to the specialist menopause clinic complaining of hot flushes that people are not always ideally qualified to be able to ascertain how significant depression is as part of that. Because if it is, I think it is an entirely reasonable thing to do, but we must not assume that every woman that comes to see us with hot flushes is necessarily depressed.

Beral: But you know, hot flushes are hot flushes, and they are treated as such. There was quite a lot of discussion in the previous days that for many women it is depression and anxiety that are prominent symptoms.

Buckler: Yes, and in fact if not treated then the hot flushes and the sleep deprivation are going to go on and cause problems. But I think it would be wrong to label all women with menopausal symptoms as necessarily being depressed as well. It would require teasing out what is most appropriate. I think the use of antidepressants for menopausal symptoms is going to increase and perhaps particularly in those patients where it is identified that there is a significant mood or depressive effect as well.

Gray: A very quick comment – many women are happy to try them out but if it is not good enough for their symptom complex they move on. We need to remember that selective serotonin reuptake inhibitors (SSRIs) have a very negative effect on sexual responsiveness and that may be the limiting factor for them.

Burger: The other problem with gabapentin, at least for us in Australia, is that it is forbiddingly expensive. It is the one drug, I think, amongst the group which is way out in front in terms of potential expense, which I had not realised until I was investigating it for this purpose.

Buckler: It is expensive here as well.

Burger: You did not comment at all about whether you think androgens have a role in the management of hot flushes and I wondered if you could comment on that.

Buckler: Yes, I did not comment on that partly because there actually is not any evidence. But of course testosterone, or testosterone implants, certainly in the UK, do have part of their licence for addition to oestrogen when vasomotor symptoms are not satisfactorily settled. But I do not think that that is based on any good evidence at all. I am not sure that we could recommend the use of testosterone at the moment for the treatment of hot flushes and I would have some concerns about giving testosterone alone to postmenopausal women without the use of oestrogen as well. I do not know if there would be risks or problems attached to it, but I think that there is just a slight feeling of not being quite sure that it would be the right thing to do, to give androgens to a woman who is oestrogen-deficient.

Burger: dehydroepiandrosterone (DHEA)?

Buckler: Again I do not think that there is any evidence for DHEA. Although there are suggestions that DHEA might be beneficial for certain things. But again, DHEA probably works either because of the fact that it is converted to testosterone and it is the testosterone-like effect or the conversion to oestrogens. So I am not sure whether that is a possibility.

Burger: In the report there should be some note about not using androgens, or a commentary of the kind.

Whitehead: Dr Buckler, the randomised controlled trials that showed that progesterone relieves flushes and sweats, is it the Leonetti data?

Buckler: Yes.

Whitehead: I had always thought that in that database there were too many perimenopausal women taking progesterone rather than being postmenopausal. There was much more bleeding in that group. I think they had spontaneous intermittent ovarian function, which caused the bleeding and also relieved their flushes and sweats and it was nothing to do with the progesterone at all.

Buckler: I think that is a very valid comment. I did not feel I had time to really analyse individual studies but I would agree with you there. It is the only study that has shown any benefit.

Whitehead: The other comment I have is that I think most clinicians found the commentary which accompanied the Million Women Study paper quite offensive. I think it was the most unpleasant piece of writing I have seen in 35 years in clinical practice. The other thing I found interesting was that I actually got the bibliographies out of the three authors. Not one of them has written anything about menopause or HRT. How were these three people chosen? Did you have any idea about this at all Professor Beral?

Beral: No, I did not see it until it was published.

Whitehead: I think we have to remember that most journals these days, the *Lancet* included, are not the nice old journals with a nice old-fashioned friendly editor. They are hard-nosed commercial businesses, and they are there to make a fast buck. If they can make a fast buck with appalling publicity, then they will do that.

Glasier: There are data on the long-term safety of progestogens on breast cancer from contraception. Professor Beral, in the 1996 paper[12] that you published about breast cancer and the combined pill, where the relative risk of breast cancer was 1.24, for progestogen only contraception it was 1.17, and it was statistically significantly increased. There are many fewer women on progestogen only methods but there are some data there for progestogen only and breast cancer.

References

1. Hoffmann J, Lichtner RB, Fuhrmann U, Michna H, Parczyk K, Neef G, *et al.* Effects of progesterone receptor antagonists on breast cancer. In: Robertson JFR, Nicholson RI, Hayes DF, editors. *Endocrine Therapy of Breast Cancer.* London: Martin Dunitz; 2002.
2. Perrault D, Eisenhauer EA, Pritchard KI, Panasci L, Norris B, Vandenberg T, *et al.* Phase II study of the progesterone antagonist mifepristone in patients with untreated metastatic breast carcinoma: a National Cancer Institute of Canada Clinical Trials Group study. *J Clin Oncol* 1996;14:2709–12.
3. Robertson JF, Willsher PC, Winterbottom L, Blamey RW, Thorpe S. Onapristone, a progesterone receptor antagonist, as first-line therapy in primary breast cancer. *Eur J Cancer* 1999;35:214–18.
4. Klijn JG, Setyono-Han B, Foekens JA. Progesterone antagonists and progesterone receptor modulators in the treatment of breast cancer. *Steroids* 2000;65:825–30.
5. Chwalisz K, Garg R, Brenner RM, Schubert G, Elger W. Selective progesterone receptor modulators (SPRMs): a novel therapeutic concept in endometriosis. *Ann N Y Acad Sci* 2002;955:373–88; discussion 389–93, 396–406.
6. Cummings SR, Eckert S, Krueger KA, Grady D, Powles TJ, Cauley JA, *et al.* The effect of raloxifene on risk of breast cancer in postmenopausal women: results from the MORE randomized trial. Multiple Outcomes of Raloxifene Evaluation. *JAMA* 1999;281:2189–97.
7. Riis BJ, Christiansen C, Johansen JS, Jacobson J. Is it possible to prevent bone loss in young women treated with luteinizing hormone-releasing hormone agonists? *J Clin Endocrinol Metab* 1990;70:920–4.
8. Bergqvist A, Jacobson J, Harris S. A double-blind randomized study of the treatment of endometriosis with nafarelin or nafarelin plus norethisterone. *Gynecol Endocrinol* 1997;11:187–94.
9. McClung M, *et al. Bone* 1998;23 Suppl:S465.
10. Jacobson JS, Troxel AB, Evans J, Klaus L, Vahdat L, Kinne D, *et al.* Randomized trial of black cohosh for the treatment of hot flashes among women with a history of breast cancer. *J Clin Oncol* 2001;19:2739–45.
11. Wuttke W, Seidlova-Wuttke D, Gorkow C. The Cimicifuga preparation BNO 1055 vs. conjugated estrogens in a double-blind placebo-controlled study: effects on menopause symptoms and bone markers. *Maturitas* 2003;44 Suppl 1:S67–77.
12. Collaborative Group on Hormonal Factors in Breast Cancer. Breast cancer and hormonal contraceptives: collaborative reanalysis of individual data on 53 297 women with breast cancer and 100 239 women without breast cancer from 54 epidemiological studies. *Lancet* 1996;347:1713–27.

SECTION 7

COMMUNICATING ISSUES ON HORMONE
REPLACEMENT WITH WOMEN

Chapter 25

The role of the general practitioner

Sarah Gray

Introduction

The title of general practitioner (GP) provides a clear job description and is far superior to the designation 'primary care physician'. The GP is a specialist in his field and he has the ability to evaluate a patient holistically. The interaction of the physiological systems with psychological and social influences results in illness behaviour and presentation in a way that is unique to the person and the event. The competent GP should be able to derive from the consultation that which is important to the person in front of him. He will determine key themes and influences and develop a risk analysis or profile. He then discusses this evaluation with his patient. A number of protocol-driven diagnostic algorithms have been produced but none work as well or as fast as the GP.

Once the GP has acknowledged and understood the problem presented, options for management will be evaluated. Diagnosis is not always possible and onward referral may be one of these options. The patient may be satisfied with a discussion and the provision of information so that she can understand and manage her own problem. Advice as to what actions to take, opinions to seek or the over-the-counter remedies to buy may be appropriate. The GP may be quite certain of his diagnosis and feel capable of providing suitable treatment. He may then prescribe medication or refer for specific therapies. He may need more information and investigate his patient further. Alternatively, he may opt simply to observe until the problem either spontaneously resolves or changes in such a way as to make definitive action justifiable, feasible or worth the risk and cost.

It can be seen that communication has to occur at many levels. The GP does not communicate only with his patient. He is the hub of the clinical network. He will establish and coordinate the primary care team. Efficient functioning at the community level depends equally on interpersonal communication and systems that are understood and used by the team members.

NHS perspective

Within the UK all residents are entitled to registration with a GP and care that is free at the point of delivery. No one is denied access through poverty. Secondary care provision does not meet demand and the British GP is encouraged to limit referral and manage many problems himself.

Patients usually seek the help of their GP in the event of acute illness. While this is recognised by the Department of Health as an essential service, the emphasis is moving towards management of chronic disease and health promotion. Menopausal health care falls naturally within this area of working practice but is not specifically recognised within the structure of the new GP contract.[1]

Patient perspective

Patients also turn to primary care for counselling and lifestyle advice. Aspects of the GP's own personality or style of working may attract patients and, in general, patients will choose whom they wish to consult. It is known that both in British and Norwegian society there is a higher rate of HRT use among female consultant gynaecologists and GPs than the general population.[2,3] Many patients express a preference for a female clinician. We do not yet know whether this affects the outcome of the consultation.

In the UK, it is usually the GP who chooses a specialist on behalf of the patient. This may involve a subtle assessment of the ability of both parties to communicate together, in conjunction with the specialist's skills and interest.

GPs work in a community setting and will thus be very aware of the demographic and cultural issues that influence their patients' lives. The GP may use local terminology to help the patient to understand and deal with their condition. He also has to be aware of the huge increase in available information offered by the Internet. He may also therefore spell out the medical name of the problem and even give an appropriate web address for reference.

Continuity of care is still considered highly desirable and many GPs spend their entire professional career in one practice, building a considerable knowledge and rapport with their patients. With a stable indigenous population, three or four generations of the same family can be cared for simultaneously. This provides great insight into the social and family pressures on the individual members of the family and is a valuable asset in communication. It is important however, that this depth of intimate knowledge does not conflict with individual confidentiality.

GP perspective

The GP may at times feel overwhelmed by the demands made upon him. He is expected to deal with the entire spectrum of human conditions with a reasonable degree of competence. Patients are encouraged to demand ever higher standards of care and resources rarely match this. Political and administrative pressure is added. Despite this, the essence of the job is fundamental. The GP aims first to understand his patient's problem and then to help the patient to understand the problem. They then go on to manage the problem together.

In the primary care setting, a woman may directly present the issue of menopausal health. She may have chosen to wait for the doctor of her choice and have prepared her agenda. In contrast, the doctor has no warning of the topic of the consultation. This variety is both stimulating and challenging and for many common problems he will have memorised, written or computerised guidance. Women's health is a substantial component of primary care. It is reasonable, therefore, to expect the GP to be able to provide a clear but simple evaluation, supply the patient with information and agree to complete the process when the patient is ready or direct her to a colleague better able to provide this service.

Post-reproductive health care requires exactly this approach. Many women accessing this service have no continuing pathological process. They seek to understand their situation and to determine what lifestyle or therapeutic interventions are available to them. They seek to make an informed choice and take control of their own health.[4,5]

International perspective

The art of general practice lies in the subtlety of communication, which involves an exchange of information, interaction and dialogue. What is required of the individual GP will alter according to the healthcare system in which he works but the need for this communication to be appropriate to the circumstance and to be effective does not.

The GP is the point of entry into the healthcare system. The 'gatekeeper' role that is imposed on the UK GP acts as a filter to control demand for secondary care. However, this is not universal. What can be generalised is that the patient will seek help from a GP not just when acutely unwell. In fact, in some countries being unwell will cause her to seek help elsewhere. She comes to discuss her general condition. Her concerns need to be interpreted, evaluated and responded to: it is impossible to be a GP and not communicate, wherever you work in the world.

In France it is possible to go to different GPs with different problems. Continuity of care is now acknowledged to be desirable and patients are encouraged to collate their own health record. Background information with respect to family or personal medical history is reliant on patient recall and honesty: completeness of account cannot always be assumed. It is therefore much more difficult for the French GP to provide a midlife analysis. However, the French secondary and investigative sectors allow rapid access with far greater availability than in the UK. Onward referral tends to occur earlier after presentation, and menopause is more likely to be managed by the gynaecologist.

In Australia there is also no system of registration, and it is possible to see a number of doctors until a desired endpoint is obtained. The doctors are reimbursed according to the number of consultations and it is not in their interests to turn patients away. This potentially exposes patients to conflicting information and advice. However, specialist practices do develop and it may be possible to choose a GP with an interest in women's health and then simply stay with that individual.

In the health maintenance organisations (HMOs) of the USA, the clinicians at the first point of contact may not be doctors but physician's assistants. These organisations are protocol-driven and audited to obtain best value for money and outcomes. Evaluation is systematic with greater use of objective measures than in the UK. Not everyone belongs to an HMO. For many perimenopausal women, an office gynaecologist will be accessed directly and will provide women's health services up to but not including surgery. A recent publication has identified that 70% of prescriptions for HRT in the USA are written by gynaecologists.[6] There is little clear information as to the generalist skills of these practitioners but the North American Menopause Society (NAMS) does offer education and assessment of knowledge in menopause.

In Japan there is no established primary care system. If unwell or concerned, the individual will directly approach a specialist in whatever area of medicine she feels is the cause of her problem. Menopausal health care is difficult to obtain.

In Italy a pelvic examination is considered beyond the capability of the GP and to require the skills of a gynaecologist.

Postmenopausal health care requires competent generalist assessment. It may draw on the opinions of experts. These opinions should be communicated and in such a way to allow integration to occur.

Women's health in primary care

Women's health has long had a low political priority in the UK and is notable for the variation in secondary care provision across the country. Some areas provide a specialist menopause referral service but many do not. The GP may have to rely on his own knowledge and experience. It is vital that issues of women's health are integrated into the routine training process for it is inevitable that these will be regularly presented in the primary care setting.

Nurses are increasingly recognised for their communication skills and ability to perform a risk:benefit analysis once training and guidance have been provided. For many practices, the nurse may become the appropriate in-house resource to counsel women through the issues of midlife. It is useful for a practice to identify and acknowledge such resources within their own team so that all members of the team can direct a patient appropriately.[7]

If a management decision to proceed with intervention is made and a therapeutic regimen devised, this should be both explained to the patient and communicated to the pharmacist with instructions that are clear, unambiguous and allow reiteration in the dispensary. The pharmacist becomes part of the clinical and communication network.

Menopausal health care

Routine screening appointments such as for cervical cytology are opportunities that primary care can use to improve knowledge about menopause. In most areas of the UK, over 80% of women respond to their invitation to attend. Menstrual cycle data is routinely sought and it would be easy for a trained nurse to provide information regarding expected changes in menstrual pattern during the menopause transition. General lifestyle advice regarding calcium intake and the need for weight-bearing exercise can also be given. Nurses are particularly skilled at health promotion and could easily incorporate this. An openness to discuss such matters will encourage the woman to return when ready.

Clinical pathways within general practice have been shown to be helpful as a method of handling particular problems.[7] For example, a perimenopausal woman wishing to discuss her symptoms might just have her current situation evaluated on presentation. If it is decided that she is significantly affected and wishes intervention she may then see the practice nurse for any tests that are indicated. The nurse might at the same time demonstrate various types of intervention and provide some written information for the woman to consider. Finally, there could be an overall review by the member of the practice with greatest specialist knowledge and interest. This might be a doctor or a nurse. Between them, a solution is negotiated.

The woman makes her choice from the management options offered. She needs to be told that if the initial choice is unsatisfactory there is considerable scope for modification. It is helpful for clinicians to familiarise themselves with a short formulary of preparations such that they can make a rational prescribing choice with confidence and logically solve problems if the response is less than satisfactory.[8,9] Lack of confidence in prescribing is easily identified by patients and has a markedly negative effect on their confidence in the clinician. Hard outcome data may take a long time to accrue and may not be appropriate. In the initial stages, evaluation is based on patient satisfaction surveys. A consistent theme from these is that effective communication is rated very highly among women. In the primary care setting it is rarely necessary or possible to complete presentation, evaluation, discussion and management in a single consultation. This is not important provided that communication is good and information consistent.

Primary care may seek to initiate contact by identifying high-risk women and offering them appointments.[10] An adequate database in the primary care setting can identify women from the registered population with any given combination of indicators. Data availability and completeness are crucial for this to work. Letters of explanation should be very carefully drafted and offer something that the woman would choose if offered the choice. In the real world, target group screening is only possible if the practice is resourced with time, facilities and staff, including trained and interested clinicians.

Information technology

A lifelong health record is created in the UK that follows the patient should they subsequently register elsewhere. Government intention is that this record be converted to a computerised version that will be password-protected and enable any entitled NHS employee access to relevant confidential health information. In theory this could, at a stroke, transform inter-professional communication. In practice it is proving difficult to achieve. Primary care is regarded as the guardian of the electronic health record and has been set the task of summarising, standardising and encoding the records of over 50 million people.[11] The programme is behind schedule and issues of resources and technology remain to be addressed. Secondary care computerisation stills lags behind that in primary care and huge issues of compatibility and confidentiality are still to be resolved.

There are a number of different IT systems currently in use in UK general practice. All are capable of collecting information but they vary in their ability to integrate data. Midlife health assessment relies crucially on the availability of information. In a service that provides short appointment times but continuing care, information collected during previous consultations must be readily accessed and clearly displayed.

Despite the logistical difficulties, the goal of an electronic personal health record that is complete and up to date has much to recommend it for post-reproductive health care. Summarised information is required in order to produce and compare a concise risk profile for all relevant physiological systems. Information technology offers the potential to integrate clearly all the information collected.

Subjective information

A key feature of a menopause consultation is the need to draw out the very personal features regarding the woman's priorities and preferences. This is not possible to computerise and relies essentially on interpersonal skills.

The skilled clinician will be able to draw information from the content and delivery of verbal communication and will be aware of any behavioural clues. In an area of medicine that aims predominantly to improve quality of life, assessment of the woman's overall situation is required. An idea of what is sought and how reasonable that aim is should also be elucidated. Comparison of the final analysis with the evidence base in existence at the time allows management options to be refined. These can be explained carefully using information drawn from the analysis, and the final decision is the result of informed patient choice.[12]

GP educational needs

The GP should have a good understanding of the physiology of the menopause transition. He requires a supply of up-to-date, balanced and nonpromotional literature, with the knowledge, willingness and skills to explain it. He should understand the current evidence base and be able to apply it to the situation of his patient. He should be able to offer options for management and understand the positive and negative implications of each. He should be able to counsel his patient through the choices put before her.[13] This is a high demand to make of the clinician as an individual and almost impossible within the confines of a ten-minute consultation. How can the GP be helped?

Traditional medical education uses pathology and systems-based training. Women's health requires a different approach, with multi-system evaluation of problems that are often not pathological in aetiology. Informed patient choice is the 'modus operandi' in all aspects of women's health, from contraceptive choices, through maternity, management of bleeding issues, menopausal symptomatology to postmenopausal osteoporosis. There is a case that exposure to this manner of working should begin at the undergraduate level and be emphasised during subspecialty training.

NAMS has a knowledge-based assessment for menopause care. In the UK there is now a formal training programme for the career gynaecologist wishing to specialise in post-reproductive health. For the aspiring GP specialist or interested primary care clinician there is also a new programme coordinated by the British Menopause Society and the Faculty of Family Planning and Reproductive Health Care (of the RCOG). This will use a core, two-day interactive course and subsequent competency-based training under the supervision of a mentor. Depending on the requirements of the individual, a basic or advanced level of competencies can be sought. The higher level is recommended for the GP specialist.

What can be done to help the GP who struggles but is not sufficiently motivated to attend a specialised training programme? A lack of knowledge may be identified via a personal learning plan or appraisal. Appropriate GP education courses including the relevant topic might be the answer. He may choose to join the specialist or GP specialist in their clinic for an update in clinical management. The local clinical network may be able to provide someone to go to his practice for an individual teaching session or one facilitated to include all members of the practice team. Recommendations from the specialist clinic should explain how and why the clinical decisions were made. The primary care trust could establish a point of contact or e-mail address so that their specialist lead can respond to any query. Networking and support have the potential to raise the standard of women's health in primary care.[14]

To illustrate this, a study in East Anglia showed that a programme of practice team education could change the management of menorrhagia within primary care.[15] A smaller study in Cornwall has shown that a similar strategy for menopause can not only improve the knowledge base and confidence of the individual clinician but also facilitate the development of clinical pathways and formularies within practices.

Written information, individual mentoring arrangements, group meetings and networking with peers all offer the potential to maintain and extend knowledge. They represent variations on the theme of communication and equip the clinician in turn to improve his communication with his patient.

The GP is increasingly expected to audit and evaluate his service, both for accreditation and to inform the agenda for development and improvement. This may be extended, published and enter the higher academic plane of research.

Investigations

The GP traditionally serves as a link between the primary and secondary sectors. It is his authority that is required to request imaging or laboratory tests. Local commissioning can ensure that the GP is able to order investigations that are clinically indicated with a delay no greater than would result from consultant request. The specialist GP is able to organise bone density measurement, thrombophilia screening, endometrial biopsy, mammography or endocrine assessment and is therefore quite able to offer a full service from within the primary care sector.

Referral

The possession of organised information, the experience of multi-system evaluation and an interactional consultation style make general practice the ideal environment for an initial menopause assessment. Should the clinician be unable to complete the analysis or be unwilling to offer definitive advice then his onward referral should carry his baseline information with it. Communication with the woman will prepare her for what to expect from the referral and help her to make best use of the opportunity.

In the field of post-reproductive health, local resources will determine whom the woman is referred to. Menopause clinics within the secondary care sector are not widely available. They rely on a lead consultant with an interest in menopause who is usually a gynaecologist. They work closely with colleagues in haematology (regarding thrombotic issues), breast units, rheumatology (osteoporosis), biochemistry (hormone profiles) and endocrinology. GPs may be employed within this specialist facility and gain experience and training which can then be used in their own practice. Familiarity with people and systems makes the process of communication much more efficient and effective.

The personal relationship between the GP and the specialist has traditionally affected the tone and nature of their communication. In the UK it is proposed that all written communication be copied to the patient. There are conflicting views as to whether this is helpful or whether by reducing the information supplied to the factual it will deprive the receiving clinician of insight into the character of the referred patient. The opposing view is that it will allow equity of access by preventing pejorative remarks or adverse subjective assessment

Possession of the computer-generated summary allows the specialist clinician to move forward rather than to have to repeat the preliminary analysis. Electronic transmission of information has the potential to be more flexible than the simple printout. The specialist recommendation could be returned in the same manner in a format to be incorporated into the continuing patient record.

GP specialist

If there is no secondary care menopause clinic then a solution is to develop the role of the GP specialist. In Cornwall this concept has been pioneered since 1998. It began as a primary care development initiative but subsequently became government policy under the NHS plan.[11] There is now formal guidance regarding the role and responsibilities of the GP with Special Interest (GPwSI) in Sexual Health.[16] In this instance a very broad definition of 'sexual health' includes a range of activities from gender assignment counselling to screening for sexually transmitted infections (STIs). Menopausal medicine is included in the list of potential activities but no more specific guidance is given. The new GP contract currently under implementation mentions menopause clinics as a potential local enhanced service. Commissioning will depend on local priorities and the availability of resources.

The low priority accorded to women's health underestimates the potential advantages of the GP specialist. This role extends the strengths of the generalist with detailed knowledge of the relevant evidence base and additional skills and competencies. This ensures that complex clinical questions can be managed. The role demands advanced communication skills, including an ability to teach. Evaluation in Cornwall has shown that a substantial number of simpler queries can be handled with a response by telephone or e-mail.[17] This saves patient travel (often over large distances with little public transport) and costs to commissioners and acts to improve the knowledge base of the referring clinician. The GP specialist supports peers in clinical management rather than assuming clinical responsibility. Audit is used to evaluate and inform the further development of the service. Research at the population level will develop from this and add to the evidence base derived from clinical trials.

Media influence

The influence of the media on GPs, the public and their ability to communicate has changed dramatically in the past decade. There is a feeling among the UK medical profession that there has been a concerted media campaign to undermine the respect that the British general public has traditionally held for its doctors.

During the early 1990s the epidemiological and biomedical evidence suggested that HRT was generally helpful. Both the medical and popular press echoed this theme. In 1997 the Collaborative Group on Hormonal Factors and Breast Cancer published their reanalysis of data examining the influence of oestrogen on breast cancer.[18] Risks were expressed in simple terms that could easily be remembered and incorporated into everyday counselling and practice. Leaflets were produced spelling out the size of the absolute risks involved. While the risks were real, a consistency of approach and information enabled women to take these at face value and trust the information they were given. They felt that they were making an informed decision.

The next significant publication was an American secondary prevention trial with respect to cardiovascular disease, the Heart and Estrogen/Progestin Replacement Study, HERS, published in the *Journal of the American Medical Association* in 1998,[19] and was discussed extensively in specialist meetings and journals. Only once consensus had been achieved was there any perception of penetration into the general medical media and even less into the public sphere. Guidance was produced both in the USA and in the UK that cardiovascular protection was not considered to be an indication for HRT. Primary care was able to adopt this advice and counsel appropriately.

Media strategy then changed. The Women's Health Initiative (WHI) initial findings were released in July 2002 in a blaze of publicity simultaneously to both the scientific community and the popular press.[20] Newspaper headlines appeared, but insufficient time was provided for a coherent response to emerge from medical and scientific experts. In the absence of such a response, GPs were unprepared. GPs do not have time to access, read and review original papers before starting a morning surgery. This is what patients were led to expect. Women were advised to discuss the findings with their GPs and the GP had no more and often less information than their patients did. This contributed to a growing distrust in the medical profession.

No suggestion of the emerging data had been given at the triennial International

Menopause Society meeting only one month before. The immediate response to the study was spontaneous and not coordinated. Leading articles in major journals such as the *BMJ* appeared the following week and UK government guidance months later. The North Americans produced guidance at an early stage[21] but the consensus opinion of UK experts was not published for almost a year.[22] This was too slow. GPs were left floundering, their ability to communicate reduced through lack of information. There is data to suggest that those women who had previously been well counselled were more able to cope with the uncertainty.[23,24] For many, however, the reflex reaction was simply to stop their treatment. This trend was seen in New Zealand and the USA, as well as in the UK. Many women did this without reference to their prescribers.

The initial findings of the Million Women Study were published in the *Lancet* in the summer holiday month of August 2003.[25] The day before, the lay press was briefed with contentious remarks drawn from the scientific paper and its accompanying commentary. Both of these were embargoed such that experts were given only a few hours to produce a response. There was inadequate time to evaluate and discuss the findings and to coordinate the response. In the absence of expert analysis, GPs were once again left to flounder. The accompanying editorial[26] was highly critical of menopause specialists and was used to generate sensationalist headlines in both the lay and medical press. GPs felt very vulnerable: the lay press was hostile, patient trust was undermined and medical publications gave the impression of huge potential liability. There was little to provide either solace or guidance. Some months later the *Lancet* published a series of correspondence critical of the study design, analysis and conclusions.[27] This reached neither the general medical nor public domains.

This is not an argument for censorship of the media. Rather, that medical research should be released first to fellow specialists for expert analysis in order that considered guidance can be provided to frontline clinicians. GPs have to understand the core findings in order to translate the evidence into something meaningful for their individual patients. They are expected to shoulder the burden of communication but need something to work with.

Flow of information

Information should also be made available directly to women. With tabloid headlines that are little more than an advertising ploy how is the average woman to make sense of what might be very important to her? Leaflets are useful, authentic and authoritative websites can help, but television and radio have the highest population penetration. There should be a public service requirement that such findings are accompanied by a balanced discussion that allows the public to make up its own mind.[28]

High-profile publication and a sensationalist media strategy result in a dearth of information in primary care. The media have shown a capability and desire to undermine the ability of primary care to communicate effectively.

Some practices have responded to the recent controversies by making a policy decision not to prescribe HRT. Does this mean they do not address issues of menopausal and post-reproductive health? What is going to be the impact on their patients, the secondary services, the health economy and, ultimately, their community?

UK government advice

In September 2003 the UK Committee on Safety of Medicines issued new guidance to

GPs incorporating the findings of the Million Women Study.[29] Concern was expressed regarding clinical input into the recommendations made. Women by this time were unsure as to who to trust. The guidance was revised again in December 2003 as a result of pan-European collaboration. The message was obscured by a further flurry of media activity that portrayed the release of this guidance as a separate and new 'scare'. The confidence of the public in their doctors and of doctors in their ability to perform risk assessment was so severely shaken by this time that the situation was exacerbated rather than helped. While this guidance is couched in necessarily generalist terms it has done little to help the clinician facing a specific clinical problem.

Conclusions

Menopausal medicine requires holistic evaluation and addresses issues faced by all female members of the population. It is strategically a primary care service. GPs are trained to evaluate all aspects of clinical presentation. Their role in the UK health system expects competency in consultation skills and a knowledge and ability to access all other health-related services. GPs represent the communication hub at the centre of the clinical network from the perspective of both the patient and the health service commissioners. Primary care has the potential to deliver health education and promote awareness of midlife changes, healthy living and appropriate use of healthcare services and medication.

Primary care team education and the development of clinical pathways should be encouraged to raise standards of communication and clinical practice in this field. The way ahead may be to develop specialist referral clinics in each primary care locality with recognition for GP specialists trained in menopausal medicine.

References

1.   *Investing in General Practice: The New General Medical Services Contract.* 2003 [http://www.nhsconfed.org/docs/contract.pdf].
2.   Isaacs AJ, Britton AR, McPherson K. Why do women doctors in the UK take hormone replacement therapy? *J Epidemiol Community Health* 1997;51:373–7.
3.   Nilsen ST, Moen MH, Iversen O-E. Norwegian gynaecologists' attitude, practice and own use of HRT. *Maturitas* 2000;35 (Suppl 1):S24.
4.   Hope S, Rees MCP. Why do British women start and stop HRT? *J Br Menopause Soc* 1995;1:26–7.
5.   Pilon D, Castilloux AM, LeLorrier J. Estrogen replacement treatment: determinants of continuation with treatment. *Obstet Gynecol* 2001;97:97–100.
6.   Hersch AL, Stefanick ML, Stafford RS. National use of postmenopausal hormone therapy: annual trends and response to recent evidence. *JAMA* 2004;291:47–53.
7.   Gray SJ. Integrating menopausal healthcare. *J Br Menopause Soc* 2001;S2:4–7.
8.   Gray SJ. HRT and the individual: developing rational decision making in general practice. *J Br Menopause Soc* 2000;6 Suppl 3:29.
9.   Gray SJ. Rational prescribing of HRT within primary care in the UK. *Maturitas* 2000;35 Suppl 1:S25.
10. Drew SV, Rowe R, Panay N, Studd JW. A general practice pilot audit study to assess advice and treatment offered to women following hysterectomy. *Climacteric* 1999;2:212–7.
11. Department of Health. *The NHS Plan.* July 2000 [www.nhs.uk/nationalplan/].
12. O'Connor AM, Legare F, Stacey D. Risk communication in practice: the contribution of decision aids. *BMJ* 2003;327:736–40.
13. Armstrong D, Reyburn H, Jones R. A study of general practitioners' reasons for changing prescribing behaviour. *BMJ* 1996;312:949–52.
14. NHS Centre for Reviews and Dissemination. *Getting Evidence into Practice. Effective Health Care.* York: University of York; 1999 [www.york.ac.uk/inst/crd/ehc51.pdf].

15. Fender GR, Prentice A, Gorst T, Nixon RM, Duffy SW, Day NE, *et al*. Randomised controlled trial of educational package on management of menorrhagia in primary care: the Anglia menorrhagia education study. *BMJ* 1999;318:1246–50.
16. Department of Health, *Guidelines for the Appointment of General Practitioners with Special Interests in the Delivery of Clinical Services: Sexual Health*. April 2003 [www.natpact.nhs.uk].
17. Gray SJ, Levine J. A specialist menopause clinic in primary care: the first year review. *J Br Menopause Soc* 2002;S2:23.
18. Beral V, Bull D, Doll R, *et al*. Breast cancer and hormone replacement therapy: collaborative reanalysis of data from 51 epidemiological studies of 52,705 women with breast cancer and 108,411 women without breast cancer. Collaborative Group on Hormonal Factors in Breast Cancer. *Lancet* 1997;350:1047–59. Erratum in: *Lancet* 1997;350:1484.
19. Hulley S, Grady D, Bush T, Furberg C, Herrington D, Riggs B, *et al*. Randomized trial of estrogen plus progestin for secondary prevention of coronary heart disease in postmenopausal women. Heart and Estrogen/progestin Replacement Study (HERS) Research Group. *JAMA* 1998;280:605–13.
20. Rossouw JE, Anderson GL, Prentice RL, LaCroix AZ, Kooperberg C, Stefanick ML, *et al.*; Writing Group for the Women's Health Initiative Investigators. Risks and benefits of estrogen plus progestin in healthy postmenopausal women: principal results fom the Women's Health Initiative randomized controlled trial. *JAMA* 2002;288:321–3.
21. North American Menopause Society. Estrogen and progestogen use in peri- and postmenopausal women: September 2003 position statement of The North American Menopause Society. *Menopause*. 2003;10:497–506 [menopause.org/HTpositionstatement.pdf].
22. Pitkin J, Rees MC, Gray S, Lumsden MA, Stevenson J, Williamson J; Writing Group for the British Menopause Society Council. Managing the menopause – British Menopause Society Council consensus statement on hormone replacement therapy. *J Br Menopause Soc* 2003;9:129–31. Update at [www.the-bms.org/conses_stat.htm].
23. Gray SJ, Newton C. Influence of the media and WHI in primary care. *J Br Menopause Soc* 2003;9:178.
24. C Newton, Gray SJ. Media scares: primary care response to the Women's Health Initiative. *Maturitas* 2003;44:S106–7.
25. Beral V; Million Women Study Collaborators. Breast cancer and hormone-replacement therapy in the Million Women Study. *Lancet* 2003;362:419–27. Erratum in: *Lancet* 2003;362:1160.
26. Lagro-Janssen T, Rosser W, van Weel C. Breast cancer and hormone-replacement therapy: up to general practice to pick up the pieces. *Lancet* 2003;362:414–15.
27. Various authors. Breast cancer and hormone replacement therapy: the Million Women Study [letters]. *Lancet* 2003;362:1328–32.
28. Quilliam S. Hormone replacement therapy (HRT). *J Fam Plann Reprod Health Care* 2004;30:59–61.
29. Committee on Safety of Medicines. HRT: update on the risk of breast cancer and long term safety. *Current Problems in Pharmacovigilance* 2003;29:1–3 [http://www.mca.gov.uk].

Chapter 26

Hormone replacement therapy – communication with the public

Heather Cubie

Reaction of women to information about HRT

It is more than 50 years since hormone replacement therapy (HRT) was first introduced[1] and one hopes that a slightly increased risk of breast cancer should have been explained to every woman who is taking it. In the early days of HRT use, the immediate benefits appeared to outweigh the risks so obviously that the choice to try HRT as a means of reducing menopausal symptoms was probably taken lightly by many. For most women, effects on cardiovascular function and osteoporosis did not come into their initial decision. Indeed, at that time, possible protection was a potential added bonus. Headline news came in 1997 when *The Sunday Times*[2] reported the interim results of the 'world's biggest study of the long-term risks of HRT' in which the risk of developing breast cancer appeared more than double that of non-users, with the overall risk higher in women taking HRT for more than ten years, although no evidence of an increase in death rates from the disease was noted. Given the introduction of mammography and the realisation that many breast lumps were being detected very early, this fairly low level of added risk was not worrying. The value of screening for pre-malignant cancers is evident from the cervical screening programme and no doubt will develop for colorectal and prostatic cancers, but unfortunately screening cannot predict which individuals will actually progress to invasive disease. In a straw poll of friends and colleagues, the main reason for not starting HRT or giving up quickly appears to have been simply a fear of breast cancer (Figure 26.1).

Over 50 forms of HRT are prescribed, with differing dosages, combinations and means of taking each of them, and it is a confusing scene even for those with some basic medical or physiological understanding. Large numbers of patient information leaflets and extensive guidelines have been produced, often with financial help from pharmaceutical companies. Many say much the same thing, usually with an underlying promotion of HRT use. Promotion relates to immediate reduction in symptoms such as hot flushes, vaginal dryness, headaches and depression, and includes subliminal messages by speaking of increased osteoporosis and coronary heart disease as hormone levels fall. However, information and documentation does not equate with knowledge and understanding (Figure 26.2).

With the high expectations of the earlier years having been severely dented recently, many women are now confused. Female doctors have been among the highest users of HRT, but there seems to be a division of opinion among them. If medical opinion is divided, even vacillating, it is not surprising that it is hard for women themselves to

> *I will not have anything to do with HRT. A friend firmly lays the blame for her breast cancer on taking HRT and this convinced me not to take it.*
>
> Colleague, aged 49
>
> *I took HRT for one month about ten years ago and developed lumps in my breasts. I stopped and would not consider it again.*
>
> Friend, aged 60

Figure 26.1 Typical reasons for not starting HRT or giving up quickly

make sensible, clear decisions about HRT. The advice given by Solomon and Dluhy in the *New England Journal of Medicine*[3] in 2003 was to use HRT short-term to limit menopausal symptoms and to stop HRT if control of symptoms is no longer necessary. This seems simple, sound and sensible.

General communication

It may be obvious to state that people are hugely diverse but, as a consequence, delivery of standard messages about a complex subject must vary. Similarly, reaction to and comprehension of such messages will be almost as varied as the individuals. In relation to their reactions to HRT information, I have divided people into three groups (Figure 26.3).

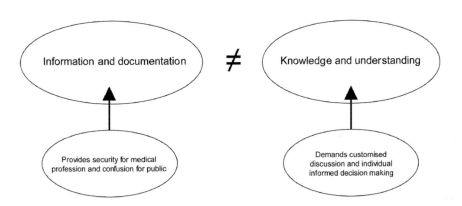

Figure 26.2 The flawed logic which matches information with knowledge

H	'Hoarders'	Read and believe everything
R	'Rovers'	Scan selected sources of information
T	'Trusters'	Listen to professionals

Figure 26.3 Communication characteristics

'Hoarders' hang on to every word of media coverage without doubting its accuracy or validity, or react to isolated pieces of information without question. They tend to embrace the most recent pronouncement. 'Rovers' inform themselves conscientiously from the many reputable sources of information available, both written and oral, and are more discerning. 'Trusters' largely believe what they are told by professional experts and I suspect that they still represent a large part of the public, despite the much greater availability of sources of information. The requirements of each group to allow them to make informed decisions will be quite different.

The public can also be divided according to background educational level and reading age, interest, and the range and accessibility of information sources. Therefore, different methods will be needed to communicate effectively with different groups. A comparative study of patient information sheets used in research studies involving human papillomavirus found that most were too academic and few were set at a reading age appropriate to the population they were designed to inform. We are all individuals with different needs when it comes to communication. It is an impossible task to satisfy or get it right for everyone, but the medical profession can and must do better.

I believe there are some generic concepts about healthcare communication that need to be understood and that go far beyond discussion of HRT. The public, both men and women, need to be better educated about the limits of healthcare provision and interventions and to understand the mismatch with their expectations. For example, the public loss of faith in whooping cough vaccine in the 1970s and the recent public 'scares' relating to the safety of MMR vaccine undermine the real benefits of

	Ongoing research provides changing evidence	
Generic – based on population	Limitations of biological interventions	
	Variation in biological responses across and within populations	
	Related to specific individual	
Specific – based on individuals	At specific time point	
	Relevance of new developments and information to that individual	

Figure 26.4 Key points in healthcare communication

protection to both individuals and the population as a whole. In the UK, if we are to continue to have a nationally provided healthcare system, we have to learn that we have a responsibility to think about our communities as well as ourselves as individuals (Figure 26.4). Large-scale epidemiological studies give us the results that refer to populations. They have considerable implications for future healthcare resource use and cost effectiveness. However, in emotive areas, it is the concerns of the individual that surface and this is just as true for HRT as it has been for vaccine coverage. Results from very large studies are averaged out and the individual response is lost. This was well summarised in 1860 by Claud Bernard who said 'variation is absolute and in physiology averages give nothing real'. More than a century later, GP Roger Henderson wrote in *The Times*[4] that women had ' very high almost unrealistic expectations of HRT' and therefore there was a great need to spend more time explaining the pros and cons for them as individuals at the same time as talking about fears and expectations. At the next level, people need to learn that the effects of new treatments will need many, many years to determine true long-term effects. Interim results of studies and follow-up of years rather than decades may fail to recognise long-term problems. The public must be patient in their healthcare demands or be willing to take the risks associated with availability of data from shorter follow-up. The choice is theirs.

Media scaremongering

Three areas of concern for women have recently hit the headlines. Firstly, the announcement in July 2002 that the Women's Health Initiative (WHI)[5] had stopped its trial of combined oestrogen and progestogen therapy because of the increased risk of breast cancer and had found an increased risk of myocardial infarction. Secondly, in August 2003 the Million Women Study (MWS)[6] reported an increased risk of breast cancer after 1–2 years of HRT use and a substantially higher risk of breast cancer in association with the use of combined therapy. Finally, the advice in December 2003[7] that HRT should not be used as a frontline treatment to prevent osteoporosis came as a shock given earlier expert opinion. Together, these led to a huge number of women stopping HRT without further consideration of its benefits.

The published research findings of both WHI and MWS in relation to breast cancer are robust. The level of evidence from such large studies is indisputable and confidence in their reproducibility must come from the similar results obtained by them. Very quickly, the Departments of Health[8] posted patient information sheets on their websites advising women to consult their doctors if they were worried. They highlighted the fact that the longer HRT is used the higher the risk of breast cancer and pointed out that this risk begins to decline when HRT is stopped, reaching the same level after five years as in women who have never taken HRT.

What about the media coverage that followed, where scaremongering headlines were as varied as political colours? According to Susan Quilliam writing in the *Journal of Family Planning and Reproductive Health Care*, it is not the facts themselves that scare women but the emotional messages interwoven with these facts.[9] While most press coverage in August 2003 attempted to reassure readers with expert quotes, celebrity endorsements of HRT and real-life stories, quite a number sounded significant notes of fear. However, even expert opinion spanned the whole range from reassurance to downright fear. Quilliam summed up the overall message as 'taking HRT can give you breast cancer; not taking it ruins your life'. She also commented that women need to be aware that media stories are 'spun' and health professionals need to be aware that women take in the emotional messages from such spin. The tendency of women to blame the scientific community and health professionals for inflicting risks and the guilt from inflicting such risks on themselves undermine self-belief and make it impossible to reach informed decisions. No wonder women can become confused and anxious when they read newspaper articles with different emphases. Clearly it takes time to reach beyond this concerning stage. Comments from my friends and colleagues at this time are shown in Figure 26.5.

The belief that HRT might reduce a woman's risk of coronary heart disease contributed considerably to its widespread use, at least in the USA. When the WHI clinical trial found that HRT had an increased risk of cardiovascular events, clinicians were surprised and disappointed. Unlike the situation with breast cancer, different observational studies and clinical trials have produced different results. The increased risk of venous thromboembolism with HRT has been recognised for some time and can be minimised by careful prescribing, but what about the hidden threats of myocardial infarction and stroke? It is not enough to explain that observed differences in studies could be attributed to numerous causes including biological, population base and hormonal preparations studied. If it is hard for the experts to understand when there is a real risk, how much harder is it for women? The advice that diet, exercise and smoking cessation are more important than HRT in reducing cardiovascular disease is straightforward and puts HRT findings into perspective.

Most women know that as they get older fractures are more common in them than in men and believe that taking HRT will protect them. I suspect that few women knew until recently that bone protection actually only lasted as long as HRT was taken and therefore lifelong use of HRT would be required to minimise the risk of hip fracture. The 2003 announcement that HRT was no longer to be used as a first-line prevention for osteoporosis sowed more seeds of doubt about its use to prevent menopausal symptoms and left unanswered questions. Nevertheless, the advice to consume adequate calcium and vitamin D and to engage in weight-bearing exercise in order to maintain bone density is again straightforward and appealing.

The advice from the Committee on the Safety of Medicines on 8 August 2003 was clear and straightforward. In contrast, the advice given on 3 December 2003 was much more alarming (Figure 26.6).

I came off HRT immediately after the scares.

Friend, aged 59

I have thought about it and I am almost ready to come off after several years of use but worry about what this will do to my tiredness levels and energy for work.

Colleague, aged 57

After six years of helpful reduction in menopausal symptoms, I no longer need HRT and now is the right time to come off.

Friend, aged 60

Figure 26.5 Typical responses to the current concerns about HRT

CSM advice on HRT, 8 August 2003

1. For short-term use of HRT for the relief of menopausal symptoms, the benefits outweigh the risks.
2. For longer-term use of HRT, women must be made aware of the increased incidence of breast cancer and other adverse effects.
3. Each decision to start HRT should be made on an individual basis and treatment should be reappraised at least once per year.
4. For combined HRT the benefits of lower risk of endometrial disorders should be weighed against the new information about the increased risk of breast cancer
5. The results of the Million Women Study do not necessitate any urgent changes to women's treatment.
6. Women who wish to stop HRT or change their current preparation should make a routine appointment to discuss their treatment options with their doctor.
7. It is important for all women to be 'breast aware' and to attend for breast screening from the age of 50 years.

CSM advice on HRT, 3 December 2003

1. The risk–benefit of HRT is favourable for the treatment of menopausal symptoms. The minimum effective dose should be used for the shortest duration.
2. The risk–benefit of HRT is unfavourable for the prevention of osteoporosis as first-line use.
3. In healthy women without symptoms, the risk:benefit of HRT is generally unfavourable.

Figure 26.6 Advice on HRT from the Committee on Safety of Medicines on 8 August 2003 and on 3 December 2003

Conclusions

Women have recently become anxious about their use of HRT following publication of the results of very large trials. Some of the subsequent media coverage was misjudged and ill-informed, resulting in heated debate among experts. Messages have been confused and responsibility for this rests jointly with healthcare professionals, newspaper and media reports and with women themselves for hoping they had found a way of extending activity and better health in middle years, if not 'the elixir of youth'.

Large studies produce population-based results and some women want lots of information to make their own decisions. Most women, however, need simple clear advice appropriate to their level of understanding and which must come from personal discussion about the risks and benefits for them as *individuals* at particular points in their lives. This may take time on the part of GPs, but many women have been given that time in the past and in light of the evidence then current felt they had then made informed choices. Others may not have been so lucky. All women need to reconsider their positions regarding HRT more frequently.

References

1.   Gebbie A. Hormone replacement therapy: a panacea or Pandora's box? *J Assoc Chart Physiother Women's Health* 2003;92:39–41.
2.   Rogers L. HRT link to breast cancer proved. *The Sunday Times* 5 October 1997.
3.   Solomon CG, Dluhy RG. Rethinking postmenopausal hormone therapy. *N Engl J Med* 2003;348:579–80.
4.   Henderson R. On call: health. *The Sunday Times* 14 September 1997.
5.   Rossouw JE, Anderson GL, Prentice RL, LaCroix AZ, Kooperberg C, Stefanick ML, *et al.*; Writing Group for the Women's Health Initiative Investigators. Risks and benefits of estrogen plus progestin in healthy postmenopausal women: principal results fom the Women's Health Initiative randomized controlled trial. *JAMA* 2002;288:321–33.
6.   Beral V; Million Women Study Collaborators. Breast cancer and hormone-replacement therapy in the Million Women Study. *Lancet* 2003;362:419–27. Erratum in: *Lancet* 2003;362:1160.
7.   Duff G, Committee on Safety of Medicines. *Use of hormone replacement therapy in the prevention of osteoporosis: important new information.* 3 December 2003 [http://medicines.mhra.gov.uk].
8.   Scottish Executive Department of Health. *Hormone replacement therapy and breast cancer – results of the UK Million Women Study.* 8 August 2003. [http://www.show.scot.nhs.uk/sehd/publications/DC20030808HRT.pdf].
9.   Quilliam S. Hormone replacement therapy (HRT). *J Fam Plann Reprod Health Care* 2004;30:59–61.

Chapter 27

Advice from the Committee on Safety of Medicines on hormone replacement therapy

Mary Armitage and Janet Nooney

Introduction

The Committee on Safety of Medicines (CSM) was established in 1970 under Section 4 of the Medicines Act 1968. It is an independent scientific committee, set up to advise the UK Licensing Authority on the quality, efficacy and safety of medicines in order to ensure that appropriate public health standards are met and maintained. Its responsibilities therefore are, broadly, two-fold:

- to provide advice to Ministers (the Licensing Authority) through the Medicines and Healthcare products Regulatory Agency (MHRA), an executive agency of the Department of Health, on whether new products should be granted a marketing authorisation (in simple terms, a licence), and on variations to the indications for existing licences
- to monitor the safety of marketed medicines and to ensure that medicines meet acceptable standards of quality, safety and efficacy and are used safely.

The commitment to safeguarding public health includes collecting and investigating information relating to adverse reactions, monitoring adverse drug reaction reporting, issuing safety warnings, acting on safety concerns after marketing and providing advice and guidance on medicines.

CSM has kept the safety of hormone replacement therapy (HRT) under careful review over many years, as new data have become available. It is interesting to note that the earliest products (Premarin Cream® and oral preparations of Premarin® and Hormonin®) were available in the 1960s and 70s and pre-date modern licensing requirements. The earliest indications of these oestrogen-only preparations were for 'endocrine therapy', including relief of menopausal symptoms. Combined HRT products followed shortly afterwards: Cyclo-Progynova® and Menophase® were available in the early 1970s and Prempak® products from around 1978. Later, several products were also licensed for the prophylaxis of postmenopausal osteoporosis. Product information contained warnings about possible adverse reactions, including venous thromboembolism (VTE), but without giving a clear view on whether it was truly causal or what the rate might be.

Early safety warnings on HRT

The first major warnings regarding safety were issued in 1996, following the publication of observational studies that suggested a two- to four-fold higher risk of VTE for current users compared with nonusers of HRT. For healthy women this resulted in one to two additional cases of VTE per 10 000 patient-years of treatment. CSM issued a warning of this increased risk for current users in an article in their safety bulletin for healthcare professionals, *Current Problems in Pharmacovigilance*, in October 1996.[1] The advice concluded that the absolute risk was small, and that there was no need for women without predisposing factors for VTE to stop taking HRT. The view expressed was 'that the new data do not change the overall positive balance between the benefits and risks of treatment for most women'. This information was incorporated into the data sheets and Summary of Product Characteristics (SPCs) under Special Warnings and Precautions. Interestingly, this update also included the comment that 'there have also been suggestions that long-term HRT may protect against ischaemic heart disease', reflecting the observational data available at the time. However, no product was, or has been, licensed for this indication.

Shortly afterwards, the CSM reviewed the findings of a major collaborative reanalysis of the data regarding the effects of hormonal factors in breast cancer, published in the *Lancet*,[2,3] which identified an increased risk of breast cancer in current users of oral contraceptive pills (OCPs) and HRT.[4]

For HRT, the key conclusion was that there was an increased risk of breast cancer while on treatment that was related to the duration of treatment. The risk declined when treatment was stopped and seemed to return to baseline about five years after HRT was discontinued. Between the ages of 50 and 70 years, the absolute risk of breast cancer was estimated to be 45 cases per 1000 women not using HRT. In 1000 HRT users, an additional 2 cases of breast cancer were expected after 5 years' use, an extra 6 cases after 10 years' use and an extra 12 cases after 15 years' use. This information was disseminated in an Epinet message (now known as Chief Medical Officer's Public Health Link) from the Chairman of CSM on 9 October 1997, two days before publication of the paper in the *Lancet*, in order to provide healthcare professionals with information to help advise their patients. The conclusion was that 'the new results did not markedly alter the balance of benefits and risks for HRT and they do not provide a reason for women to stop their treatment'. A patient information sheet was included, which commented: 'The benefits of HRT: HRT is effective in relieving unpleasant symptoms of the menopause and when taken for several years, prevents fractures which are caused by thinning of the bones (osteoporosis). It may also reduce heart disease.'

In terms of regulatory action, the numerical information on the risks of breast cancer was incorporated into the product information (SPCs for prescribers and the Patient Information Leaflets, PILs, for users) for all licensed systemic HRT products. The text also included the statement: 'The findings may be due to the biological effects of HRT, an earlier diagnosis, or a combination of both' to reflect the uncertainty regarding causality. Much of the information (approximately 80%) was derived from women treated with oestrogen-only therapy. At that time no conclusions could be drawn regarding different regimens or products and some speculated that the addition of progestogen could reduce the risks, although there was no evidence to support this from the limited data available.

Thus although there were concerns in the mid-1990s about increased risks of VTE and breast cancer, the absolute risks were viewed as small and were not sufficient to change the overall positive balance between the benefits and risks of treatment for most women.

Medical examination and the CSM Expert Working Group

Originally, product information for both OCPs and HRT had recommended routine breast and pelvic examination before starting treatment and at regular intervals thereafter. However, in February 1998 a professional letter from the UK Chief Medical (CMO) and Nursing Officers stated that 'there was no evidence to support the efficacy of breast examination by health professionals of the well woman'. A *CMO's Update* in May 1998 confirmed that women taking oral contraceptives and HRT were included in the category of 'well women', but acknowledged that the advice given earlier in the year conflicted with the manufacturers' advice regarding routine examination in these women. Consequently, in 1999 CSM reviewed the available evidence and, in line with earlier guidance published by the Faculty of Family Planning and Reproductive Health Care, advised that routine pelvic and breast examination was not necessary in all women taking the OCP, but that some women may require examination on clinical grounds.[5]

The CMO requested that a similar review be undertaken for women on HRT. The population of women taking HRT is older and has different incidences of both breast and pelvic disease than the younger population taking OCPs. In addition, the effect of HRT on both pelvic and breast disease may differ from the effect of OCPs. The key issue was whether routine examination provided any benefit (or harm) in terms of screening for disease, taking into account the existing screening programme. An *ad hoc* CSM Expert Working Group (EWG) on HRT was set up specifically to consider the issues. This Group, which included expertise from general practice, gynaecology, bone disease, endocrinology, public health and epidemiology and clinical trials expertise, met in February 2001.

Having considered the evidence, CSM advised that clinical examination of the breasts and pelvis was not routinely necessary in all women taking HRT, but should be performed when clinically indicated. The SPCs for all the nationally licensed HRT products were amended to include the following statement in the Warnings and Precautions section:

> Assessment of each woman prior to taking hormone replacement therapy (and at regular intervals thereafter) should include a personal and family medical history. Physical examination should be guided by this and by the contraindications (section 4.3) and warnings (section 4.4) for this product. During assessment of each individual woman clinical examination of the breasts and pelvis should be performed where clinically indicated rather than as a routine procedure. Women should be encouraged to participate in the national breast cancer screening programme (mammography) and in the national cervical screening programme (cervical cytology) as appropriate for their age. Breast awareness should also be encouraged and women advised to report any changes in their breasts to their doctor or nurse.

This advice was communicated in a *CMO's Update* in October 2001.[6]

Subsequently, as other issues have arisen, the CSM has referred them to the reconvened EWG (expanded to include expertise in haematology, pharmaco-epidemiology and a lay representative) for detailed review.

Consistency of product information – a Core SPC for HRT products

While the majority of HRT products are authorised through the national procedure in the UK, an increasing number are being authorised through the Mutual Recognition Procedure (across Europe). As a result, considerable inconsistency arose in the SPCs and PILs for different HRT products, even though they contained the same hormones. To provide consistent information, several European member states (including the UK) developed a European Core SPC for HRT products, on behalf of the Mutual Recognition Facilitation Group (MRFG). The EWG considered that it was preferable to have harmonised product information for both European and UK SPCs, and endorsed the concept of the Core SPC. The EWG met in September 2001 to review the draft Core SPC and make recommendations to the MRFG working group. Following consultation with industry, who also supported this initiative, the final draft was agreed in March 2002. The Core SPC has since been implemented in the UK and across Europe, via a Class Action Variation Procedure.

During consideration of the draft Core SPC, the EWG reviewed various safety aspects of HRT, including evidence relating to endometrial hyperplasia and carcinoma, breast cancer and VTE. The review also included emerging evidence on cardiovascular disease that suggested that the previously hoped for cardiovascular benefits had not been found in controlled trials. The overall conclusion of CSM and its EWG was that 'The benefits of HRT use outweigh the risks, but care in prescribing must always be taken, particularly with long-term (over 5 years) use.' Information regarding the new product information for HRT and the risks of cardiovascular disease and cancer was communicated in *Current Problems in Pharmacovigilance* in April 2002.[7] The specific advice that was given is discussed below.

Cardiovascular disease

Cardiovascular benefit unproven

Prescribers are reminded that all HRT products have an indication for treatment of menopausal symptoms, and some products are also authorised for prevention of osteoporosis. However, HRT products do not have an indication for the prevention of cardiovascular disease. It is commonly believed that HRT prevents Coronary Heart Disease (CHD), based on previous observational studies and on potentially favourable effects on lipids and the development of atherosclerosis. Recently conducted Randomised Controlled Trials (RCTs) have failed to show any benefit in CHD, both in women with and without previous CHD. The overall results so far show neither benefit nor harm in heart disease.

From this it was recommended that 'The initiation and continuation of HRT should be based on established indications. HRT has not been proven to be beneficial in preventing CHD.' This advice reflected that of the American Heart Association in 2001; the AHA have since reconfirmed and strengthened this advice.

While HRT products in the UK do not include prevention of cardiovascular disease in the therapeutic indications, it was noted that the pharmacodynamics section of many SPCs contained claims that HRT could be beneficial in protecting against developing vascular disease. For example, the SPC for Premarin used to read:

Further information: After the menopause the protective effect that endogenous oestrogens appear to have on the female cardiovascular system is lost, and the risk of women developing cardiovascular disease rises to become similar to that in men. Most studies show that oral administration of conjugated equine oestrogens to postmenopausal women increases serum high density lipoprotein (HDL-cholesterol) and decreases the potentially atherogenic low density lipoprotein (LDL-cholesterol) levels. This improves the lipid profile and is recognised as a factor contributing to the beneficial effect of conjugated equine oestrogens on the risk of coronary heart disease in postmenopausal women.

The Premique® SPC stated:

Although some of the effects may be modified by the addition of MPA [medroxyprogesterone acetate], clinical trial results suggest that the combination of conjugated oestrogens with MPA show similar beneficial effects on lipid parameters to that seen during treatment with conjugated oestrogen therapy alone.

Many other SPCs referred to metabolic benefits, such as reducing total cholesterol, LDL-cholesterol (LDL-C) and lipoprotein (a).

The EWG supported the exclusion of any claims, based on surrogate endpoints, that HRT is protective against vascular disease in the Core SPC.

Venous thromboembolism

Recently conducted RCTs had confirmed the previously observed increased relative risk of VTE in HRT users compared with nonusers. These latest studies suggested that the absolute risk of VTE in all women using HRT was higher than that shown in previous observational studies. This discrepancy was thought to be due to the exclusion of women with a known previous risk factor for VTE in the observational studies. The absolute risks of VTE caused by HRT are age-dependent, increasing in older women, and in those with other risk factors for VTE. The warnings about the risk of VTE following surgery or other periods of immobilisation were reinforced.

Breast cancer

Following the CSM advice concerning the increased risk of diagnosis of breast cancer in long-term users of HRT in 1997, details of the increased numbers at risk were included in the SPCs. The Core SPC now made it clear that there is numerical uncertainty in these values:

Section 4.8 Undesirable Effects:

> The risk of breast cancer increases with the number of years of HRT usage. According to data from epidemiological studies – 51 epidemiological studies performed during the 1970s to the early 1990s and reported in a re-analysis, and from more recent studies – the best estimate of the risk is that for women not using HRT, in total about 45 women in every 1000 women are expected to have breast cancer diagnosed over the period from ages 50 to 70 years. It is estimated that, among those with current or recent use of HRT, the total number of additional cases during the corresponding period will be between 1 and 3 (best estimate = 2) extra cases per 1000 for those using HRT for 5 years, between 3 and 9 (best estimate = 6) extra cases per 1000 for using HRT for 10 years and between 5 and 20 (best estimate = 12) per 1000 treated women for those using HRT for 15 years (see section 4.4).

In 1997 it was not clear whether combined HRT had the same or possibly lower risk than oestrogen alone, but preliminary evidence suggested that it may have at least as high a risk. The *Current Problems in Pharmacovigilance* article emphasised that the addition of a progestogen does not confer protection against the increased risk of developing breast cancer and might increase it. Likewise, the Core SPC now made it clear that the risk applies to combined HRT as well as to oestrogen alone:

Section 4.4 Special Warnings and Precautions for use:

> Women using oestrogen-progestogen combined HRT had a similar or possibly higher risk as compared with women who used oestrogens alone.

Endometrial cancer

It had been well known that there is an important increase in risk of endometrial cancer with oestrogen-only HRT. The advice confirmed that long-term oestrogen-only HRT should not be used in women with an intact uterus and that the addition of a progestogen reduces, but does not eliminate, this risk. It was additionally noted that unopposed oestrogen may stimulate residual foci of endometriosis and that addition of progestogen was recommended in women with residual disease, even after hysterectomy.

In summary, following the review of the evidence available until 2001 for the development of a Core SPC for HRT products, the implications for prescribing concluded that:

> HRT should not be initiated for the prevention of CHD and consideration should be given to stopping HRT after any cardiovascular event. Previous confirmed VTE, active or recent arterial thromboembolic disease (e.g. angina or MI) are each contraindications for use of HRT. Women with an intact uterus should be given HRT containing progestogen to reduce the risk of endometrial cancer. For women who have had full hysterectomy, a progestogen should not be added, because this does not reduce the risk of developing breast cancer.

This advice was reiterated in the *CMO's Update* in May 2002.[8]

Long-term risks reappraisal following early termination of the combined HRT arm of the Women's Health Initiative

The EWG met again in July and September 2002, to consider the findings of one arm of the Women's Health Initiative (WHI) following its premature termination and publication in *JAMA*.[9] In this part of the WHI trial, women were taking a particular continuous combined HRT, Prempro®, which is not marketed in the UK but has the same active ingredients as Premique, i.e. conjugated equine oestrogen (CEE) and MPA. Following careful consideration of these new data and further review of other recent relevant studies,[10–15] CSM issued further advice which was communicated to prescribers via the CMO's Public Health Link (an e-mail and fax cascade, previously termed Epinet). More detailed advice followed in *Current Problems in Pharmacovigilance* in October 2002[16] and was reiterated in the *CMO's Update* in January 2003.[17] The Core SPC for HRT products was also revised in light of the new evidence.

The update highlighted the fact that the RCT findings mostly related to the use of one particular HRT regimen (CEE 0.625 mg plus MPA 2.5 mg) and that comparable long-term safety data for other HRT regimens were less complete. Accordingly, it emphasised that: 'From the evidence currently available, it is not known whether all the risks outlined extend to other HRT products, although the available data do not suggest substantial variation between products.' The key findings for long-term use of these particular HRT regimens were:

- Coronary heart disease (CHD): the anticipated benefit of long-term HRT use in preventing CHD, as suggested by observational studies, had not been supported by RCT data.
- Stroke: overall results from RCTs had shown an increase in the risk of stroke in HRT users. For women aged 50–59 years, this corresponded to one extra stroke per 1000 women using HRT for 5 years and, because the risk increases with age, about 4 extra strokes per 1000 women for those aged 60–69 years taking HRT for 5 years.

- VTE: the relative risk of VTE compared with nonusers remained unchanged, however the baseline risk, and hence the absolute risk associated with HRT, was found to be higher in RCTs than previously estimated. The risk would correspond to approximately 4 extra cases per 1000 women aged 50–59 years using HRT for 5 years, and 9 extra cases per 1000 women aged 60–69 years.
- Cancer: the new data confirmed previous estimates of the increased risks associated with HRT for breast cancer. The CSM noted that a number of observational studies in oestrogen-only HRT have suggested a small increased risk in ovarian cancer.

The Women's Health Initiative – implications for prescribing

In the light of the WHI findings the following implications for prescribing were highlighted:

- For short-term (e.g. 2–3 years) use of HRT for the relief of menopausal symptoms, the benefits are considered to outweigh the risks for most women who use it.
- Longer-term use of HRT is licensed for the prevention of osteoporosis. However women should be aware of the increased incidence of some conditions with long-term HRT use and of alternative treatment options for the prevention of osteoporosis.
- The decision to use HRT should be discussed with each woman on an individual basis, taking into account her history, risk factors and personal preferences.
- In addition, an individual's risks and benefits should be regularly reappraised (e.g. at least yearly) with continued HRT use.
- HRT should not be prescribed for the prevention of CHD.

Updated breast cancer warnings – the Million Women Study

In August 2003 the Group met to review the most recent data on the risks of breast cancer from the Million Women Study[18] and its implications for prescribing.

The publication of two high-quality studies, the UK's Million Women Study and further results of the WHI trial,[19] had provided important new evidence with respect to the risk of breast cancer in association with the use of HRT. The finding that oestrogen-only treatment is associated with a small duration-dependent increase in the risk of breast cancer (RR = 1.3) that returned to baseline within 5 years of stopping was not new, and warnings had been previously communicated and incorporated into the SPCs. However the findings that the risk associated with combined HRT (RR = 2.0) was substantially higher than oestrogen alone was new. The use of tibolone conferred an intermediate risk. Additionally, the study found that the increased risks were evident within 1–2 years of initiation of treatment, which is earlier than recognised previously. Absolute numbers of excess cases were calculated as 1.5 and 5 additional cases per 1000 women over 5 and 10 years' use of oestrogen-only HRT, respectively, compared with 6 and 19 additional cases for combined HRT over the same time periods. There was no evidence of a difference in risk between specific preparations or the route of administration, and no support for the previous observation that the tumours in HRT users were less likely to have spread at the time of diagnosis.

The Million Women Study – implications for prescribing

The results of the Million Women Study did not necessitate any urgent changes to women's treatment and did not change the advice regarding short-term use of HRT for the relief of menopausal symptoms. However, for longer-term use of HRT, prescribers were advised that women must be made aware of the increased incidence of breast cancer and other adverse effects.

Prescribers were reminded that oestrogen-only HRT is associated with a clinically significant increase in risk of endometrial disorders, including cancer. For combined HRT the benefits of a lower risk of endometrial disorders, including cancer, would need to be weighed against the new information about the increased risk of breast cancer. For women with a uterus it was recognised that this would be a difficult decision for the women and their doctors to make. The importance of treating each woman as an individual, and reappraising regularly (at least once a year) was emphasised.

In view of the predicted public interest in the results, advice from CSM was issued in an urgent communication via the CMO's Public Health Link as well as through information on the MHRA and CSM websites. The advice included an information sheet for doctors to give to women. Women who wished to stop HRT, or change their current preparation were advised to make a routine appointment to see their doctor to discuss their individual needs. This advice was also published in *Current Problems in Pharmacovigilance* in September 2003.[20]

Endometrial safety of topical vaginal oestrogens

The same issue of *Current Problems in Pharmacovigilance* contained a brief article on the endometrial safety of topical vaginal oestrogens.[21] The limited data on this had been reviewed by the EWG in January 2003, following concerns that women may use topical vaginal oestrogen products repeatedly over a long term (although they are licensed for short-term use only) and the product information of these preparations was inconsistent in the advice on whether a progestogen needed to be added. The article advised that an added progestogen was not generally needed with these products but emphasised the uncertainty regarding systemic availability and the lack of data on their long-term endometrial safety. Prescribers were reminded that where these products were used repeatedly, women should be reassessed regularly and that any signs of endometrial symptoms should be promptly investigated.

Reappraisal of the balance of risks and benefits of long-term HRT use

In mid-2003, at the request of various European member states, the Committee for Proprietary Medicinal Products (CPMP) set up an *ad hoc* Expert Group to review recent published studies and advise whether the data raised public health concerns with regard to the safe and effective use of HRT, in particular for the long-term use in the indication for the prevention of osteoporosis. The CPMP (now the CHMP, the Committee for Human Medicinal Products) is the scientific committee that advises the European Commission through the European Agency for the Evaluation of Medicinal Products (EMEA, now known as the European Medicines Agency).

The *ad hoc* Expert Group was required to provide advice to the CPMP in relation to the following aspects of HRT:

- the evidence for risk associated with long-term use of various HRT products
- the efficacy of HRT in the prevention and treatment of postmenopausal osteoporosis

- the risk–benefit balance for the use of HRT in relation to the duration of treatment.

The group comprised 18 nominated specialists from across European member states, including members from the UK EWG, and met twice to review the data. Based on the available data the group concluded that:

- The risk–benefit of HRT is favourable for the treatment of menopausal symptoms. The minimum effective dose should be used for the shortest duration.
- The risk–benefit of HRT is unfavourable for the prevention of osteoporosis as first-line use.
- In healthy women without symptoms, the risk–benefit of HRT is generally unfavourable.

Interestingly, these conclusions were in line with the published consensus statement from the Consensus Conference on Hormone Replacement Therapy at the Royal College of Physicians of Edinburgh (October 2003), which concluded 'the benefit for fracture prevention for most women is outweighed by the overall risks of HRT. Therefore HRT cannot be recommended as a first-line therapy for the prevention and treatment of osteoporosis except for women requiring treatment for menopausal symptoms.'

The Group reported their recommendation to CPMP in November 2003 that the risk–benefit balance was not favourable for use as first-line treatment for the indication for the prevention of osteoporosis. This recommendation was endorsed by CPMP and the heads of all the European regulatory agencies and resulted in Europe-wide coordinated regulatory action to restrict the indication of prevention of osteoporosis to second-line therapy and to communicate the new advice.

In the UK the advice was cascaded using the CMO's Public Health Link, in a letter from the Chairman of CSM to healthcare professionals and an information sheet for women, with further information available on the MHRA, EMEA and the heads of European medicines regulatory agencies websites. The advice concluded that the outcome of the review did not have any implications for women who are using HRT for the short-term treatment of menopausal symptoms, as the benefits are still considered to outweigh the risks for the majority of women.

Specifically, CSM gave the following advice for prescribers:

- For the treatment of menopausal symptoms that adversely affect quality of life, the balance of risk and benefits of HRT is generally favourable. However, the lowest effective dose should be used for the shortest possible duration, each decision to start HRT should be made on an individual basis with a fully informed woman, and any treatment should be re-evaluated at least annually in light of new knowledge and any changes in a woman's risk factors.
- HRT should not be considered first-line therapy for the long-term prevention of osteoporosis in women aged over 50 years and at an increased risk of fractures. HRT remains an option for those who are intolerant of other osteoporosis prevention therapies, for whom these are contraindicated, or for whom there is evidence of a lack of response to other therapies. In such cases, the individual risk–benefit balance should be carefully assessed. This new advice does not necessitate any urgent changes but women currently receiving HRT as long-term prophylaxis should have their treatment reviewed at the next appointment.
- HRT may be used in younger women who have experienced a premature menopause (due to ovarian failure, surgery or other causes) for treating their

menopausal symptoms and for preventing osteoporosis until the age of 50 years, when the therapy should be reviewed and HRT considered a second-line choice for the prevention of osteoporosis.

The indications sections of all the affected products were subsequently amended. In addition, the Core SPC was revised to include expanded warnings on the risks of breast cancer, including a statement on the effects of HRT on mammography, more detailed information on the risk of endometrial cancer with oestrogen-only HRT, and expanded information on osteoporosis/fracture prevention, including the duration of the protective effects. These changes were reviewed and endorsed by the CSM EWG in January and April 2004, respectively.

The oestrogen-only arm of the Women's Health Initiative

In April 2004 the preliminary results from the oestrogen-only arm of the WHI trial were published.[22] These have been reviewed by the CSM EWG. Although there were some differences between the findings of this and the continuous combined HRT arm, this arm of the trial confirmed an increased risk of stroke and VTE in association with oestrogen-only HRT and no benefit in preventing CHD. In line with previous evidence, the risk of breast cancer was confirmed as being lower than that associated with combined HRT. However, the absolute risk was lower than previously estimated in observational studies and the CSM considered that further information is required before any firm conclusions can be drawn. The data currently available do not change the present advice.

Extrapolating safety data?

One of the greatest difficulties in assessing the long-term risk and benefit balance is that many of the observational studies included 'generic HRT' without distinguishing between the routes of administration, the different products, or even whether oestrogen alone or in combination with progestogen was used. Additionally, many RCTs are too small in size and/or too short in duration to assess the risks of rare events accurately. In contrast, the findings on safety and efficacy from large long-term RCTs relate to the use of specific HRT regimens. This raises the question as to whether risks associated with one product can, or indeed should, be extrapolated to other products, i.e. is any increased risk a class effect or product-specific? Both the route of administration (oral or transdermal) and the various progestogens, doses and combinations will have different metabolic effects. However, long-term safety data on every possible combination are never likely to be available.

Therefore, while the CSM and its EWG on HRT, in close liaison with the European regulatory and scientific bodies, keep the safety of HRT under careful review as new data become available, in the absence of evidence that other products are safer, current advice remains.

Acknowledgements

The authors wish to thank Dr Jane Woolley for her helpful comments on the manuscript.

References

1.   MCA/CSM. Risks of venous thromboembolism with hormone replacement therapy. New evidence suggests a small increase in risk. *Current Problems in Pharmacovigilance* 1996;22:9.
2.   Collaborative Group on Hormonal Factors in Breast Cancer. Breast cancer and hormonal contraceptives: collaborative reanalysis of individual data on 53 297 women with breast cancer and 100 239 women without breast cancer from 54 epidemiological studies. *Lancet* 1996;347:1713–27.
3.   Collaborative Group on Hormonal Factors in Breast Cancer. Breast cancer and hormone replacement therapy: collaborative reanalysis of data from 51 epidemiological studies of 52,705 women with breast cancer and 108,411 women without breast cancer. *Lancet* 1997;350:1047–59. Erratum in: *Lancet* 1997;350:1484.
4.   MCA/CSM. Oral contraceptives and breast cancer. *Current Problems in Pharmacovigilance* 1998;24:2.
5.   MCA/CSM. Breast and pelvic examination in women taking oral contraceptives. *Current Problems in Pharmacovigilance* 2000;26:5.
6.   Chief Medical Officer. Breast and pelvic examination in women taking HRT. *CMO's Update* 2001;31:8.
7.   MCA/CSM. New product information for hormone replacement therapy. *Current Problems in Pharmacovigilance* 2002;28:1–2.
8.   Chief Medical Officer. Hormone replacement therapy – product information update. *CMO's Update* 2002;33:6.
9.   Rossouw JE, Anderson GL, Prentice RL, LaCroix AZ, Kooperberg C, Stefanick ML, *et al.*; Writing Group for the Women's Health Initiative Investigators. Risks and benefits of estrogen plus progestin in healthy postmenopausal women: principal results fom the Women's Health Initiative randomized controlled trial. *JAMA* 2002;288:321–33.
10. Grady D, Herrington D, Bittner V, Blumenthal R, Davidson M, Hlatky M, *et al.*; HERS Research Group. Cardiovascular disease outcomes during 6.8 years of hormone therapy: Heart and Estrogen/progestin Replacement Study follow-up (HERS II). *JAMA* 2002;288:49–57. Erratum in: *JAMA* 2002;288:1064.
11. Lacey JV Jr, Mink PJ, Lubin JH, Sherman ME, Troisi R, Hartge P, *et al.* Menopausal hormone replacement therapy and risk of ovarian cancer. *JAMA* 2002;288:334–41. Erratum in: *JAMA* 2002;288:2544.
12. Riman T, Dickman PW, Nilsson S, Correia N, Nordlinder H, Magnusson CM, *et al.* Hormone replacement therapy and the risk of invasive epithelial ovarian cancer in Swedish women. *J Natl Cancer Inst* 2002;94:497–504.
13. Rodriguez C, Patel AV, Calle EE, Jacob EJ, Thun MJ. Estrogen replacement therapy and ovarian cancer mortality in a large prospective study of US women. *JAMA* 2001;285:1460-5.
14. Viscoli CM, Brass LM, Kernan WN, Sarrel PM, Suissa S, Horwitz RI. A clinical trial of estrogen-replacement therapy after ischemic stroke. *N Engl J Med* 2001;345:1243–9.
15. Beral V, Banks E, Reeves G. Evidence from randomised trials on the long-term effects of hormone replacement therapy. *Lancet* 2002;360:942–4.
16. MCA/CSM. Safety update on long-term HRT. *Current Problems in Pharmacovigilance* 2002;28:11–12.
17. Chief Medical Officer. Hormone replacement therapy – safety information update. *CMO's Update* 2003;35:8.
18. Beral V; Million Women Study Collaborators. Breast cancer and hormone-replacement therapy in the Million Women Study. *Lancet* 2003;362:419–27. Erratum in: *Lancet* 2003;362:1160.
19. Chlebowski RT, Hendrix SL, Langer RD, Stefanick ML, Gass M, Lane D, *et al.*; WHI Investigators. Influence of estrogen plus progestin on breast cancer and mammography in healthy postmenopausal women: the Women's Health Initiative Randomized Trial. *JAMA* 2003;289:3243–53.
20. MHRA/CSM. HRT: update on the risk of breast cancer and long-term safety. *Current Problems in Pharmacovigilance* 2003;29:1–3.
21. MHRA/CSM. Topical vaginal oestrogens: endometrial safety. *Current Problems in Pharmacovigilance* 2003;29:3.
22. Anderson GL, Limacher M, Assaf AR, Bassford T, Beresford SA, Black H, *et al.*; Women's Health Initiative Steering Committee. Effects of conjugated equine estrogen in postmenopausal women with hysterectomy: the Women's Health Initiative randomized controlled trial. *JAMA* 2004;291:1701–12.

Communicating issues on hormone replacement with women

Discussion

Discussion following Dr Gray's paper

Barlow: It is interesting how, in the last decade or so, evidence-based medicine and the role of randomised controlled trials has made us think hard about what is evidence. This has largely come through the rigour of the publishing process. However, I think the process of how editorials are chosen, in other words, how an editorial writer is chosen by the editor-in-chief of a journal, and then the degree to which there is any adjudication or refereeing process of any kind on the editorial content, is an area that has never been very much discussed. I think the editorial end remains still a very personalised and potentially flamboyant aspect of the whole publishing process. Of course the media can easily catch on to that end of it.

Buckler: Well, the media were given key excerpts from it. It was not that they picked up on it – they were fed with some of the more extreme recommendations and that was the perceived message.

Barlow: Despite all the rigour nowadays, I have never seen any questions being asked as to whether there should be a very rigorous process for how editorials are made secure.

Prentice: Dr Gray, I very much enjoyed your comment. Could you just explain how the HERS result rolled out in a manner that was helpful to you? Whereas, regarding the Women's Health Initiative and Million Women Study, how did that information get to you?

Gray: It never really made headlines. It came out very gradually after the experts sat down and talked about it. From memory, HERS published in about October of 1998 and there were a number of scientific meetings after that where it gradually got filtered out, rather than being a shock–horror headline.

Prentice: So it was the absence of media attention, rather than any organised effort to get the information?

Gray: Yes, and we went through our education profiles and we were informed about the changes. We were actually able to get the message out in a balanced fashion rather than have to retract from sensation all the time.

Studd: I am very pleased that Dr Gray has brought up the point about communication through press conferences, rather through medical meetings. It does not happen very often, but it did happen with the Women's Health Initiative and the Million Women Study and it caused great concern. Dr Buckler spoke about progesterone and we have data after a long study of many years, 200 patients, and I can answer all of your questions but I will not do so because we are waiting for a press release to get maximum benefit from our story. If I said that, I hope you would throw the book at me. Although yesterday we mentioned this, we asked about the data about incontinence in the Women's Health Initiative and Dr Prentice could not tell us. He knows but he cannot tell us because it is information that is privileged. I just do think that this is a great manipulation of the data, to get the best out of your data before it is analysed by experts who see the faults in the papers. Suddenly it is on the front page of all the newspapers and although there may be enormous faults with the study, it is now in the public memory and you cannot get rid of it.

Prentice: Our motivations are quite different from trying to maximise the press coverage. It is just like we hear from the GPs, everybody feels they are a sector that is oppressed in some fashion. These complicated clinical trials with a lot of investigators need to have their own discipline to allow the committees to decide who gets to take which roles. The people that get a lead role at a given time, we have to respect their chance to have the first opportunity to describe and defend results. Also the journal will be upset if information on results that they are publishing for the first time are widely disseminated prior to the paper coming out.

Studd: Today's news on the 30 cloned embryos occurred in the press at the same time as appearing with the journal. At the same time there is a clinical conference, and that is how it should be done. Not a press conference preceding the publication by three days while the rest of us have embargoed copies.

Prentice: I think there is a lot of room for improvement.

Armitage: Dr Gray, your issues about communication have real resonance for us. I think one of our recommendations might be around the role of the media. The problem is that the media like relative risks. They do not like to say the absolute risk is a very tiny increase. They like to say there is a doubling of risk. The problem is that very often the information is leaked to them before the Committee on Safety of Medicines (CSM) and the Medicines and Healthcare Products Regulatory Agency (MHRA) have had a chance to look at this. So, we have a very short timescale and you will see that when I present that in all cases we emphasise the very small absolute risks. But that is not the message that gets into the media. It does not sell papers and it could be one of the things that we could have as our recommendations, about the shared responsibility with the media for not scaremongering.

Lowe: Dr Gray, following on from what we might do about the medical media as distinct from the lay media, I think many of us sympathise with drastic editorials often commissioned from idiosyncratics, which are generally unhelpful. I wonder whether, as a positive recommendation, this group might consider learning from the experiences that you reminded us about. If we could suggest to the editors of major medical journals that if they are publishing something likely to have an immediate and potentially deleterious effect upon clinical practice through over-hasty judgement, then the onus should be on the editor to commission several people giving different viewpoints. One of these could be the CSM, for example, so that you come up with a more balanced editorial. I would suggest what we should do is to recommend that to COPE – the Committee on Publication Ethics – which an editor will know about. I wondered if we might asked Professor Barlow to take this to the next meeting of COPE in October and ask the editors of the *Lancet* and *BMJ* if they could consider, for example, having a clinical problem with a variety of specialist GPs or whatever commenting upon how they would see it. That surely is an example of good practice that they could put into their editorial commissioning.

Rees: I would suggest that to WAME, the World Association of Medical Editors, as well.

Discussion following Dr Cubie's paper and Dr Armitage's paper

Burger: Dr Armitage, I wanted to ask you about the phenomenon of, on the one hand, a consideration that the results of the trials refer to one single combination of hormones and that you would be a bit cautious about saying that it would necessarily apply to everything else. But, on the other hand, there seems to have been no emphasis or discussion at all about the problem of extrapolating data from one population treated in a randomised controlled trial, the Women's Health Initiative, to a different population, the target population of symptomatic women who are usually treated with HRT. The risks and benefits were taken from the older, well and truly postmenopausal population in general and completely applied to a younger symptomatic population in terms of saying these are the benefits and these are the risks. Why has there been no emphasis on that difference?

Armitage: Well, I suppose that at a clinical level, does it make a lot of difference? Because the younger women we are treating for vasomotor symptoms. If you are trying to protect against osteoporosis we have heard that you have to continue it for a long time, that as soon as you stop you lose the benefit, so by definition if you were giving it to young women for a long time, they would become older women and they would then fall into that group. I try to keep it clear in my mind as to why I am treating a woman, and if it is a vasomotor symptom in young women, then we said absolutely and categorically it is effective and the benefits outweigh the risks. But we do not have long-term data in young women.

Burger: But in that risk–benefit equation there were things such as increased incidence of cardiovascular events, increased stroke events, where, as far as I know, the data does not apply to younger women.

Armitage: In fact, the tables are age-related. Professor Evans can confirm that. We actually demonstrated them for the 50–59 and the 60–69 year olds – we clearly showed that the absolute risks are very age-dependent for stroke and cardiovascular problems. Therefore, we give the absolute risks which are very helpful to women. Professor Evans, are you going to rescue me?

Evans: Can I just step back with a brief bit of information and that is that the original core SPC (summary of product characteristics) group in Europe was particularly concerned over the breast warning. We in the UK did not feel that this was a clinically sensible thing to be doing or evidence-based. But the companies, the manufacturers and the European regulatory authorities all wanted to have those sorts of warnings in there. So we often end up in great difficulty because the SPC is set in one country to have that thing.

Armitage: Professor Evans, Professor Beral and Professor Purdie went to the European group.

Evans: But the core SPC group was even before that in some sense. In terms of applying those risks to younger women, what we do have very clearly from the Women's Health Initiative is that there is no evidence at all that the relative risk of breast cancer, let us say, changes with age. There are data down to women in their 50s. We have no evidence that that relative risk is changing with age. The idea that you could say that the risk of breast cancer does not apply to women in their 50s just could not happen. We saw that very clearly from the collaborative re-analysis,[1] we did have quite a lot of data from women in their 50s, and so that would apply. Now in terms of the coronary heart disease and stroke risks, there again there is no evidence that that relative risk is changing with age. What is changing is the absolute risk and of course the absolute risk of stroke to women in their 50s is very low. The absolute risk of myocardial infarction is notably higher, and what I think, again, is that to most women in their 50s smoking is the most important thing. We made that point earlier with regard to combined oral contraceptives (COCs) over the third-generation issue that myocardial infarction is not the big issue to a woman in her 50s. We had emphasised that. So the numbers of women in their 50s are very small and to say that we are extrapolating without any data is not quite fair. We had actually looked at the interaction test and I think Dr Prentice can confirm that that was commented on, that the relative risk did not vary with age. Is that fair?

Prentice: True, the P value is 0.36 for coronary heart disease, for example, in by-age strata.

Lowe: I support everything Professor Evans says. The idea of a class effect of oral oestrogens extending to younger woman is entirely supported by all the data on COCs. There is an increased risk of myocardial infarction, there is an increased risk of stroke, the relative risk is about 1.8 or so in the first year or two of use, entirely consistent with the class effect on early risk. Now except that that again is COCs, but I think the total evidence does support the idea of an early myocardial infarction and stroke risk with oral oestrogens.

Evans: For oestrogen only we do have evidence on the overall cardiovascular risk and certainly conditions such as venous thromboembolism. We do not find those varied by whether it is combined or not very strongly. What we do not have and where I would agree it is very much more difficult, is when you come to transdermal preparations. There, there may be some difficulties. That particularly applies to effects on the cardiovascular system. It probably seems to apply rather less to breast cancer. Similarly, it could be that 17β-oestradiol has a different cardiovascular effect. That is much less certain, but again from the other trials we do not see cardiovascular benefit with 17β-oestradiol. So I think that extrapolating to 17β-oestradiol in terms of clinical events, we do not have that data. But again I accept that there could be a difference in terms of the risk. We have not emphasised anywhere in any of the advice that coronary heart disease risk is really a big issue. But there could be a risk in the first year and we are all quite cautious about that.

Cubie: Dr Armitage, I was interested in what you were saying about the European expert working group. Clearly, it is important that we have European harmonisation as far as possible and there are lots of areas where that is going to impinge, increasingly, over the next year or two. But you made a comment about the urgent safety restriction causing some rush. That you either had to publish very quickly or it would take years. That is really what has caused quite a bit of damage, it seems to me.

Armitage: I cannot defend that or comment on that.

Cubie: Well, I think it is important.

Armitage: My understanding is that is why it had to happen, because it does not make a lot of clinical sense that it was urgent.

Cubie: It does not make any clinical sense! That is what worries me most of all, coming from the outside. We can talk in this area about very specific and expert elements, but it is that bureaucratic control over professional and clinical recommendations that is the most destructive of all.

Armitage: That point is very well made. In fact, when we had our expert working group in January, because we could not get it in beforehand in December, as a group we made that point to the agency and they undertook to take it back to Europe. We said that we did not have the opportunity to deal with the communication in the way that we would have wished to, and they said they did not think that Europe had really understood that, and they were going to take that message back.

Stevenson: There are a number of issues that I would like to raise, in terms of the recommendations from the European Committee for Proprietary Medicinal Products (CPMP). First of all, I was concerned because I asked at the meeting of the European Medicines Agency (EMEA) recently who was their expert advisory group for HRT, and I recognised three of the names out of maybe 18 or 20 on the committee. I recognised three of them as being active experts in the field of HRT. Who the others were I do not know. I think it is rather important that if we are going to regulate practice of medicine, it should primarily done by those who practise medicine. In terms of their advice on HRT that it should be second-line therapy because the risks outweigh the benefits for osteoporosis, I do not know where they got their evidence from. We treat, and prevent, osteoporosis with HRT in those who are at increased risk of the disease. I think that is just standard clinical practice. There is no big long-term prospective randomised clinical trial looking at HRT in terms of risks and benefits in that population. So to say that the risks outweigh benefits cannot be supported. So I have major concern about that recommendation and thankfully the EMEA have agreed to take out the bit about second-line. That is a bit of window-dressing, however, because they said they will remove the phrase 'second-line' but they intend to retain the advice that 'HRT should be used only if alternative therapies have not proven suitable'.

The other issue that concerns me is that the ways you have, or your committee has, been communicating is through the *Current Problems in Pharmacovigilance* bulletin. There have been a few things that have been in there that I did not think were correct or were truly supported. I have written on three occasions about this and I got bland answers back from, presumably, one of the administrators. I do not know whether my comments have been passed on to anyone else, but I feel that there is not much two-way communication going on. I last wrote to the CSM in my capacity as chairman of a charity in October of last year and I have not even had the courtesy of an acknowledgement of the letter. I do not think it got lost in the post because it was hand-delivered. So I have concerns that the lines of communication do not seem to be quite as open as I would like them to be. The representation does not seem to me to be absolutely balanced and I would like to know whether there are ways of improving this. I would like to see, for example, involvement of the British Menopause Society on issues of HRT, or the European Menopause Society for the European agencies. It would seem to me that that would be a sensible move because they are expert groups, yet they are not involved.

Armitage: I can only apologise if you did not get a reply. Letters are not sent around to individual members of the CSM, obviously, but I am sure the chairman would normally reply. Three of the members on the European group are here, so I am sure those are the three you are referring to as the experts.

Stevenson: I meant the clinical experts.

Armitage: I do not know who else was there. Were there clinical experts from Europe?

Evans: I would not know the exact constitution of and background of those people but I recall that they were clinicians, certainly from some of the other countries. But, of course, I think, being honest, the kind of menopause group that is here is one spectrum of the people who are involved in HRT. There are other groups of people with different interests in the area and there are advocacy groups who are pro- or anti-HRT. I think that the difficulty is that we all end up talking only to the people we are involved with.

But if I can just go back to the urgent safety restriction and the CPMP, I have very great concerns about the constitution of the CPMP and European drug regulation. First of all, European drug regulation comes under the remit of the Directorate General for industry, it does not come under the Directorate General for public health. There is great deal of concern by a very large number of people that drug regulation in Europe has been driven by the pharmaceutical industry and not by public health. For example, many of you will be aware of the European directive on clinical trials, that there has been immense concern that publicly funded trials are going to come to an end virtually as a result of that. I chaired the Medical Research Council working group on that. So there is a great deal of concern that what has happened in drug regulation has been driven by industry, and industry interest.

The next thing that I think one needs to appreciate in context is that the CPMP is supposedly a committee like the CSM, but it is not. It is meant to be an independent scientific committee but it is not. It is largely people who are employed in the drug regulatory agencies in Europe. So the two UK representatives on that, and we are about to lose them because with the enlargement of the European Union, we will only have one representative, they are people from the regulatory authority. They are therefore not independent. They again have enormous pressure put on them, in some instances through No. 10 and the heads of the pharmaceutical industry to do the things that they say. They are not independent. Nobody can pressurise Dr Armitage, as a member of the CSM, to have an opinion that she must have, and she is not under government employ, whereas if you are a government employee you are required to do what ministers say. So there is a major problem at CPMP. Now one of the consequences of that is that their reaction to that has to be very defensive, and so they try and say, if you have got any financial interest, we are not going to touch you. Professor Purdie encountered major problems in terms of the running of that, and I think that is then very dangerous.

Whereas at the CSM if you have an interest then they are able to be declared and under certain circumstances you have to leave the room, under others you can remain and only be spoken to, and under others you can fully participate. But because I think that the CPMP is regulatory-driven, that the whole structure comes under the industry in order to try to appear to be whiter than white, they then brought on these interests. The consequence is, I suspect, that a lot of the people in the Menopause Society would not be allowed to appear, because of their interests, but yet they are the experts. So that is a major problem and, I think it is very important that you realise the context.

But the urgent safety restriction is again that the legislation in Europe which allows you to do things on drug safety has major problems with it and there is nothing we are able to do right now about that. It means that the opportunities that are available to you are very, very limited in terms of changing information to practitioners. They do have the opportunities that we have in the UK and so you say that the second-line aspect, where was the evidence of that? Well you could say the exact same thing to the Royal College of Physicians of Edinburgh, and a large number of the people who were around here were at that meeting and that was the consensus then.

Pitkin: Not all countries in Europe have followed the European regulations, have they? Italy has decided not to?

Evans: All countries in Europe are meant to do so, but they do not all, just as not all countries in Europe followed accepting British beef when the European Union said they had to. They did not all do so, so countries can decide not to, and the European Commission will take them to the European Court of Justice in The Hague for what are called infraction proceedings. In terms of the licences for Europe that were mutually recognised, they are by law required to change that. It may take them a little while; they may not do it quite as quickly.

Armitage: I would like to emphasise, and all clinicians know this, that at the end of the day we do the best for our patients. We do use drugs all the time outside licence. I have become more cautious about doing this since I sat on the CSM, but I still do it. You do it when the individual patient in front of you has different needs. What you have to be sure about is that if you are using it outwith the licence, that you are able to defend that practice and that you have also shared with your patient that it is outside the recommendations and that you have documented it carefully. But at the end of the day, certainly in this country, clinicians are free to practise as they think best.

Reference

1.   Collaborative Group on Hormonal Factors in Breast Cancer. Breast cancer and hormone replacement therapy: collaborative reanalysis of data from 51 epidemiological studies of 52,705 women with breast cancer and 108,411 women without breast cancer. *Lancet* 1997;350:1047–59. Erratum in: *Lancet* 1997;350:1484.

SECTION 8

CONSENSUS VIEWS

Chapter 29

Consensus views arising from the 47th Study Group: Menopause and Hormone Replacement

Clinical practice

1. Hormone replacement therapy (HRT) is effective for symptomatic relief of menopausal symptoms and its use for this is justified when symptoms adversely affect quality of life. The lowest effective dose for a particular woman should be used for the shortest period necessary and treatment reappraised at least annually. If menopausal symptoms return after stopping HRT, women may wish to consider restarting it and, provided they are fully informed of the risks, it should not be withheld.
2. 'Short-duration' HRT may be considered to be use of HRT for up to five years and is usually aimed at relief of menopausal symptoms in women in their early 50s. In some women, symptoms may persist considerably longer than this. If a decision is made to stop HRT, it should be phased out slowly in symptomatic women.
3. HRT can be used in younger women who have experienced a premature menopause (younger than 40 years), unless contraindicated, for treating menopausal symptoms and preventing osteoporosis until the age of normal menopause, when the therapy should be reviewed.
4. HRT can be used as 'add-back' therapy when gonadotrophin-releasing hormone (GnRH) agonists are administered to avoid menopausal symptoms.
5. Local oestrogen replacement may be required for the long term to reverse the symptoms of urogenital atrophy, which is a late manifestation of oestrogen deficiency. It appears to be more effective than systemic therapy. Low-dose vaginal oestrogens can also be used in the management of postmenopausal women with recurrent urinary tract infection once underlying pathology has been excluded. There is no evidence that local vaginal oestrogen treatment is associated with significant risks.
6. While irritative urinary symptoms such as urgency, urge incontinence and frequency and nocturia may be improved by oestrogens, stress incontinence cannot be treated effectively by oestrogens alone, although it may be a beneficial adjunct to surgery.

7.   Women who have experienced a surgical menopause with bilateral oopho-rectomy may benefit from testosterone replacement in addition to oestrogen specifically to improve libido. The place of testosterone in ovary-intact women with low libido requires further evaluation. Testosterone replacement may be associated with adverse clinical and metabolic side effects and long-term consequences are unknown.

8.   The overall risk–benefit balance for HRT in women without menopausal symptoms is not generally favourable.

9.   HRT prevents osteoporotic fractures while it is taken although the benefit declines soon after stopping. Its use for this alone is, for most women, not recommended. However, its use in women at very high risk of osteoporosis could be carefully considered, particularly if other therapeutic agents are unsuitable.

10. Raloxifene, a selective oestrogen receptor modulator (SERM), reduces the incidence of vertebral fractures in women with osteoporosis. There is no current evidence of protection against fractures at the hip or at other sites. Use of raloxifene is associated with reduced risk of breast cancer but increased incidence of vasomotor symptoms.

11. Most randomised trials and observational studies have indicated that current or recent use of HRT increases risk of breast cancer. However, the risk returns to that of women who have never used HRT soon after it is discontinued. Women must be carefully counselled regarding this increased risk, which appears to be directly related to duration of therapy, not to dose. The evidence suggests that combined oestrogen and progestogen preparations increase the risk of breast cancer more than oestrogen alone. Women taking HRT should be advised to attend regularly for mammographic screening. HRT is contraindicated in women with previous breast cancer.

12. Women being prescribed, or already taking, combined oestrogen and progestogen preparations should be informed that this therapy may increase the likelihood of both false positive and false negative mammographic screening and that mammography may not detect breast cancer. Approximately one-quarter of women taking combined oestrogen and progestogen preparations will show a significant increase in mammographic density. This increase in density has been shown to reduce the sensitivity of screening mammography and to increase the likelihood that women are recalled for further investigations after mammography (even if they are not found to have breast cancer).

13. Tibolone has oestrogenic, progestogenic and androgenic properties. It appears to be effective in the treatment of vasomotor symptoms. Recent data suggest that tibolone may also be associated with an increased risk of breast cancer, but less than that associated with combined oestrogen and progestogen preparations.

14. HRT has been demonstrated in randomised trials not to confer either primary or secondary prevention against ischaemic heart disease or stroke. There is increased risk of stroke and an early excess risk of myocardial infarction in HRT users. The absolute risk of these conditions increases with age. HRT is contraindicated in women with clinical evidence of ischaemic heart disease, cerebrovascular disease or peripheral arterial disease.

15. The metabolic effect of oestrogen can be influenced by the route of administration.

16. All women commencing HRT should be counselled about the risk of venous thromboembolism (VTE), should be aware of the signs and symptoms of VTE, and should be able to access medical help rapidly if they suspect that they have developed a thrombus. Prior to commencing HRT, a personal history and a family

history assessing the presence of VTE in a first- or second-degree relative should be obtained. HRT should be avoided in women with multiple pre-existing risk factors for VTE. Non-oral oestrogen may be associated with lower risk of VTE, compared with oral oestrogen therapy.

17. Testing for thrombophilia should be discussed with and be available for women with a personal or family history of VTE. It is recommended that, in women with a previous VTE, with or without an underlying heritable thrombophilia, oral HRT should usually be avoided in view of the relatively high risk of recurrent VTE. Universal screening of women for thrombophilic defects prior to or continuing the prescription of HRT is inappropriate. In women without a personal history of VTE but with an underlying thrombophilic trait that is identified through screening, HRT is not recommended in high risk situations such as type 1 antithrombin deficiency or with combinations of defects or additional risk factors for VTE, and specialist advice should be sought.

18. It is recommended that, when a woman who is on HRT develops a VTE, HRT should be discontinued. It is recommended that, if a woman requires to continue on HRT after a VTE, long-term anticoagulation should be considered.

19. HRT should be considered a risk factor for VTE when assessing women preoperatively. However, HRT does not require to be routinely stopped prior to surgery provided that appropriate thromboprophylaxis, such as low-dose unfractionated or low-molecular-weight heparin, with or without thromboembolic deterrent stockings, is used.

20. Recent randomised controlled trials in women of 65 years or older reported that HRT does not have a beneficial effect on cognitive function. Also, HRT does not appear to be an effective treatment of established Alzheimer's disease. There is some evidence that use of HRT in women older than 75 years may increase the risk of developing dementia.

21. HRT should not be used, and is not licensed, as a primary treatment for clinically significant depression or dementia. Some, but not all, studies have shown that HRT appears to improve depressed mood in women with menopausal symptoms.

22. In women with a uterus, oestrogen-only therapy is associated with a significantly increased risk of developing endometrial hyperplasia and, with continued use, of endometrial carcinoma. This risk remains beyond cessation of therapy.

23. The addition of progestogen to oestrogen therapy reduces the risk of endometrial disease, but regimens should usually include at least 10 days in each monthly cycle. Postmenopausal women who have been taking sequential oestrogen-progestogen therapy for more than five years and wish to continue are at increased risk of endometrial carcinoma. They should consider changing to a continuous combined regimen, which appears to confer no increased risk.

24. Progestogens* alone may be effective in treating hot flushes and may be considered a therapeutic option for women who do not want to take, or cannot take, oestrogen. However some evidence suggests that progestogens might increase breast cancer risk even when prescribed without oestrogen. In addition, high-dose progestogens may be associated with increased risk of VTE.

25. There are differences between the progestogens in their metabolic and physiological effects but it is not known if these differences are clinically significant.

---

* indicates an unlicensed indication

26. Small research studies suggest that the antidepressants venlafaxine*, paroxetine* and fluoxetine* are options for women with hot flushes who are not candidates for oestrogen therapy. These are not contraindicated in women with breast cancer. The additional antidepressant effect of these agents may be beneficial in women who also suffer from mood disorders although they may be associated with loss of libido.

27. A benefit of up to 50% is seen in trials of many 'alternative' preparations prescribed for vasomotor symptoms, even in placebo groups. Data are lacking regarding the efficacy and safety of topical natural progesterone cream and it cannot be recommended at present for the treatment of hot flushes. Similarly, there is no convincing evidence to support the use of food supplements and herbs.

Education

1. The distinction between short-term HRT use for acute relief of menopausal symptoms and the risks and benefits of long-term use should be clarified.

2. Where appropriate, women should be advised in terms of absolute risks of the known adverse and beneficial effects of HRT, rather than relative risks.

3. With HRT use, women should appreciate the concept of individual needs and risk assessment coupled with population-based evidence.

4. Balanced information on HRT should be readily available to both clinicians and the public. Women with menopausal symptoms who choose to take HRT should be supported by well-informed healthcare professionals.

5. Accurate information should be available for women and primary care staff on the management of premature menopause.

6. The terminology for HRT preparations should be clarified and universally adopted.

7. Education at undergraduate level should introduce the communication skills necessary to enable doctors to deal with areas of medicine that are not disease-related, such as menopausal problems.

8. The primary care team should be able to respond to the challenge of evaluating and treating menopausal women. There are a number of GPs who have extended their knowledge and skills in the area of women's health and should be considered GP specialists. Further expansion of the GP specialist concept is important and should be supported by the academic colleges and central government.

9. Information technology offers enormous potential benefit for service delivery and communication. Investment in this field could assist information flow and decision support and provide for much-needed population-based research in areas such as menopausal medicine.

10. The media should make efforts to convey the key messages of the new results from research on HRT accurately.

11. New information regarding HRT should be released to experts sufficiently early so that findings can be put into context and cascaded down in sufficient time to allow clinicians to respond appropriately.

12. Editors of major medical journals should commission balanced editorials to accompany new research findings.

---

* indicates an unlicensed indication

Research is recommended in the following areas:

1. To study the natural history of menopausal symptoms.
2. To ascertain more precisely the relationship between declining steroid hormone levels accompanying the menopause and menopausal symptoms and quality of life issues.
3. To clarify further the mechanisms that lead to menstrual cycle disturbance during the menopausal transition and the cessation of menstruation at the end of the transition.
4. To formulate internationally acceptable definitions for the onset of the menopausal transition, with a precise definition of menstrual irregularity.
5. To develop and assess treatment strategies in women with premature menopause.
6. To investigate the link between sex hormones, mental health and cognitive function.
7. To look at the effect of oestrogen on mood disorders as distinct from vasomotor symptoms and insomnia.
8. To define quality of life issues in menopausal women using appropriately validated quality of life tools.
9. To consider the holistic needs of women and their expectations and goals, including lifestyle and impact of symptoms on ability to function normally.
10. To identify further areas where HRT may have an impact on quality of life, e.g. urogenital prolapse, urinary incontinence and sexual dysfunction.
11. To identify the optimum regimen of HRT for women with endometriosis following hysterectomy and bilateral oophorectomy.
12. To study the benefit and optimum type of 'add-back' hormone therapy in women receiving long-term (more than 6 months) GnRH regimens.
13. To evaluate the role of intrauterine delivery of progestogen for providing long-term protection of the endometrium in an HRT regimen and its effect on breast cancer risk.
14. To evaluate the long-term effects of treatments for osteoporosis other than HRT, so that the benefits and any associated risks can be compared.
15. To ascertain what the optimum treatment is for women in their 50s with osteopenia and a family history of osteoporotic fracture in a first-degree relative. In particular, to identify agents other than HRT that can be used by women before they actually sustain an osteoporotic fracture.
16. To identify dosages and routes of administration of oestrogen alone or combined oestrogen plus progestogen preparations that do not increase breast cancer risk, while still retaining fracture benefit.
17. To identify novel oestrogenic agents that do not bind oestrogen receptors in breast and endometrium, while maintaining bone protection.
18. To examine the effects of progesterone and synthetic progestogens on the breast.
19. To define factors and mechanisms that control proliferation and involution of terminal ductal-alveolar units within the breast.
20. To develop model systems that more accurately reflect the structure, activity, sensitivity and hormonal environment of postmenopausal breast, recognising that risk of breast cancer may be more dependent upon local influences within the breast than factors circulating in blood.
21. To examine whether women shown to have increased mammographic density as a result of HRT should consider temporarily stopping treatment for a period of time before attending for mammographic screening.
22. To ascertain whether cessation of a selective oestrogen receptor modulator

(SERM) such as raloxifene, which reduces breast cancer risk in healthy but 'high-risk' women, is followed by a 'rebound' increase in risk.

23. To examine the effects of oestrogen alone and oestrogen plus progestogen in relation to cardiovascular disease risk, with emphasis on preparation, dosage and route of administration among younger, recently postmenopausal women.

24. To identify alternative agents and non-hormonal ways of alleviating menopausal symptoms. In particular, the potential roles of phyto-oestrogens and black cohosh need careful evaluation and the quality assurance of these agents during manufacture should be assessed.

Index